Case Studies in
Certified Quantitative Risk Management (CQRM)

Applying Monte Carlo Risk Simulation,
Strategic Real Options, Stochastic Forecasting,
Portfolio Optimization, Data Analytics,
Business Intelligence, and Decision Modeling

Johnathan Mun, Ph.D.

California, USA

For Jayden, Emma, and Penny.

In a world where risk and uncertainty abound,
you are the only constants in my life.

Dedicated in loving memory of my mom.

*Delight yourself in the Lord and He will
give you the desires of your heart.*

Psalm 37:4

INTRODUCTION

This case studies book was created specifically to cover the real-life applications of the knowledge gained in the Certified Quantitative Risk Management (CQRM) program. It is based on the author's book, *Modeling Risk: Applying Monte Carlo Risk Simulation, Strategic Real Options, Stochastic Forecasting, Portfolio Optimization, Data Analytics, Business Intelligence, and Decision Modeling,* Third Edition (2015). This current case studies book is not required for the CQRM examination; but it nonetheless, provides valuable insights into how the Integrated Risk Management (IRM) process is applied in real-life situations by multinational corporations. This book mirrors the contents of the *Modeling Risk* book's Chapters 7 and 14 case study applications, and can be used in conjunction with *Readings in Certified Quantitative Risk Management (CQRM).*

We live in an environment fraught with risk and operate our businesses in a risky world, as higher rewards only come with risks. It is unimaginable if the element of risk is not considered when corporate strategy is framed and when tactical projects are implemented. *Modeling Risk* provides a novel view of evaluating business decisions, projects, and strategies by taking into consideration a unified strategic portfolio analytical process. The book provides a qualitative and quantitative description of risk, as well as introductions to the Integrated Risk Management methods used in identifying, quantifying, applying, predicting, valuing, hedging, diversifying, and managing risk, through rigorous examples of the methods' applicability in the decision-making process.

Pragmatic applications are emphasized in order to demystify the many elements inherent in risk analysis. A black box will remain a black box if no one can understand the concepts despite its power and applicability. It is only when the black box becomes transparent so that analysts can understand, apply, and convince others of its results, value-add, and applicability, that the approach will receive widespread influence. This is done through step-by-step applications of risk analysis as well as presenting multiple cases, and discussing real-life applications.

This book is targeted at those individuals who have completed the CQRM certification program but can also be used by those well-versed in risk analysis—there is something for everyone. It is also applicable for use as a second-year M.B.A.-level or introductory Ph.D. textbook.

Additional information on the CQRM program can be obtained at:

www.iiper.org and *www.realoptionsvaluation.com* or *www.rovusa.com*

ACKNOWLEDGEMENTS

The author is greatly indebted to David Mercier, Robert Fourt, Professor Morton Glantz, Dr. Charles Hardy, Steve Hoye, Professor Bill Rodney, Larry Pixley, Dr. Tom Housel, Lt. Commander Cesar Rios, Ken Cobleigh, Pat Haggerty, Larry Blair, Andy Roff, Tony Jurado, Commander Mark Rhoades, Dr. Nelson Albuquerque, Thomas Schmidt, Alfredo Roisenzvit, and David Bittlingmeier for their business case contributions. Finally, an extra special thanks to Bernice Pettinato for her incredible efforts and editing skills.

ABOUT THE AUTHOR

Dr. Johnathan C. Mun is the founder, chairman, and CEO of Real Options Valuation, Inc. (ROV), a consulting, training, and software development firm specializing in strategic real options, financial valuation, Monte Carlo risk simulation, stochastic forecasting, optimization, decision analytics, business intelligence, healthcare analytics, enterprise risk management, project risk management, and risk analysis located in northern Silicon Valley, California. ROV has partners around the world including Argentina, Beijing, Chicago, China, Colombia, Hong Kong, India, Italy, Japan, Malaysia, Mexico City, New York, Nigeria, Peru, Puerto Rico, Russia, Saudi Arabia, Shanghai, Singapore, Slovenia, South Korea, Spain, Venezuela, Zurich, and others. ROV also has a local office in Shanghai.

Dr. Mun is also the chairman of the International Institute of Professional Education and Research (IIPER), an accredited global organization staffed by professors from named universities from around the world that provides the Certified Quantitative Risk Management (CQRM) and Certified Risk Management (CRM) designations, among others. He is the creator of many different powerful software tools including Risk Simulator, Real Options SLS Super Lattice Solver, Modeling Toolkit, Project Economics Analysis Tool (PEAT), Credit Market Operational Liquidity Risk (CMOL), Employee Stock Options Valuation, ROV BizStats, ROV Modeler Suite (Basel Credit Modeler, Risk Modeler, Optimizer, and Valuator), ROV Compiler, ROV Extractor and Evaluator, ROV Dashboard, ROV Quantitative Data Miner, and other software applications, as well as the risk-analysis training DVD. He holds public seminars on risk analysis and CRM programs. He has over 21 registered patents and patents pending globally. He has authored 13 books published by John Wiley & Sons, Elsevier Science, and ROV Press, including *Modeling Risk: Applying Monte Carlo Simulation, Real Options, Optimization, and Forecasting,* First Edition (Wiley, 2006), Second Edition (Wiley, 2010), and Third Edition (ROV Press, 2015); *The Banker's Handbook on Credit Risk* (2008); *Advanced Analytical Models: 250 Applications from Basel II Accord to Wall Street and Beyond* (2008); *Real Options Analysis: Tools and Techniques,* First Edition (2003) and Second Edition (2005); *Real Options Analysis Course: Business Cases* (2003); *Applied Risk Analysis: Moving Beyond Uncertainty* (2003); and *Valuing Employee Stock Options* (2004). His books and software are being used at over 350 top universities around the world, including the Bern Institute in Germany, Chung-Ang University in South Korea, Georgetown University, ITESM in Mexico, Massachusetts Institute of Technology, U.S. Naval Postgraduate School, New York University, Stockholm University in Sweden, University of the Andes in Chile, University of Chile, University of Pennsylvania Wharton School, University of York in the United Kingdom, and Edinburgh University in Scotland, among others.

Currently a risk, finance, and economics professor, Dr. Mun has taught courses in financial management, investments, real options, economics, and statistics at the undergraduate and the graduate MBA levels. He teaches and has taught at universities all over the world, from the U.S. Naval Postgraduate School (Monterey, California) and University of Applied Sciences (Switzerland and Germany) as full professor, to Golden Gate University (California) and St. Mary's College (California), and has chaired many graduate research MBA thesis and Ph.D. dissertation committees. He also teaches weeklong Risk Analysis, Real Options Analysis, and Risk Analysis for Managers public courses where participants can obtain the CRM and CQRM designations on completion. He is a senior fellow at the Magellan Center and sits on the board of standards at the American Academy of Financial Management.

He was formerly the Vice President of Analytics at Decisioneering, Inc., where he headed the development of options and financial analytics software products, analytical consulting, training, and technical support, and where he was the creator of the Real Options Analysis Toolkit software, the older and much less powerful predecessor of the Real Options Super Lattice software. Prior to joining Decisioneering, he was a Consulting Manager and Financial Economist in the Valuation Services and Global Financial Services practice of KPMG Consulting and a Manager with the Economic Consulting Services practice at KPMG LLP.

He has extensive experience in econometric modeling, financial analysis, real options, economic analysis, and statistics. During his tenure at Real Options Valuation, Inc., Decisioneering, and KPMG Consulting, he taught and consulted on a variety of real options, risk analysis, financial forecasting, project management, and financial valuation issues for more than 100 multinational firms (current and former clients include 3M, Airbus, Boeing, BP, Chevron Texaco, Financial Accounting Standards Board, Fujitsu, GE, Goodyear, Microsoft, Motorola, Pfizer, Timken, U.S. Department of Defense, U.S. Navy, Veritas, and many others). His experience prior to joining KPMG included being department head of financial planning and analysis at Viking Inc. of FedEx, performing financial forecasting, economic analysis, and market research. Prior to that, he did financial planning and freelance financial consulting work.

Dr. Mun received a Ph.D. in finance and economics from Lehigh University, where his research and academic interests were in the areas of investment finance, econometric modeling, financial options, corporate finance, and microeconomic theory. He also has an MBA in business administration, an MS in management science, and a BS in biology and physics. He is Certified in Financial Risk Management, Certified in Financial Consulting, and Certified in Risk Management. He is a member of the American Mensa, Phi Beta Kappa Honor Society, and Golden Key Honor Society as well as several other professional organizations, including the Eastern and Southern Finance Associations, American Economic Association, and Global Association of Risk Professionals.

In addition, he has written many academic articles published in the *Journal of Expert Systems with Applications; Defense Acquisition Research Journal; American Institute of Physics Proceedings; Acquisitions Research (U.S. Department of Defense); Journal of the Advances in Quantitative Accounting and Finance; Global Finance Journal; International Financial Review; Journal of Financial Analysis; Journal of Applied Financial Economics; Journal of International Financial Markets, Institutions and Money; Financial Engineering News;* and *Journal of the Society of Petroleum Engineers.* Finally, he has contributed chapters in dozens of books and written over a hundred technical whitepapers, newsletters, case studies, and research papers for Real Options Valuation, Inc.

JohnathanMun@cs.com

San Francisco, California

SUMMARY PRAISES FOR *MODELING RISK*

… powerful toolset for portfolio/program managers to make rational choices among alternatives…
Rear Admiral James Greene (Ret.), Naval Postgraduate School, Acquisitions Chair (USA)

…unavoidable for any professional…logical, concrete and conclusive approach…
Jean Louis Vaysse, Vice President, Airbus (France)

…proven, revolutionary approach to quantifying risks and opportunities in an uncertain world…
Mike Twyman, Executive Vice President, Cubic Global Defense, Inc. (USA)

…must read for anyone running investment economics…best way to quantify risk and strategic options…
Mubarak A. Alkhater, Executive Director, New Business, Saudi Electric Co. (Saudi Arabia)

… pragmatic powerful risk techniques, valuable theoretical insights and analytics useful in any industry…
Dr. Robert S. Finocchiaro, Director, Corporate R&D Services, 3M (USA)

…most important risk tools in one volume, definitive source on risk management with vivid examples…
Dr. Ricardo Valerdi, Engineering Systems, Massachusetts Institute of Technology (USA)

…step-by-step complex concepts with unmatched ease and clarity…a "must read" for all professionals…
Dr. Hans Weber, Product Development Leader, Syngenta AG (Switzerland)

…clear step-by-step approach…latest technology in decision making for real-world business…
Dr. Paul W. Finnegan, Vice President, Alexion Pharmaceuticals (USA)

…clear roadmap and breadth of topics to create dynamic risk-adjusted strategies and options…
Jeffrey A. Clark, Vice President Strategic Planning, The Timken Company (USA)

…clearly organized and tool-supported exploration of real-life business risks, options, strategy…
Robert Mack, Vice President, Distinguished Analyst, Gartner Group (USA)

...full range of methodologies for quantifying and mitigating risk for effective enterprise management...

Raymond Heika, Director of Strategic Planning, Northrop Grumman Corporation (USA)

...a must-read for product portfolio managers...captures risk exposure of strategic investments...

Rafael Gutierrez, Executive Director Strategic Marketing Planning, Seagate Tech. (USA)

...complex topics exceptionally explained...can understand and practice...

Agustín Velázquez, Senior Economist, Venezuela Central Bank (Venezuela)

...constant source of practical applications with risk management theory...simply excellent!

Alfredo Roisenzvit, Executive Director/Professor, Risk-Business Latin America (Argentina)

...the best risk modeling book is now better...required reading by all executives...

David Mercier, Vice President Corporate Dev., Bonanza Creek Energy [Oil & Gas] (USA)

...bridge of theory and practice, intuitive, understandable interpretations...

Luis Melo, Senior Econometrician, Colombia Central Bank (Colombia)

...valuable tools for corporations to deliver value to shareholders and society even in rough times...

Dr. Markus Götz Junginger, Lead Partner, Gallup (Germany)

...innovative approach bridging the gap between theory and practice...

Dr. Richard J. Kish, Chair and Professor of Finance, Lehigh University (USA)

...absolutely the best book in risk...allows even mere mortals to do it...useful in all industries...

Dr. Thomas Housel, Professor, U.S. Naval Postgraduate School (USA)

...best theoretical and practical support for risk managers in all industries facing today's complex risks...

Dr. Timotej Jagric, Professor/Head, Finance and Banking, University of Maribor (Slovenia)

...a simple and very intuitive approach in explaining the technical aspects of quantitative risk analysis...
Dr. Zaidi Isa, Professor/Chief Risk Officer, UKM, Malaysian National University (Malaysia)

...integrates advanced theories of mathematical statistics with user-friendly practical techniques...
Dr. Takao Fujiwara, Management Professor, Toyohashi Univ. of Technology (Japan)

...a "must have" for first-hand experience with cutting-edge, high-productivity analytical tools...
Dr. Roberto Santillan-Salgado, Professor/Director, EGADE-ITESM, Monterrey (Mexico)

...brilliantly clear exposition of nontrivial subjects, combination of theory and real-world practice...
Dr. Evaristo Diz, Professor and Director of Risk, Universidad Católica UCAB (Venezuela)

...conceptualizes and measures risk...great value to professionals, venture capitalists, investors...
Dr. Charles T. Hardy, Principal, Hardy and Associates (USA)

...combines practical application with intellectual and academic rigor...
Paul Siegel, Chief Executive Officer, The Globecon Group (USA)

...pioneering the application of financial analytics and real options with healthcare data...
Thomas Schmidt, CEO, Health Quant, Inc. (USA)

...the most comprehensive, understandable, practical and indispensable in valuation...a tour-de-force...
Jay B. Abrams, Author and President, Abrams Valuation Group (USA)

...helps managers make informed, disciplined, replicable, defensible choices...
CAPT Mark D. Wessman (US Navy, Ret.), President, Wessman Consultancy (USA)

...powerful and practical with an elegant balance between theory and practice...
Kim Kovacs, CEO, OptionEase, Inc. (USA)

...my favorite writer...a sparkling jewel... complex concepts with lucid explanations and examples...
Janet Tavakoli, President, Tavakoli Structured Finance (USA)

CONTENTS

CASE STUDY 1: PHARMACEUTICAL AND BIOTECH—HIGH PRECISION QUANTITATIVE DEAL STRUCTURING IN THE BIOTECHNOLOGY AND PHARMACEUTICAL INDUSTRIES

This business case is contributed by Dr. Charles Hardy, principal of BioAxia Incorporated of Foster City, California, a consulting firm specializing in valuation and quantitative deal structuring for bioscience firms. He is also chief financial officer and director of business development at Panorama Research, a biotechnology incubator in the San Francisco/Bay Area. Dr. Hardy has a Ph.D. in Pathobiology from the University of Washington in Seattle, Washington, and an MBA in Finance and Entrepreneurship from the University of Iowa in Iowa City, Iowa. He has functioned in a variety of roles for several start-up companies, including being CEO of Pulmogen, an early-stage medical device company. Dr. Hardy lives and works in the San Francisco/Bay Area.

Smaller companies in the biotechnology industry rely heavily on alliances with pharmaceutical and larger companies to finance their R&D expenditures. Pharmaceutical and larger organizations, in turn, depend on these alliances to supplement their internal R&D programs. In order for smaller organizations to realize the cash flows associated with these alliances, they must have a competent and experienced business development component to negotiate and structure these crucial deals. In fact, the importance of these business collaborations to the survival of most young companies is so great that deal-making experience, polished business-development skills, and a substantial network of contacts are all frequent assets of the most successful executives of start-up and early-stage biotechnology companies.

Although deal-making opportunities for biotech companies are abundant because of the pharmaceutical industry's need to keep a healthy pipeline of new products in development, in recent years deal-making opportunities have lessened. Intuitively, then, firms have to be much more careful in the way they structure and value the deals they do get the opportunity to participate. However, despite this importance, a large number of executives prefer to go with comparable business deal structures for these collaborations in the hope of maximizing shareholder value for their firms, or by developing deal terms using their own intuition rather than developing a quantitative methodology for deal valuation and optimization to supplement their negotiation skills and strategies. For companies doing only one deal or fewer a year, perhaps the risk might be lower by structuring a collaboration based on comparable deal structures; at least they will get as much as the average company, or will they?

As described in this case study, *Monte Carlo simulation, stochastic optimization,* and *real options* are ideal tools for valuing and optimizing the financial terms of collaborative biomedical business deals focused on the development of human therapeutics. A large amount of data associated with clinical trial stage lengths and completion probabilities are publicly available. By quantitatively valuing and structuring deals, companies of all sizes can gain maximum shareholder value at all stages of development, and most importantly future cash flows can be defined based on expected cash-flow needs and risk preference.

Deal Types

Most deals between two biotechnology companies or a biotechnology company and pharmaceutical company are strategic alliances where a cooperative agreement is made between two organizations to work together in defined ways with the goal of successfully developing or commercializing products. As the following list describes, there are several different types of strategic alliances:

- *Product Licensing*—A highly flexible and widely applicable arrangement where one party wishes to access the technology of another organization with no other close cooperation. This type of alliance carries very low risk and these types of agreements are made at nearly every stage of pharmaceutical development.

- *Product Acquisition*—A company purchases an existing product license from another company and thus obtains the right to market a fully or partially developed product.

- *Product Fostering*—A short-term exclusive license for a technology or product in a specific market and will typically include hand-back provisions.

- *Co-Marketing*—Two companies market the same product under different trade names.

- *Co-Promotion*—Two parties promote the same product under the same brand name.

- *Minority Investment Alliance*—One company buys stock in another as part of a mutually desired strategic relationship.

The historical agreement valued and optimized in this case study is an example of a product-licensing deal.

Financial Terms

Each business deal is decidedly unique, which explains why no "generic" financial model is sufficient to value and optimize every opportunity and collaboration. A biomedical collaborative agreement is the culmination of the combined goals, desires, requirements, and pressures from both sides of the bargaining table, possibly biased in favor of one party by exceptional negotiating skills, good preparation, more thorough due diligence, and accurate assumptions, and less of a need for immediate cash.

The financial terms agreed on for licensing or acquiring a new product or technology depends on a variety of factors, most of which impact the value of the deal. These include but are not limited to:

- Strength of the intellectual property position,

- Exclusivity of the rights agreed on,

- Territorial exclusivity granted,

- Uniqueness of the technology transferred,

- Competitive position of the company,

- Stage of technology developed,

- Risk of the project being licensed or sold.

Although every deal is different, most include: (1) licensing and R&D fees, (2) milestone payments, (3) product royalty payments, and (4) equity investments.

Primary Financial Models

All calculations described in this case study are based on discounted cash flow (DCF) principals using risk-adjusted discount rates. Here, assets under uncertainty are valued using the following basic financial equation:

$$NPV = \sum_{i=0}^{n} \frac{E(CF_t)}{(1 + r_t + \pi_t)^t}$$

where NPV is the net present value, $E(CF_t)$ is the expected value of the cash flow at time t, r_t is the risk-free rate, and π_t is the risk premium appropriate for the risk of CF_t.

All subcomponents of models described here use different discount rates if they are subject to different risks. In the case of biomedical collaborative agreements, all major subcomponents (licensing fees, R&D costs and funding, clinical costs, milestone payments, and royalties) are frequently subject to many different distinct risks, and thus are all assigned their own discount rates based on a combination of factors, with the subject company's weighted average cost of capital (WACC) used as the base value. To incorporate the uncertain and dynamic nature of these risk assumptions into the model, all of these discount rates are themselves Monte Carlo variables. This discounting supplementation is critical to valuing the deal accurately, and most importantly for later stochastic optimization.

Historical Deal Background and Negotiated Deal Structure

The deal valued and optimized in this case study was a preclinical, exclusive product-licensing agreement between a small biotechnology company and a larger organization. The biopharmaceutical being valued had one major therapeutic indication; with an estimated market size of $1 billion at the date the deal was signed. The licensee negotiated the right to sublicense. The deal had a variety of funding provisions, with a summary of the financial terms presented in Table 1. The licensor estimated they were approximately 2 years away from filing an investigational new drug (IND) application that would initiate clinical trials in humans. For the purposes of the deal valuation and optimization described here, it is assumed that no information asymmetries exist between the companies forming the collaboration (i.e., both groups feel there is an equally strong likelihood their candidate biopharmaceutical will be a commercial success).

Table 1: Historical Financial Terms Granted to the Licensor of the Signed Biomedical Collaborative Deal Valued and Optimized in this Case Study

Component	Deal Scenario			Timing
	Historical	Higher Value Lower Risk	Higher Value Higher Risk	
Licensing Fees	$100,000	$125,000	$85,000	30-days from effective date
Licensing Maintenance Fees	$100,000	$125,000	$75,000	First Anniversary
	200,000	250,000	150,000	Second Anniversary
	300,000	375,000	225,000	Third Anniversary
	400,000	500,000	300,000	Fourth Anniversary
	500,000	500,000	300,000	Fifth Anniversary
Research & Development Funding	$250,000	$275,000	$165,000	Per Year
Milestone Payments	$500,000	$660,000	$910,000	First IND[1] filing in U.S. or European equivalent.
		895,000		Successful conclusion of Phase I clinical trials in the U.S. or European equivalent
		1,095,000	1,400,000	Successful conclusion of Phase II clinical trials in the U.S. or European equivalent
	1,500,000	1,375,000	1,650,000	First PLA[2] (or NDA[3]) filing or European equivalent.
	4,000,000	1,675,000	1,890,000	NDA approval in the U.S. or European equivalent
Royalties	2.0% Net Sales	0.5% Net Sales	5.5% Net Sales	

[1]Investigational New Drug (application)
[2]Product License Application
[3]New Drug Application

Licensing fees for the historical deal consisted of an up-front fee followed by licensing maintenance fees including multipliers (Table 1). Licensing maintenance fees will terminate upon any one of the following events: (*i*) first IND filing by licensor, (*ii*) tenth anniversary of the effective date, (*iii*) and termination of the agreement. Milestone values for the historical deal numbered only three, with a $500,000 payment awarded on IND filing, a $1,500,000 payment on new drug application (NDA) filing, and a $4,000,000 payment on NDA approval (Table 1). The negotiated royalties for the historical deal were a flat 2.0 percent of net sales.

As described later in this case, two additional deal scenarios were constructed and stochastically optimized from the historical structure: a higher-value, lower-risk (HVLR) scenario and a higher-value, higher-risk (HVHR) scenario (Table 1).

Major Assumptions

Figure 1 shows a time line for all three deal scenarios evaluated. Also shown are the milestone schedules for all three scenarios, along with major assumption data. The total time frame for all deal calculations was 307.9 months, where the candidate pharmaceutical gains a 20 percent maximum market share of a 1 billion dollar market, with a 20 percent standard deviation during the projected 15-year sales period of the pharmaceutical. The market is assumed to grow 1.0 percent annually starting at the effective date of the agreement and throughout the valuation period. The manufacturing and marketing costs of the potential pharmaceutical were estimated to be 58 percent, an important assumption considering that royalties are paid on net sales, not gross sales. The total market size, market growth rate, maximum market share, and manufacturing and marketing offset are all Monte Carlo variables following lognormal distributions where extreme values are unlikely. Assumptions regarding clinical trial length, completion probabilities, and major variables in the valuation model are also shown in Figure 1. All of these values are Monte Carlo assumptions. Throughout this case study, deal values were based on royalties from 15 years of net sales. Royalties were paid on a quarterly basis, not at the end of each sales year. Total R&D costs for the licensor were $200,000 annually, again estimated with a Monte Carlo assumption.

Inflation during the period was assumed to be 1.95 percent annually and average annual pharmaceutical price increases (APPIs) were assumed to be 5.8 percent. Thus, milestones were deflated in value, and royalties inflated by APPI less inflation. For the deal valuation described here, the licensor was assumed to be unprofitable preceding and during the clinical trial process and milestone payments were not subject to taxes. However, royalties from the licensee paid to the licensor were taxed at a 33.0 percent rate.

Deal Valuations

Historical Deal Valuation

Figure 2 shows a comparative illustration of each major component of the historical scenario while Figure 3 shows the HVLR deal scenario, and Figure 4 shows the HVHR deal scenario. Next, Figure 5 illustrates the Monte Carlo summary of the historical deal. Mean deal present value was $1,432,128 with a standard deviation of $134,449 (Figure 5). The distribution describing the mean was relatively symmetric with a skewness of 0.46. The kurtosis of the distribution, the "peakedness," was 3.47 (excess kurtosis of 0.47), limiting the deal range from $994,954 to $2,037,413. The coefficient of variation (CV), the primary measure of risk for the deal, was low at 9.38 percent. R&D/licensing contributed the most to total deal value with a mean present value of $722,108, while royalties contributed the least with a mean value of $131,092 (Figure 2). Milestones in the historical scenario also contributed greatly to the historical deal value with a mean present value of $578,927.

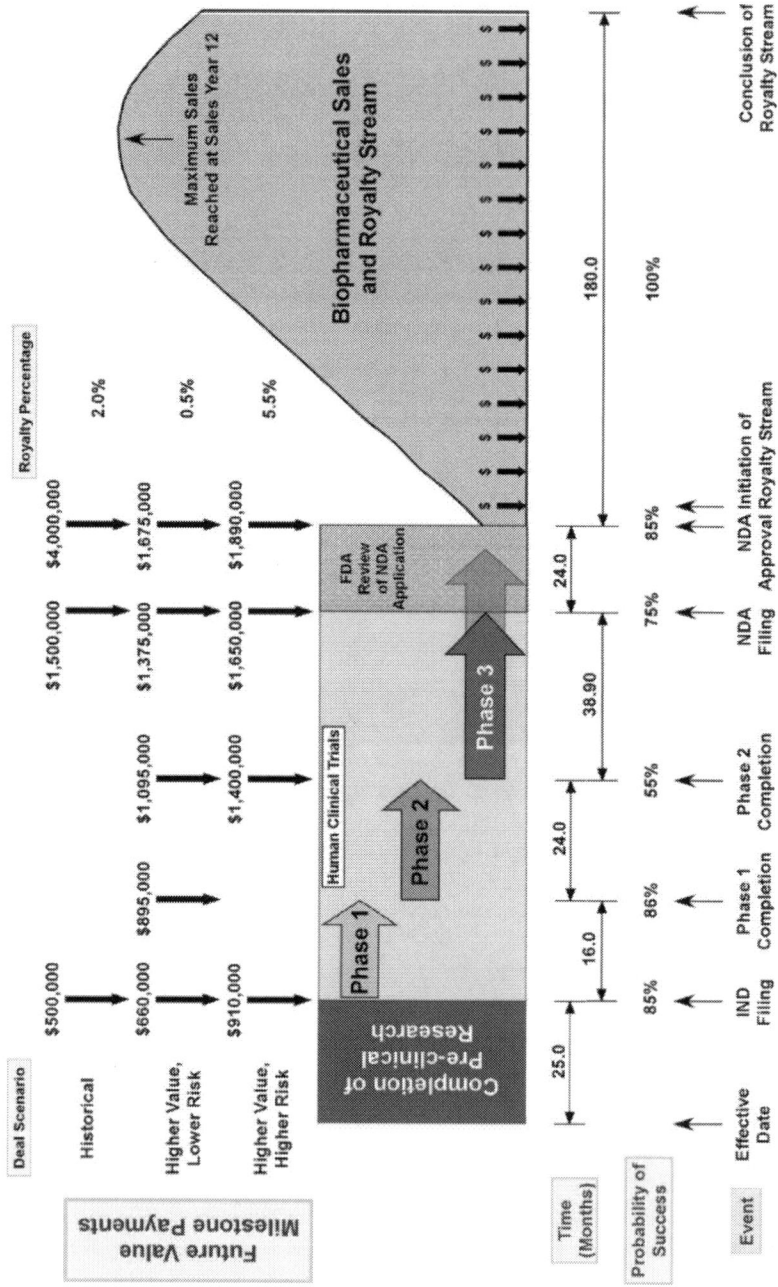

Figure 1: Timeline for the Biomedical Licensing Deal

Milestone and royalty values for all deal scenarios evaluated are shown. R&D, licensing, and licensing maintenance fees are not shown.

Historical Deal

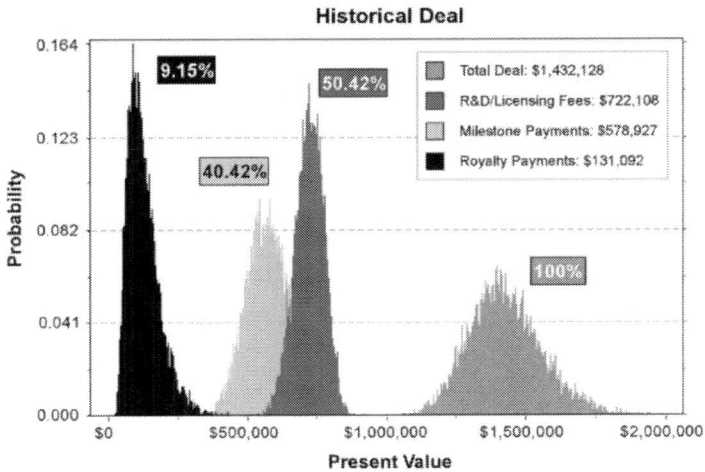

Figure 2: A Comparative Illustration I

Figure 2 illustrates the Monte Carlo distributions of the cash-flow present value of the historical deal scenario, along with the distributions of the deal's individual components. Each component has a clearly definable distribution that differs considerably from other deal components, both in value and risk characteristics. The percentage of each component to total deal present value is also shown.

The riskiness of the cash flows varied greatly among individual historical deal components. R&D/licensing cash flows varied the least and had by far the lowest risk with a CV of only 7.48 percent and proportional to the distribution's mean had the smallest range among any deal component (data not shown). The present value of milestone cash flows was much more volatile, with a CV of 14.58 percent. Here the range was greater ($315,103 to $1,004,563) with a symmetric distribution having a skewness of only 0.40 (data not shown).

Royalty present value was by far the most volatile with a CV of 45.71 percent (data not shown). The kurtosis of royalty present value was large (5.98; data not shown), illustrating the proportionally wide distribution to the small royalty mean ($131,093; Figure 2). These data should not be surprising as the royalty cash flows are subject to variability of nearly all Monte Carlo assumptions in the model and are thus highly volatile.

Monte Carlo Assumption and Decision Variable Sensitivities

Figures 5–10 illustrate the Monte Carlo simulation results and sensitivities of the three deal scenarios. For instance, Figure 5 shows the simulation results of the historical deal, followed by its sensitivity analysis in Figure 6. In contrast, Figure 7 shows the simulation results of the HVLR deal scenario, followed by its sensitivity analysis in Figure 8. Finally, Figure 9 shows the HVHR deal scenario, followed by its sensitivity analysis in Figure 10.

Figure 6 shows a tornado chart of historical deal assumptions and decision variables. The probability of IND filing had the largest influence on variation of total deal present value, as all milestones and royalties are dependent on this variable. Interestingly, next came the annual research cost for each full-time equivalent (FTE) for the licensor performing the remaining preclinical work in preparation for an IND filing, followed by the negotiated funding amount of each FTE (Figure 6). Thus, an area for the licensor to create shareholder value is to overestimate R&D costs in negotiating the financial terms for the deal, considering

19

R&D/licensing funding contributed 50.42 percent of total deal present value (Figure 2). Variables impacting royalty cash flows, such as the royalty discount rate and manufacturing and marketing offset percentages, were more important than the negotiated milestone amounts, although the milestone discount rate was 10th in contribution to variance to the historical deal (Figure 6).

Higher-Value, Lower-Risk (HVLR) Deal Valuation

Changes in Key Assumptions and Parameters Differing from the Historical, Signed Deal

The financial structure for the HVLR deal scenario was considerably different from the historical deal (Table 1). Indeed, R&D and licensing funding were significantly increased and the milestone schedule was reorganized with five payments instead of the three in the historical deal. In the HVLR scenario, the value of each individual milestone was stochastically optimized using individual restrictions for each payment. While the future value of the milestone payments was actually $300,000 less than the historical deal (Table 1), the present value as determined by Monte Carlo analysis was 93.6 percent higher. In devising this scenario, to compensate the licensee for increased R&D/licensing fees and milestone restructuring, the royalty value in the HVLR scenario was reduced to only a 0.5 percent flat rate (Table 1).

Deal Valuation, Statistics, and Sensitivities

Figure 7 shows the Monte Carlo summary of the HVLR scenario, and Figure 3 shows an illustration of present value of the HVLR deal and its three components. The Monte Carlo mean deal value for this scenario was $2,092,617, an increase of 46.1 percent over the historical deal, while total risk was reduced by 16.3% as measured by changes in the coefficient of variation (CV) of cash flow present value (Figures 5 and 7). This gain in total deal value was achieved by a 93.6 percent increase in the present value of milestone payments (Figure 2 and 7.3) along with a 9.6 percent reduction in milestone risk (data not shown). The present value of R&D/licensing funding also increased (30.1 percent) while there is a 22.5 percent reduction in risk. These gains came at the cost of royalty income being reduced by 75.1 percent (Figures 2 and 3).

The royalty component was so small and the mean so tightly concentrated, that the other distributions were comparatively distorted (Panel A, Figure 3). If the royalty component is removed, the total deal, milestone, and R&D/licensing distributions are more clearly presented (Panel B, Figure 3). The milestone percentage of the total HVLR scenario was much higher than the milestone component of the historical deal, while the R&D/licensing fees of the HVLR structure were less than the historical structure (Figures 2 and 4).

Cumulatively, the HVLR scenario had a 16.9 percent reduction in risk in comparison to the historical deal (Figures 5 and 7), where the R&D/licensing and milestone cash flows of HVLR structure were considerably less risky than the historical scenario (data not shown). However, not surprisingly, the risk for the royalty cash flows of the HVLR structure remained nearly identical to that of the historical deal's royalties (data not shown).

Monte Carlo Assumption and Decision Variable Sensitivities

The tornado chart for the HVLR deal is presented in Figure 8. As with the historical deal, the probability of IND filing produced the largest variation in the HVLR deal. The annual research cost for each FTE for the licensor performing the remaining preclinical work in preparation for IND filing was third while the negotiated annual funding amount for each FTE was fourth. The value of each milestone was listed earlier in importance in comparison to the historical deal (Figures 6 and 8). This result should not be surprising as the present value of total milestones increased 93.6 result over the historical structure.

The figures illustrate the Monte Carlo distributions for cash-flow present value of the HVLR deal scenario along with the distributions of the deal's individual components. Because the royalty cash flows greatly distort the other distributions (Panel A), removing the royalties from the overlay chart allows the other distributions to be more clearly presented (Panel B). The data in Panel B is comparable to a similar representation of the historical deal (Figure 2). Here, proportionally, milestones contributed the most to deal value (53.56 percent), followed by R&D/licensing (44.88 percent), while royalties contributed very little (1.56 percent; Panel A).

The probabilities of completing various clinical trial stages were not clustered as with the historical deal (Figures 6 and 8). Indeed, the probability of completing Phase 1 was Second, the probability of Phase 2 completion 5th, and the probability of Phase 3 completion 10th in predicting variation in total HVLR deal value (Figure 8), whereas in the historical deal, these three variables were clustered and ranked 4th through 6th (Figure 6). This reorganization is probably because of milestone restructuring where, in the HVLR deal structure; early milestone payments are worth much more (Table 1 and Figure 1). Among the top 20 most important variables inducing variation in the HVLR deal, are the lengths of Phase 1, Phase 2, and Phase 3 clinical trials (13th-15th; Figure 8), although their importance was considerably less than the historical deal (Figure 6). This is probably because of the reduced royalty component of the HVLR scenario (Table 1).

Higher-Value, Higher-Risk (HVHR) Deal Valuation

Changes in Key Assumptions and Parameters Differing from the Historical and HVLR Deal Structures

A variety of financial terms were changed for the HVHR deal structure. First, licensing and licensing maintenance fees were reduced, sometimes substantially (Table 1). R&D fees were reduced across the board from the historical deal and the milestone schedule was completely restructured. The historical structure had three payments, the HVLR structure five, with the HVHR deal having only four (Figure 1). As shown, the milestone future value for the HVHR deal was reduced to $5,850,000 from $6,000,000 in the historical deal. Like the HVLR deal, the milestone values for the HVHR scenario were stochastically optimized based on specific ranges. The sacrifices gained by lower licensing fees, R&D funding, and milestone restructuring were compensated for by a higher flat royalty rate of 5.5 percent of net sales (Table 1).

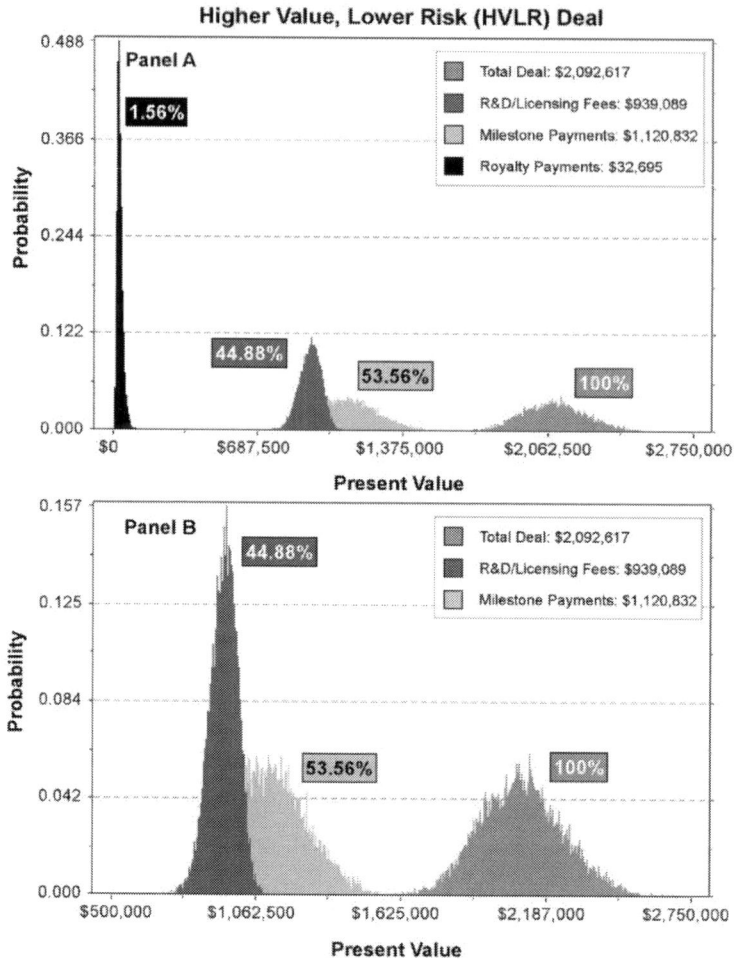

Figure 3: A Comparative Illustration II

Deal Valuation, Statistics, and Sensitivities

Figure 4 shows an illustration of the total HVHR deal along with its three components. Total deal value for the HVHR scenario was $1,739,028, a 21.4 percent increase from the historical deal and 16.9 percent decrease from the HVLR structure. R&D/licensing present value decreased by 44.7 percent and 57.4 percent from the historical and HVLR deals, respectively (Figures 2–4).

The royalty distribution is much more pronounced and noticeably positively skewed, and illustrates the large downside potential of this deal component. Changes in the royalty percentage also significantly expanded the range maximum for the total deal ($3,462,679) with a range width of $2,402,076, a 130.4 percent increase from the historical and 84.6 percent increase over the HVLR deal widths respectively (Table 2).

Milestone present value increased by 69.1 percent from the historical deal and decreased 12.6 percent from the HVLR scenario, while royalty present value increased 175 percent and 1,002% percent respectively (Figures 2–4). Both the skewness and kurtosis of total deal value under the HVHR scenario was greater than the other deal structures evaluated (Figures 2–4).

This result has to do with the greater royalty component in the HVHR scenario and its associated large cash-flow volatility.

The overall deal risk under the HVHR scenario was the greatest (14.33 percent) in comparison to the historical deal's 9.38 percent and the HVLR scenario's 7.85 percent cash-flow CV, again illustrating the strong royalty component of this deal structure with its greater volatility. With the HVHR deal, R&D/licensing cash flows had much higher risk than either the historical or HVLR deals (data not shown). This increased risk is surely because negotiated R&D funding per FTE and licensing fees were considerably less than the estimated cost per FTE, resulting in more R&D/licensing cash-flow volatility in the HVHR structure. This result again shows the importance of accurate accounting and finance in estimating R&D costs for maximizing this type of licensing deal value.

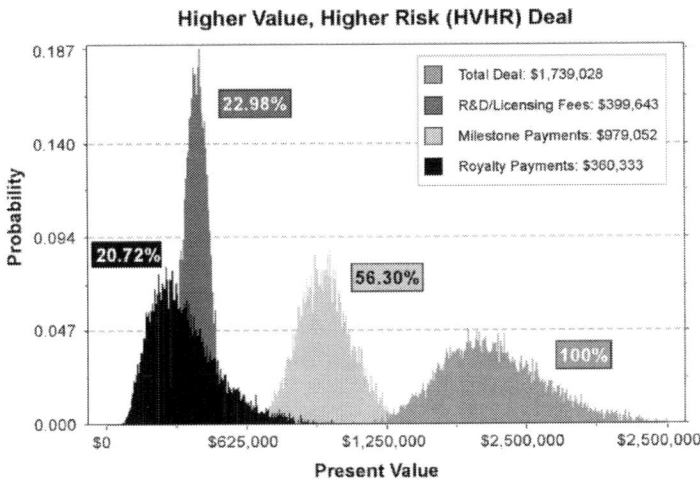

Figure 4: A Comparative Illustration III

Figure 4 illustrates the Monte Carlo distributions for cash-flow present value of the HVLR deal scenario along with the distributions of the deal's individual components. Here, proportionally, milestones contributed the most to deal value (56.30 percent), followed by R&D/licensing (22.98 percent), while royalties contributed 20.72 percent to total deal value.

Monte Carlo Assumption and Decision Variable Sensitivities

The tornado chart for the HVHR deal scenario emphasized the importance of variables directly impacting royalty cash flows (Figure 10). Here, the royalty discount rate was 4th, manufacturing and marketing offset 5th, and maximum market share capture 6th in impacting total deal present value variation. Total market size and the average APPI were 11th and 12th, respectively. Interestingly, the negotiated royalty percentage was only 19th in contribution to deal variance. Cost per FTE ranked 8th showing this assumption is important in all deal scenarios (Figures 6, 8, and 10). The negotiated first milestone value was the only milestone listed on the sensitivity chart (13th, Figure 10), illustrating the importance of milestone structuring (Table 1 and Figure 1). The first milestone is impacted the least by the time value of money and the probability of completion of each clinical trial stage.

A Structural Comparison of Deal Scenario Returns and Risks

Total deal expected value and risk as measured by the CV of cash flow present value are shown in Table 2. As illustrated here, higher expected value is not necessarily correlated with higher risk, which is contrary to a basic principal in finance where investments of higher risk should always yield higher returns. Thus, these data show why quantitative deal valuation and optimization is critical for *all* companies as higher deal values can be constructed with significantly less risk.

Table 2: Deal Scenario Summary Table as Calculated by Monte Carlo Analysis

Deal Structure	Expected Value	CV	Range Minimum	Range Maximum	Range Width
Historical	$1,432,128	9.38%	$994,954	$2,037,413	$1,042,459
Higher-Value, Lower-Risk	2,092,617	7.85	1,475,620	2,777,047	1,301,427
Higher-Value, Higher-Risk	1,739,028	14.33	1,060,603	3,462,679	2,402,076

Also shown in Table 2 are the range minimums, maximums, and widths of the total deal value distributions as calculated by Monte Carlo analysis for each scenario evaluated. The range minimum is the smallest number and the range maximum the largest number in a distribution, while the range width is the difference between the range minimum and maximum.

Collaborative business deals in the biotechnology and pharmaceutical industries formed during strategic alliances, such as the one described here, are, in fact, risky asset portfolios. As such, the standard deviation of a portfolio of assets is less than the weighted average of the component asset standard deviations. To view the impact of diversification of cash-flow streams with the various deal scenarios evaluated in this case study, the weight of each deal component was determined and the weighted average CV of cash-flow present value calculated for each deal scenario (Table 3). The CV is used as the primary risk measure because of differences in the scale of the cash flows from individual deal components.

Table 3: Deal Component Weights, CVs, Weighted Average CVs and Calculated CVs

Deal Structure	Weights			Coefficient of Variation (CV)				
	$W_{R\&D}$[1]	W_{Mi}[2]	W_{Ry}[3]	R&D[4]	Milestone	Royalty	W. Avg.[5]	Calculated[6]
Historical	50.42%	40.42%	9.17%	7.47%	14.57%	45.70%	13.84%	9.38%
Higher-Value Lower-Risk	44.88	53.56	1.56	5.79	13.18	45.95	10.38	7.85
Higher-Value Higher-Risk	22.98	56.30	20.72	13.40	12.69	46.21	19.80	14.33

[1]Proportion of total deal present value attributable to R&D and licensing fees.
[2]Proportion of total deal present value attributable to milestone payments.
[3]Proportion of total deal present value attributable to royalty payments.
[4]CV in the present value of cash flows from R&D and licensing fees.
[5]Weighted average of the CV of total deal value.
[6]Calculated deal CV by Monte Carlo simulation.

As expected with a portfolio of risky assets, the weighted average of the CV of individual deal components (R&D/licensing funding, milestone payments, and royalties) was always greater than the CV of the total deal present value, illustrating the impact of diversification (Table 3). Thus, portfolios of less than perfectly correlated assets always offer better risk-return opportunities than the individual component assets on their own. As such, companies would probably not want to completely forgo receiving milestone payments and royalties for only R&D funding and licensing fees, *if* these deal components can be valued and optimized with reasonable accuracy as described here. By combining assets whose returns are uncorrelated or partially correlated, such as cash flows from milestone payments, royalties, licensing, and R&D funding, risk is reduced (Table 3). Risk can be eliminated most rapidly while keeping expected returns as high as possible if a company's cumulative deal repertoire is valued, structured, and balanced from the beginning of a company's evolution and development.

Discussion and Conclusion

The historical deal evaluated in this case study was a preclinical, product-licensing deal for a biopharmaceutical with one major therapeutic indication. For collaborative deal structures containing licensing fees, R&D funding, milestone payments, and royalties, each deal component has definable expected values, variances, and widely varying risk characteristics. Alternative deal structures were developed and optimized, all of which had different expected returns and risk levels with the primary risk measure being the CV of cash-flow present value. Thus, nearly any biomedical collaborative deal with the types of financial terms described here can be quantitatively valued, structured, and optimized using financial models, Monte Carlo analysis, stochastic optimization, real options, and portfolio theory.

During this study, the author was at a considerable disadvantage because the historical deal valued and optimized here had already been signed, and he was not present during the negotiation process. Therefore, the author had to make a large number of assumptions when restructuring the financial terms of the agreement. Considering these limitations, this case is not about what is appropriate in the comparative financial terms for a biomedical licensing deal and what is not; rather the data described here is valuable in showing the quantitative influence of different deal structures on the overall valuation of a biomedical collaborative agreement, and most importantly on the level of overall deal risk, as well as the risk of the individual deal components. The most effective approach using this technique is to work with a negotiator during the development, due diligence, and through the closing process of a collaborative agreement. During this time, data should be continually gathered and the financial models refined as negotiations and due diligence proceeds.

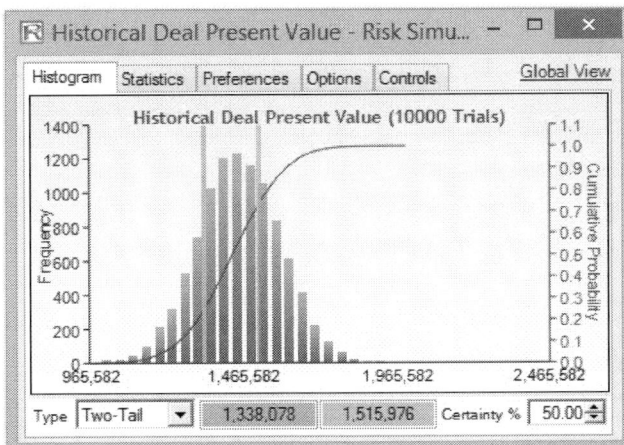

Certainty is 50.00% from $1,338,078 and $1,515,976

Summary Simulation Statistics

Trials	10,000
Mean	$1,432,128
Median	$1,422,229
Standard Deviation	$134,449
Skewness	0.46
Kurtosis	0.47
Coefficient of Variability	9.38%
Minimum	$994,954
Maximum	$2,037,413
Width Range	$1,042,459

Figure 5: Historical Deal Scenario Monte Carlo Summary

Historical Deal Present Value

	$1,200,000	$1,300,000	$1,400,000	$1,500,000	$1,600,000

Monte Carlo & Decision Variable

Variable	Downside	Upside
1. Probability of IND Filling	74.1%	95.9%
2. Costs Per FTE	$226,146	$175,126
3. Funding Per FTE	$230,000	$270,000
4. Probability of Phase 1 Completion	75.0%	97.0%
5. Probability of Phase 2 Completion	48.0%	62.0%
6. Probability of Phase 3 Completion	65.4%	84.6%
7. Licensing Fee Per Year	$92,000	$108,000
8. Probability of NDA Approval	74.1%	95.9%
9. Royalty Discount Rate	24.5%	20.5%
10. Milestone Discount Rate	17.7%	15.3%
11. Manufacturing & Marketing Offset	65.6%	50.8%
12. Maximum Market Share	15.2%	25.3%
13. Phase 3 Length (Mths)	43.99	34.06
14. Milestone 1 Value	$460,000	$540,000
15. Months to IND Filing	27.00	23.00
16. Market Size	$875,629,995	$1,130,727,608
17. Phase 2 Length (Mths)	27.14	21.02
18. APPI[1]	5.06%	6.54%
19. Milestone 3 Value	$3,680,000	$4,320,000
20. Average Annual Inflation Rate	2.20%	1.70%

Downside / Upside

[1]Average Annual Pharmaceutical Price Increase

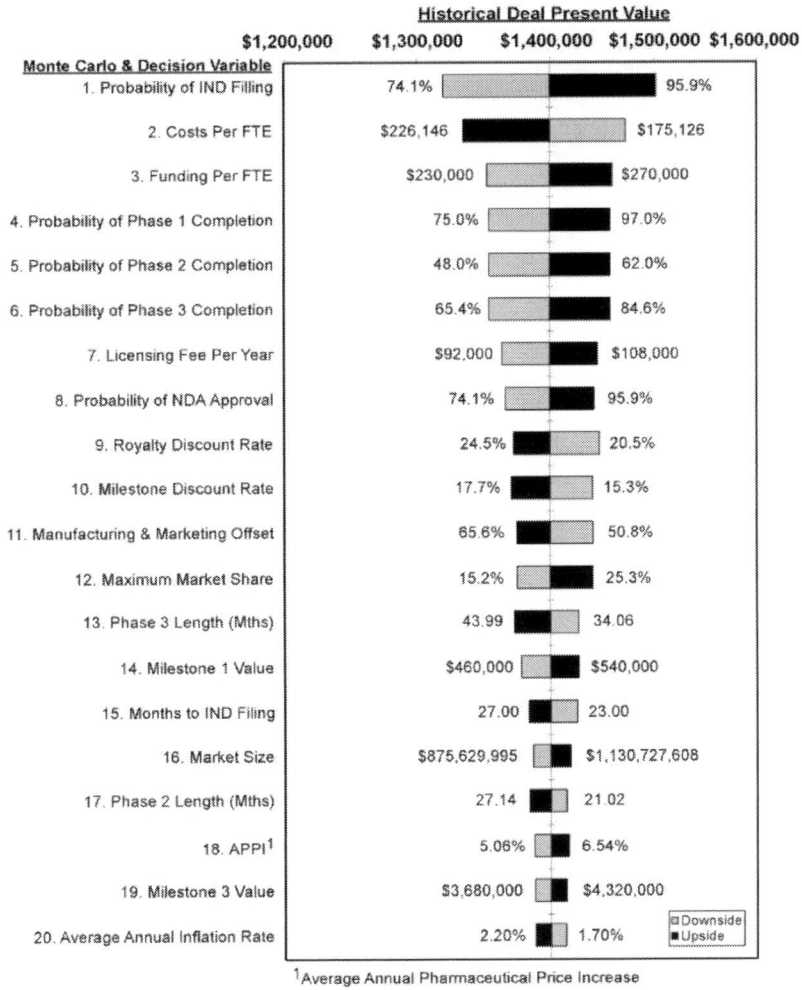

Figure 6: Historical Deal Monte Carlo and Decision Variable Tornado Chart

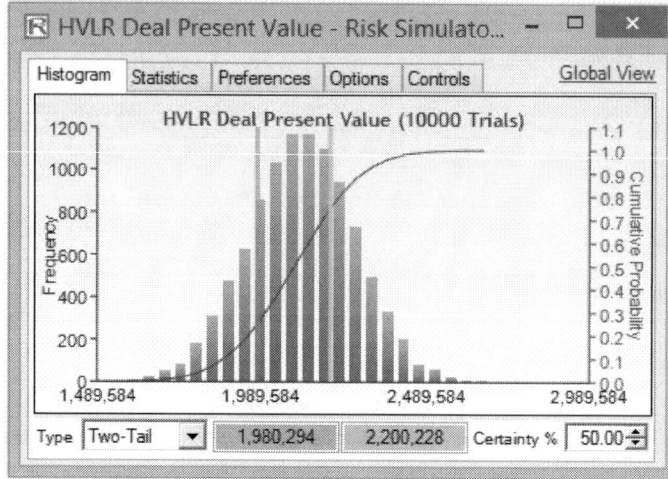

Certainty is 50.00% from $1,980,294 and $2,200,228

Summary Simulation Statistics

Trials	10,000
Mean	$2,092,617
Median	$2,087,697
Standard Deviation	$164,274
Skewness	0.18
Kurtosis	0.06
Coefficient of Variability	7.85%
Minimum	$1,475,620
Maximum	$2,777,047
Width Range	$1,301,427

Figure 7: Higher-Value, Lower-Risk (HVLR) Deal Scenario Monte Carlo

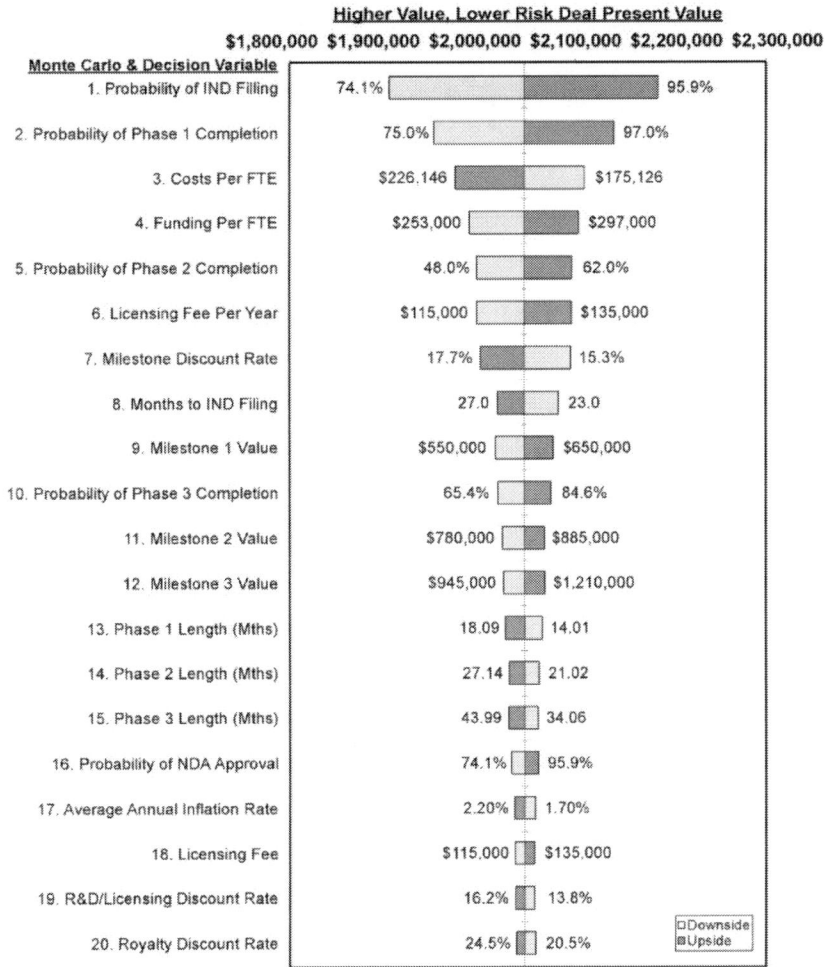

Figure 8: Higher-Value, Lower-Risk (HVLR) Deal Scenario Monte Carlo Tornado

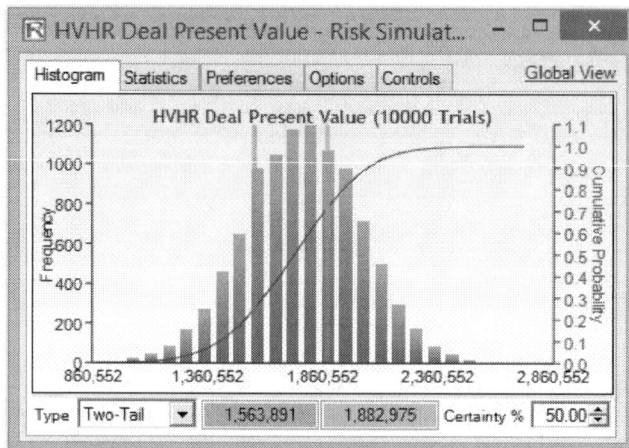

Certainty is 50.00% from $1,563,891 and $1,882,975

Summary Simulation Statistics

Trials	10,000
Mean	$1,739,028
Median	$1,712,532
Standard Deviation	$249,257
Skewness	0.77
Kurtosis	1.39
Coefficient of Variability	14.33%
Minimum	$1,060,603
Maximum	$3,462,679
Width Range	$2,402,076

Figure 9: Higher-Value, Higher-Risk (HVHR) Deal Scenario Monte Carlo Summary

Higher Value, Higher Risk Deal Present Value

Monte Carlo & Decision Variable	$1,400,000	$1,600,000	$1,800,000	$2,000,000
1. Probability of IND Filling	74.1%		95.9%	
2. Probability of Phase 1 Completion	75.0%		97.0%	
3. Probability of Phase 2 Completion	48.0%		62.0%	
4. Royalty Discount Rate	24.5%		20.5%	
5. Manufacturing & Marketing Offset	65.6%		50.8%	
6. Maximum Market Share	15.2%		25.3%	
7. Probability of Phase 3 Completion	65.4%		84.6%	
8. Costs Per FTE	$226,146		$175,126	
9. Probability of NDA Approval	74.1%		95.9%	
10. Milestone Discount Rate	17.7%		15.3%	
11. Market Size	$875,629,995		$1,130,727,608	
12. APPI[1]	5.06%		6.54%	
13. Milestone 1 Value	$760,000		$890,000	
14. Phase 3 Length (Mths)	43.99		34.06	
15. Funding Per FTE	$151,800		$178,200	
16. Licensing Fee Per Year	$78,200		$91,800	
17. Months to IND Filing	27.00		23.00	
18. Phase 2 Length (Mths)	27.14		21.02	
19. Royalty Percentage (%)	5.1%		6.0%	
20. Average Annual Inflation Rate	2.20%		1.70%	

Downside
Upside

[1]Average Annual Pharmaceutical Price Increase

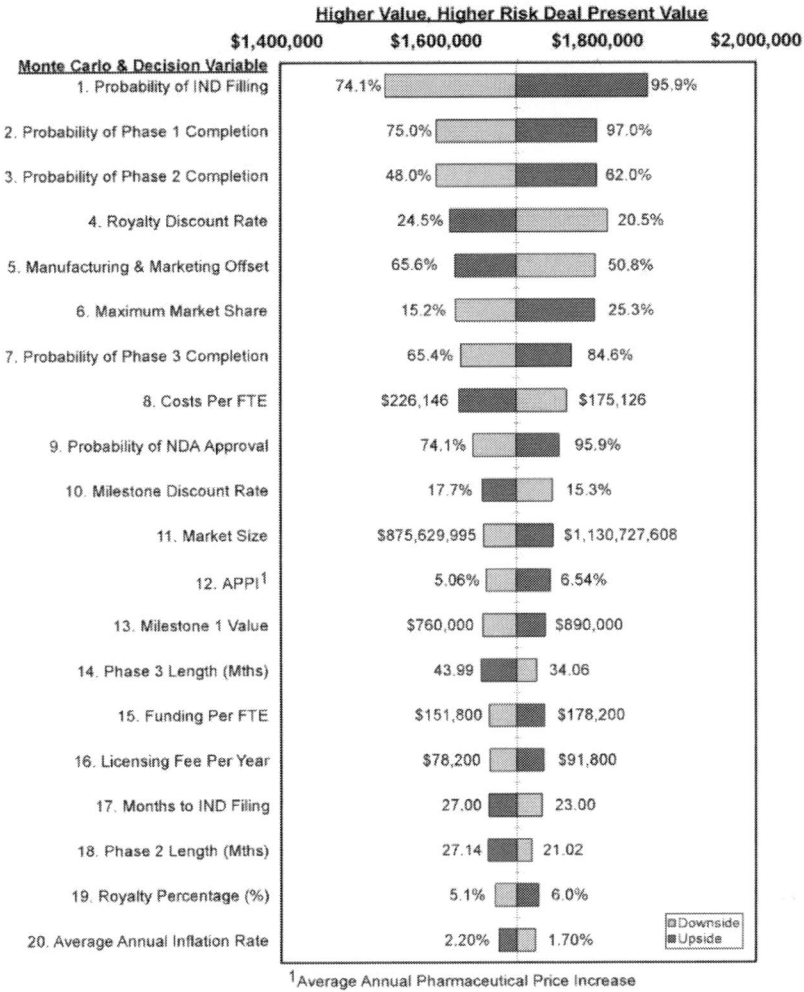

Figure 10: Higher-Value, Higher-Risk (HVHR) Deal Scenario Monte Carlo Tornado

CASE STUDY 2: OIL AND GAS EXPLORATION AND PRODUCTION

This case study is contributed by Steve Hoye. Steve is an independent business consultant with more than 23 years of oil and gas industry experience, specializing in Monte Carlo simulation for the oil and gas industry. Starting with a Bachelor of Science degree from Purdue University in 1980, he served as a geophysicist with Texaco in Houston, Denver, and Midland, Texas, before earning an MBA degree from the University of Denver in 1997. Since then, Steve has held leadership roles with Texaco as the mid-continent BU technology team leader, and as asset team manager in Texaco's Permian Basin business, before starting his consultancy.

The oil and gas industry is an excellent place to examine and discuss techniques for analyzing risk. The basic business model discussed involves making investments in land rights, geologic data, drilling (services and hardware), and human expertise in return for a stream of oil or gas production that can be sold at a profit. This model is beset with multiple, significant risk factors that determine the resulting project's profitability, including:

- *Dry-Hole Risk*—Investing drilling dollars with no resulting revenue from oil or gas because none is found in the penetrated geologic formation.

- *Drilling Risk*—High drilling costs can often ruin a project's profitability. Although companies do their best to estimate them accurately, unforeseeable geological and/or mechanical difficulties can cause significant variability in actual costs.

- *Production Risk*—Even when oil or gas reservoirs are discovered by drilling, there is a high probability that point estimates of the size and recoverability of the hydrocarbon reserves over time are wrong.

- *Price Risk*—Along with the cyclical nature of the oil & gas industry, product prices can also vary unexpectedly during significant political events such as war in the Middle East, overproduction and cheating by the OPEC cartel, interruptions in supply such as large refinery fires, labor strikes or political uprisings in large producing nations (e.g., Venezuela in 2002), and changes in world demand.

- *Political Risk*—Significant amounts of the world's hydrocarbon reserves lie in nations with unstable governments. Companies who invest in projects in these countries take significant risks that the governments and leaders with whom they have signed contracts will no longer be in power when earned revenue streams should be shared contractually. In many well-documented cases, corporate investments in property, plants, and equipment (PPE) are simply nationalized by local governments, leaving companies without revenue or the equipment and facilities that they built to earn that revenue.

Oil and gas investments generally are very capital-intensive, often making these risks more than just of passing interest. Business units and entire companies stake their survival on their ability to properly account for these risks as they apportion their capital budgets in a manner that ensures value to their stakeholders. To underline the importance of risk management in the industry, many large oil companies commission high-level corporate panels of experts to review and endorse risk assessments done across all of their business units for large capital projects. These reviews attempt to ensure consistency of risk assessment across departments and divisions that are often under pressure to make their investment portfolios look attractive to corporate leadership as they compete for capital.

Monte Carlo simulation is a preferred approach to the evaluation of the multiple, complex risk factors in the model we discuss. Because of the inherent complexity of these risk factors and their interactions, deterministic solutions are not practical, and point forecasts are of limited use and, at worst, are misleading. In contrast, Monte Carlo simulation is ideal for economic evaluations under these circumstances. Domain experts can individually quantify and describe the project risks associated with their areas of expertise without having to define their overall effect on project economics.[26] Cash-flow models that integrate the diverse risk assumptions for each of the prospect team's experts are relatively straightforward to construct and analyze. Most importantly, the resulting predictions of performance do not result in a simple single-point estimate of the profitability of a given oil and gas prospect. Instead, they provide management with a spectrum of possible outcomes and their related probabilities. Best of all, Monte Carlo simulation provides estimates of the sensitivities of their investment outcomes to the critical assumptions in their models, allowing them to focus money and people on the critical factors that will determine whether they meet the financial goals defined in their business plans. Ultimately, Monte Carlo simulation becomes a project management tool that decreases risk while increasing profits.

In this case study, we explore a practical model of an oil-drilling prospect, taking into account many of the risk factors described earlier. While the model is hypothetical, the general parameters we use are consistent with those encountered drilling in a mature, oil-rich basin in the United States (e.g., Permian Basin of West Texas) in terms of the risk factors and related revenues and expenses. This model is of greater interest as a framework and approach than it is as an evaluation of any particular drilling prospect. Its value is in demonstrating the approach to quantifying important risk assumptions in an oil prospect using Monte Carlo simulation, and analyzing their effects on the profitability forecasts of the project. The techniques described herein are extensible to many other styles and types of oil and gas prospects.

Cash-Flow Model

The model was constructed using Risk Simulator, which provides all of the necessary Monte Carlo simulation tools as an easy-to-use, comprehensive add-in to Microsoft Excel. The model simulates the drilling outcome as being a dry hole or an oil discovery using dry-hole risk factors for the particular geologic formation and basin. Drilling, seismic, and land-lease costs are incurred whether the well is dry or a discovery. If the well is a discovery, a revenue stream is computed for the produced oil over time using assumptions for product price, and for the oil production rate as it declines over time from its initial value. Expenses are deducted for royalty payments to landowners, operating costs associated with producing the oil, and severance taxes levied by states on the produced oil. Finally, the resulting net cash flows are discounted at the weighted average cost of capital (WACC) for the firm and summed to a net present value (NPV) for the project. Each of these sections of the model is now discussed in more detail.

Dry-Hole Risk

Companies often have proprietary schemes for quantifying the risk associated with not finding any oil or gas in their drilled well. In general, though, there are four primary and independent conditions that must all be encountered in order for hydrocarbons to be found by the drill bit:

1. Hydrocarbons must be present.

2. A reservoir must be developed in the rock formation to hold the hydrocarbons.

3. An impermeable seal must be available to trap the hydrocarbons in the reservoir and prevent them from migrating somewhere else.

4. A structure or closure must be present that will cause the hydrocarbons (sealed in the reservoir) to pool in a field where the drill bit will penetrate.

Because these four factors are independent and must each be true in order for hydrocarbons to be encountered by the drill bit (and a dry hole to be avoided), the probability of a producing well is defined as:

$$P_{Producing\ Well} = P_{Hydrocarbons} * P_{Reservoir} * P_{Seal} * P_{Structure}$$

Figure 11 shows the model section labeled "dry-hole risk, "along with the probability distributions for each factor's Monte Carlo assumption. While a project team most often describes each of these factors as a single-point estimate, other methods are sometimes used to quantify these risks. The most effective process the author has witnessed involved the presentation of the geological, geophysical, and engineering factors by the prospect team, to a group of expert peers with wide experience in the proposed area. These peer experts then rated each of the risk factors. The resulting distribution of risk factors often appeared near-normally distributed, with strong central tendencies and symmetrical tails. This approach was very amenable to Monte Carlo simulation. It highlighted those factors where there was general agreement about risk and brought the riskiest factors to the foreground where it was examined and specifically addressed.

Accordingly, the assumptions regarding dry-hole risk in this model reflect a relatively low risk profile.[27] Each of the four risk factor assumptions in Figure 11 (dark shaded area) are described as normally distributed variables, with the mean and standard deviations for each distribution to the right of the assumption fields. The ranges of these normal distributions are confined and truncated between the *min* and *max* fields, and random samples for any simulation trial outside this range are ignored as unrealistic.

Dry-Hole Risk					
Risk Factor	Prob. of Success	Mean	Stdev	Min	Max
Hydrocarbons	89.7%	99.0%	5.0%	0%	100%
Structure	89.7%	100.0%	0.0%	0%	100%
Reservoir	89.7%	75.0%	10.0%	0%	100%
Seal	89.7%	100.0%	0.0%	0%	100%
Net Producing Well Prob.:	64.8%				
Producing Well [0=no,1=yes]	1				

Figure 11: Dry-Hole Risk

As described earlier, the *Net Producing Well Probability* field in the model corresponds to the product of the four previously described risk factors. These four risk factors are drawn as random samples from their respective normal distributions for each trial or iteration of the simulation. Finally, as each iteration of the Monte Carlo simulation is conducted, the field labeled *Producing Well* generates a random number between zero and one to determine if that simulation resulted in a discovery of oil or a dry hole. If the random number is less than the *Net Producing Well Probability*, it is a producing well and shows the number one. Conversely, if the random number is greater than the *Net Producing Well Probability*, the simulated well is a dry hole and shows zero.

Production Risk

A multi-year stream of oil can be characterized as an initial oil production rate (measured in barrels of oil per day, BOPD), followed by a decline in production rates as the natural reservoir energy and volumes are depleted over time. Reservoir engineers can characterize production declines using a wide array of mathematical models, choosing those that most closely match the geology and producing characteristics of the reservoir. Our hypothetical production stream is described with two parameters:

- *IP*—The initial production rate tested from the drilled well.

- *Decline Rate*—An exponentially declining production rate that describes the annual decrease in production from the beginning of the year, to the end of the same year. Production rates in BOPD for our model are calculated by:

Rate (Year End) = (1 − *Decline Rate*) * *Rate(Year Begin)*

Yearly production volumes in Barrels of Oil are approximated as:

Oil Volume (Year) = 365 * (*Rate (Year Begin)* + *Rate (YearEnd)*) / 2

For Monte Carlo simulation, our model represents the IPs with a lognormal distribution with a mean of 441 BOPD, and a standard deviation of 165 BOPD. The decline rate was modeled with a uniform probability of occurrence between 15 percent and 28 percent. To add interest and realism to our hypothetical model, we incorporated an additional constraint in the production model that simulates a situation that might occur for a particular reservoir where higher IPs imply that the production decline rate will be higher. This constraint is implemented in Risk Simulator by imposing a correlation coefficient of 0.60 between the IP and decline rate assumptions that are drawn from their respective distributions during each trial of the simulation.

The production and operating expense sections of the model are shown in Figure 12. Although only the first 3 years are shown, the model accounts for up to 25 years of production. However, when production declines below the economic limit,[28] it will be zeroed for that year and every subsequent year, ending the producing life of the well. As shown, the IP is assumed to occur at the end of Year 0, with the first full year of production accounted for at the end of Year 1.

Revenue Section

Revenues from the model flow literally from the sale of the oil production computed earlier. Again there are two assumptions in our model that represent risks in our prospect:

- *Price*—Over the past two decades, oil prices have varied from $13.63/barrel in 1998 to nearly $30/barrel in 2000.[29] Consistent with the data, our model assumes a normal price distribution with a mean of $20.14 and a standard deviation of $4.43/barrel. For simplicity, we used a normal distribution. Clearly, a geometric Brownian motion stochastic process can be modeled and simulated instead.

- *Net Revenue Interest*—Oil companies must purchase leases from mineral interest holders. Along with paying cash to retain the drilling and production rights to a property for a specified time period, the lessee also generally retains some percentage of the oil revenue produced in the form of a royalty. The percentage that the producing company retains after paying all royalties is the net revenue interest (NRI). Our model represents a typical West Texas scenario with an assumed NRI distributed normally with a mean of 75 percent and a standard deviation of 2 percent.

The revenue portion of the model is also shown in Figure 12 immediately below the production stream. The yearly production volumes are multiplied by sampled price per barrel, and then multiplied by the assumed NRI to reflect dilution of revenues from royalty payments to lessees.

	Decline Rate	End of Year: 0	1	2	3
BOPD	21.5%	442	347	272	214
Net BBLS/Yr.			143,866	112,924	88,636
Price/Bbl.			$20.14	$20.14	$20.14
Net Revenue Interest	77.4%		77.4%	77.4%	77.4%
Revenue			$2,242,311	$1,760,035	$1,381,487
Operating Costs [$/Barrel]	$4.80		$(690,558)	$(542,033)	$(425,453)
Severance Taxes [$]	6.0%	rate	$(134,539)	$(105,602)	$(82,889)
Net Sales			$1,417,214	$1,112,400	$873,145

Figure 12: Decline Rate

Operating Expense Section

Below the revenue portion are operating expenses, which include two assumptions:

- Operating Costs—Companies must pay for manpower and hardware involved in the production process. These expenses are generally described as a dollar amount per barrel. A reasonable West Texas cost would be $4.80 per barrel with a standard deviation of $0.60 per barrel. These can be simulated if desired.

- Severance Taxes—State taxes levied on produced oil and gas are assumed to be a constant value of 6 percent of revenue.

Operating expenses are subtracted from the gross sales to arrive at net sales (Figure 12).

Year 0 Expenses

Figure 13 shows the Year 0 expenses assumed to be incurred before oil production from the well (and revenue) is realized.

Drilling Costs	$ 1,209,632
Completion Cost	$ 287,000
Professional Overhead	$ 160,000
Lease Costs/Well	$ 469,408
Seismic Costs/Well	$ 81,195

Figure 13: Year Zero Expenses

These expenses are:

- Drilling Costs—These costs can vary significantly as previously discussed, due to geologic, engineering, and mechanical uncertainty. It is reasonable to skew the distribution of drilling costs to account for a high-end tail consisting of a small number of wells with very large drilling costs due to mechanical failure and unforeseen geologic or serendipitous occurrences. Accordingly, our distribution is assumed to be lognormal, with a mean of $1.2 million and a standard deviation of $200,000.

- Completion Cost(s)—If it is determined that there is oil present in the reservoir (and we have not drilled a dry hole), engineers must prepare the well (mechanically/chemically) to produce oil at the optimum sustainable rates.[30] For this particular well, we hypothesize our engineers believe this cost is normally distributed with a mean of $287,000 and a standard deviation of $30,000.

- Professional Overhead—This project team costs about $320,000 per year in salary and benefits, and we believe the time they have spent is best represented by a triangular distribution, with a most likely percentage of time spent as 50 percent, with a minimum of 40 percent, and a maximum of 65 percent.

- Seismic and Lease Costs—To develop the proposal, our team needed to purchase seismic data to choose the optimum well location, and to purchase the right to drill on much of the land in the vicinity of the well. Because this well is not the only well to be drilled on this seismic data and land, the cost of these items is distributed over the planned number of wells in the project. Uncertain assumptions are shown in Figure 14, and include leased acres, which were assumed to be normally distributed with a mean of 12,000 and a standard deviation of 1,000 acres. The total number of planned wells over which to distribute the costs was assumed to be uniform between 10 and 30. The number of seismic sections acquired was also assumed to be normally distributed with a mean of 50 sections and a standard deviation of 7. These costs are represented as the final two lines of Year 0 expenses in Figure 13.

Lease Expense		Comments
Project Lease Acres	12,800	20 Sections
Planned Wells	20.0	
Acres/Well	640	
Acreage Price	$733.45	$/Acre
Acreage Cost/Well	$469,408	
Seismic Expense		
Seismic Sections Acquired	50.0	
Seismic Sections/Well	2.50	
Seismic Cost	$32,478.18	$/Section
Seismic Cost/Well	$81,195	

Figure 14: Uncertain Assumptions

Net Present Value Section

The final section of the model sums all revenues and expenses for each year starting at Year 0, discounted at the weighted average cost of capital (WACC—which we assume for this model is 9 percent per year), and summed across years to compute the forecast of NPV for the project. In addition, NPV/I is computed,[31] as it can be used as a threshold and ranking mechanism for portfolio decisions as the company determines how this project fits with its other investment opportunities given a limited capital budget.

Monte Carlo Simulation Results

As we assess the results of running the simulation with the assumptions defined previously, it is useful to define and contrast the point estimate of project value that is computed from our model using the mean or most likely values of the earlier assumptions. The expected value of the project is defined as:

$$E(Project) = E(Dry\ Hole) + E(Producing\ Well)$$

$$E(Project) = P(Dry\ Hole) \times NPV(Dry\ Hole) + P(Producing\ Well) \\ \times NPV(Producing\ Well)$$

$$where\ P(Producing\ Well) = Probability\ of\ Producing\ a\ Well$$

$$and\ P(Dry\ Hole) = Probability\ of\ a\ Dry\ Hole = 1 - P(Producing\ Well)$$

Using the mean or most likely point estimate values from our model, the expected NPV of the project is $1,250,000, which might be a very attractive prospect in the firm's portfolio.

In contrast, we can now examine the spectrum of outcomes and their probability of occurrence. Our simulation was run with 8,450 trials (trial size selected by precision control) to forecast NPV, which provided a mean NPV plus or minus $50,000 with 95 percent confidence. Figure 15 is the frequency distribution of NPV outcomes. The distribution is obviously bimodal, with the large, sharp negative NPV peak to the left representing the outcome of a dry hole. The smaller, broader peak toward the higher NPV ranges represents the wider range of more positive NPVs associated with a producing well.

All negative NPV outcomes are to the left of the $NPV = 0$ line (with a lighter shade) in Figure 15, while positive outcome NPVs are represented by the area to the right of the $NPV = 0$ line (with a darker shade), with the probability of a positive outcome (breakeven or better) shown as 69.33 percent. Of interest, the negative outcome possibilities include not only the dry-hole population of outcomes as shown, but also a small but significant portion of producing-well outcomes that could still lose money for the firm. From this information, we can conclude that there is a 30.67 percent chance that this project will have a negative NPV.

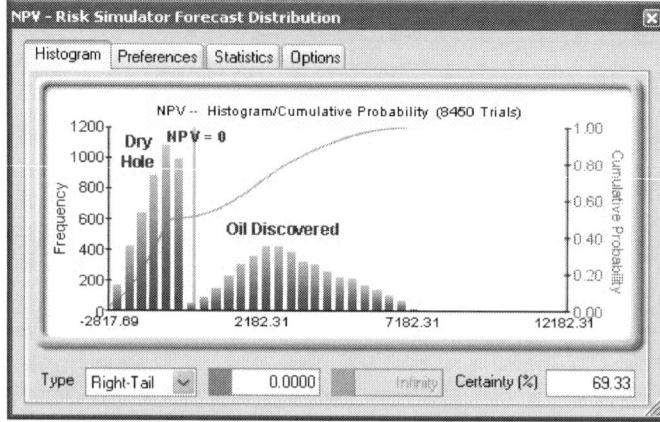

Figure 15: Frequency Distribution of NPV Outcomes

It is obviously not good enough for a project of this sort to avoid a negative NPV. The project must return to shareholders something higher than its cost of capital, and further, must be competitive with other investment opportunities that the firm has. If our hypothetical firm had a hurdle rate of NPV/I greater than 25 percent for its yearly budget, we would want to test our simulated project outcomes against the probability that the project could clear that hurdle rate.

Figure 16 shows the forecast distribution of outcomes for NPV/I. The large peak at negative 100 percent again represents the dry-hole case, where, in fact, the NPV of the outcome is negative in the amount of Year 0 costs incurred, making NPV/I equal to –1. All outcomes for NPV greater than the hurdle rate of 25 percent show that there is a 64 percent probability that the project will exceed that rate. To a risk-sensitive organization, this outcome implies a probability of greater than one in three that the project will fail to clear the firm's hurdle rate, a significant risk indeed.

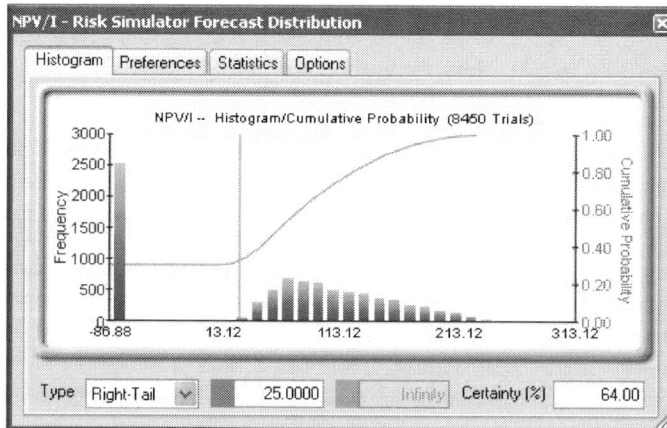

Figure 16: Forecast Distribution of NPV to I Ratio

Finally, our simulation gives us the power to explore the sensitivity of our project outcomes to the risks and assumptions that have been made by our experts in building the model.

Figure 17 shows a sensitivity analysis of the NPV of our project to the assumptions made in our model. This chart shows the correlation coefficient of the top 10 model assumptions to the NPV forecast in order of decreasing correlation.

At this point, the project manager is empowered to focus resources on the issues that will have an impact on the profitability of this project. Given the information from Figure 17, we could hypothesize the following actions to address the top risks in this project in order of importance:

- *IP*—The initial production rate of the well has a driving influence on value of this project, and our uncertainty in predicting this rate is causing the largest swing in predicted project outcomes. Accordingly, we could have our team of reservoir and production engineers further examine known production IPs from analogous reservoirs in this area, and perhaps attempt to stratify the data to further refine predictions of IPs based on drilling or completion techniques, geological factors, or geophysical data.

- *Reservoir Risk*—This assumption is the driver of whether the well is a dry hole or producer, and as such is not surprising that it is a major driving factor. Among many approaches, the project team could investigate the possibility that inadequate analysis of subsurface data is causing many companies to declare dry holes in reservoirs that have hidden producing potential.

- *Oil Price (Year 1) and Drilling Costs*—Both of these items are closely related in their power to affect NPV. Price uncertainty could best be addressed by having a standard price prediction for the firm against that all projects would be compared.[32] Drilling costs could be minimized by process improvements in the drilling team which would tighten the variation of predicted costs from actual costs. The firm could seek out companies with strong track records in their project area for reliable, low cost drilling.

- *Decline Rate*—The observant reader will note a positive-signed correlation between decline rate and project NPV. At first glance this is unexpected, because we would normally expect that a higher decline rate would reduce the volumes of oil to be sold and hurt the revenue realized by our project. Recall, however, that we correlated higher IPs with higher decline rates in our model assumptions, which is an indirect indication of the power of the IP on the NPV of our project: Despite higher decline rates, the positive impact of higher IPs on our project value is overriding the lost production that occurs because of the rapid reservoir decline. We should redouble our efforts to better predict IPs in our model.

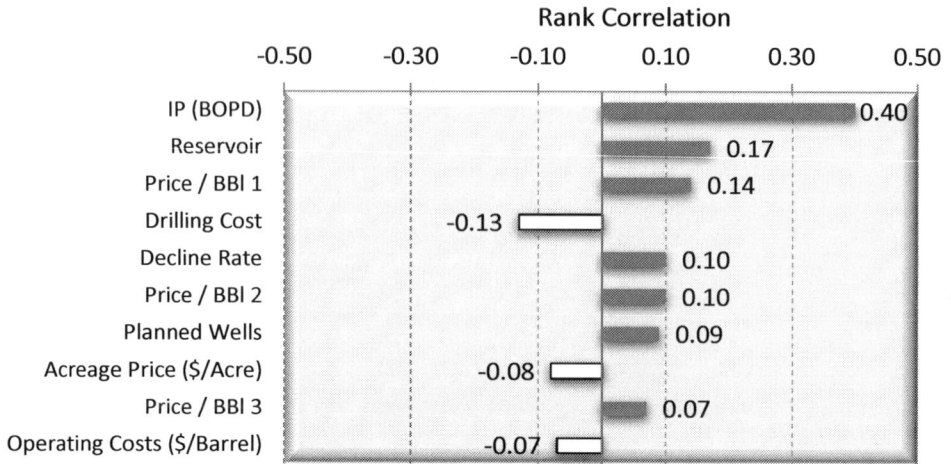

Figure 17: NPV Sensitivity Analysis

Conclusion

Monte Carlo simulation can be an ideal tool for evaluating oil and gas prospects under conditions of significant and complex uncertainty in the assumptions that would render any single-point estimate of the project outcome nearly useless. The technique provides each member of multidisciplinary work teams a straightforward and effective framework for quantifying and accounting for each of the risk factors that will influence the outcome of his or her drilling project. In addition, Monte Carlo simulation provides management and team leadership something much more valuable than a single forecast of the project's NPV: it provides a probability distribution of the entire spectrum of project outcomes, allowing decision makers to explore any pertinent scenarios associated with the project value. These scenarios could include break-even probabilities as well as scenarios associated with extremely poor project results that could damage the project team's credibility and future access to capital, or outcomes that resulted in highly successful outcomes. Finally, Monte Carlo simulation of oil and gas prospects provides managers and team leaders critical information on which risk factors and assumptions are driving the projected probability of project outcomes, giving them the all-important feedback they need to focus their people and financial resources on addressing those risk assumptions that will have the greatest positive impact on their business, improving their efficiency and adding profits to their bottom line.

CASE STUDY 3: FINANCIAL PLANNING WITH SIMULATION

Tony Jurado is a financial planner in northern California. He has a BA from Dartmouth College and is a candidate for the Certified Financial Planner designation. Tony specializes in the design and implementation of comprehensive financial plans for high net-worth individuals.

Corporate America has increasingly altered the retirement landscape by shifting from defined benefit to defined contribution plans. As the baby boomers retire, they will have different financial planning needs than those of previous generations because they must manage their own retirement funds. A thoughtful financial planner has the ability to positively impact the lives of these retirees.

A Deterministic Plan

Today was the last day of work for Henry Tirement and until just now, he and his financial planner, Mr. Determinist, had never seriously discussed what do to with his 401k rollover. After a moment of fact gathering with Henry, Mr. D obtains the following information:

- Current assets are $1,000,000 in various mutual funds

- Current age is 65

- Desired retirement salary is $60,000 before-tax

- Expected return on investments is 10%

- Expected inflation is 3%

- Life expectancy is age 95

- No inheritance considerations

With his financial calculator, Mr. D concludes that Henry can meet his retirement goals and, in fact, if he died at age 95 he'd have over $3.2 million in his portfolio. Mr. D knows that past performance does not guarantee future results, but past performance is all that we have to go by. With the stock market averaging over 10% for the past 75 years, Mr. D feels certain that this return is reasonable. As inflation has averaged 3% over the same time period, he feels that this assumption is also realistic. Mr. D delivers the good news to Henry and the plan is put into motion (Table 4).

Table 4: The Deterministic Plan

Year	Returns	Beginning Balance	Withdrawal	Ending Balance
1	10.00%	$1,000,000.00	$60,000.00	$1,034,000.00
2	10.00%	$1,034,000.00	$61,800.00	$1,069,420.00
3	10.00%	$1,069,420.00	$63,654.00	$1,106,342.60
4	10.00%	$1,106,342.60	$65,563.62	$1,144,856.88
5	10.00%	$1,144,856.88	$67,530.53	$1,185,058.98
6	10.00%	$1,185,058.98	$69,556.44	$1,227,052.79
7	10.00%	$1,227,052.79	$71,643.14	$1,270,950.62
8	10.00%	$1,270,950.62	$73,792.43	$1,316,874.01
9	10.00%	$1,316,874.01	$76,006.20	$1,364,954.58
10	10.00%	$1,364,954.58	$78,286.39	$1,415,335.01
11	10.00%	$1,415,335.01	$80,634.98	$1,468,170.03
12	10.00%	$1,468,170.03	$83,054.03	$1,523,627.60
13	10.00%	$1,523,627.60	$85,545.65	$1,581,890.14
14	10.00%	$1,581,890.14	$88,112.02	$1,643,155.93
15	10.00%	$1,643,155.93	$90,755.38	$1,707,640.60
16	10.00%	$1,707,640.60	$93,478.04	$1,775,578.81
17	10.00%	$1,775,578.81	$96,282.39	$1,847,226.07
18	10.00%	$1,847,226.07	$99,170.86	$1,922,860.73
19	10.00%	$1,922,860.73	$102,145.98	$2,002,786.22
20	10.00%	$2,002,786.22	$105,210.36	$2,087,333.45
21	10.00%	$2,087,333.45	$108,366.67	$2,176,863.45
22	10.00%	$2,176,863.45	$111,617.67	$2,271,770.35
23	10.00%	$2,271,770.35	$114,966.20	$2,372,484.56
24	10.00%	$2,372,484.56	$118,415.19	$2,479,476.31
25	10.00%	$2,479,476.31	$121,967.65	$2,593,259.53
26	10.00%	$2,593,259.53	$125,626.68	$2,714,396.14
27	10.00%	$2,714,396.14	$129,395.48	$2,843,500.73
28	10.00%	$2,843,500.73	$133,277.34	$2,981,245.73
29	10.00%	$2,981,245.73	$137,275.66	$3,128,367.08
30	10.00%	$3,128,367.08	$141,393.93	$3,285,670.46

Fast forward to ten years later. Henry is not so thrilled anymore. He visits the office of Mr. D with his statements in hand and they sit down to discuss the portfolio performance. Writing down the return of each of the past ten years, Mr. D calculates the average performance of Henry's portfolio (Table 5).

"You've averaged 10% per year!" Mr. D tells Henry. Befuddled, Henry scratches his head. He presents his last statement to Mr. D that shows a portfolio balance is $501,490.82. Once again, Mr. D uses his spreadsheet program and obtains the results in Table 6.

Mr. D is not certain what has happened. Henry took out $60,000 at the beginning of each year and increased this amount by 3% annually. The portfolio return averaged 10%. Henry should have over $1.4 million by now.

Table 5: The Actual Results

Year	Return
1	-20.00%
2	-10.00%
3	9.00%
4	8.00%
5	12.00%
6	-10.00%
7	-2.00%
8	25.00%
9	27.00%
10	61.00%
Average Return	10.00%

Table 6: Portfolio Balance Analysis

Year	Returns	Withdrawal	Ending Balance
1	-20.00%	$60,000.00	$752,000.00
2	-10.00%	$61,800.00	$621,180.00
3	9.00%	$63,654.00	$607,703.34
4	8.00%	$65,563.62	$585,510.90
5	12.00%	$67,530.53	$580,138.01
6	-10.00%	$69,556.44	$459,523.41
7	-2.00%	$71,643.14	$380,122.67
8	25.00%	$73,792.43	$382,912.80
9	27.00%	$76,006.20	$389,771.37
10	61.00%	$78,286.39	$501,490.82

Sequence of Returns

Sitting in his office later that night, Mr. D thinks hard about what went wrong in the planning. He wonders what would have happened if the annual returns had occurred in reverse order (Table 7).

Table 7: Reversed Returns

Year	Return	Withdrawal	Ending Balance
1	61.00%	$60,000.00	$1,513,400.00
2	27.00%	$61,800.00	$1,843,532.00
3	25.00%	$63,654.00	$2,224,847.50
4	-2.00%	$65,563.62	$2,116,098.20
5	-10.00%	$67,530.53	$1,843,710.91
6	12.00%	$69,556.44	$1,987,053.00
7	8.00%	$71,643.14	$2,068,642.65
8	9.00%	$73,792.43	$2,174,386.74
9	-10.00%	$76,006.20	$1,888,542.48
10	-20.00%	$78,286.39	$1,448,204.87

The average return is still 10% and the withdrawal rate has not changed, but the portfolio ending balance is now $1.4 million. The only difference between the two situations is the sequence of returns. Enlightenment overcomes Mr. D, and he realizes that he has been employing a deterministic planning paradigm during a period of withdrawals.

Withdrawals versus No Withdrawals

Most financial planners understand the story of Henry. The important point of Henry's situation is that he took withdrawals from his portfolio during an unfortunate sequence of returns. During a period of regular withdrawals, it doesn't matter that his portfolio returns averaged 10% over the long run. It is the sequence of returns combined with regular withdrawals that was devastating to his portfolio. To illustrate this point, imagine that Henry never took withdrawals from his portfolio (Table 8).

Table 8: Returns Analysis Without Withdrawals

Actual return sequence with no withdrawals

Year	Return	Ending Balance
1	-20.00%	$800,000.00
2	-10.00%	$720,000.00
3	9.00%	$784,800.00
4	8.00%	$847,584.00
5	12.00%	$949,294.08
6	-10.00%	$854,364.67
7	-2.00%	$837,277.38
8	25.00%	$1,046,596.72
9	27.00%	$1,329,177.84
10	61.00%	$2,139,976.32
Average Return	10.00%	

Reverse return sequence with no withdrawals

Year	Return	End Balance
1	61.00%	$1,610,000.00
2	27.00%	$2,044,700.00
3	25.00%	$2,555,875.00
4	-2.00%	$2,504,757.50
5	-10.00%	$2,254,281.75
6	12.00%	$2,524,795.56
7	8.00%	$2,726,779.20
8	9.00%	$2,972,189.33
9	-10.00%	$2,674,970.40
10	-20.00%	$2,139,976.32
Average Return	10.00%	

The time value of money comes into play when withdrawals are taken. When Henry experienced negative returns early in retirement while taking withdrawals, he had less money in his portfolio to grow over time. To maintain his inflation-adjusted withdrawal rate, Henry needed a bull market at the beginning of retirement.

Henry's retirement plan is deterministic because it assumes that returns will be the same each and every year. What Henry and Mr. D didn't understand was that averaging 10% over time is very different than getting 10% each and every year. As Henry left the office, Mr. D wished he had a more dynamic retirement planning process; one that allowed for varying variables.

Stochastic Planning Using Monte Carlo Simulation

Monte Carlo is a stochastic tool that helps people think in terms of probability and not certainty. As opposed to using a deterministic process, financial planners can use Monte Carlo to simulate risk in investment returns. A financial plan's probability of success can be tested by simulating the variability of investment returns. Typically, to measure this variability, the expected mean and standard deviation of the portfolio's investment returns are used in a Monte Carlo model. What would Mr. D have told Henry had this approach been used? Using Henry's same information but an expected return of 10% with a standard deviation of 17.5%, Mr. D can assign success probabilities for how long Henry's money will last. Henry has a 64% chance that his portfolio will last 30 years (Figure 18). If Henry is not comfortable with that success rate, then Mr. D can increase both expected return and standard deviation, or decrease withdrawals. Mr. D could change the return to 20%, but this is obviously not realistic. In Henry's case, it makes more sense to decrease the withdrawal rate. Assuming that Henry will be comfortable with a 70% chance of success, then Mr. D needs to lower the annual withdrawal to $55,000 (Figure 19).

Expenses Lower Returns

It is truly a misuse of Monte Carlo and unfair to the client to illustrate a plan without fees if an advisory fee is to be charged. If Mr. Determinist charges Henry a 1% advisory fee, then this figure must be deducted from the annual return assumption, which will lower the plan's 30-year success probability to 54%. In Henry's case, the standard deviation will still be 17.5%, which is higher than a standard deviation of a portfolio that averages 9%. One can simply modify the Monte Carlo simulation to allow an advisory fee to be included by maintaining the return and standard deviation assumptions and deducting the advisory fee. For Henry's plan to still have a 70% success ratio after a 1% fee, he can withdraw an inflation-adjusted $47,000 annually, which is notably different from the $55,000 withdrawal rate before fees.

Success Probability

Monte Carlo educates the client about the trade-off between risk and return with respect to withdrawals. The risk is the success probability with which the client is comfortable. The return is the withdrawal rate. The financial planner should understand that a higher success rate amounts to lower withdrawals. A by-product of this understanding is that a higher success rate also increases the chance of leaving money in the portfolio upon the client's death. In other words, Henry may be sacrificing lifestyle for an excessive probability of success.

For Henry to have a 90% chance that his portfolio will last 30 years, he needs to lower his withdrawals to $32,000 (Figure 20). An equally important interpretation of this result is that Henry has a 90% chance of dying with money in his portfolio. This is money he could have used for vacation, fancy dinners, gifts for his family, or circus tickets.

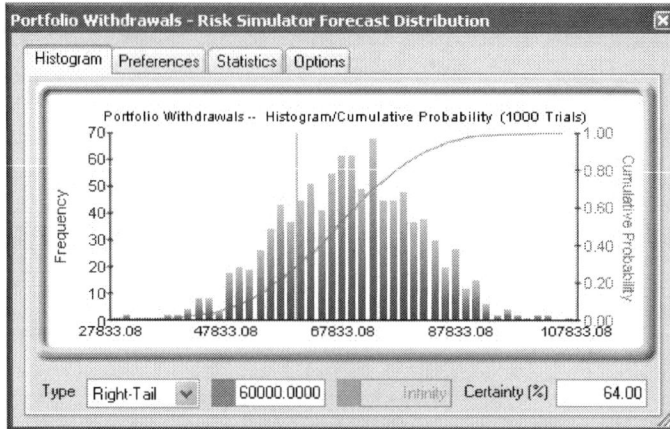

Figure 18: 64% Chance of Portfolio Survival at $60,000 Withdrawals

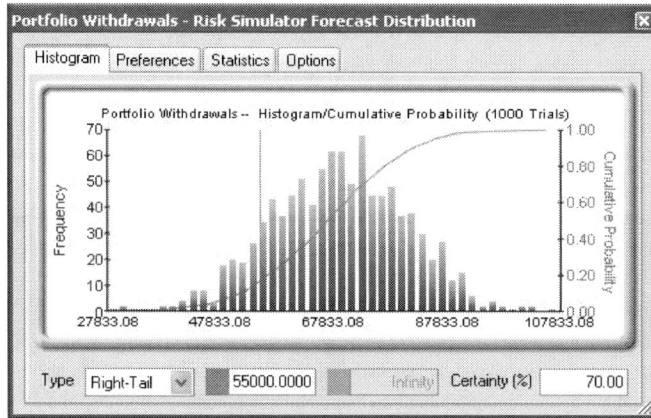

Figure 19: 70% Chance of Portfolio Survival at $55,000 Withdrawals

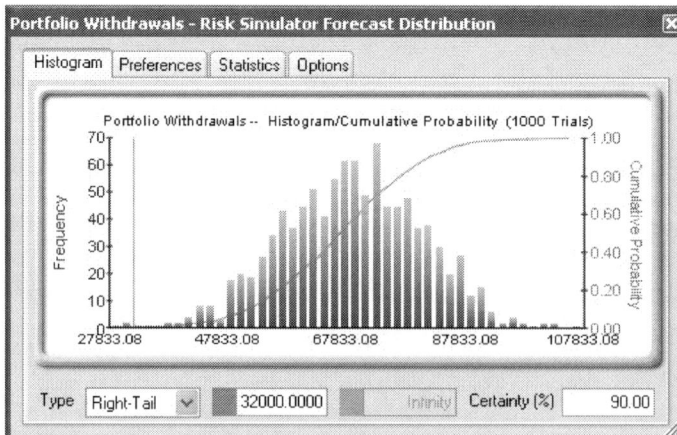

Figure 20: 90% Chance of Portfolio Survival at $32,000 Withdrawals

Success Tolerance

Going back to Henry's example of withdrawing $47,000 each year, if 5,000 simulation trials are run, a 70% success rate means that 3,500 times the plan worked. The 1,500 times the plan failed resulted in a withdrawal amount marginally less than $47,000. What is unclear about the 1,500 failures is how many of these resulted in Henry only being able to withdraw $46,000 each year. If Henry takes out $47,000 for 29 years and then only withdraws $46,000 in the last year, is this a failure? Monte Carlo says yes. Most people are more flexible.

Establishing a success tolerance alleviates this problem. If Henry's goal is to take out $47,000, but he would be quite happy with $42,000, then he has a success tolerance of $5,000. This is the same as running a simulation using $42,000 with a zero success tolerance; however, the purpose of the success tolerance is to clearly illustrate to Henry the likelihood that a range of withdrawals will be achieved. By accounting for both the complexities of the market and the flexibility of human response to those complexities, Monte Carlo helps Henry understand, prepare for, and properly choose his risk tolerance.

Bear Markets and Monte Carlo

No matter what financial planning method is used, the reality is that a bear market early in retirement will drastically affect the plan. If Mr. D had used Monte Carlo when Henry first came to him and Henry took out $47,000 in Year 1 and $48,410 in Year 2, the portfolio balance at the end of the second year would be $642,591. For the portfolio to last another 28 years and to preserve a 70% success rate, Henry must reduce his withdrawal amount to $31,500! The difficulty of this situation is obvious; however, Mr. D is in a position to help Henry make a decision about maintaining his standard of living versus increasing the chances of running out of money.

Table 9 illustrates running a Monte Carlo simulation at the end of each year to determine the withdrawal amount that preserves a 70% success rate for Henry's plan.

Table 9: Simulation-based Withdrawal Rates

Year	Return	Beg Balance	End Balance	Monte Carlo Withdrawal	Withdrawal Change	Remaining Years
1	-20.00%	$1,000,000	$762,400	$47,000	0%	29
2	-10.00%	$762,400	$653,310	$36,500	-22%	28
3	9.00%	$653,310	$676,683	$32,500	-11%	27
4	8.00%	$676,683	$693,558	$34,500	6%	26
5	12.00%	$693,558	$735,904	$36,500	6%	25
6	-10.00%	$735,904	$627,214	$39,000	7%	24
7	-2.00%	$627,214	$580,860	$34,500	-12%	23
8	25.00%	$580,860	$685,137	$32,750	-5%	22
9	27.00%	$685,137	$819,324	$40,000	22%	21
10	61.00%	$819,324	$1,239,014	$49,750	24%	20

Henry, like most people, will not be enthusiastic about lowering his retirement salary by as much as 22% in any year. Without changing the return assumption, Henry's alternative is to accept a lower success rate. If Henry never adjusted his withdrawal rate from the initial $47,000, after 10 years his portfolio value would be $856,496 and his withdrawal would be $61,324 ($47,000 x 1.03 ^{9}). The success probability is 60% for a portfolio life of 20 years.

Other Monte Carlo Variables

Monte Carlo can simulate more than just investment returns. Other variables that are frequently simulated by financial planners using Monte Carlo include inflation and life expectancy.

Inflation

Since 1926, inflation has averaged approximately 3% annually with a standard deviation of 4.3%. In a plan with inflation-adjusted withdrawals, the change in inflation is significant. According to Ibbotson and Associates, inflation averaged 8.7% from the beginning of 1973 until the end of 1982. If such a period of inflation occurred at the beginning of retirement, the effects on a financial plan would be terrible.

Life Expectancy

Using mortality tables, a financial planner can randomize the life expectancy of any client to provide a more realistic plan. According to the National Center for Health Statistics, the average American born in 2002 has a life expectancy of 77.3 years with a standard deviation of 10. However, financial planners should be more concerned with the specific probability that their client will survive for the duration of the plan.

Monte Carlo Suggestions

Financial plans created using Monte Carlo should not be placed on autopilot. As with most forecasting methods, Monte Carlo is not capable of simulating real-life adjustments that individuals make. As previously discussed, if a portfolio experienced severe negative returns early in retirement, the retiree can change the withdrawal amount. It is also important to realize that Monte Carlo plans are only as good as the input assumptions.

Distributions

If Henry is invested in various asset classes, it is important for Mr. D to determine the distinct distribution characteristics of each asset class. The most effective approach to modeling these differences is by utilizing a distribution fitting analysis in Risk Simulator.

Taxes

Henry Tirement's situation involved a tax-deferred account and a pre-tax salary. For individuals with nontaxable accounts, rebalancing may cause taxes. In this case, a financial planner using Monte Carlo might employ a tax-adjusted return and a post-tax salary might be used. The after-tax account balance should be used in the assumptions for clients with highly concentrated positions and a low tax basis who plan to diversify their investments.

Correlations

It is important to consider any correlations between variables being modeled within Monte Carlo. Cross-correlations, serial correlations, or cross-serial correlations must be simulated for realistic results. For example, it may be shown that a correlation exists between investment returns and inflation. If this is true, then these variables should not be treated as independent of each other.

CASE STUDY 4: HOSPITAL RISK MANAGEMENT

This case is contributed by Lawrence Pixley, a founding partner of Stroudwater Associates, a management consulting firm for the healthcare industry. Larry specializes in analyzing risk and uncertainty for hospitals and physician practices in the context of strategic planning and operational performance analyses. His expertise includes hospital facility planning, hospital/physician joint ventures, medical staff development, physician compensation packages utilizing a balanced scorecard approach, practice operations assessment, and practice valuations. Larry spent 15 years in healthcare management, and has been a consultant for the past three decades, specializing in demand forecasting using scientific management tools including real options analysis, Monte Carlo simulation, simulation-optimization, data envelopment analysis (DEA), queuing theory, and optimization theory. He can be reached at lpixley@stroudwaterassociates.com.

Hospitals today face a wide range of risk factors that can determine success or failure, including:

- Competitive responses both from other hospitals and physician groups.

- Changes in government rules and regulations.

- Razor-thin profit margins.

- Community relations as expressed through zoning and permitting resistance.

- State of the bond market and the cost of borrowing.

- Oligopsony (market with a few buyers) of a few large payers, e.g., the state and federal governments.

- Success at fund-raising and generating community support.

- Dependence on key physicians, admitting preferences, and age of medical staff.

- High fixed cost structure.

- Advances in medical technology and their subsequent influence on admissions and lengths of stay.

In addition, hundreds of hospitals across the country are faced with aging facilities. Their dilemma is whether to renovate or relocate to a new site and build an entirely new facility. Many of these hospitals were first constructed in the early 1900s. Residential neighborhoods have grown up around them, locking them into a relatively small footprint, which severely hampers their options for expansion.

The Problem

Located in a large metropolitan area, CMC is a 425-bed community hospital. The region is highly competitive, with 12 other hospitals located within a 20-mile radius. Like most hospitals of similar size, CMC consists of a series of buildings constructed over a 50-year time span, with three major buildings 50, 30, and 15 years old respectively. All three facilities house patients in double occupancy (or two-bed) rooms.

The hospital has been rapidly outgrowing its current facilities. In the last year alone, CMC had to divert 450 admissions to other hospitals, which meant a loss of $1.6 M in incremental revenue. Figure 21 shows CMC's average daily census and demonstrates why the hospital is running out of bed space.

CMC Average Daily Census

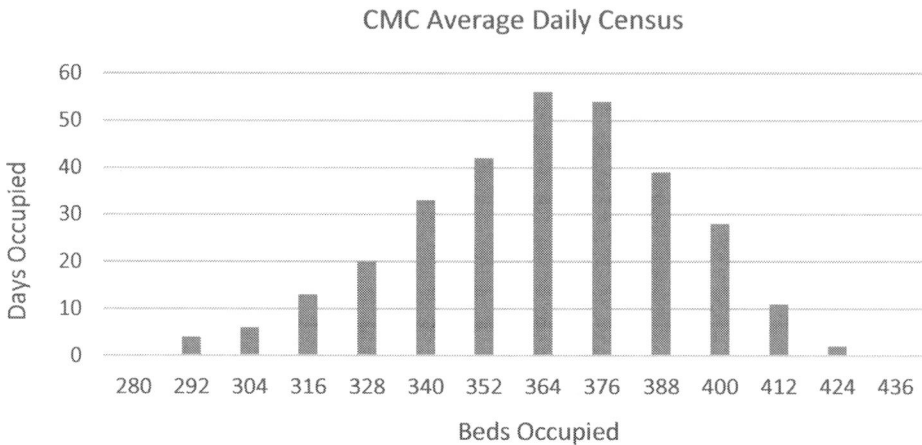

Figure 21: Histogram of CMC Bed Occupancy by Number of Days Beds Were Occupied

Because of this growing capacity issue, the hospital CEO asked his planning team to project discharges for the next 10 years. The planning department performed a trend line analysis using the linear regression function in Excel and developed the chart shown in Figure 22. They projected the number of discharges in 2014 to be 35,000.

Applying a Poisson distribution to the projected 35,000 discharges, the planners projected a total bed need of 514 (Figure7.23). They made no adjustment for a change in the average length of stay over that 10-year period, assuming that it would remain constant.

Confronted with the potential need to add 95 beds, the board of directors asked the CEO to prepare an initial feasibility study. To estimate the cost of adding 95 beds to the existing campus, the administrative staff first consulted with a local architect who had designed several small projects for the hospital. The architect estimated a cost of $260M to renovate the existing structure and build a new addition, both of which were required to fit 95 more beds within the hospital's current footprint. To accommodate the additional beds on the current site, however, all beds would have to be double occupancy. Single occupancy rooms—the most marketable today—simply could not be accommodated on the present campus.

Discharge Projections

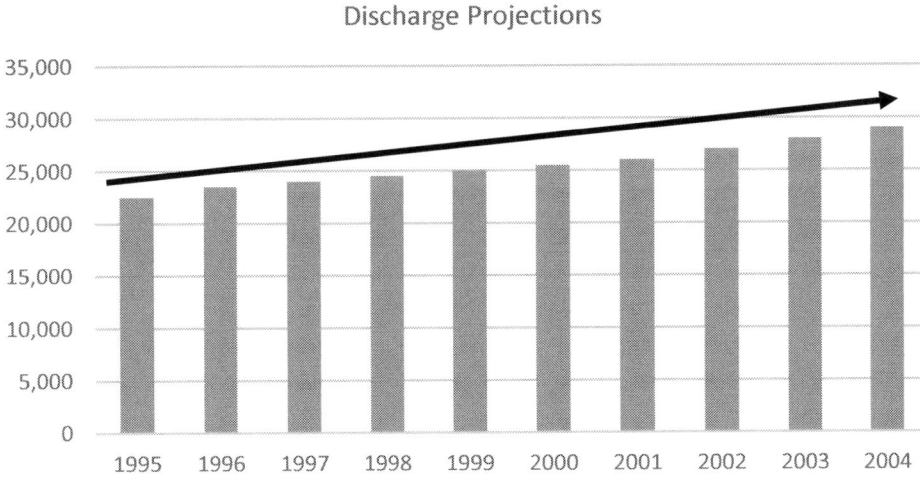

Figure 22: Trend Line Projections of CMC Discharges for Next 10 years (Provided by CMC Planning Department)

CMC Projected Bed Need for Average Daily Census of 463 (Poisson Distribution)

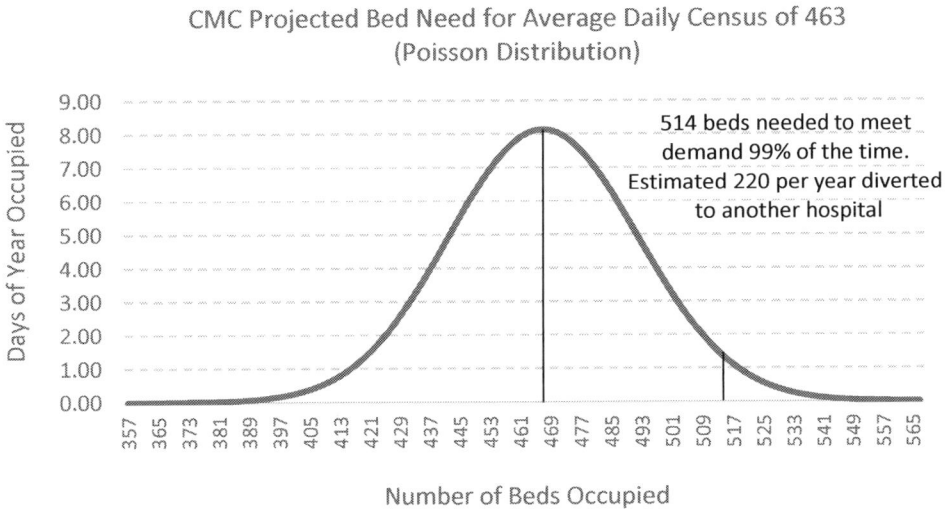

Figure 23: Projected CMC Beds Needs Based on Estimated Average Daily Census of 463 Patients for Year 2014 (Provided by CMC Planning Department)

In 1990, the hospital board faced a similar decision, whether to build a needed addition on the present campus or to relocate. The board opted to invest $90 million in a major expansion on the current site. Faced with the current dilemma, many of those same board members wished that in 1990 they had been able to better analyze their future options. A number of them expressed regrets that they did not relocate to another campus then. They clearly understood that that their current decision—to renovate and add to the existing campus—or to relocate—would be a decision the hospital would live with for the next 30 to 50 years.

There was no available site in the town (25 acres minimum), but there was space available in the adjacent town near a new $110 million ambulatory care center the hospital built five years ago. Yet, given the amount invested in the current campus, and the uncertainty of how a new location would affect market share, there was real hesitancy to relocate.

The board had other considerations as well. Historically there had been litigation involved every time the hospital tried to expand. The neighboring property owners unsuccessfully opposed the Emergency Department expansion in 1999, but had managed through various legal actions, to delay the construction three years. This delay added significantly to the cost of construction, in addition to the revenue lost from not having the modernized facility available as projected.

Two members of the board had attended a conference on the future of hospitals and noted that building more double occupancy rooms was not a good decision for the following reasons:

- By the time the facility was ready for construction, code requirements for new hospital construction would likely dictate single occupancy rooms.
- Patients prefer single rooms and CMC would be at a competitive disadvantage with other hospitals in the area that were already converting to single occupancy.
- Single occupancy rooms require fewer patient transfers and therefore fewer staff.
- Rates of infection were found to be considerably lower.

After receiving a preliminary cost estimate from the architect on a replacement hospital, the CFO presented the analysis shown in Figure 24 to the Finance Committee as an initial test of the project's viability.

Initial Capital Analysis for New Hospital ($ in M)		
Cost of Project	$	670
less: unrestricted cash	$	(150)
: deferred maintanence	$	(50)
: existing debt capacity	$	(100)
: future debt capacity-based on new volume	$	(95)
: sale of assets	$	(56)
: capital campaign	$	(150)
Capital 'Shortfall'	$	69

Figure 24: Capital Position Analysis for New Hospital as Prepared by CMC Chief Financial Officer

The initial projections for a new hospital estimated construction costs at $670 million. The study estimated a $50 million savings by not funding further capital improvements in the existing buildings. The CFO projected that the hospital would have a debt service capacity of an additional $95 million, assuming that the planning department's volume projections were accurate and that revenue and expense per admission remained static. The balance would have to come from the sale of various properties owned by the hospital and a major capital campaign. Over the years, the hospital had acquired a number of outlying buildings for administrative functions and various clinics that could be consolidated into a new facility. In addition, there was a demand for additional residential property within the town limits, making the hospital's current site worth an estimated $17 million. Although skeptical, the CFO felt that with additional analysis, it could be possible to overcome the projected $69 million shortfall.

The board authorized the administration to seek proposals from architectural firms outside their area. The Selection Committee felt that given the risks of potentially building the wrong-sized facility in the wrong location, they needed firms that could better assess both risks and options. At the same time, as a hedge pending the completion of the analysis, the committee took a one-year option on the 25-acre property in the adjacent town. After a nationwide review, CMC awarded the project analysis to a nationally recognized architectural firm and Stroudwater Associates, with the strategic planning and analytics in Stroudwater's hands.

The Analysis

Stroudwater first needed to test the trendline projections completed by CMC's planning department. Rather than taking simple trendline projections based on past admissions, Stroudwater used a combination of both qualitative and quantitative forecasting methodologies. Before financial projections could be completed, a better estimate of actual bed need was required. Stroudwater segmented the bed need calculation into five key decision areas: population trends, utilization changes, market share, length of stay, and queuing decisions. Given the rapid changes in healthcare technology in particular, it was determined that forecasting beyond ten years was too speculative, and the Board agreed that 10 years was an appropriate period for the analysis. In addition, the hospital wanted to project a minimum of three years beyond completion of hospital construction. Because projections were required for a minimum of 10 years, and because of the large number of variables involved, Stroudwater employed Monte Carlo simulation techniques each of these five decision areas (Figure 25).

Projecting Bed Need

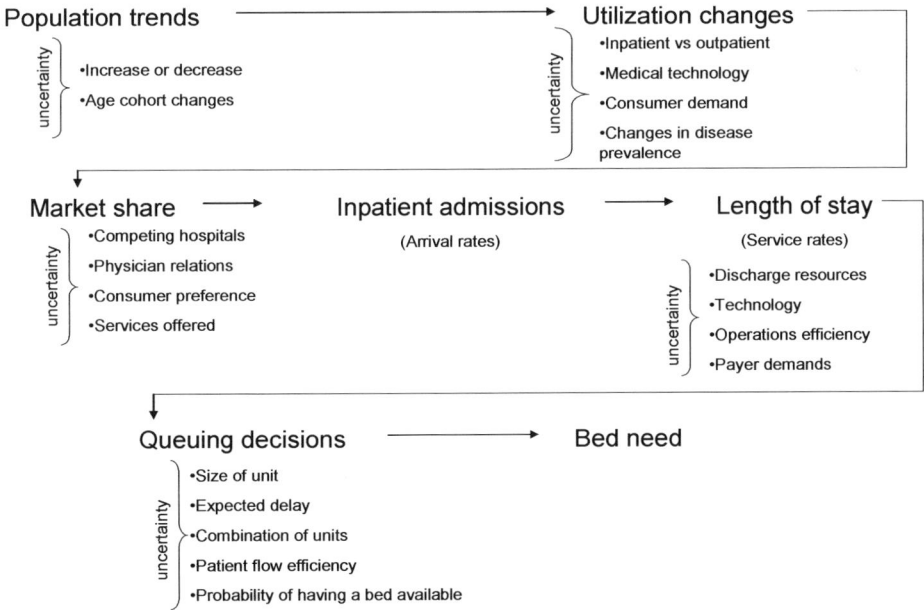

Figure 25: Stroudwater Associates' Methodology for Forecasting Hospital Bed Requirements

For qualitative input to this process, the hospital formed a 15-person steering committee composed of medical staff, board directors, and key administrative staff. The committee met every three weeks during the four-month study and was regularly polled by Stroudwater on key decision areas through the entire process.

In addition, Stroudwater conducted 60 interviews with physicians, board members, and key administrative staff. During the interviews with key physicians in each major service line, Stroudwater consultants were struck by the number of aging physicians in solo practice and not planning to replace themselves, a significant risk factor for CMC. The CFO identified another issue: A majority of physicians in key specialties had recently stopped accepting insurance assignments, further putting the hospital at risk vis-à-vis its major competitor whose employed physicians accepted assignment from all payers.

To understand better what service lines were at risk, Stroudwater developed a bubble diagram (Figure 26) to highlight areas that needed further business planning before making market share estimates. The three variables were net revenue, operating margin, and a subjective risk factor rating system.

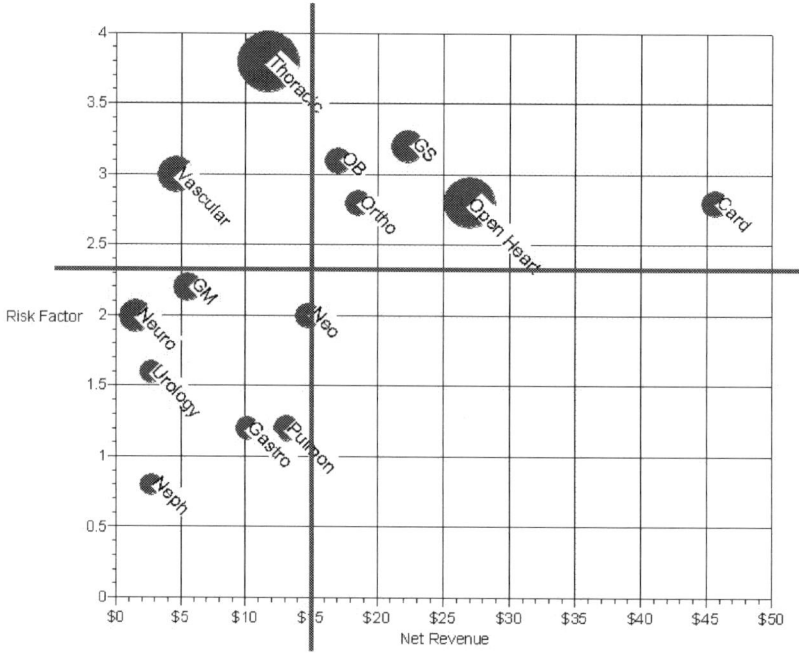

Figure 26: Bubble Chart Highlighting Service Lines Considered Most at Risk (Upper Right Quadrant) and Operating Margin is Represented by the Size of the Bubble

The following risk factors were identified, assigned a weight, rated on a scale of one to five, and plotted on the y-axis.

- Size of practice—percentage of solo and two-physician practices in specialty.

- Average age of physicians in specialty.

- Potential competitive threat from other hospitals.

- Percentage of admissions coming from outside of service area.

- Percentage of physicians in the specialty accepting assignment from major insurance carriers.

The analysis revealed five key specialties—orthopedics, obstetrics, general surgery, open-heart surgery and cardiology—in which CMC's bottom line was at risk, but which also afforded the greatest opportunity for future profitability. To better inform market share estimates, Stroudwater then developed mini business plans for each of the areas identified in the upper right-hand quadrant of Figure 26.

Population Trends

To determine future population numbers in the CMC service area, Stroudwater depended upon nationally recognized firms that specialize in population trending. Because hospital utilization is three times higher for over-65 populations, it was important to factor in the ongoing effect of the baby boomers. Stroudwater also asked members of the Steering Committee to review the 2014 population projections and determine what local issues not factored into the professional projections should be considered.

The committee members raised several concerns. There was a distinct possibility of a major furniture manufacturer moving its operations to China, taking some 3,000 jobs out of the primary service area. However, there was also the possibility of a new computer chip factory coming to the area. Stroudwater developed custom distributions to account for these population/employment contingencies.

Utilization Projections

Upon completion of its population forecasting, Stroudwater turned its attention to calculating discharges per 1,000 people, an area of considerable uncertainty. To establish a baseline for future projections, 2004 discharge data from the state hospital association were used to calculate the hospitalization use rates (discharges per 1,000) for CMC's market. Stroudwater calculated use rates for 34 distinct service lines (Figure 27).

Product Line	Discharges	Length of Stay	Population	Discharges / 1000	Days/ 1000	Ave. Length of Stay	Population	Change in Utilization	Estimated Total Market Discharges
ABORTION	137	213	1,193,436	0.12	0.18	1.6	1,247,832	0	150
ADVERSE EFFECTS	878	2,836	1,193,436	0.74	2.40	3.2	1,247,832	0	923
AIDS & RELATED	358	3,549	1,193,436	0.30	3.00	9.9	1,247,832	0	374
BURNS	86	859	1,193,436	0.07	0.73	10.0	1,247,832	0	87
CARDIOLOGY	19,113	75,857	1,193,436	16.17	64.19	4.0	1,247,832	18%	20,177
DERMATOLOGY	435	3,446	1,193,436	0.37	2.92	7.9	1,247,832	0	462
ENDOCRINOLOGY	3,515	18,248	1,193,436	2.97	15.44	5.2	1,247,832	5%	3,706
GASTROENTEROLOGY	9,564	46,103	1,193,436	8.09	39.01	4.8	1,247,832	5%	10,095
GENERAL SURGERY	7,488	51,153	1,193,436	6.34	43.28	6.8	1,247,832	9%	7,911
GYNECOLOGY	3,056	8,633	1,193,436	2.59	7.31	2.8	1,247,832		3,232
HEMATOLOGY	1,362	10,325	1,193,436	1.15	8.74	7.6	1,247,832	8%	1,435
INFECTIOUS DISEASE	2,043	15,250	1,193,436	1.73	12.90	7.5	1,247,832	0%	2,159
NEONATOLOGY	1,721	20,239	1,193,436	1.46	17.13	11.8	1,247,832	4%	1,822
NEUROLOGY	5,338	34,873	1,193,436	4.52	29.51	6.5	1,247,832	12%	5,640
NEUROSURGERY	3,042	13,526	1,193,436	2.57	11.45	4.4	1,247,832	12%	3,207
NEWBORN	11,197	25,007	1,193,436	9.47	21.16	2.2	1,247,832	-5%	11,817
OBSTETRICS	13,720	36,962	1,193,436	11.61	31.28	2.7	1,247,832	-5%	14,487
ONCOLOGY	1,767	11,563	1,193,436	1.50	9.78	6.5	1,247,832	15%	1,872

Figure 27: Utilization Trends for 2014 by Service Line (Source: State Hospital Discharge Survey)

Stroudwater factored a number of market forces affecting hospital bed utilization into the utilization trend analyses. The consultants considered the following key factors that might decrease facility utilization:

- Better understanding of the risk factors for disease, and increased prevention initiatives (e.g., smoking prevention programs, cholesterol-lowering drugs).

- Discovery/implementation of treatments that cure or eliminate diseases.

- Consensus documents or guidelines that recommend decreases in utilization.

- Shifts to other sites causing declines in utilization in the original sites.

    o As technology allows shifts (e.g., ambulatory surgery).

    o As alternative sites of care become available (e.g., assisted living).

- Changes in practice patterns (e.g., encouraging self-care and healthy lifestyles, reduced length of hospital stay).

- Changes in technology.

Factors that may increase hospital bed utilization:

- Growing elderly population.

- New procedures and technologies (e.g., hip replacement, stent insertion, MRI).

- Consensus documents or guidelines that recommend increases in utilization.

- New disease entities (e.g., HIV/AIDS, bioterrorism).

- Increased health insurance coverage.

- Changes in consumer preferences and demand (e.g., bariatric surgery, hip and knee replacements).

In all key high volume services, Stroudwater consultants made adjustments for utilization changes and inserted them into the spreadsheet model, using a combination of uniform, triangular, and normal distributions.

Market Share

The Steering Committee asked Stroudwater to model two separate scenarios, one for renovations and an addition to the current campus, and the second for an entirely new campus in the adjacent town. To project the number of discharges that CMC was likely to experience in the year 2014, market share assumptions for both scenarios were made for each major service line.

A standard market share analysis aggregates zip codes into primary and secondary service markets depending on market share percentage. Instead, Stroudwater divided the service area into six separate market clusters using market share, geographic features and historic travel patterns.

Stroudwater selected eight major service areas that represented 80% of the admissions for further analysis and asked committee members and key physicians in each specialty area to project market share. The committee members and participating physicians attended one large meeting where CMC planning department members and Stroudwater consultants jointly presented results from the mini business plans. Local market trends and results of past patient preference surveys were considered in a discussion that followed. As an outcome from the meeting, participants agreed to focus on specific factors to assist them in estimating market share, including:

- Change in patient preference.

- Proximity of competing hospitals.

- New hospital halo effect.

- Change in "hospital of choice" preferences by local physicians.

- Ability to recruit and retain physicians.

Using a customized survey instrument, Stroudwater provided those participating in the exercise with four years of trended market share data, challenging them to create a worst-case, most-likely, and best-case estimate for (1) each of the six market clusters in (2) each of the eight service lines for (3) each campus scenario.

After compiling the results of the survey instrument, Stroudwater assigned triangular distributions to each variable. An exception to the process occurred in the area of cardiac surgery. There was considerable discussion over the impact of a competing hospital potentially opening a cardiothoracic surgery unit in CMC's secondary service market. For the "current campus" scenario, the steering committee agreed that if a competing unit were opened it would decrease their market share to the 15% to 19% range, and they assigned a 20% probability that their competitor would open the unit. Should the competitor not build the unit, a minority of the group felt that CMC's market share would increase significantly to the 27% to 30% range; a 30% probability was assigned. The remaining members were more conservative and estimated a 23% to 25% market share. Similarly, estimates were made for the new campus in which participants felt there were better market opportunities and where losses would be better mitigated should the competing hospital open a new cardiothoracic unit. Stroudwater used the custom distributions shown in Figure 28.

Average Length of Stay

Stroudwater performed length of stay estimates for 400 diagnostic groupings (DRG) using a combination of historic statistics from the National Hospital Discharge Survey of the National Center for Health Statistics and actual CMC data.

Key CMC physicians participated in estimating length of stay based on the benchmark data, their knowledge of their respective fields, and historic CMC data. Stroudwater consultants separately trended historic lengths of stay and developed an algorithm for weighting benchmark data and CMC physician estimates. Length of stay estimates were rolled up into one distribution for each of the major service lines.

At this point, Stroudwater performed a sensitivity analysis (Figure 29) to determine which assumptions were driving the forecasts. Based on the relative unimportance population had on outcome, the population distribution assumptions were dropped in favor of single-point estimates.

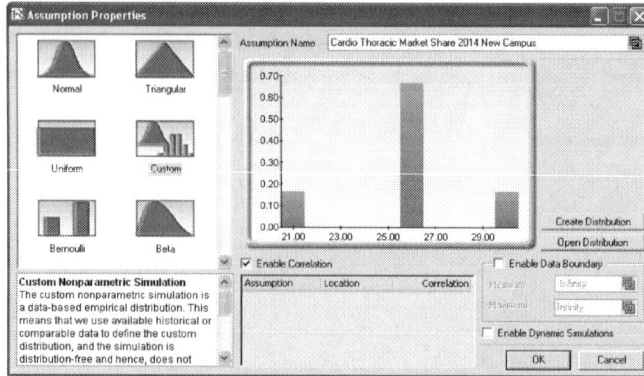

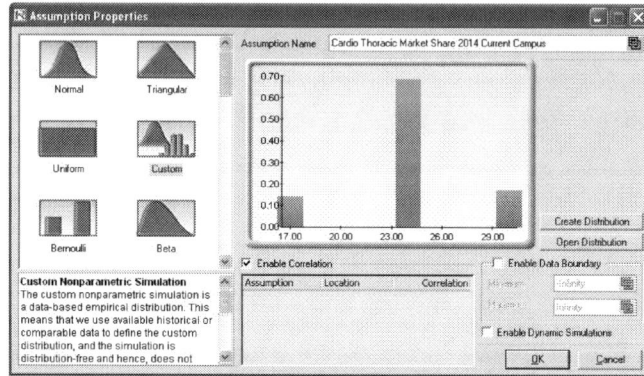

Figure 28: Cardiothoracic Market Share Using Custom Distributions Comparing Market Share Assumptions for Both Current and New Campus

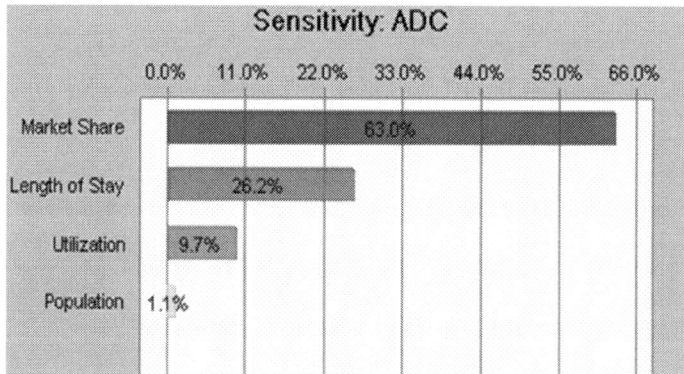

Figure 29: Sensitivity Analysis of Key Variables in Monte Carlo Simulation

Queuing Decisions

A typical approach to determining bed need, and the one used by the CMC planning department, is to multiply projections for single-point admissions by those for single-point lengths of stay to determine the total number of patient days. Patient days are divided by 365 to determine the average daily census (ADC). A Poisson distribution is then applied to the ADC to determine the total number of beds required. In addition to the problems of single-point estimates, Poisson distributions assume that all arrivals are unscheduled and thus overstate the bed need if any of the services have elective or urgent admissions.

Because CMC had categorized all of its admissions by urgency of the need for a bed, Stroudwater was able to conduct an analysis for each unit and found wide differences in the timing needs for beds ranging from OB with 100% emergency factor to Orthopedics with 57% of its admissions classified as elective (Figure 30).

Orthopedics/Neurosurgery

	Emergency	Urgent	Elective	Total
Total Days	5,540	415	7,894	13,849
Total Admissions	1,497	112	2,133	3,743
Percentage (Admits)	40%	3%	57%	100%

Figure 30: Orthopedic/Neurosurgery Admissions Classified by Admission Priority

To deepen the analysis, the physician members of the committee met separately to determine which units could be combined because of natural affinities and similar nursing requirements. The Steering Committee then met to discuss service targets for each category of admission. They agreed that "Emergencies" had to have a bed available immediately, "Urgent" within 48 hours and "Elective" within 72 hours. Using a multiple channel queuing model jointly developed by Dr. Johnathan Mun and Lawrence Pixley, bed needs were determined for each of the major unit groupings (Figure 31 and 7.32).

				Bed Needs Service Target		
				Emergency	Urgent	Elective
Unit	Discharges Arrival Rates	Service Rate 1/ALOS	CV	<1 day	1-2 days	2-3 days
Medical Cardiology	8.6301	0.0606	142.3973	71%	25%	4%
General Surgery	10.9315	0.0741	147.5753	49%	2%	49%
Orthopedics/Neuro	17.9795	0.0901	199.5719	40%	3%	57%

Figure 31: MGK Blocking Model Showing Bed Need Service Targets

Period/Day 3

MGK Blocking Model

No. Beds Per Day	No. Beds Per Period	Beds Busy	Prob Busy	Prob Served <1 Day	Prob Served 1-2 Days	Prob Served 2-3 Days
102	34	34	76.3%	99.4%	100.0%	100.0%
66	22	22	84.7%	89.6%	100.0%	100.0%
78	26	26	81.9%	96.0%	100.0%	100.0%
	82					

Figure 32: MGK Blocking Model with Beds Forecast and Probability of Availability

Distributions had been set for utilization and market share by service line to determine the arrival rates needed for the queuing model. Length of stay distributions by service line had been determined for the service rate input to the model. Forecast cells for Monte Carlo simulation were set for "Probability of Being Served" for <1, 1-2, and 2-3 days for each of the units respectively. As its planning criteria, the committee decided on a target rate of 95% confidence in having a bed available with a greater than 50% certainty. Stroudwater employed an iterative process to the model, rerunning the Monte Carlo simulation until the performance criteria were met. For example, the first run for Orthopedics at 75 beds had a certainty of 47.8% at 95% confidence level compared to a later run of 78 beds with a certainty of 60.57%. The 78-bed figure was adopted (Figure 33).

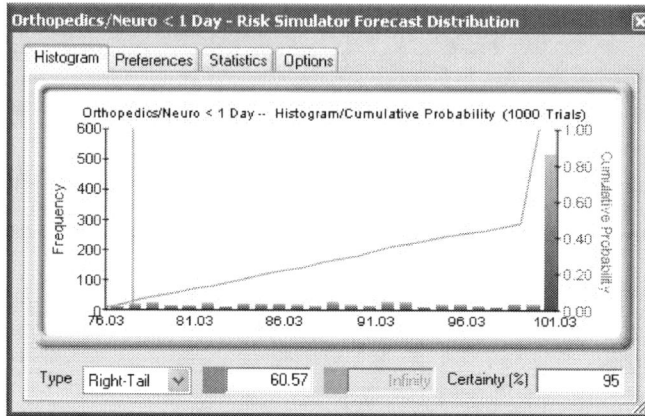

Figure 33: Frequency Distribution for 78 Orthopedic Beds at New Campus Site

Results of the Analysis

The committee's perception was that a new hospital located in a neighboring community closer to its target markets would improve market share in key specialties. That perception was reinforced by Stroudwater's findings in the projected differences in bed need between the two sites (Figure 34).

Service Line	Current Campus 2004	Current Campus 2014	New Campus Projection
Obstetrics	47	48	49
Cardiology	41	43	47
Pumonary	50	55	56
Infectious Disease	18	20	19
Ortho/Neurosurgery	49	69	73
Rahabilitation	16	18	18
Hematology/Oncology	14	15	16
General Surgery	38	41	42
Vascular/Cardiac Surgery	64	60	68
Urology	14	14	16
Gastroenterology	18	21	21
Neurology	18	20	21
Other Medical	12	14	15
Other Surgical	26	26	28
TOTAL BEDS	425	464	489

Figure 34: Results of Bed Need Projections for Both Current and
New Campus Solutions

The project architects utilized the bed demand information and completed construction cost projections for each of the two scenarios (Figures 35 and 36). With a need for only 39 additional beds on the current campus compared to the original projection of the need for 95 additional beds, the architects were able design space that afforded 92 private rooms.

The architects estimated the project cost for the new replacement facility at $587 million compared to $285 million for the renovation/addition option for the current campus. The new campus solution afforded an estimated increase in capital campaign contributions of $125 million and income from sale of assets of $56 million, bringing the borrowing required to an estimated $231 million. Borrowing for the current campus option was estimated to be $110 million. The pro formas reflected the following advantages to the new campus solution:

- Revenue per admission and per bed was higher with the new campus scenario because of the expected increase in higher margin specialty admissions. Cardio-thoracic surgery, for example, contributed $11,600 per case in margin compared to $2,200 for Urology.

- CMC was averaging 6.1 full time equivalent (FTE) employees per bed in the current facility, much of it due to facility inefficiencies. Stroudwater projected that a renovated campus could bring down the FTE to occupied bed ratio to 6.0 but projected the new facility at 5.8.

- Utility costs were projected to drop from the current $4.51 to $4.08 per square foot and maintenance costs were expected to drop from $2.46 to $1.40 per square foot.

- Loss of revenue from disruption of operations would be minimized with the new campus solution.

- The adjacent communities provided assurances to CMC that it would not experience zoning difficulties should the hospital choose to relocate, whereas because of ongoing community opposition to further construction on the existing campus, a three-year delay in construction was expected.

Financial Projections for New Hospital

	FY2006	FY2007	FY2008	FY2009	FY2010	FY2011	FY2012	FY2013	FY2014
Total Operating Revenue	$ 338,250,000	$ 350,550,000	$ 358,360,000	$ 330,000,000	$ 364,000,000	$ 361,088,000	$ 382,720,000	$ 425,700,000	$ 455,225,000
Total Expenses	$ 314,215,000	$ 325,641,000	$ 332,003,200	$ 309,100,000	$ 336,336,000	$ 320,762,624	$ 328,852,160	$ 364,854,600	$ 388,220,050
EBIDA	$ 31,613,900	$ 32,487,900	$ 33,935,700	$ 28,478,900	$ 35,242,900	$ 44,325,376	$ 57,867,840	$ 64,845,400	$ 71,004,950
EBIDA Margin	9.2%	9.1%	9.3%	8.5%	9.5%	12.2%	15.1%	15.2%	15.5%
Total Capital and Other Costs	$ 10,602,167	$ 10,774,367	$ 10,883,707	$ 41,544,014	$ 10,962,667	$ 34,891,167	$ 36,583,630	$ 34,532,014	$ 34,335,657
Operating Income/(Loss)	$ 13,432,833	$ 14,134,633	$ 15,473,093	$ (20,644,014)	$ 16,701,333	$ 5,434,209	$ 17,284,210	$ 26,313,386	$ 32,669,293
Operating Margin	4.0%	4.0%	4.3%	-6.3%	4.6%	1.5%	4.5%	6.2%	7.2%
Contributions and Investment Income	$ 7,578,900	$ 7,578,900	$ 7,578,900	$ 7,578,900	$ 7,578,900	$ 4,000,000	$ 4,000,000	$ 4,000,000	$ 4,000,000
Net Income/(Loss)	$ 21,011,733	$ 21,713,533	$ 23,051,993	$ (13,065,114)	$ 24,280,233	$ 9,434,209	$ 21,284,210	$ 30,313,386	$ 36,669,293
Profit Margin	6.1%	6.1%	6.3%	-3.9%	6.5%	2.6%	5.5%	7.1%	8.0%
Income Available for Capital	$ 31,613,900	$ 32,487,900	$ 33,935,700	$ 28,478,900	$ 35,242,900	$ 44,325,376	$ 57,867,840	$ 64,845,400	$ 71,004,950
Debt Service Coverage Ratio	6.1	6.1	6.2	1.7	3.3	1.3	3.5	3.9	4.3

Figure 35: Pro Forma for New Hospital Scenario

Financial Projections for Current Campus

	FY2006	FY2007	FY2008	FY2009	FY2010	FY2011	FY2012	FY2013	FY2014
Total Operating Revenue	$338,250,000	$350,550,000	$358,360,000	$330,000,000	$364,000,000	$361,088,000	$370,760,000	$387,500,000	$409,500,000
Total Expenses	$314,215,000	$325,641,000	$332,003,200	$309,100,000	$336,336,000	$321,845,888	$326,759,160	$340,612,500	$359,014,500
EBIDA	$ 31,613,900	$ 32,487,900	$ 33,935,700	$ 28,478,900	$ 35,242,900	$ 43,242,112	$ 48,000,840	$ 50,887,500	$ 54,485,500
EBIDA Margin	9.2%	9.1%	9.3%	8.5%	9.5%	11.9%	12.9%	13.1%	13.3%
Total Capital and Other Costs	$ 10,602,167	$ 10,774,367	$ 10,883,707	$ 22,711,484	$ 10,962,667	$ 23,318,486	$ 23,370,578	$ 23,516,484	$ 23,724,575
Operating Income/(Loss)	$ 13,432,833	$ 14,134,633	$ 15,473,093	$ (1,811,484)	$ 16,701,333	$ 15,923,626	$ 20,630,262	$ 23,371,016	$ 26,760,925
Operating Margin	4.0%	4.0%	4.3%	-0.5%	4.6%	4.4%	5.6%	6.0%	6.5%
Contributions and Investment Income	$ 7,578,900	$ 7,578,900	$ 7,578,900	$ 7,578,900	$ 7,578,900	$ 4,000,000	$ 4,000,000	$ 4,000,000	$ 4,000,000
Net Income/(Loss)	$ 21,011,733	$ 21,713,533	$ 23,051,993	$ 5,767,416	$ 24,280,233	$ 19,923,626	$ 24,630,262	$ 27,371,016	$ 30,760,925
Profit Margin	6.1%	6.1%	6.3%	1.7%	6.5%	5.5%	6.6%	7.0%	7.4%
Income Available for Capital	$ 31,613,900	$ 32,487,900	$ 33,935,700	$ 28,478,900	$ 35,242,900	$ 43,242,112	$ 48,000,840	$ 50,887,500	$ 54,485,500
Debt Service Coverage Ratio	6.1	6.1	6.2	3.6	3.3	2.7	6.1	6.4	6.9

Figure 36: Pro Forma for Current Campus Scenario

In addition to the foregoing pro forma presentations, Stroudwater provided the board with the Monte Carlo simulation results for projected profit margin in the year 2014 as shown in Figure 37.

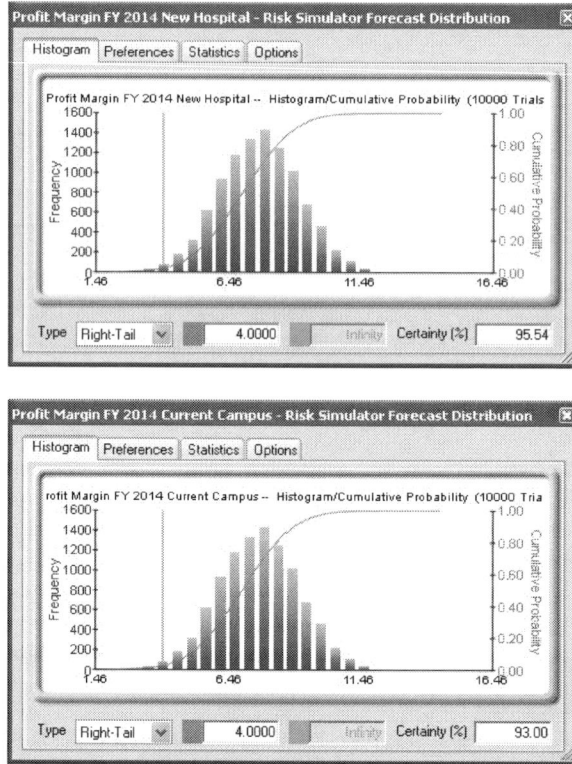

Figure 37: Frequency Distribution of Profit Margin Comparing Alternative Scenarios

Interestingly, the profit margins projected for the two scenarios were remarkably similar, with the new hospital scenario having a slightly higher probability of exceeding a 4% profit margin. Given the similar outcomes of the pro formas, the board elected to proceed with the new campus solution. They felt that even though moving to the adjacent community was a risk, the risk of remaining on the current site was even greater. They realized that their future expansion options were limited should the projections prove to underrepresent future demand for services, whereas the new campus afforded them a great deal of flexibility for unanticipated events.

A bond rating agency rewarded CMC's approach to risk assessment with a favorable rating. Its opinion letter reflected the following observations:

- CMC received high marks for the decision-making process. The agency appreciated the alternative analysis of comparing building on the present campus compared to a new campus and the unique approach of incorporating uncertainty into the calculation of bed need. It noted that the original projections for a 515-bed facility were scaled back to 489 beds as a result of the analysis.

- CMC received points for involving the physicians in the steering committee, and for the fact that CMC administration continually met with the medical staff to provide updates on the analysis.

- The agency felt that the relocation to the new campus was a risk by moving away from existing physician offices but the risk was not only mitigated but enhanced by a privately owned and developed 300,000 square foot. medical office building as part of the new campus. (It noted the lack of room for medical office facilities on the existing campus.) It also accepted the argument that CMC's long-term financial viability was improved by the future ability to recruit and retain physicians, particularly in large group practices.

- The fact that the new hospital would be located adjacent to CMC's ambulatory care center that had already been in full operation for six years was also viewed positively as patients were accustomed to traveling to this site.

- The agency found that management had compellingly examined all reasonable scenarios for patient volume and third-party reimbursement and their impact on earnings and liquidity.

The following were the principal advantages of using applied risk analysis in this case:

- Board members, many of whom were familiar with applied risk analysis in their own industries, were more comfortable making a major relocation decision based on a range of probable outcomes rather than on previously employed single-point estimates.

- The bond-rating agency awarded the hospital a favorable bond rating because "what if" scenarios were employed and because of the methods utilized in both identifying and mitigating risk factors.

- The hospital also was able to reduce the number of projected beds and, hence, its overall construction cost because of the more sophisticated queuing methodology employed.

CASE STUDY 5: RISK-BASED EXECUTIVE COMPENSATION VALUATION

This case was written by Patrick Haggerty, a Principal at the executive compensation consulting firm James F. Reda & Associates, LLC. As independent advisors to management and boards, the firm assists companies with designing and implementing executive compensation programs. The firm has significant expertise in valuing long-term incentive awards using guidance provided by FASB Statement No. 123 (Revised 2004), Share-Based Payment (FAS 123R), and related interpretations. Through partnering with Dr. Mun and using his option valuation software packages, James F. Reda & Associates, LLC helps clients determine and understand the compensation expense impact of selecting alternative long-term incentive designs.

This case is based on actual projects performed, but for the purposes of maintaining proprietary information, we use a fictitious entity named Boris Manufacturing, Inc. (Boris). This case study is about the process that Boris used to evaluate alternative long-term incentive (LTI) plan designs and determine the fair value for expensing purposes, as required by the new financial accounting standards. Through the following steps, the management team and the compensation committee worked together to evaluate the advantages and disadvantages of the various LTI vehicles available. The steps undertaken included:

- Reviewing the historical LTI awards made to employees.

- Reviewing the company's LTI plan.

- Conducting a market study.

- Evaluating advantages and disadvantages of each LTI vehicle available.

Ultimately, Boris decided to award restricted stocks that vest on achieving a total shareholder return target. Because the performance condition is total shareholder return, an option-pricing model can be used to determine fair value based on a barrier option, where the stock vests only after breaching a predetermined upper performance barrier. A simple Black–Scholes is not designed to value these types of awards. Instead, Monte Carlo and binomial lattice models like Dr. Mun's Real Options Super Lattice Solver and Risk Simulator software are most appropriate because they include the necessary input factors. FAS 123(R) considers the vesting criteria on Boris's restricted stock award a "market condition," meaning it is stock-price related. This distinction is important because if Boris designed a plan that vests on achieving a non-stock price-related measure (i.e., earnings per share or EPS, and earnings before interest, taxes, depreciation, and amortization or EBITDA) the company could not factor the performance condition into the fair value of the award (FAS 123(R) calls this type of performance measure a "performance condition"). For more technical details on valuing regular employee stock options based on the 2004 revised FAS 123, see Dr. Johnathan Mun's Case Study 14 on valuing employee stock options.

Background

Boris Manufacturing, Inc., is a publicly traded billion-dollar manufacturer of chemical products. The company has 2,000 employees with approximately 200 management- and executive-level employees. The compensation committee at Boris is responsible for determining executive pay levels and awarding LTIs to all employees. The compensation committee evaluated pay practices among its peer group companies and determined that LTIs should be a significant and important part of total compensation. Accordingly, the company has awarded its management- and executive-level employees LTIs. Historically, Boris awarded stock options to employees because prior to FAS 123(R) the expense was zero—under previous accounting rules, compensation expense was zero for at-the-money stock options if the number of shares awarded are known on the grant date.

Boris's stock option awards have not provided the incentive or link to shareholders that the compensation committee expected. Over the past four years, Boris's stock price has been relatively volatile and has generally decreased. Roughly half of the stock options Boris awarded to employees have an exercise price higher than the current stock price or are *underwater*. Further, the company kept awarding more stock options because the stock price continued to fall. As a result, the company has unproductive stock overhang, employees with minimal linkage to shareholders, and few shares remaining in their stock pool. As described next, the compensation committee decided to undertake a study to evaluate these issues.

Compensation Committee Process

To review alternative LTI designs, the compensation committee conducted the following:

    1.   Reviewed Historical LTI Awards Made to Employees

Purpose: To understand what employees had received in the past—such as type of award, current fair value of award, and any gains received.

Result: Over the past three years, Boris awarded approximately 900,000 stock options to employees each year (2.7 million in total). Unfortunately, roughly half are underwater, and very few employees were able to exercise and sell with any gain.

    2.   Reviewed Company's Long-Term Incentive Plan

Purpose: To understand types of LTI vehicles that Boris shareholders approved in its LTI plan and how many shares are available for awards.

Result: Boris's LTI Plan is very flexible and allows for all types of LTI vehicles, including:

- Non-Qualified Stock Options (NQSO)

- Incentive Stock Options (ISO)

- Stock-Settled Stock Appreciations Rights (Stock SAR)

- Restricted Stock and Restricted Stock Units (RSU)

- Performance Shares and Performance Units

Due to higher than expected stock option grants made over the past 3 years, the company has only 500,000 shares available for future grants. It is likely that Boris will need to go back to shareholders next year so they want to use the remaining shares wisely.

3. Conducted a Market Study

Purpose: To determine competitive practices for LTI awards, costs, and LTI designs (vesting, performance measures, termination provisions, and holding periods).

Result: Based on an analysis of industry competitors, the company determined that historical stock option awards were above market levels—on an individual position level, overhang basis, and cost basis. Also, it was determined that many peer group companies are awarding full value shares (i.e., restricted stock and performance shares) rather than stock options. Among the peer group companies that are awarding full value shares with performance conditions, the most common performance conditions were total shareholder return, earnings per share, and EBITDA.

4. Evaluated Advantages and Disadvantages of each LTI Vehicle Available. Table 10 summarizes the compensation committee's findings.

Table 10: Advantages and Disadvantages of LTI Vehicles

LTI Vehicle	FAS 123R Measurement Approach	Key Employee Tax Issue	Key Advantage	Key Disadvantage
NQSOs	Fixed: grant date fair value[1]	Ordinary income tax at exercise	Determine taxable event, upside potential	Potential underwater, highly dilutive
ISOs	Fixed: grant date fair value	Capital gains tax at sale[2]	Capital gains, upside potential	No company tax deduction, ISO rules
Stock SARs	Fixed: grant date fair value	Ordinary income tax at exercise	Limits dilution, upside potential	Potential underwater
Restricted Stock	Fixed: grant date face value[3]	Ordinary income when vested	Retention, no cost to employee	Pay tax when vested, not 162(m) qualified
Restricted Stock Units (paid in stock)	Fixed: grant date face value	Ordinary income when delivered	Flexibility, can include performance	Flexibility subject to 409A rules
Performance Shares	Fixed/variable: stock price fixed, shares adjusted[4]	Ordinary income when vested	Add'l shares and higher stock price	Setting performance measures
Performance Units (paid in cash)	Variable[5]: adjusted until paid	Ordinary income when vested	Receive cash, diversify	Cash flow, variable accounting

[1] Fair Value based on an option-pricing model, such as Black-Scholes.
[2] If requisite holding periods are met, otherwise same as NQSOs.
[3] Face Value equals stock price on grant date.
[4] Stock price fixed on grant date; shares are variable until measurement period is complete.
[5] Mark-to-market accounting until award is paid.

Compensation Committee Decision

The compensation committee decided to award restricted stock that vests on achieving a predefined total shareholder return (TSR) target. Key factors that influenced the Committee to select this LTI plan included:

- Reduction in overhang and run rate.
- Better link to shareholders.
- Requires minimum acceptable level of performance before payout.
- Promotes stock ownership because executives don't have to sell shares to exercise.

Details of the design include:

Type:	Restricted stock
Vesting criteria:	Vests on achieving 6% annual TSR
Performance period:	3 years (average cumulative TSR must exceed 6%)
Dividend rights:	Participants do not receive dividends until stock vests

Number of shares is all-or-nothing award, no adjustment in number of shares if TSR is below or above 6%

Before selecting the 6% TSR target, the compensation committee reviewed Boris's historical TSR. Based on this review, it was determined that Boris's 3-year historical average annualized return is 5.2% and using this and the volatility estimates, we were able to compute the expected distribution of future returns (see Figure 38). The Committee considered this and set the TSR target and expected range TSR performance at:

TSR Target:	6%
Minimum Expected:	0%
Most Likely:	5%
Max Expected:	9%

Distribution of IP Returns at Horizon

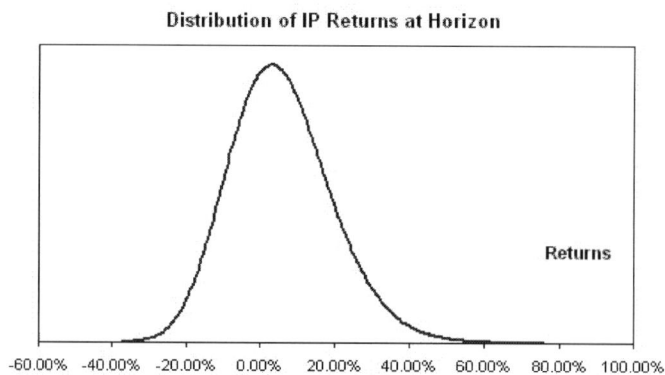

Returns

-60.00% -40.00% -20.00% 0.00% 20.00% 40.00% 60.00% 80.00% 100.00%

Figure 38: Boris's Projected Returns Based on Historical Performance

The compensation committee considered and analyzed, but ultimately decided against the following alternative plan designs. Each one of these alternatives would result in a different fair value calculation.

- Increasing duration of performance period from 3 years to 5 years.

- Vesting award based on company TSR performance against a peer group rather than a predetermined target.

- Awarding performance shares rather than restricted stock (note, this change does not impact the fair value but impacts the number of shares that will vest).

Compensation Cost Determination

Using FAS 123(R) guidance, Boris determined the fair value of the restricted stock award for expense recognition. Compensation cost for the award will equal the fair value multiplied by the number of restricted shares granted. Determining the fair value for its restricted stock awards is similar to the process Boris had used to determine fair value of its stock option awards under the pro forma disclosure rules of FAS 123. However, a simple Black–Scholes model cannot be used to determine the fair value of an award with a TSR target. Instead, a Monte Carlo simulation model coupled with a binomial lattice model must be used with inputs as detailed next. A Monte Carlo Simulation model coupled with a binomial model is more appropriate than other closed-form option-pricing models because this analysis has a barrier associated with the payoff structure (i.e., TSR targets), which means only a binomial lattice can be used to model such barrier options. In addition, the potential that Boris's TSR will exceed these targets is highly uncertain and thus, we need to run a Monte Carlo simulation to capture its expected value. Therefore, we couple Risk Simulator's Monte Carlo simulation capabilities with the Employee Stock Options Valuation and Real Options SLS software to perform the computations. See the chapters on real options analysis for more details on running the SLS software, or refer to the author's *Real Options Analysis,* Second Edition, (Wiley Finance, 2005). The following are assumptions used in the model:

- Grant date. This assumption determines the grant date stock price and interest rates.

- Grant date stock price. Equals the closing stock price on the grant date, or $20.00 for this example.

- Purchase price. Typically $0 for restricted stock awards.

- Volatility. Calculated based on historical stock prices, 30% for this example. Significant guidance for determining this assumption is provided in FAS 123(R) and SEC's Staff Accounting Bulletin No. 107.

- Contractual period. Equals duration of performance period, 3 years for this example.

- Dividend yield. Calculated based on Boris's historical dividend yield, 1%:

Dividend Payment Date	Dividend Amount	Stock Price	Quarterly Dividend Yield
3/15/2005	$0.04	$15.00	0.27%
6/15/2005	$0.04	$15.50	0.26%
9/15/2005	$0.04	$15.75	0.25%
12/15/2005	$0.04	$16.00	0.25%
Sum of quarterly dividend yields			1.03%

- Interest rate. Based on the U.S. Treasury rates available on the grant date with a maturity equaling the contractual term. For this example, we used a 4% interest rate.

- TSR target. Boris's compensation committee set the target at 6% based on the company's 3-year historical average annualized return of 5.2%.

- Expected range TSR performance. Sets the parameters for determining the likelihood of achieving the TSR Target. The Committee thought it would be reasonable to assume a minimum expected TSR of 0% and a stretch TSR of 9%.

- Suboptimal exercise multiple. Set the price at which the participant is expected to exercise. This assumption is set at 10,000, which theoretically renders it unattainable. If this award were a stock option, this assumption could be used if employee exercise behavior indicated a lower level.

The results generated using Risk Simulator's Monte Carlo simulation coupled with the Real Options SLS provides a fair value of $10.27 (Figure 39). Real Options SLS software was used to obtain the restricted stock's fair-market valuation, while Risk Simulator was used to simulate the potential TSR values. Thus if Boris awards 400,000 restricted shares to employees, the compensation cost equals 400,000 x $10.27 = $4,108,000, which is accrued over the performance period of 3 years. If the Monte Carlo simulation model were not used, Boris would be required to use the grant date stock price, $20, resulting in an expense of 400,000 x $20 = $8,000,000. Therefore, by applying the right methodologies as well as the right engineered LTI grants, Boris was able to reduce its expenses by almost 50%.

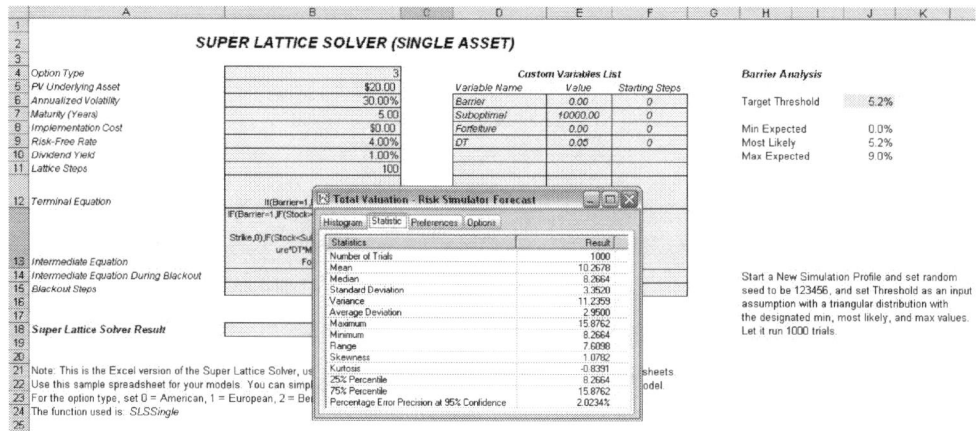

Figure 39: Total Valuation Results (Sample Only) for Boris's LTI

Conclusion

Monte Carlo Simulation models can be used to help design the LTI award by understanding the impact that certain changes have on fair value, and to determine the fair value of the LTI award for expense purposes under FAS 123(R). Without the use of such sophisticated methodologies, the fair value would never have been computed correctly and the decision to undertake the right LTI would have been flawed. In addition, such methodologies outlined here can also be used for multiple other applications such as engineering LTIs and stock-based compensations that are tied to say, a market index such as the S&P 500, or a company's performance (i.e., we can use financial metrics such as net profit margin, gross profits, EBITDA, and the like), or perhaps to some commodity price (e.g., price of gold or oil). For technical and application details on FAS 123(R) and running the Employee Stock Options Valuation software, please refer to the author's book, *Valuing Employee Stock Options (Under 2004 FAS 123)*, (Wiley Finance, 2004).

CASE STUDY 6: RISK-BASED SCHEDULE PLANNING WITH SIMULATION

Mark Rhoades is a lecturer at the Naval Postgraduate School at Monterey, California. He is a former U.S. Navy Commander and has served as the Deputy Program Manager at the NAVSTAR Global Positioning System Joint Program Office, a systems engineer at the Naval Air Systems Command, and the Program Manager of the Naval Aviation Depot Field Service Repair Teams. Mark has had years of experience in program management, program planning, reliability, and logistics. In addition to teaching graduate-level classes in risk management, he currently runs his own consulting business, Risk and Opportunity Management.

All organizations depend heavily on project planning tools to forecast when various projects will complete. Completing projects within specified times and budgets is critical to facilitate smooth business operations. In our high-technology environment, many things can impact schedule. Technical capabilities can often fall short of expectations. Requirements are insufficient in many cases and need further definition. Tests can bring surprising results—good or bad. A whole host of other reasons can lead to schedule slips. On rare occasions, we may run into good fortune and the schedule can be accelerated. Project schedules are inherently uncertain and change is normal. Therefore, we should expect changes and find the best way to deal with them. So why do projects always take longer than anticipated? The following discussion presents a description on shortcomings in the traditional methods of schedule estimation and how Risk Simulator can be applied to address these shortcomings.

Traditional Schedule Management

Traditional schedule management typically starts with a list of tasks. Next these tasks are put in order and linked from the predecessor to successor for each task. They are typically displayed in either a Gantt chart form or a network. For our discussion, we concentrate on the network. The duration for each task within the network is then developed. The estimated duration for each task is given a single-point estimate, even though we know from experience that this estimate should be a range of values. The first error is using a single-point estimate. In addition, many people who provide duration estimates try to put their best foot forward and give an optimistic or best-case estimate. If we assume that the probability of achieving this best-case estimate for one task is 20 percent, then the likelihood of achieving the best case for two tasks is merely 4 percent (20 percent of 20 percent), and three tasks yields only 0.8 percent. Within a real project with many more tasks, there is only an infinitesimal chance of making the best-case schedule.

Once the task duration estimates have been developed, the network is constructed and the various paths through the network are traced. The task durations are summed along each of these paths, and the one that takes the longest is identified as the critical path. Figure 40 illustrates an example network and critical path. The sum of task durations along the critical path is listed as the project completion date. In Figure 40, there are four paths through the network from beginning to end. The shortest/quickest path is Tasks 1-2-3-10-11 with a total duration of 22 days. The next shortest path is tasks 1-7-8-9-10-11 at 34 days, and then path 1-4-5-6-10-11 at 36 days. Finally, the path 1-4-8-9-10-11 takes the longest at 37 days and is the critical path for this network.

So let us assume that this network of tasks is our part of a larger effort and some other effort upstream of ours has overrun by a day. Our boss has asked us to shorten our schedule by one or two days to get the overall effort back on track. Traditional schedule management has one target: shorten the longest duration item in the critical path. Another approach is to shorten every task on the entire critical path. Because the first technique is more focused, more prone to success, and creates fewer conflicts on our team, let us assume that we will use that one. Hence, we will want to reduce Task 8 from 10 days to 9 days to shorten our schedule and we will satisfy our boss or our customer. Let us leave the traditional methodology at this stage feeling satisfied with our efforts.

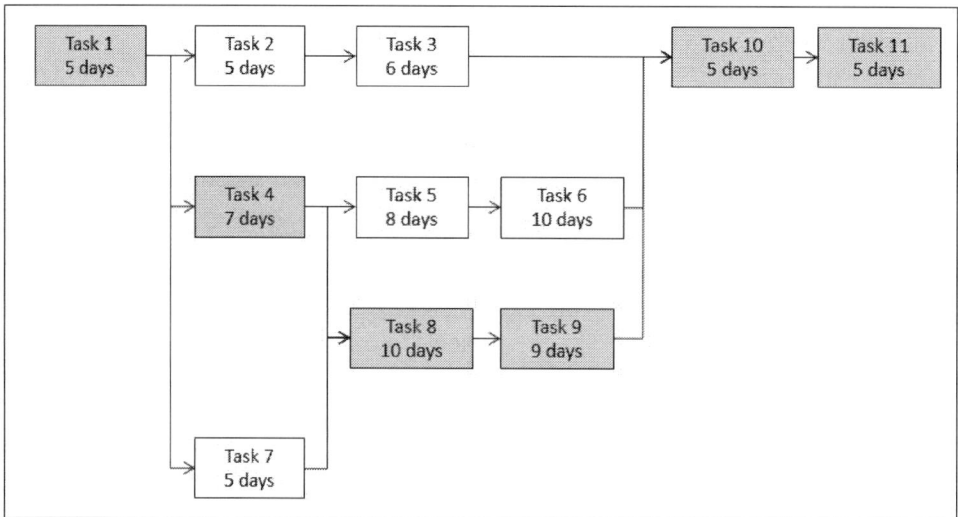

Figure 40: Schedule Network

Probabilistic Schedule Management

If we agree that task durations can vary, then that uncertainty should be taken into account in schedule models. A schedule model can be developed by creating a probability distribution for each task, representing the likelihood of completing the particular task at a specific duration. Monte Carlo simulation techniques can then be applied to forecast the entire range of possible project durations.

A simple triangular distribution is a reasonable probability distribution to use to describe the uncertainty for a task's duration. It is a natural fit because if we ask someone to give a range of duration values for a specific task, he or she usually supplies two of the elements: the minimum duration and the maximum duration. We need only ask or determine the most likely duration to complete the triangular distribution. The parameters are simple, intuitively easy to understand, and readily accepted by customers and bosses alike. Other more complex distributions could be used such as the Beta or Weibull but little, if anything, is gained because the determination of the estimated parameters for these distributions is prone to error and the method of determination is not easily explainable to the customer or boss.

To get the best estimates, we should use multiple sources to get the estimates of the minimum, most likely, and maximum values for the task durations. We can talk to the contractor, the project manager, and the people doing the hands-on work and then compile a list of duration estimates. Historical data can also be used, but with caution because many efforts may be similar to past projects but usually contain several unique elements or combinations. We can use Figure 41 as a guide. Minimum values should reflect optimal utilization of resources. Maximum values should take into account substantial problems, but it is not necessary to account for the absolute worst case where everything goes wrong and the problems compound each other. Note that the most likely value will be the value experienced most often, but it is typically less than the median or mean in most cases.

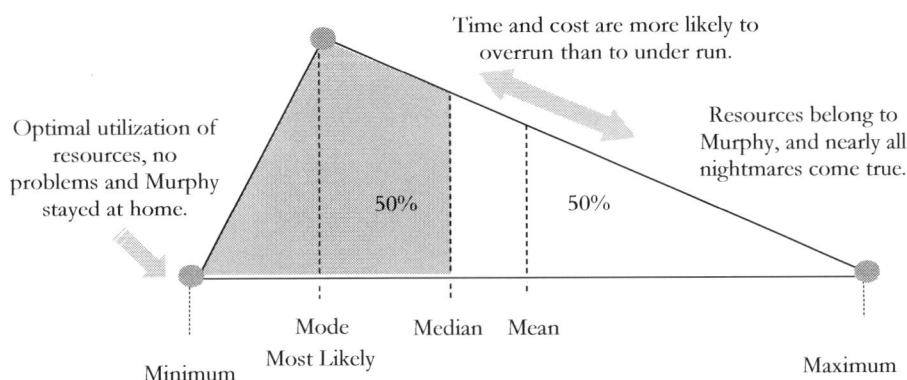

Figure 41: Triangular Distribution

For our example problem, shown in Figure 40, the minimum, most likely, and maximum values given in Table 11 will be used. We can use Risk Simulator's input assumptions to create triangular distributions based on these minimum, most likely, and maximum parameters. The column of dynamic duration values shown in the table was created by taking one random sample from each of the associated triangular distributions.

After the triangular distributions are created, the next step is to use the schedule network to determine the paths. For the example problem shown Figure 40, there are four paths through the network from beginning to end. These paths are shown in Table 12 with their associated durations. (Note: When setting up the spreadsheet for the various paths, it is absolutely essential to use the input assumptions for the task durations and then reference these task duration cells when calculating the duration for each path. This method ensures that duration of individual tasks is the same regardless of which path is used.) The overall schedule total duration is the maximum of the four paths. In Risk Simulator, we would designate that cell as an Output Forecast. In probabilistic schedule analysis, we are not concerned with the critical path/near-critical path situations because the analysis automatically accounts for all path durations through the calculations.

Table 11: Range of Task Durations

Task #	Task Name	Dynamic Duration	Minimum	Most Likely	Maximum	Point Estimate
1	Stakeholder Analysis	5.78	4.5	5	6	5
2	Objectives Hierarchy	4.79	4.5	5	6	5
3	Decision Metrics Development	6.16	5.5	6	7	6
4	Functional Analysis	7.78	6	7	9	7
5	Primary Module Rqmts	9.22	7	8	10	8
6	Primary Module Development	10.12	9	10	13	10
7	Secondary Module Functional Analysis	5.42	4.5	5	6	5
8	Secondary Requirements Allocation	10.05	9	10	12	10
9	Secondary Module Development	9.40	8	9	10	9
10	Trade Studies	3.33	2.5	3	4	3
11	Final Development Specification	3.76	2.5	3	4	3

Table 12: Paths and Durations for Example Problem

Path1	Duration1	Path2	Duration2	Path3	Duration3	Path4	Duration4
1	5.78	1	5.78	1	5.78	1	5.78
2	4.79	4	7.78	4	7.78	7	5.42
3	6.16	5	9.22	8	10.05	8	10.05
10	3.33	6	10.12	9	9.40	9	9.40
11	3.76	10	3.33	10	3.33	10	3.33
		11	3.76	11	3.76	11	3.76
Total1	23.81	Total2	39.99	Total3	40.10	Total4	37.73

Overall Schedule Total   >>>>>>   40.0968125 =MAX(Total1,Total2,Total3,Total4)

We can now use Risk Simulator and run a Monte Carlo simulation to produce a forecast for schedule duration. Figure 42 shows the results for the example problem. Let us return to the numbers given by the traditional method. The original estimate stated the project would be complete in 37 days. If we use the left-tail function on the forecast chart, we can determine the likelihood of completing the task in 37 days based on the Monte Carlo simulation. In this case, there is a mere 8.27 percent chance of completion within the 37 days. This result illustrates the second shortcoming in the traditional method: Not only is the point estimate incorrect, but it puts us in a high-risk overrun situation before the work even has started! As shown in Figure 42, the median value is 38.5 days. Some industry standards recommend using the 80 percent certainty value for most cases, which equates to 39.5 days in the example problem.

Now let us revisit the boss's request to reduce the overall schedule by one day. Where do we put the effort to reduce the overall duration? If we are using probabilistic schedule management, we do not use the critical path; so where do we start? Using Risk Simulator's *Tornado Analysis* and *Sensitivity Analysis* tools, we can identify the most effective targets for reduction efforts. The tornado chart (Figure 43) identifies the most influential variables (tasks) to the overall schedule. This chart provides the best targets to reduce the mean/median values. We cannot address the mean/median without addressing the variation, however. The *Sensitivity Analysis* tool shows what variables (tasks) contribute the most to the variation in the overall schedule output (see Figure 44). In this case, we can see that the variation in Task 4 is the major contributor to the variation in the overall schedule. Another interesting observation is the variation in Task 6, a task not on the critical path, is also contributing nearly 9 percent of the overall variation.

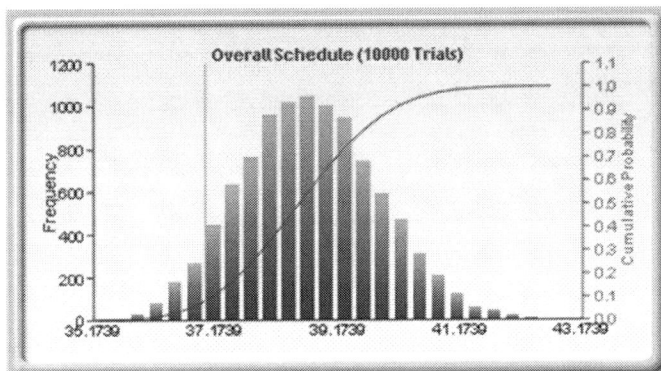

Type: Left-Tail ≤, Lower: -Infinity, Upper: 37.0000, Certainty: 8.2700%

Figure 42: Results of Monte Carlo Risk Simulation

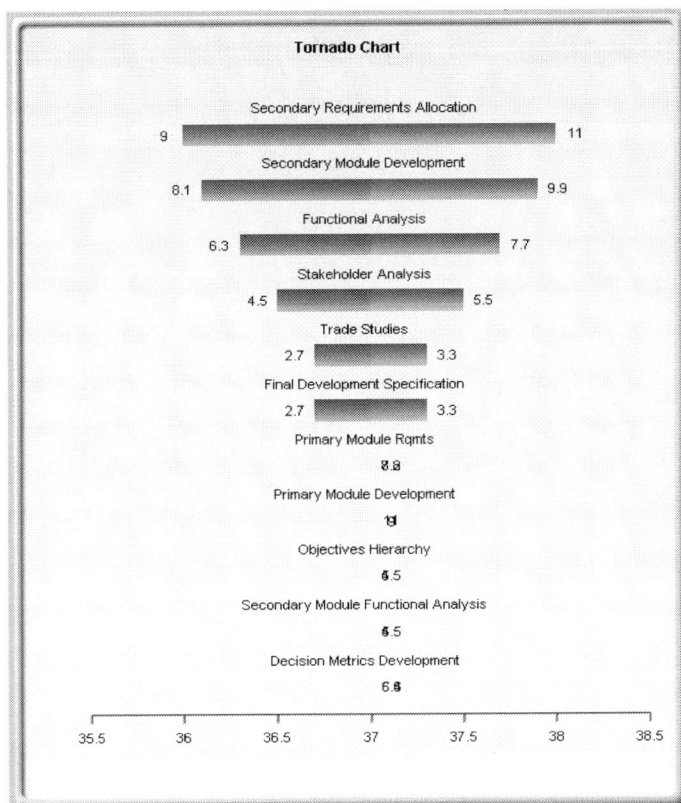

Figure 43: Tornado Chart

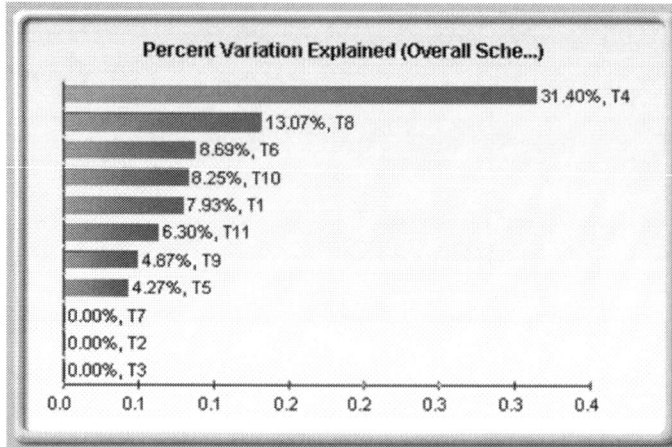

Figure 44: Sensitivity Analysis Chart

In this example, reducing the schedule duration for Task 4, Task 8, and Task 9 would pay the most dividends as far as reducing the overall schedule length. Determining the underlying reasons for the substantial variation in Tasks 4, 6, and 8 would likely give better insight into these processes. For example, the variation in Task 4 may be caused by the lack of available personnel. Management actions could be taken to dedicate personnel to the effort and reduce the variation substantially, which would reduce the overall variation and enhance the predictability of the schedule. Digging into the reasons for variation will lead to targets where management actions will be most effective, much more so than simply telling the troops to reduce their task completion time.

Using the network schedule model, we can also experiment to see how different reduction strategies may pay off. For example, taking one day out of Tasks 4, 8, and 9 under the traditional method would lead us to believe that a three-day reduction has taken place, but if we reduce the Most Likely value for Tasks 4, 8, and 9 by one day and run the Monte Carlo risk simulation, we find that the median value is still 37.91, or only a 0.7 day reduction. This small reduction proves that the variation must be addressed. If we reduce the variation by 50 percent, keeping the original minimum and the most likely values, but reducing the maximum value for each distribution, then we reduce the median from 38.5 to 37.91—about the same as reducing the Most Likely values. Taking both actions (reducing the Most Likely and Maximum values) reduces the median to 36.83, giving us a 55 percent chance of completing within 37 days. This analysis proves that reducing the most likely value and the overall variation is the most effective action.

To get to 36 days, we need to continue to work down the list of tasks shown in the sensitivity and tornado charts addressing each task. If we give Task 1 the same treatment, reducing its most likely and maximum values, then completion within 36 days can be accomplished with a 51 percent certainty, and a 79.25 percent certainty of completing within 37 days. The maximum value for the overall schedule is reduced from more than 42 days to less than 40 days. Substantial management efforts would be needed, however, to reach 36 days at the 80 percent certainty level.

Rules for Schedule Risk Management

When managing the production schedule, use the best-case numbers. If we use the most likely values or, worse yet, the maximum values, production personnel will not strive to hit the best-case numbers thus implementing a self-fulfilling prophecy of delayed completion. When budgeting, we should create the budget for the median outcome but recognize that there is uncertainty in the real world as well as risk. When advertising the schedule to the customer, provide the values that equate to the 75 percent to 80 percent certainty level. In most cases, customers prefer predictability (on-time completion) over potential speedy completion that includes significant risk. Lastly, acknowledge that the "worst case" can conceivably occur and create contingency plans to protect your organization in case it does occur. If the "worst case"/maximum value is unacceptable, then make the appropriate changes in the process to reduce the maximum value of the outcome to an acceptable level.

How to Apply This Method to Larger Networks

Some could argue that this methodology is only good for small networks because it appears that you have to trace all of the paths from beginning to end. We can, however, break up the schedule network to make the problem easier for larger cases. In our example problem, all of the paths came together at Task 10. We can call Task 10 a Merge Event. We can break a large network up into smaller pieces utilizing the merge points to define the boundaries. To further illustrate this technique, we will use the schedule network shown in Figure 45.

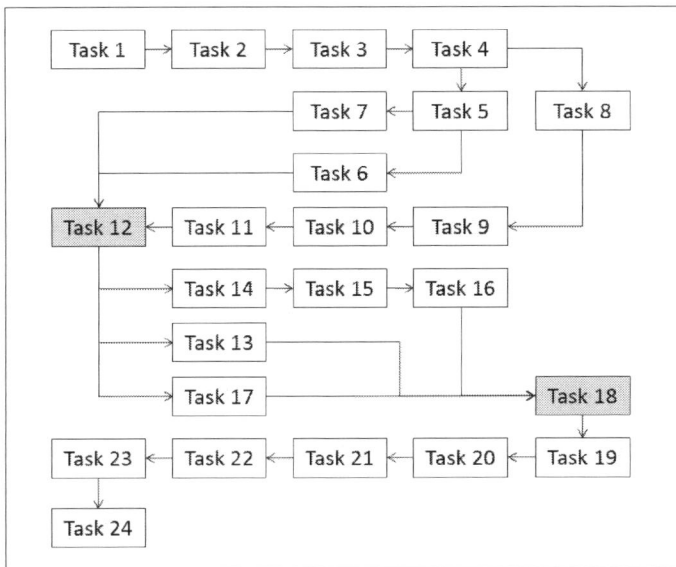

Figure 45: Example Schedule Network with Multiple Merge Points

In Figure 45, there are two merge points—Task 12 and Task 18. After we have created Input Assumptions for each task, we can set up our calculations. For this example, we should create the sum of the durations for tasks 1-2-3-4 as our first subtotal since these tasks are in series. The second subtotal would be equal to the maximum duration among Tasks 5-6, Task 5-7, and Tasks 8-9-10-11. We would then add the duration of Task 12 as the third subtotal. The fourth subtotal would be the maximum duration among Task 13, Tasks 14-15-16, and Task 17. Lastly we sum the durations of Tasks 18 through 24 as the fifth subtotal. We can then sum all of the five subtotals to determine the overall schedule duration. The spreadsheet cell that sums all five subtotals is set as the Output Forecast for our entire schedule network. The calculations are demonstrated in the spreadsheet shown in Figure 46.

	A	B	C	D	E	F	G	H	I	J
1	Task	MIN	ML	MAX	Input Assumption		Summations	Value	Formulas	Description
2	1	2	5	10	5.33		Subtotal1 =	76.03	=SUM(E3:E6)	Tasks 1-2-3-4
3	2	5	10	15	10.48		Subtotal2 =	108.13	=MAX(SUM(E7:E8),SUM(E7,E9),SUM(E10:E13))	Max of (Task 5-6,Tasks 5-7,Tasks 8-9-10-11)
4	3	30	45	90	47.12		Subtotal3 =	18.98	=E14	Task 12
5	4	5	10	15	13.11		Subtotal4 =	88.21	=MAX(E15,SUM(E16:E18),E19)	Max of (Task 13, Task 14-15-16, Task 17)
6	5	30	45	90	74.60		Subtotal5 =	165.52	=SUM(E20:E26)	Tasks 18-19-20-21-22-23-24
7	6	5	10	15	14.04					
8	7	15	25	60	33.53		Total	456.87	=SUM(H3:H7)	Output Forecast
9	8	10	20	60	16.05					
10	9	5	15	30	16.31		Forecasts			
11	10	5	10	15	9.88					
12	11	15	25	45	39.91					
13	12	15	20	30	18.98					
14	13	20	30	45	37.55					
15	14	30	45	60	50.76					
16	15	15	30	45	29.34					
17	16	5	10	20	8.11					
18	17	10	15	25	11.13					
19	18	15	30	60	33.60					
20	19	10	15	30	11.40					
21	20	15	30	60	40.63					
22	21	5	10	15	12.09					
23	22	30	60	90	44.41					
24	23	5	10	15	11.70					
25	24	5	8	12	11.70					

Forecasts

Name	Total		
Enabled	Yes	Number of Datapoints	5000
Cell	H9	Mean	460.5237
		Median	459.7741
Forecast Precision		Standard Deviation	27.7741
Precision Level	—	Variance	771.3997
Error Level	—	Coefficient of Variation	0.0603
		Maximum	557.3585
		Minimum	366.8121
		Range	190.5464
		Skewness	0.1385
		Kurtosis	-0.0754
		25% Percentile	441.0357
		75% Percentile	478.8738
		Error Precision at 95%	0.0017

Type: Two-Tail, Lower: -Infinity, Upper: Infinity, Certainty: 100.0000%

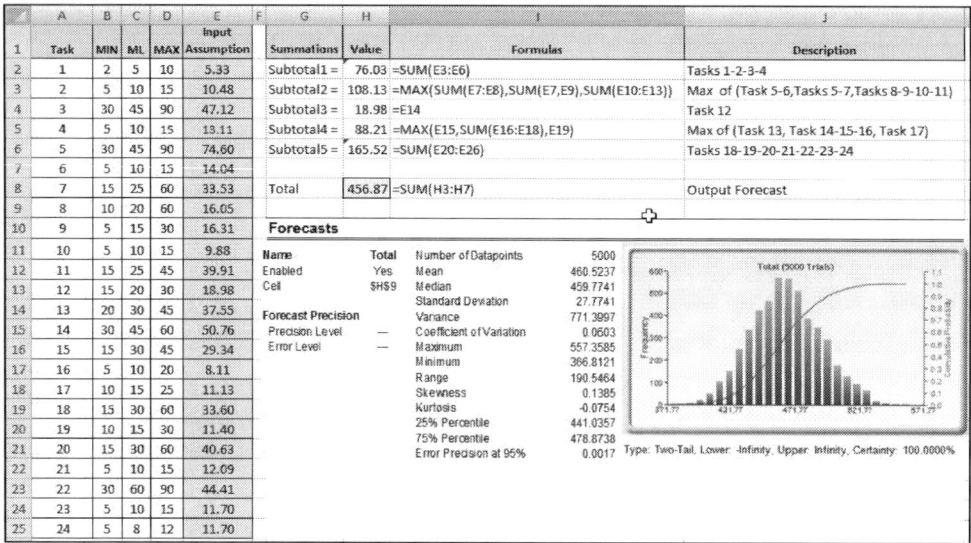

Figure 46: Example Schedule Spreadsheet with Multiple Merge Points

Risk Simulator can also be used to take into account correlations between tasks. After we create the Input Assumptions, we can go back and use the *Risk Simulator | Analytical Tools | Edit Correlations* to account for correlations among tasks. For example, if previous experience or data indicates that as Task 8 takes longer the duration for Task 9 will also increase, then there is likely a correlation between those two tasks. If we have paired data, then we can use Risk Simulator's Distribution Fitting (Multi-Variable) tool to determine the correlation values between the two items. This tool also works with more than two items. If we have data from several previous cases, we can use this tool to determine the correlation matrix for all of the tasks. To build the most accurate forecast, we should account for correlations whenever we know they exist.

Conclusion

With traditional schedule management, there is only one answer for the scheduled completion date. Each task gets one duration estimate and that estimate is accurate only if everything goes according to plan, not a likely occurrence. With probabilistic schedule management, thousands of trials are run exploring the range of possible outcomes for schedule duration. Each task in the network receives a time estimate distribution, accurately reflecting each task's uncertainty. Correlations can be entered to more accurately model real-world behavior. Critical paths and near critical paths are automatically taken into account, and the output forecast distribution will accurately reflect the entire range of possible outcomes. Using tornado and sensitivity analyses, we can maximize the effectiveness of our management actions to control schedule variations and reduce the overall schedule at high certainty levels.

7

CASE STUDY 7: EXTREME VALUE THEORY AND APPLICATION TO MARKET SHOCKS FOR STRESS TESTING AND EXTREME VALUE AT RISK

This case study is written by the author, Dr. Johnathan Mun.

Economic Capital is highly critical to banks (as well as central bankers and financial regulators who monitor banks) as it links a bank's earnings and returns on investment tied to risks that are specific to an investment portfolio, business line, or business opportunity. In addition, these measurements of Economic Capital can be aggregated into a portfolio of holdings. To model and measure Economic Capital, the concept of Value at Risk (VaR) is typically used in trying to understand how the entire financial organization is affected by the various risks of each holding as aggregated into a portfolio, after accounting for pairwise cross-correlations among various holdings. VaR measures the maximum possible loss given some predefined probability level (e.g., 99.90%) over some holding period or time horizon (e.g., 10 days). Senior management and decision makers at the bank usually select the probability or confidence interval, which reflects the board's risk appetite, or it can be based on Basel III capital requirements. Stated another way, we can define the probability level as the bank's desired probability of surviving per year. In addition, the holding period usually is chosen such that it coincides with the time period it takes to liquidate a loss position.

VaR can be computed several ways. Two main families of approaches exist: *structural closed-form models* and *Monte Carlo risk simulation* approaches. We showcase both methods later in this case study, starting with the structural models. The second and much more powerful of the two approaches is the use of Monte Carlo risk simulation. Instead of simply correlating individual business lines or assets in the structural models, entire probability distributions can be correlated using more advanced mathematical Copulas and simulation algorithms in Monte Carlo risk simulation methods by using the Risk Simulator software. In addition, tens to hundreds of thousands of scenarios can be generated using simulation, providing a very powerful stress-testing mechanism for valuing VaR. Distributional fitting methods are applied to reduce the thousands of historical data into their appropriate probability distributions, allowing their modeling to be handled with greater ease.

There is, however, one glaring problem. Standard VaR models assume an underlying normal distribution. Under the normality assumption, the probability of extreme and large market movements is largely underestimated and, more specifically, the probability of any deviation beyond 4 sigma is basically zero. Unfortunately, in the real world, 4-sigma events do occur, and they certainly occur more than once every 125 years, which is the supposed frequency of a 4-sigma event (at a 99.995% confidence level) under the normal distribution. Even worse, the 20-sigma event corresponding to the 1987 stock crash is supposed to happen not even once in trillions of years.

The VaR failures led the Basel Committee to encourage banks to focus on rigorous stress testing that will capture *extreme tail events* and integrate an appropriate risk dimension in banks' risk management. For example, the Basel III framework affords a bigger role for stress testing governing capital buffers. In fact, a 20-sigma event, under the normal distribution, would occur once every *googol*, which is 1 with 100 zeroes after it, years. In 1996, the Basel Committee had already imposed a multiplier of four to deal with model error. The essential non-normality of real financial market events suggests that such a multiplier is not enough. Following this conclusion, regulators have said VaR-based models contributed to complacency, citing the inability of advanced risk management techniques to capture tail events.

Hervé Hannoun, Deputy General Manager of the Bank for International Settlements, reported that during the crisis, VaR models "severely" underestimated the tail events and the high loss correlations under systemic stress. The VaR model has been the pillar for assessing risk in normal markets but it has not fared well in extreme stress situations. Systemic events occur far more frequently and the losses incurred during such events have been far heavier than VaR estimates have implied. At the 99% confidence level, for example, you would multiply sigma by a factor of 2.33.[1]

While a normal distribution is usable for a multitude of applications, including in computing the standard VaR where the normal distribution might be a good model near its mean or central location, it might not be a good fit to real data in the tails (extreme highs and extreme lows), and a more complex model and distribution might be needed to describe the full range of the data. If the extreme tail values (from either end of the tails) that exceed a certain threshold are collected, you can fit these extremes to a separate probability distribution. There are several probability distributions capable of modeling these extreme cases, including the Gumbel distribution (also known as the extreme value distribution type I), the generalized Pareto distribution, and the Weibull distribution. These models usually provide a good fit to extremes of complicated data.

Figure 47 illustrates the shape of these distributions. Notice that the Gumbel Max (extreme value distribution type I, right skew), Weibull 3, and generalized Pareto all have a similar shape, with a right or positive skew (higher probability of a lower value, and a lower probability of a higher value).

Typically, we would have potential losses listed as positive values (a potential loss of ten million dollars, for instance, would be listed as $10,000,000 *losses* instead of –$10,000,000 in *returns*) as these distributions are unidirectional. The Gumbel Min (extreme value distribution type I, left skew), however, would require negative values for losses (e.g., a potential loss of ten million dollars would be listed as –$10,000,000 instead of $10,000,000). (See Figure 50 for an example dataset of extreme losses.) This small but highly critical way of entering the data to be analyzed will determine which distributions you can and should use.

---

[1] The Basel III Capital Framework: A Decisive Breakthrough, Hervé Hannoun, Deputy General Manager, Bank for International Settlements, BoJ-BIS High Level Seminar on Financial Regulatory Reform: Implications for Asia and the Pacific Hong Kong SAR, 22 November 2010.

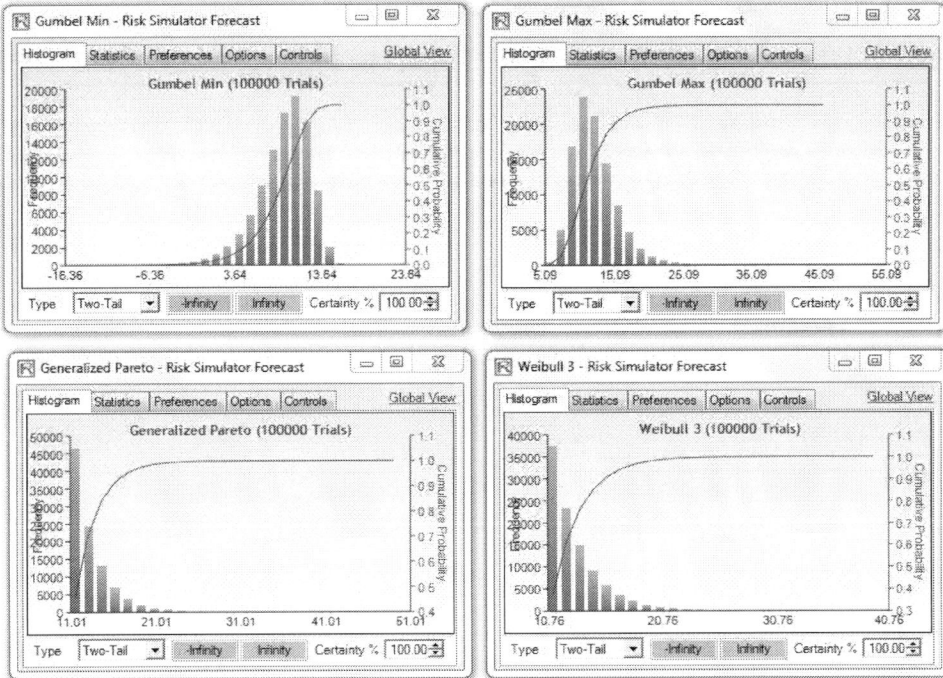

Figure 47: Sample Probability Distribution Function Shapes of the Common Extreme Value Distributions

The probability distributions and techniques shown in this case study can be used on a variety of datasets. For instance, you can use extreme value analysis on stock prices (Figure 48) or any other macroeconomic data such as interest rates or price of oil, and so forth (Figure 49 illustrates historical data on U.S. Treasury rates and global Crude Oil Prices for the past 10 years). Typically, macroeconomic shocks (extreme shocks) can be modeled using a combination of such variables. For illustration purposes, we have selected Google's historical stock price to model. The same approach can be applied to any time-series macroeconomic data.

Macroeconomic shocks can sometimes be seen on time-series charts. For instance, in Figures 48 and 49, we see the latest U.S. recession at or around January 2008 to June 2009 on all three charts (highlighted vertical region).

	A	B	C	D	E	F	G	H	I	J	K	L
1	HISTORICAL STOCK PRICES (WEEKLY) FOR GOOGLE											
2	Date	Open	High	Low	Close	Volume	Adj Close		Absolute	Relative	LN Relative	GARCH (1,1)
3	8/19/2004	100.00	109.08	95.96	108.31	16890200	108.31		Returns %	Returns	Returns	Volatility
									-1.99%	0.9801	-0.0201	
4	8/23/2004	110.75	113.48	103.57	106.15	5605400	106.15		-5.78%	0.9422	-0.0596	32.54%
5	8/30/2004	105.28	105.49	98.94	100.01	3956300	100.01		5.32%	1.0532	0.0518	33.93%
6	9/7/2004	101.01	106.56	99.61	105.33	2952100	105.33		11.54%	1.1154	0.1093	34.33%
7	9/13/2004	106.63	117.49	106.46	117.49	4817300	117.49		1.99%	1.0199	0.0197	41.64%
8	9/20/2004	116.95	124.10	116.77	119.83	4314100	119.83		10.64%	1.1064	0.1011	39.19%
9	9/27/2004	119.56	135.02	117.80	132.58	8347800	132.58		3.88%	1.0388	0.0381	43.99%
10	10/4/2004	135.25	139.88	132.24	137.73	6662800	137.73		4.63%	1.0463	0.0453	42.01%
11	10/11/2004	137.00	145.50	133.40	144.11	6560600	144.11		19.65%	1.1965	0.1794	40.71%
12	10/18/2004	143.20	180.17	139.60	172.43	15788600	172.43		10.56%	1.1056	0.1004	57.45%
13	10/25/2004	176.40	199.95	172.55	190.64	20887400	190.64		-11.17%	0.8883	-0.1184	58.37%
14	11/1/2004	193.55	201.60	168.55	169.35	14340500	169.35		7.47%	1.0747	0.0720	61.01%
15	11/8/2004	170.93	189.80	165.27	182.00	12926300	182.00		-6.92%	0.9308	-0.0717	58.99%
16	11/15/2004	180.45	188.32	165.73	169.40	15270100	169.40		5.90%	1.0590	0.0573	57.21%
17	11/22/2004	164.47	180.03	161.31	179.39	11635600	179.39		0.56%	1.0056	0.0056	54.70%
18	11/29/2004	180.36	183.00	177.51	180.40	7672100	180.40		-4.85%	0.9515	-0.0497	50.69%
19	12/6/2004	179.13	180.70	168.47	171.65	6527500	171.65		4.91%	1.0491	0.0479	48.54%
20	12/13/2004	172.17	180.69	169.45	180.08	8667400	180.08		4.34%	1.0434	0.0425	46.55%
21	12/20/2004	182.00	188.60	181.87	187.90	5718100	187.90		2.60%	1.0260	0.0257	44.50%
22	12/27/2004	189.15	199.88	189.10	192.79	5300100	192.79		0.55%	1.0055	0.0055	41.92%
23	1/3/2005	197.40	203.64	187.72	193.85	11577300	193.85		3.16%	1.0316	0.0311	39.17%
24	1/10/2005	194.50	200.01	190.50	199.97	7833100	199.97		-5.85%	0.9415	-0.0602	37.43%
25	1/18/2005	200.97	205.30	188.12	188.28	10672500	188.28		1.09%	1.0109	0.0109	37.99%
26	1/24/2005	188.69	194.70	176.29	190.34	11165000	190.34		7.37%	1.0737	0.0711	35.72%
27	1/31/2005	193.69	216.80	190.63	204.36	17808400	204.36		-8.30%	0.9170	-0.0866	37.67%
28	2/7/2005	205.26	206.40	185.25	187.40	14742100	187.40		5.63%	1.0563	0.0548	41.00%
29	2/14/2005	182.85	199.84	181.00	197.95	19955500	197.95		-6.10%	0.9390	-0.0630	40.51%
30	2/22/2005	196.50	198.90	182.23	185.87	16214300	185.87		0.02%	1.0002	0.0002	40.79%
31	2/28/2005	186.00	189.87	182.00	185.90	7759500	185.90					

Figure 48: Google's Historical Stock Prices & Returns, GARCH (1,1) Volatility, and Time-series Chart

Daily Treasury Long Term Rate Data

DATE	LT COMPOSITE (>10 yrs)	TREASURY 20-yr CMT
3/11/2003	4.50	4.64
3/12/2003	4.48	4.62
3/13/2003	4.61	4.75
3/14/2003	4.59	4.73
3/17/2003	4.68	4.82
3/18/2003	4.76	4.89
3/19/2003	4.81	4.94
3/20/2003	4.86	4.99
3/21/2003	4.95	5.08
3/24/2003	4.84	4.97
3/25/2003	4.83	4.97
3/26/2003	4.83	4.96
3/27/2003	4.82	4.96
3/28/2003	4.80	4.93
3/31/2003	4.71	4.84
4/1/2003	4.71	4.85
4/2/2003	4.80	4.94
4/3/2003	4.81	4.95
4/4/2003	4.83	4.97
4/7/2003	4.88	5.01
4/8/2003	4.80	4.93
4/9/2003	4.78	4.92
4/10/2003	4.80	4.94

U.S. Daily Treasury Long Term Rate Data

Date	NYMEX LS Crude
1/2/2003	31.85
1/3/2003	33.03
1/6/2003	32.1
1/7/2003	31.08
1/8/2003	30.56
1/9/2003	31.99
1/10/2003	31.99
1/13/2003	32.26
1/14/2003	32.37
1/15/2003	33.2
1/16/2003	33.91
1/20/2003	33.91
1/21/2003	34.61
1/22/2003	32.85
1/23/2003	32.25
1/24/2003	33.28
1/27/2003	33.6
1/28/2003	32.67
1/29/2003	33.63
1/30/2003	33.85
1/31/2003	33.51
2/3/2003	32.76
2/4/2003	33.58

NYMEX Crude Oil Price (USD)

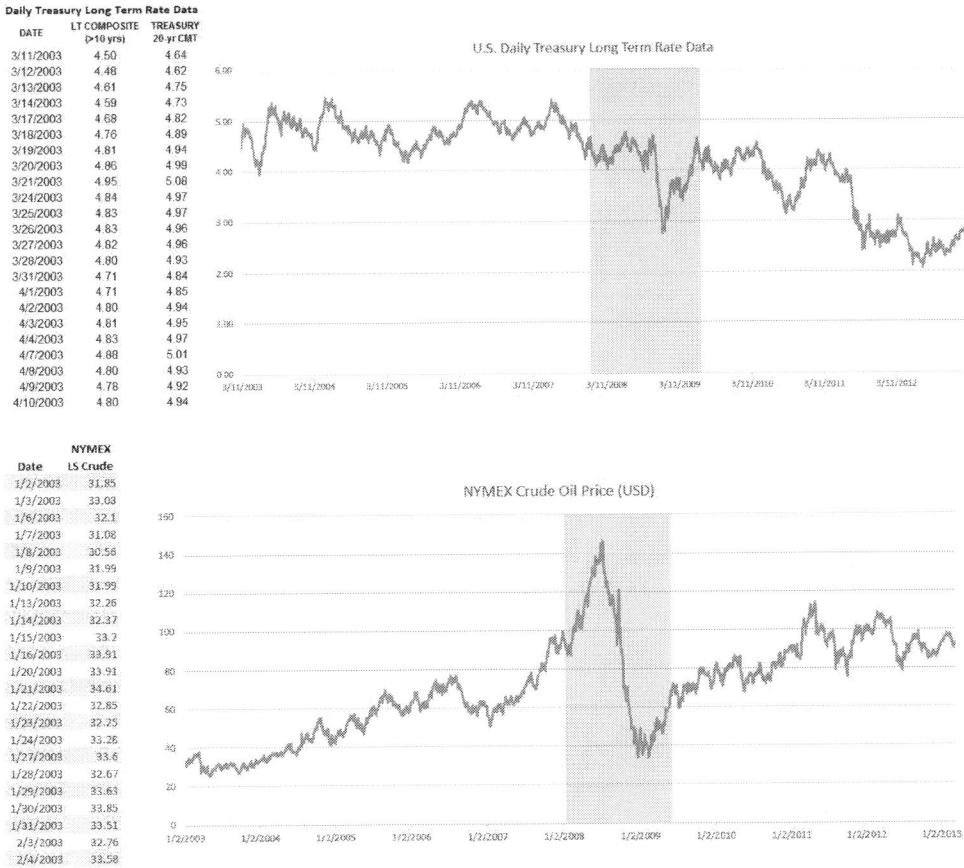

Figure 49: Historical U.S. Treasury Interest Rates and Global Crude Oil Prices

Therefore, the first step in extreme value analysis is to download the relevant time-series data on the selected macroeconomic variable. The second step is to determine the threshold, which is data above and beyond this threshold is deemed as extreme values (tail ends of the distribution), where these data will be analyzed separately.

Figure 50 shows the basic statistics and confidence intervals of Google stock's historical returns. As an initial test, we select the 5th percentile (−6.61%) as the threshold. That is, all stock returns at or below this −6.00% (rounded) threshold are considered potentially extreme and significant. Other approaches can also be used such as (i) running a GARCH model, where this Generalized Autoregressive Conditional Heteroskedasticity model (and its many variations) is used to model and forecast volatility of the stock returns, thereby smoothing and filtering the data to account for any autocorrelation effects; (ii) creating Q-Q quantile plots of various distributions (e.g., Gumbel, Generalized Poisson, or Weibull) and visually identifying at what point the plot asymptotically converges to the horizontal; and (iii) testing various thresholds to see at what point these extreme value distributions provide the best fit. Because the last two methods are related, we only illustrate the first and third approaches.

Figure 50 shows the filtered data where losses exceed the desired test threshold. Losses are listed as both negative values as well as positive (absolute) values. Figure 51 shows the distributional fitting results using *Risk Simulator's* distributional fitting routines applying the Kolmogorov–Smirnov test.

Absolute Returns %	Relative Returns	LN Relative Returns	GARCH (1,1) Volatility
-1.99%	0.9801	-0.0201	
-5.78%	0.9422	-0.0596	32.54%
5.32%	1.0532	0.0518	33.93%
11.54%	1.1154	0.1093	34.33%
1.99%	1.0199	0.0197	41.64%
10.64%	1.1064	0.1011	39.19%
3.88%	1.0388	0.0381	43.99%
4.63%	1.0463	0.0453	42.01%
19.65%	1.1965	0.1794	40.71%
10.56%	1.1056	0.1004	57.45%
-11.17%	0.8883	-0.1184	58.37%
7.47%	1.0747	0.0720	61.01%
-6.92%	0.9308	-0.0717	58.99%
5.90%	1.0590	0.0573	57.21%
0.56%	1.0056	0.0056	54.70%
-4.85%	0.9515	-0.0497	50.69%
4.91%	1.0491	0.0479	48.54%
4.34%	1.0434	0.0425	46.55%
2.60%	1.0260	0.0257	44.50%
0.55%	1.0055	0.0055	41.92%
3.16%	1.0316	0.0311	39.17%
-5.85%	0.9415	-0.0602	37.43%
1.09%	1.0109	0.0109	37.99%
7.37%	1.0737	0.0711	35.72%
-8.30%	0.9170	-0.0866	37.67%
5.63%	1.0563	0.0548	41.00%
-6.10%	0.9390	-0.0630	40.51%
0.02%	1.0002	0.0002	40.79%
-4.36%	0.9564	-0.0445	38.13%

	Absolute Returns %	Relative Returns	GARCH (1,1) Volatility
Average	0.57%	1.0057	33.25%
Stdev	4.76%	0.0476	8.39%
1% Percentile	-11.62%	0.8838	23.71%
5% Percentile	-6.61%	0.9339	24.32%
50% Percentile	0.68%	1.0068	30.52%
95% Percentile	8.18%	1.0818	51.29%
99% Percentile	13.88%	1.1368	59.18%
Minimum	-15.35%	0.8465	22.69%
Maximum	19.65%	1.1965	63.73%
Threshold	-6.00%		

Returns >6% Threshold	ABS Returns >6% Threshold	Returns >4% Threshold	Returns >7% Threshold
-15.35%	15.35%	-5.78%	-15.35%
-14.32%	14.32%	-15.35%	-14.32%
-14.19%	14.19%	-14.32%	-14.19%
-12.92%	12.92%	-14.19%	-12.92%
-11.98%	11.98%	-12.92%	-11.98%
-11.17%	11.17%	-11.98%	-11.17%
-10.76%	10.76%	-11.17%	-10.76%
-10.24%	10.24%	-10.76%	-10.24%
-9.83%	9.83%	-10.24%	-9.83%
-8.93%	8.93%	-9.83%	-8.93%
-8.92%	8.92%	-8.93%	-8.92%
-8.70%	8.70%	-8.92%	-8.70%
-8.45%	8.45%	-8.70%	-8.45%
-8.30%	8.30%	-8.45%	-8.30%
-8.21%	8.21%	-8.30%	-8.21%
-8.03%	8.03%	-8.21%	-8.03%
-7.85%	7.85%	-8.03%	-7.85%
-7.64%	7.64%	-7.85%	-7.64%
-7.21%	7.21%	-7.64%	-7.21%
-6.99%	6.99%	-7.21%	
-6.92%	6.92%	-6.99%	
-6.79%	6.79%	-6.92%	
-6.65%	6.65%	-6.79%	
-6.48%	6.48%	-6.65%	
-6.38%	6.38%	-6.48%	
-6.24%	6.24%	-6.38%	
-6.19%	6.19%	-6.24%	
-6.11%	6.11%	-6.19%	
-6.10%	6.10%	-6.11%	

Figure 50 Extreme Losses (Negative Returns) Statistics and Values Above a Threshold

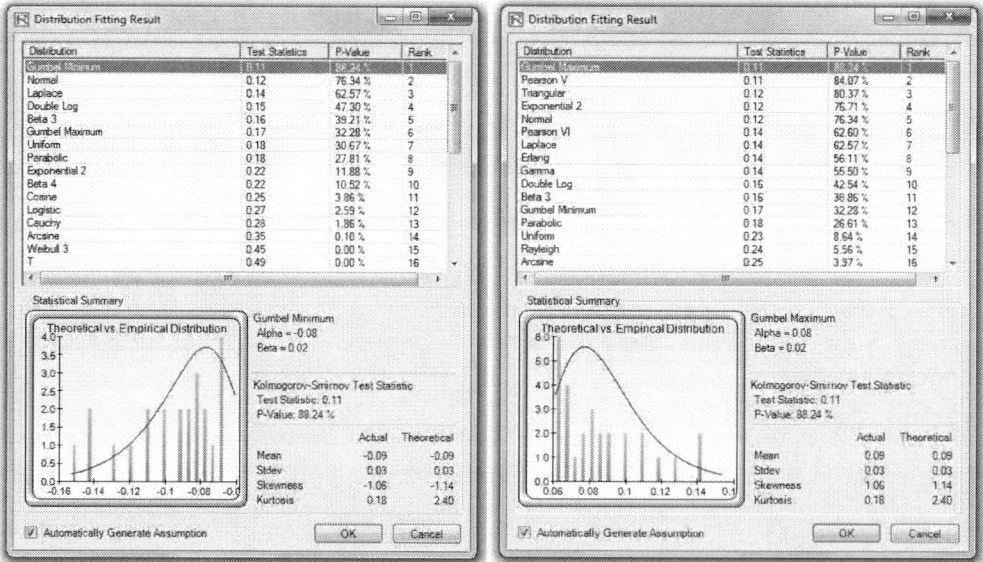

Figure 51: Distributional Fitting on Negative and Positive Absolute Values of Losses (6% Loss Threshold)

We see in Figure 51 that the negative losses fit the Gumbel minimum distribution the best, whereas the absolute positive losses fit the Gumbel maximum distribution the best. These two probability distributions are mirror images of each other and, therefore, using either distribution in your model would be fine. Figure 52 shows two additional sets of distributional fit on data with 4% and 7% loss thresholds, respectively. We see that the best-fitting dataset for the extreme value is at the 7% loss threshold (a higher p-value means a better fit, and a p-value of 93.71% on the 7% threshold data returns the best fit among the three).[2]

We recommend using the Kolmogorov–Smirnov method as it is a nonparametric test and would be best suited for fitting extreme value tail events. You can also try the other fitting methods available in Risk Simulator, including Anderson–Darling, Akaike Information Criterion, Schwartz/Bayes Criterion, Kuiper's Statistics, and so forth.

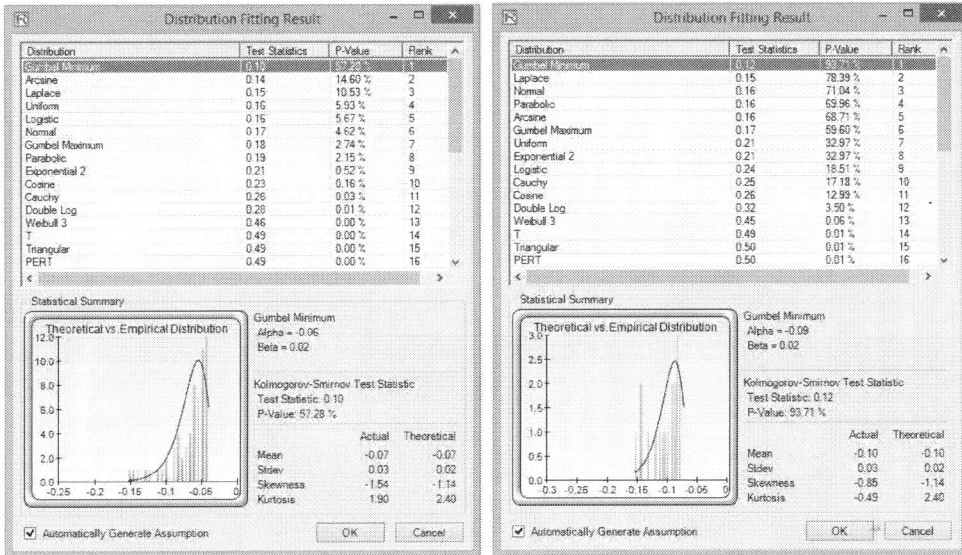

Figure 52: Distributional Fitting on 4% and 7% Loss Thresholds

To illustrate another method of data filtering, Figure 53 shows how a GARCH model can be run on the historical macroeconomic data. See the technical section later in this case study for the various GARCH model specifications (e.g., GARCH, GARCH-M, TGARCH, EGARCH, GJR-GARCH, etc.). In most situations, we recommend using either GARCH or EGARCH for extreme value situations. The generated GARCH volatility results can also be charted, and we can visually inspect the periods of extreme fluctuations and refer back to the data to determine what those losses are. The volatilities can also be plotted as control charts in the Risk Simulator's BizStats module (Figure 54) in order to determine at what point the volatilities are deemed statistically *out of control*, that is, extreme events.

---

[2] The null hypothesis tested is that the theoretically fitted distribution is the correct distribution, or that the error between the theoretical distribution tested and the empirical distribution of the data is zero, indicating a good fit. Therefore, a high p-value would allow us to not reject this null hypothesis and accept that the distribution tested is the correct distribution (any fitting errors are statistically insignificant).

HISTORICAL STOCK PRICES (WEEKLY) FOR GOOGLE

Date	Open	High	Low	Close	Volume	Adj Close
8/19/2004	100.00	109.08	95.96	108.31	16890200	108.31
8/23/2004	110.75	113.48	103.57	106.15	5605400	106.15
8/30/2004	105.28	105.49	98.94	100.01	3956300	100.01
9/7/2004	101.01	106.56	99.61	105.33	2952100	105.33
9/13/2004	106.63	117.49	106.46	117.49	4817300	117.49
9/20/2004	116.95	124.10	116.77	119.83	4314100	119.83
9/27/2004	119.56	135.02	117.80	132.58	8347800	132.58
10/4/2004	135.25	139.88	132.24	137.73	6662800	137.73
10/11/2004	137.00	145.50	133.40	144.11	6560600	144.11
10/18/2004	143.20	180.17	139.60	172.43	15788600	172.43
10/25/2004	176.40	199.95	172.55	190.64	20887400	190.64
11/1/2004	193.55	201.60	168.55	169.35	14340500	169.35
11/8/2004	170.93	189.80	165.27	182.00	12926300	182.00
11/15/2004	180.45	188.32	165.73	169.40	15270100	169.40
11/22/2004	164.47	180.03	161.31	179.39	11635600	179.39
11/29/2004	180.36	183.00	177.51	180.40	7672100	180.40
12/6/2004	179.13	180.70	168.47	171.65	6527500	171.65
12/13/2004	172.17	180.69	169.45	180.08	8667400	180.08
12/20/2004	182.00	188.60	181.87	187.90	5718100	187.90
12/27/2004	189.15	199.88	189.10	192.79	5300100	192.79
1/3/2005	197.40	203.64	187.72	193.85	11577300	193.85
1/10/2005	194.50	200.01	190.50	199.97	7833100	199.97
1/18/2005	200.97	205.30	188.12	188.28	10672500	188.28
1/24/2005	188.69	194.70	176.29	190.34	11165000	190.34

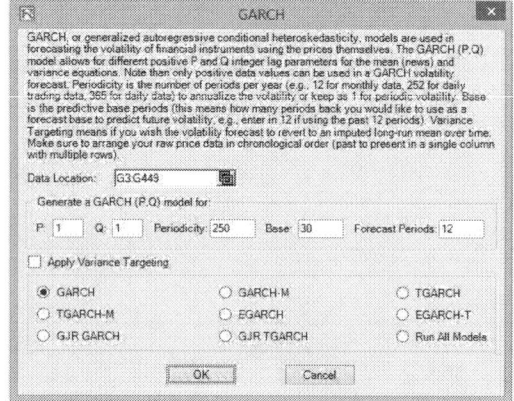

GARCH: Generalized Autoregressive Conditional Heteroskedasticity (Volatility Forecast)

GARCH models are used mainly for computing the volatility on liquid and tradable assets such as stocks in financial options; this model is sometimes used for other traded assets such as price of oil and price of electricity. The drawback is that a lot of data is required, advanced econometric modeling expertise is required, and this approach is highly susceptible to user manipulation. The benefit is that rigorous statistical analysis is performed to find the best-fitting volatility curve, providing different volatility estimates over time. GARCH is a term that incorporates a family of models that can take on a variety of forms, known as GARCH (P,Q), where P and Q are positive integers that define the resulting GARCH model and its forecasts. In most cases for financial instruments, a GARCH (1,1) is sufficient and is most generally used.

GARCH Model (P, Q)	1,1	Periodicity (Periods/Year)	52
Optimized Alpha	0.1107	Predictive Base	12
Optimized Beta	0.8386	Forecast Periods	12
Optimized Omega	0.0001	Variance Targeting	FALSE

	Period	Data	Volatility
8/19/2004	0	108.31	
8/23/2004	1	106.15	
8/30/2004	2	100.01	32.54%
9/7/2004	3	105.33	33.93%
9/13/2004	4	117.49	34.33%
9/20/2004	5	119.83	41.64%
9/27/2004	6	132.58	39.19%
10/4/2004	7	137.73	43.99%
10/11/2004	8	144.11	42.01%
10/18/2004	9	172.43	40.71%
10/25/2004	10	190.64	57.45%
11/1/2004	11	169.35	58.37%
11/8/2004	12	182.00	61.01%
11/15/2004	13	169.40	58.99%
11/22/2004	14	179.39	57.21%
11/29/2004	15	180.40	54.70%
12/6/2004	16	171.65	50.69%
12/13/2004	17	180.08	48.54%
12/20/2004	18	187.90	46.55%
12/27/2004	19	192.79	44.50%
1/3/2005	20	193.85	41.92%
1/10/2005	21	199.97	39.17%
1/18/2005	22	188.28	37.43%
1/24/2005	23	190.34	37.99%

GARCH or generalized autoregressive conditional heteroskedasticity models are used in forecasting the volatility of financial instruments, using the prices themselves. The GARCH (P,Q) model allows for different positive P and Q integer lag parameters for the mean (news) and variance equations. Note than only positive data values can be used in a GARCH volatility forecast. Periodicity is the number of periods per year (e.g., 12 for monthly data, 252 for daily trading data, 365 for daily data) to annualize the volatility or keep as 1 for periodic volatility. Base is the predictive base periods (this means how many periods back you would like to use as a forecast base to predict future volatility, and is typically between 1 and 12). Variance Targeting means if you wish the volatility forecast to revert to an imputed long-run mean over time. Make sure to arrange your raw price data in chronological order (past to present in a single column with multiple rows).

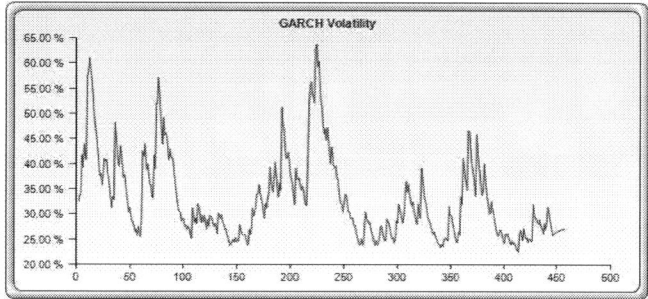

Figure 53: Generalized Autoregressive Conditional Heteroskedasticity (GARCH) Model

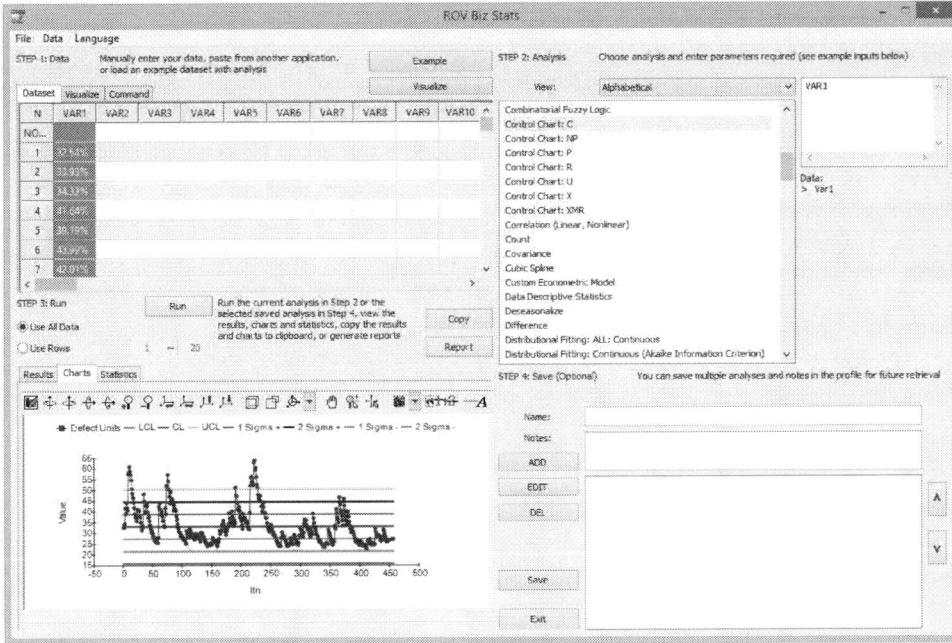

Figure 54: Time-series Control Charts on GARCH Volatility Estimates

Single Variable Distributional Fitting

Statistical Summary

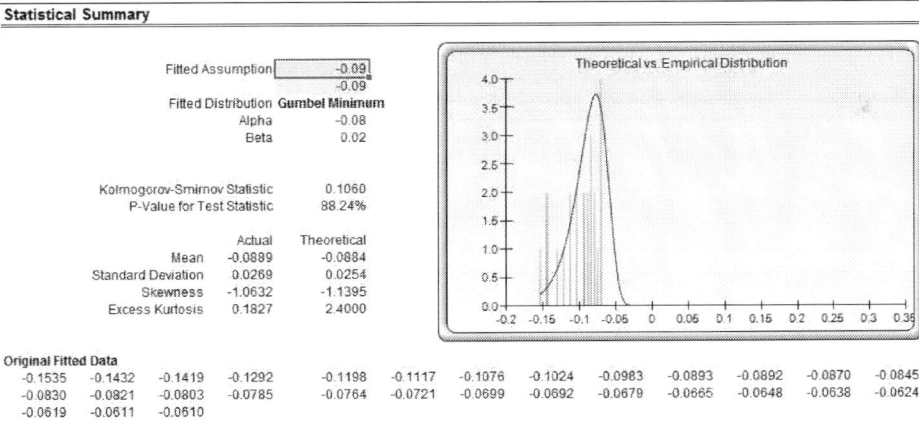

	Actual	Theoretical
Fitted Assumption	-0.09	
	-0.09	
Fitted Distribution	Gumbel Minimum	
Alpha	-0.08	
Beta	0.02	
Kolmogorov-Smirnov Statistic	0.1060	
P-Value for Test Statistic	88.24%	
Mean	-0.0889	-0.0884
Standard Deviation	0.0269	0.0254
Skewness	-1.0632	-1.1395
Excess Kurtosis	0.1827	2.4000

Original Fitted Data

-0.1535	-0.1432	-0.1419	-0.1292	-0.1198	-0.1117	-0.1076	-0.1024	-0.0983	-0.0893	-0.0892	-0.0870	-0.0845
-0.0830	-0.0821	-0.0803	-0.0785	-0.0764	-0.0721	-0.0699	-0.0692	-0.0679	-0.0665	-0.0648	-0.0638	-0.0624
-0.0619	-0.0611	-0.0610										

Figure 55: Distributional Fitting and Setting Simulation Assumptions in Risk Simulator

Figure 55 shows the distributional fitting report from Risk Simulator. If we run a simulation for 100,000 trials on both the Gumbel minimum and Gumbel maximum distributions, we obtain the results shown in Figure 56. The VaR at 99% is computed to be a loss of –16.75% (averaged and rounded, taking into account both simulated distributions' results). Compare this –16.75% value, which accounts for extreme shocks on the losses, to, say, the empirical historical (1% worst case or 99% VaR) which is a value of –11.62% loss (Figure 50), only accounting for a small window of actual historical returns, which may or may not include any extreme loss events. The VaR at 99.9% is computed as –21.35% (Figure 56).

Further, as a comparison, if we assumed and used only a normal distribution to compute the VaR, the results would be significantly below what the extreme value stressed results should be. Figure 57 shows the results from the normal distribution VaR, where the 99% and 99.9% VaR show a loss of –8.99% and –11.99%, respectively, a far cry from the extreme values of –16.75% and –21.35%.

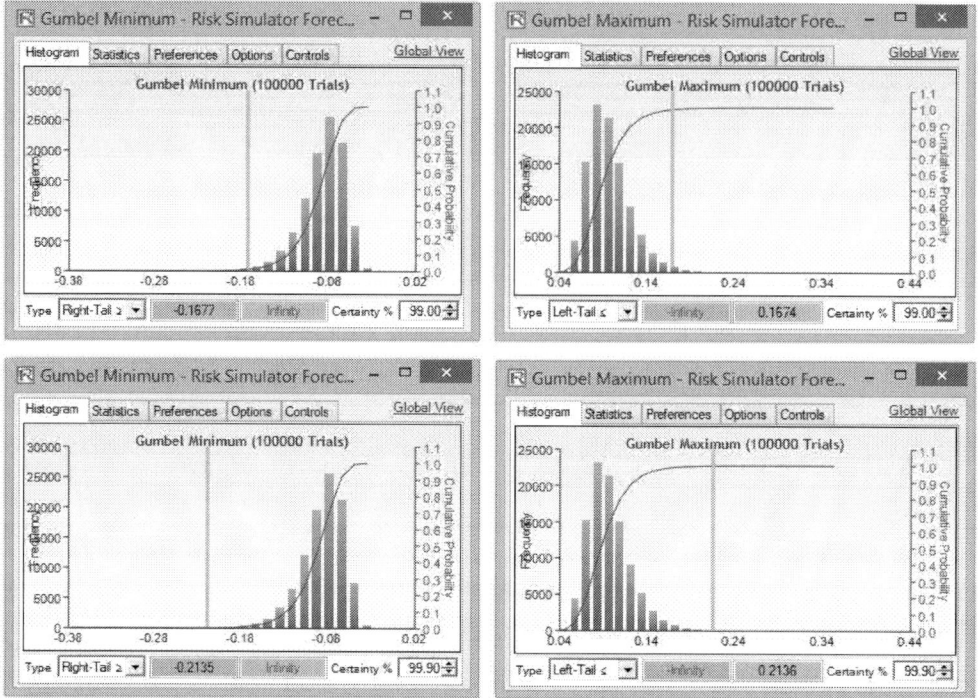

Figure 56: Gumbel Minimum and Gumbel Maximum Sample Simulated Results

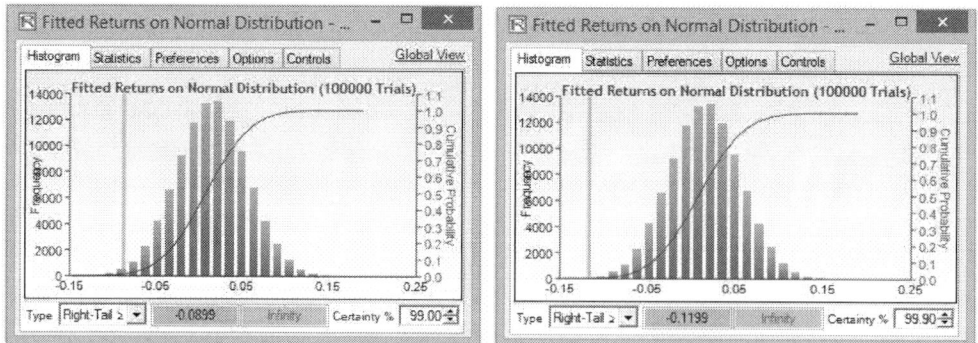

Figure 57: Similar Analysis using Normal Distributions

Another approach to predict, model, and stress test extreme value events is to use a jump-diffusion stochastic process with a Poisson jump probability. Such a model will require historical macroeconomic data to calibrate its inputs. For instance, using Risk Simulator's *Statistical Analysis* module, the historical Google stock returns were subjected to various tests and the stochastic parameters were calibrated as seen in Figure 58. Stock returns were used as the first-differencing creates added stationarity to the data. The calibrated model has a 50.99% fit (small probabilities of fit are to be expected because we are dealing with real-life nonstationary data with high unpredictability). The inputs were then modeled in *Risk Simulator | Forecast | Stochastic Processes* module (Figure 59). The results generated by Risk Simulator are shown in Figure 60. As an example, if we use the end of Year 1's results and set an assumption, in this case, a normal distribution with whatever mean and standard deviation is computed in the results report (Figure 60), a Monte Carlo risk simulation is run and the forecast results are shown in Figure 61, indicating that the VaR at 99% for this holding period is a loss of –11.33%. Notice that this result is consistent with Figure 50's 1% percentile (left 1% is the same as right tail 99%) of –11.62%. In normal circumstances, this stochastic process approach is valid and sufficient, but when extreme values are to be analyzed for the purposes of extreme stress testing, the underlying requirement of a normal distribution in stochastic process forecasting would be insufficient in estimating and modeling these extreme shocks. And simply fitting and calibrating a stochastic process based only on extreme values would also not work as well as using, say, the extreme value Gumbel or generalized Poisson distributions.

Stochastic Process - Parameter Estimations

Statistical Summary

A stochastic process is a sequence of events or paths generated by probabilistic laws. That is, random events can occur over time but are governed by specific statistical and probabilistic rules. The main stochastic processes include Random Walk or Brownian Motion, Mean-Reversion, and Jump-Diffusion. These processes can be used to forecast a multitude of variables that seemingly follow random trends but yet are restricted by probabilistic laws. The process-generating equation is known in advance but the actual results generated is unknown.

The Random Walk Brownian Motion process can be used to forecast stock prices, prices of commodities, and other stochastic time-series data given a drift or growth rate and a volatility around the drift path. The Mean-Reversion process can be used to reduce the fluctuations of the Random Walk process by allowing the path to target a long-term value, making it useful for forecasting time-series variables that have a long-term rate such as interest rates and inflation rates (these are long-term target rates by regulatory authorities or the market). The Jump-Diffusion process is useful for forecasting time-series data when the variable can occasionally exhibit random jumps, such as oil prices or price of electricity (discrete exogenous event shocks can make prices jump up or down). Finally, these three stochastic processes can be mixed and matched as required.

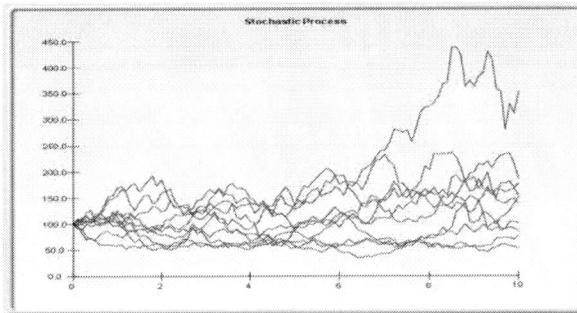

Statistical Summary

The following are the estimated parameters for a stochastic process given the data provided. It is up to you to determine if the probability of fit (similar to a goodness-of-fit computation) is sufficient to warrant the use of a stochastic process forecast, and if so, whether it is a random walk, mean-reversion, or a jump-diffusion model, or combinations thereof. In choosing the right stochastic process model, you will have to rely on past experiences and a priori economic and financial expectations of what the underlying data set is best represented by. These parameters can be entered into a stochastic process forecast (**Risk Simulator I Forecasting I Stochastic Processes**).

(Annualized)

Drift Rate*	0.60%	Reversion Rate**	N/A	Jump Rate**	12.13%
Volatility*	48.79%	Long-Term Value**	1.01	Jump Size**	0.07
		Probability of stochastic model fit	50.99%		

Figure 58: Stochastic Process Parameter Estimates from Raw Returns

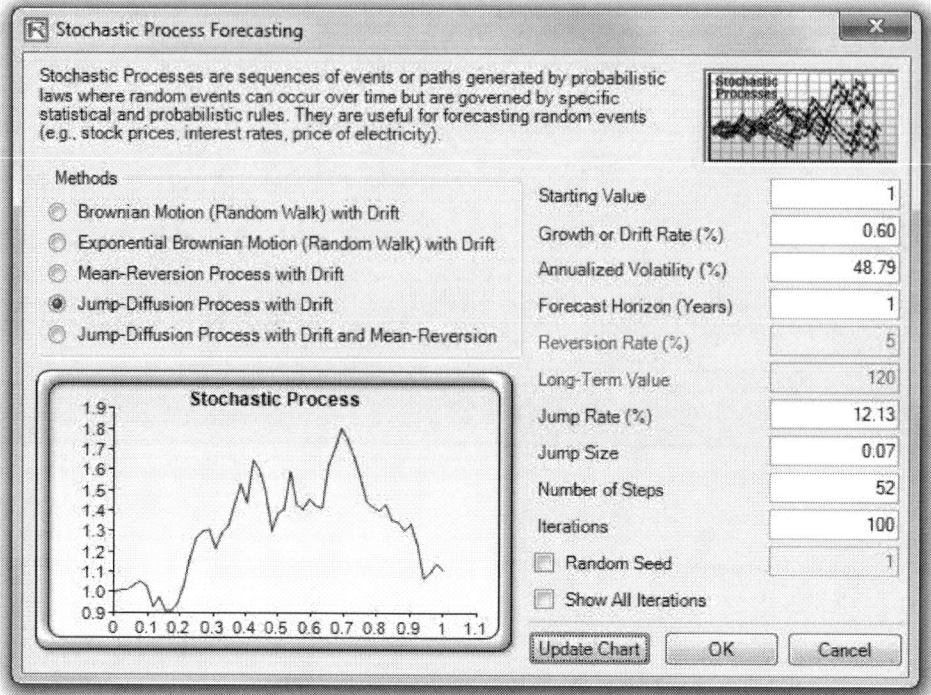

Figure 59: Modeling a Jump-diffusion Stochastic Process

Stochastic Process Forecasting: Jump Diffusion with Poisson Process

Statistical Summary

A stochastic process is a sequence of events or paths generated by probabilistic laws. That is, random events can occur over time but are governed by specific statistical and probabilistic rules. The main stochastic processes include Random Walk or Brownian Motion, Mean-Reversion, and Jump-Diffusion. These processes can be used to forecast a multitude of variables that seemingly follow random trends but yet are restricted by probabilistic laws.

The Random Walk Brownian Motion process can be used to forecast stock prices, prices of commodities, and other stochastic time-series data given a drift or growth rate and a volatility around the drift path. The Mean-Reversion process can be used to reduce the fluctuations of the Random Walk process by allowing the path to target a long-term value, making it useful for forecasting time-series variables that have a long-term rate such as interest rates and inflation rates (these are long-term target rates by regulatory authorities or the market). The Jump-Diffusion process is useful for forecasting time-series data when the variable can occasionally exhibit random jumps, such as oil prices or price of electricity (discrete exogenous event shocks can make prices jump up or down). Finally, these three stochastic processes can be mixed and matched as required.

The results on the right indicate the mean and standard deviation of all the iterations generated at each time step. If the Show All Iterations option is selected, each iteration pathway will be shown in a separate worksheet. The graph generated below shows a sample set of the iteration pathways.

Time	Mean	Stdev
0.0000	1.0000	0.0000
0.0192	1.0069	0.0684
0.0385	1.0135	0.0845
0.0577	1.0194	0.1166
0.0769	1.0049	0.1300
0.0962	1.0080	0.1587
0.1154	1.0142	0.1738
0.1346	1.0134	0.1828
0.1538	1.0209	0.1962
0.1731	1.0281	0.2056
0.1923	1.0364	0.2151
0.2115	1.0291	0.2204
0.2308	1.0300	0.2400
0.2500	1.0325	0.2363
0.2692	1.0205	0.2442
0.2885	1.0353	0.2626
0.3077	1.0293	0.2743
0.3269	1.0387	0.2808
0.3462	1.0388	0.2843
0.3654	1.0430	0.2864
0.3846	1.0552	0.3048
0.4038	1.0501	0.3062
0.4231	1.0668	0.3368
0.4423	1.0624	0.3357
0.4615	1.0622	0.3428
0.4808	1.0592	0.3453
0.5000	1.0657	0.3576
0.5192	1.0729	0.3713
0.5385	1.0782	0.3874
0.5577	1.0917	0.4084
0.5769	1.0993	0.4151
0.5962	1.1051	0.4194
0.6154	1.1071	0.4311
0.6346	1.0942	0.4353
0.6538	1.0990	0.4516
0.6731	1.0988	0.4688
0.6923	1.1024	0.4815
0.7115	1.0870	0.4707
0.7308	1.0930	0.4704
0.7500	1.0971	0.4663
0.7692	1.0984	0.4653
0.7885	1.1056	0.4671
0.8077	1.1118	0.4788

Stochastic Process: Jump-Diffusion Process with Drift

Start Value	1	Steps	52.00	Jump Rate	12.13%	
Drift Rate	0.60%	Iterations	100.00	Jump Size	0.07	
Volatility	48.79%	Reversion Rate	N/A	Random Seed	1091287598	
Horizon	1	Long-Term Value	N/A			

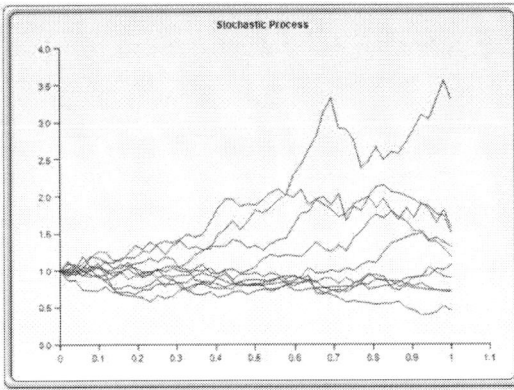

Figure 60: Stochastic Process Time-series Forecasts for a Jump-diffusion Model with a Poisson Process

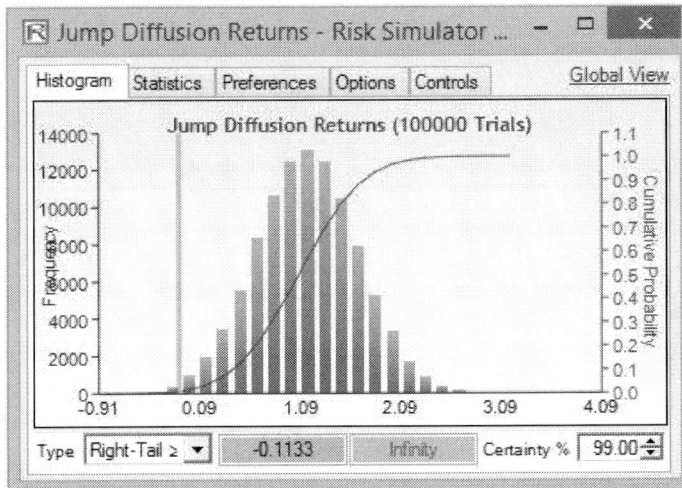

Figure 61: Risk Simulated Results from the Jump-diffusion Stochastic Process

Joint Dependence and T-Copula for Correlated Portfolios

Extreme co-movement of multiple variables occurs in the real world. For example, if the U.S. S&P 500 index is down 25% today, we can be fairly confident that the Canadian market suffered a relatively large decline as well. If we modeled and simulated both market indices with a regular Normal Copula to account for their correlations, this extreme co-movement would not be adequately captured. The most extreme events for the individual indices in a Normal Copula require that they be independently and identically distributed with respect of each other (*i.i.d. random*). The T-Copula, in contrast, includes a degrees-of-freedom input parameter to model the co-tendency for extreme events that can and do occur jointly. The T-Copula enables the modeling of a co-dependency structure of the portfolio of multiple individual indices. The T-Copula also allows for better modeling of fatter-tails extreme events as opposed to the traditional assumption of jointly normal portfolio returns of multiple variables.

The approach to run such a model is fairly simple. Analyze each of the independent variables using the methods described above, and when these are inputted into a portfolio, compute the pairwise correlation coefficients, and then apply the T-Copula in Risk Simulator available through the *Risk Simulator | Options* menu (Figure 62). The T-Copula method employs a correlation matrix you enter, computes the correlation's Cholesky-decomposed matrix on the inverse of the t-distribution, and simulates the random variable based on the selected distribution (e.g., Gumbel Max, Weibull 3, or generalized Pareto distribution).

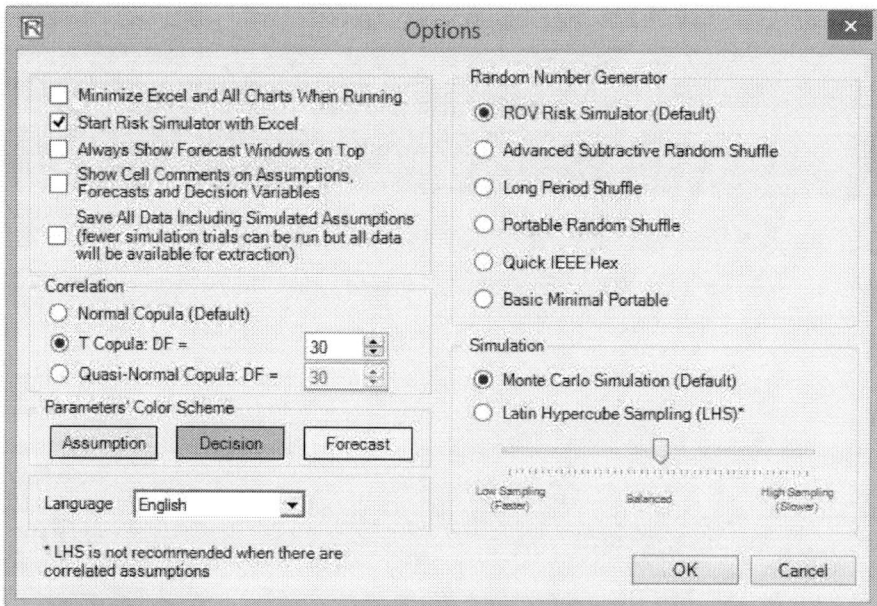

Figure 62: T-Copula

Technical Details: Extreme Value Distribution or Gumbel Distribution

The extreme value distribution (type 1) is commonly used to describe the largest value of a response over a period of time, for example, in flood flows, rainfall, and earthquakes. Other applications include the breaking strengths of materials, construction design, and aircraft loads and tolerances. The extreme value distribution is also known as the Gumbel distribution. The mathematical constructs for the extreme value distribution are as follows:

$$f(x) = \frac{1}{\beta} z e^{-z} \; where \; z = e^{\frac{x-\alpha}{\beta}} \quad for \; \beta > 0; \; and \; any \; value \; of \; x \; and \; \alpha$$

$$Mean = \; \alpha + 0.577215\beta$$

$$Standard \; Deviation = \; \sqrt{\frac{1}{6}\pi^2\beta^2}$$

$$Skewness = \; \frac{12\sqrt{6}(1.2020569)}{\pi^3} = 1.13955 \;\; \text{(this applies for all values of mode and scale)}$$

Excess Kurtosis = 5.4 (this applies for all values of mode and scale)

Mode (α) and scale (β) are the distributional parameters.

Calculating Parameters

There are two standard parameters for the extreme value distribution: mode and scale. The mode parameter is the most likely value for the variable (the highest point on the probability distribution). After you select the mode parameter, you can estimate the scale parameter. The scale parameter is a number greater than 0. The larger the scale parameter, the greater the variance.

The Gumbel maximum distribution has a symmetrical counterpart, the Gumbel minimum distribution. Both are available in Risk Simulator. These two distributions are mirror images of each other where their respective standard deviations and kurtosis are identical, but the Gumbel maximum is skewed to the right (positive skew, with a higher probability on the left and lower probability on the right) as compared to the Gumbel minimum, where the distribution is skewed to the left (negative skew). Their respective first moments are also mirror images of each other along the scale (β) parameter.

Figures 63 to 66 illustrate the distributional properties of the Gumbel minimum and Gumbel maximum.

Input requirements:

Mode alpha can be any value.

Scale beta > 0.

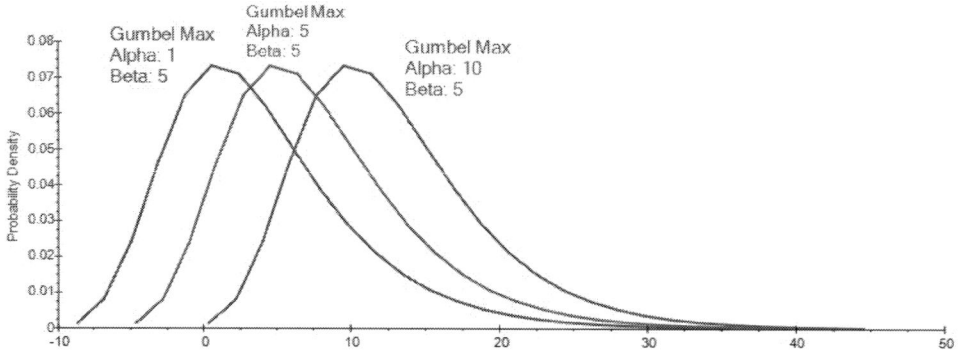

Figure 63: Gumbel Maximum Distribution with Different Alpha (Mode) Values

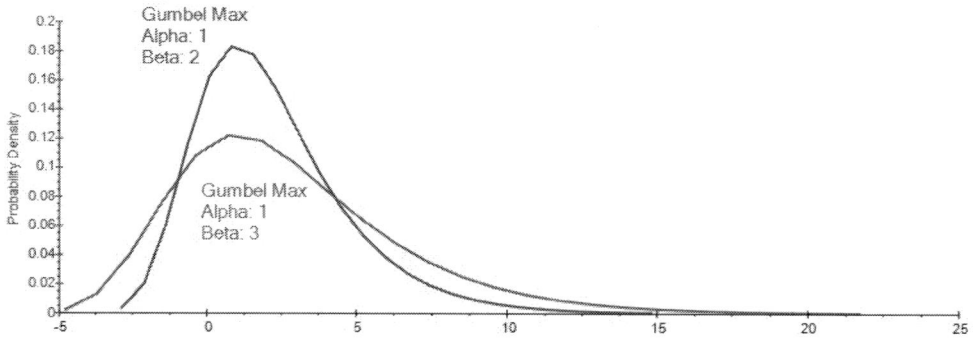

Figure 64: Gumbel Maximum Distribution with Different Beta (Scale) Values

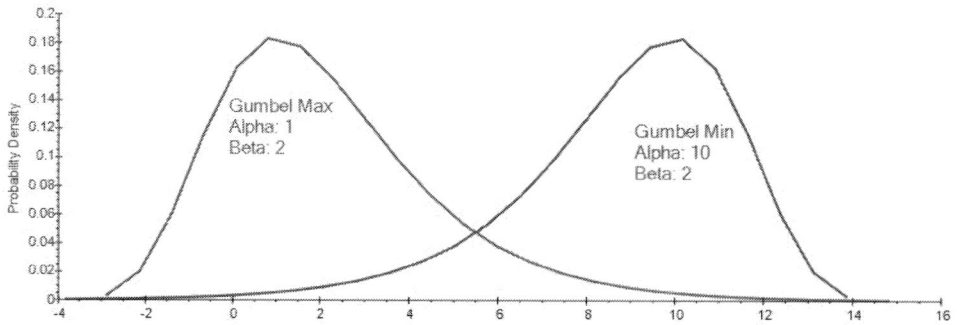

Figure 65: Gumbel Maximum versus Gumbel Minimum Distributions

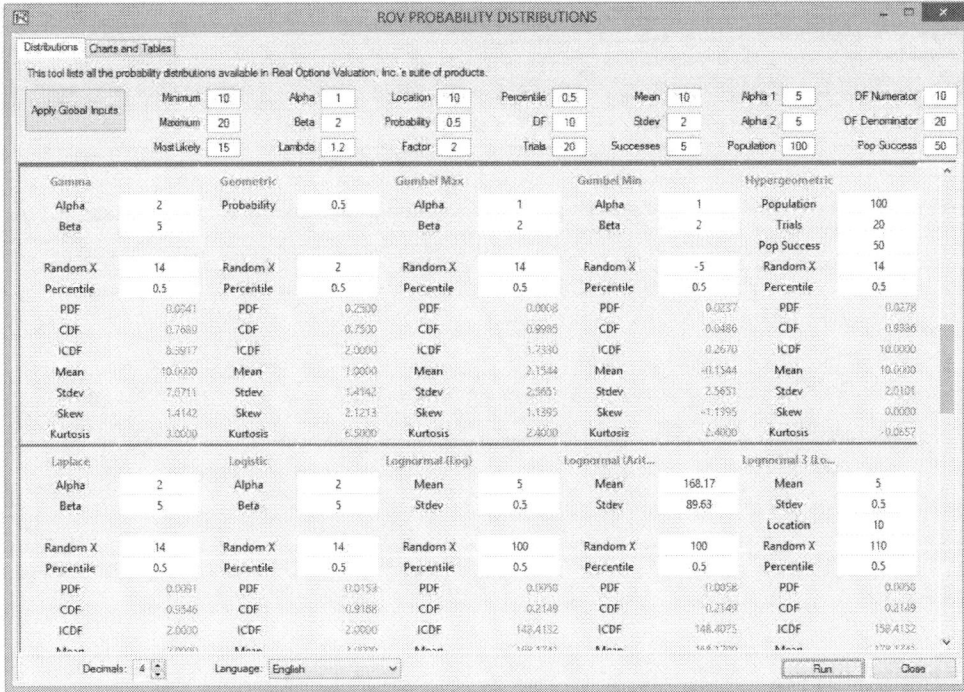

**Figure 66: Gumbel Maximum versus Gumbel Minimum Distributions'
Statistics and Moments**

Generalized Pareto Distribution

The generalized Pareto distribution is often used to model the tails of another distribution. The mathematical constructs for the generalized Pareto distribution are as follows:

$$f(x) = \frac{1}{\sigma}\left[1 + \frac{\varepsilon(x-\mu)}{\sigma}\right]\exp\left(-\frac{1}{\varepsilon}-1\right) \text{ for all nonzero } \varepsilon \text{ else } f(x) = \frac{1}{\sigma}\exp\left(\frac{-(x-\mu)}{\sigma}\right)$$

$$Mean = \mu + \frac{\sigma}{1-\varepsilon} \text{ if } \varepsilon < 1$$

$$Standard\ Deviation = \sqrt{\frac{\sigma^2}{(1-\varepsilon)^2(1-2\varepsilon)}} \text{ if } \varepsilon < 0.5$$

Location (μ), scale (σ), and shape (ε) are the distributional parameters.

Input requirements:

Location mu can be any value.

Scale sigma > 0.

Shape epsilon can be any value; $\varepsilon < 0$ would create a long-tailed distribution with no upper limit, whereas $\varepsilon > 0$ would generate a short-tailed distribution with a smaller variance and thicker right tail, where $\mu \le x < \infty$. If shape epsilon and location mu are both zero, then the distribution reverts to the exponential distribution. If the shape epsilon is positive and location mu is exactly the ratio of scale sigma to shape epsilon, we have the regular Pareto distribution. The location mu is sometimes also known as the threshold parameter.

Distributions whose tails decrease exponentially, such as the normal distribution, lead to a generalized Pareto distribution's shape epsilon parameter of zero. Distributions whose tails decrease as a polynomial, such as Student's t-distribution, lead to a positive shape epsilon parameter. Finally, distributions whose tails are finite, such as the beta distribution, lead to a negative shape epsilon parameter.

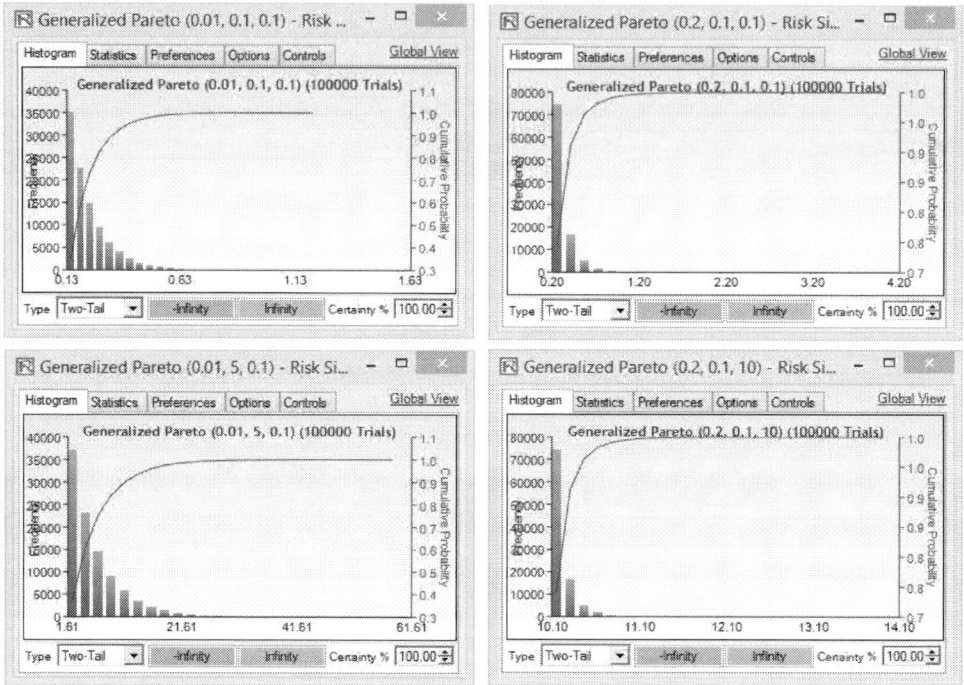

Figure 67: Generalized Pareto Distributions with Different Parameters (Shape Alpha, Scale Beta, Location)

Weibull Distribution (Rayleigh Distribution)

The Weibull distribution describes data resulting from life and fatigue tests. It is commonly used to describe failure time in reliability studies as well as the breaking strengths of materials in reliability and quality control tests. Weibull Distributions are also used to represent various physical quantities, such as wind speed.

The Weibull distribution is a family of distributions that can assume the properties of several other distributions. For example, depending on the shape parameter you define, the Weibull distribution can be used to model the exponential and Rayleigh distributions, among others. The Weibull distribution is very flexible. When the Weibull shape parameter is equal to 1.0, the Weibull distribution is identical to the exponential distribution. The Weibull location parameter lets you set up an exponential distribution to start at a location other than 0.0. When the shape parameter is less than 1.0, the Weibull distribution becomes a steeply declining curve. A manufacturer might find this effect useful in describing part failures during a burn-in period.

The mathematical constructs for the Weibull distribution are as follows:

$$f(x) = \frac{\alpha}{\beta} \left[\frac{x}{\beta} \right]^{\alpha-1} e^{-\left(\frac{x}{\beta}\right)^{\alpha}}$$

$Mean = \beta \Gamma (1 + \alpha^{-1})$

$Standard\ Deviation = \beta^2 \left[\Gamma(1 + 2\alpha^{-1}) - \Gamma^2(1 + \alpha^{-1}) \right]$

$$Skewness = \frac{2\Gamma^3(1 + \beta^{-1}) - 3\Gamma(1 + \beta^{-1})\Gamma(1 + 2\beta^{-1}) + \Gamma(1 + 3\beta^{-1})}{\left[\Gamma(1 + 2\beta^{-1}) - \Gamma^2(1 + \beta^{-1}) \right]^{3/2}}$$

$Excess\ Kurtosis =$

$$\frac{-6\Gamma^4(1 + \beta^{-1}) + 12\Gamma^2(1 + \beta^{-1})\Gamma(1 + 2\beta^{-1}) - 3\Gamma^2(1 + 2\beta^{-1}) - 4\Gamma(1 + \beta^{-1})\Gamma(1 + 3\beta^{-1}) + \Gamma(1 + 4\beta^{-1})}{\left[\Gamma(1 + 2\beta^{-1}) - \Gamma^2(1 + \beta^{-1}) \right]^2}$$

Shape (α) and central location scale (β) are the distributional parameters, and Γ is the gamma function.

Input requirements:

Shape alpha ≥ 0.05.

Scale beta > 0 and can be any positive value.

The Weibull 3 distribution uses the same constructs as the original Weibull distribution but adds a location, or shift, parameter. The Weibull distribution starts from a minimum value of 0, whereas this Weibull 3, or shifted Weibull, distribution shifts the starting location to any other value. Figures 68–70 illustrate the distributional characteristics of the Weibull.

Alpha, beta, and location or shift are the distributional parameters.

Input requirements:

Alpha (shape) ≥ 0.05.

Beta (central location scale) > 0 and can be any positive value.

Location can be any positive or negative value including zero.

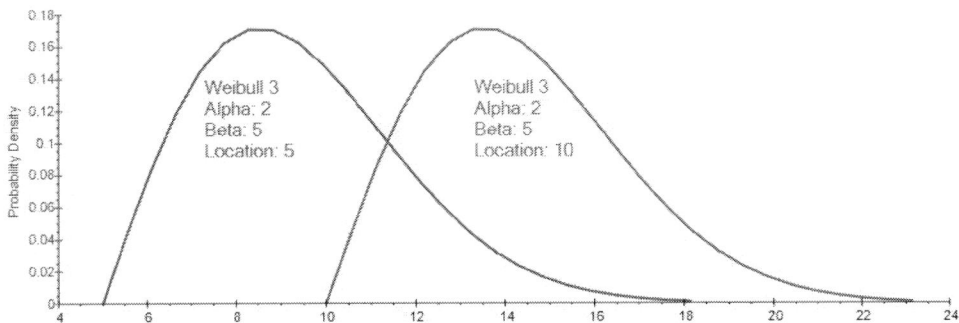

Figure 68: Weibull with Different Location Parameters

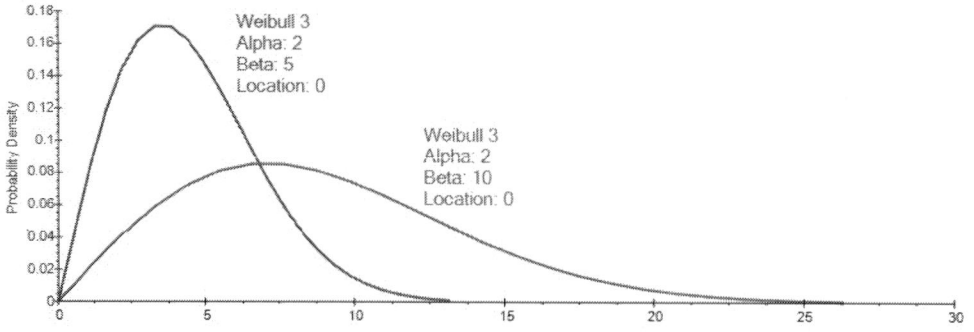

Figure 69: Weibull with Different Scaled Central Location (Beta) Parameters

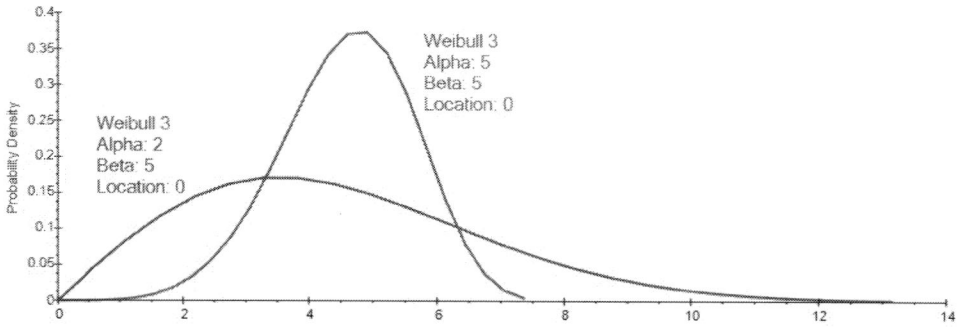

Figure 70: Weibull with Different Shape (Alpha) Parameters

8

CASE STUDY 8: BASEL II AND BASEL III CREDIT, MARKET, OPERATIONAL, AND LIQUIDITY RISKS WITH ASSET LIABILITY MANAGEMENT

This case study was written by the author and Alfredo B. Roisenzvit. Alfredo is a partner at RiskBusiness Latin America and a strategic partner of Real Options Valuation, Inc. He is currently acting as Invited Professor for ERM & Operational Risk and Financial Regulation for the Masters in Finance of Universidad de San Andrés in Buenos Aires, Argentina; Risk Management for the Program in Bank Administration developed for the Argentine Banking Association (ADEBA) by Universidad Torcuato Di Tella in Buenos Aires, Argentina; and the Risk Management Module for the Program for Professional Development of the Business School and the Risk Management class for the graduate program for Sustainable Economic Development at the Pontifica Universidad Católica Argentina. He is also a Guest Professor for the exchange program with Frankfurt University. Formerly, he has been an instructor for various programs in Banking Supervision at the Toronto Centre and Lead Lecturer of the Master Class for Operational Risk in Spanish at The Annual Op Risk Conference of the Risk Management Association. Previously he worked for over 12 years in various roles at the Central Bank of the Argentine Republic, including Board Advisor, Economic Research, and Director of Supervision Coordination in charge of developing and enforcing supervision manuals and supervisory procedures. Alfredo also presided over the CAMEL committee of bank evaluation, with the responsibility of representing the Central Bank before the Basel Committee and the International Supervisory Associations, which activity coincided with the drafting of working groups and the implementation discussions of Basel II. He participated in the drafting of the initial regulations of Basel II for Argentina, and he coordinated the multidisciplinary group that performed the Self-Assessment of the Core Principles of the Basel Committee, and as counterpart of the FSAP Mission led by the World Bank and the IMF.

It is often said that the Basel Committee Standards, formally called Capital Accords, constitute the bible for banking regulators (Central Banks) everywhere. In addition to the Accords, the Basel Committee has also framed 29 principles for effective banking supervision known as the Core Principles for Effective Banking Supervision. The standards encompassed by the Capital Accord and the Core Principles have become the source of banking regulation in every country in the world. As is widely known, these standards have evolved from Basel I to Basel II and III, reflecting the evolution of the financial industry (from Basel I to II) and the lessons from the financial crisis of 2008 (from Basel II to III). The most noticeable financial regulation paradigm changes captured and fostered by the Basel standards' evolution are risk management and capital allocation. These most important changes in the international standards, and, therefore, in virtually every country´s financial regulatory framework, relate to the manner in which risks are managed and capital is calculated. By the general definition, as stated in Core Principle 15, Risk Management is the process to be used by banks to "identify, measure, evaluate, monitor, report and control or mitigate all material risks on a timely basis and to assess the adequacy of their capital and liquidity in relation to their risk profile." This process has been presented as the IMMM process: Identify, Measure, Monitor, and Mitigate each risk. In practice, the way to manage risks, and, hence, comply with the new Basel regulations, is to introduce or enhance the IMMM process for each material risk the financial institution faces.

Along with the aforementioned international standards, there are tools that facilitate the implementation or enhancement of the IMMM processes. Briefly, these are Formal Policies, Key Risk Indicators, Capital Models, and MIS/Reports.

This case study looks at the practical tools—quantitative models, Monte Carlo risk simulations, credit models, and business statistics—utilized to model and quantify regulatory and economic capital, measure and monitor key risk indicators, and report all the obtained data in a clear and intuitive manner. It relates to the modeling and analysis of asset liability management, credit risk, market risk, operational risk, and liquidity risk for banks or financial institutions, allowing these firms to properly identify, assess, quantify, value, diversify, hedge, and generate periodic regulatory reports for supervisory authorities and Central Banks on their credit, market, and operational risk areas, as well as for internal risk audits, risk controls, and risk management purposes.

In banking finance and financial services firms, *economic capital* is defined as the amount of risk capital, assessed on a realistic basis based on actual historical data, the bank or firm requires to cover the risks as a going concern, such as market risk, credit risk, liquidity risk, and operational risk. It is the amount of money that is needed to ensure survival in a worst-case scenario. Financial services regulators such as Central Banks, Bank of International Settlements, and other regulatory commissions should then require banks to hold an amount of risk capital equal at least to its economic capital times some holding multiple. Typically, economic capital is calculated by determining the amount of capital that the firm needs to ensure that its realistic balance sheet stays solvent over a certain time period with a prespecified probability (e.g., usually defined as 99.00%). Therefore, economic capital is often calculated with *Value at Risk* (VaR) type models.

Capital modeling in banks surged as a necessity for the larger international financial institutions, which discovered that the regulatory approaches taken by regulators were too basic and mainly not risk based. For example, credit risk capital requirements under Basel I were just a percentage (8% times another multiplier) of the volume of operations. This measure, which was very easy to calculate, was not risk sensitive, other than the differentiation of broad asset types. Therefore, complex banks found these capital requirements to be very inefficient in terms of capital planning, pricing, and leveraging limits and targets. With the evolution of the use of statistical models and available data—especially in market risk measurement—regulators started accepting internal capital models developed by the big international financial institutions. Accordingly, in 1996, an amendment was introduced to the Basel Accord (still Basel I) that allowed certain qualifying banks to calculate and hold capital in line with their internal models. To differentiate these measures of capital, banks started calling these internal calculations "economic capital," because it had a very close relationship with the real economics of the business, whereas "regulatory capital" was the requirement mandated by regulators. As the business evolved, and regulations became more ample, complex financial institutions started relying more on their economic capital models for the measurement and management of risks, while simultaneously having to hold regulatory capital. In most cases, the differences between these two kinds of capital for the same risk were very significant. This fact was one of the main motivators of Basel II, prompted mainly by a request from the more complex banks that the International Standards and, hence, banking regulations allow them to use their economic capital models to allocate regulatory capital. In other words, one of the outright motivations for the Basel II reforms was to close the practical gap between economic and regulatory capital.

As Basel II started to be implemented in most countries, the new regulatory paradigm established that banks—not just complex international financial institutions—must have IMMM processes for all material risks, and calculate and allocate economic capital for each and every one of these risks. For any given bank, these risks are defined by regulations as identified in the above-mentioned Core Principles: credit, market, operational, liquidity, interest rate, strategic, reputational, securitization, and so on. In this light, banks of any size, in virtually every country, need to identify, measure, monitor, and mitigate all these risks, and calculate, evaluate, and allocate economic capital for each. This case discusses a set of simple approaches with straightforward tools that allow banks of any size and complexity to generate information for the management (the IMMM process) of these risks, and for the calculation of economic capital based on available balance sheet and regulatory information. In light of these International Standards, which are now formal regulations in virtually every country in the world, we utilize a spectrum of basic and more complex approaches to generate an economic capital model calculated on the formally defined risk drivers in each case and providing for risk-sensitive capital results for each relevant risk. Additionally, for each risk, through a set of basic information, a set of key risk indicators is generated and combined with the capital model results to produce relevant risk reports. Since regulations still require many instances of regulatory capital, such calculation is still provided along with Basel Standards as another useful output of the designed tools. Finally, The Basel Committee differentiates credit, market, and operational risks from the rest, defining these three as the most relevant in any given financial institution. According to the Three Pillar design of Basel II, these are known as Pillar I risks. Under Basel II and III, economic and regulatory capital can be unified for Pillar I risks. In other words, for these three risks (credit, market and operational), economic capital models are given by the Basel Accord as a way to generate some standardization of methodologies and comparison among banks and countries.

For credit risk, the traditional approach for Basel I regulatory capital (still available as a basic choice in Basel III) is to calculate 8% of outstanding loan volume, multiplied by a factor depending of the type of asset treated (100% for uncollateralized loans, 50% for mortgages, 20% for interbank, etc.). This approach, however, does not differentiate by risk within each category. In order to create a more risk-sensitive approach, Basel II incorporated the main logic of portfolio models, where capital is the amount required to cover unexpected losses. Unexpected losses, in turn, are calculated as the residual given by the difference between the mean and the confidence interval of a loss distribution function.

Project Economic Analysis Tool on Modeling Banking Risk

Figure 71 illustrates the PEAT utility's ALM-CMOL module for Credit Risk—Economic Regulatory Capital (ERC) Global Settings tab. This current analysis is performed on credit issues such as loans, credit lines, and debt at the commercial, retail, or personal levels. To get started with the utility, existing files can be opened or saved, or a default sample model can be retrieved from the menu. However, to follow along, we recommend opening the default example (click on the menu icon on the top right corner of the software, then select *Load Example*).

The number of categories of loans and credit types can be set as well as the loan or credit category names, a *Loss Given Default* (LGD) value in percent, and the Basel credit type (*residential mortgages, revolving credit, other miscellaneous credit,* or *wholesale corporate and sovereign debt*). Each credit type has its required Basel III model that is public knowledge, and the software uses the prescribed models per Basel regulations. Further, historical data can be manually entered by the user into the utility or via existing databases and data files. Such data files may be large and, hence, stored either in a single file or multiple data files where each file's contents can be mapped to the list of required variables (e.g., credit issue date, customer information, product type or segment, Central Bank ratings, amount of the debt or loan, interest payment, principal payment, last payment date, and other ancillary information the bank or financial services firm has access to) for the analysis, and the successfully mapped connections are displayed. Additional information such as the required VaR percentiles, average life of a commercial loan, and historical data period on which to run the data files to obtain the *Probability of Default* (PD) is entered. Next, the *Exposure at Default* (EAD) analysis periodicity is selected as is the date type and the Central Bank ratings. Different Central Banks in different nations tend to have similar credit ratings but the software allows for flexibility in choosing the relevant rating scheme (i.e., Level 1 may indicate on-time payment of an existing loan whereas Level 3 may indicate a late payment of over 90 days, which, therefore, constitutes a default). All these inputs and settings can be saved either as stand-alone settings and data or including the results. Users would enter a unique name and notes and save the current settings (previously saved models and settings can be retrieved, edited, or deleted; a new model can be created; or an existing model can be duplicated). The saved models are listed and can be rearranged according to the user's preference.

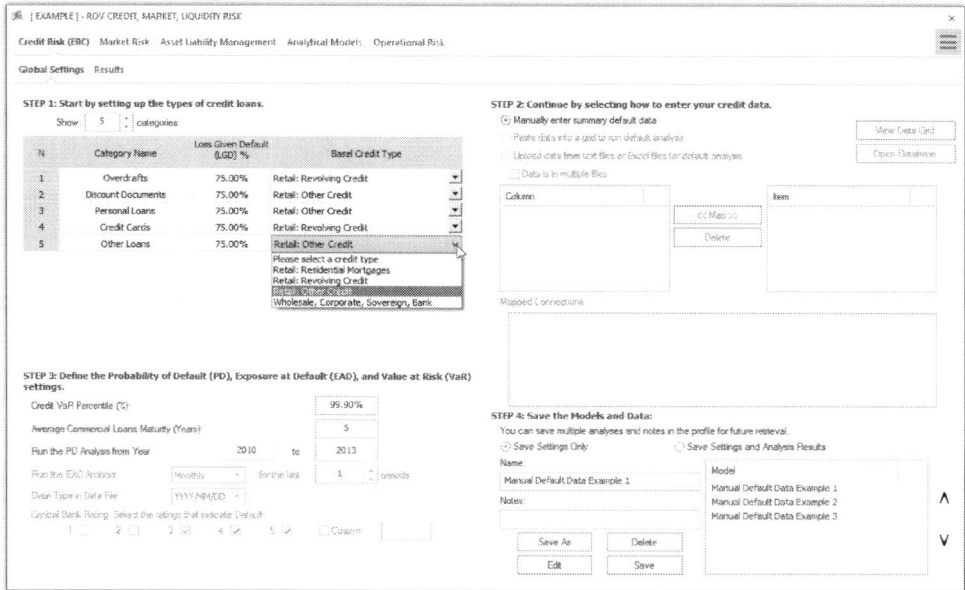

Figure 71: Credit Risk Settings

Credit Economic and Regulatory Capital

Figure 72 illustrates the PEAT utility's ALM-CMOL module for Credit Risk—Economic Regulatory Capital's Results tab. The results are shown in the grid if data files were loaded and preprocessed and results were computed and presented here (the loading of data files is discussed in connection with Figure 71). However, if data are to be manually entered (as previously presented in Figure 71), then the grey areas in the data grid are available for manual user input, such as the number of clients for a specific credit or debt category, the number of defaults for said categories historically by period, and the exposure at default values (total amount of debt issued within the total period). One can manually input the number of clients and number of credit and loan defaults within specific annual time-period bands. The utility computes the percentage of defaults (number of credit or loan defaults divided by number of clients within the specified time periods), and the average percentage of default is the proxy used for the PD. If users have specific PD rates to use, they can simply enter any number of clients and number of defaults as long as the ratio is what the user wants as the PD input (e.g., a 1% PD means users can enter 100 clients and 1 as the number of defaults). The LGD can be user inputted in the global settings as a percentage (LGD is defined as the percentage of losses of loans and debt that cannot be recovered when they are in default). The EAD is the total loans amount within these time bands. These PD, LGD, and EAD values can also be computed using structural models as is discussed later. *Expected Losses* (EL) is the product of *PD × LGD × EAD*. *Economic Capital* (EC) is based on Basel II and Basel III requirements and is a matter of public record. *Risk Weighted Average* (RWA) is a regulatory requirement per Basel II and Basel III such as *12.5 × EC*. The change in *Capital Adequacy Requirement* (ΔCAR @ 8%) is simply the ratio of the EC to EAD less the 8% holding requirement. In other words, the *Regulatory Capital* (RC) is 8% of EAD.

The results obtained by the model allow for the construction of key risk indicators, comparing basic regulatory capital requirements with these economic capital requirements. Additionally, when coupled with the internal or external rating models (or credit scores) a profile of expected and unexpected losses for each product or asset type can be constructed. This is also the basis for the application of RAROC indicators, and the effective allocation of economic capital, in line with the international standards and local regulatory requirements.

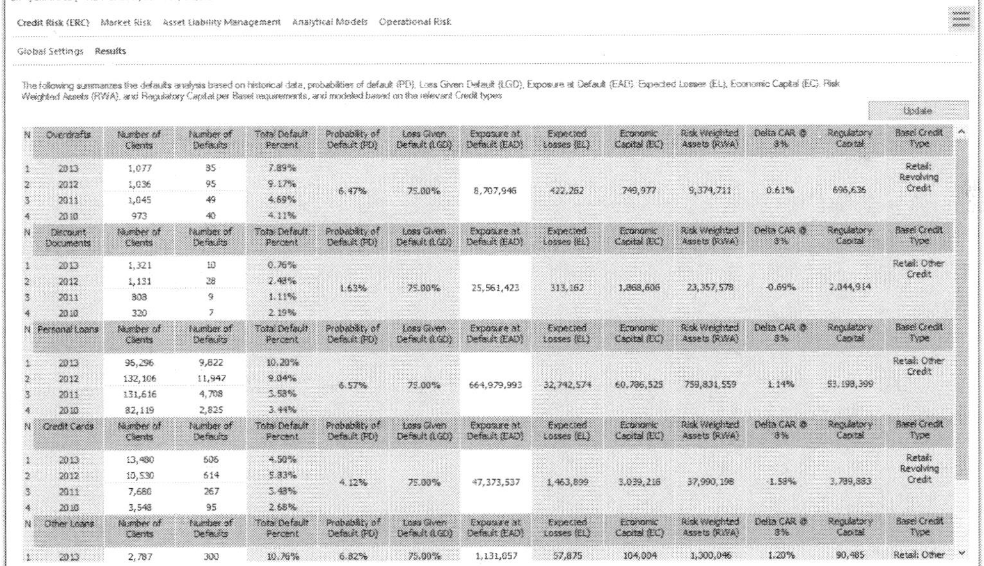

N	Overdrafts	Number of Clients	Number of Defaults	Total Default Percent	Probability of Default (PD)	Loss Given Default (LGD)	Exposure at Default (EAD)	Expected Losses (EL)	Economic Capital (EC)	Risk Weighted Assets (RWA)	Delta CAR @ 8%	Regulatory Capital	Basel Credit Type
1	2013	1,077	85	7.89%	6.47%	75.00%	8,707,946	422,262	749,977	9,374,711	0.61%	696,636	Retail: Revolving Credit
2	2012	1,036	95	9.17%									
3	2011	1,045	49	4.69%									
4	2010	973	40	4.11%									
N	Discount Documents	Number of Clients	Number of Defaults	Total Default Percent	Probability of Default (PD)	Loss Given Default (LGD)	Exposure at Default (EAD)	Expected Losses (EL)	Economic Capital (EC)	Risk Weighted Assets (RWA)	Delta CAR @ 8%	Regulatory Capital	Basel Credit Type
1	2013	1,321	10	0.76%	1.63%	75.00%	25,561,423	313,162	1,868,606	23,357,578	-0.69%	2,044,914	Retail: Other Credit
2	2012	1,131	28	2.48%									
3	2011	808	9	1.11%									
4	2010	320	7	2.19%									
N	Personal Loans	Number of Clients	Number of Defaults	Total Default Percent	Probability of Default (PD)	Loss Given Default (LGD)	Exposure at Default (EAD)	Expected Losses (EL)	Economic Capital (EC)	Risk Weighted Assets (RWA)	Delta CAR @ 8%	Regulatory Capital	Basel Credit Type
1	2013	96,296	9,822	10.20%	6.57%	75.00%	664,979,993	32,742,574	60,786,525	759,831,559	1.14%	53,198,399	Retail: Other Credit
2	2012	132,106	11,947	9.04%									
3	2011	131,616	4,708	3.58%									
4	2010	82,119	2,825	3.44%									
N	Credit Cards	Number of Clients	Number of Defaults	Total Default Percent	Probability of Default (PD)	Loss Given Default (LGD)	Exposure at Default (EAD)	Expected Losses (EL)	Economic Capital (EC)	Risk Weighted Assets (RWA)	Delta CAR @ 8%	Regulatory Capital	Basel Credit Type
1	2013	13,480	606	4.50%	4.12%	75.00%	47,373,537	1,463,899	3,039,216	37,990,198	-1.58%	3,789,883	Retail: Revolving Credit
2	2012	10,530	614	5.83%									
3	2011	7,680	267	3.48%									
4	2010	3,548	95	2.68%									
N	Other Loans	Number of Clients	Number of Defaults	Total Default Percent	Probability of Default (PD)	Loss Given Default (LGD)	Exposure at Default (EAD)	Expected Losses (EL)	Economic Capital (EC)	Risk Weighted Assets (RWA)	Delta CAR @ 8%	Regulatory Capital	Basel Credit Type
1	2013	2,787	300	10.76%	6.82%	75.00%	1,131,057	57,875	104,004	1,300,046	1.20%	90,485	Retail: Other

Figure 72: Economic Regulatory Capital (ERC)

Basel Credit Risk Models and Economic Capital

The CMOL software applies Basel II and Basel III requirements and definitions on regulatory capital. For instance, the Economic Capital is defined as Value at Risk (i.e., the Total Risk Amount) less any Expected Losses. There are 4 categories of equations based on the type of credit and loans: 3 types of Retail Loans plus a category for Corporate Loans.

Retail Loans: Residential Mortgage Exposures

$$Correlation\ (R) = 0.15$$

$$Capital\ Requirement\ (K) = \left[LGD \times \Phi \left(\frac{\phi^{-1}(PD) + \sqrt{R}\phi^{-1}(99.9\%)}{\sqrt{1-R}} \right) - LGD \times PD \right]$$

$$Economic\ Capital\ (EC) = EAD \times K$$

$$= EAD \times \left[LGD \times \Phi \left(\frac{\phi^{-1}(PD) + \sqrt{R}\phi^{-1}(99.9\%)}{\sqrt{1-R}} \right) - LGD \times PD \right]$$

Retail Loans: Qualifying Revolving Retail Exposures

$$Correlation\ (R) = 0.04$$

$$Capital\ Requirement\ (K) = \left[LGD \times \Phi \left(\frac{\phi^{-1}(PD) + \sqrt{R}\phi^{-1}(99.9\%)}{\sqrt{1-R}} \right) - LGD \times PD \right]$$

$$Economic\ Capital\ (EC) = EAD \times K$$

$$= EAD \times \left[LGD \times \Phi \left(\frac{\phi^{-1}(PD) + \sqrt{R}\phi^{-1}(99.9\%)}{\sqrt{1-R}} \right) - LGD \times PD \right]$$

$$Risk\ Weighted\ Assets\ (RWA) = 12.5 \times EC = 12.5 \times EAD \times K$$

Retail Loans: Other Retail Exposures

$$Correlation\ (R) = \frac{0.03 \times (1 - e^{-35 \times PD})}{(1 - e^{-35})} + 0.16 \times \left[1 - \frac{(1 - e^{-35 \times PD})}{(1 - e^{-35})} \right]$$

$$Capital\ Requirement\ (K) = \left[LGD \times \Phi \left(\frac{\phi^{-1}(PD) + \sqrt{R}\phi^{-1}(99.9\%)}{\sqrt{1-R}} \right) - LGD \times PD \right]$$

$$Economic\ Capital\ (EC) = EAD \times K$$

$$= EAD \times \left[LGD \times \Phi \left(\frac{\phi^{-1}(PD) + \sqrt{R}\phi^{-1}(99.9\%)}{\sqrt{1-R}} \right) - LGD \times PD \right]$$

$$Risk\ Weighted\ Assets\ (RWA) = 12.5 \times EC = 12.5 \times EAD \times K$$

Corporate Loans: Corporate, Sovereign, Bank, and Corporate Loans

$$Correlation\ (R) = \frac{0.12 \times (1 - e^{-50 \times PD})}{(1 - e^{-50})} + 0.24 \times \left[1 - \frac{(1 - e^{-50 \times PD})}{(1 - e^{-50})} \right]$$

$$Maturity\ Adjustment\ (B) = [0.11852 - 0.05478 \times \ln(PD)]^2$$

$$Capital\ Requirement\ (K)$$

$$= \left[LGD \times \Phi \left(\frac{\phi^{-1}(PD) + \sqrt{R}\phi^{-1}(99.9\%)}{\sqrt{1-R}} \right) - LGD \times PD \right]$$

$$\times \left[\frac{1 + (M - 2.5) \times b}{1 - 1.5 \times b} \right]$$

$$Economic\ Capital\ (EC) = EAD \times K$$

$$Economic\ Capital\ (EC)$$

$$= EAD \times \left[LGD \times \Phi\left(\frac{\phi^{-1}(PD) + \sqrt{R}\phi^{-1}(99.9\%)}{\sqrt{1-R}} \right) - LGD \times PD \right]$$

$$\times \left[\frac{1 + (M-2.5) \times B}{1 - 1.5 \times B} \right]$$

$$Risk\ Weighted\ Assets\ (RWA) = 12.5 \times EC = 12.5 \times EAD \times K$$

$$Risk\ Weighted\ Assets\ (RWA) = 12.5 \times EC = 12.5 \times EAD \times K$$

$$The\ Phi\ function\ \Phi\ is\ the\ CDF\ of\ Normal\ (0,1), and\ \phi^{-1}\ is\ the\ ICDF\ of\ Normal\ (0,1)$$

Market Risk

For market risk, as a Pillar I risk, has requirements similar to those for economic regulatory capital. The particularities of market risk make it, possibly, the one that is easier to model and calculate, and the one that has had more tool development so far. This is explained by the fact that the main input for market risk measurement and modeling is market prices of assets or, more practically, their volatilities. Therefore, there is great public availability of data, as opposed to the other Pillar I risks that do not have daily prices publically available. As an example, there is no public pricing of a particular group of retail loans issued by a private bank. Yet, modeling tools for both market and credit risk are based on the same approach: utilizing past stylized data to project future behavior under certain assumptions and within a confidence interval. Logically then, market risk has a great bundle of information available and the potential to better test and calibrate models. As presented, market risk models take on a Value at Risk (VAR) approach.

Figure 73 illustrates the PEAT utility's ALM-CMOL module for Market Risk where Market Data is entered. Users start by entering the global settings, such as the number of investment assets and currency assets the bank has in its portfolio, that require further analysis; the total number of historical data that will be used for analysis; and various VaR percentiles to run (e.g., 99.00% and 95.00%). In addition, the volatility method of choice (industry standard volatility or Risk Metrics volatility methods) and the date type (mm/dd/yyyy or dd/mm/yyyy) are entered. The amount invested (balance) of each asset and currency is entered and the historical data can be entered, copy and pasted from another data source, or uploaded to the data grid, and the settings as well as the historical data entered can be saved for future retrieval and further analysis in subsequent subtabs.

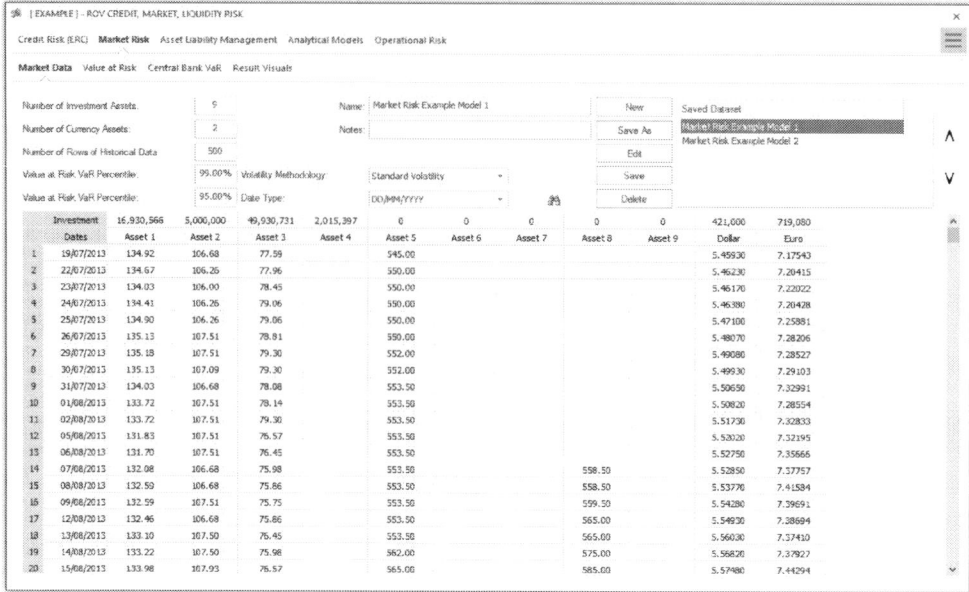

Figure 73: Market Risk Data

Figure 74 illustrates the computed results for the Market VaR. Based on the data entered in the interface shown as Figure 73, the results are computed and presented in two separate grids: the VaR results and asset positions and details. The computations can be triggered to be rerun or Updated, and the results can be exported to an Excel report template if required. The results computed in the first grid are based on user input market data. For instance, the VaR calculations are simply the *Asset Position × Daily Volatility × Inverse Standard Normal Distribution of VaR Percentile × Square Root of the Horizon in Days.*

In other words, we have:

$$VaR\ X\% = Asset\ \times\ Daily\ Volatility\ \times\ \sqrt{Days}\ \times Inverse\ Standard\ Normal\ of\ X\%$$

$$VaR_{X\%} = A\sigma\sqrt{D}\Phi^{-1}(x)$$

Therefore, the Gross VaR is simply the summation of all VaR values for all assets and foreign exchange–denominated assets. In comparison, the Internal Historical Simulation VaR uses the same calculation based on the historically simulated time-series of asset values. The historically simulated time-series of asset values is obtained by the *Asset's Investment × Asset Price$_{t-1}$ × Period-Specific Relative Returns – Asset's Current Position.* The Asset's Current Position is simply the *Investment × Asset Price$_t$.* From this simulated time series of asset flows, the $(1 - X\%)$ percentile asset value is the *VaR X%.* Typically, *X%* is 99.00% or 95.00% and can be changed as required by the user based on the regional or country-specific regulatory agency's statutes.

This can be stated as:

$$Historical\ Simulation\ (HSS)\ VaR\ X\%$$
$$= (1 - X\%)\ Percentile\ of\ Historically\ Simulated\ Series\ (HSS)$$

$$HSS = Investment \times Price_{t-1} \times Exp(LNRR) - Investment \times Price_t$$

[EXAMPLE] - ROV CREDIT, MARKET, LIQUIDITY RISK

Credit Risk (ERC) **Market Risk** Asset Liability Management Analytical Models Operational Risk

Market Data Value at Risk Central Bank VaR Result Visuals

Horizon	Gross Value at Risk (VaR)		Internal Historical Simulation Value at Risk (VaR) 99.00%			Internal Historical Simulation Value at Risk (VaR) 95.00%		
	VaR 99.00%	VaR 95.00%	Total Values	Bonds Only	Currency Only	Total Values	Bonds Only	Currency Only
1 Day	2,679,921	1,894,349	1,784,836	1,817,804	55,871	1,352,838	1,348,769	38,157
5 Day	5,992,486	4,237,012	3,991,015	4,064,733	124,932	3,025,037	3,015,939	85,323
10 Day	8,474,655	5,992,040	5,644,147	5,748,400	176,681	4,278,049	4,265,182	120,565

[Update]

Asset Positions and Details

Asset	Daily Volatility	Current Position	Current Weight	99.00% VaR 1 Day	99.00% VaR 5 Day	99.00% VaR 10 Day	95.00% VaR 1 Day	95.00% VaR 5 Day	95.00% VaR 10 Day
Asset 1	1.06%	26,073,072	30.65%	643,403	1,438,693	2,034,620	454,921	1,017,234	1,438,586
Asset 2	2.61%	3,187,500	3.75%	193,273	432,173	611,184	136,655	305,569	432,140
Asset 3	1.50%	28,710,170	33.75%	999,427	2,234,787	3,160,466	706,649	1,580,115	2,234,620
Asset 4	1.78%	15,720,097	18.48%	652,132	1,458,212	2,062,323	461,093	1,031,035	1,458,103
Asset 5	1.26%	0	0.00%	0	0	0	0	0	0
Asset 6	1.29%	0	0.00%	0	0	0	0	0	0
Asset 7	1.03%	0	0.00%	0	0	0	0	0	0
Asset 8	1.15%	0	0.00%	0	0	0	0	0	0
Asset 9	1.39%	0	0.00%	0	0	0	0	0	0
Dollar	0.68%	3,456,494	4.06%	54,809	122,557	173,322	38,753	86,654	122,548
Euro	0.74%	7,908,463	9.30%	135,876	306,065	432,841	96,779	216,404	306,042

Figure 74: Market Value at Risk

Many countries issue regulations for market risk measurement and capital allocation, whereby some standardized models are suggested or even imposed, in line with the Basel Standards. We analyze such an example in Figure 75, where the regulatory model can be obtained by utilizing the parameters given by the regulator (i.e., volatilities and holding periods for given common assets). The structure of the tool allows for the comparison of regulatory, internal, and stressed scenarios, giving the analysts a large array of results to better interpret risk measurement, capital allocation, and future projections.

Central Bank Market Risk

Figure 75 illustrates the Central Bank VaR method and results in computing VaR based on user settings (e.g., the VaR percentile, time horizon of the holding period in days, number of assets to analyze, and the period of the analysis) and the assets' historical data. The VaR computations are based on the same approach as previously described, and the inputs, settings, and results can be saved for future retrieval.

ROV CREDIT, MARKET, LIQUIDITY RISK - [C:\Users\Dr. Johnathan Mun\Desktop\ROV Credit Market and Liquidity Example.rovcml]

Credit Risk (ERC) **Market Risk** Asset Liability Management Analytical Models Operational Risk

Market Data Value at Risk **Central Bank VaR** Result Visuals

Value at Risk (VaR) %: 99.00%
Time Horizon (Days): 5
Number of Assets: 20
Analysis is for Month/Year:

Name of Dataset:
Sample of Central Bank VaR
List of Saved Datasets: Save As
Dataset
Sample of Central Bank VaR

New   Delete
Edit   Save

Asset Type	T02405	Asset Type	SX240S	Asset Type	MU2405	Asset Type
Volatility	1.0000%	Volatility	1.0500%	Volatility	1.1100%	Volatility
Day	NPV of Position	Value at Risk	NPV of Position	Value at Risk	NPV of Position	Value at Risk
1	11,042.50	575.32	11,009.00	601.76	10,985.00	635.28
2	11,444.82	996.28	11,115.00	608.05	11,458.00	662.63
3	11,534.80	600.97	11,534.80	631.02	11,534.80	667.07
4	11,596.80	604.20	11,596.80	634.41	11,625.00	672.29
5	11,596.80	604.20	11,596.80	634.41	11,596.80	670.66
6	11,596.80	604.20	11,596.80	634.41	11,996.80	670.66
7	11,651.16	607.03	11,651.16	637.38	11,651.16	673.80
8	11,698.25	609.48	11,698.25	639.96	11,698.25	676.53
9	11,698.25	609.48	11,698.25	639.96	11,698.25	676.53
10	16,541.80	861.83	16,541.80	904.83	16,541.80	956.64
11	17,290.98	900.87	17,290.98	945.91	17,290.98	999.96
12	17,290.98	900.87	17,290.98	945.91	17,290.98	999.96
13	17,290.98	900.87	17,290.98	945.91	17,290.98	999.96
14	17,346.15	903.74	17,346.15	948.93	17,346.15	1,003.15
15	24,343.58	1,268.31	24,343.58	1,331.73	24,343.58	1,407.82
16	24,457.51	1,274.25	24,457.51	1,337.96	24,457.51	1,414.41
17	22,445.01	1,169.39	22,445.01	1,227.86	22,445.01	1,298.03
18	22,549.57	1,174.84	22,549.57	1,233.58	22,549.57	1,304.07
19	22,549.57	1,174.84	22,549.57	1,233.58	22,549.57	1,304.07
20	22,549.57	1,174.84	22,549.57	1,233.58	22,549.57	1,304.07
21	23,984.37	1,249.59	23,984.37	1,312.07	23,984.37	1,387.05
22	23,610.71	1,230.13	23,610.71	1,291.63	23,610.71	1,365.44
23	23,798.73	1,239.92	23,798.73	1,301.92	23,798.73	1,376.31
24	22,359.26	1,164.93	22,359.26	1,223.17	22,359.26	1,293.07
25	18,958.36	987.74	18,958.36	1,037.12	18,958.36	1,096.39

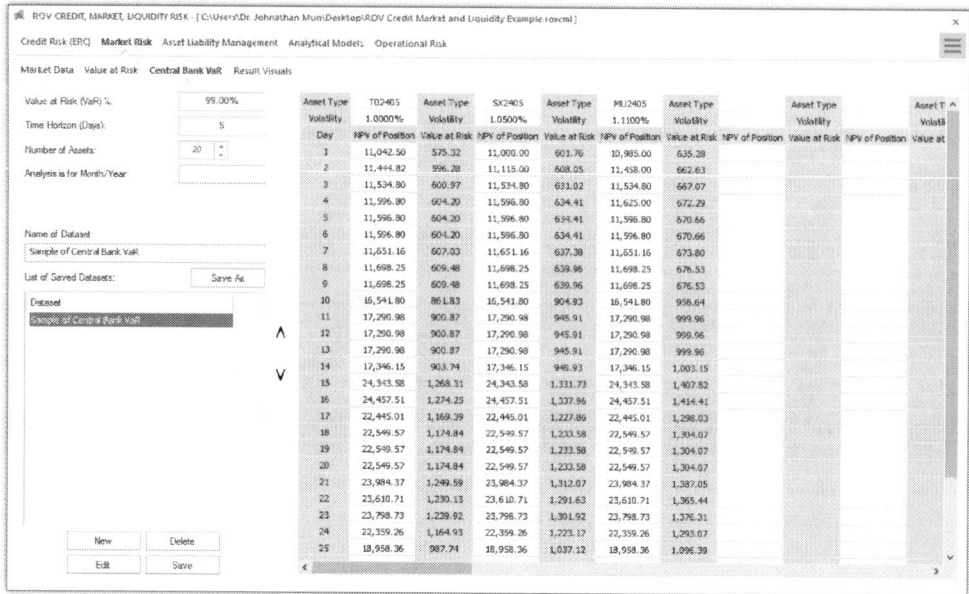

Figure 75: Market Central Bank VaR

Asset Liability Management

As with any other Basel-defined risk, KRIs are constructed based on the inputs and results of the modeling tool, and can be duly monitored and reported, in line with the IMMM process. Liquidity and interest rate risk are usually managed together in a function called ALM, short for Asset Liability Management. These two risks are closely intertwined, since liquidity risk monitors the availability of liquid funds to confront disbursement requirements (usually in three time horizons: immediate and intraday, short-term structure, and long-term structure), while interest rate risk measures the impact of the difference in maturities, or duration, for assets and liabilities.

Figure 76 illustrates the PEAT utility's ALM-CMOL module for Asset Liability Management—Interest Rate Risk's Input Assumptions and general Settings tab. This segment represents the analysis of Asset Liability Management (ALM) computations. ALM is the practice of managing risks that arise due to mismatches between the maturities of assets and liabilities. The ALM process is a mix of risk management and strategic planning for a bank or financial institution. It is about offering solutions to mitigate or hedge the risks arising from the interaction of assets and liabilities as well as the success in the process of maximizing assets to meet complex liabilities such that it will help increase profitability. The current tab starts by obtaining, as general inputs, the bank's regulatory capital obtained earlier from the credit risk models. In addition, the number of trading days in the calendar year of the analysis (e.g., typically between 250 and 253 days), the local currency's name (e.g., U.S. Dollar or Argentinian Peso), the current period when the analysis is performed and results reported to the regulatory agencies (e.g., January 2015), the number of VaR percentiles to run (e.g., 99.00%), number of scenarios to run and their respective basis point sensitivities (e.g., 100, 200, and 300 basis points, where every 100 basis points represent 1%), and number of foreign currencies in the bank's investment portfolio. As usual, the inputs, settings, and results can be saved for future retrieval. Figure 76 further illustrates the PEAT utility's ALM-CMOL module for Asset Liability Management. The tab is specifically for Interest Rate Sensitive Assets and Liabilities data where historical impacts of interest-rate sensitive assets and liabilities, as well as foreign currency–denominated assets and liabilities are entered, copy and pasted, or uploaded from a database. Historical Interest Rate data is uploaded where the rows of periodic historical interest rates of local and foreign currencies can be entered, copy and pasted, or uploaded from a database.

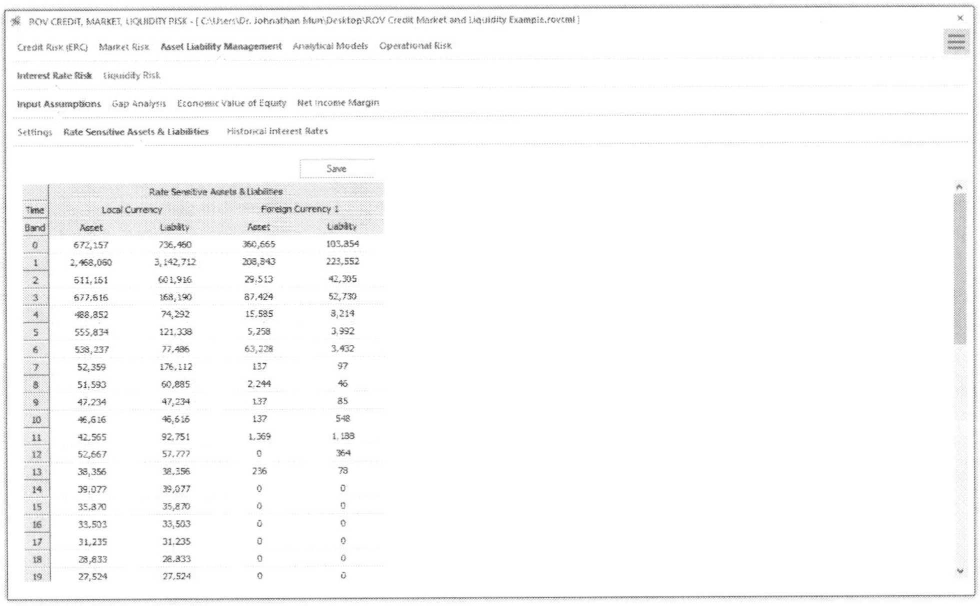

	Rate Sensitive Assets & Liabilities			
Time	Local Currency		Foreign Currency 1	
Band	Asset	Liability	Asset	Liability
0	672,157	736,460	360,665	103,854
1	2,468,060	3,142,712	208,843	223,552
2	611,161	601,916	29,513	42,305
3	677,616	168,190	87,424	52,730
4	488,852	74,292	15,585	8,214
5	555,834	121,338	5,258	3,992
6	538,237	77,486	63,228	3,432
7	52,359	176,112	137	97
8	51,593	60,885	2,244	46
9	47,234	47,234	137	85
10	46,616	46,616	137	548
11	42,565	92,751	1,369	1,188
12	52,667	57,777	0	364
13	38,356	38,356	236	78
14	39,077	39,077	0	0
15	35,870	35,870	0	0
16	33,503	33,503	0	0
17	31,235	31,235	0	0
18	28,833	28,833	0	0
19	27,524	27,524	0	0

Figure 76: Asset Liability Management—Interest Rate Risk (Asset and Liability Data)

ALM: Net Interest Margin and Economic Value of Equity

The most straightforward way to present ALM structures for liquidity and interest-rate risk management is through the utilization of Gap charts. A Gap chart is simply the listing of all assets and liabilities as affected by interest rate movements or liquidity movements, respectively, ordered on time-defined buckets (i.e., days, weeks, months, or years). Typically, for interest rate risk there are two main management approaches: a shorter-term structure analysis based on a more accounting-side perspective, usually referred to as the NIM (Net Interest Margin) approach, and a longer-term structure analysis based on a more economic-side perspective, usually referred to as the EVE (Economic Value of Equity) approach. The NIM approach rests on the logic that the natural mismatch between assets and liabilities has an impact on earnings, through the net interest margin, and such impact can be measured through given deltas (variations) in the referential market interest rate. In this case, the impact is measured through the Gap chart, as applied to balance sheet items of the asset and liability sides, respectively. So, on the one hand, a natural NIM approach would deliver a balance sheet impact on earnings, based on the structure and maturity of assets and liabilities, when subjected to a 100 basis point increase in the referential market interest rate risk. Because the Gap analysis defines which side of the balance sheet (assets or liabilities) the cash flow is on, as well as accounting for each time bucket, analysts can define which sign would apply to earnings should interest rates go up or down. Therefore, the combination of these two tools allows for the establishment of different business and stress scenarios and, hence, the determination of targets and limits on the structure and duration of assets and liabilities. The EVE approach, on the other hand, is a long-term evaluation tool, by which analysts can determine the impact on capital (or equity, defined as assets minus liabilities) of referential market interest rate valuations, as it affects the net present value and duration of the described balance sheet items.

By this approach, the system can calculate the deltas in durations and in net present value of assets, liabilities, and equity, as measured in the Gap charts. Therefore, such variations allow for the construction of scenarios for the different impacts on equity value and duration of changes in the referential market interest rate. These results are then fed into different KRIs for monitoring, defining, and calibrating targets and limits, in line with the IMMM risk management structure.

Figure 77 illustrates the Gap Analysis results of Interest Rate Risk. The results are shown in different grids for each local and foreign currency. Gap Analysis is, of course, one of the most common ways of measuring liquidity position and represents the foundation for scenario analysis and stress testing, which will be executed in subsequent tabs. The Gap Analysis results are from user inputs in the input assumptions tab. The results are presented for the user again for validation and in a more user-friendly tabular format. The Economic Value of Equity results are based on interest-rate risk computations in previous tabs. The impacts on regulatory capital as denoted by VaR levels on local and foreign currencies are computed, as are the duration gaps and basis point scenarios affecting the cash flows of local and foreign currencies.

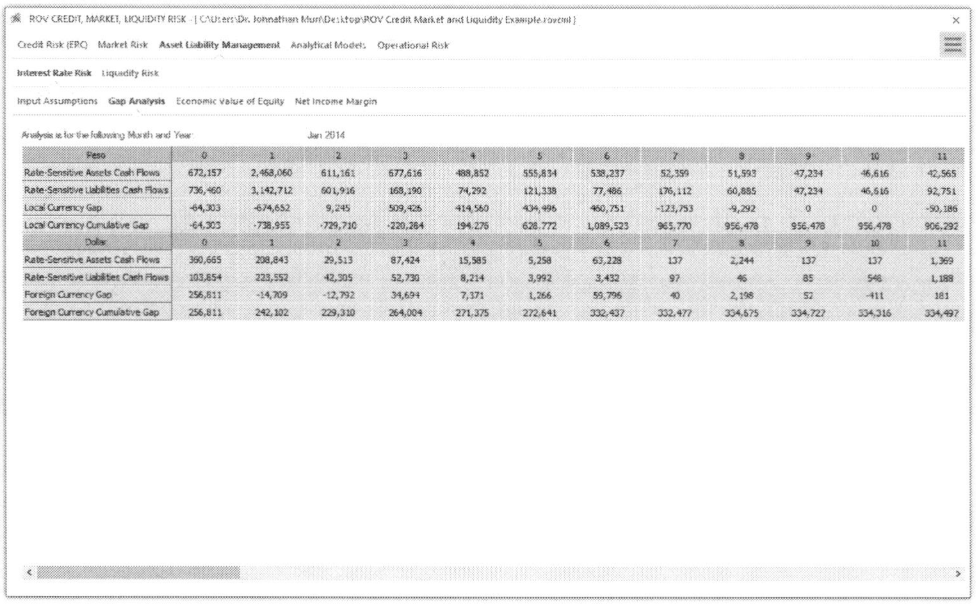

Peso	0	1	2	3	4	5	6	7	8	9	10	11
Rate-Sensitive Assets Cash Flows	672,157	2,468,060	611,161	677,616	488,852	555,834	538,237	52,359	51,593	47,234	46,616	42,565
Rate-Sensitive Liabilities Cash Flows	736,460	3,142,712	601,916	168,190	74,292	121,338	77,486	176,112	60,885	47,234	46,616	92,751
Local Currency Gap	-64,303	-674,652	9,245	509,426	414,560	434,496	460,751	-123,753	-9,292	0	0	-50,186
Local Currency Cumulative Gap	-64,303	-738,955	-729,710	-220,284	194.276	628.772	1,089,523	965.770	956.478	956.478	956.478	906.292
Dollar	0	1	2	3	4	5	6	7	8	9	10	11
Rate-Sensitive Assets Cash Flows	360,665	208,843	29,513	87,424	15,585	5,258	63,228	137	2,244	137	137	1,369
Rate-Sensitive Liabilities Cash Flows	103,854	223,552	42,305	52,730	8,214	3,992	3,432	97	46	85	548	1,188
Foreign Currency Gap	256,811	-14,709	-12,792	34,694	7,371	1,266	59,796	40	2,198	52	-411	181
Foreign Currency Cumulative Gap	256,811	242,102	229,310	264,004	271,375	272,641	332,437	332,477	334,675	334,727	334,316	334,497

Figure 77: Asset Liability Management—Interest Rate Risk: Gap Analysis

Figure 78 illustrates the *Net Income Margin* (NIM) Input Assumptions requirements based on interest-rate risk analysis. The highlighted cells in the data grid represent user input requirements for computing the NIM model. The Economic Value of Equity and Gap Analysis calculations described above are for longer-term interest-rate risk analysis, whereas the NIM approach is for shorter-term (typically 12 months) analysis of liquidity and interest-rate risk effects on assets and liabilities. In the gap analysis and stress testing analysis, we proceed using:

$$Cash\ Flows\ on\ Basis\ Points\ BP = -Modified\ Duration \times Asset \times \Delta BP\ in\ \%$$

$$Modified\ Duration = Duration\ Gap\ \div (1 + Interest\ Rate)$$

$$Duration\ Gap = \sum \frac{PVCF_A}{V_A} \times \frac{Monthly\ Time\ Band}{12} - Liability\ Duration \times \frac{NPV_L}{NPV_A}$$

$$Duration\ Gap = Asset\ Duration - Liability\ Duration \times \frac{NPV_L}{NPV_A}$$

$$Duration = \sum_{i=1}^{n} \frac{PVCF_t}{V}\ time$$

$$Modified\ Duration = \frac{Macaulay\ Duration}{\left(1 + \frac{YTM}{\#\ Coupons}\right)}$$

$$Convexity = \frac{d^2p}{di^2} = \frac{\sum_{i=1}^{n} \frac{CF}{(1+i)^t}(t^2 + t)}{(1+i)^2}$$

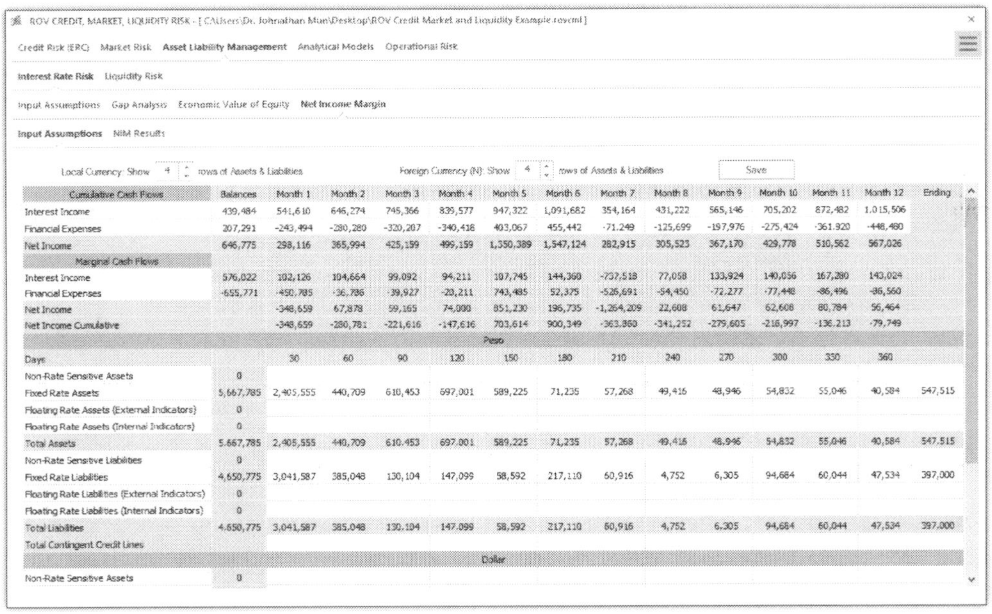

Figure 78: Net Income Margin (NIM): Input Assumptions and Model

In NIM calculations, we use:

$$Gap = Asset - Liability + Contingency\ Cash$$

$$\Delta NIM = Change\ in\ Net\ Interest\ Margin$$
$$= Monthly\ Gap\ \times\ \Delta\ Basis\ Points \times \%\ Days\ Left\ to\ Maturity \div 10000$$

$$Total\ NIM = \Sigma\Delta NIM$$

$$Financial\ Margin = Total\ NIM\ \div\ Net\ Income$$

Figure 79 illustrates the PEAT utility's ALM-CMOL module for Asset Liability Management—Liquidity Risk Input Assumptions tab on the historical monthly balances of interest-rate sensitive assets and liabilities. The typical time horizon is monthly for one year (12 months) where the various assets such as liquid assets (e.g., cash), bonds, and loans are listed, as well as other asset receivables. On the liabilities side, regular short-term deposits and timed deposits are listed, separated by private versus public sectors, as well as other payable liabilities (e.g., interest payments and operations). Adjustments can also be made to account for rounding issues and accounting issues that may affect the asset and liability levels (e.g., contingency cash levels, overnight deposits, etc.). The data grid can be set up with some basic inputs as well as the number of subsegments or rows for each category. As usual, the inputs, settings, and results can be saved for future retrieval.

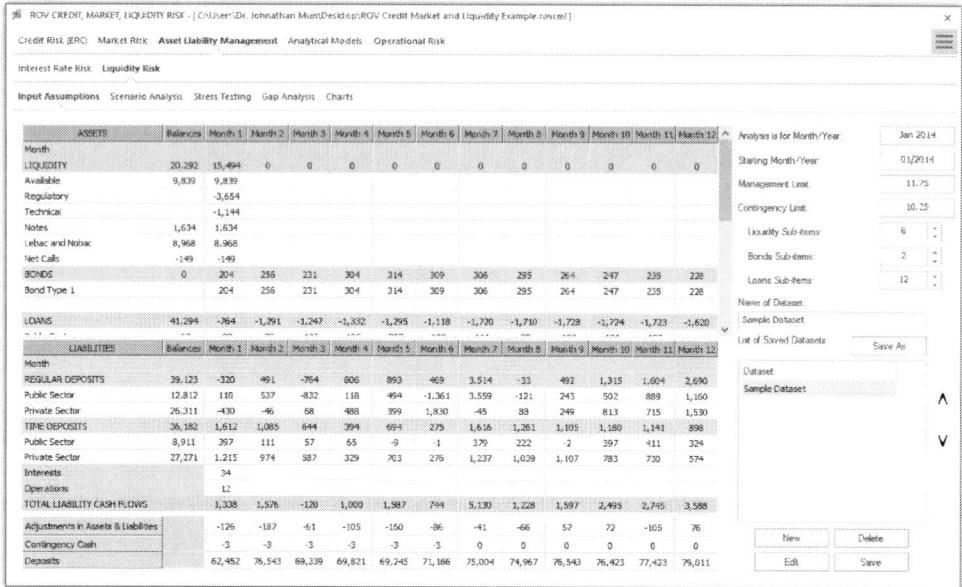

Figure 79: Asset Liability Management—Liquidity Risk Model and Assumptions

Scenario Analysis and Stress Testing

The Liquidity Risk's Scenario Analysis and Stress Testing settings can be set up to test interest-rate sensitive assets and liabilities. The scenarios to test can be entered as data or percentage changes. Multiple scenarios can be saved for future retrieval and analysis in subsequent tabs as each saved model constitutes a stand-alone scenario to test. Scenario analysis typically tests both fluctuations in assets and liabilities and their impacts on the portfolio's ALM balance, whereas stress testing typically tests the fluctuations on liabilities (e.g., runs on banks, economic downturns where deposits are stressed to the lower limit) where the stressed limits can be entered as values or percentage change from the base case. Multiple stress tests can be saved for future retrieval and analysis in subsequent tabs as each saved model constitutes a stand-alone stress test.

Figure 80 illustrates the Liquidity Risk's Gap Analysis results. The data grid shows the results based on all the previously saved scenarios and stress test conditions. The *Gap* is, of course, calculated as the *difference between Monthly Assets and Liabilities, accounting for any Contingency Credit Lines*. The gaps for the multitude of Scenarios and Stress Tests are reruns of the same calculation based on various user inputs on values or percentage changes as described previously in the Scenario Analysis and Stress Testing sections.

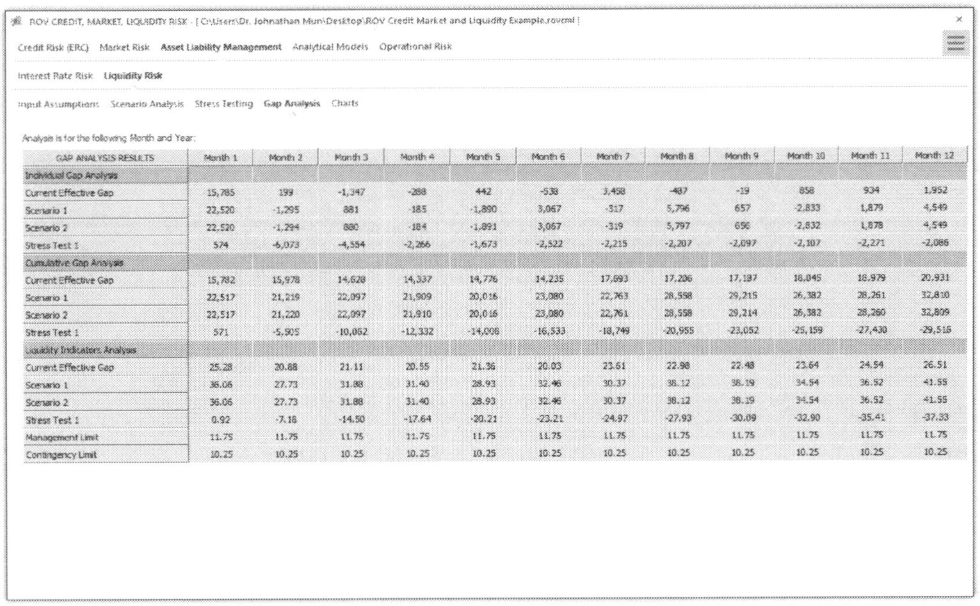

GAP ANALYSIS RESULTS	Month 1	Month 2	Month 3	Month 4	Month 5	Month 6	Month 7	Month 8	Month 9	Month 10	Month 11	Month 12
Individual Gap Analysis												
Current Effective Gap	15,785	199	-1,347	-288	442	-538	3,458	-487	-19	858	934	1,952
Scenario 1	22,520	-1,295	881	-185	-1,890	3,067	-317	5,796	657	-2,833	1,879	4,549
Scenario 2	22,520	-1,294	880	-184	-1,891	3,067	-319	5,797	656	-2,832	1,878	4,549
Stress Test 1	574	-6,073	-4,554	-2,266	-1,673	-2,522	-2,215	-2,207	-2,097	-2,107	-2,271	-2,086
Cumulative Gap Analysis												
Current Effective Gap	15,782	15,978	14,628	14,337	14,776	14,235	17,693	17,206	17,187	18,045	18,979	20,931
Scenario 1	22,517	21,219	22,097	21,909	20,016	23,080	22,763	28,558	29,215	26,382	28,261	32,810
Scenario 2	22,517	21,220	22,097	21,910	20,016	23,080	22,761	28,558	29,214	26,382	28,260	32,809
Stress Test 1	571	-5,505	-10,062	-12,332	-14,008	-16,533	-18,749	-20,955	-23,052	-25,159	-27,430	-29,516
Liquidity Indicators Analysis												
Current Effective Gap	25.28	20.88	21.11	20.55	21.36	20.03	23.61	22.98	22.48	23.64	24.54	26.51
Scenario 1	36.06	27.73	31.88	31.40	28.93	32.46	30.37	38.12	38.19	34.54	36.52	41.55
Scenario 2	36.06	27.73	31.88	31.40	28.93	32.46	30.37	38.12	38.19	34.54	36.52	41.55
Stress Test 1	0.92	-7.18	-14.50	-17.64	-20.21	-23.21	-24.97	-27.93	-30.09	-32.90	-35.41	-37.33
Management Limit	11.75	11.75	11.75	11.75	11.75	11.75	11.75	11.75	11.75	11.75	11.75	11.75
Contingency Limit	10.25	10.25	10.25	10.25	10.25	10.25	10.25	10.25	10.25	10.25	10.25	10.25

Figure 80: Asset Liability Management—Liquidity Risk: Gap Analysis

Credit and Market Risk Analytical Models

The Analytical Models modules contain models on estimating and valuing PD, EAD, LGD, Volatility, Credit Exposures, Options-based Asset Valuation, Debt Valuation, Credit Conversion Factors (CCF), Loan Equivalence Factors (LEQ), Options Valuation, Hedging Ratios, and multiple other models. In Basel II/III, the regulations specifically state that all Over the Counter (OTC) options, options-embedded instruments, and other exotic options need to also be valued and accounted for. This requirement is why CMOL has devoted an entire module to modeling and valuing these exotic nonlinear instruments. The module is divided into four categories depending on their required inputs and structure of the model. In other words, you might see analytical types like Probability of Default or Volatility traversing multiple tabs or analytical segments.

Figure 81 illustrates the Analytical Models tab with input assumptions and results. This analytical models segment is divided into Structural, Time-Series, Portfolio, and Analytics models. The current figure shows the Structural models tab where the computed models pertain to credit risk–related model analysis categories such as PD, EAD, LGD, and Volatility calculations. Under each category, specific models can be selected to run. Selected models are briefly described and users can select the number of model repetitions to run and the decimal precision levels of the results. The data grid in the Computations tab shows the area in which users would enter the relevant inputs into the selected model and the results would be computed. As usual, selected models, inputs, and settings can be saved for future retrieval and analysis.

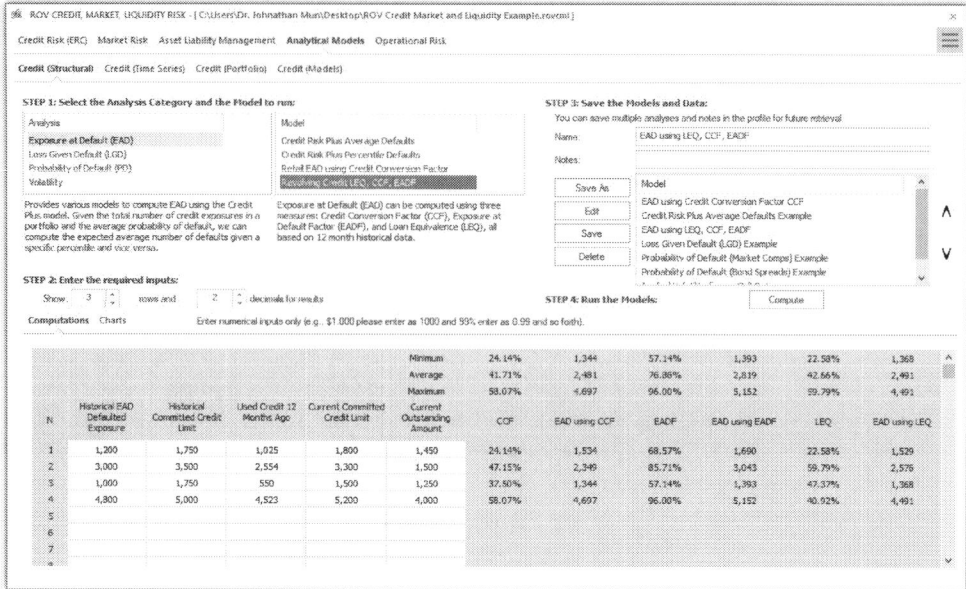

Figure 81: Structural Credit Risk Models

Figure 81 illustrates the Structural Analytical Models tab with visual chart results. The results computed are displayed as various visual charts such as bar charts, control charts, Pareto charts, and time-series charts. Figure 82 illustrates the Time-Series Analytical Models tab with input assumptions and results. The analysis category and model type is first chosen where a short description explains what the selected model does, and users can then select the number of models to replicate as well as decimal precision settings. Input data and assumptions are entered in the data grid provided (additional inputs can also be entered if required), and the results are computed and shown. As usual, selected models, inputs, and settings can be saved for future retrieval and analysis. Figure 83 illustrates the Portfolio Analytical Models tab with input assumptions and results. The analysis category and model type is first chosen where a short description explains what the selected model does, and users can then select the number of models to replicate as well as decimal precision settings. Input data and assumptions are entered in the data grid provided (additional inputs such as a correlation matrix can also be entered if required), and the results are computed and shown.

Additional models are available in the Credit Models tab with input assumptions and results. The analysis category and model type are first chosen and input data and assumptions are entered in the required inputs area (if required, users can Load Example inputs and use these as a basis for building their models), and the results are computed and shown. Scenario tables and charts can be created by entering the From, To, and Step Size parameters, where the computed scenarios will be returned as a data grid and visual chart. As usual, selected models, inputs, and settings can be saved for future retrieval and analysis.

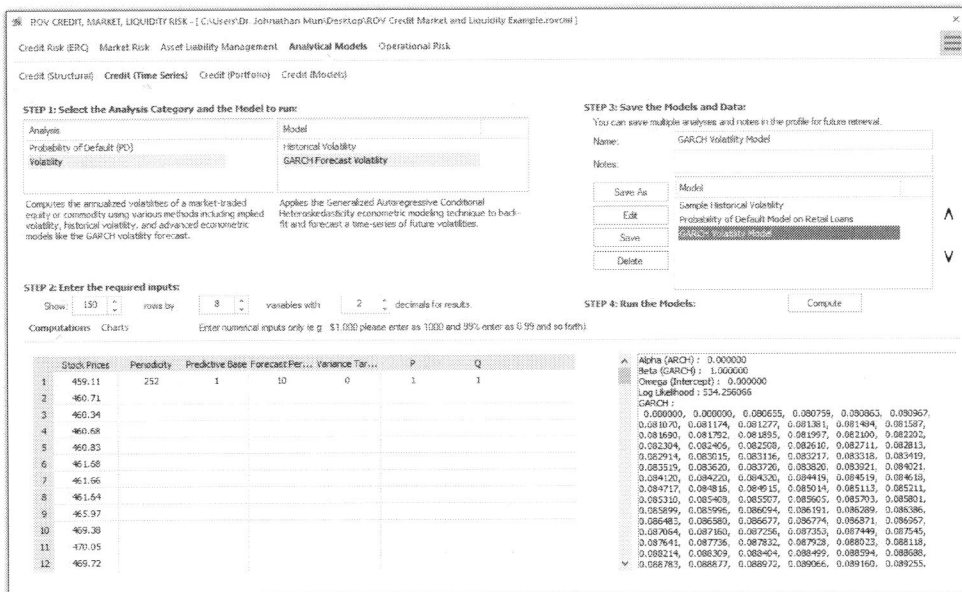

Figure 82: Time-Series Credit and Market Models

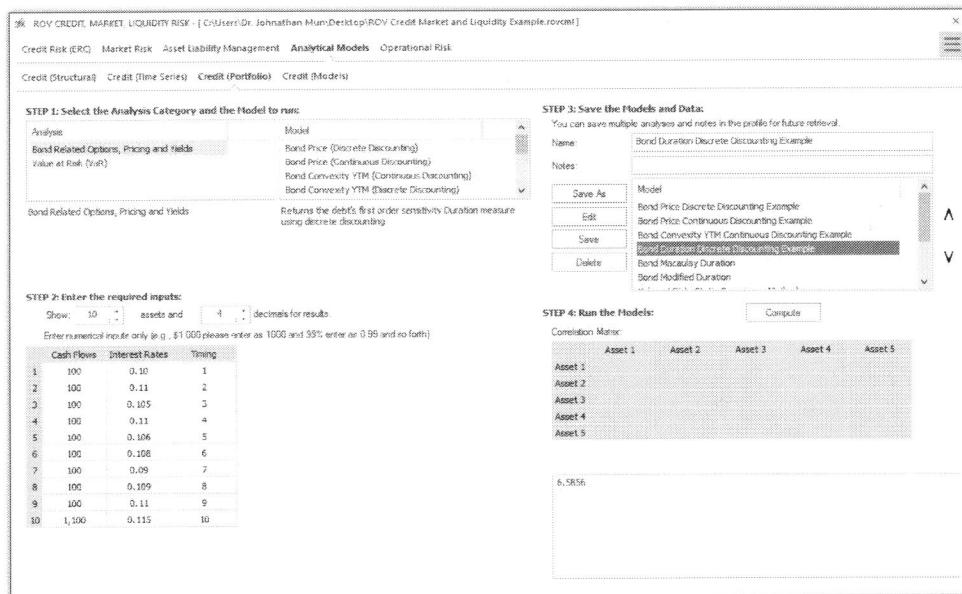

Figure 83: Credit Portfolio Models

Operational Risk

The case of operational risk is undoubtedly the most difficult to measure and model. The opposite of market risk, by its definition, operational risk data is not only scarce, but biased, unstable, and unchecked in the sense that the most relevant operational risk events do not come identified in the balance sheet of any financial institution. Since the modeling approach is still based on VaR logic, whereby the model utilizes past empirical data to project expected results, modeling operational risk is a very challenging task. As stated, market risk offers daily, publicly audited information to be used and modeled. Conversely, operational risk events are, in most cases, not public, not identified in the general ledger, and, in many instances, not identified at all. But the utmost difficulty comes from the proper definition of operational risk. Even if we managed to go about the impossible task of identifying each and every operational risk event of the past five years, we would still have very incomplete information. The definition of operational risk entails events generated by failure in people, processes, systems, and external events. With market risk, asset prices can either go up or down, or stay unchanged. With operational risk, an unknown event that has never occurred before can take place in the analysis period and materially affect operations even without it being an extreme tail event. So the logic of utilizing similar approaches for such different information availability and behavior requires very careful definitions and assumptions. With this logic in mind, the Basel Committee has defined that in order to model operational risk properly, banks need to have four sources of operational risk data: internal losses, external losses, business environment and internal control factors, and stressed scenarios. These are known as the four elements of operational risk, and the Basel Committee recommends that they are taken into account when modeling. For smaller banks, and smaller countries, this recommendation poses a definitive challenge, because many times these elements are not developed enough, or not present at all. In this light, most banks have resorted to just using internal data to model operational risk. This approach comes with some shortcomings and more assumptions, and should be taken as an initial step that considers the later development of the other elements as they become available. The example shown in Figure 84 looks at the modeling of internal losses as a simplified approach usually undertaken by smaller institutions. Since operational risk information is scarce and biased, it is necessary to "complete" the loss distributions with randomly generated data. The most common approach for the task is the use of Monte Carlo risk simulations (Figures 85, 86, and 87) that allow for the inclusion of more stable data and for the fitting of the distributions into predefined density functions.

Basel II and Basel III regulations allow for the use of multiple approaches when it comes to computing capital charge on operational risk, defined by the Basel Committee as losses resulting from inadequate or failed internal processes, people, and systems or from external events, which includes legal risk, but excludes any strategic and reputational risks.

- *Basic Indicator Approach* (BIA) uses positive Gross Income of the last 3 years applied to an Alpha multiplier.

- *The Standardized Approach* (TSA) uses positive Gross Income of 8 distinct business lines with its own Beta risk-weighted coefficients.

- *Alternate Standardized Approach* (ASA) is based on the TSA method and uses Gross Income but applies Total Loans and Advances for the Retail and Commercial business lines, adjusted by a multiplier, prior to using the same TSA beta risk-weighted coefficients.

- *Revised Standardized Approach* (RSA) uses Income and Expenses as proxy variables to obtain the *Business Indicator* required in computing the risk capital charge.

- *Advanced Measurement Approach* (AMA) is open-ended in that individual banks can utilize their own approaches subject to regulatory approval. The typical approach, and the same method used in the ALM-CMOL software application, is to use historical loss data, perform probability distribution-fitting on the frequency and severity of losses, which is then convoluted through Monte Carlo Risk Simulation to obtain probability distributions of future expected losses. The tail event VaR results can be obtained directly from the simulated distributions.

Figure 84 illustrates the BIA, TSA, ASA, and RSA methods as prescribed in Basel II/III. The BIA uses total annual gross income for the last 3 years of the bank and multiplies it with an Alpha coefficient (15%) to obtain the capital charge. Only positive gross income amounts are used. This is the simplest method and does not require prior regulatory approval. In the TSA method, the bank is divided into 8 business lines (*corporate finance, trading and sales, retail banking, commercial banking, payment and settlement, agency services, asset management,* and *retail brokerage*) and each business line's positive total annual gross income values for the last 3 years are used, and each business line has its own beta coefficient multiplier. These beta values are proxies based on industry-wide relationships between operational risk loss experience for each business line and aggregate gross income levels. The total capital charge based on the TSA is simply the sum of the weighted average of these business lines for the last 3 years. The ASA is similar to the TSA except that the retail banking and commercial banking business lines use *total loans and advances* instead of using annual total gross income. These total loans and advances are first multiplied by a 3.50% factor prior to being beta-weighted, averaged, and summed. The ASA is also useful in situations where the bank has extremely high or low net interest margins (NIM), whereby the gross income for the retail and commercial business lines are replaced with an asset-based proxy (total loans and advances multiplied by the 3.50% factor). In addition, within the ASA approach, the 6 business lines can be aggregated into a single business line as long as it is multiplied by the highest beta coefficient (18%), and the 2 remaining loans and advances (retail and commercial business lines) can be aggregated and multiplied by the 15% beta coefficient. In other words, when using the ALM-CMOL software, you can aggregate the 6 business lines and enter it as a single row entry in Corporate Finance, which has an 18% multiplier, and the 2 loans and advances business lines can be aggregated as the Commercial business line, which has a 15% multiplier.

The main issue with BIA, TSA, and ASA methods is that, on average, these methods are undercalibrated, especially for large and complex banks. For instance, these three methods assume that operational risk exposure increases linearly and proportionally with gross income or revenue. This assumption is invalid because certain banks may experience a decline in gross income due to systemic or bank-specific events that may include losses from operational risk events. In such situations, a falling gross income should be commensurate with a higher operational capital requirement, not a lower capital charge. Therefore, the Basel Committee has allowed the inclusion of a revised method, the RSA. Instead of using gross income, the RSA uses both income and expenditures from multiple sources, as shown in Figure 84. The RSA uses inputs from an *interest* component (interest income less interest expense), a *services* component (sum of fee income, fee expense, other operating income, and other operating expense), and a *financial* component (sum of the absolute value of net profit and losses on the trading book, and the absolute value of net profit and losses on the banking book). The calculation of capital charge is based on the calculation of a *Business Indicator* (BI), where the BI is the sum of the absolute values of these three components (thereby avoiding any counterintuitive results based on negative contributions from any component). The purpose of a BI calculation is to promote simplicity and comparability using a single indicator for operational risk exposure that is sensitive to the bank's business size and business volume, rather than static business line coefficients regardless of the bank's size and volume. Using the computed BI, the risk capital charge is determined from 5 predefined buckets from Basel II/III, increasing in value from 10% to 30%, depending on the size of the BI (ranging from €0 to €30 billion). These Basel predefined buckets are denoted in thousands of Euros, with each bucket having its own weighted beta coefficients. Finally, the risk capital charge is computed based on a marginal incremental or layered approach (rather than a full cliff-effect when banks migrate from one bucket to another) using these buckets.

Figures 85, 86, and 87 illustrate the Operational Risk Loss Distribution analysis when applying the AMA method. Users start at the Loss Data tab where historical loss data can be entered or pasted into the data grid. Variables include losses in the past pertaining to operational risks, segmentation by divisions and departments, business lines, dates of losses, risk categories, and so on. Users then activate the controls to select how the loss data variables are to be segmented (e.g., by risk categories and risk types and business lines), the number of simulation trials to run, and seed values to apply in the simulation if required, all by selecting the relevant variable columns. The distributional fitting routines can also be selected as required. Then the analysis can be run and distributions fitted to the data. As usual, the model settings and data can be saved for future retrieval.

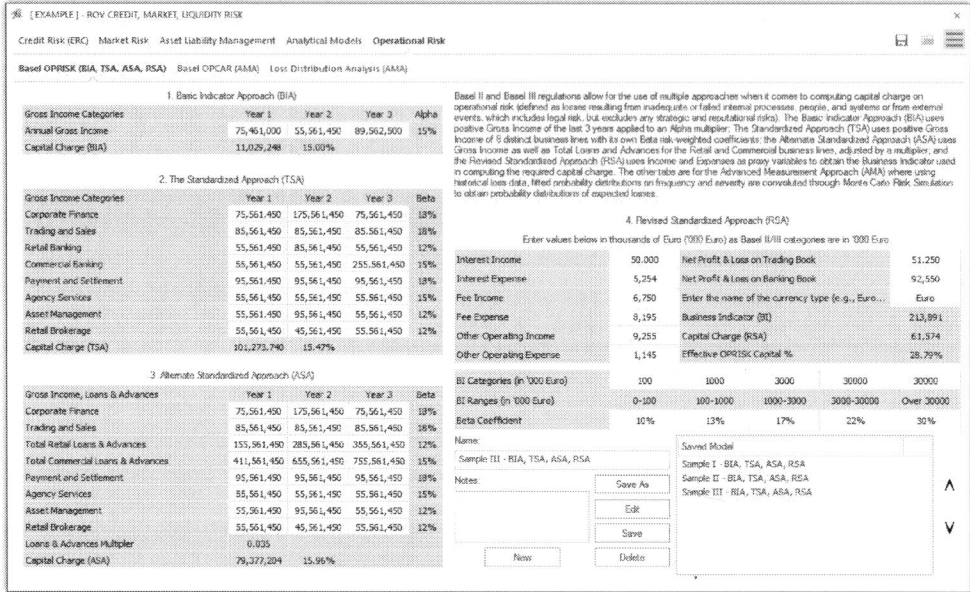

Figure 84: Basel II/III BIA, TSA, ASA, RSA Methods

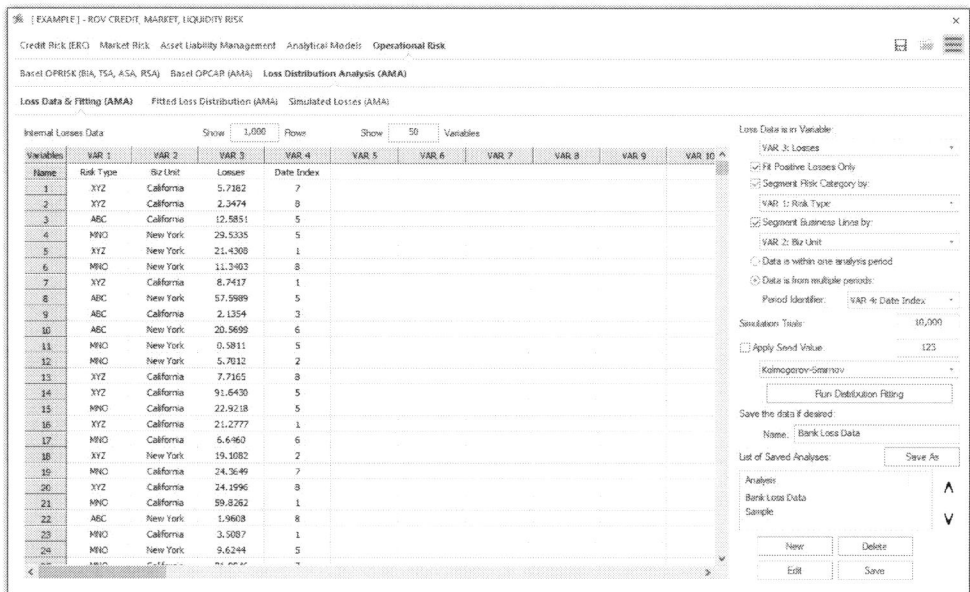

Figure 85: Operational Risk Data in Advanced Measurement Approach (AMA)

Figure 86 illustrates the Operational Risk—Fitted Loss Distribution subtab. Users start by selecting the fitting segments for setting the various risk category and business line segments, and, based on the selected segment, the fitted distributions and their p-values are listed and ranked according to the highest p-value to the lowest p-value, indicating the best to the worst statistical fit to the various probability distributions. The empirical data and fitted theoretical distributions are shown graphically, and the statistical moments are shown for the actual data versus the theoretically fitted distribution's moments. After deciding on which distributions to use, users can then run the simulations.

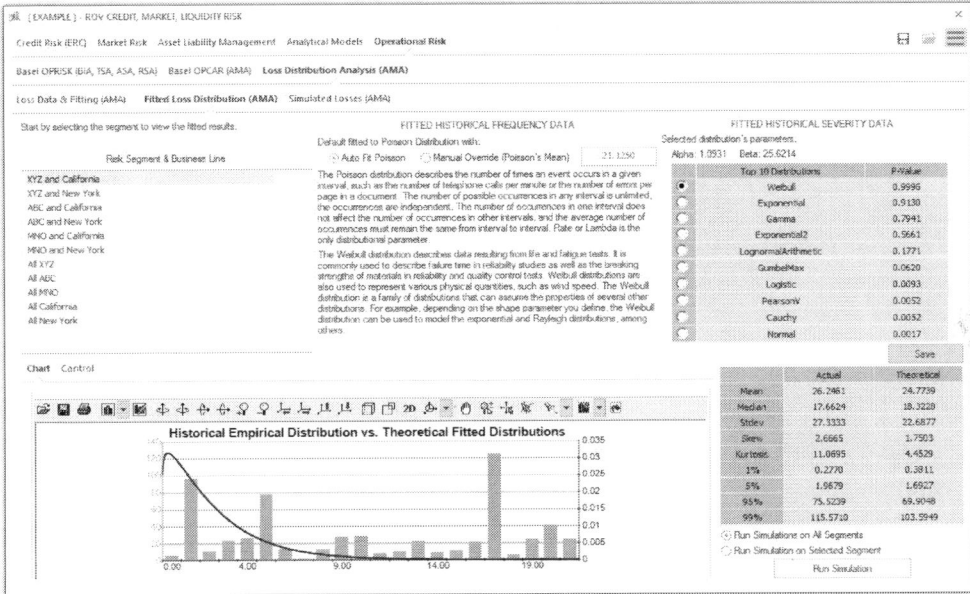

Figure 86: Fitted Distributions on Operational Risk Data

Figure 87 illustrates the Operational Risk—Risk Simulated Losses subtab using convolution of frequency and severity of historical losses, where, depending on which risk segment and business line was selected, the relevant probability distribution results from the Monte Carlo risk simulations are displayed, including the simulated results on Frequency, Severity, and the multiplication between frequency and severity, termed Expected Loss Distribution, as well as the Extreme Value Distribution of Losses (this is where the extreme losses in the dataset are fitted to the extreme value distributions—see the case study for details on extreme value distributions and their mathematical models). Each of the distributional charts has its own confidence and percentile inputs where users can select one-tail (right-tail or left-tail) or two-tail confidence intervals and enter the percentiles to obtain the confidence values (e.g., user can enter right-tail 99.90% percentile to receive the VaR confidence value of the worst-case losses on the left tail's 0.10%).

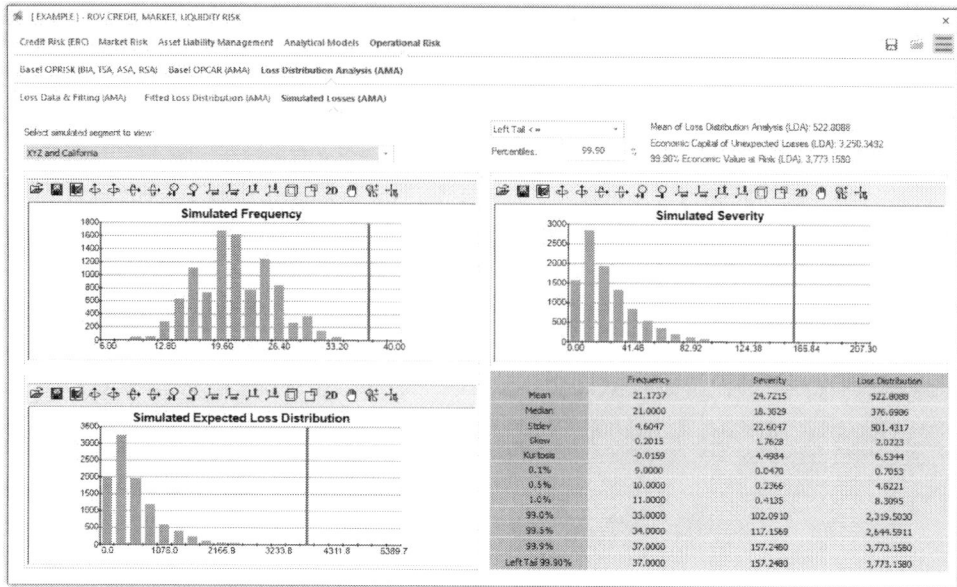

Figure 87: Monte Carlo Risk Simulated Operational Losses

Figure 88 shows the computations of Basel II/III's OPCAR (Operational Capital at Risk) model where the probability distribution of risk event Frequency is multiplied by the probability distribution of Severity of operational losses, the approach where Frequency × Severity is termed the Single Loss Approximation (SLA) model. The SLA is computed using convolution methods of combining multiple probability distributions. SLA using convolution methods is complex and very difficult to compute and the results are only approximations, and valid only at the extreme tails of the distribution (e.g., 99.9%). However, as can be seen in the Technical Note 2, Monte Carlo Risk Simulation provides a simpler and more powerful alternative when convoluting and multiplying two distributions of random variables to obtain the combined distribution. Clearly the challenge is setting the relevant distributional input parameters. This is where the data-fitting and percentile-fitting tools come in handy, as will be explained later.

Figure 89 shows the convolution simulation results where the distribution of loss frequency, severity, and expected losses are shown. The resulting Expected Losses (EL), Unexpected Losses (UL), and Total Operational Capital at Risk (OPCAR) are also computed and shown. EL is, of course, the mean value of the simulated results, OPCAR is the tail-end 99.90th percentile, and UL is the difference between OPCAR and EL.

Figure 90 shows the loss severity data fitting using historical loss data. Users can paste historical loss data, select the required fitting routines (Kolmogorov–Smirnov, Akaike Criterion, Bayes Information Criterion, Anderson–Darling, Kuiper's Statistic, etc.) and run the data fitting routines. When in doubt, use the Kolmogorov–Smirnov routine. The best-fitting distributions, p-values, and their parameters will be listed, and the same interpretation applies as previously explained.

Figure 91 shows the loss severity percentile fitting instead, which is particularly helpful when there are no historical loss data and where there only exists high-level management assumptions of the probabilities certain events occur. In other words, by entering a few percentiles (%) and their corresponding values, one can obtain the entire distribution's parameters.

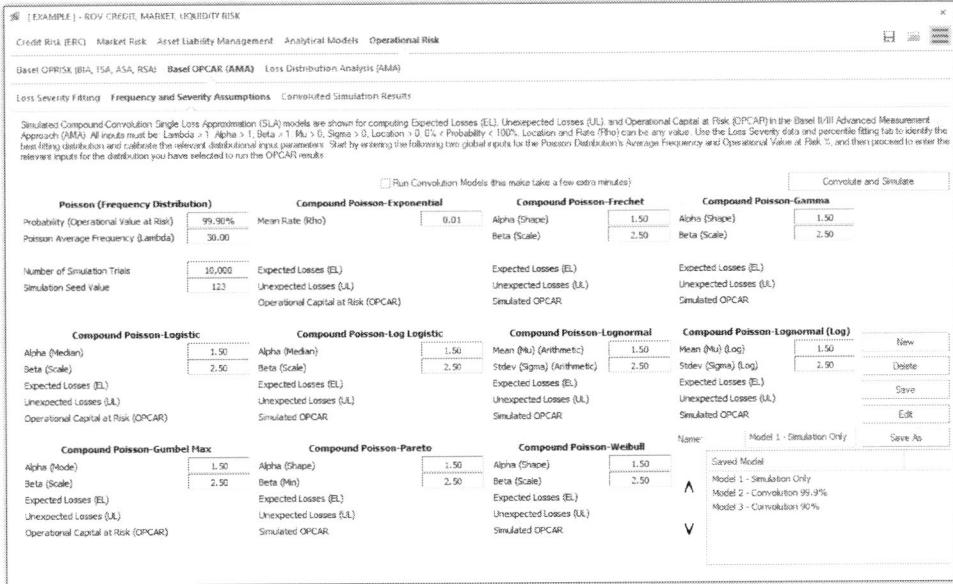

Figure 88: Basel OPCAR Frequency and Severity Assumptions

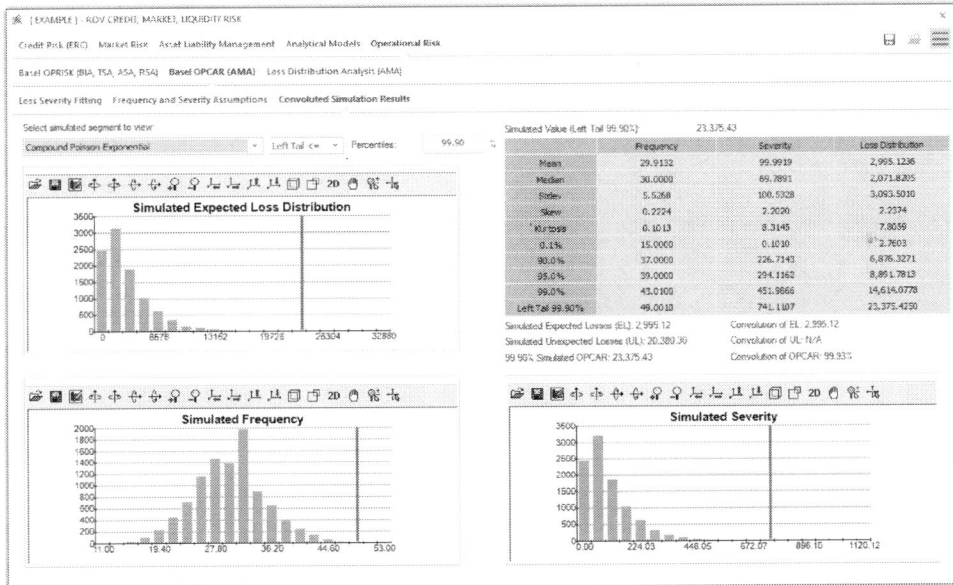

Figure 89: Basel OPCAR Convoluted Simulation Results

These modeling tools allow smaller banks to have a first approach at more advanced operational risk management techniques. The use of internal models allows for a better calibration of regulatory capital that knowingly overestimated for operational risk. The use of different scenarios providing various results can allow smaller banks to have a much more efficient capital allocation for operational risk that, being a Pillar I risk, tends to be quite expensive in terms of capital, and quite dangerous at the same time if capital was severely underestimated. Together with the traditional operational risk management tools, such as self-assessment and KRIs, these basic models allow for a proper IMMM risk management structure, aligned with the latest international standards.

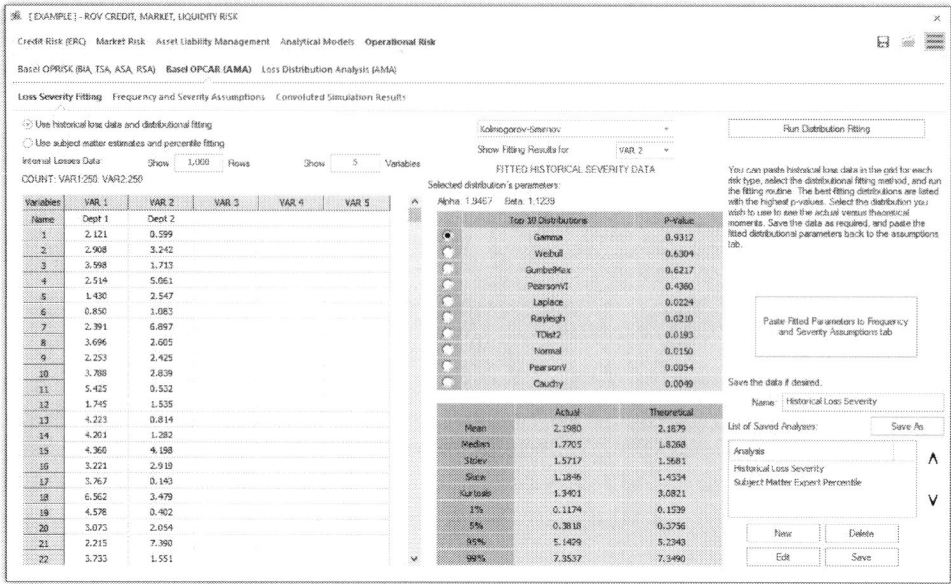

Figure 90: Basel OPCAR Loss Severity Data Fitting

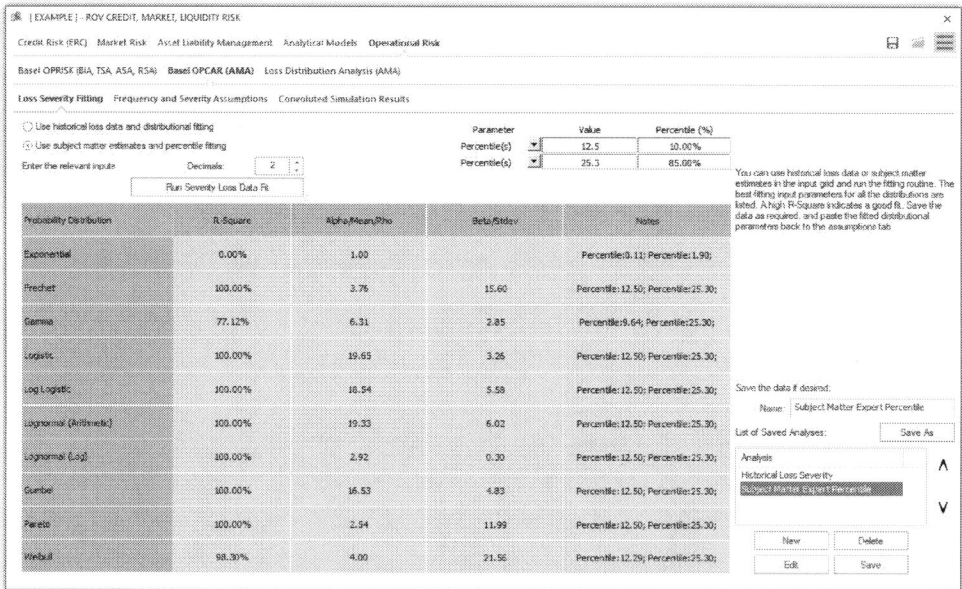

Figure 91: Basel OPCAR Loss Severity Percentile Fitting

CASE STUDY 9: UNDERSTANDING RISK AND OPTIMAL TIMING IN A REAL ESTATE DEVELOPMENT USING REAL OPTIONS ANALYSIS

This case study is contributed by Robert Fourt (contact: Gerald Eve, 7 Vere Street, London W1G OJB, UK, +44(0)2074933338, rfourt@geraldeve.com) and Bill Rodney (contact: Cass Business School, 106 Bunhill Row, London, EC1Y8TZ, UK, +44(0)2070408600, whr@dial.pipex.com.). Robert is a partner within the planning & development team of UK-based real estate consultants, Gerald Eve. He specializes in development consultancy, providing advice on a wide range of schemes to corporate and public sector clients with a particular emphasis on strategy, finance, and project management. Gerald Eve is a multidisciplinary practice employing more than 300 people operating from a head office in central London and a regional network that spans the United Kingdom. The firm provides specialist advice in all real estate sectors. Bill is a senior lecturer in real estate finance at the Cass Business School, as well as undertaking research and providing advice to a number of institutions on real estate risk analysis, financing strategies and the risk pricing of PPP/PFI projects. The Cass Business School (part of the City University) is a leading European center for finance research, investment management, and risk assessment and benefits from its location in the heart of the London's financial district and involvement of leading practitioners in its teaching and research.

Consideration of risk and its management is key in most real estate investment and development opportunities. Recognition of this, particularly in recent years, has led to various financial techniques being employed, including simulation analysis and Value at Risk (VaR), to assess various proposed transactions. The UK Investment Property Forum has sought to establish a real estate sector standard for risk. This standard for risk has provided a greater insight into the risk structure and returns on investments for management to review. Notwithstanding these approaches, they have nevertheless largely relied on traditional deterministic appraisals as a basis for assessing risk and return.

An addition to understanding the risks and returns of a project is to apply a real options analysis (ROA). In commercial real estate, the application of an ROA to date has largely been academically driven. While this has provided a strong theoretical base with complex numerical and analytical techniques employed, there has been limited practical application. This lack in some respects is surprising, given that real estate contains a multiplicity of embedded real options due to its intrinsic nature and that the sector operates under conditions of uncertainty.

In particular, real estate development provides flexibility in deferring, commencing, or abandoning a project, which in turn are options that convey value.

This case example, which focuses on a large site in the town center of Croydon, 20 minutes from central London in the United Kingdom, highlights the differences of an investments risk structure and average return when comparing a static net present value (NPV) to an ROA approach. It also illustrates the apparent irrationality of why land is left undeveloped in downtown locations despite the apparent redevelopment potential, an issue that has been the subject of several seminal real option real estate papers (see Notes at the end of this case).

The ROA approach for this example initially formed the basis for advice to the Council (local authority) who were working closely with an investor developer. For this case study, the analysis is from the perspective of the investor in seeking to understand the optimal timing for development and its associated risk structure. In order to maintain confidentiality and simplify certain steps, prices and issues referred to have been adapted.

The right or flexibility to develop (i.e., construct) land is a real option and this often comes in the form of an American call option. This case study utilizes a binomial lattice approach and methodology. The call option is combined with an American put to sell the site either to the Council at open market value (OMV) or as a result of compulsory purchase order (CPO). Therefore, the strategic decision is whether to defer, sell (i.e., abandon), or develop. This flexibility conveys value, which is not captured by a conventional deterministic or NPV appraisal.

A five step ROA approach was adopted and comprised:

- Stage I: Mapping or framing the problem.

- Stage II: Base-scoping appraisal (deterministic).

- Stage III: Internal and external uncertainty inputs.

- Stage IV: Real options quantitative analysis.

- Stage V: Explanation and strategic decisions.

Three quantitative variations using a lattice approach were considered: a binomial lattice; state pricing; and a binomial lattice with two volatility variables. The reasoning for this is explained later. A Monte Carlo analysis was undertaken at both the deterministic (Stage II) and with the ROA (Stage IV), which further illustrates the risk profile comparison between real options and NPV.

The lattice approach allows for decisions to be taken at each node. This provides an investor with the ability to determine the optimal timing with respect to development, or to defer, or to abandon (disposal of the property).

The basic simplified details of this case study are as follows:

- An undeveloped town center site of approximately 2.43 ha (6 acres) adjacent to a major public transport interchange.

- A comprehensive mixed-use scheme has been granted planning permission comprising: a supermarket (7,756 sq m, 83,455 sq ft); retail units (6,532 sq m, 68,348 sq ft); restaurants and bar (7,724sq m, 83,110 sq ft); health club and swimming pool (4,494 sq m, 48,355 sq ft); night club (3,718 sq m, 40,006 sq ft); casino (2,404 sq m, 25,867 sq ft); offices (12,620 sq m, 135,791 sq ft); and a car park (500 spaces).

- A Fund acquired part of the site (in a larger portfolio acquisition) at a book (accounting) cost of £8m, reflecting the development potential. It also inherited option agreements with other adjoining landowners in order to assemble the entirety of the site, which would result in a total site acquisition cost of £12.75m, thereby enabling the implementation of a comprehensive scheme.

- The costs of holding the site and keeping the options open with the other landowners are £150,000pa. Income from a car park on the site is £50,000pa. Therefore, net outgoings are £100,000pa (totaling £500k over 5 years that is, this is assumed to be an intrinsic sunk cost in developing the site).

- The Council wishes to see the site comprehensively developed for the scheme and have granted permission. They also have a long-held objective of developing a sports and entertainment arena in the center of Croydon. Under an agreement with the investor in conjunction with granting the planning permission, the Council has said it would acquire the land at OMV (i.e., equivalent to the book cost) at any time up to 5 years from grant of planning permission should the investor wish to sell and not implement the scheme. Thereafter, the Council would acquire the site using CPO powers (a statutory procedure) if comprehensive development has not been started. The case for granting a CPO is believed to be given, among other reasons, due to the fragmented ownership and that this high-profile site has lain undeveloped for many years. Compensation from the Council to the Fund in acquiring the site via a CPO based on a *no scheme* world (i.e., ignoring any development potential) has been calculated at £5m.

Stage I: Mapping the Problem

Three basic real options were identified that conveyed *flexibility* in terms of optionality in real estate development. They were the option to abandon (i.e., sell), the option to defer investment, and the option to execute (i.e., implement the development). Any of these should be exercised prior to the expiration of 5 years given that the site would be compulsorily acquired at what the Fund estimated as being at subbook value under a CPO. In addition to these options, the option to alter the planning permission subject to market circumstances could also be added. While this would often occur in practice, it is not examined in this instance. The optionality of achieving an optimal tenant mix could also be considered.

As indicated earlier, these options are American (two calls and one put), although the decision just prior to the expiration of 5 years or the CPO could be considered a European put and therefore should be calculated as such.

The Croydon market was considered uncertain in terms of occupier requirements and rental levels, which were sensitive to general real estate market movements for both offices and retail. The ability to attract a supermarket operator and a major office pre-let were seen as key prerequisites prior to implementation of construction. The scheme would not be developed speculatively.

It is evident from Table 13 that even in applying a qualitative analysis, values may evolve asymmetrically. There could be a considerable upside relative to the downside. It was a characteristic of the Croydon office market for example that other competitor office schemes, if implemented, could encourage office sector activity and upward pricing of space with a high probability of occupier relocations. In this instance the investor did not have other real estate holdings in the town center. If the investor did, implementation of the scheme may also be considered a strategic (growth) option and could be analyzed as such. An ROA strategy matrix was prepared. Table 13 provides a simplified summary.

Table 13: ROA Development Strategy Matrix

Strategy/ Approach	Type	Market Factors	Planning Issues	Timing	Embedded Option Appraisal
Pessimistic	Comprehensive Development	Poor office market; uncertain retail requirements	Reduce office content; reconfigure retail	3–5 yrs	Defer or sell
Cautious		Occupiers require 50% of offices; anchor retail tenant but at low rent	Consider phasing offices and retail (review planning gain obligations)	2–4 yrs	Defer or develop/ expansion option
Optimistic		Major office pre-let; quality anchor retailers secured; demand is high for all uses in the scheme	Consider increasing office content	1–3 yrs	Develop and expansion option

Stage II: Base-Scoping Approach

A cash-flow residual development appraisal was produced, with key value drivers of the scheme being the supermarket and office components accounting for 47.15 percent of the expected capital value of the entire project. An overall blended yield of 7.8 percent was expected, which in market terms was considered cautious. An office rent of £215 per sq m (£20 per sq ft) was applied, although this was considered to have underperformed London's (and United Kingdom) office growth as illustrated in the two graphs in Figure 92.

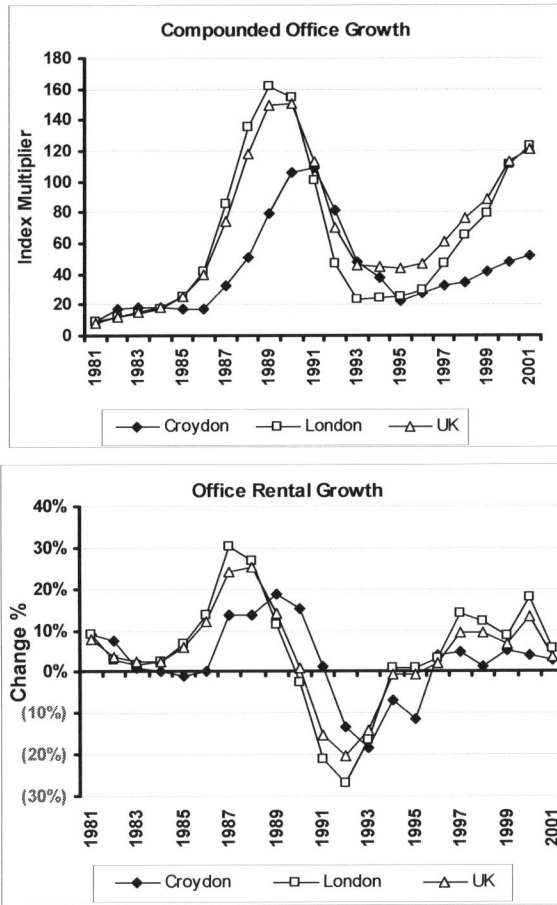

Figure 92: Croydon Office Rental & Compounded Growth (Data Source: IPD 2001)

Total office returns also underperformed London (and the United Kingdom), which is in line with historic patterns for Croydon.

Costs comprised land acquisition, construction, professional fees, other agents' fees and costs, and finance (rolled up interest on costs). Land and construction costs excluding profit totaled £90.48m. The gross development value (GDV) of the scheme was £105.76m. It was considered by the investor that, for a project of this scale, a developer's profit on cost of 17.5 percent would be required (although profit on land was acceptable at 10 percent). The scheme on this basis outlined previously was marginally producing a total profit of £15.28m, in other words, a deterministic (NPV) measure of development profit. The next stage was to consider the project risks in a state without strategic flexibility.

A Monte Carlo simulation analysis was undertaken based on key input variables of supermarket and office rents and yields and office construction costs (a fuller analysis with other variables was initially undertaken and then narrowed down to key variables together with preliminary sensitivity and scenario analysis). The results are shown in the frequency chart in Figure 93.

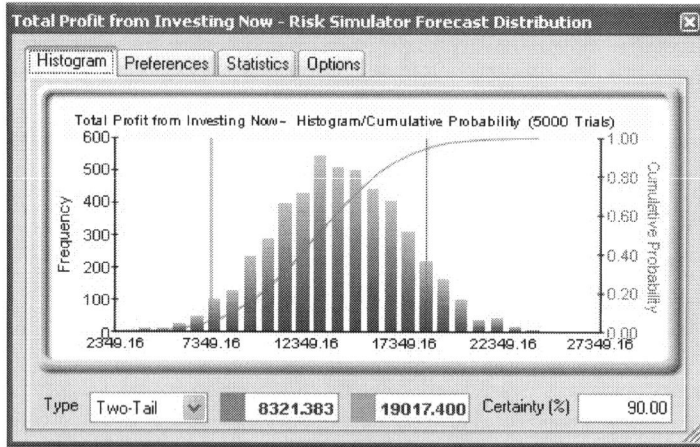

Figure 93: Base-scoping Monte Carlo Analysis

Figure 93 shows a mean total profit return of £13.7m (90 percent certainty range of £8.3m to £19.0m) against a minimum required return of £14.7m (assuming 10 percent and 17.5 percent profit on land and construction cost respectively). These returns can be compared with the ROA and explanation that incorporate a simulation of the option values in Figure 98 and Table 15. It should be noted that the project risk testing and use of simulation analysis, as illustrated earlier is in itself a complex area, as highlighted earlier in this book.

Stage III: Internal and External Uncertainty Inputs

The base scoping provided a useful measure of the financial internal uncertainties and their inter-dependencies. In addition, it was necessary to regard specialist reports concerning construction constraints, cost variables, and programming. These also aided the simulation analysis in Stage II.

An ROA requires an assessment of volatility, a key input into the risk-neutral framework of real options pricing. In this instance state pricing was also used. An assessment of the magnitude of the upside and downside within an underlying lattice in order to capture the likely asymmetry of the Croydon market was therefore undertaken.

As volatility is key to ROA, research and subsequent analysis are critical in obtaining suitable input data and then reviewing the resultant computations in Stage V. Indexes, as outlined later, are based on professional valuations as opposed to market transactions. Academic papers have highlighted the potential for what is known as valuation "smoothing" within the indexes with the result that volatility of real estate may be understated. Various techniques and data sources have been used for backing out true, historic, implied, and expected volatility in real estate over alternative timeframes. This however remains a significant area of research. The following approach has been simplified for practical reasons in obtaining appropriate volatility rates for this case study.

The U.K. Investment Property Databank (IPD) data on office and retail rental growth and total returns for Croydon, London, and the United Kingdom between 1981 and 2002 were analyzed. As investment performance is judged on total returns these volatility figures were used with respect to the underlying asset value. Volatility of total returns for office and retail for three periods: 1981-2002(1); 1991-2002(2); and 1995-2001(3) are shown in Figure 94—both graphs show volatility decreasing over the three periods from a range of 8.6 percent to 12.1 percent (offices) and 6.4 percent to 8.7 percent (retail) to 2.4 percent to 3.3 percent (offices) and 1.15 percent to 3.4 percent (retail). These appear to be low volatility rates compared to empirical research. Another way of considering the volatility over this period for offices and retail is on a 5-year rolling basis as shown in the two charts in Figure 95.

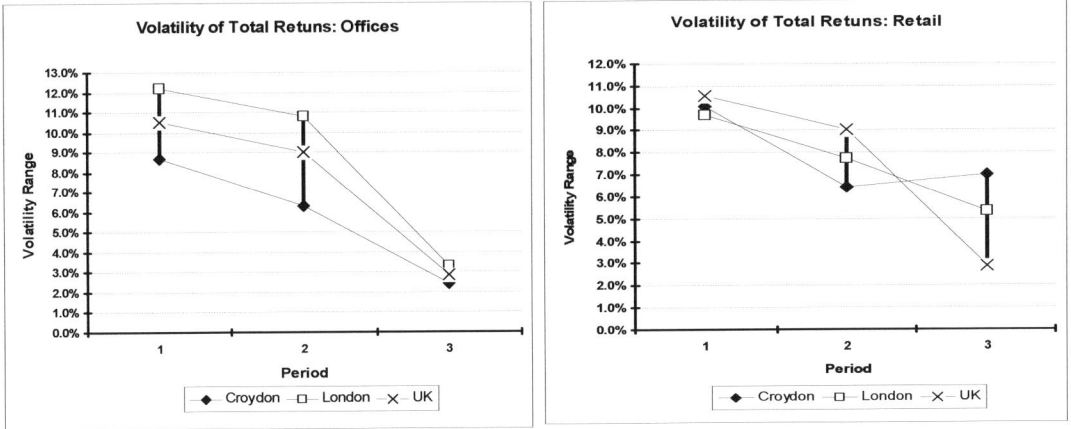

Figure 94: Croydon Retail & Office Volatility of Total Returns (Data Source: IPD 2001)

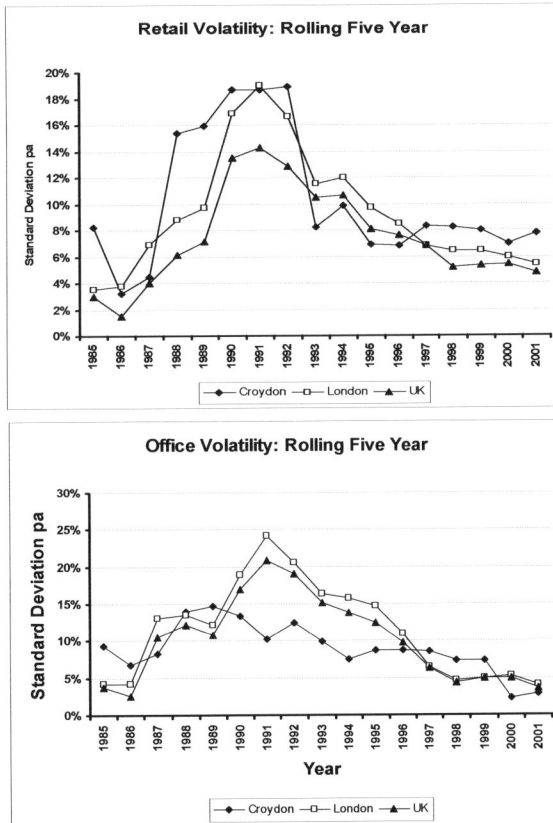

Figure 95: Croydon Retail & Office Returns—Five-year Rolling Volatility
(Data Source: IPD 2001)

From Figure 95 we see that the Croydon office market showed an average volatility of 8.95 percent (range 2.2 percent to 14.7 percent). This was below both London (average 11.39 percent – range 4.1 percent to 24.1 percent) and the UK (average 10.12 percent – range 2.6 percent to 10.9 percent).

For retail (except in Croydon) the volatility levels were generally lower than offices with the Croydon market showing an average of 10.27 percent (range 3.2 percent to 18.9 percent) compared with a London average of 9.29 percent (range 3.5 percent to 19 percent) and the UK average of 7.46 percent (range 1.5 percent to 14.3 percent).

It is necessary for the underlying asset to arrive at a single volatility that is, combining retail and offices. Further research and analysis in practice was undertaken, including cross correlations. For the purposes here a figure of 10 percent with an analysis range of between 5 percent and 35 percent is utilized. Taking account of sector empirical studies and desmoothing of base indexes.

So far as the price probability falls under the real options analysis approach of state pricing, this has regard to compounded growth in capturing the asymmetry of future underlying asset changes. Again, further research in practice was undertaken. Indeed, an alternative approach in option pricing would be via a jump-diffusion whereby an initial jump (i.e., upside) could be followed by a reversion to appropriate volatility levels. Nonrecombining lattices or multiple recombining lattices with changing volatilities could also achieve similar results. For state pricing, the upstate was assumed at 15 percent and downstate 5 percent.

So far as costs were concerned, cost inflation was set at 5 percent; and cost volatility at 5 percent. The latter was considered low in comparison to empirical examples and therefore, was analyzed within a range of 5 percent to 25 percent. U.K. published construction cost indexes have been criticized as not reflecting the true volatility found in the sector. This criticism has again led to other alternative measures and proxies being sought and analyzed, including traded call options of construction companies.

Stage IV: Real Options Quantitative Analysis

The three lattice approaches together with the inputs and assumptions outlined earlier were computed. The cost of implementation input excluded profit on cost and land in order to directly compare the option price to development profit. The value input was that derived from the deterministic appraisal. Under each approach, the lattices were as follows:

- An underlying asset pricing lattice (P), the price evolution.

- An underlying cost lattice (C), the cost growth or evolution.

- The value of exercising the development (P – C), in simple terms the NPV in each moment of time of making an investment.

- A valuation (V) lattice (V = maximum (P – C), (D – M), A), where the value would be the maximum of: price less cost (P – C); the option to defer less the intrinsic sunk costs (D – M); or the offer to be acquire by the Council (A). The termination boundary (year 5) would be the maximum of the underlying price less costs or the offer to be acquired by the Council (V = maximum ((P – C), A)).

- A decision lattice, which was based on the valuation lattice in determining at each node whether to defer, sell, or develop.

Option values were calculated under each of the three approaches, which were then compared to the development profit of the deterministic approach, as shown in Table 14.

Table 14: A Comparison of Real Option Values with NPV

NPV (£m)	ROA		
	Binomial (£m)	State Pricing (£m)	Binomial (Dual Volatility) (£m)
15.28	18.13	18.09	23.77
Additional Value Created by ROA	2.85	2.81	8.49

The NPV of 15.28 represents the total profit of investing now of which £14.7m would be the minimum required return. In each case the value (profit) of the option to defer (i.e., now or later) is higher than the current or expected profit of investing immediately. The difference in the real option values results from the evolution of the lattice and risk-neutral pricing of each approach.

Stage V: Explanation and Strategic Decisions

The option price takes into account all possible future outcomes under the three ROA approaches that were not captured by the deterministic analysis. It was, however, necessary to consider the sensitivity of the inputs particularly with respect to volatility (price and cost) and price probabilities under state pricing as well as the impact on the decision lattice at the different nodes. The decision lattices in Figure 96 (with time in years in bold) are set out for comparative purposes.

Taking an overview with regard to all of the approaches, development should probably be deferred in years 1 and 2; deferral or selling were the dominant options in year 3; and development should only probably be envisaged in years 4 or 5. This scheme essentially provided an analytical underpinning for a professional judgment and decision framework. The surface graphs in Figure 97 illustrated the sensitivity for each approach.

Binomial

0	1	2	3	4	5
					Develop
				Develop	
			Develop		Develop
		Defer		Defer	
	Defer		Defer		Sell
Defer		Defer		Sell	
	Defer		Sell		Sell
		Sell		Sell	
			Sell		Sell
				Sell	
					Sell

State Pricing

0	1	2	3	4	5
					Develop
				Develop	
			Develop		Develop
		Develop		Develop	
	Defer		Develop		Develop
Defer		Defer		Defer	
	Defer		Defer		Sell
		Defer		Sell	
			Sell		Sell
				Sell	
					Sell

Price & Cost Volatility

0	1	2	3	4	5
					Develop
				Defer	
			Defer		Develop
		Defer		Defer	
	Defer		Defer		Develop
Defer		Defer		Defer	
	Defer		Defer		Develop
		Defer		Defer	
			Sell		Sell
				Sell	
					Sell

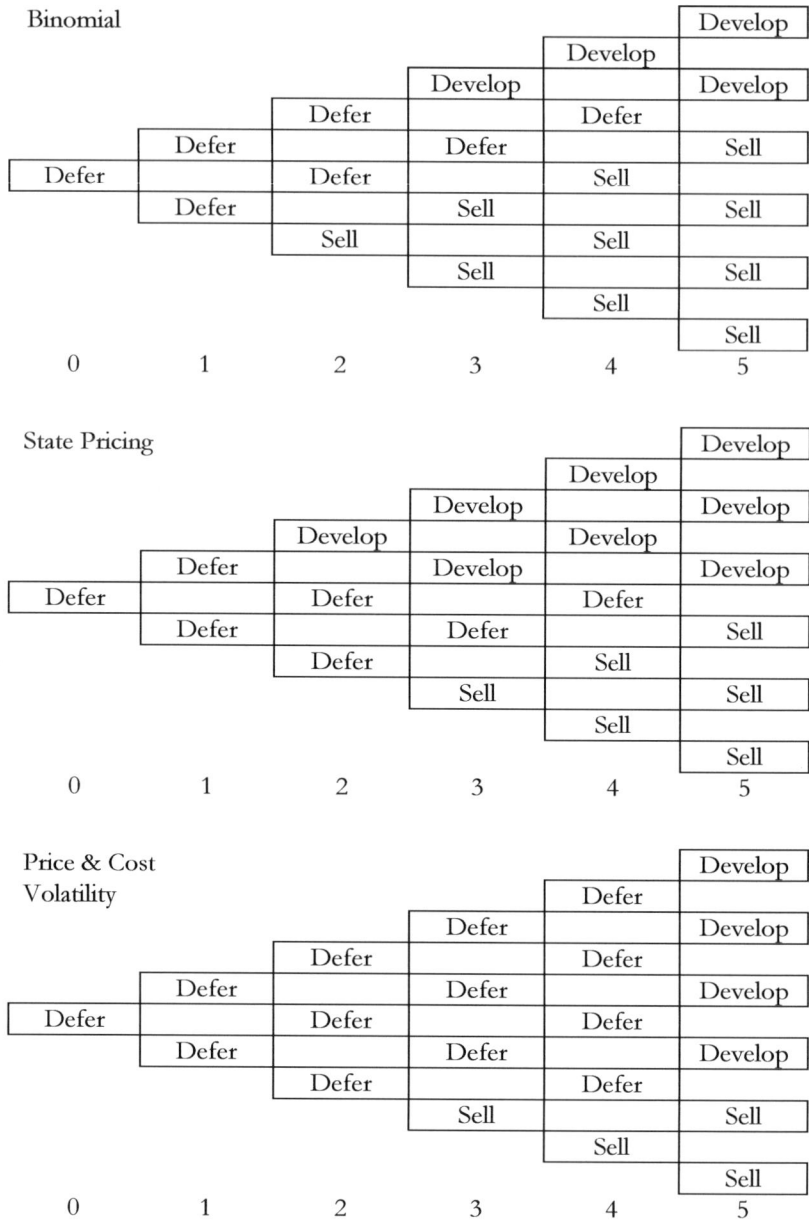

Figure 96: Binomial Lattices

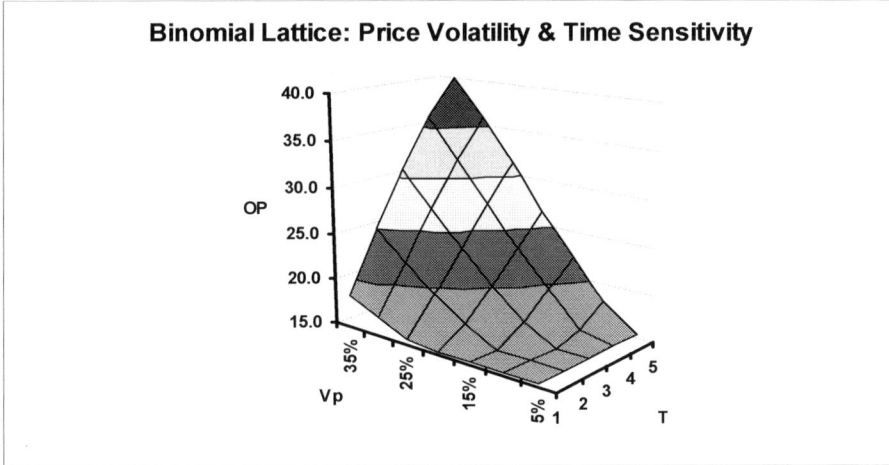

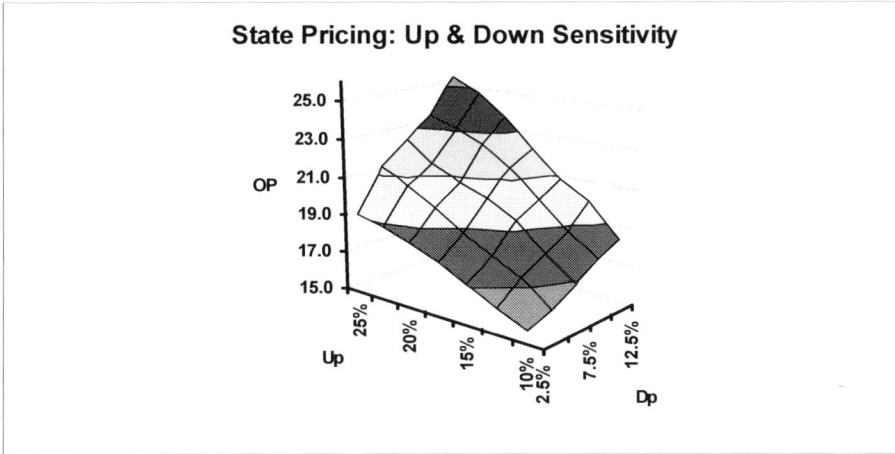

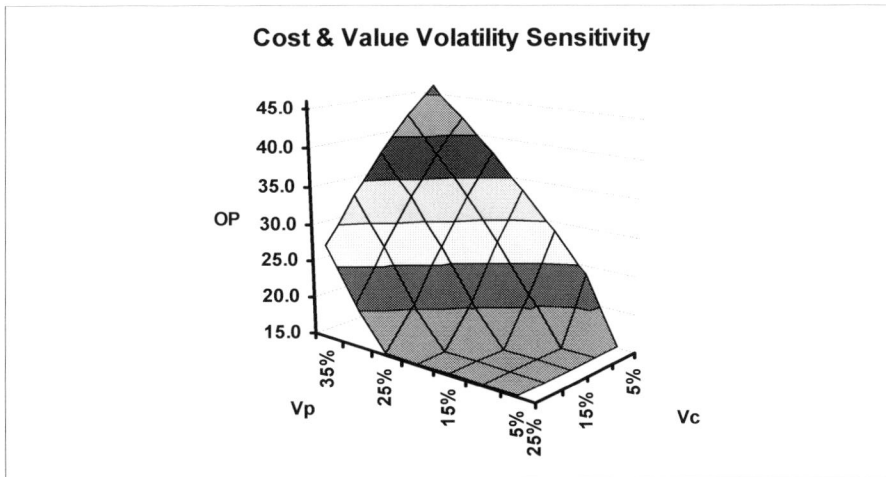

Figure 97: Croydon ROA Sensitivity Graphs

Figure 97 clearly indicated the effect and interaction of volatility on the option price (OP), which again emphasized the importance attached to establishing base volatility inputs as discussed earlier in Stage II. This analysis in practice was analyzed and reported on further. A Monte Carlo analysis of each option price was undertaken and the frequency charts are set out in Figure 98 together with a certainty level of 90 percent. These charts can be compared to the base-scoping frequency chart (Figure 93) and illustrate the narrowing (particularly with state pricing) of the risk structure and higher average return.

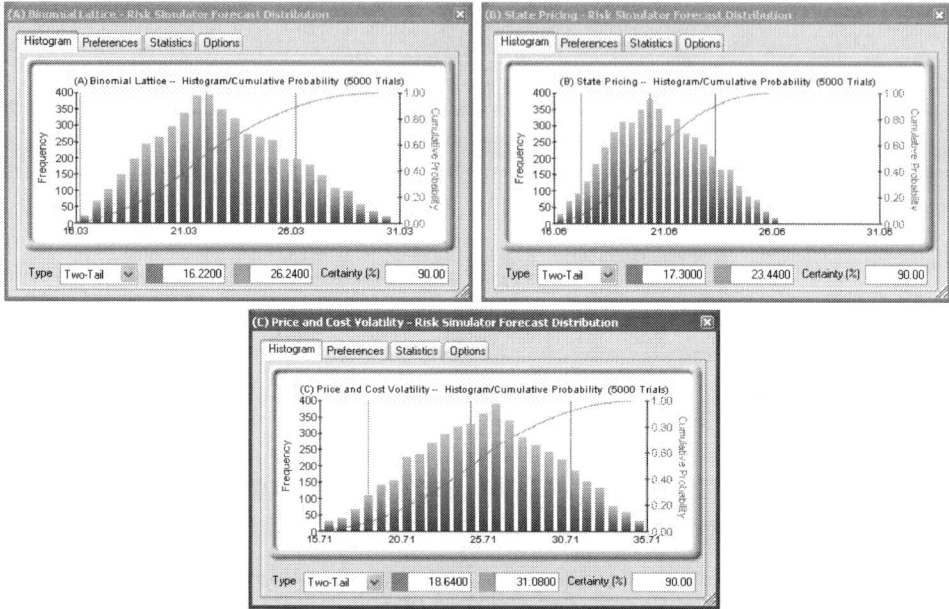

Figure 98: ROA Monte Carlo Application

Table 15: Simulated NPV and Option Values Croydon (Average & Range)

	Average Return (£m)	Risk Structure Range 90% (£m)	Percentage Above Required Return
NPV	13.7	8.3–19.0	(6.8%)
Binomial Lattice	21.1	16.2–26.2	43.5%
State Pricing	20.6	17.3–23.4	40.0%
Binomial (Cost/Price Volatility)	25.1	18.6–31.1	70.7%

It was notable that the risk structure range's downside of the three approaches was relatively similar, being between £16.2m and £18.6m (see Table 15). In this particular instance the downsides provided useful benchmarks to the minimum required return of £14.7m under an NPV approach, as an alternative measure to comparing average returns. Notwithstanding this NPV result, the upsides under the three approaches were significant.

The investor, as a result of an ROA, could clearly form a strategy in terms of optimal timing or whether to invest at all. The flexibility of this decision created additional value over and above a conventional valuation of the development. This additional value would perhaps be incorporated within a price, if the investor were to dispose of the opportunity to a third party at the beginning of the period.

The real option paradigm when applied to real estate potentially highlights, on one hand the seemingly intuitive action of investors and, on the other hand, undervalues investment opportunities and suboptimal decisions. As such the ROA, as illustrated previously, therefore provides another approach and valuable layer to the risk analysis and potential returns of real estate investment and development.

Bibliography: The following papers provide further reading on the subjects of investment risk, volatility measures, and real options in real estate development.

Brown, G. and Matysiak G. *Real Estate Investment, A Capital Market Approach*. Financial Times Prentice Hall, 2000.

Grenadier, S. "The Strategic Exercise of Options: Development Cascades and Overbuilding in Real Estate Markets," *Journal of Finance* 51, no. 5 (1996): 1653-1679.

Quigg, L. "Empirical Testing of Real Option-Pricing Models." *Journal of Finance* 68, no. 2 (1993): 621-639.

Sing T. "Optimal Timing of Real Estate Development under Uncertainty." *Journal of Property Investment & Finance*, Special Issue: Real Options, 19, no. 1 (2001): 35-52.

Titman, S. "Urban Land Prices under Uncertainty." *The American Economic Review* 75, no. 3 (1985): 505-514.

Ward C. "Arbitrage and Investment in Commercial Property." *Journal of Business & Accounting* 9, no. 1 (1982): 93-108.

Williams, J. "Real Estate Development as an Option." *Journal of Real Estate Finance and Economics* 4, no. 2 (1991): 191-208.

CASE STUDY 10: USING STOCHASTIC OPTIMIZATION AND VALUATION MODELS TO EVALUATE THE CREDIT RISK OF CORPORATE RESTRUCTURING

This business case is contributed by Professor Morton Glantz. Professor Glantz is on the finance faculty of Fordham Graduate Business School in New York. He is widely published in financial journals and has authored a number of books including Optimal Trading Strategies, Managing Bank Risk, Scientific Financial Management, *and* Loan Management Risk. *He is a financial advisor to government and business.*

Companies restructure their product mix to boost sales and profits, increase shareholder value, or to survive when the corporate structure becomes impaired. In successful restructurings, management not only actualizes lucrative new projects, but abandons existing projects when they no longer yield sufficient returns, thereby channeling resources to more value-creating uses.

At one level, restructuring can be viewed as changes in financing structures and management. At another level, restructuring may be operational—in response to production overhauls, market trends, technology, and industry or macroeconomic disturbances. It is often the essence of strategy formulation, that is, management's response to changes in the environment to creatively deploy internal resources that improves the firm's competitive position. Indeed, changing operating and financial structures in pursuit of a long-run strategy is a key corporate goal—the most direct path to shareholder value.

For banks called on to finance corporate restructurings, things are a bit different. For example, most loans provide a fixed return over fixed periods that are dependent on interest rates and the borrower's ability to pay. A good loan will be repaid on time and in full. It is hoped that the bank's cost of funds will be low, with the deal providing attractive risk-adjusted returns. If the borrower's business excels, *the bank will not participate in upside corporate values* (except for a vicarious pleasure in the firm's success). However, if a borrower ends up financially distressed, lenders share much, perhaps most, of the pain.

Two disparate goals—controlling default (credit) risk, the bank's objective, and value maximization, a traditional corporate aspiration—are often at odds, particularly if borrowers want term money to finance excessively aggressive projects. In the vast majority of cases of traditional credit analysis, where the spotlight focuses on deterministically drawn projections, hidden risks are often exceedingly difficult to uncover. Devoid of viable projections, bankers will time and again fail to bridge gaps between their agendas and client aspirations.

This case study offers ways for bankers to advance both their analytics and communication skills—senior bank officials and clients alike to "get the deal done" and insure risk/reward agendas are set in equilibrium. Undeniably, the direct way to achieve results is to take a stochastic view of strategic plans rather than relying inappropriately on deterministic base case or conservative scenarios. Let us start with the following fundamentals:

- Stochastically driven optimization models allow bankers to more realistically represent the flow of random variables.

- In negotiating restructuring loans, borrowers (and bankers) can determine under stochastic assumptions optimal amounts to invest in or borrow to finance projects.

- McKinsey & Company, Inc. suggests that business units should be defined and separated into lines of business. Business units should be broken down into the smallest components and analyzed at the base level first.

- Consolidating financials, rather than consolidated reports, should be used to perform business-unit valuations.

- Knowing the market value and volatility of the borrower's assets is crucial in determining the probability of default.

- A firm's leverage has the effect of magnifying its underlying asset volatility. As a result, industries with low-asset volatility can take on larger amounts of leverage, whereas industries with high-asset volatility tend to take on less.

- After restructuring is optimized at the unit stage, unit level valuations are linked to the borrower's consolidated worksheet to process corporate valuations.

The Business Case

Consider the data in Excel spreadsheets depicted in Figures 99–101. The worksheets depict management's original restructuring plan. ABC Bank is asked to approve a $3,410,000 loan facility for the hypothetical firm RI Furniture Manufacturing LTD. Management wants to restructure four of its operating subsidiaries. In support of the facility, the firm supplied the bank with deterministic base case and conservative consolidating and consolidated projections—income statement, balance sheet, and cash flows.

The deterministic or static forecasts tendered the bank limited the variability of outcomes. From a banker's perspective it is often difficult to single out which of a series of strategic options the borrower should pursue if the bank fails to understand differences in the range and distribution shape of possible outcomes and the most likely result associated with each option. Indeed an overly aggressive restructuring program might reduce the firm's credit grade and increase default probabilities. We will not let this happen. Undeniably, this deal deserves stochastic analytics rather than a breadbasket consisting of passé deterministic tools.

From deterministic consolidating projections, bankers developed a stochastic spreadsheet depicted in Figure 101. This spreadsheet included maximum/minimum investment ranges supporting restructuring in each of four product lines. Using Risk Simulator along with the deterministic McKinsey DCF Valuation 2000 Model, the firm's bankers came up with a stochastic solution. On a unit level, they developed a probability distribution assigned to each uncertain element in the forecast, established an optimal funding array for the various business combinations, held cash-flow volatility to acceptable levels preserving the credit grade (again at the unit level). Finally, the last optimization (worksheet) was linked to the consolidating and consolidated DCF valuation worksheet(s). The firm's bankers then determined postrestructuring equity values, specific confidence levels, and probabilities that asset values fall below debt values.

Business History

RI Furniture started operations in 1986. The firm manufactures a full line of indoor and outdoor furniture. Operating subsidiaries targeted for restructuring, depicted later, represent approximately 65 percent of consolidated operations.

All-Weather Resin Wicker Sets

This furniture comes with a complete aluminum frame with handwoven polypropylene resin produced to resist weather. Operating profit margin distributions and investment ranges for each subsidiary are shown in Figures 99–101.

Commuter Mobile Office Furniture

The commuter rolls from its storage location to any work area and sets up in minutes. It integrates computer peripherals (monitor, CPU tower, keyboard, and printer) in a compact, secure mobile unit.

Specialty Furniture

After restructuring, this business segment will include production of hotel reception furniture, cafe furniture, canteen furniture, restaurant seating, and banqueting furniture.

The Analysis

Furniture will be custom built in the firm's own workshop or sourced from a host of reputable manufacturers both at home and abroad.

This analysis was run by placing a constraint on $3,410,000 investment—that is, the bank's facility cannot exceed $3,410,000. Later we place an additional constraint: the forecast variable's volatility. From the information in Figures 99 and 100, the bank developed the spreadsheet depicted in Figure 101.

	Distribution	Operating Profit Margin Range	Operating Profit Margin Most Likely
All Weather Resin Wicker Sets	Triangular	5.5% – 12..6%	11.0%
Commuter Mobile Office Furniture	Triangular	6.5% – 8.7%	7.5%
Specialty Furniture	Triangular	0.5% – 5.3%	4.7%
Custom Built Furniture	Uniform	3.3% – 6.6%	None

Figure 99: Distributional Assumptions

Product Line	Lower Bound	Upper Bound
All Weather Resin Wicker Sets	1,000,000	1,250,000
Commuter Mobile Office Furniture	600,000	1,000,000
Specialty Furniture	570,000	1,100,000
Custom Built Furniture	400,000	900,000

Figure 100: Investment Boundaries

	B	C	D	E	F
1	**RI Furniture Co. Limited: Strategic Plan**				
2					
3		Annual	Lower	Upper	
4	Proposed New Product Lines	operating return	bound	bound	
5	All Weather Resin Wicker Sets	9.7%	$1,000,000	$1,250,000	
6	Commuter Mobile Office Furniture	7.6%	$600,000	$1,000,000	
7	Specialty Furniture	3.5%	$570,000	$1,100,000	
8	Custom Built Furniture	5.0%	$400,000	$900,000	
9					
10					
11		Amount		Constraint	
12	Decision variables	invested			
13	All Weather Resin Wicker Sets	$1,125,000		Decision Variables	
14	Commuter Mobile Office Furniture	$800,000		prior to optimization	
15	Specialty Furniture	$835,000			Total amount
16	Custom Built Furniture	$650,000			invested
17	Total expected return	$231,058		Objective	$3,410,000
18	(Annual operating return X Amount invested)				

Figure 101: Borrower's Original Strategic Restructuring Plan
(reworked by the bank in a stochastic mode, not yet optimized)

Using optimization, a constraint on investment/loan facility was entered:

All Weather Resin Wicker Sets + Commuter Mobile Office Furniture + Specialty Furniture + Custom Built Furniture <= 3410000.

Risk Simulator macros were used to copy results to the original spreadsheet with results depicted in Figure 102. Note that investment falls to within the constraint boundary, while expected return increased.

Simulation statistics reveal that volatility of the expected return (the forecast variable), as measured by the standard deviation, was $20,000. Again, *volatility of operating results affects the volatility of assets.* This point is important. Suppose we determine the market value of a corporation's assets as well as the volatility of that value. Moody's KMV demonstrates that volatility measures the propensity of asset values to change within a given time period. This information determines the probability of default, given the corporation's obligations. For instance, KMV suggests that if the current asset market value is $150 million and a corporation's debt is $75 million and is due in 1 year, then default will occur if the asset value turns out to be less than $75 million in 1 year.

Thus, as a prudent next step, bankers discuss the first optimization run (Figure 102) with management on three levels: (1) maximum expected return, (2) optimal investments/loan facility, and (3) volatility of expected return. If volatility is unacceptable, the standard deviation must be reduced to preserve credit grade integrity. We assume the bank requires project standard deviation to be equal to or below $17,800.

The final simulation shown in Figure 103 produced an optimization that reconciled both risk/reward agendas discussed earlier. The loan facility effectively reduces to (optimized) $3,331,102, and because the firm requires less money, financial leverage improves. We note that $227,889 is the maximized expected return, lower than the $245,757 produced with no volatility constraint—lower risk reduces rewards.

	A	B	C	D	E	F
10						
11			Amount		Constraint	
12		Decision variables	invested			
13		All Weather Resin Wicker Sets	$1,247,100		Decision Variables	
14		Commuter Mobile Office Furniture	$993,671		prior to optimization	
15		Specialty Furniture	$570,000			Total amount
16		Custom Built Furniture	$598,998			invested
17		Total expected return	$245,757		Objective	$3,409,769
18		(Annual operating return X Amount invested)				
19						

Total Expected Return – Risk Simulator Forecast Distribution ☒

Histogram | Preferences | Statistics | Options

Statistics	Result
Number of Trials	1000
Mean	248378.1019
Median	248845.3630
Standard Deviation	20278.0716
Variance	411200188.4180
Average Deviation	15951.5389
Maximum	314095.8767
Minimum	176695.9212
Range	137399.9555
Skewness	-0.0396
Kurtosis	0.2564
25% Percentile	234474.0950
75% Percentile	261455.6607
Error Precision at 95% confidence	0.5060%

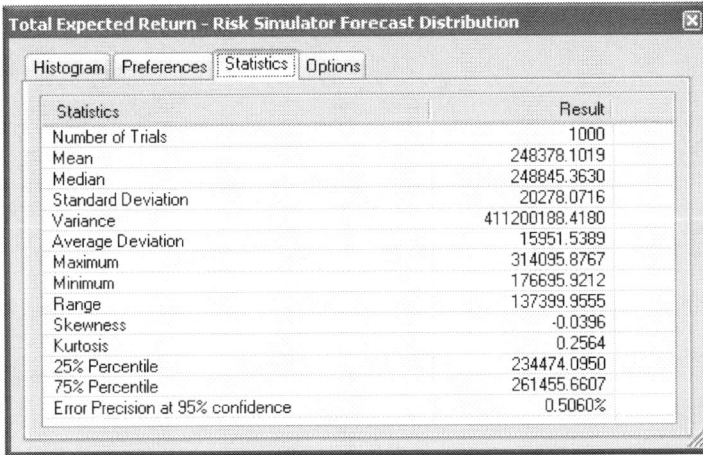

Figure 102: Run Two Optimization Results

	B	C	D	E	F
10					
11		Amount		Constraint	
12	Decision variables	invested			
13	All Weather Resin Wicker Sets	$1,000,000		Decision Variables	
14	Commuter Mobile Office Furniture	$993,225		prior to optimization	
15	Specialty Furniture	$723,457			Total amount
16	Custom Built Furniture	$614,420			invested
17	Total expected return	$227,889		Objective	$3,331,102
18	(Annual operating return X Amount invested)				
19		Expected	Total		
20	Summary	Return	Investment	Standard Deviation	
21	Borrower's Original Projections	$231,058	$3,410,000	n/a	
22	Run One: Original Projections Optimized	$245,757	$3,409,769	$20,373	
23	Run Two: Project Volitility Constraint	$227,889	$3,331,102	$17,800	
24	Run Two: Project Volitility Actual			$17,701	
25	Expected Return and Loan Reduction	$17,868	$78,667		
26	(Bank Requirement: Reduce Project Risk)				
27					
28			Run One	Run Two	
29	Investment (Loan Amounts)	Original Strategy	Optimized; No	Optimized; Risk	
30		Not Optimized	Risk Constraint	Constraint	
31	All Weather Resin Wicker Sets	$1,125,000	$1,247,100	$1,000,000	
32	Commuter Mobile Office Furniture	$800,000	$993,671	$993,225	
33	Specialty Furniture	$835,000	$570,000	$723,457	
34	Custom Built Furniture	$650,000	$598,998	$614,420	
35	Total	$3,410,000	$3,409,769	$3,331,102	

Figure 103: Final Optimization Results

The story does not end here; our analysis up to now was restricted to the unit level—that is, business segments involved in the restructuring. While the spreadsheet in Figure 103 worked its stochastic wonders, it *must now link to consolidating and consolidated discounted cash-flow (DCF) valuation worksheets.*

Consolidated DCF valuations provide a *going-concern* value—the value driven by a company's future economic strength. RI Furniture's value is determined by the present value of future cash flows for a specific forecast horizon (projection period) plus the present value of cash flow *beyond* the forecast horizon (residual or terminal value). In other words, the firm's value depends on cash-flow potential and the risks (threats) of those future cash flows. It is these perceived risks or threats that help define the discounting factor used to measure cash flows in present value terms. Cash flow depends on the industry and the economic outlook for the RI Furniture's products, current and future competition, sustainable competitive advantage, projected changes in demand, and this borrower's capacity to grow in light of its past financial and operating performance. Risk factors that the firm's bankers will examine carefully include their borrower's financial condition, quality, magnitude, and volatility of cash flows, financial and operating leverage, and management's capacity to sustain operations on a profitable basis. *These primary attributes cannot be ignored when bankers determine distributions associated with assumption variables.* Risk Simulator embedded into powerful valuation models provides an intuitive advantage; utilizing Risk Simulator is a decidedly efficient and precise way to get deals analyzed, done, and sold.

CASE STUDY 11: REAL OPTIONS AND KVA IN MILITARY STRATEGY AT THE UNITED STATES NAVY

This case was written by Lieutenant Commander Cesar Rios in collaboration with Dr. Tom Housel and Dr. Johnathan Mun. Lieutenant Commander Rios is an intelligence officer for the U.S. Navy assigned to the third Expeditionary Strike Group in San Diego, California. Dr. Tom Housel is a Professor of Information Sciences at the Naval Postgraduate School in Monterey, California. Please contact Dr. Housel with any questions about the case at tjhousel@nps.edu.

Millions of dollars are spent by the United States military for information technology (IT) investments on Quick Reaction Capability Information Warfare (IW) and intelligence collection systems. To evaluate and select projects yielding maximum benefits to the government, valuation tools are critical to properly define, capture, and measure the total value of those investments. This case study applies Knowledge Value Added (KVA) and Real Options valuation techniques to the Naval Cryptologic Carry-On Program (CCOP) systems used in the intelligence collection process, with particular focus on human capital and IT processes. The objective is to develop a model and methodology to assist in the budgeting process for IW systems. The methodology had to be capable of producing measurable objectives so existing and future CCOP systems could be evaluated.

The Challenge

The Chief of Naval Operations directed its CCOP Office to focus on three goals for fiscal year 2005: Efficiencies, Metrics, and Return on Investment. Given this mandate, CCOP Program Manager Lieutenant Commander (LCDR) Brian Prevo had the difficult choice of how much funding to allocate among the 12 IW CCOP systems currently in his portfolio. Should he merely allocate an equal amount of continuous funding? Should he ask which ones needed the most funding to continue or upgrade? Should he ask the users which ones they preferred? To make appropriate budget decisions, LCDR Prevo had to analyze the operating performance of each CCOP program by developing metrics, measuring efficiencies, and calculating the return on investment. Moreover, he had to identify which investment options supported the United States Navy's Global Intelligence, Surveillance, and Reconnaissance (ISR) mission. LCDR Prevo teamed with researchers at the Naval Postgraduate School (NPS). He enlisted Professor Thomas Housel and Professor Johnathan Mun (the author) at NPS's Graduate School of Operations and Information Sciences to identify valuation techniques to help manage his CCOP portfolio. LCDR Prevo also sought the aid of NPS student LCDR Cesar Rios, a Naval Cryptologist and Information Warfare Officer. Rios had operated CCOP systems and other IW systems while conducting ISR missions from various Navy platforms, including ships and aircraft. As the team lead and subject matter expert, LCDR Rios worked with Dr. Housel and Dr. Mun to conduct the analysis required to make the optimal portfolio management decision in his CCOP strategies.

Background

Intelligence is a critical component of the United States Security Strategy. It is the first line of defense against threats posed by hostile states and terrorists, according to the National Security Strategy (NSS) of the United States.[1] After the tragic events of September 11, 2001, a new world emerged where intelligence techniques from the Cold War era were inadequate to meet the new and complex security threats to the United States. Several initiatives were launched to transform the country's intelligence capabilities to keep pace with emerging threats, including:

- Establishing a new framework for intelligence warning providing seamless and integrated warning across the spectrum of threats facing the nation and its allies.

- Developing new methods for collecting information to sustain intelligence advantage.

- Investing in future capabilities while working to protect them through a more vigorous effort to prevent the compromise of intelligence capabilities.

- Collecting intelligence against the terrorist danger across the government with all-source analysis.[2]

Expenditures on U.S. intelligence activities are estimated at $40 billion annually and a significant amount of that total is spent on Intelligence, Surveillance, and Reconnaissance (ISR) activities. The ISR are the systems that gather, process, and disseminate intelligence. In addition, these ISR systems cover a multitude of systems and programs for acquiring and processing information needed by national security decision makers and military commanders. ISR systems range in size from small, hand-held cameras to billion-dollar satellites. Some ISR programs collect basic information for a wide range of analytical products while others are designed to acquire data for specific weapons systems. Some are "national" systems, collecting information for government agencies whereas others are "tactical" systems intended to support military commanders on the battlefield. The ISR programs are currently grouped into three major categories: the National Intelligence Program (NIP), the Joint Military Intelligence Program (JMIP), and Tactical Intelligence and Related Activities (TIARA).

Most intelligence used by the military comes from the Defense Intelligence Agency (DIA), which produces some HUMINT, MASINT, and a large portion of the Department of Defense's (DoD) strategic, long-term analysis; the National Security Agency (NSA), which produces most SIGINT; and the National Imagery and Mapping Agency (NIMA), which produces most IMINT.[3] To a lesser extent, the military intelligence community also consists of the Central Intelligence Agency (CIA), State Department, Department of Energy, Department of Justice, and Department of Treasury.

Navy ISR

The Naval Transformation Roadmap of 2003 calls for the reengineering of maritime ISR to align with the DoD's 5000 Series and joint warfighting concepts. Goals are to redefine standards and metrics and ensure interoperability while providing the warfighter required capabilities in a timely, cost-effective, and efficient manner. Maritime ISR lies at the core of the Naval Operational Doctrine and is an essential element in improving the speed and effectiveness of naval and joint operations. With today's security threats, it is necessary to expand the range of ISR options available to the commander and ensure decision superiority across the range of military operations in accordance with the NSS.

The Intelligence Collection Process (ICP) is the way tactical Navy ISR units of ships, aircraft, and other platforms complete intelligence requests. Once requests are received, human disciplines and IT technologies are used together to search, acquire, process and report results back to tactical users (i.e., fleet staffs and strike groups), and national-level consumers (i.e., NSA). The generalized process is shown in Figure 104.

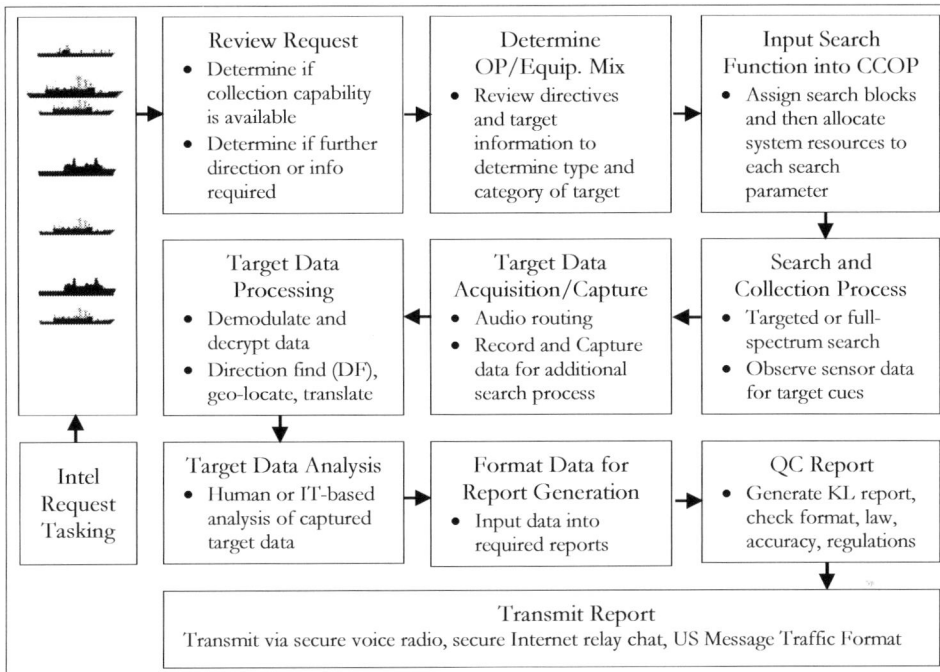

Figure 104: The U.S. Navy ISR Intelligence Collection Process

Each subprocess is further broken down into individual actions that may be required to perform the subprocess in the ICP. For example, the subprocess "Target Data Processing" can be broken down into a number of tasks:

1. Human-based (no automation required)

    a. Manual copy directly into report

    b. Human translation & processing

2. IT-based

    a. Direct transfer into report

        i. Demodulate

            1. All IT-based

            2. Human-enabled

  ii. Decrypt

    1. All IT-based

    2. Human-enabled

 b. Direction finding

  i. Automatic - Local Line Of Bearing (LOB)

  ii. Human-enabled - local LOB

  iii. Human-enabled - B-rep request

 c. Geolocation

  i. Special processing

Established in 1994, CCOP developed state-of-the-art ISR capabilities for Combatant Command requirements for a quick-reaction surface, subsurface, and airborne cryptologic carry-on capability. Approximately 100 cryptologic-capable surface ships are currently in the U.S. Navy inventory. Each one is a potential user of carry-on equipment, along with numerous subsurface and air platforms. Although CCOP systems have broad scope and functions, basic capabilities include:

- Tactical surveillance, targeting.

- Passive detection, classification, tracking, enemy intent at extended range.

- Analysis tools allowing interpretation and reporting of the potential or known meaning of intercepted data.

- Correlation and tracking.

As part of the Advanced Cryptologic Systems Engineering program, CCOP utilizes Commercial Off-The-Shelf (COTS) technology, Government Off-The-Shelf (GOTS) technology and modular, Open Systems architectures. COTS and GOTS technologies, when applied to ISR system functionalities, typically require various levels of integration to leverage on-board capabilities to provide system and mission management, product reporting, and data analysis support. COTS and GOTS also require some level of adaptation or modification to meet fleet requirements. Before deployment for operational use, systems must be systematically tested to ensure suitable and reliable operation. They must also be tested for network vulnerabilities (if connected to Navy or Joint networks), and tested against joint interoperability requirements.

Valuation Techniques

Assessing information technology investments is a daunting challenge. Although several valuation methods are used to measure and justify IT investments, return on investment (ROI) is the most widely used metric to measure past, present, and potential future performance. Other techniques are used to measure the impact of IT on organizations at the corporate and subcorporate levels. Although approaches differ, the objectives are similar and that is to provide managers with metrics to measure tangible IT investments and intangible knowledge assets. Corporate-level approaches determine the contribution of both IT and knowledge assets on the overall performance of the organization. Subcorporate-level approaches look internally at the subprocesses involved in the production of organizational output and attempt to establish a measure for the benefits of knowledge and IT assets within each subprocess.

ROI in the Public Sector

ROI yields insights for managers and investors making high-level strategic business decisions, yet what if an organization does not produce measurable revenues such as the U.S. DoD? Traditional ROI metrics cannot measure the total value of IT investments made by public sector entities. When conducting an ROI analysis for the public sector, there are several considerations:

- Lack of measurable revenues and profits makes it challenging to determine the overall benefit stream produced by the organization.

- Concrete data is often difficult to collect amid an abundance of seemingly intangible soft data.

- ROI depends on costs and benefits; recipients of benefits or stakeholders are not easily identifiable because potential beneficiaries are program participants, managers of participants, program sponsors, or taxpayers.

- Certain government services are essential for the public good and must be provided, regardless of the accountability or cost.

Budgets of public sector organizations are under increased scrutiny, with stakeholders, managers and taxpayers demanding higher levels of accountability and transparency of public investment. Compounding the problem further are increased regulations such as the Government Performance Results Act of 1993 (GPRA), requiring the establishment of strategic planning and performance measurement in programs for the accountability of their expenditures. These challenges have forced public sector organizations to adopt quantifiable methods to produce the required metrics for measuring the *total value* of services and products.

ROI in DoD Programs

Funding for many intelligence programs comes from the DoD, which requires all IT programs be managed as investments and not acquisitions. To achieve this goal and meet other government regulations and legislation such as the Government Performance and Results Act (GPRA) and the Information Technology Management and Results Act (ITMRA), the DoD has established performance measures in the IT investment process. Although profitability is not the primary goal of the DoD and other nonprofit organizations, there is pressure to ensure efficient use of taxpayers' money and deliver maximum value to citizens and communities.

Many issues are inherent in determining overall value and risks with ISR systems acquisitions. Technological complexities from the use of COT/GOTS systems, open architectures systems, evolving software standards, shortened acquisitions timelines and funding instability all contribute to risks in Navy ISR systems. Although the DoD has instituted rigorous types of testing and evaluation (T&E) for all of its programs and projects to mitigate risk, metrics for IT systems have lacked the requisite depth for meaningful valuation. Crucial to successful T&E is the development of measurable Key Performance Parameters (KPPs) and Measures of Effectiveness (MOEs) to provide accurate projections of system performance in a variety of operational environments.

Another issue in the DoD case is the translation of outputs into monetary benefits. Whereas in the commercial case, a price per unit is assigned to the outputs, there is no equivalent pricing mechanism in the DoD or non-profit case. This presents a problem when conducting empirical financial analysis and in particular when seeking a baseline from which to formulate sound fiscal decisions. Valuation methodologies used by DoD for acquisitions must include a common framework for understanding, evaluating, and justifying the impact of government IT investments on the overall successful completion of the national security mission of the United States. KVA methodology is a viable valuation technique for that purpose.

Knowledge Value-Added (KVA) Methodology

KVA was developed by Dr. Thomas Housel and Dr. Valery Kanevsky 15 years ago to estimate the value added by knowledge assets, both human and IT. It is based on the premise that businesses and other organizations produce outputs (e.g., products and services) through a series of processes and subprocesses which changes into raw inputs (i.e., labor into services, information into reports). Changes made on the inputs by organizational processes to produce outputs are the equivalent corresponding changes in entropy. Entropy is defined in the American Heritage Dictionary as a "measure of the degree of disorder [or change] in a closed system." In the business context, it can be used as a surrogate for the amount of changes that a process makes to inputs to produce the resulting outputs.[4]

Describing all process outputs in common units allows managers to assign revenues and costs to those units at any given point in time. With the resulting information, traditional accounting and financial performance and profitability metrics can be applied at the suborganizational level. KVA differs from other financial models in two important respects: It provides a method to analyze the metrics at a suborganizational level and allows for the allocation of cost and revenue across subprocesses for accounting purposes.

KVA uses a knowledge-based metaphor to operationalize the relationship between change in entropy and value added. The units of change induced by a process to produce an output are described in terms of the knowledge required to make the changes. More specifically, the time it takes the average learner "to acquire the procedural knowledge required to produce a process output provides a practical surrogate for the corresponding changes in entropy."[5]

KVA, Monte Carlo simulation, and real options methodologies are applied to the USS *Readiness* in this case study to demonstrate how program managers can build metrics to conduct a financial analysis of each CCOP system at the process and subprocess level. Managers and senior decision makers can thereby establish monetary values to traditionally intangible assets such as knowledge.

The USS *Readiness*

The goal of this case study is to assess the effectiveness and efficiency of CCOP systems in the Navy ISR mission. With KVA methodology, metrics are produced and the CCOP portfolio can be compared on existing and future programs. This section reviews how KVA is applied in two of the subprocesses in the CCOP program: Search/Collection Process (P4) and Format Data for Report Generation (P8).

The USS *Readiness* is a fictitious U.S. Navy warship outfitted to conduct ISR missions.[6] Along with the general manning, the ship has a contingent of IW operators performing intelligence collection processes utilizing CCOP systems. The ship is on a typical six-month deployment and receives daily tasking for ISR collection at national and tactical levels. Onboard the USS *Readiness* is an ISR crew of IW Officers: Division Officer, Division Leading Petty Officer, Signals Operators, and Comms Operators. Each IW officer performs certain processes in the ICP. After a request is received, the ISR crew produces a variety of reports which include raw intelligence reports, technical reports, analyst-to-analyst exchanges and daily collection summaries. USS *Readiness* is outfitted with four CCOP systems (A, B, C, and D).

As shown in Table 16, CCOP systems may be used in a single subprocess or across multiple subprocesses along with the existing infrastructure available in each particular platform. Additionally, some systems such as CCOP A are highly complex and comprised multiple subsystems. With the help of KVA, the proxy revenues and costs are obtained and are shown in Table 17. Clearly, in the corporate setting, revenues and costs can be obtained quickly and easily but KVA is required when applied to the public sector.

Table 18 lists the preliminary results where ROK is the Return on Knowledge (a productivity ratio), ROKA is the Return on Knowledge Assets, a profitability ratio, and ROKI is the Return on Knowledge Investment, the value equation.

Table 16: USS READINESS CCOP Systems

	SUBPROCESS NAME	CCOP A	CCOP B	CCOP C	CCOP D
P1	Review Request/Tasking	X			
P2	Determine Op/Equip Mix	X			
P3	Input Search Function/Coverage Plan	X			
P4	Search/Collection Process	X	X		
P5	Target Data Acquisition/Capture	X	X		
P6	Target Data Processing	X	X	X	X
P7	Target Data Analysis	X		X	X
P8	Format Data for Report Generation	X			
P9	QC Report	X			
P10	Transmit Report	X			

Table 17: P4 and P8 Cost Allocation for CCOP C, D, and Fixed IT Infrastructure

Proxy Revenue Assigned to CCOP C Process K ($US)	Cost Assigned to CCOP C Process K ($US)	Proxy Revenue of CCOP D Process K ($US)	Cost Assigned to CCOP D Process K ($US)	Proxy Revenue Assigned to Fixed Infrastructure Process K ($US)	Cost Assigned to Fixed Infras Process K ($US)
$ -		$ -		$ 28,156	$ 10,250
$ -		$ -		$ 13,868	$ 10,250
$ 58,253	$ 12,000	$ 19,906	$ 63,462	$ 241,667	$ 102,500

Table 18: P4 and P8 KVA Metrics

KVA Metrics for Total K					
	Subprocess Name	ROK as Ratio	ROK as %	ROKA	ROKI
P4	Search/Collection	3.39	339.01%	70.50%	239.01%
P8	Format Data for Report Generation	0.80	79.63%	-25.59%	-20.37%
Metrics for Aggregated		14.10	1410.20%	157.31%	410.20%

KVA provides the structured data required to perform various methods of risk analysis and performance projections such as real options analysis. This combination of KVA historical performance metrics, simulation, and real options analysis will enable the CCOP Program Office and the U.S. Navy to estimate and compare the future value added of different mixes of human assets and systems as well as a range of new initiatives for the deployment and employment options of both.

Analyzing Real Options

A real options analysis was performed to determine the prospective value of three basic options over a three year period (Figure 105). The eight-step Integrated Risk Management process with KVA data was used to estimate the value of the options.

The first option (A – Remote to Shore) was to use the various CCOP systems in a way that would allow all the data they generated to be viewed by a geographically remote center, the idea being that if all the intelligence collection processing could be done remotely in a consolidated center, fewer intelligence personnel would be required on ships. The idea of remoting capabilities to a consolidated center is a popular movement in the military to cut costs and provide more shore-based operations to support warfighting capabilities. This is akin to the consolidation of service operations in businesses for example in larger, but fewer, call centers.

The second option (B – Direct Support) focused on how the CCOP's equipment and operators could be moved from ship to ship. When a ship came into port for maintenance, repair, or modernization, the idea was to move the CCOP equipment and operators to ships that were about to be deployed. This way, fewer sets of CCOP equipment and operators would be needed to service the intelligence gathering needs of the fleet.

The third option (C – Permanent SSES) basically kept the CCOP systems and operators assigned to given ships at all times. This approach required more operators and CCOP systems raising the potential costs but providing more control of the intelligence capability by the ships and fleet commanders.

The results of the analysis (Figure 106) indicated that the highest value was for option C. The result ran contrary to the expected cost savings of options A and B. However, because KVA provided a monetized numerator in the form of surrogate revenue, it was possible to see the effects of greater outputs-revenue for option C. Option C is the preferred option of the commanders of the fleet and ships because it affords greater control of the intelligence assets for their specific operations. So, intuitively, these commanders favored option C but prior to the real options with KVA data analysis, they had no relatively objective way to support their intuitions.

It is possible that with time and experience, the remoting option would provide greater benefits-revenue per cost than data collection techniques because remoting provides more robust operations from ship platforms. But, the current bandwidth limitations of the Naval operating environment, mitigate against remoting systems that have high bandwidth requirements.

The CCOPs program office has asked for further analysis using the KVA and real options methodologies. Software that applies KVA, simulation, and real options analysis are routinely in the process of being deployed with a Naval strike group to enable ongoing monitoring of the performance of the data collection process and its supporting CCOP systems. The next step will be to include the use of these software to enable the commanders and program executives to make projections about the best options for deploying the CCOP systems to support the intelligence needs of the Naval commanders and other intelligence gathering and analysis agencies in the federal government.

NOTES

1. United States. President. The National Security Strategy of the United States of America. Washington, White House, 2002. Internet: 1 June, 2005: http://www.whitehouse.gov/nsc/nss.pdf p. 30.

2. Ibid.

3. Chizek, Judy G., "Military Transformation: Intelligence, Surveillance and Reconnaissance," Congressional Research Services, Jan. 17, 2003, p. 2.

4. Housel, T., El Sawy, O., Zhong, J., and Rodgers, W. "Models for Measuring the Return on Information Technology: A Proof of Concept Demonstration," Second International Conference on Information Systems. December, 2001, p. 13.

5. Ibid.

6. The ISR Mission is generally conducted at a highly classified level so specifics of the ICP and CCOP are not available to the public. For the purpose of this academic research, much of the data was estimated or inferred based on realistic sampling of unclassified process information. Information on human capital, such as salaries and operator training, are public information and were gathered from sources such as the Stay Navy website and the Center for Information Dominance (CID) training documentation. The equipment data was also derived or inferred from documentation provided by the OPNAV N20 staff and the Space and Naval Warfare Command (SPAWAR). Other information such as number of process outputs and executions were extrapolated from samples gathered via interviews with ISR crews currently operating onboard, deployed U.S. Navy surface ships.

12

CASE STUDY 12: MANUFACTURING AND SALES IN THE AUTOMOTIVE AFTERMARKET

This case study was written by Andy Roff and Larry Blair with modelling assistance from the author. Both Andy and Larry are executives from the automotive aftermarket who have owned and managed several businesses. They each have over 30 years of experience, specifically in the provision of information systems for the shared benefit of both suppliers and distributors. They can be contacted at lcblair@goalshq.com.

Background and History of the Automotive Aftermarket

The Automotive Aftermarket (AAM) came into existence soon after the first horseless carriage made its way onto the world's roads over a century ago, perhaps within a couple of days when the original dog-clutch succumbed to the abuse of its erstwhile horse-driving operator and certainly the moment the first screw needed replacement. As makes and models of automobiles multiplied over time, so did the manufacturers of parts to repair and keep them running— some commissioned by the vehicle manufacturers (VMs)—with various manufacturing patterns and varying quality and durability. In fact, the relationship of AAM suppliers to the VMs started out as adversarial (i.e., taking a major portion of the lucrative service and repair business away from the authorized dealerships using only VM/OEM parts). However, it has evolved into strategic partnerships in which advanced designs sanctioned by the VMs have become the source of supply of components for the base vehicles. This situation has not precluded the continued manufacture of parts by the AAM supplier for the independent repair market. At the time of this writing, the global AAM total revenues are approximately $800 billion per year, with a 3% expected annual growth rate going forward. In North America alone, 80% of all parts used in vehicle repair is consumed not by a dealership but by an AAM service provider. This is generally true because of convenience, lower cost, and comparable quality of repair. The point is that both the VM and AAM sectors are viable markets and can be approached by common products serving both interests. While the level of business for both VM and AAM is significant, each is based on very different market demands, and, hence, there exist fundamental differences in risk.

The Analytical Complexity

This case study is based on Caskey Automotive Electrics, Inc., a fictitious privately held company that is a leader in the design and manufacturing of automotive products in support of the VM sector of the automotive industry and sales to the AAM. Caskey's specialty is rotating electrics, commonly known as *alternators* and *starters*. The company has close ties to Detroit with both Ford and General Motors (GM), and these firms have provided Caskey with a basis for growing its business in North America and Europe. As a development partner to two of the world's largest VMs, Caskey has supported the development programs of both companies with engineering expertise that has led to manufacturing contracts for starter motors of some of the most recognized car models on the road. Those relationships have also led to contracts for some of the newest "hi-bred" models in which fuel efficiency is maximized. These models place an even greater burden on the starter motor and therefore increase its cost and complexity. Caskey has won a contract for the starter motor for the new Phalanx hi-bred mini-van that will be introduced by GM within the near future. GM has placed orders for the units that will be fitted to the cars during their assembly. However, Caskey has also won the contract for the service support of the dealer network for replacement of starters as required by service demands. The nature of automotive service falls into several categories. As an industry, it is one of the largest (considering both economic value and employment) in those countries having a high vehicle registration. Certainly North America and Europe continue to account for a majority of the vehicle registrations in the world and the highest per capita ratios of car registrations in comparison to the general population. (As a side note, emerging economies in Asia, such as China and India, are gaining larger market shares of the general vehicle population but these markets are mostly dominated by indigenous vehicle makes.)

Initial total sales of the Phalanx are predicted to be 100,000 units per year, rising to 150,000 units in year 2 and reducing to 100,000 units in year 3. Sales predictions for similar models in the past have been accurate to ±5%. The vehicle will be manufactured in mainland Europe and primarily marketed in Europe and North America. The eventual population of the model will vary across the European and North American states but will aggregate 55% and 45% in the two markets respectively. Vehicle population statistics will be available annually from various external suppliers. A face-lift, as opposed to an all new model, will be marketed in year 4 and sales are predicted to recover to 150,000 units before declining steadily to 75,000 units in year 5 prior to an all-new model launch. The total predicted model population will, therefore, be 575,000 units with an annual scrap rate—attrition through either insurance total loss or being uneconomical to repair—of 2% compounded annually. There are two petrol and one diesel versions with a prediction of equal demand for all three engine variations across the model range with these engines serving both the original and face-lift versions, but not the all-new model.

Caskey was chosen to provide the starter motor for all three engines. It supplies only new units, as opposed to reconditioned units, both to GM and the AAM. Each starting motor unit is different, having been designed for a specific model, and has different wear characteristics with a Mean Time Between Failure (MTBF) of 100,000 miles for the smaller petrol engine, 85,000 miles for the larger petrol engine, and 100,000 miles for the diesel version. The average annual user mileage is predicted to be 12,000 for the smaller petrol engine and 15,000 for both the larger petrol engine and the diesel. There is a 2-year warranty on the units sold in mainland Europe versus 3 years in the UK, Ireland, and North America.

There is a demand from GM to have sufficient stock on hand for one week's production with a zero failure rate at fitting. The unexpected failure rate (i.e., before MTBF and therefore resulting in a warranty claim) is 1:10,000. GM's retail service network has 250 outlets in Europe and 150 in North America, where each location must hold at least two of each unit at the model launch date. Caskey has three European and two North American distribution warehouses that service both GM's retail network and the AAM through both independent and chain parts retailers. The margin is the least on sales to GM, with a +20% markup to the chains and +25% markup to the independents.

Caskey expects to supply 90% of the units sold through GM's service network outside of warranty claims, but competes in year 4 and forward with other *new unit* manufacturers and in year 5 onwards with unit reconditioners. There is a single European new-unit manufacturer with a distribution network in North America who introduces a modified starter motor that also fits another model with an existing and out-of-warranty model with a similar population and engine mix. This new-unit manufacturer expects to gain an initial 10% of the market for the new model, increasing by 2% compound and 50% of the additional model where it was one of two vehicle parts manufacturers (VPMs) selected for the original equipment. Two unit reconditioners enter the market in North America and three in Europe, each expecting a 5% share of the market and each distributing only to the AAM. The reconditioners' ability to service the market is directly related to the return of worn units, which in the first year of their operation (year 5 of production) are 100% from GM, reducing in subsequent years as more units from the other new-unit VPM wear out. The MTBF for the reconditioned units is only 66% of that for the all-new units.

The Analytical Framework Applying Risk Analysis, Simulation, Forecasting, and Optimization

Setting up and solving the problem is not a trivial task, requiring facility with Risk Simulator's Monte Carlo simulation, forecasting, and optimization routines. Figure 107 illustrates a forecast model of the automobile demand based on the assumptions listed previously. Minimum, maximum, and most likely value ranges are also listed and each of the period's demand values is simulated (Figure 108). That is, the Europe and U.S. demands for each quarter are simulated such that the expected values of each year are in line with the foregoing assumptions of 100, 150, 100, 150, and 75 thousand vehicles, respectively.

Expected Auto Demand Forecast

						Possible Ranges for Actual Auto Demand					
Period	Europe	USA	Total	Running Total	Annual Totals	Minimum Europe	Likely Europe	Maximum Europe	Minimum USA	Likely USA	Maximum USA
Year 1 Q1	11,001	8,996	20,000	20,000		10,451	11,001	11,551	8,546	8,996	9,445
Year 1 Q2	13,767	11,242	25,000	45,000		13,079	13,767	14,455	10,680	11,242	11,804
Year 1 Q3	19,266	15,763	35,000	80,000		18,303	19,266	20,230	14,974	15,763	16,551
Year 1 Q4	10,998	8,999	20,000	100,000	100,000	10,448	10,998	11,547	8,549	8,999	9,449
Year 2 Q1	16,497	13,504	30,000	130,000		15,672	16,497	17,322	12,828	13,504	14,179
Year 2 Q2	20,615	16,902	37,500	167,500		19,584	20,615	21,646	16,057	16,902	17,747
Year 2 Q3	28,892	23,629	52,500	220,000		27,447	28,892	30,336	22,448	23,629	24,810
Year 2 Q4	16,499	13,503	30,000	250,000	150,000	15,674	16,499	17,324	12,828	13,503	14,178
Year 3 Q1	10,997	8,995	20,000	270,000		10,447	10,997	11,547	8,546	8,995	9,445
Year 3 Q2	13,746	11,246	25,000	295,000		13,059	13,746	14,434	10,684	11,246	11,809
Year 3 Q3	19,253	15,737	35,000	330,000		18,290	19,253	20,216	14,951	15,737	16,524
Year 3 Q4	11,004	9,007	20,000	350,000	100,000	10,453	11,004	11,554	8,557	9,007	9,458
Year 4 Q1	16,500	13,498	30,000	380,000		15,675	16,500	17,325	12,823	13,498	14,173
Year 4 Q2	20,619	16,890	37,500	417,500		19,588	20,619	21,650	16,046	16,890	17,735
Year 4 Q3	28,882	23,637	52,500	470,000		27,438	28,882	30,326	22,455	23,637	24,819
Year 4 Q4	16,487	13,504	30,000	500,000	150,000	15,663	16,487	17,311	12,828	13,504	14,179
Year 5 Q1	8,246	6,757	15,000	515,000		7,834	8,246	8,658	6,419	6,757	7,094
Year 5 Q2	10,307	8,433	18,750	533,750		9,792	10,307	10,823	8,012	8,433	8,855
Year 5 Q3	14,434	11,802	26,250	560,000		13,712	14,434	15,156	11,212	11,802	12,392
Year 5 Q4	8,255	6,746	15,000	575,000	75,000	7,843	8,255	8,668	6,409	6,746	7,083
Grand Total	316,266	258,790	575,000			300,452	316,266	332,079	245,850	258,790	271,729

Figure 107: Automobile Demand Forecast

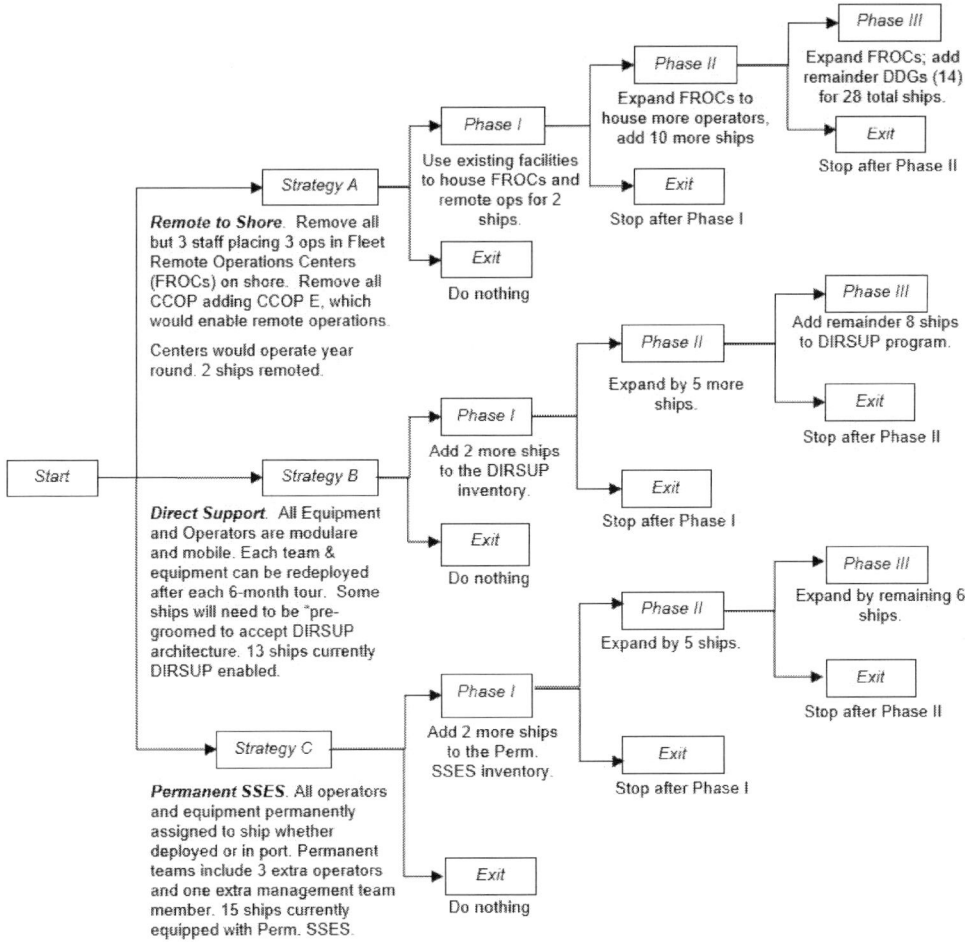

Figure 105: Staging Three Path-dependent Real Options Strategies for CCOPs

Summary Results	Strategy A	Strategy B	Strategy C
PV Option Cost (Year 1)	$348,533	$1,595,697	$1,613,029
PV Option Cost (Year 2)	$4,224,487	$3,043,358	$4,494,950
PV Option Cost (Year 3)	$3,688,994	$10,105,987	$8,806,643
PV Revenues	$24,416,017	$33,909,554	$38,820,096
PV Operating Costs	$16,220,188	$16,765,513	$9,951,833
PV Net Benefit	$8,195,829	$17,144,041	$28,868,264
PV Cost to Purchase Option	$425,000	$169,426	$72,611
Maturity in Years	3.00	3.00	3.00
Average Risk-Free Rate	3.54%	3.54%	3.54%
Dividend Opportunity Cost	0.00%	0.00%	0.00%
Volatility	26.49%	29.44%	15.04%
Total Strategic Value with Options	$1,386,355	$4,466,540	$15,231,813

Figure 106: Summary Real Options Analysis Results

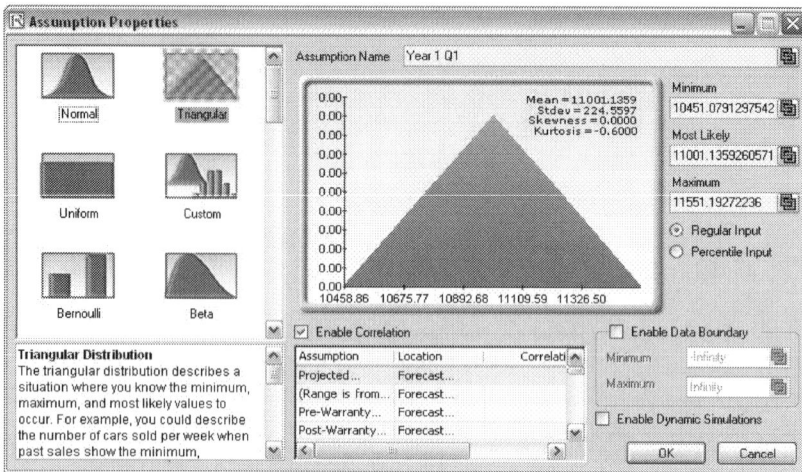

Figure 108: Monte Carlo Risk Simulation of Demand Forecast

Initial Projected Scrap Rate	1.99%	(Range is from 1.50% to 2.5% per year)
Post-Warranty Scrap Rate	10.82%	(Range is from 8% to 15% per year)
Projected Miles Driven Per Year	12,000	(Range is from 10,000-14,000 for small petrol engines)
	15,000	(Range is from 13,000-17,000 for large petrol engines)
	14,989	(Range is from 13,000-17,000 for diesel engines)
Average Warranty	100,000	(miles)
Pre-Warranty Failure Rate	0.01%	(Range is from 0.01% to 0.02% per week)
Post-Warranty Failure Rate	0.15%	(Range is from 0.05% to 0.20% per week)

Figure 109: Additional Requirements

Figure 109 illustrates the modeling of the additional requirements and restrictions of the demand forecasts, such as failure rates of the parts, scrap rates of the automobile model, and average miles driven per year. Note that all the highlighted cells in Figures 107 and 109 are simulation assumptions and each value is simulated thousands of times in the model. Next, an optimization model is developed based on these uncertainties in demand levels, as shown in Figure 110. In this model, we see that the decision variables are the quantity to manufacture. That is, to find the optimal quantity to manufacture given the uncertainty-based forecasted demand levels. Price per unit, failure rates, and average driving distance per year for a vehicle are all accounted for in the model. The analysis provides the optimal quantity to manufacture such that the total net profits are maximized, subject to excess costs of surplus and shortages in quantity on hand.

| Expected Auto Parts Demand Forecast | | | | Miles | Quantity to | Required | | Amount Shortage/ | Marginal | Total | Price | Required Min | Max | Stochastic |
Period	Europe	USA	Total	Driven	Manufacture	Min	Max	Surplus	Cost	Sales	Unit	Price	Price	Sales
Year 1 Q1	83	68	152	3,747	400	200	500	248	$ (248.21)	$ 1,138	$ 7.44	$ 5.00	$10.00	$ 1,129
Year 1 Q2	188	154	342	7,495	400	200	500	58	$ (58.46)	$ 2,562	$ 7.48	$ 5.00	$10.00	$ 2,554
Year 1 Q3	334	273	607	11,242	224	200	500	-383	$ (459.81)	$ 1,680	$ 7.51	$ 5.00	$10.00	$ 1,681
Year 1 Q4	417	342	759	14,989	225	200	500	-534	$ (640.76)	$ 1,688	$ 7.46	$ 5.00	$10.00	$ 1,680
Year 2 Q1	543	444	987	18,736	977	300	2,000	-10	$ (11.59)	$ 10,991	$ 11.23	$ 7.50	$15.00	$ 10,973
Year 2 Q2	699	572	1,271	22,484	978	300	2,000	-293	$ (351.93)	$ 11,003	$ 11.20	$ 7.50	$15.00	$ 10,954
Year 2 Q3	918	751	1,670	26,231	978	300	2,000	-692	$ (830.08)	$ 11,003	$ 11.26	$ 7.50	$15.00	$ 11,008
Year 2 Q4	1,044	854	1,897	29,978	978	300	2,000	-919	$ (1,103.31)	$ 11,003	$ 11.13	$ 7.50	$15.00	$ 10,885
Year 3 Q1	1,127	922	2,049	33,725	1,586	500	4,000	-463	$ (555.86)	$ 23,790	$ 14.89	$10.00	$20.00	$ 23,616
Year 3 Q2	1,231	1,008	2,239	37,473	1,586	500	4,000	-653	$ (783.55)	$ 23,790	$ 15.10	$10.00	$20.00	$ 23,955
Year 3 Q3	1,378	1,127	2,505	41,220	1,586	500	4,000	-919	$ (1,102.32)	$ 23,790	$ 14.80	$10.00	$20.00	$ 23,472
Year 3 Q4	1,461	1,195	2,656	44,967	1,587	500	4,000	-1,069	$ (1,283.27)	$ 23,805	$ 14.84	$10.00	$20.00	$ 23,558
Year 4 Q1	1,586	1,298	2,884	48,715	2,251	500	4,000	-633	$ (759.70)	$ 33,765	$ 14.91	$10.00	$20.00	$ 33,567
Year 4 Q2	1,743	1,426	3,169	52,462	2,252	500	4,000	917	$ (1,100.04)	$ 33,780	$ 15.20	$10.00	$20.00	$ 34,240
Year 4 Q3	1,962	1,605	3,567	56,209	2,252	500	4,000	-1,315	$ (1,578.19)	$ 33,780	$ 15.02	$10.00	$20.00	$ 33,824
Year 4 Q4	2,087	1,708	3,795	59,956	2,252	500	4,000	-1,543	$ (1,851.42)	$ 33,780	$ 15.05	$10.00	$20.00	$ 33,890
Year 5 Q1	2,150	1,759	3,909	63,704	2,782	500	4,000	-1,127	$ (1,352.04)	$ 41,730	$ 15.12	$10.00	$20.00	$ 42,055
Year 5 Q2	2,228	1,823	4,051	67,451	2,782	500	4,000	-1,269	$ (1,522.80)	$ 41,730	$ 15.07	$10.00	$20.00	$ 41,928
Year 5 Q3	2,338	1,913	4,250	71,198	2,782	500	4,000	-1,468	$ (1,761.88)	$ 41,730	$ 15.00	$10.00	$20.00	$ 41,738
Year 5 Q4	2,400	1,964	4,364	74,946	2,782	500	4,000	-1,582	$ (1,898.49)	$ 41,730	$ 14.90	$10.00	$20.00	$ 41,439
Year 6 Q1	2,353	1,925	4,277	78,693	2,706	500	4,000	-1,491	$ (1,789.63)	$ 41,790	$ 15.10	$10.00	$20.00	$ 42,067
Year 6 Q2	2,306	1,887	4,192	82,440	2,786	500	4,000	-1,406	$ (1,687.63)	$ 41,790	$ 14.92	$10.00	$20.00	$ 41,572
Year 6 Q3	2,260	1,849	4,109	86,187	2,787	500	4,000	-1,322	$ (1,586.46)	$ 41,805	$ 14.88	$10.00	$20.00	$ 41,470
Year 6 Q4	2,215	1,812	4,027	89,935	2,787	500	4,000	-1,240	$ (1,488.47)	$ 41,805	$ 14.89	$10.00	$20.00	$ 41,506
Year 7 Q1	2,171	1,776	3,947	93,682	3,947	500	4,000	0	$ (0.43)	$ 59,205	$ 14.92	$10.00	$20.00	$ 58,874
Year 7 Q2	2,128	1,741	3,869	97,429	3,869	500	4,000	0	$ (0.08)	$ 58,034	$ 15.05	$10.00	$20.00	$ 58,229
Year 7 Q3	9,871	8,076	17,948	101,176	4,000	500	4,000	-13,948	$ (16,737.06)	$ 60,000	$ 14.84	$10.00	$20.00	$ 59,380
Year 7 Q4	8,804	7,203	16,006	104,924	4,000	500	4,000	-12,006	$ (14,407.69)	$ 60,000	$ 15.09	$10.00	$20.00	$ 60,366
Year 8 Q1	7,851	6,424	14,275	108,671	4,000	500	4,000	-10,275	$ (12,330.26)	$ 60,000	$ 15.11	$10.00	$20.00	$ 60,428
Year 8 Q2	7,002	5,729	12,731	112,418	4,000	500	4,000	-8,731	$ (10,477.52)	$ 60,000	$ 15.09	$10.00	$20.00	$ 60,371
Year 8 Q3	6,245	5,109	11,354	116,166	4,000	500	4,000	-7,354	$ (8,825.16)	$ 60,000	$ 14.95	$10.00	$20.00	$ 59,802
Year 8 Q4	5,569	4,557	10,126	119,913	4,000	500	4,000	-6,126	$ (7,351.51)	$ 60,000	$ 15.12	$10.00	$20.00	$ 60,499
Year 9 Q1	4,967	4,064	9,031	123,660	4,000	500	4,000	-5,031	$ (6,037.25)	$ 60,000	$ 15.03	$10.00	$20.00	$ 60,132
Year 9 Q2	4,430	3,624	8,054	127,407	4,000	500	4,000	4,054	$ (4,865.13)	$ 60,000	$ 15.08	$10.00	$20.00	$ 60,315
Year 9 Q3	3,951	3,232	7,183	131,155	4,000	500	4,000	-3,183	$ (3,819.79)	$ 60,000	$ 15.02	$10.00	$20.00	$ 60,067
Year 9 Q4	3,523	2,883	6,406	134,902	4,000	500	4,000	-2,406	$ (2,887.50)	$ 60,000	$ 14.91	$10.00	$20.00	$ 59,639
Year 10 Q1	3,142	2,571	5,713	138,649	3,850	500	4,000	-1,855	$ (2,226.45)	$ 57,870	$ 15.01	$10.00	$20.00	$ 57,925

Figure 110: Optimization Model

For instance, say we have a marginal holding or carrying cost of $1.00 for each surplus unit manufactured versus a cost of $1.20 marginal excess net losses in sales if there is a shortage in manufactured parts with respect to sales demand. In addition, at least 800 units must be available within the first 6 months to cover the two-unit minimum per outlet for the 400 outlets worldwide. Finally, the manufactured output cannot exceed 1.50 times the forecasted values per year, to prevent any glut in the market. Monte Carlo simulation and forecasting methodologies were applied as well as dynamic optimization techniques. The actual part quantities that should be manufactured that maximizes net profits, minimizes excess losses, and all the while subject to the relevant minimum and maximum manufactured parts are illustrated in Figure 110 and charted in Figure 111. As can be seen in the chart, it is optimal to start with a small quantity initially when the Phalanx is introduced and, gradually but with a stepwise progression, increase the number of parts as the car gets older. The quantity peaks between years 7 and 10 when warranties expire and when the parts are most needed, and then gradually decreases over time as the cars are decommissioned, sold or scrapped.

Using these advanced risk analysis techniques, we are able to predict the optimal manufacturing output and the life cycle of a specific part based on historical data and simulating thousands of potential outcomes and scenarios in an optimization model. In fact, we can take this one step further and on completion of the optimization analysis, reapply simulation and obtain the probabilities of the net revenues for this particular part, as seen in Figures 112–114.

However, we require 2 parts per outlet for
250 outlets in Europe and 150 outlets in the USA
So, the first period requires 800 units.

Assumed Cost of a Surplus unit: $1.00   (Additional carrying cost losses per unit)
Assumed Cost of a Shortage unit: $1.20   (Additional sales loss per unit)

Constraints:
1. First 6 months must be at least 800 units: 800
2. Each year we cannot manufacture more
   than 1.5 times the forecasted demands:

Year	Manufactured	Limit
1	1,249	1,859
2	3,911	5,825
3	6,345	9,449
4	9,007	13,415
5	11,128	16,574
6	11,146	16,606
7	15,816	41,770
8	16,000	48,487
9	16,000	30,675
10	15,434	19,406
11	10,126	12,277
12	6,644	7,767
13	2,000	4,914

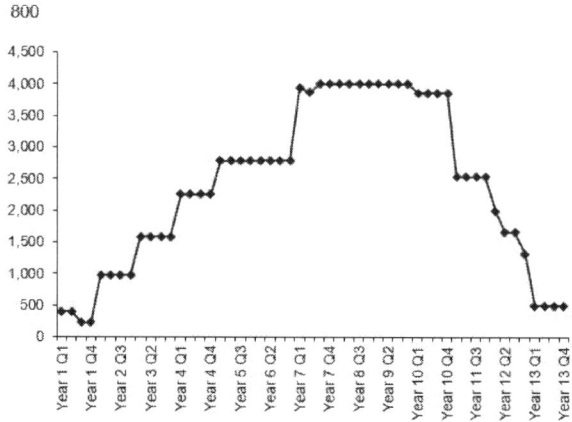

Figure 111: Optimal Quantity and Manufacturing Constraints

Figure 112 shows that the 90 percent confidence interval of the net profits for this particular part is between $15.64 and $18.87 million over its lifetime. In fact, the expected value or mean net profit is $17.54 million (Figure 113). Finally, using the simulated results, we can compare the profitability of one part versus another. For instance suppose we have an alternative part that the company is deciding on manufacturing, and the expected net profit payoff is $15.0 million, we can determine that by manufacturing the current parts, there is a 92.60 percent probability that this current part's net profits will exceed the alternative business line.

In contrast, had optimization and simulation risk analysis not been performed, the results would have been a highly suboptimal set of results. For instance, based on the minimum and maximum production required in each period, say we manufacture at the average of the forecasted values, the total net profits would have been $13.43 million or manufacturing at the minimum required values returns $0.71 million in net profits. Therefore, given such huge swings in values, running optimization guarantees the maximum possible net profits of $17.54 million subject to the uncertainties and risks inherent in the demand forecasts.

To conclude, Monte Carlo simulation, forecasting, and optimization are crucial in determining the risk elements and uncertainties of pricing and demand levels. In addition, the analysis provides a set of valid optimal quantities to manufacture given these uncertainty demand levels, all the while considering the risk of the business line. Thus, using risk analysis, decision makers can not only decide which business lines or parts to manufacture, but how much to manufacture, when to manufacture them, and if required, to decide the optimal price points to sell the parts, to maximize profits, and minimize any losses and risks.

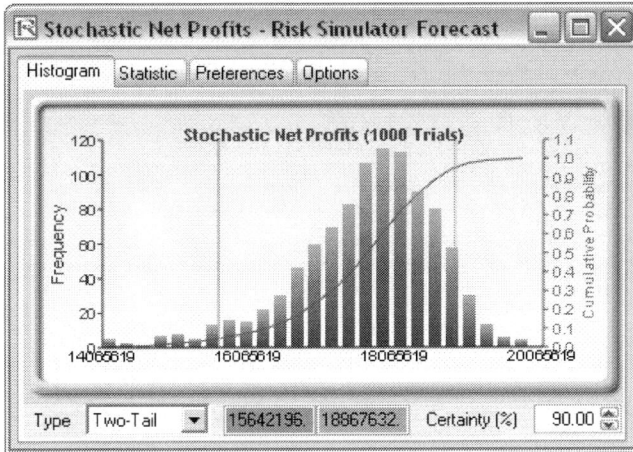

Figure 112: The 90% Confidence Interval

Figure 113: The Simulated Statistics

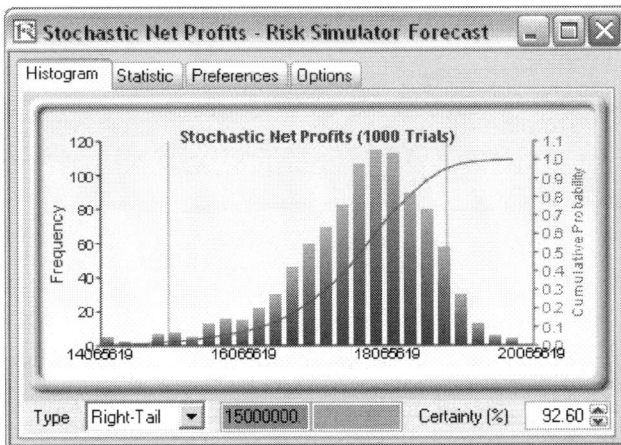

Figure 114: Sample Breakeven Points

13

CASE STUDY 13: THE BOEING COMPANY'S STRATEGIC ANALYSIS OF THE GLOBAL EARTH OBSERVATION SYSTEM OF SYSTEMS

This case study was written by Ken Cobleigh, Dan Compton, and Bob Wiebe, from the Boeing Company in Seattle, Washington, with assistance from the author. This is an actual consulting project performed by Ken, Dan, Bob and the author on the GEOSS system. Although the facts are correct at the time of writing, the analysis has been significantly simplified for the purposes of this case study.

A Background on the Global Earth System of Systems (GEOSS)

On February 16, 2005, 61 countries agreed to a plan that, over the next 10 years, humanity will revolutionize its understanding of the earth and how it works. Agreement for a 10-year implementation plan for a Global Earth Observation System of Systems, known as GEOSS, was reached by member countries of the Group on Earth Observations at the Third Observation Summit held in Brussels. Nearly 40 international organizations also support the emerging global network. The number of participating countries has nearly doubled, and interest has accelerated since the December 2004 tsunami devastated parts of Asia and Africa. In the coming months, more countries and global organizations are expected to join the historic initiative. The GEOSS project will help all nations involved produce and manage their information in a way that benefits the environment and humanity by taking the pulse of the planet. The beneficiaries are divided into nine major categories, as depicted in Figure 115.

The data can come from satellites, airplanes, balloons, ships, radars, river gauges, ground weather stations, buoys, and field data collected on recorders as well as data collected with pencil and paper. An end-to-end architecture was derived from the basic needs of the system and defined into three groups: the observations systems and other domain data; the GEOSS information architecture; and the user communities. This is shown in Figures 116–117. Some of the applications can be as basic as measuring an ecosystem's biodiversity of animal life to measuring, capturing, analyzing, and better predicting natural disasters like tsunamis, earthquakes, hurricanes, and so forth, providing a global early warning system, saving lives in the process.

Figure 115: Societal Benefits from Earth Observations

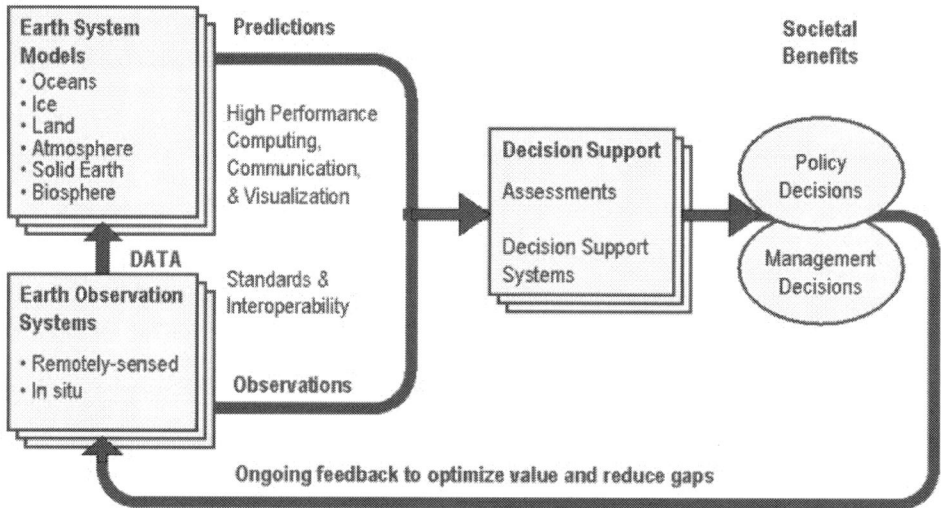

Figure 116: GEOSS Dynamic Decision Process

Currently, several issues must be overcome in order to allow a long-term high-level vision such as the GEOSS to become a reality. An assessment was made with the technical GEOSS community, which comprised several subcommittees; the one the authors consulted with was the architecture subcommittee. The major issues are summarized in the following list:

- Capability of supporting multiple data formats and exchanging between formats.

- Agree on a new standard format for raw and processed data for new systems.

- Provide information assurance (knowing the data will arrive uncorrupted).

- Provide data, information security, controlled access (country restrictions, classified data).

- Assure easy use of data and information including training, data mining, and usability tools.

- Enable the creation and use of decision support tools.

- Allow data and knowledge products (higher-level processed products through the use of multiple sensor fusing).

- Assure easy global access.

- Allow data and knowledge products (higher level processed products through the use of multiple sensor and nonsensor fusing).

- Provide high throughput end to end.

- Support nonelectronic transfer of data and information.

- Provide low latency.

As can be seen, many of these high-level issues are going to be politically and economically charged. For instance, is the economic benefit decided by the country's gross domestic product or wealth, or by the countries that are in the most need of the benefits? Clearly, a lot of discussions and negotiations need to occur before such a system can be realized. And most likely, it will happen in stages.

One current problem is that many systems are built as stand-alone or stovepipe systems. Their data does not easily register, correlate, or fuse with data from other systems, although in a few cases this is not true as in some of the National Oceanographic and Atmospheric Administration (NOAA) applications. Another key issue is that many countries simply are not open to sharing their data with the world, even though there are obvious advantages to doing so. They may feel their national security or exclusive economic zones (the 200 nautical miles offshore areas from most countries) are at risk. These issues will need to be resolved before a working implementation can occur. Once these issues are resolved, it is obvious how powerful such a system of systems will be.

Observation Systems & Other Domain data	GEOSS Information Architecture	User Communities
Spacecraft Aircraft UAVs Radiosondes Buoys River gauges Weather stations Weather radars Ships Seismograph nets Human reports Other in-situ Demographic data Geopolitical data Maps Economic data Health/disease data, etc.	Comprised of: Communications systems Archives Distribution systems (e.g. AWIPS) Geo Portals (gateways) Internet Intelligent search engines Data mining tools Evaluation tools Fusion tools Decision support tools (usually an end-user app) Data format transforms MMIs Provides: Information assurance QoS, security… Low latency where needed High throughput where needed Man–machine interface	Governments Civil Military Emergency Managers Research Orgs Academia Individuals VARs (Commercial) K-12

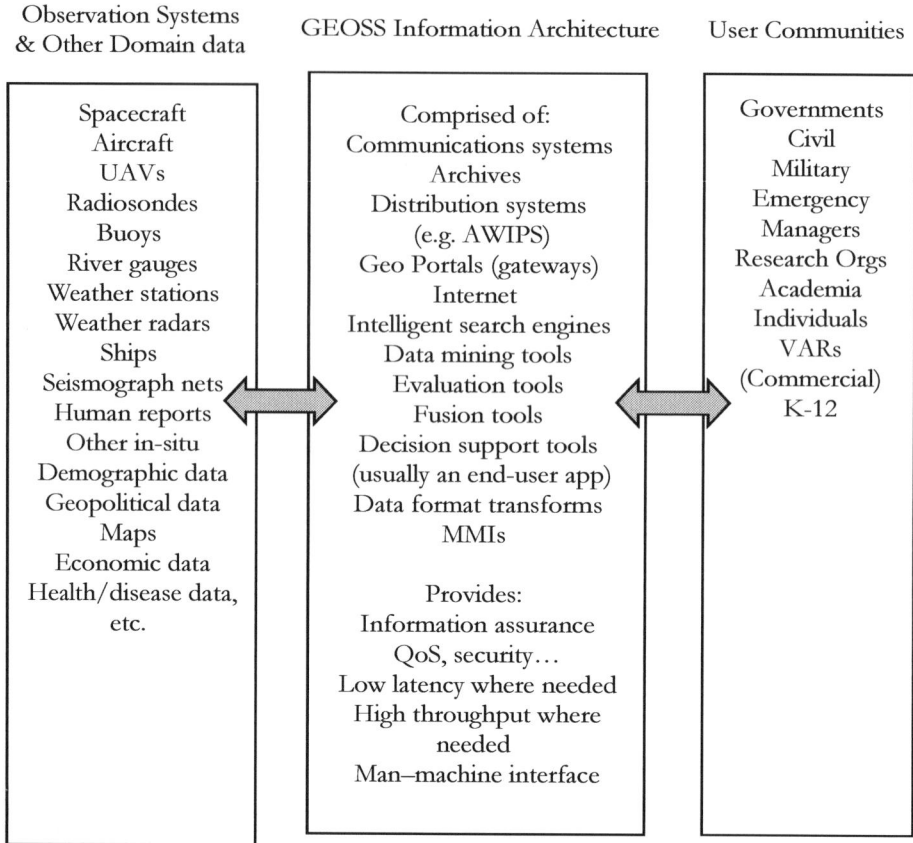

Figure 117: GEOSS End-to-end Architecture

A Background on Systems Dynamics

In order to perform a strategic analysis of the GEOSS system, we need to apply Monte Carlo simulation, real options analysis, and couple them with a systems dynamics model. Therefore a quick aside is required here to briefly explain the basics of systems dynamics.

Although systems engineering is a disciplined approach to identifying and specifying requirements as well as architecting systems, systems dynamics allows one to observe the behavior of a system under given circumstances. One such model that makes this possible is the Ventana Vensim model, which allows one to conceptualize, document, simulate, analyze, and optimize models of dynamic systems. Systems dynamics models allow models to be built from causal loops or stocks and flow diagrams. By connecting words with arrows, relationships among system variables are entered and recorded as causal connections. This information is used by the mathematical equations in the model to help form a complete simulation model. The model can be analyzed through the building process, looking at the causes and uses of a variable, and the loops involving the variable. When you have built a model that can be simulated, systems dynamics let you thoroughly explore the behavior of the model.

As a simple example, Figure 118 shows the rabbit and fox population behavior and the interaction between the two populations within a systems dynamics model.

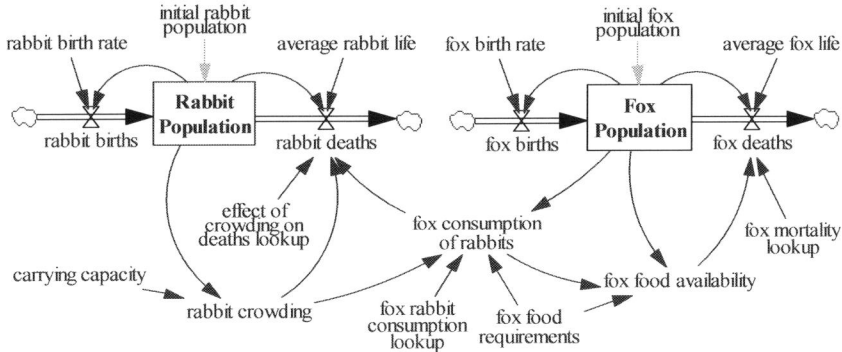

Figure 118: Sample Fox-Rabbit Population Systems Dynamics Model

The model has slider bars built into the birth rates, the initial population, and the average life for the rabbit and fox populations, as well as the fox food requirements and the carrying capacity of the rabbit population. As these bars are adjusted, the remaining variables change the number of births (population and deaths of rabbits and foxes, rabbit crowding, fox consumption of rabbits, and fox food availability). Variables can also be expressed as lookup tables. In this way, we can investigate the behavior of the rabbit and fox population and their interrelationships.

Of course, a model is only as good as its builder and the underlying assumptions. However, systems dynamics have built-in tools that help the builder assess if the model makes sense and the units are correct.

Creation of GEOSS Systems Dynamics Model

Next, the GEOSS model was created using systems dynamics concepts and based on the U.S. military's Office of Force Transformation's model of Network Centric Operations (NCO) as shown in Figure 119.

- A robustly networked force improves information sharing.

- Information sharing and collaboration enhance the quality of information and shared situational awareness.

- Shared situational awareness enables collaboration and self-synchronization, and enhances sustainability and speed of command.

- These, in turn, dramatically increase mission effectiveness.

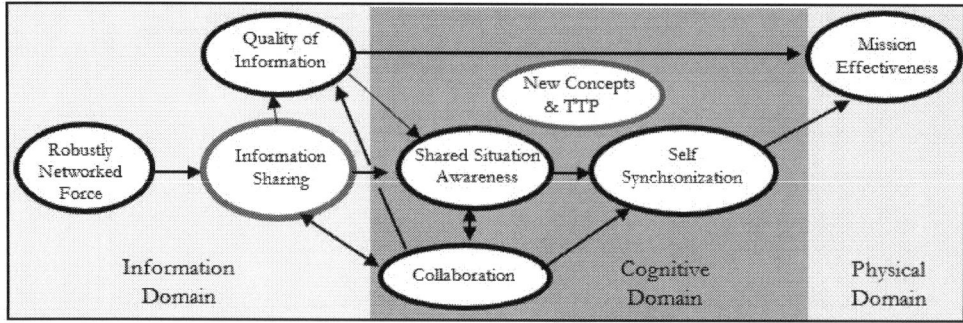

Figure 119: The Office of Force Transformation NCO Model Tenets

The tenets of the NCO model were then modeled. When presented to the GEOSS experts, it was noticed that the tenets of NCO could be slightly modified to fit the GEOSS model, as shown in Figure 120.

Seventy-four technology areas were identified as required for this large-scale System of Systems (SoS) architecture to operate. An optimization run was then done to determine the most influential technologies in determining system effectiveness, which is largely driven by collaboration. Next, the link to real options analysis was accomplished so the relative value of each technology area could be assessed.

Real Options Valuation Integration and Cost-Benefit Results

The social and economic benefits of a fully developed GEOSS system are very substantial. For instance, according to the U.S. Environmental Protection Agency (EPA), the following is only a small list of the potential benefits:

- We could more accurately know the severity of next winter's weather, with strong implications for emergency managers, transportation, energy and medically personnel, farmers, families, manufacturers, store owners, etc. Weather- and climate-sensitive industries account for one-third of the nation's gross domestic product or $3 trillion.

- We could forecast weather with one degree Fahrenheit more accurately, saving at least $1 billion annually in U.S. electricity costs.

- With coastal storms reflecting 71 percent or $7 billion of U.S. disaster losses every year, improved forecasting would have a major favorable impact on preparedness.

- In the U.S., at a cost of $4 billion annually, weather is responsible for about two-thirds of aviation delays—$1.7 billion of which would be avoidable with better observations and forecasts.

- Benefits from more effective air quality monitoring could provide real-time information as well as accurate forecasts that, days in advance, could enable us to mitigate the effects of poor quality through proper transportation and energy use.

- Benefits from ocean instrumentation that, combined with improved satellite earth observing coverage, could provide revolutionary worldwide and regional climate forecasts, enabling us, for example, to predict years of drought.

- Benefits from real-time monitoring and forecasting of the water quality in every watershed and accompanying coastal areas could provide agricultural interests with immediate feedback and forecasts of the correct amount of fertilizers and pesticides to apply to maximize crop generation at minimum cost, helping to support both healthy ecosystems and greatly increased U.S. fishery output and value from coastal tourism.

- Globally, an estimated 300-500 million people worldwide are infected with malaria each year and about one million die from this largely preventable disease. With a linked international system, we could pinpoint where the next outbreak of SARS, or bird flu, or West Nile virus, or malaria is likely to hit.

- Natural hazards such as earthquakes, volcanoes, landslides, floods, wildfires, extreme weather, coastal hazards, sea ice and space weather, plus major pollution events, impose a large burden on society. In the United States, the economic cost of disasters averages tens of billions of dollars per year. Disasters are a major cause of loss of life and property. The ability of GEOSS to predict, monitor, and respond to natural and technological hazards is a key consideration in reducing the impact of disasters.

Currently, thousands of individual pieces of technology are gathering earth observations globally. These individual pieces of technologies are demonstrating their value in estimating crop yields, monitoring water and air quality, and improving airline safety. For instance, according to the EPA, U.S. farmers gain about $15 of value for each $1 spent on weather forecasting. Benefits to U.S. agriculture from altering planting decisions are estimated at more than $250 million. The annual economic return to the U.S. from the NOAA's El Nino ocean-observing and forecast system is between 13 and 26 percent. In the meantime, there are thousands of moored and free floating data buoys in the world's oceans, thousands of land-based environmental stations, and more than 50 environmental satellites orbiting the globe, all providing millions of datasets, but most of these technologies do not yet talk to each other. Until they do, as in a comprehensive GEOSS system, there will always be blind spots and scientific uncertainty. Scientists really cannot know what is happening on our planet without taking the earth's pulse everywhere it beats, all around the globe. Therefore, the challenge is to connect the scientific dots—to build a system of systems that will yield the science on which sound policy must be built.

Strategic Option Pathways

Due to the nature and scope of the project being a global effort, this case study does not expound on all the numerical analyses involved in the quantification of the strategic real options and risk analysis currently being performed. However, a sample strategic tree used for framing real options analysis is provided next to illustrate some of the potential options that GEOSS has. Of course, the entire universe of strategic option pathways and courses of action are a lot more significant than the simple examples illustrated next. See the author's other books on real options for more details on generating strategy trees, as well as modeling and quantifying the real options values using the SLS software (e.g., see *Real Options Analysis: Tools and Techniques,* Second Edition (Wiley 2005) by Dr. Johnathan Mun).

To illustrate the basics of the GEOSS options, Figure 121 shows three sample pathways of the technology development required as part of a global earth observation system.

Strategy A is to invest heavily in the single most required technology area, the Courses of Action Decision Support tools. It has been determined that Courses of Action technology development builds future options at a faster rate than other technology development because of their influence on collaboration. Collaboration is required for technology diffusion, building situational awareness, and building a whole systems view. The main benefit of this strategic pathway is the speed to a collaborative environment, with the potential drawback of not having any focus on the remaining technology areas.

Strategy B is to invest in the top three technology areas, namely, the Courses of Action Decision Support tools; Modeling and Simulation Decision Support Tools; and Resource Allocation Tools. One set of technology combinations enables the development of certain follow-on options and activities. So, if Courses of Action tools are unsuccessful, there are two more technology areas that are being developed to take over, providing a risk-hedging mechanism. However, the disadvantage is that the other 8 technology areas are temporarily abandoned, and with global events consistently changing, we may unknowingly have reduced our ability to handle a new global crisis.

Strategy C is to invest in the top 11 technology areas but scale them so the more important technologies get a proportionately higher percentage of the overall investment funding. The advantage is that all technology areas will be funded and developed, creating a portfolio effect for downstream strategic options of newer applications, and mitigating any downside risks of failures of any one technology. However, the disadvantage is that the critical need for global collaboration will be significantly delayed as focus is diffused over many technology areas.

Each of these simple example strategic paths has exit points and each also has an option of whether the technology should be tackled in-house or by some large integrator such as the Boeing Company or by smaller vendors with other expertise in these areas. These are nested options or options within options.

Of course, the efforts are ongoing and would pose rather significant analytical and resource challenges. However, with the combinations of simulation, real options, systems dynamics and optimization tools, the analysis methodology and results can become more valid and robust.

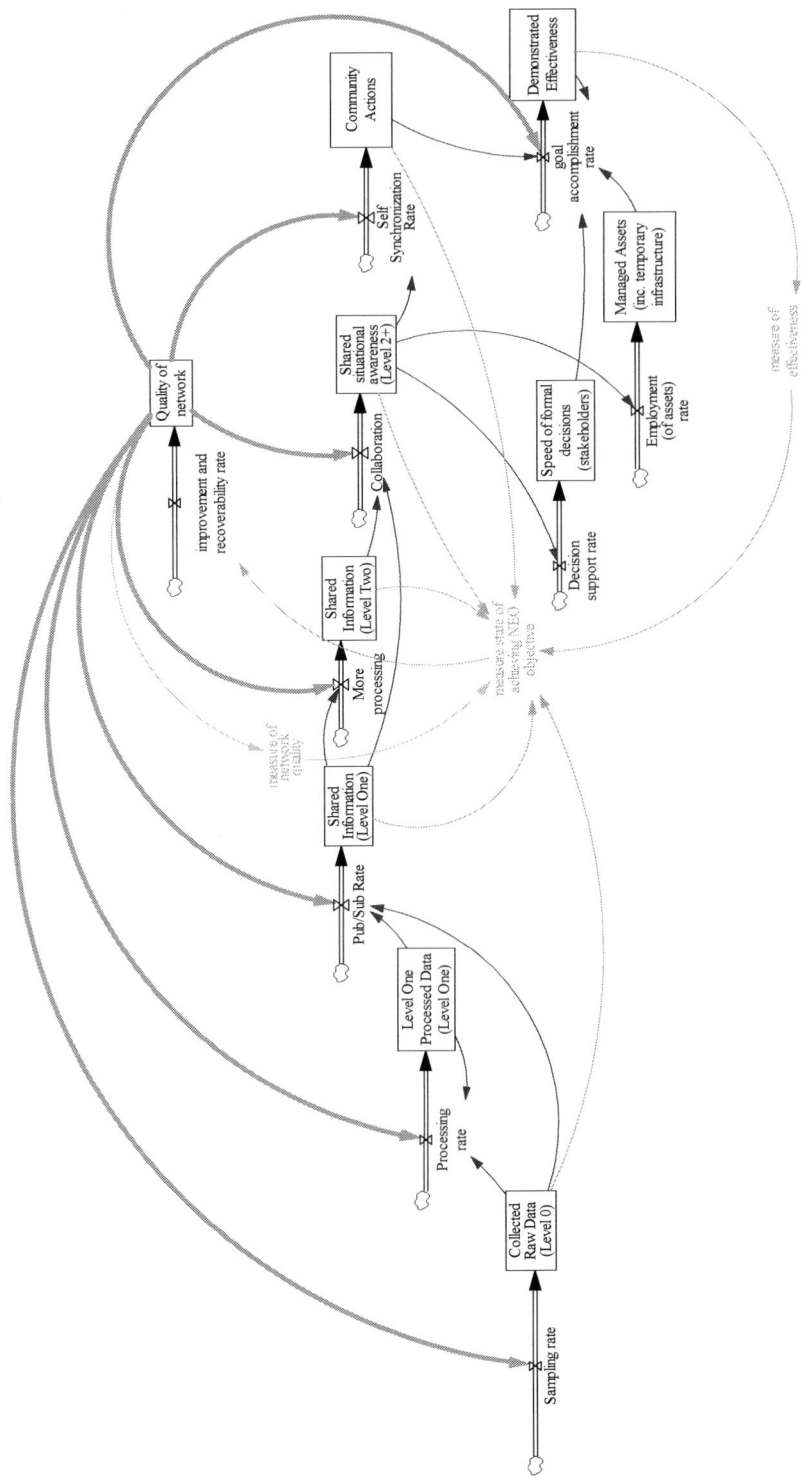

Figure 120: Systems Dynamics Model of GEOSS

Advantage: Collaboration is required for technology diffusion, building situational awareness, and building a whole systems view. So, the main benefit of this strategic pathway is speed to a collaborative environment, with the potential drawback of not having any focus on the remaining technology areas.

Disadvantage: The other 10 technology areas are temporary abandoned, and with global events consistently changing, we may unknowingly have reduced our ability to handle a new global crisis.

Advantage: If Courses of Action tools are unsuccessful, there are two more technology areas that are being developed to take over, providing a risk-hedging mechanism.

Disadvantage: The other 8 technology areas are temporarily abandoned, and with global events consistently changing, we may unknowingly have reduced our ability to handle a new global crisis.

Advantage: All technology areas will be funded and developed, creating a portfolio effect for downstream strategic options of newer applications, and mitigating any downside risks of failures of any one technology.

Disadvantage: The critical need for global collaboration will be significantly delayed as focus is diffused over many technology areas.

Strategy A — Invest heavily in the single most required technology area, the Course of Action Decision Support Tool, with a future option to add in Collaboration

Phase I — Invest 100% on COA Decision Tools

Expand — Add in Collaboration capabilities

Switch — Reallocate resources to other technology areas

Exit — Do nothing

Strategy B — Invest in the top three technology areas: Course of Action Decision Support Tool, Modeling and Simulation, and Resource Allocation

Phase I — Invest in top three technology areas

Execute — Add on additional technologies as required

Expand — Add on Collaboration capabilities

Exit — Do nothing

Strategy C — Invest in all top 11 technology areas with the ability to reallocate resources as required

Phase I — Invest in all 11 technologies

Switch — Option to Switch and reallocate resources to the successful and key technology areas

Abandon — Option to Abandon nonviable and lagging technologies

Expand — Pursue collaboration

Exit — Discontinue efforts and avoid collaboration

Exit — Do nothing

Start

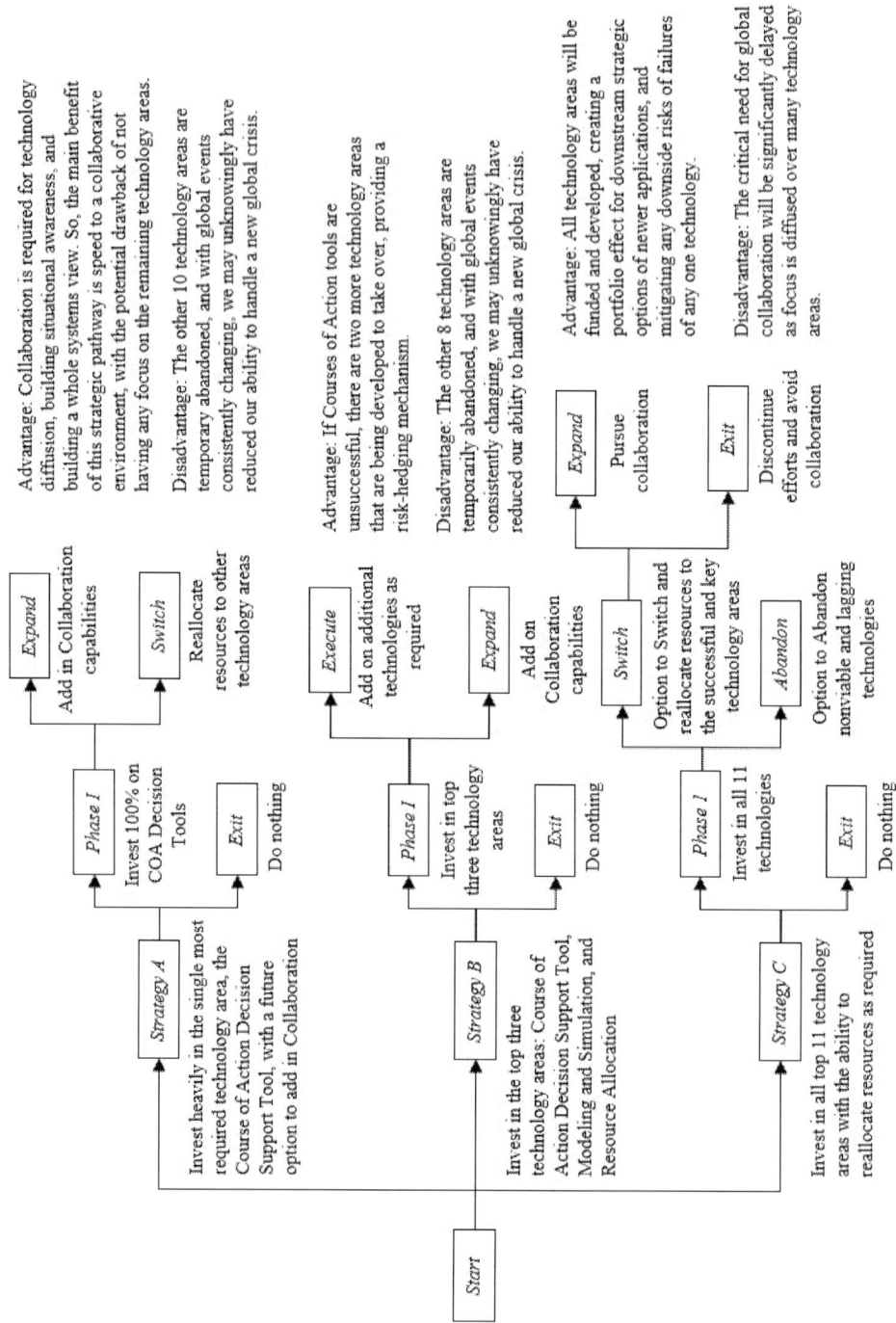

Figure 121: Sample Real Options Strategies for GEOSS

CASE STUDY 14: VALUING EMPLOYEE STOCK OPTIONS UNDER THE 2004 FAS 123R

This case study is based on the author's other book, Valuing Employee Stock Options: Under 2004 FAS 123R *(Wiley Finance, 2004). This case study and book applies the same software FASB used to create the valuation examples in FAS 123's section A87. It was this software application and the training seminars provided by the author for the Board of Directors at FASB, and one-on-one small group trainings for the project managers and research fellows at FASB, which convinced them of the pragmatic applications of ESO valuation. The author consulted for and taught FASB about employee stock options valuation and also the creator of the ESO Valuation Toolkit software used by FASB as well as many corporations and consultants.*

Executive Summary

In what the *Wall Street Journal* calls "among the most far-reaching steps that the Financial Accounting Standards Board (FASB) has made in its 30 year history,"[3] in December, 2004, FASB released a final revised Statement of Financial Accounting Standard 123 (FAS 123R or simply denoted as FAS 123) on Share-Based Payment amending the old FAS 123 and 95 issued in October 1995.[4] Basically, the proposal states that starting June 15, 2005, all new and portions of existing employee stock option (ESO) awards that have not yet vested will have to be expensed. In anticipation of the Standard, many companies such as GE and Coca-Cola have already voluntarily expensed their ESOs at the time of writing, while hundreds of other firms are now scrambling to look into valuing their ESOs.

The goal of this case study is to provide the reader a better understanding of the valuation applications of FAS 123's preferred methodology—the binomial lattice—through a systematic and objective assessment of the methodology and comparing its results with the Black–Scholes model (BSM). It is shown in this paper that with care, FAS 123 valuation can be implemented accurately. The analysis performed uses a customized binomial lattice that takes into account real-life conditions such as vesting, employee suboptimal exercise behavior, forfeiture rates, blackouts, as well as changing dividends, risk-free rates, and volatilities over the life of the ESO. This case study introduces the FAS 123 concept, followed by the different ESO valuation methodologies (closed-form BSM, binomial lattices, and Monte Carlo simulation) and their impacts on valuation. It is shown here that by using the right methodology that still

---

[3] *Wall Street Journal,* April 21, 2004.

[4] Financial Accounting Standards Board website: www.fasb.org.

conforms to the FAS 123 requirements, **firms can potentially reduce their expenses by millions of dollars a year by avoiding the unnecessary over-valuation of the naïve BSM, by using a modified and customized binomial lattice model that takes into account suboptimal exercise behavior, forfeiture rates, vesting, blackout dates, and changing inputs over time.**

Introduction

One of the areas of concern is the fair-market valuation of ESOs. The binomial lattice is the preferred method in the FAS 123 requirements, but critics argue that companies do not necessarily have the resources in-house or the data availability to perform complex valuations that are both consistent with these new requirements as well as still be able to pass an audit. Based on a prior published study by the author that was presented to the FASB Board in 2003, it is concluded that the BSM, albeit theoretically correct and elegant, is insufficient and inappropriately applied when it comes to quantifying the fair-market value of ESOs.[5] This is because the BSM is applicable only to European options without dividends, where the holder of the option can exercise the option only on its maturity date and the underlying stock does not pay any dividends.[6] However, in reality, most ESOs are American-type[7] options with dividends, where the option holder can execute the option at any time up to and including the maturity date while the underlying stock pays dividends. In addition, under real-world conditions, ESOs have a time to *vesting* before the employee can execute the option, which may also be contingent upon the firm and/or the individual employee attaining a specific performance level (e.g., profitability, growth rate, or stock price hitting a minimum barrier before the options become live), and subject to *forfeitures* when the employee leaves the firm or is terminated prematurely before reaching the vested period. In addition, certain options follow a *tranching* or graduated scale, where a certain percentage of the stock option grants become exercisable every year.[8] Also, employees exhibit erratic exercise behavior where the option will be executed only if it exceeds a particular multiple of the strike price. This is termed the *suboptimal exercise behavior multiple*. Next, the option value may be sensitive to the expected economic environment, as characterized by the term structure of interest rates (i.e., the U.S. Treasuries yield curve) where the risk-free rate changes during the life of the option. Finally, the firm may undergo some corporate restructuring (e.g., divestitures, or mergers and acquisitions that may require a stock swap that changes the volatility of the underlying stock). All these real-life scenarios make the BSM insufficient and inappropriate when used to place a fair-market value on the option grant.[9] In summary, firms can implement a variety of

---

[5] See Johnathan Mun's *Real Options Analysis,* Second Edition (Wiley Finance 2005) for details on the case study.

[6] The GBM accounts for dividends on European options but the basic BSM does not.

[7] American options are exercisable at any time up to and including the expiration date. European options are exercisable only at termination or maturity expiration date. Most ESOs are a mixture of both—European option during the vesting period (the option cannot be exercised prior to vesting) and reverts to an American option after the vesting period.

[8] These could be cliff vesting (the options are all void if the employee leaves or is terminated before this cliff vesting period) or graded monthly/quarterly/annually vesting (a certain proportion of the options vest after a specified period of employment service to the firm).

[9] The BSM described in this paper refers to the original model developed by Fisher Black, Myron Scholes, and Robert Merton. Although significant advances have been made such that

provisions that affect the fair value of the options where the list above is only a few examples. The closed-form models such as the BSM or the Generalized Black–Scholes (GBM)—the latter accounts for the inclusion of dividend yields—are inflexible and cannot be modified to accommodate these real-life conditions. Hence, the binomial lattice approach is preferred.

Under very specific conditions (European options without dividends) the binomial lattice and Monte Carlo simulation approaches yield identical values to the BSM, indicating that the two former approaches are robust and exact at the limit. However, when specific real-life business conditions are modeled (i.e., probability of forfeiture, probability the employee leaves or is terminated, time-vesting, suboptimal exercise behavior, and so forth), only the binomial lattice with its highly flexible nature will provide the true fair-market value of the ESO. The BSM only takes into account the following inputs: stock price, strike price, time to maturity, a single risk-free rate, and a single volatility. The GBM accounts for the same inputs as well as a single dividend rate. Hence, in accordance to the FAS 123 requirements, the BSM and GBM fail to account for real-life conditions. On the contrary, the binomial lattice can be customized to include the stock price, strike price, time to maturity, a single risk-free rate and/or multiple risk-free rates changing over time, a single volatility and/or multiple volatilities changing over time, a single dividend rate and/or multiple dividend rates changing over time, plus all the other real-life factors including but not limited to: vesting periods, suboptimal early exercise behavior, blackout periods, forfeiture rates, stock price and performance barriers, and other exotic contingencies. Note that the binomial lattice results revert to the GBM if these real-life conditions are negligible.

The two most important and convincing arguments for using binomial lattices are: FASB requires it and states that the binomial lattice is the preferred method for ESO valuation. The second argument is that lattices can substantially reduce the cost of the ESO by more appropriately mirror real-life conditions. Below is a sample of FAS 123's requirements discussing the use of binomial lattices.

> B64. As discussed in paragraphs A10–A17, closed-form models are one acceptable technique for estimating the fair value of employee share options. However, a lattice model (or other valuation technique, such as a Monte Carlo simulation technique, that is not based on a closed-form equation) can accommodate the term structures of risk-free interest rates and expected volatility, as well as expected changes in dividends over an option's contractual term. A lattice model also can accommodate estimates of employees' option exercise patterns and post-vesting employment termination during the option's contractual term, and thereby can more fully reflect the effect of those factors than can an estimate developed using a closed-form model and a single weighted-average expected life of the options.

> A15. The Black–Scholes–Merton formula assumes that option exercises occur at the end of an option's contractual term, and that expected volatility, expected dividends, and risk-free interest rates are constant over the option's term. If used to estimate the fair value of instruments in the scope of this Statement, the Black–Scholes–Merton formula must be adjusted to take account of certain characteristics of employee share options and similar instruments that are not consistent with the model's assumptions (for example, the ability to exercise before the end of the option's contractual term). Because of the nature of the formula, those adjustments take the form of weighted average assumptions about those characteristics. In contrast, a lattice model can be designed to accommodate dynamic assumptions of expected volatility and dividends over the option's contractual term, and estimates of expected option exercise patterns during the option's contractual term, including

the BSM can be modified to take into consideration some of the exotic issues discussed in this paper, it is mathematically very complex and is highly impractical for use.

the effect of blackout periods. Therefore, the design of a lattice model more fully reflects the substantive characteristics of a particular employee share option or similar instrument. Nevertheless, both a lattice model and the Black–Scholes–Merton formula, as well as other valuation techniques that meet the requirements in paragraph A8, can provide a fair value estimate that is consistent with the measurement objective and fair-value-based method of this Statement. However, if an entity uses a lattice model that has been modified to take into account an option's contractual term and employees' expected exercise and post-vesting employment termination behavior, the expected term is estimated based on the resulting output of the lattice. For example, an entity's experience might indicate that option holders tend to exercise their options when the share price reaches 200 percent of the exercise price. If so, that entity might use a lattice model that assumes exercise of the option at each node along each share price path in a lattice at which the early exercise expectation is met, provided that the option is vested and exercisable at that point. Moreover, such a model would assume exercise at the end of the contractual term on price paths along which the exercise expectation is not met but the options are in-the-money at the end of the contractual term. That method recognizes that employees' exercise behavior is correlated with the price of the underlying share. Employees' expected post-vesting employment termination behavior also would be factored in. Expected term, which is a required disclosure (paragraph A240), then could be estimated based on the output of the resulting lattice.

In fact, some parts of the FAS 123 Final Requirements cannot be modeled with a traditional Black–Scholes model. A lattice is required to model items such as suboptimal exercise behavior multiple, forfeiture rates, vesting, blackout periods, and so forth. This case study and the software used to compute the results, will use both a binomial (and trinomial) lattice as well as closed-form Black–Scholes models to compare the results. The specific paragraphs describing the use of lattices include:

> A27. However, if an entity uses a lattice model that has been modified to take into account an option's contractual term and employees' expected exercise and post-vesting employment termination behavior, the expected term is estimated based on the resulting output of the lattice. For example, an entity's experience might indicate that option holders tend to exercise their options when the share price reaches 200 percent of the exercise price. If so, that entity might use a lattice model that assumes exercise of the option at each node along each share price path in a lattice at which the early exercise expectation is met, provided that the option is vested and exercisable at that point.

> A28. Other factors that may affect expectations about *employees' exercise and post-vesting employment termination behavior* include the following:

> o The vesting period of the award. An option's expected term must at least include the vesting period.

> o Employees' historical exercise and post-vesting employment termination behavior for similar grants.

> o Expected volatility of the price of the underlying share.

> o Blackout periods and other coexisting arrangements such as agreements that allow for exercise to automatically occur during blackout periods if certain conditions are satisfied.

> o Employees' ages, lengths of service, and home jurisdictions (that is, domestic or foreign).

Therefore, based on the justifications above, and in accordance to the requirements and recommendations set forth by the revised FAS 123, which prefers the binomial lattice, it is hereby concluded that the customized binomial lattice is the best and preferred methodology to calculate the fair-market value of ESOs.

Application of the Preferred Method

In applying the customized binomial lattice methodology, several inputs have to be determined:

- Stock price at grant date;
- Strike price of the option grant;
- Time to maturity of the option;
- Risk-free rate over the life of the option;
- Dividend yield of the option's underlying stock over the life of the option;
- Volatility over the life of the option;
- Vesting period of the option grant;
- Suboptimal exercise behavior multiples over the life of the option;
- Forfeiture and employee turnover rates over the life of the option; and
- Blackout dates post-vesting when the options cannot be exercised.

The analysis assumes that the employee cannot exercise the option when it is still in the vesting period. Further, if the employee is terminated or decides to leave voluntarily during this vesting period, the option grant will be forfeited and presumed worthless. In contrast, after the options have been vested, employees tend to exhibit erratic exercise behavior where an option will be exercised only if it breaches the suboptimal exercise behavior multiple.[10] However, the options that have vested must be exercised within a short period if the employee leaves voluntarily or is terminated, regardless of the suboptimal behavior threshold—that is, if forfeiture occurs (measured by the historical option forfeiture rates as well as employee turnover rates). Finally, if the option expiration date has been reached, the option will be exercised if it is in-the-money, and expire worthless if it is at-the-money or out-of-the-money. The next section details the results obtained from such an analysis.

ESO Valuation Toolkit Software

It is theoretically impossible to solve a large binomial lattice ESO valuation without the use of software algorithms.[11] The analyses results in this case study were performed using the author's *Employee Stock Options Valuation Toolkit 1.1 software* (Figure 122), which is the same software used by FASB to convince themselves that ESO valuation is pragmatic and manageable. In fact, FASB used this software to calculate the valuation example in the Final FAS 123 release in sections A87-A88 (to be illustrated later). Figure 123 shows a sample module for computing the Customized American Option using binomial lattices with vesting, forfeiture rate, suboptimal exercise behavior multiple, and changing risk-free rates and volatilities over time. The Real Options *Super Lattice Solver* software also can be used to create any customized ESO model using binomial lattices, FASB's favored method.

---

[10] This multiple is the ratio of the stock price when the option is exercised to the contractual strike price, and is tabulated based on historical information. Post- and near-termination exercise behaviors are excluded.

[11] For instance, a 1,000-step nonrecombining binomial lattice will require 2×10^{301} computations, and even after combining all of the world's fastest supercomputers together, will take longer than the lifetime of the sun to compute!

The software shows the applications of both closed-form models such as the BSM/GBM as well as binomial lattice methodologies. By using binomial lattice methodologies, more complex ESOs can be solved. For instance, the Customized Advanced Option (Figure 123) shows how multiple variables can be varied over time (risk-free, dividend, volatility, forfeiture rate, suboptimal exercise behavior multiple, and so forth). In addition, for added flexibility, the *Super Lattice Solver* module allows the expert user to create and solve his/her own customized ESO. This feature allows management to experiment with different flavors of ESO as well as to engineer one that would suit their needs, by balancing fair and equitable value to employees, with cost minimization to its shareholders.

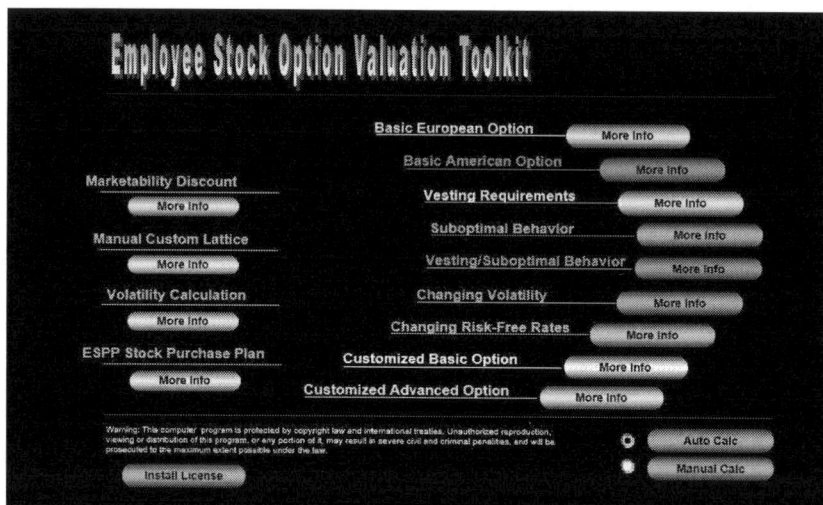

Figure 122: ESO Valuation Toolkit Software

Figure 123 shows the solution of the case example provided in section A87 of the Final 2004 FAS 123 standards. Specifically, A87-A88 states:

> A87. The following table shows assumptions and information about the share options granted on January 1, 20X5.
> Share options granted 900,000
> Employees granted options 3,000
> Expected forfeitures per year 3.0%
> Share price at the grant date $30
> Exercise price $30
> Contractual term (CT) of options 10 years
> Risk-free interest rate over CT 1.5 to 4.3%
> Expected volatility over CT 40 to 60%
> Expected dividend yield over CT 1.0%
> Suboptimal exercise factor 2
>
> A88. This example assumes that each employee receives an equal grant of 300 options. Using as inputs the last 7 items from the table above, Entity T's lattice-based valuation model produces a fair value of $14.69 per option. A lattice model uses a suboptimal exercise factor to calculate the expected term (that is, the expected term is an output) rather than the expected term being a separate input. If an entity uses a Black–Scholes–Merton option-pricing formula, the expected term would be used as an input instead of a suboptimal exercise factor.

Figure 123 shows the result as $14.69, the answer that FASB uses in its example. The forfeiture rate of 3 percent used by FASB's example is applied outside of the model to discount for the quantity reduced over time. The software allows the ability to input the forfeiture rates (pre- and post-vesting) inside or outside of the model. In this specific example, we set forfeiture rate to zero in Figure 123 and adjust the quantity outside, just as FASB does, in A91:

The number of share options expected to vest is estimated at the grant date to be 821,406 (900,000 × .97³).

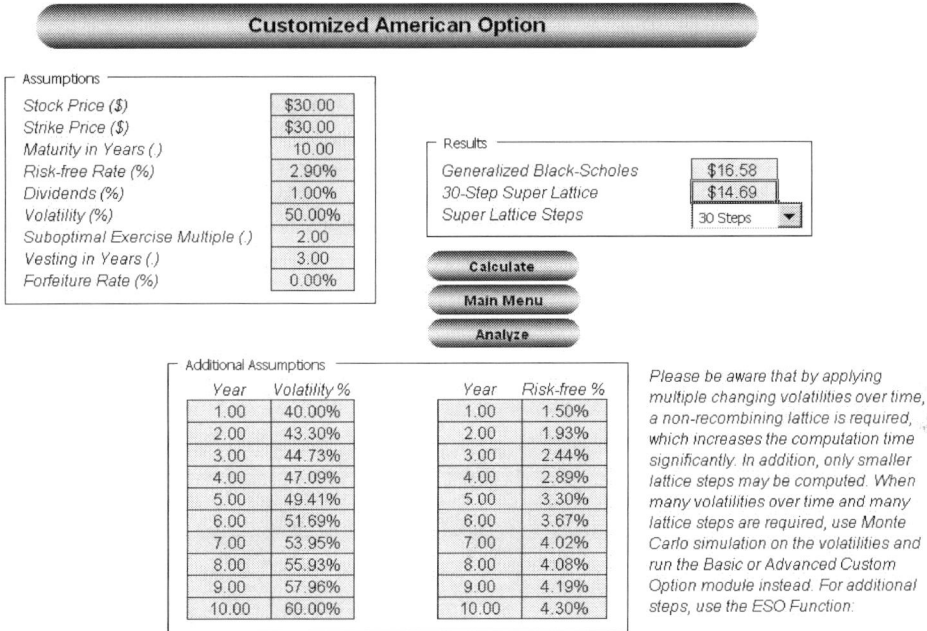

Customized American Option

Assumptions

Stock Price ($)	$30.00
Strike Price ($)	$30.00
Maturity in Years (.)	10.00
Risk-free Rate (%)	2.90%
Dividends (%)	1.00%
Volatility (%)	50.00%
Suboptimal Exercise Multiple (.)	2.00
Vesting in Years (.)	3.00
Forfeiture Rate (%)	0.00%

Results

Generalized Black-Scholes	$16.58
30-Step Super Lattice	$14.69
Super Lattice Steps	30 Steps

Calculate

Main Menu

Analyze

Additional Assumptions

Year	Volatility %	Year	Risk-free %
1.00	40.00%	1.00	1.50%
2.00	43.30%	2.00	1.93%
3.00	44.73%	3.00	2.44%
4.00	47.09%	4.00	2.89%
5.00	49.41%	5.00	3.30%
6.00	51.69%	6.00	3.67%
7.00	53.95%	7.00	4.02%
8.00	55.93%	8.00	4.08%
9.00	57.96%	9.00	4.19%
10.00	60.00%	10.00	4.30%

Please be aware that by applying multiple changing volatilities over time, a non-recombining lattice is required, which increases the computation time significantly. In addition, only smaller lattice steps may be computed. When many volatilities over time and many lattice steps are required, use Monte Carlo simulation on the volatilities and run the Basic or Advanced Custom Option module instead. For additional steps, use the ESO Function:

Figure 123: Customized Advanced Option Model

In fact, using the ESO Valuation Toolkit software and Excel's goal seek function, we can find that the expected life of this option is 6.99 years. We can then justify the use of 6.99 years as the input into a modified GBM to obtain the same result at $14.69, something that cannot be done without the use of the binomial lattice approach.

Technical Justification of Methodology Employed

This section illustrates some of the technical justifications that make up the price differential between the GBM and the customized binomial lattice models. Figure 124 shows a tornado chart and how each input variable in a customized binomial lattice drives the value of the option.[12] Based on the chart, it is clear that volatility is not the single key variable that drives option value. In fact, when vesting, forfeiture, and suboptimal behavior elements are added to the model, their effects dominate that of volatility. The chart illustrated is based on a typical case and cannot be generalized across all cases.

---

[12] A tornado chart lists all the inputs that drive the model, starting from the input variable that has the most effect on the results. The chart is obtained by perturbing each input at some consistent range (e.g., ±10% from the base case) one at a time, and comparing their results to the base case.

In contrast, volatility is a significant variable in a simple BSM as can be seen in Figure 125. This is because there is less interaction among input variables due to the fewer input variables, and for most ESOs that are issued at-the-money, volatility plays an important part when there are no other dominant inputs.

In addition, the interactions among these new input variables are nonlinear. Figure 126 shows a spider chart [13] and it can be seen that vesting, forfeiture rates, and suboptimal exercise behavior multiples have nonlinear effects on option value. That is, the lines in the spider chart are not straight but curve at certain areas, indicating that there are nonlinear effects in the model. This means that we cannot generalize these three variables' effects on option value (for instance, we cannot generalize that if a 1 percent increase in forfeiture rate will decrease option value by 2.35 percent, it means that a 2 percent increase in forfeiture rate drives option value down 4.70 percent, and so forth). This is because the variables interact differently at different input levels. The conclusion is that we really cannot say *a priori* what the direct effects are of changing one variable on the magnitude of the final option value. More detailed analysis will have to be performed in each case.

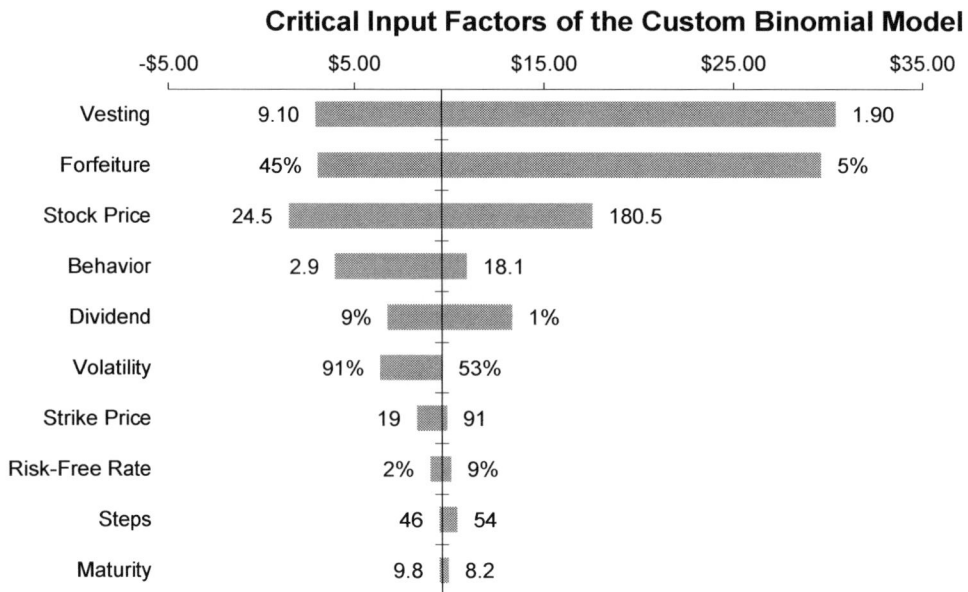

Critical Input Factors of the Custom Binomial Model

	-$5.00	$5.00	$15.00	$25.00	$35.00

Vesting: 9.10 — 1.90
Forfeiture: 45% — 5%
Stock Price: 24.5 — 180.5
Behavior: 2.9 — 18.1
Dividend: 9% — 1%
Volatility: 91% — 53%
Strike Price: 19 — 91
Risk-Free Rate: 2% — 9%
Steps: 46 — 54
Maturity: 9.8 — 8.2

Figure 124: Tornado Chart Listing the Critical Input Factors of a Customized Binomial Model

Although the tornado and spider charts illustrate the impact of each input variable on the final option value, its effects are static. That is, one variable is tweaked at a time to determine its ramifications on the option value. However, as shown, the effects are sometimes nonlinear, which means we need to change all variables simultaneously to account for their interactions. Figure 127 shows a Monte Carlo simulated dynamic sensitivity chart where forfeiture, vesting,

---

[13] A spider chart looks like a spider with a central body and its many legs protruding. The positively sloped lines indicate a positive relationship (e.g., the higher the stock price, the higher the option value), while a negatively sloped line indicates a negative relationship. Further, spider charts can be used to visualize linear and nonlinear relationships.

and suboptimal exercise behavior multiple are determined to be important variables, while volatility is again relegated to a less important role. The dynamic sensitivity chart perturbs all input variables simultaneously for thousands of trials, and captures the effects on the option value. This approach is valuable in capturing the net interaction effects among variables at different input levels.

From this preliminary sensitivity analysis, we conclude that incorporating forfeiture rates, vesting, and suboptimal exercise behavior multiple is vital to obtaining a fair-market valuation of ESOs due to their significant contributions to option value. In addition, we cannot generalize each input's effects on the final option value. Detailed analysis has to be performed to obtain the option's value every time.

Black–Scholes Critical Input Factors

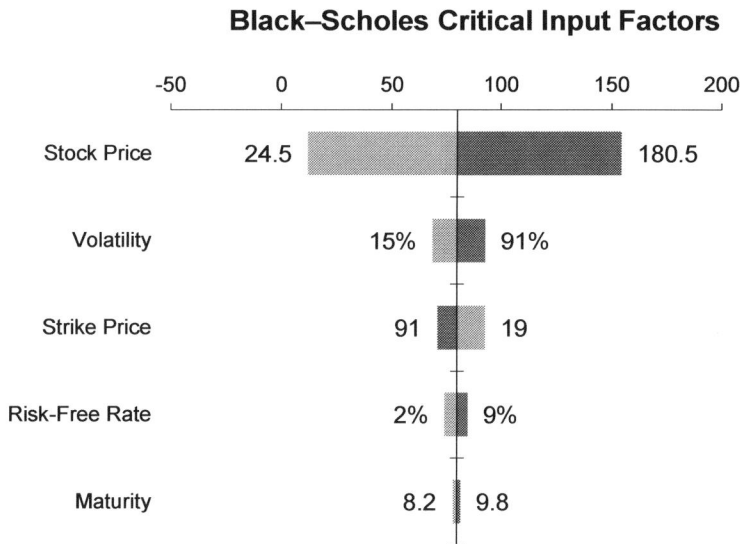

Figure 125: Tornado Chart Listing the Critical Input Factors of the BSM

Non-Linear Critical Input Factors

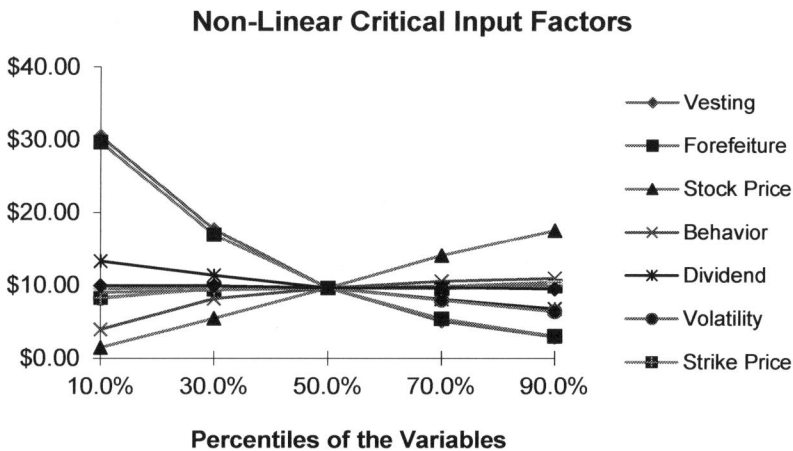

Figure 126: Spider Chart Showing the Nonlinear Effects of Input Factors in the Binomial Model

Dynamic Rank Correlation

Stock Price	0.66
Forfeiture	-0.45
Vesting	-0.33
Dividend	-0.15
Strike Price	-0.13
Behavior	0.10
Maturity	0.09
Risk Free Rate	0.02
Steps	0.02
Volatility	0.01

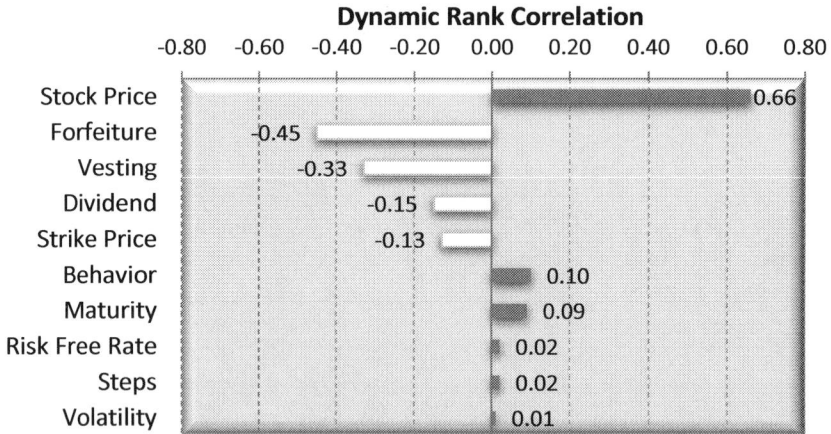

Figure 127: Dynamic Sensitivity with Simultaneous Changing Inputs in Binomial

Options with Vesting and Suboptimal Behavior

Further investigation into the elements of suboptimal behavior and vesting yields the chart shown in Figure 128. Here we see that at lower suboptimal exercise behavior multiples (within the range of 1 to 6) the stock option value can be significantly lower than that predicted by the BSM. With a 10-year vesting stock option, the results are identical regardless of the suboptimal exercise behavior multiple—its flat line bears the same value as the BSM result. This is because for a 10-year vesting of a 10-year maturity option, the option reverts to a European option, exercisable only at expiration. The BSM provides the correct result here.

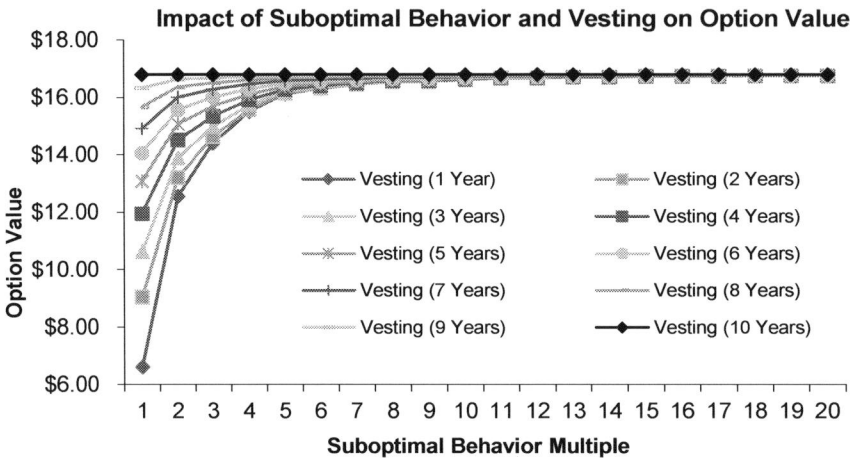

Impact of Suboptimal Behavior and Vesting on Option Value

Vesting (1 Year)	Vesting (2 Years)
Vesting (3 Years)	Vesting (4 Years)
Vesting (5 Years)	Vesting (6 Years)
Vesting (7 Years)	Vesting (8 Years)
Vesting (9 Years)	Vesting (10 Years)

Suboptimal Behavior Multiple

Figure 128: Impact of Suboptimal Exercise Behavior and Vesting on Option Value[14]

---

[14] Assumptions used: stock and strike price of $25, 10-year maturity, 5% risk-free rate, 50% volatility, 0% dividends, suboptimal exercise behavior multiple range of 1–20, vesting period of 1–10 years, and tested with 100–5,000 binomial lattice steps.

However, when suboptimal exercise behavior multiple is low, the option value decreases. This is because employees holding the option will tend to exercise the option suboptimally—that is, the option will be exercised earlier and at a lower stock price than optimal. Hence, the option's upside value is not maximized. As an example, suppose an option's strike price is $10 while the underlying stock is highly volatile. If an employee exercises the option at $11 (this means a 1.10 suboptimal exercise multiple), he or she may not be capturing the entire upside potential of the option as the stock price can go up significantly higher than $11 depending on the underlying volatility. Compare this to another employee who exercises the option when the stock price is $20 (suboptimal exercise multiple of 2.0) versus one who does so at a much higher stock price. Thus, lower suboptimal exercise behavior means a lower fair-market value of the stock option. This suboptimal exercise behavior has a higher impact when stock prices at grant date are forecast to be high. Figure 129 shows that (at the lower end of the suboptimal multiples) a steeper slope occurs the higher the initial stock price at grant date.

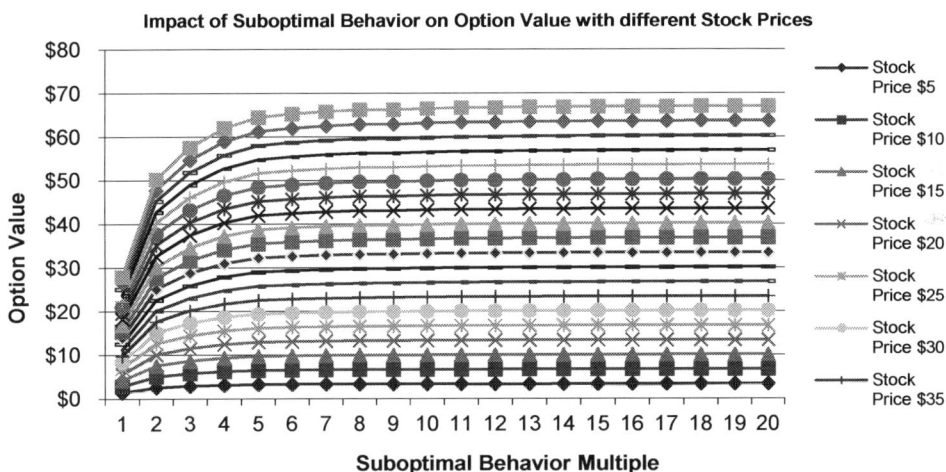

Figure 129: Impact of Suboptimal Exercise Behavior and Stock Price on Option Value in the Binomial Model [15]

Figure 130 shows that for higher volatility stocks, the suboptimal region is larger and the impact to option value is greater, but the effect is gradual. For instance, for the 100 percent volatility stock (Figure 130), the suboptimal region extends from a suboptimal exercise behavior multiple of 1.0 to approximately 9.0 versus from 1.0 to 2.0 for the 10 percent volatility stock. In addition, the vertical distance of the 100 percent volatility stock extends from $12 to $22 with a $10 range, as compared to $2 to $10 with an $8 range for the 10 percent volatility stock. Therefore, the higher the stock price at grant date and the higher the volatility, the greater the impact of suboptimal behavior will be on the option value. *In all cases, the BSM results are the horizontal lines in the charts (Figures 129 and 130). That is, the BSM will always generate the maximum option value assuming optimal behavior, and over-expense the option significantly.* A GBM or BSM cannot be modified to account for this suboptimal exercise behavior. Only the binomial lattice can be used.

---

[15] Assumptions used: stock and strike price range of $5–$100, 10-year maturity, 5% risk-free rate, 50% volatility, 0% dividends, suboptimal exercise behavior multiple range of 1–20, 4-year vesting, and tested with 100–5,000 binomial lattice steps.

Impact of Suboptimal Behavior on Option Value with different Volatilities

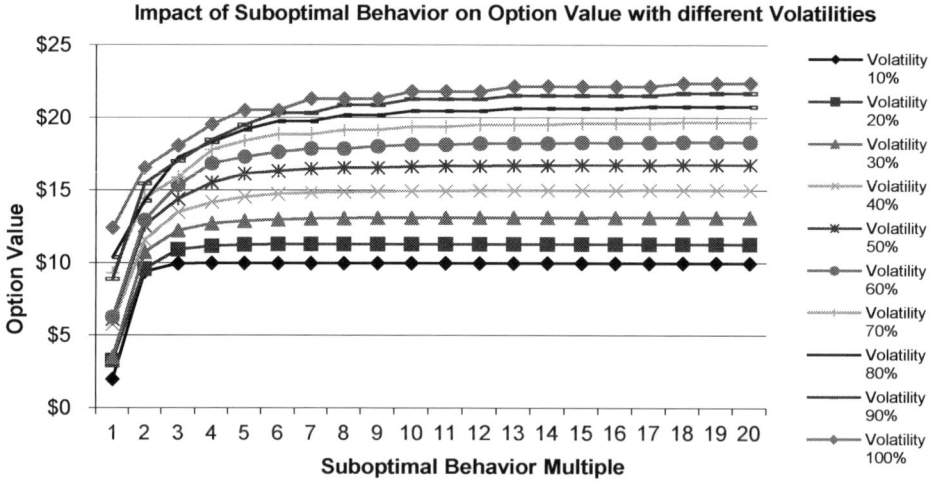

Figure 130: Impact of Suboptimal Exercise Behavior and Volatility on Option Value (Binomial) [16]

Options with Forfeiture Rates

Figure 131 illustrates the reduction in option value when the forfeiture rate increases. The rate of reduction changes depending on the vesting period. The longer the vesting period, the more significant the impact of forfeitures will be. This illustrates once again the nonlinear interacting relationship between vesting and forfeitures (that is, the lines in Figure 131 are curved and nonlinear). This is intuitive because the longer the vesting period, the lower the compounded probability that an employee will still be employed in the firm and the higher the chances of forfeiture, reducing the expected value of the option.

Again, we see that the BSM result is the highest possible value assuming a 10-year vesting in a 10-year maturity option with zero forfeiture (Figure 131). In addition, forfeiture rates can be negatively correlated to stock price—if the firm is doing well, its stock price usually increases, making the option more valuable and making the employees less likely to leave and the firm less likely to lay off its employees. Because the rate of forfeitures is uncertain (forfeiture rate fluctuations typically occur in the past due to business and economic environments, and will most certainly fluctuate again in the future) and is negatively correlated to the stock price, we can also apply a correlated Monte Carlo simulation on forfeiture rates in conjunction with the customized binomial lattices—this is shown later in this case study. **The BSM will always generate the maximum option value assuming all options will fully vest, and overexpense the option significantly.** The ESO Valuation software can account for forfeiture rates, while the accompanying *Super Lattice Solver* can account for different pre-vesting and post-vesting forfeiture rates in the lattices.

---

[16] Assumptions used: stock and strike price of $25, 10-year maturity, 5% risk-free rate, annualized 10%–100% volatility range, 0% dividends, suboptimal exercise behavior multiple range of 1–20, 1–year vesting, and tested with 100-5,000 binomial lattice steps.

Impact of Forefeitures and Vesting on Option Value

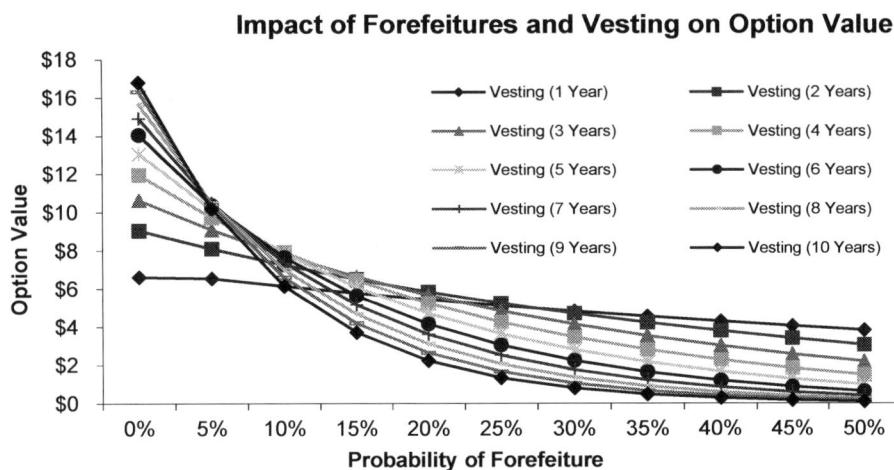

Figure 131: Impact of Forfeiture Rates and Vesting on Option Value in the Binomial Model [17]

Options Where Risk-free Rate Changes Over Time

Another input assumption is the risk-free rate. Figure 132 illustrates the effects of changing risk-free rates over time on option valuation. When other exotic inputs are added, the changing risk-free lattice model has an overall lower valuation. In addition, due to the time-value-of-money, discounting more heavily in the future will reduce the option's value. In other words, Figure 132 compares an upward sloping yield curve, a downward sloping yield curve, risk-free rate smile, and risk-free rate frown. When the term structure of interest rates increases over time, the option value calculated using a customized changing risk-free rate binomial lattice is lower than that calculated using an average of the changing risk-free rates base case. The reverse is true for a downward-sloping yield curve. In addition, Figure 132 shows a risk-free yield curve frown (low rates followed by high rates followed by low rates) and a risk-free yield curve smile (high rates followed by low rates followed by high rates). The results indicate that using a single average rate will overestimate an upward-sloping yield curve, underestimate a downward-sloping yield curve, underestimate a yield curve smile, and overestimate a yield curve frown. Therefore, whenever appropriate, use all available information in terms of forward risk-free rates, one rate for each year. The results illustrate a typical case and should not be generalized across all cases.

---

[17] Assumptions used: stock and strike price of $25, 10-year maturity, 5% risk-free rate, 50% volatility, 0% dividends, suboptimal behavior 1.01, vesting period of 1–10 years, forfeiture range 0%–50%, and tested with 100–5,000 binomial lattice steps.

Basic Input Parameters		Year	Static Base Case	Increasing Risk-free Rates	Decreasing Risk-free Rates	Risk-free Rate Smile	Risk-free Rate Frown
Stock Price	$100	1	5.50%	1.00%	10.00%	8.00%	3.50%
Strike Price	$100	2	5.50%	2.00%	9.00%	7.00%	4.00%
Maturity	10	3	5.50%	3.00%	8.00%	5.00%	5.00%
Volatility	45%	4	5.50%	4.00%	7.00%	4.00%	7.00%
Dividend Rate	4%	5	5.50%	5.00%	6.00%	3.50%	8.00%
Lattice Steps	100	6	5.50%	6.00%	5.00%	3.50%	8.00%
Suboptimal Behavior	100	7	5.50%	7.00%	4.00%	4.00%	7.00%
Vesting Period	0	8	5.50%	8.00%	3.00%	5.00%	5.00%
Forfeiture Rate	0%	9	5.50%	9.00%	2.00%	7.00%	4.00%
		10	5.50%	10.00%	1.00%	8.00%	3.50%
		Average	5.50%	5.50%	5.50%	5.50%	5.50%
		BSM using 5.50% Average Rate	$37.45	$37.45	$37.45	$37.45	$37.45
		Forfeiture Modified BSM using 5.50% Average Rate	$37.45	$37.45	$37.45	$37.45	$37.45
		Changing Risk-free Binomial Lattice	$37.41	$37.39	$37.41	$37.40	$37.41

Figure 132: Effects of Changing Risk-free Rates on Option Value

Options Where Volatility Changes Over Time

Figure 133 illustrates the effects of changing volatilities on an ESO. If volatility changes over time, the BSM ($71.48) using the average volatility over time will overestimate the true option value when there are other exotic inputs. In addition, compared to the $70.34 base case, slowly increasing volatilities over time from a low level has lower option values, while a decreasing volatility from high values and volatility smiles and frowns have higher values than using the average volatility estimate.

Basic Input Parameters		Year	Static Base Case	Increasing Volatilities	Decreasing Volatilities	Volatility Smile	Volatility Frown
Stock Price	$100.00	1	55.00%	10.00%	100.00%	80.00%	35.00%
Strike Price	$100.00	2	55.00%	20.00%	90.00%	70.00%	40.00%
Maturity	10.00	3	55.00%	30.00%	80.00%	50.00%	50.00%
Risk-free Rate	5.50%	4	55.00%	40.00%	70.00%	40.00%	70.00%
Dividend Rate	0.00%	5	55.00%	50.00%	60.00%	35.00%	80.00%
Lattice Steps	10.00	6	55.00%	60.00%	50.00%	35.00%	80.00%
Suboptimal Behavior	100.00	7	55.00%	70.00%	40.00%	40.00%	70.00%
Vesting Period	0.00	8	55.00%	80.00%	30.00%	50.00%	50.00%
Forfeiture Rate	0.00%	9	55.00%	90.00%	20.00%	70.00%	40.00%
		10	55.00%	100.00%	10.00%	80.00%	35.00%
		Average	55.00%	55.00%	55.00%	55.00%	55.00%
		BSM using 55% Average Rate	$71.48	$71.48	$71.48	$71.48	$71.48
		Forfeiture Modified BSM using 5.50% Average Rate	$71.48	$71.48	$71.48	$71.48	$71.48
		Changing Volatilities Binomial Lattice	$70.34	$75.68	$75.67	$73.04	$73.03

Figure 133: Effects of Changing Volatilities on Option Value

Options Where Dividend Yield Changes Over Time

Dividend yield is a simple input that can be obtained from corporate dividend policies or publicly available historical market data. Dividend yield is the total dividend payments computed as a percentage of stock price that is paid out over the course of a year. The typical dividend yield is between 0 percent and 7 percent. In fact, about 45 percent of all publicly traded firms in the U.S. pay dividends. Of those who pay a dividend, 85 percent of them have a yield of 7 percent or below, and 95 percent of them have a yield of 10 percent or below.[18] Dividend yield is an interesting variable with very little interaction with other exotic input variables. Dividend yield has a close-to-linear effect on option value, whereas the other exotic input variables do not. For instance, Figure 134 illustrates the effects of different maturities on the same option.[19] The higher the maturity, the higher the option value but the option value increases at a decreasing rate.

1.8 Behavior Multiple,
1-Year Vesting, 10%
Forfeiture Rate

Maturity	Option Value	Change
1	$25.16	
2	$32.41	28.84%
3	$35.35	9.08%
4	$36.80	4.08%
5	$37.87	2.91%
6	$38.41	1.44%
7	$38.58	0.43%

Figure 134: Nonlinear Effects of Maturity

In contrast, Figure 135 illustrates the near-linear effects of dividends even when some of the exotic inputs have been changed. Whatever the change in variable is, the effects of dividends are always very close to linear. While Figure 135 illustrates many options with unique dividend rates, Figure 136 illustrates the effects of changing dividends over time on a single option. That is, Figure 133's results are based on comparing different options with different dividend rates, whereas Figure 136's results are based on a single option whose underlying stock's dividend yields are changing over the life of the option.[20]

Options Where Blackout Periods Exist

Another item of interest is blackout periods. These are the dates that ESOs cannot be executed. These dates are usually several weeks before and several weeks after an earnings announcement (usually on a quarterly basis). In addition, only senior executives with fiduciary responsibilities have these blackout dates, and hence, their proportion is relatively small compared to the rest of the firm.

---

[18] Of the 6,553 stocks analyzed, 2,924 of them pays dividends, 2,140 of them yielding at or below 5%, 2,282 at or below 6%, 2,503 at or below 7%, and 2,830 at or below 10%.

[19] Stock price and strike price are set at $100, 5% risk-free rate, 75% volatility, and 1,000 steps in the customized lattice. Other exotic variable inputs are listed in Figure 134.

[20] Stock price and strike price are set at $100, 5-year maturity, 5% risk-free rate, 75% volatility, 1,000 steps in the customized lattice, 1.8 behavior multiple, 10% forfeiture rate, and 1-year vesting.

Figure 137 illustrates the calculations of a typical ESO with different blackout dates.[21] In the case where there are only a few blackout days a month, there is little difference between options with blackout dates and those without blackout dates. In fact, if the suboptimal exercise behavior multiple is small (a 1.8 ratio is assumed in this case), blackout dates at strategic times will actually prevent the option holder from exercising suboptimally and sometimes even increase the value of the option ever so slightly.

Clearly, a changing-dividend option has some value to add in terms of the overall option valuation results. Therefore, if the firm's stock pays a dividend, then the analysis should also consider the possibility of dividend yields changing over the life of the option.

Dividend Rate	1.8 Behavior Multiple, 4-Year Vesting, 10% Forfeiture Rate		1.8 Behavior Multiple, 1-Year Vesting, 10% Forfeiture Rate		3.0 Behavior Multiple, 1-Year Vesting, 10% Forfeiture Rate	
	Option Value	Change	Option Value	Change	Option Value	Change
0%	$42.15		$42.41		$49.07	
1%	$39.94	-5.24%	$41.47	-2.20%	$47.67	-2.86%
2%	$37.84	-5.27%	$40.55	-2.22%	$46.29	-2.89%
3%	$35.83	-5.30%	$39.65	-2.24%	$44.94	-2.92%
4%	$33.92	-5.33%	$38.75	-2.26%	$43.61	-2.95%
5%	$32.10	-5.37%	$37.87	-2.28%	$42.31	-2.98%

Dividend Rate	$50 Stock Price, 1.8 Behavior Multiple, 1-Year Vesting, 10% Forfeiture Rate		1.8 Behavior Multiple, 1-Year Vesting, 5% Forfeiture Rate	
	Option Value	Change	Option Value	Change
0%	$21.20		$45.46	
1%	$20.74	-2.20%	$44.46	-2.20%
2%	$20.28	-2.22%	$43.47	-2.23%
3%	$19.82	-2.24%	$42.49	-2.25%
4%	$19.37	-2.26%	$41.53	-2.27%
5%	$18.93	-2.28%	$40.58	-2.29%

Figure 135: Near-linear Effects of Dividends

Scenario	Option Value	Change	Notes
Static 3% Dividend	$39.65	0.00%	*Dividends are kept steady at 3%*
Increasing Gradually	$40.94	3.26%	*1% to 5% with 1% increments (average of 3%)*
Decreasing Gradually	$38.39	-3.17%	*5% to 1% with -1% increments (average of 3%)*
Increasing Jumps	$41.70	5.19%	*0%, 0%, 5%, 5%, 5% (average of 3%)*
Decreasing Jumps	$38.16	-3.74%	*5%, 5%, 5%, 0%, 0% (average of 3%)*

Figure 136: Effects of Changing Dividends Over Time

---

[21] Stock and strike price of $100, 75% volatility, 5% risk-free rate, 10-year maturity, no dividends, 1-year vesting, 10% forfeiture rate, and 1,000 lattice steps.

Blackout Dates	Option Value
No Blackouts	$43.16
Every 2 years evenly spaced	$43.16
First 5 years annual blackouts only	$43.26
Last 5 years annual blackouts only	$43.16
Every 3 months for 10 years	$43.26

Figure 137: Effects of Blackout Periods on Option Value

Figure 137's analysis assumes only a small percentage of blackout dates in a year (for example, during several days in a year, the ESO cannot be executed). This may be the case for certain so-called brick-and-mortar companies, and as such, blackout dates can be ignored. However, in other firms such as those in the biotechnology and high-tech industries, blackout periods play a more significant role. For instance, in a biotech firm, blackout periods may extend 4–6 weeks every quarter, straddling the release of its quarterly earnings. In addition, blackout periods prior to the release of a new product may exist. Therefore, the proportion of blackout dates with respect to the life of the option may reach upward of 35 percent to 65 percent per year. In such cases, blackout periods will significantly affect the value of the option. For instance, Figure 138 illustrates the differences between a customized binomial lattice with and without blackout periods. By adding in the real-life elements of blackout periods, the ESO value is further reduced by anywhere between 10 percent and 35 percent depending on the rate of forfeiture and volatility. As expected, the reduction in value is nonlinear, as the effects of blackout periods will vary depending on other input variables in the analysis.

% Difference between no blackout periods versus significant blackouts	Volatility (25%)	Volatility (30%)	Volatility (35%)	Volatility (40%)	Volatility (45%)	Volatility (50%)
Forfeiture Rate (5%)	-17.33%	-13.18%	-10.26%	-9.21%	-7.11%	-5.95%
Forfeiture Rate (6%)	-19.85%	-15.17%	-11.80%	-10.53%	-8.20%	-6.84%
Forfeiture Rate (7%)	-22.20%	-17.06%	-13.29%	-11.80%	-9.25%	-7.70%
Forfeiture Rate (8%)	-24.40%	-18.84%	-14.71%	-13.03%	-10.27%	-8.55%
Forfeiture Rate (9%)	-26.44%	-20.54%	-16.07%	-14.21%	-11.26%	-9.37%
Forfeiture Rate (10%)	-28.34%	-22.15%	-17.38%	-15.35%	-12.22%	-10.17%
Forfeiture Rate (11%)	-30.12%	-23.67%	-18.64%	-16.45%	-13.15%	-10.94%
Forfeiture Rate (12%)	-31.78%	-25.11%	-19.84%	-17.51%	-14.05%	-11.70%
Forfeiture Rate (13%)	-33.32%	-26.48%	-21.00%	-18.53%	-14.93%	-12.44%
Forfeiture Rate (14%)	-34.77%	-27.78%	-22.11%	-19.51%	-15.78%	-13.15%
Forfeiture Rate (14%)	-34.77%	-27.78%	-22.11%	-19.51%	-15.78%	-13.15%

Figure 138: Effects of Significant Blackouts (Different Forfeiture Rates & Volatilities) [22]

Figure 139 shows the effects of blackouts under different dividend yields and vesting periods, while Figure 140 illustrates the results stemming from different dividend yields and suboptimal exercise behavior multiples. Clearly, it is almost impossible to predict the exact impact unless a detailed analysis is performed, but the range can be generalized to be typically between 10 percent and 20 percent. Blackout periods can only be modeled in a binomial lattice and not in the BSM/GBM.

---

[22] Stock and strike price range of $30-$100, 45% volatility, 5% risk-free rate, 10-year maturity, dividend range 0%–10%, vesting of 1–4 years, 5%–14% forfeiture rate, suboptimal exercise behavior multiple range of 1.8–3.0, and 1,000 lattice steps.

% Difference between no blackout periods versus significant blackouts	Vesting (1)	Vesting (2)	Vesting (3)	Vesting (4)
Dividends (0%)	-8.62%	-6.93%	-5.59%	-4.55%
Dividends (1%)	-9.04%	-7.29%	-5.91%	-4.84%
Dividends (2%)	-9.46%	-7.66%	-6.24%	-5.13%
Dividends (3%)	-9.90%	-8.03%	-6.56%	-5.43%
Dividends (4%)	-10.34%	-8.41%	-6.90%	-5.73%
Dividends (5%)	-10.80%	-8.79%	-7.24%	-6.04%
Dividends (6%)	-11.26%	-9.18%	-7.58%	-6.35%
Dividends (7%)	-11.74%	-9.58%	-7.93%	-6.67%
Dividends (8%)	-12.22%	-9.99%	-8.29%	-6.99%
Dividends (9%)	-12.71%	-10.40%	-8.65%	-7.31%
Dividends (10%)	-13.22%	-10.81%	-9.01%	-7.64%

Figure 139: Effects of Significant Blackouts (Different Dividend Yields and Vesting Periods)

% Difference between no blackout periods versus significant blackouts	Dividends (0%)	Dividends (1%)	Dividends (2%)	Dividends (3%)	Dividends (4%)	Dividends (5%)	Dividends (6%)	Dividends (7%)	Dividends (8%)	Dividends (9%)	Dividends (10%)
Suboptimal Behavior Multiple (1.8)	-1.01%	-1.29%	-1.58%	-1.87%	-2.16%	-2.45%	-2.75%	-3.06%	-3.36%	-3.67%	-3.98%
Suboptimal Behavior Multiple (1.9)	-1.01%	-1.29%	-1.58%	-1.87%	-2.16%	-2.45%	-2.75%	-3.06%	-3.36%	-3.67%	-3.98%
Suboptimal Behavior Multiple (2.0)	-1.87%	-2.29%	-2.72%	-3.15%	-3.59%	-4.04%	-4.50%	-4.96%	-5.42%	-5.90%	-6.38%
Suboptimal Behavior Multiple (2.1)	-1.87%	-2.29%	-2.72%	-3.15%	-3.59%	-4.04%	-4.50%	-4.96%	-5.42%	-5.90%	-6.38%
Suboptimal Behavior Multiple (2.2)	-4.71%	-5.05%	-5.39%	-5.74%	-6.10%	-6.46%	-6.82%	-7.19%	-7.57%	-7.95%	-8.34%
Suboptimal Behavior Multiple (2.3)	-4.71%	-5.05%	-5.39%	-5.74%	-6.10%	-6.46%	-6.82%	-7.19%	-7.57%	-7.95%	-8.34%
Suboptimal Behavior Multiple (2.4)	-4.71%	-5.05%	-5.39%	-5.74%	-6.10%	-6.46%	-6.82%	-7.19%	-7.57%	-7.95%	-8.34%
Suboptimal Behavior Multiple (2.5)	-6.34%	-6.80%	-7.28%	-7.77%	-8.26%	-8.76%	-9.27%	-9.79%	-10.32%	-10.86%	-11.41%
Suboptimal Behavior Multiple (2.6)	-6.34%	-6.80%	-7.28%	-7.77%	-8.26%	-8.76%	-9.27%	-9.79%	-10.32%	-10.86%	-11.41%
Suboptimal Behavior Multiple (2.7)	-6.34%	-6.80%	-7.28%	-7.77%	-8.26%	-8.76%	-9.27%	-9.79%	-10.32%	-10.86%	-11.41%
Suboptimal Behavior Multiple (2.8)	-6.34%	-6.80%	-7.28%	-7.77%	-8.26%	-8.76%	-9.27%	-9.79%	-10.32%	-10.86%	-11.41%
Suboptimal Behavior Multiple (2.9)	-8.62%	-9.04%	-9.46%	-9.90%	-10.34%	-10.80%	-11.26%	-11.74%	-12.22%	-12.71%	-13.22%
Suboptimal Behavior Multiple (3.0)	-8.62%	-9.04%	-9.46%	-9.90%	-10.34%	-10.80%	-11.26%	-11.74%	-12.22%	-12.71%	-13.22%

Figure 140: Effects of Significant Blackouts (Different Dividend Yields and Exercise Behaviors)

Nonmarketability Issues

The 2004 FAS 123 revision does not explicitly discuss the issue of nonmarketability. That is, ESOs are neither directly transferable to someone else nor freely tradable in the open market. Under such circumstances, it can be argued based on sound financial and economic theory that a non-tradable and nonmarketable discount can be appropriately applied to the ESO. However, this is not a simple task as will be discussed.

A simple and direct application of a discount should not be based on an arbitrarily chosen percentage *haircut* on the resulting binomial lattice result. Instead, a more rigorous analysis can be performed using a *put option*. A call option is the contractual right, but not the obligation, to *purchase* the underlying stock at some predetermined contractual strike price within a specified time, while a put option is a contractual right, but not the obligation, to *sell* the underlying stock at some predetermined contractual price within a specified time. Therefore, if the holder of the ESO cannot sell or transfer the rights of the option to someone else, then the holder of the option has given up his or her rights to a put option (that is, the employee has written or sold the firm a put option). Calculating the put option and discounting this value from the call option provides a theoretically correct and justifiable nonmarketability and nontransferability discount to the existing option. However, care should be taken in analyzing this haircut or discounting feature. The same inputs that go into the customized binomial lattice to calculate a call option should also be used to calculate a customized binomial lattice for a put option. That is, the put option must also be under the same risks (volatility that can change over time), economic environment (risk-free rate structure that can change over time), corporate financial policy (a static or changing dividend yield over the life of the option), contractual obligations (vesting, maturity, strike price, and blackout dates), investor irrationality (suboptimal exercise behavior), firm performance (stock price at grant date), and so forth. Albeit nonmarketability discounts or haircuts are not explicitly discussed in FAS 123, the valuation analysis is performed below anyway, for the sake of completeness. It is up to each firm's management to decide if haircuts should and can be applied. Figure 141 shows the customized binomial lattice valuation results of a typical ESO.[23]

Customized Binomial Lattice (Option Valuation)	Behavior (1.20)	Behavior (1.40)	Behavior (1.60)	Behavior (1.80)	Behavior (2.00)	Behavior (2.20)	Behavior (2.40)	Behavior (2.60)	Behavior (2.80)	Behavior (3.00)
Forfeiture (0.00%)	$24.57	$30.53	$36.16	$39.90	$43.15	$45.87	$48.09	$49.33	$50.40	$51.31
Forfeiture (5.00%)	$22.69	$27.65	$32.19	$35.15	$37.67	$39.74	$41.42	$42.34	$43.13	$43.80
Forfeiture (10.00%)	$21.04	$25.22	$28.93	$31.29	$33.27	$34.88	$36.16	$36.86	$37.45	$37.94
Forfeiture (15.00%)	$19.58	$23.13	$26.20	$28.11	$29.69	$30.94	$31.93	$32.46	$32.91	$33.29
Forfeiture (20.00%)	$18.28	$21.32	$23.88	$25.44	$26.71	$27.70	$28.48	$28.89	$29.23	$29.52
Forfeiture (25.00%)	$17.10	$19.73	$21.89	$23.17	$24.20	$25.00	$25.61	$25.93	$26.19	$26.41
Forfeiture (30.00%)	$16.02	$18.31	$20.14	$21.21	$22.06	$22.70	$23.19	$23.44	$23.65	$23.82
Forfeiture (35.00%)	$15.04	$17.04	$18.61	$19.51	$20.20	$20.73	$21.12	$21.32	$21.49	$21.62
Forfeiture (40.00%)	$14.13	$15.89	$17.24	$18.00	$18.58	$19.01	$19.33	$19.49	$19.63	$19.73

Figure 141: Customized Binomial Lattice Valuation Results

Figure 142 shows the results from a nonmarketability analysis performed using a down-and-in upper barrier modified put option with the same exotic inputs (vesting, blackouts, forfeitures, suboptimal behavior, and so forth) calculated using the customized binomial lattice model.[24] The discounts range from 22 percent to 53 percent. These calculated discounts look somewhat significant but is actually in line with market expectations.[25] As these discounts are not explicitly sanctioned by FASB, the author cautions its use in determining the fair-market value of the ESOs.

---

[23] Assumptions used: stock and strike price of $100, 10-year maturity, 1-year vesting, 35% volatility, 0% dividends, 5% risk-free rate, suboptimal exercise behavior multiple range of 1.2 to 3.0, forfeiture range of 0% to 40%, and 1,000 step customized lattice.

[24] An alternative method is to calculate the relevant carrying cost adjustment by artificially inserting an inflated dividend yield to convert the ESO into a "soft option," thereby discounting the value of the ESO. This method is more difficult to apply and is susceptible to more subjectivity than using a put option.

[25] Cedric Jolidon finds the mean values of marketability discounts to be between 20% and 35% in his article, "The Application of the Marketability Discount in the Valuation of Swiss Companies" (Swiss Private Equity Corporate Finance Association). A typical marketability range of 10%–40% was found in several discount court cases. In the *CPA Journal* (Feb. 2001), M. Greene and D. Schnapp found that a typical range was somewhere between 30% and 35%. Another article in the *Business Valuation Review* finds that 35% is the typical value (Jay Abrams, "Discount for Lack of Marketability"). In the *Fair Value* newsletter, Michael Paschall finds that 30%–50% is the typical marketability discount used in the market.

Haircut (Customized Binomial Lattice Modified Put)	Behavior (1.20)	Behavior (1.40)	Behavior (1.60)	Behavior (1.80)	Behavior (2.00)	Behavior (2.20)	Behavior (2.40)	Behavior (2.60)	Behavior (2.80)	Behavior (3.00)
Forfeiture (0.00%)	$11.33	$11.33	$11.33	$11.33	$11.33	$11.33	$11.33	$11.33	$11.33	$11.33
Forfeiture (5.00%)	$10.76	$10.76	$10.76	$10.76	$10.76	$10.76	$10.76	$10.76	$10.76	$10.76
Forfeiture (10.00%)	$10.23	$10.23	$10.23	$10.23	$10.23	$10.23	$10.23	$10.23	$10.23	$10.23
Forfeiture (15.00%)	$9.72	$9.72	$9.72	$9.72	$9.72	$9.72	$9.72	$9.72	$9.72	$9.72
Forfeiture (20.00%)	$9.23	$9.23	$9.23	$9.23	$9.23	$9.23	$9.23	$9.23	$9.23	$9.23
Forfeiture (25.00%)	$8.77	$8.77	$8.77	$8.77	$8.77	$8.77	$8.77	$8.77	$8.77	$8.77
Forfeiture (30.00%)	$8.34	$8.34	$8.34	$8.34	$8.34	$8.34	$8.34	$8.34	$8.34	$8.34
Forfeiture (35.00%)	$7.92	$7.92	$7.92	$7.92	$7.92	$7.92	$7.92	$7.92	$7.92	$7.92
Forfeiture (40.00%)	$7.52	$7.52	$7.52	$7.52	$7.52	$7.52	$7.52	$7.52	$7.52	$7.52

Nonmarketability and Nontransferability Discount (%)	Behavior (1.20)	Behavior (1.40)	Behavior (1.60)	Behavior (1.80)	Behavior (2.00)	Behavior (2.20)	Behavior (2.40)	Behavior (2.60)	Behavior (2.80)	Behavior (3.00)
Forfeiture (0.00%)	46.09%	37.09%	31.32%	28.39%	26.25%	24.69%	23.55%	22.96%	22.47%	22.07%
Forfeiture (5.00%)	47.43%	38.92%	33.43%	30.62%	28.57%	27.08%	25.98%	25.42%	24.95%	24.57%
Forfeiture (10.00%)	48.60%	40.55%	35.35%	32.68%	30.73%	29.32%	28.28%	27.75%	27.31%	26.95%
Forfeiture (15.00%)	49.62%	42.01%	37.08%	34.57%	32.73%	31.40%	30.43%	29.93%	29.53%	29.19%
Forfeiture (20.00%)	50.52%	43.31%	38.66%	36.29%	34.57%	33.33%	32.42%	31.96%	31.59%	31.28%
Forfeiture (25.00%)	51.32%	44.48%	40.09%	37.86%	36.25%	35.10%	34.26%	33.84%	33.49%	33.22%
Forfeiture (30.00%)	52.03%	45.53%	41.38%	39.29%	37.79%	36.72%	35.95%	35.56%	35.25%	35.00%
Forfeiture (35.00%)	52.67%	46.48%	42.56%	40.60%	39.20%	38.21%	37.50%	37.15%	36.86%	36.63%
Forfeiture (40.00%)	53.24%	47.34%	43.64%	41.80%	40.49%	39.57%	38.92%	38.60%	38.34%	38.14%

Figure 142: Nonmarketability and Nontransferability Discount

Expected Life Analysis

As seen previously, the 2004 Final FAS 123, Sections A15 and B64 expressly prohibit the use of a modified BSM with a single expected life. This means that instead of using an expected life as the *input* into the BSM to obtain the similar results as in a customized binomial lattice, the analysis should be done the other way around. That is, using vesting requirements, suboptimal exercise behavior multiples, forfeiture or employee turnover rates, and the other standard option inputs, calculate the valuation results using the customized binomial lattice. This result can then be compared with a modified BSM and the expected life can then be *imputed*. Excel's goal-seek function can be used to obtain the imputed expected life of the option by setting the BSM result equal to the customized binomial lattice. The resulting expected life can then be compared with historical data as a secondary verification of the results, i.e., if the expected life falls within reasonable bounds based on historical performance. This is the correct approach because measuring the expected life of an option is very difficult and inaccurate.

Figure 143 illustrates the use of Excel's goal-seek function on the ESO Valuation Toolkit software to impute the expected life into the BSM model by setting the BSM results equal to the customized binomial lattice results.

Customized Binomial Lattice Results to Impute the Expected Life for BSM
Applying Different Suboptimal Behavior Multiples

Stock Price	$20.00	$20.00	$20.00	$20.00	$20.00	$20.00	$20.00
Strike Price	$20.00	$20.00	$20.00	$20.00	$20.00	$20.00	$20.00
Maturity	10.00	10.00	10.00	10.00	10.00	10.00	10.00
Risk-Free Rate	3.50%	3.50%	3.50%	3.50%	3.50%	3.50%	3.50%
Dividend	0.00%	0.00%	0.00%	0.00%	0.00%	0.00%	0.00%
Volatility	50.00%	50.00%	50.00%	50.00%	50.00%	50.00%	50.00%
Vesting	4.00	4.00	4.00	4.00	4.00	4.00	4.00
Suboptimal Behavior	**1.10**	**1.50**	**2.00**	**2.50**	**3.00**	**3.50**	**4.00**
Forfeiture Rate	0.00%	0.00%	0.00%	0.00%	0.00%	0.00%	0.00%
Lattice Steps	1000	1000	1000	1000	1000	1000	1000
Binomial	$8.94	$10.28	$11.03	$11.62	$11.89	$12.18	$12.29
BSM	$12.87	$12.87	$12.87	$12.87	$12.87	$12.87	$12.87
Expected Life	*4.42*	*5.94*	*6.95*	*7.83*	*8.26*	*8.74*	*8.93*
Modified BSM	$8.94	$10.28	$11.03	$11.62	$11.89	$12.18	$12.29

Figure 143: Imputing the Expected Life for the BSM Using the Binomial Lattice Results

Figure 144 illustrates another case where the expected life can be imputed, but this time the forfeiture rates are not set at zero. In this case, the BSM results will need to be modified. For example, the customized binomial lattice result of $5.41 is obtained with a 15 percent forfeiture rate. This means that the BSM result needs to be BSM(1–15%) = $5.41 using the modified expected life method. The expected life that yields the BSM value of $6.36 ($5.41/85% is $6.36, and $6.36(1–15%) is $5.41) is 2.22 years.

Customized Binomial Lattice Results to Impute the Expected Life for BSM
Applying Different Forfeiture Rates

Stock Price	$20.00	$20.00	$20.00	$20.00	$20.00	$20.00	$20.00
Strike Price	$20.00	$20.00	$20.00	$20.00	$20.00	$20.00	$20.00
Maturity	10.00	10.00	10.00	10.00	10.00	10.00	10.00
Risk-Free Rate	3.50%	3.50%	3.50%	3.50%	3.50%	3.50%	3.50%
Dividend	0.00%	0.00%	0.00%	0.00%	0.00%	0.00%	0.00%
Volatility	50.00%	50.00%	50.00%	50.00%	50.00%	50.00%	50.00%
Vesting	4.00	4.00	4.00	4.00	4.00	4.00	4.00
Suboptimal Behavior	1.50	1.50	1.50	1.50	1.50	1.50	1.50
Forfeiture Rate	**0.00%**	**2.50%**	**5.00%**	**7.50%**	**10.00%**	**12.50%**	**15.00%**
Lattice Steps	1000	1000	1000	1000	1000	1000	1000
Binomial	$10.28	$9.23	$8.29	$7.44	$6.69	$6.02	$5.41
BSM	$12.87	$12.87	$12.87	$12.87	$12.87	$12.87	$12.87
Expected Life	*5.94*	*4.71*	*3.77*	*3.03*	*2.45*	*1.99*	*1.61*
Modified BSM*	$10.28	$9.23	$8.29	$7.44	$6.69	$6.02	$5.41
Expected Life	*5.94*	*4.97*	*4.19*	*3.55*	*3.02*	*2.59*	*2.22*
Modified BSM**	$10.28	$9.23	$8.29	$7.44	$6.69	$6.02	$5.41

*Note: Uses the binomial lattice result to impute the expected life for a modified BSM
**Note: Uses the binomial lattice but also accounts for the Forfeiture rate to modify the BSM

Figure 144: Imputing BSM Expected Life using Lattices under Non-zero Forfeitures

Dilution

In most cases, the effects of dilution can be safely ignored as the proportion of ESO grants is relatively small compared to the total equity issued by the company. In investment finance theory, the market has already anticipated the exercise of these ESOs and the effects have already been accounted for in the stock price. Once a new grant is announced, the stock price will immediately and fully incorporate this news and account for any dilution that may occur. This means that as long as the valuation is performed after the announcement is made, then the effects of dilution are nonexistent. The 2004 FAS 123 revisions do not explicitly provide guidance in this area. Given that FASB only provides little guidance on dilution (Section A39), and because forecasting stock prices (as part of estimating the effects of dilution) is fairly difficult and inaccurate at best, plus the fact that the dilution effects are minimal (small in proportion compared to all the equity issued by the firm), the effects of dilution are assumed to be minimal, and can be safely ignored.

Applying Monte Carlo Simulation for Statistical Confidence and Precision Control

Next, Monte Carlo simulation can be applied to obtain a range of calculated stock option fair values. That is, any of the inputs into the stock options valuation model can be chosen for Monte Carlo simulation if they are uncertain and stochastic. Distributional assumptions are assigned to these variables, and the resulting option values using the BSM, GBM, path simulation, or binomial lattices are selected as forecast cells. These modeled uncertainties include the probability of forfeiture and the employees' suboptimal exercise behavior.

The results of the simulation are essentially a distribution of the stock option values. Keep in mind that the simulation application here is used to vary the inputs to an options valuation model to obtain a range of results, not to model and calculate the options themselves. However, simulation can be applied both to simulate the inputs to obtain the range of options results and also to solve the options model through path-dependent simulation. For instance, the simulated input assumptions are those inputs that are highly uncertain and can vary in the future, such as stock price at grant date, volatility, forfeiture rates, and suboptimal exercise behavior multiples. Clearly, variables that are objectively obtained, such as risk-free rates (U.S. Treasury yields for the next 1 month to 20 years are published), dividend yield (determined from corporate strategy), vesting period, strike price, and blackout periods (determined contractually in the option grant) should not be simulated. In addition, the simulated input assumptions can be correlated. For instance, forfeiture rates can be negatively correlated to stock price—if the firm is doing well, its stock price usually increases, making the option more valuable thus making the employees less likely to leave and the firm less likely to lay off its employees. Finally, the output forecasts are the option valuation results. In fact, Monte Carlo simulation is allowed and recommended in FAS 123 (Section B64, B65, and footnotes 48, 52, 74, and 97).

Figure 145 shows the results obtained using the customized binomial lattices based on single-point inputs of all the variables. The model takes exotic inputs such as vesting, forfeiture rates, suboptimal exercise behavior multiples, blackout periods, and changing inputs (dividends, risk-free rates, and volatilities) over time. The resulting option value is $31.42. This analysis can then be extended to include simulation. Figure 146 illustrates the use of simulation coupled with customized binomial lattices.

Risk-Free Rate		Volatility		Dividend Yield		Suboptimal Behavior	
Year	Rate	Year	Rate	Year	Rate	Year	
1	3.50%	1	35.00%	1	1.00%	1	1.80
2	3.75%	2	35.00%	2	1.00%	2	1.80
3	4.00%	3	35.00%	3	1.00%	3	1.80
4	4.15%	4	45.00%	4	1.50%	4	1.80
5	4.20%	5	45.00%	5	1.50%	5	1.80

		Forfeiture Rate		Blackout Dates	
Stock Price	$100				
Strike Price	$100	Year	Rate	Month	Step
Time to Maturity	5	1	5.00%	12	12
Vesting Period	1	2	5.00%	24	24
Lattice Steps	60	3	5.00%	36	36
		4	5.00%	48	48
Option Value	$31.42	5	5.00%	60	60

Figure 145: Single-point Result Using a Customized Binomial Lattice

Rather than randomly deciding on the correct number of trials to run in the simulation, statistical significance and precision control are setup to run the required number of trials automatically. A 99.9 percent statistical confidence on a $0.01 error precision control was selected and 145,510 simulation trials were run.[26] This highly stringent set of parameters means that an adequate number of trials will be run to ensure that the results will fall within a $0.01 error variability 99.9 percent of the time. For instance, the simulated average result was $31.32 (Figure 146). This means that 999 out of 1,000 times, the true option value will be accurate to within $0.01 of $31.32. These measures are statistically valid and objective.[27]

Statistic	Value	Precision
Trials	145,510	
Mean	$31.32	$0.01
Standard Deviation	$1.75	$0.01
Skewness	-0.21	
Kurtosis	2.43	

Figure 146: Options Valuation Result at $0.01 Precision with 99.9% Confidence

Number of Steps

The higher the number of lattice steps, the higher the precision of the results. Figure 147 illustrates the convergence of results obtained using a BSM closed-form model on a European call option without dividends, and comparing its results to the basic binomial lattice. Convergence is generally achieved at 1,000 steps. As such, the analysis results will use 1,000 steps whenever possible.[28] Due to the high number of steps required to generate the results,

---

[26] Any level of precision and confidence can be chosen. Here, the 99.9% statistical confidence with a $0.01 error precision ($0.01 fluctuation around the average option value) is fairly restrictive. Of course the level of precision attained is contingent upon the inputs and their distributional parameters being accurate.

[27] This assumes that the inputs are valid and accurate.

[28] A 1,000-step customized binomial lattice is generally used unless otherwise noted. Sometimes increments from 1,000 to 5,000 steps may be used to check for convergence. However, due to the nonrecombining nature of changing volatility options, a lower number of steps may have to be employed.

software-based mathematical algorithms are used.[29] For instance, a nonrecombining binomial lattice with 1,000 steps has a total of 2 x 10[301] nodal calculations to perform, making manual computation impossible without the use of specialized algorithms.[30] Figure 148 illustrates the calculation of convergence by using progressively higher lattice steps. The progression is based on sets of 120 steps (12 months per year multiplied by 10 years). The results are tabulated and the median of the average results are calculated. It shows that 4,200 steps is the best estimate in this customized binomial lattice, and this input is used throughout the analysis.[31]

Conclusion

It has been over 30 years since Fisher Black, Myron Scholes and Robert Merton derived their option pricing model and significant advancements have been made; therefore, do not restrict stock option pricing to one specific model (the BSM/GBM) while a plethora of other models and applications can be explored. The three mainstream approaches to valuing stock options are closed-form models (e.g., BSM, GBM, and American option approximation models), Monte Carlo simulation, and binomial lattices. This case study details the impacts of using a customized binomial lattice and is based on the author's book, *Valuing Employee Stock Options: Under 2004 FAS 123 Requirements* (Wiley Finance, 2004). The BSM and GBM will typically *overstate* the fair value of ESOs where there is suboptimal early exercise behavior coupled with vesting requirements and option forfeitures. *In fact, firms using the BSM and GBM to value and expense ESOs may be significantly overstating their true expense.* The BSM requires many underlying assumptions before it works, and as such, has significant limitations, including being applicable only for European options without dividends. In addition, American option approximation models are very complex and difficult to create in a spreadsheet. The BSM *cannot* account for American options, options based on stocks that pay dividends (the GBM model can however, account for dividends in a European option), forfeitures, underperformance, stock price barriers, vesting periods, changing business environments and volatilities, suboptimal early exercise behavior, and a sleuth of other conditions. Monte Carlo simulation when used alone is another option valuation approach, but is restricted only to European options. Simulation can be used in two different ways: solving the option's fair-market value through path simulations of stock prices, or used in conjunction with other approaches (e.g., binomial lattices and closed-form models) to capture multiple sources of uncertainty in the model.

---

[29] This proprietary algorithm was developed by Dr. Johnathan Mun based on his analytical work with FASB in 2003–2004; his books: *Valuing Employee Stock Options Under the 2004 FAS 123 Requirements* (Wiley, 2004), *Real Options Analysis,* Second Edition (Wiley, 2005), *Real Options Analysis Course* (Wiley, 2003), *Applied Risk Analysis: Moving Beyond Uncertainty* (Wiley, 2003); creation of his software, "Real Options Super Lattice Solver" (versions 1.0 and 2.0); academic research; and previous valuation consulting experience at KPMG Consulting.

[30] A nonrecombining binomial lattice bifurcates (splits into two) every step it takes, so starting from one value, it branches out to two values on the first step (2^1), two becomes four in the second step (2^2), and four becomes eight in the third step (2^3) and so forth, until the 1,000th step (2^{1000} or over 10[301] values to calculate, and the world's fastest supercomputer won't be able to calculate the result within our lifetimes).

[31] The Law of Large Numbers stipulates that the central tendency (mean) of a distribution of averages is an unbiased estimator of the true population average. The results from 4,200 steps show a mean value that is comparable to the median of the distribution of averages, and hence, 4,200 steps is chosen as the input into the binomial lattice.

Binomial lattices are flexible and easy to implement. They are capable of valuing American-type stock options with dividends but require computational power. Software applications should be used to facilitate this computation. Binomial lattices can be used to calculate American options paying dividends and can be easily adapted to solve ESOs with exotic inputs and used in conjunction with Monte Carlo simulation to account for the uncertain input assumptions (e.g., probabilities of forfeiture, suboptimal exercise behavior, vesting, underperformance, and so forth) and to obtain a high precision at statistically valid confidence intervals. Based on the analyses throughout the case study, it is recommended that the use of a model that assumes an ESO is European style, when in fact the option is American style with the other exotic variables, should not be permitted as this substantially overstates compensation expense. Many factors influence the fair-market value of ESOs, and a binomial lattice approach to valuation that considers these factors should be used. With due diligence, real-life ESOs can absolutely be valued using the customized binomial lattice approach as shown in this paper, where the methodology employed is pragmatic, accurate, and theoretically sound.

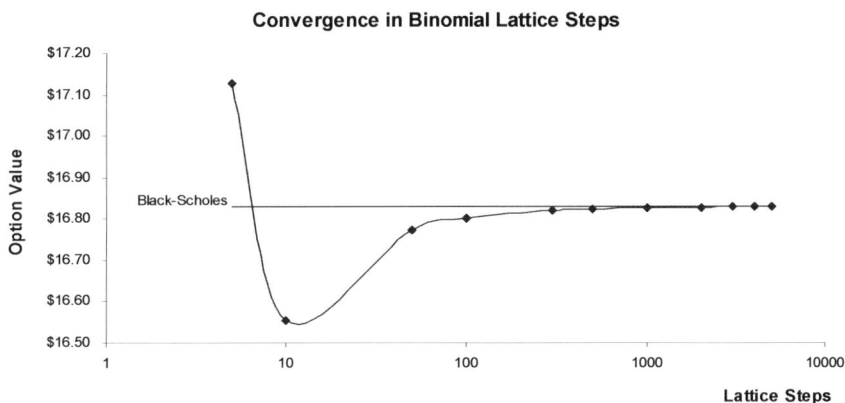

Figure 147: Convergence of the Binomial Lattice to Closed-form Solutions

Stock Price	$45.17	$45.17	$45.17	$45.17	$45.17	$45.17	$45.17	$45.17	$45.17	$45.17	$45.17	$45.17	$45.17	$45.17
Strike Strike	$45.17	$45.17	$45.17	$45.17	$45.17	$45.17	$45.17	$45.17	$45.17	$45.17	$45.17	$45.17	$45.17	$45.17
Maturity	10	10	10	10	10	10	10	10	10	10	10	10	10	10
Risk-Free Rate	1.21%	1.21%	1.21%	1.21%	1.21%	1.21%	1.21%	1.21%	1.21%	1.21%	1.21%	1.21%	1.21%	1.21%
Volatility	49.91%	49.91%	49.91%	49.91%	49.91%	49.91%	49.91%	49.91%	49.91%	49.91%	49.91%	49.91%	49.91%	49.91%
Dividend	0%	0%	0%	0%	0%	0%	0%	0%	0%	0%	0%	0%	0%	0%
Lattice Steps	10	50	100	120	600	1200	1800	2400	3000	3600	4200	4800	5400	6000
Suboptimal Behavior	1.8531	1.8531	1.8531	1.8531	1.8531	1.8531	1.8531	1.8531	1.8531	1.8531	1.8531	1.8531	1.8531	1.8531
Vesting	0.08	0.08	0.08	0.08	0.08	0.08	0.08	0.08	0.08	0.08	0.08	0.08	0.08	0.08
Option Value	$20.55	$17.82	$17.32	$18.55	$17.55	$13.08	$13.11	$12.93	$12.88	$12.91	$12.98	$13.08	$12.93	$13.06

Segment	Steps	Results	Average
1	120	$18.55	$13.91
5	600	$17.55	$13.45
10	1200	$13.08	$13.00
15	1800	$13.11	$12.99
20	2400	$12.93	$12.97
25	3000	$12.88	$12.97
30	3600	$12.91	$12.99
35	4200	$12.98	$13.01
40	4800	$13.08	$13.02
45	5400	$12.93	$12.99
50	6000	$13.06	$13.06
		Median	$13.00

Figure 148: Convergence of the Customized Binomial Lattice

CASE STUDY 15: OIL AND GAS ROYALTY LEASE NEGOTIATION

This case is contributed by David Mercier, vice president of corporate development at Bonanza Creek Energy. Mr. Mercier has executive experience in starting, financing, and selling businesses. As the chief of finance, economics, and accounting for the California State Lands Commission Mineral Resources Division, he was responsible for maximizing the value of more than 20,000 barrel of oil per day. His responsibilities included profit-sharing negotiations, crude oil and natural gas marketing, royalty accounting, financial review of lease assignments, financial risk management, and revenue forecasting and budgeting. In short, with more than 20 years of experience, Mr. Mercier has worked in every aspect of the energy business. He has published and presented numerous technical papers and has written case studies for risk modeling text books. He has presented many papers throughout the United States on maximizing value using a royalty rate that slides with oil price. California was the first state to employ this type of royalty. He is a member of the Society of Petroleum Engineers and was a California Natural Gas Committee member. Prior to joining the State Lands Commission, Mr. Mercier worked as an environmental consultant for TRC, a process engineer for Mobil Oil Company, and a commodity trader. He is an active member of and donor to the Autism Society of America. He holds a BS degree in petroleum engineering, University of Southern California (USC) and an MBA degree in finance, is Certified in Risk Management (CRM); and has completed the Strategic Decision and Risk Management six class certification program at Stanford University.

Background

Since 1938, the California State Lands Commission (SLC, or "Commission") has had exclusive jurisdiction over the leasing of oil and gas from offshore state lands. In March 2005, Plains Exploration & Production Company (PXP) applied to the California State Lands Commission and County of Santa Barbara for a new state lease and onshore permits to allow development of the Tranquillon Ridge field, located in state waters offshore from Vandenberg Air Force Base. PXP plans to use an existing platform, Platform Irene, which is currently used to produce oil and gas from the adjacent Pt. Pedernales field, in federal waters (Figure 149). Like the oil produced from Pt. Pedernales, oil produced from Tranquillon Ridge would be sent to shore by pipeline and processed at the Lompoc Oil and Gas Plant (LOGP); therefore, no new construction. However, the project requires a new state lease to allow "extended reach drilling" from Platform Irene into the Tranquillon Ridge field.

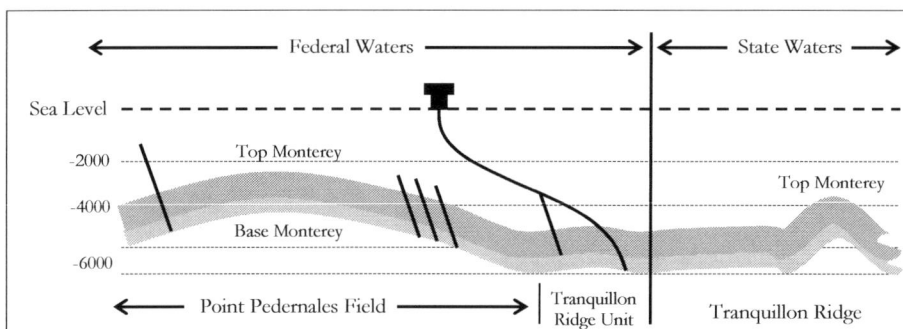

Figure 149: Picture of the Development

The lease could be issued under an exception to the California Coastal Sanctuary Act (1984), which allows a new lease if oil or gas from state-owned tide and submerged lands "are being drained by means of producing wells upon adjacent federal lands and the lease is in the best interests of the state" (Pub. Res. Code §6244.). In this case, PXP is draining oil and gas from state tide and submerged lands from wells drilled on Platform Irene. The parties to the Settlement Agreement believe the provisions that have been negotiated are in the best interests of the state, not only because they provide specific environmental benefits, but also because they set a new precedent for full mitigation of the impact of industrial development in the county and the state.

The Agreement

A previous proposal to develop the Tranquillon Ridge Field, by Nuevo Energy Company, was opposed by local environmental groups and denied by the County of Santa Barbara in 2002. When PXP made a similar proposal, the environmental groups again raised objections, based on the fact that the drilling operations would extend the life of the existing facilities. PXP responded by agreeing to include a termination date for the Tranquillon Ridge Project. This commitment goes well beyond any legal requirements, which allow oil companies to continue operations so long as they are producing commercially viable quantities of oil and gas.

The Environmental Defense Center (EDC), Get Oil Out! (GOO!), and Citizens Planning Association of Santa Barbara (CPA) signed an historic and unprecedented agreement in Santa Barbara, California. The agreement allowed for development by PXP of the Tranquillon Ridge Oil and Gas Field offshore Lompoc, while curtailing the life of existing oil and gas operations.

In addition to the royalty schedule, PXP agreed to the following:

- The Tranquillon Ridge Project will include an "end date" that will prohibit any extension of the life of existing oil and gas operations.

- PXP will phase out other oil and gas production operations in the county, both offshore near Pt. Arguello and Pt. Conception and onshore near Lompoc.

- All greenhouse gas emissions from the Tranquillon Ridge Project will be mitigated or offset, resulting in carbon neutrality.

- PXP will donate an additional $1,500,000 to reduce greenhouse gas emissions in the county.

- PXP will convey approximately 3,900 acres of land, including approximately 3,700 acres adjacent to the Burton Mesa Ecological Reserve in the Lompoc Valley and up to 200 acres on the Gaviota Coast, for the benefit of the public.

The Negotiated Royalty Rate Schedule

The California State Lands Commission (CSLC) finance and economics chief, David Mercier, together with Dr. Johnathan Mun ("Consultant"), designed, evaluated, and negotiated the royalty schedule illustrated in Figure 150 with PXP.

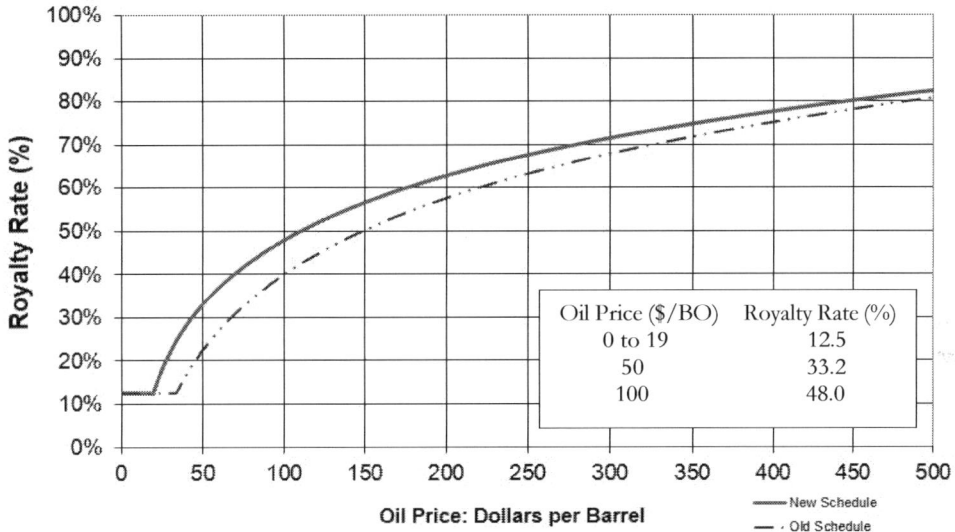

Oil Price ($/BO)	Royalty Rate (%)
0 to 19	12.5
50	33.2
100	48.0

Figure 150: State Royalty Rate versus Oil Price

Why Use a Priced-Based Sliding Scale Royalty?

In the United States, oil and gas property owners typically charge the producer a royalty rate, with the most common being 16.7 percent of the gross revenue. The initial analysis illustrated the benefits of using an oil price-based sliding scale royalty: The royalty rate is low when the price is low and vice versa. This type of royalty schedule can benefit both the royalty owner and operator by encouraging operator investment, mitigating royalty-induced production drops, and lowering the likelihood of abandonment. Increasing the amount of investment in development projects will likely increase the production rate, field value, and royalty revenue:

Royalty Revenue = Oil Price ∗ Production Rate ∗ Rate Rate

Traditionally, many royalty owners have tried to get the highest fixed royalty rate possible, thinking that a higher rate naturally translates into more royalty revenue. This approach has resulted in royalties that need to be renegotiated when the oil price goes lower than predicted to prevent premature abandonment. Negotiating the highest possible royalty rate the producer will accept should never be the royalty owner's strategy. High royalty rates do not necessarily maximize royalty revenue.

In any profit-sharing agreement the (royalty owner–operator) economic interdependence is large; these negotiations should not be treated as a zero-sum game (like chess) where someone wins and the other loses. When the royalty rate is high and the oil price is low, a royalty owner–operator win-lose relationship usually ends up lose-lose in the long term. The only way the royalty owner can win in the long term is to make sure the royalty rate is low when the price is low and vice versa. This arrangement ensures that the royalty rate is not so high at low oil prices that it triggers premature field abandonment or royalty-induced production drops (lose-lose).

To better understand how the royalty rate effects an operation, it is important to note that an X percent royalty rate has the same effect on an operator's shut-in, drilling, and well-work decisions as an X percent reduction in oil price or an X percent increase in operating costs.

Net profits sharing contracts are progressive systems employed in many places around the world; however, typically, these contracts require the mineral owner to be constantly evaluating the details of the operation. For many operations this additional accounting expense is cost-prohibitive. This continuous auditing of the operation to ensure proper payment can be costly for both the mineral owner and operator. Accounting disputes can often lead to expensive litigation and a serious deterioration of the mineral owner–operator relationship. Huge amounts of value can be lost (for both parties) if the operation's human and financial resources shift focus from optimizing the value of the field to expensive litigation/arbitration. Also, net profit contracts, as compared with royalty contracts, may expose the mineral owner to increased financial liability—the risk of negative cash flow or negative balance. Increased financial risk is not bad when it comes with a proportionate amount of increased benefit. However, because of the strong correlation between operator profits and oil price, a royalty schedule that tracks oil price can provide the same or better (if designed properly) revenue stream without all the administrative costs associated with the typical net-profits types of agreements.

Royalty Design Strategy

The royalty schedule (Figure 150) is the result of thousands of scenario combinations and permutations of royalty rates and PXP's IRR as well as other metrics. This royalty schedule was developed to maximize the total NPV of the project, and to the state. At the same time, the constraint is that PXP needs to be profitable given these royalty rates. At royalty rates that are too high, PXP will find the project unprofitable and not proceed with development.

Analysis Steps and Modeling

Building the Decision Model

The first step to develop the optimal royalty schedule was building the financial model in Excel. Before building the model, some time was taken to plan the model's structure. A decision diagram provided a high-level blueprint of the models structure. The decision diagram emphasizes which inputs are used to calculate the results and how the uncertain inputs may be interdependent on each other.

The model flow is sequential, first identifying the input variables (oil price, expense, etc.) then setting up the calculations, and then providing the summary output metrics.

Evaluating the Tornado Diagram

After the model was built, a tornado diagram was generated. This is actually a great debugging tool because it varies all of the inputs. The example tornado summary shown in Figure 151 details how each input variable affected the state's and PXP's NPV, and which inputs were the most important.

Tornado Summary

CSLC	Base Value: 2766.89539618279			Input Changes		
Precedent Cell	Output Downside	Output Upside	Effective Range	Input Downside	Input Upside	Base Case Value
Royalty Function (H7)	$ 2,199	$ 3,335	$ 1,137	0.19	0.24	0.21
Oil Price	$ 2,373	$ 3,173	$ 800	90.00	110.00	100.00
Royalty Function (H6)	$ 3,059	$ 2,475	$ 583	0.46	0.56	0.51
Volume Risking	$ 2,490	$ 3,044	$ 553	0.90	1.10	1.00
SLC Discount Rate	$ 2,919	$ 2,625	$ 294	7.2%	8.8%	8.0%
			$ 3,367			

PXP	Base Value: 1786.5447300599			Input Changes		
Precedent Cell	Output Downside	Output Upside	Effective Range	Input Downside	Input Upside	Base Case Value
Royalty Function (H7)	$ 2,262	$ 1,311	$ 952	0.19	0.24	0.21
Royalty Function (H6)	$ 1,542	$ 2,031	$ 488	0.46	0.56	0.51
Volume Risking	$ 1,550	$ 2,023	$ 473	0.90	1.10	1.00
Oil Price	$ 1,648	$ 1,915	$ 267	$ 90	$ 110	$ 100
PXP Discount Rate	$ 1,911	$ 1,673	$ 238	9.7%	11.8%	10.8%
			$ 2,418			

Figure 151: Tornado Summary and Chart

Not surprisingly, the main critical success factors in this project are:

- Oil price
- Royalty rates
- Volume/production risk
- Discount or hurdle rate

Distributional Analysis

After identifying which input variables affect the state's and PXP's NPV, the oil price history uncertainty was captured into the model using distributional analysis.

Single Variable Distributional Fitting

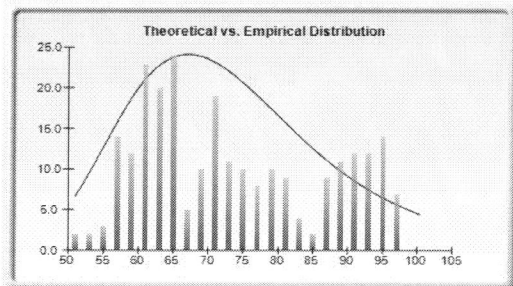

Figure 152: Historical Oil Price Distribution

Preliminary Analysis: GARCH Volatility Estimates

After understanding the key impact drivers in the model, the focus was on calibrating these variables .Thousands of simulation trials and scenarios were run on these key impact drivers to determine the outcome of the project. In other words, less attention was paid to those variables that have very little impact on the outcome of the project. After all, why spend too much time calibrating the inputs to the variables that have very negligible effects on the NPV of the project (e.g., the variables at the bottom of the tornado chart)?

As oil price is the major impact driver, our next step was to determine the risk and volatility of this variable by looking at historical oil prices (Figure 152). Figure 153 shows the results from a GARCH (generalized autoregressive conditional heteroskedasticity) model that was run to forecast the volatility of the price of oil using historical price levels. Figure 154 shows some sample oil price data coupled with macroeconomic variables such as gross domestic product and variables such as inflation and interest rates. These were entered into some advanced econometric models in order to forecast the levels of oil prices and their uncertainties (Figure 155 shows some sample results from ARIMA, or autoregressive integrated moving average, models). The results from these analyses were then used to recalibrate the cash flow models, where tens of thousands of simulation trials were run to determine the returns and risks of the project both to the state and PXP.

GARCH: Generalized Autoregressive Conditional Heteroskedasticity (Volatility Forecast)

GARCH models are used mainly for computing the volatility on liquid and tradable assets such as stocks in financial options; this model is sometimes used for other traded assets such as price of oil and price of electricity. The drawback is that a lot of data is required, advanced econometric modeling expertise is required, and this approach is highly susceptible to user manipulation. The benefit is that rigorous statistical analysis is performed to find the best-fitting volatility curve, providing different volatility estimates over time. GARCH is a term that incorporates a family of models that can take on a variety of forms, known as GARCH (P,Q), where P and Q are positive integers that define the resulting GARCH model and its forecasts. In most cases for financial instruments, a GARCH

GARCH Model (P, Q)	1,1	Periodicity (Periods/Year)	12
Optimized Alpha	0.3243	Predictive Base	1
Optimized Beta	0.5756	Forecast Periods	3
Optimized Omega	0.0009	Variance Targeting	FALSE

Real Options Valuation
www.realoptionsvaluation.com

Period	Data	Volatility
0	59.40	
1	58.26	
2	59.45	23.43%
3	60.47	20.83%
4	60.91	19.06%
5	59.44	17.70%
6	57.73	17.47%
7	56.76	17.64%
8	55.36	17.10%
9	55.92	17.17%
10	56.45	16.60%
11	57.59	16.26%
12	57.07	16.43%
13	56.39	16.15%
14	55.34	16.06%
15	53.00	16.26%
16	53.57	18.08%
17	53.40	17.17%
18	52.10	16.50%
19	50.85	16.81%
20	48.77	16.96%
21	46.21	18.32%
22	48.73	20.22%
23	50.39	21.14%
24	51.26	20.08%
25	48.74	18.59%
26	47.83	20.00%
27	47.84	18.60%
28	48.31	17.36%

GARCH or generalized autoregressive conditional heteroskedasticity models are used in forecasting the volatility of financial instruments, using the prices themselves. The GARCH (P,Q) model allows for different positive P and Q integer lag parameters for the mean (news) and variance equations. Note than only positive data values can be used in a GARCH volatility forecast. Periodicity is the number of periods per year (e.g., 12 for monthly data, 252 for daily trading data, 365 for daily data) to annualize the volatility or keep as 1 for periodic volatility. Base is the predictive base periods (this means how many periods back you would like to use as a forecast base to predict future volatility, and is typically between 1 and 12). Variance Targeting means if you wish the volatility forecast to revert to an imputed long-run mean over time. Make sure to arrange your raw price data in chronological order (past to present in a single

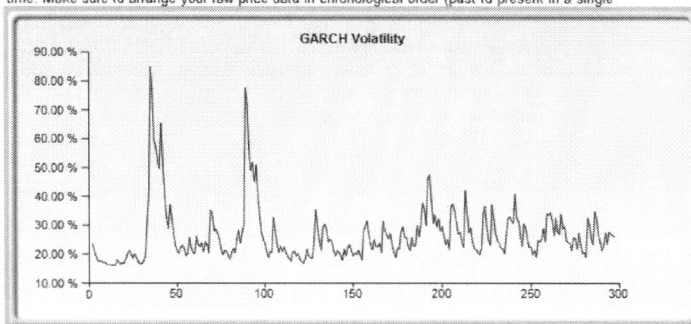

GARCH Volatility

Figure 153: Generalized Autoregressive Conditional Heteroskedasticity (Volatility Forecast)

	A	B	C	D	E	F	G	H	I
1	Date	U.S. Natural Gas Wellhead Price (Dollars per Thousand Cubic Feet)		Date	Cushing, OK Crude Oil Future Contract 1 (Dollars per Barrel)	CPI	Adjusted Contract Crude Oil Price	Adjusted Natural Gas Wellhead Price	PXP contract Crude Oil Price
392	Jul-2005	6.71		Jul-2005	59.03	201.4		7.31	55.94
393	Aug-2005	6.48		Aug-2005	64.99	203.1		7.00	61.07
394	Sep-2005	8.95		Sep-2005	65.55	205.8		9.54	60.79
395	Oct-2005	10.33		Oct-2005	62.27	206.9		10.95	57.44
396	Nov-2005	9.89		Nov-2005	58.34	205.6		10.55	54.16
397	Dec-2005	9.08		Dec-2005	59.45	203.9		9.77	55.65
398	Jan-2006	8.02		Jan-2006	65.54	206		8.54	60.72
399	Feb-2006	6.86		Feb-2006	61.93	207.5		7.25	56.96
400	Mar-2006	6.44		Mar-2006	62.97	208.5		6.78	57.64
401	Apr-2006	6.38		Apr-2006	70.16	210.5		6.65	63.61
402	May-2006	6.24		May-2006	70.96	212.4		6.44	63.76
403	Jun-2006	5.78		Jun-2006	70.97	211.1		6.01	64.16
404	Jul-2006	5.92		Jul-2006	74.46	211.4		6.14	67.22
405	Aug-2006	6.56		Aug-2006	73.08	211.9		6.79	65.82
406	Sep-2006	6.06		Sep-2006	63.9	212.9		6.24	57.28
407	Oct-2006	5.09		Oct-2006	59.14	211.4		5.28	53.39
408	Nov-2006	6.72		Nov-2006	59.4	211.1		6.98	53.70
409	Dec-2006	6.76		Dec-2006	62.09	210.6		7.04	56.27
410	Jan-2007	5.92		Jan-2007	54.35	212.584		6.11	48.79
411	Feb-2007	6.66		Feb-2007	59.39	214.76		6.80	52.78
412	Mar-2007	6.56		Mar-2007	60.74	216.5		6.65	53.55
413	Apr-2007	6.84		Apr-2007	64.04	217.845		6.89	56.11
414	May-2007	6.98		May-2007	63.53	218.596		7.00	55.47
415	Jun-2007	6.86		Jun-2007	67.53	217.273		6.93	59.32
416	Jul-2007	6.19		Jul-2007	74.15	217.454		6.24	65.08
417	Aug-2007	5.9		Aug-2007	72.36	217.33		5.96	63.54
418	Sep-2007	5.61		Sep-2007	79.63	217.697		5.65	69.81
419	Oct-2007	6.25		Oct-2007	85.66	218.696		6.27	74.75
420				Nov-2007	94.63	219.943			82.11
421				Dec-2007	91.74	219.373			79.81

Figure 154: Oil Price Forecasts Using Macroeconomic Factors

AUTO-ARIMA (Autoregressive Integrated Moving Average)

Regression Statistics

R-Squared (Coefficient of Determination)	0.9633	Akaike Information Criterion (AIC)	4.7115
Adjusted R-Squared	0.9630	Schwarz Criterion (SC)	4.7695
Multiple R (Multiple Correlation Coefficient)	0.9815	Log Likelihood	-692.59
Standard Error of the Estimates (SEy)	13.33	Durbin-Watson (DW) Statistic	2.0070
Number of Observations	294	Number of Iterations	6

Autoregressive Integrated Moving Average or ARIMA(p,d,q) models are the extension of the AR model that use three components for modeling the serial correlation in the time-series data. The first component is the autoregressive (AR) term. The AR(p) model uses the p lags of the time series in the equation. An AR(p) model has the form: $y(t)=a(1)*y(t-1)+...+a(p)*y(t-p)+e(t)$. The second component is the integration (d) order term. Each integration order corresponds to differencing the time series. I(1) means differencing the data once. I(d) means differencing the data d times. The third component is the moving average (MA) term. The MA(q) model uses the q lags of the forecast errors to improve the forecast. An MA(q) model has the form: $y(t)=e(t)+b(1)*e(t-1)+...+b(q)*e(t-q)$. Finally, an ARMA(p,q) model has the combined form: $y(t)=a(1)*y(t-1)+...+a(p)*y(t-p)+e(t)+b(1)*e(t-1)+...+b(q)*e(t-q)$.

The R-Squared, or Coefficient of Determination, indicates the percent variation in the dependent variable that can be explained and accounted for by the independent variables in this regression analysis. However, in a multiple regression, the Adjusted R-Squared takes into account the existence of additional independent variables or regressors and adjusts this R-Squared value to a more accurate view the regression's explanatory power. However, under some ARIMA modeling circumstances (e.g., with nonconvergence models), the R-Squared tends to be unreliable.

The Multiple Correlation Coefficient (Multiple R) measures the correlation between the actual dependent variable (Y) and the estimated or fitted (Y) based on the regression equation. This correlation is also the square root of the Coefficient of Determination (R-Squared).

The Standard Error of the Estimates (SEy) describes the dispersion of data points above and below the regression line or plane. This value is used as part of the calculation to obtain the confidence interval of the estimates later.

The AIC and SC are often used in model selection. SC imposes a greater penalty for additional coefficients. Generally, the user should select a model with the lowest value of the AIC and SC.

The Durbin-Watson statistic measures the serial correlation in the residuals. Generally, DW less than 2 implies positive serial correlation.

Regression Results

	Intercept	AR(1)	MA(1)
Coefficients	0.7421	0.9796	0.2874
Standard Error	0.5320	0.0147	0.0571
t-Statistic	1.3950	66.6201	5.0313
p-Value	0.1641	0.0000	0.0000
Lower 5%	1.6199	1.0038	0.3816
Upper 95%	-0.1357	0.9553	0.1931

Degrees of Freedom		Hypothesis Test	
Degrees of Freedom for Regression	2	Critical t-Statistic (99% confidence with df of 291)	2.5928
Degrees of Freedom for Residual	291	Critical t-Statistic (95% confidence with df of 291)	1.9681
Total Degrees of Freedom	293	Critical t-Statistic (90% confidence with df of 291)	1.6501

Autocorrelation

Time Lag	AC	PAC	Lower Bound	Upper Bound	Q-Stat	Prob
1	0.9583	0.9583	(0.1164)	0.1164	272.7748	-
2	0.9117	(0.0826)	(0.1164)	0.1164	520.4740	-
3	0.8706	0.0489	(0.1164)	0.1164	747.1625	-
4	0.8296	(0.0316)	(0.1164)	0.1164	953.6689	-
5	0.7968	0.0841	(0.1164)	0.1164	1,144.7658	-
6	0.7690	0.0325	(0.1164)	0.1164	1,323.4421	-
7	0.7453	0.0404	(0.1164)	0.1164	1,491.8865	-
8	0.7234	0.0081	(0.1164)	0.1164	1,651.1049	-
9	0.7029	0.0171	(0.1164)	0.1164	1,801.9631	-
10	0.6859	0.0422	(0.1164)	0.1164	1,946.1286	-
11	0.6590	(0.1255)	(0.1164)	0.1164	2,079.6593	-
12	0.6307	0.0003	(0.1164)	0.1164	2,202.4156	-
13	0.6051	0.0067	(0.1164)	0.1164	2,315.7966	-
14	0.5800	0.0049	(0.1164)	0.1164	2,420.3514	-
15	0.5484	(0.1111)	(0.1164)	0.1164	2,514.1731	-
16	0.5187	0.0099	(0.1164)	0.1164	2,598.3934	-
17	0.4962	0.0544	(0.1164)	0.1164	2,675.7356	-
18	0.4737	(0.0197)	(0.1164)	0.1164	2,746.4771	-
19	0.4500	(0.0362)	(0.1164)	0.1164	2,810.5473	-
20	0.4316	0.0379	(0.1164)	0.1164	2,869.6993	-

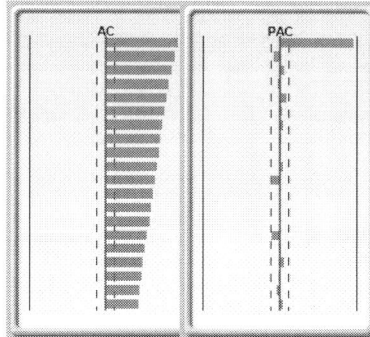

Forecasting

Period	Actual (Y)	Forecast (F)	Error (E)
2	58.2609	58.9272	(0.6664)
3	59.4452	57.6212	1.8240
4	60.4724	59.4971	0.9753
5	60.9053	60.2593	0.6460
6	59.4446	60.5888	(1.1442)
7	57.7311	58.6435	(0.9124)
8	56.7621	57.0316	(0.2695)
9	55.3630	56.2671	(0.9042)
10	55.9174	54.7142	1.2032
11	56.4486	55.8629	0.5857
12	57.5938	56.2058	1.3880
13	57.0702	57.5582	(0.4880)
14	56.3888	56.5061	(0.1173)
15	55.3367	55.9452	(0.6085)
16	52.9967	54.7735	(1.7768)
17	53.5671	52.1455	1.4216
18	53.4029	53.6234	(0.2205)
19	52.1006	52.9906	(0.8901)
20	50.8523	51.5225	(0.6702)
21	48.7739	50.3629	(1.5890)
22	46.2088	48.0630	(1.8542)

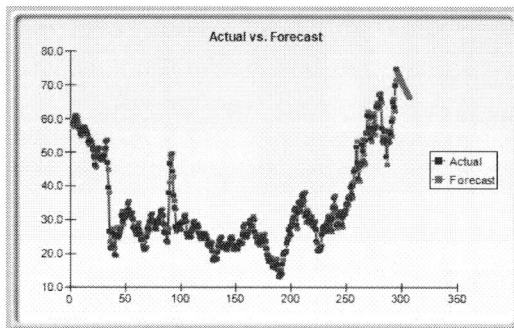

Figure 155: Oil Price Forecasts Using Advanced Econometric ARIMA Models

206

accounting, and the economic Consultant, Dr. Johnathan Mun, performed the real options analysis whereby PXP can start with three wells as a proof of concept to delineate the reservoir. If done properly, these three wells (limited total costs to drill, as compared to the total number of wells and injectors required in a full development) will help limit the downside risks and losses to PXP, while providing a significant upside. Therefore, the risks are mitigated, and, depending on the results of the three test wells, PXP can decide if it wants to pursue developing and completing all additional wells. Thus, the risks specified using simulation as previously illustrated would be diminished to a level that is close to zero, with the total loss being the expenses used to drill the three wells. The upside leverage is significant. For instance, say the total cost of drilling the three test wells is $53M. In the best-case scenario where 90 percent of the time at full production yields an NPV of $2.28B, PXP has leveraged its upside by almost 43 times. In the absolute worst-case scenario, the total losses for PXP will be the $53M spent on test drilling the three wells.

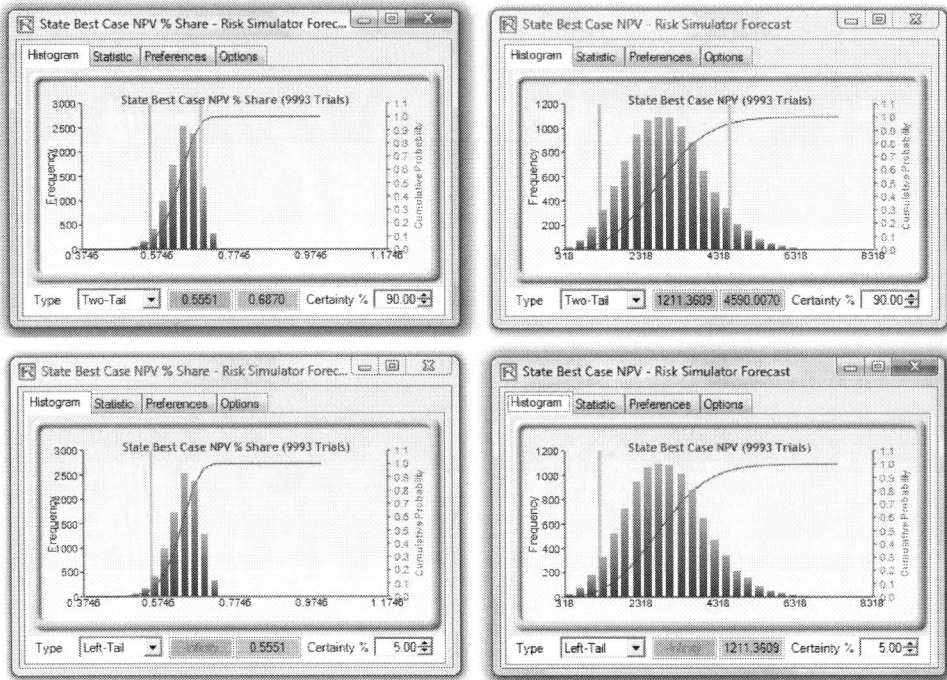

Figure 156: A Sample of the State's Risk Profile I (Simulation Results)

State Best Case NPV % Share - Risk Simulator Forec...

Histogram | Statistic | Preferences | Options

Statistics	Result
Number of Trials	9993
Mean	0.6274
Median	0.6317
Standard Deviation	0.0413
Variance	0.0017
Coefficient of Variation	0.0658
Maximum	1.0000
Minimum	0.3579
Range	0.6421
Skewness	-0.5370
Kurtosis	1.6773
25% Percentile	0.6028
75% Percentile	0.6564
Percentage Error Precision at 95% Confidence	0.1291%

State Best Case NPV - Risk Simulator Forecast

Histogram | Statistic | Preferences | Options

Statistics	Result
Number of Trials	9993
Mean	2803.5461
Median	2752.6546
Standard Deviation	1027.9473
Variance	1.056676E+006
Coefficient of Variation	0.3667
Maximum	7403.9008
Minimum	128.4847
Range	7275.4161
Skewness	0.3451
Kurtosis	0.0925
25% Percentile	2075.0334
75% Percentile	3461.4980
Percentage Error Precision at 95% Confidence	0.7189%

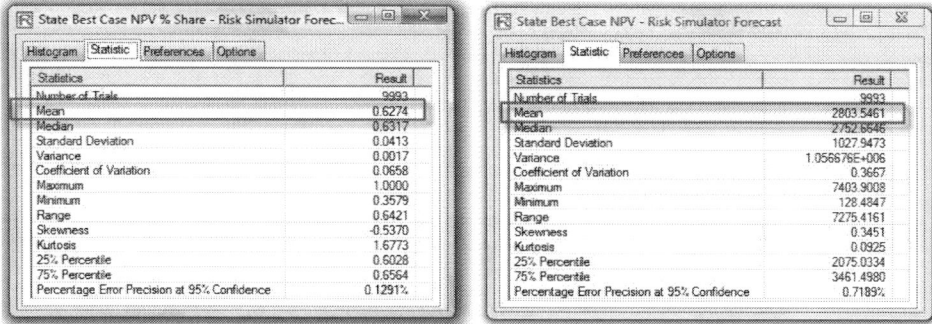

Figure 157: A Sample of the State's Risk Profile II (Simulation Results)

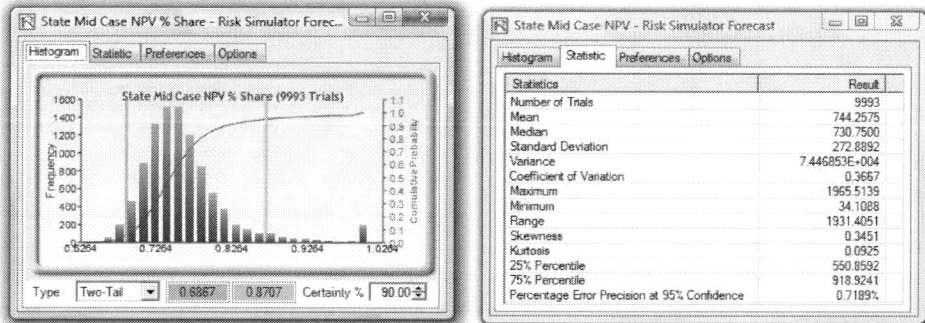

State Mid Case NPV % Share - Risk Simulator Forec...

State Mid Case NPV - Risk Simulator Forecast

Histogram | Statistic | Preferences | Options

Statistics	Result
Number of Trials	9993
Mean	744.2575
Median	730.7500
Standard Deviation	272.8892
Variance	7.446853E+004
Coefficient of Variation	0.3667
Maximum	1965.5139
Minimum	34.1088
Range	1931.4051
Skewness	0.3451
Kurtosis	0.0925
25% Percentile	550.8592
75% Percentile	918.9241
Percentage Error Precision at 95% Confidence	0.7189%

Figure 158: A Sample of the State's Risk Profile III (Simulation Results)

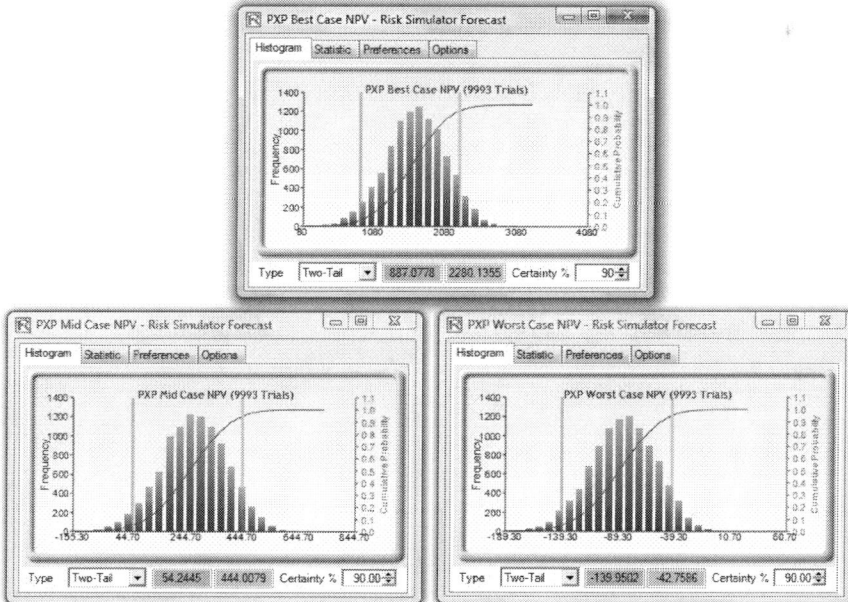

Figure 159: PXP's Risk Profile I (Simulation Results)

209

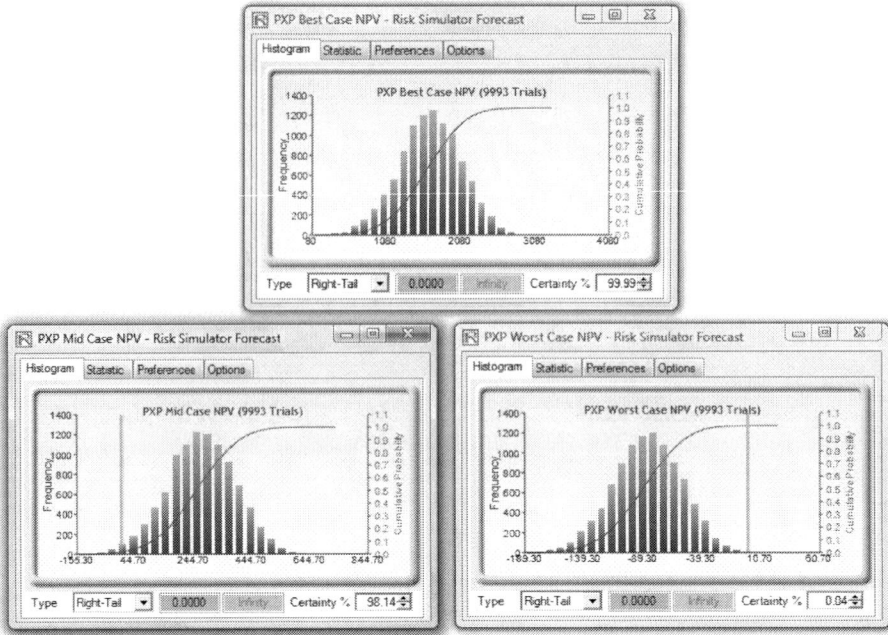

Figure 160: PXP's Risk Profile II (Simulation Results)

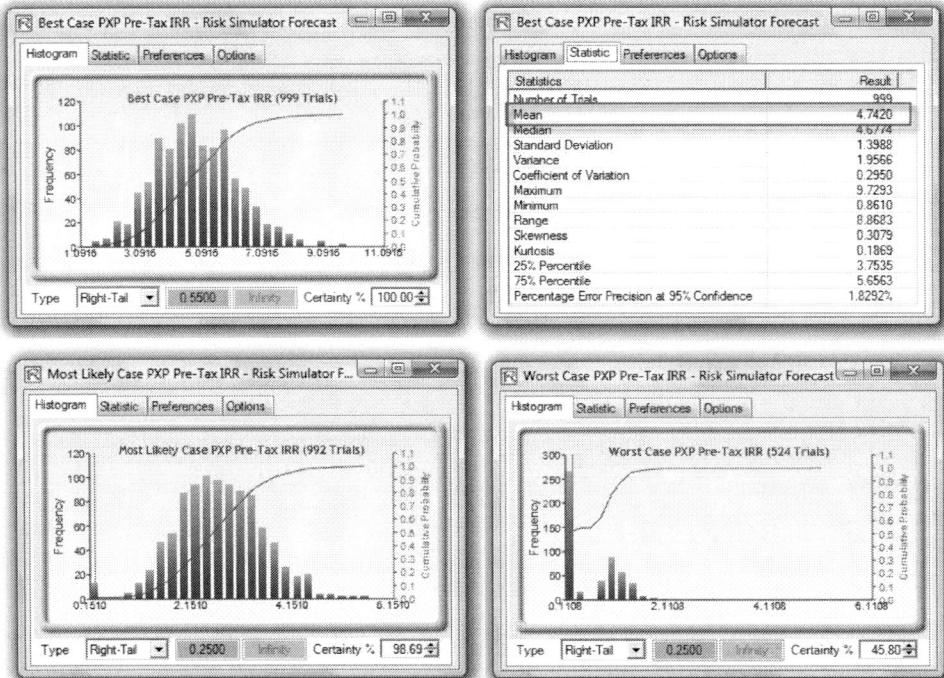

Figure 161: PXP's Risk Profile III (Simulation Results)

Strategic Real Options Analysis (Risk Mitigation)

For PXP, if the best-case or most likely mid-case scenario occurs, its NPV value is still highly positive, indicating a profitable project in general. However, if the worst-case scenario occurs, with limited production, the project might end up being unprofitable. This is clearly a risk that PXP has to undertake, even with up to a projected 30 percent geological chance of failure (dry hole). To mitigate this risk, PXP can first drill three exploratory wells (Phase I in Figure 162). On the one hand, if these three wells prove to be successful (the reservoir is clearly delineated and the geological uncertainties of the reservoir are resolved and known), then PXP can pursue additional or large-scale drilling of the other wells in Phase II. On the other hand, if Phase I proves that there are issues with the reservoir, PXP can simply exit and abandon the drilling altogether. By creating a Phase I and Phase II development process, PXP can delineate the wells and reduce its risks. Instead of paying all of the capital expenditures immediately, the maximum that will be lost will be the cost to drill the three exploratory wells.

This risk mitigation technique is known in real options analysis as a sequential compound or phased option. This stage-gate process allows PXP to reduce its total losses should the worst-case scenario become reality, capping the total loss at three wells drilled, as compared to a large-scale development. By using this technique, the uncertainty and risks become resolved over the passage of actions, time, and events. PXP will and should optimally execute Phase II only if Phase I proves to be highly successful. Figure 163 illustrates the analysis performed to value the strategic option.

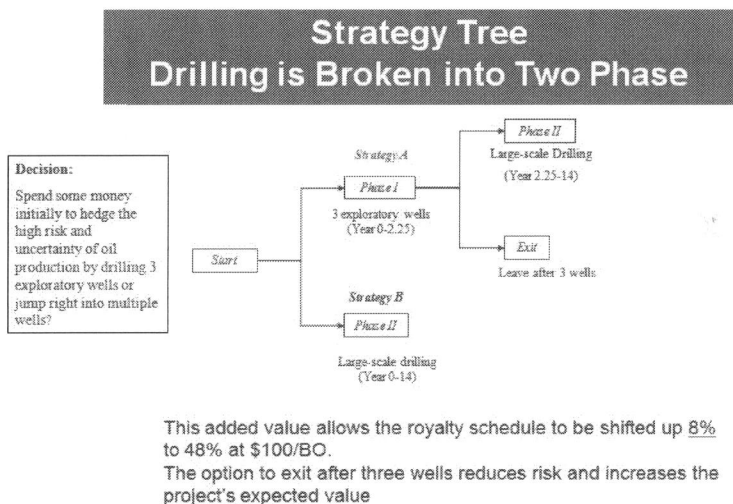

This added value allows the royalty schedule to be shifted up 8% to 48% at $100/BO.
The option to exit after three wells reduces risk and increases the project's expected value

Figure 162: Sequential Compound Two-phased Option

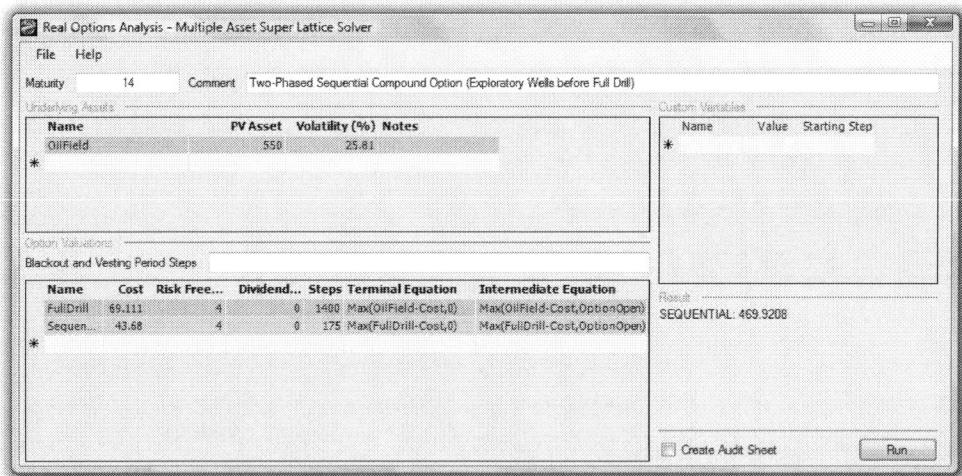

Figure 163: Real Options Valuation Results

Optimal Royalty Rate Determination (Optimization and Scenario Analysis)

The next part of the analysis is the determination of the optimal royalty rate schema. The approach used was that of an optimization, where thousands of scenario combinations and permutations of royalty rates and PXP's IRR were determined, and the optimal confidence band was determined. This band was developed to maximize the total NPV of the project while maximizing the returns to the state without leaving additional money on the negotiation table. At the same time, the constraint is such that PXP will still be profitable given these royalty rates. At rates higher than those in the optimal band, PXP will find the project unprofitable and the optimal decision is to abandon it. It is important to note that IRR was evaluated along with the many other financial metrics[32]. PXP's' NPV was also considered in the sample optimization to ensure that it increases with increasing oil price. Figure 164 illustrates a small subset of these scenarios.

---

[32] A smaller investment and a better rate of return may have a higher IRR, but an investor's total wealth may be increased more with a larger investment and a lower IRR. Therefore, IRR doesn't provide any insight into the magnitude of the investment.

Risk Analysis (Monte Carlo Risk-Based Simulation)

To properly determine the risks and uncertainties involved in the project, we employed Monte Carlo risk simulation and ran 1,000 to 100,000 simulation trials on the financial and economic models to account for all possible outcomes. The variables we simulated were those found to be the most sensitive in driving the NPV and IRR of the project. These critical success factors (e.g., price of oil and oil production) were very difficult to forecast with any certainty, hence we employed simulation techniques to handle these uncertainties. Figures 156–162 illustrate a small sample set of the analysis performed, and the descriptions of our findings are listed here:

- Figure 156 shows simulation forecast results that indicate the state's NPV levels and NPV share of the total NPV of the project, assuming that the best-case scenario occurs. The 90 percent confidence interval means that 90 percent of the time, given all that can occur in terms of price of oil and actual production as well as other uncertainties (assuming that production is at full capacity), the state will yield an NPV of between $1.21B and $4.59B, which is equivalent to obtaining between 55.51 percent and 68.70 percent of the total NPV. This result also means that in the 5 percent worst-case scenario, if production is at full capacity, the state will yield at least $1.21B (55.51 percent NPV share). This amount increases the possibility that the state will not get any more than $4.59B (68.70 percent NPV share) 5 percent of the time (that the state will only be able to beat these values at the absolute best-case scenario will occur less than 5 percent of the time).

- Figure 157 shows the same analysis as done for Figure 156 with the average NPV at $2.80B, or 62.74 percent NPV share if the production is at full capacity.

- Figure 158 shows the results of the analysis when the level of production is at the most likely middle-case scenario, where the state will be receiving an expected average of $744M and between 68.67 percent and 87.07 percent of the NPV share. The worse the situation, the higher the percentage NPV share the state receives because it carries no risk whereas PXP takes all the risk (although both the state and PXP will have reduced NPV dollar values).

- Figure 159 illustrates the results for PXP. In the best-case and most likely mid-case scenarios, the NPV on a 90 percent confidence interval shows that PXP will always have a significant NPV. The only way PXP will not obtain positive NPV values is when production is super low and close to a standstill, under the worst-case scenario.

- Figure 160 illustrates PXP's probability of success in generating a positive NPV for the entire project, at the sliding royalty rate proposed by the state. There is a 99.99 percent and 98.14 percent chance that NPV will be positive in the best- and most likely mid-case scenarios for PXP. This result indicates that there is less than a 2 percent chance that the project will be unprofitable, whereas 98.14 percent of the time, this project is lucrative and profitable for PXP. The only exception, again, is when production is at the worst-case scenario and output is close to a standstill.

- Figure 161, in contrast to the preceding figures, illustrates PXP's IRR on a pretax level. In the best-case scenario, PXP's IRR has a 100 percent chance of exceeding 55 percent, the required threshold for most high-risk projects such as undefined oil and gas exploration projects. Even in the most likely case, there is more than a 98 percent probability that the IRR exceeds PXP's hurdle rate of 25 percent, and in the worst-case scenario, a 45.80 percent chance of that occurring.

In summary, PXP's risks were nominal and the upside potential very significant. To further decrease PXP's downside risks, David Mercier, chief of finance, economics and

Sample PXP IRR

Scenario Analysis Table

Output Variable: PXP AVG IRR   Initial Base Case Val   0.47
Column Variable: Oil Price   Min: 0.00 Max: 1.00 Steps: —   Steps 0.04 Initial Base Case Value:
Row Variable: Royalty Rate   Min: 0.00 Max: 500.00 Steps: —   Steps 20.00 Initial Base Case Value:

	12%	16%	20%	24%	28%	32%	36%	40%	44%	48%	52%	56%	60%	64%	68%	72%	76%	80%	Calculated Royalty (%)
0	—	—	—	—	—	—	—	—	—	—	—	—	—	—	—	—	—	—	12.5%
20	-0.65	-0.68	-0.72	-0.75	-0.79	-0.83	-0.97	—	—	—	—	—	—	—	—	—	—	—	13.5%
40	-0.04	-0.10	-0.15	-0.21	-0.26	-0.32	-0.38	-0.43	-0.49	-0.55	-0.61	-0.68	-0.74	-0.82	—	—	—	—	28.4%
60	0.53	0.45	0.37	0.29	0.21	0.13	0.05	-0.03	-0.12	-0.20	-0.28	-0.37	-0.46	-0.54	-0.64	-0.73	-0.86	—	37.1%
80	1.10	0.99	0.89	0.78	0.67	0.57	0.46	0.35	0.25	0.14	0.03	-0.08	-0.19	-0.30	-0.42	-0.54	-0.66	-0.80	43.2%
100	1.66	1.53	1.40	1.26	1.13	1.00	0.87	0.74	0.60	0.47	0.33	0.20	0.06	-0.07	-0.21	-0.35	-0.50	-0.65	48.0%
120	2.21	2.06	1.90	1.74	1.59	1.43	1.27	1.11	0.95	0.80	0.64	0.47	0.31	0.15	-0.01	-0.18	-0.35	-0.52	51.9%
140	2.77	2.58	2.40	2.22	2.04	1.85	1.67	1.49	1.30	1.12	0.93	0.75	0.56	0.37	0.19	-0.01	-0.20	-0.40	55.2%
160	3.32	3.11	2.90	2.69	2.49	2.28	2.07	1.86	1.65	1.44	1.23	1.02	0.81	0.60	0.38	0.17	-0.05	-0.28	58.1%
180	3.87	3.64	3.40	3.17	2.94	2.70	2.47	2.23	2.00	1.76	1.53	1.29	1.05	0.82	0.58	0.33	0.09	-0.16	60.6%
200	4.42	4.16	3.90	3.64	3.38	3.12	2.86	2.60	2.34	2.08	1.82	1.56	1.30	1.03	0.77	0.50	0.23	-0.04	62.8%
220	4.97	4.68	4.40	4.11	3.83	3.54	3.26	2.97	2.69	2.40	2.12	1.83	1.54	1.25	0.96	0.67	0.37	0.08	64.9%
240	5.51	5.21	4.90	4.59	4.28	3.97	3.65	3.34	3.03	2.72	2.41	2.10	1.78	1.47	1.15	0.84	0.52	0.19	66.7%
260	6.06	5.73	5.39	5.06	4.72	4.39	4.05	3.71	3.38	3.04	2.70	2.36	2.02	1.68	1.34	1.00	0.66	0.31	68.5%
280	6.61	6.25	5.89	5.53	5.17	4.81	4.44	4.08	3.72	3.36	2.99	2.63	2.27	1.90	1.53	1.17	0.80	0.42	70.0%
300	7.16	6.77	6.38	6.00	5.61	5.22	4.84	4.45	4.06	3.67	3.29	2.90	2.51	2.12	1.72	1.33	0.93	0.54	71.5%
320	7.70	7.29	6.88	6.47	6.06	5.64	5.23	4.82	4.41	3.99	3.58	3.16	2.75	2.33	1.91	1.49	1.07	0.65	72.9%
340	8.25	7.81	7.38	6.94	6.50	6.06	5.62	5.19	4.75	4.31	3.87	3.43	2.99	2.55	2.10	1.66	1.21	0.76	74.2%
360	8.80	8.33	7.87	7.41	6.94	6.48	6.02	5.55	5.09	4.62	4.16	3.69	3.23	2.76	2.29	1.82	1.35	0.88	75.4%
380	9.34	8.86	8.37	7.88	7.39	6.90	6.41	5.92	5.43	4.94	4.45	3.96	3.47	2.97	2.48	1.99	1.49	0.99	76.6%
400	9.89	9.38	8.86	8.35	7.83	7.32	6.80	6.29	5.77	5.26	4.74	4.22	3.71	3.19	2.67	2.15	1.63	1.10	77.7%
420	10.44	9.90	9.36	8.82	8.28	7.74	7.20	6.66	6.11	5.57	5.03	4.49	3.95	3.40	2.86	2.31	1.76	1.21	78.7%
440	10.98	10.42	9.85	9.29	8.72	8.15	7.59	7.02	6.46	5.89	5.32	4.75	4.19	3.62	3.05	2.47	1.90	1.32	79.7%
460	11.53	10.94	10.35	9.76	9.16	8.57	7.98	7.39	6.80	6.20	5.61	5.02	4.42	3.83	3.23	2.64	2.04	1.44	80.7%
480	12.07	11.46	10.84	10.22	9.61	8.99	8.37	7.76	7.14	6.52	5.90	5.28	4.66	4.04	3.42	2.80	2.18	1.55	81.6%
500	12.62	11.98	11.34	10.69	10.05	9.41	8.77	8.12	7.48	6.84	6.19	5.55	4.90	4.26	3.61	2.96	2.31	1.66	82.5%

Figure 164: Sample Optimal Royalty Rates by Running Thousands of Alternate Scenarios

Analysis Conclusion

Based on the detailed economic and financial modeling performed by Staff and the economic Consultant, we came to the conclusion that the sliding royalty rate is the best and most optimal scheme for the PXP project. The analysis took into consideration the risk and volatility of oil price and production decline rates, running stochastic simulations covering hundreds of thousands of potential outcomes, creating an optimization frontier of all possible combinations and permutations of oil prices and royalty rates. Other nonfinancial factors as well as factors such as the land donation, potential payment of additional county taxes, tax rebates and incentives, donation to develop certain green technology or environmental offsets (hybrid buses, parks, and the like) were outside the purview of this financial analysis, but are nonetheless important aspects in the negotiations.

On January 29, 2009, the State Lands Commission voted down the project two (Lt. Governor Garamendi and State Controller John Chiang) against one (Deputy Finance Director Tom Sheehy). As of writing this case study, PXP has appealed to the State Legislature to get the State Lands Commission's vote overturned.

CASE STUDY 16: HOW REAL OPTIONS ENSURES IT ENTERPRISE RISK SECURITY

This case was written by David M. Bittlingmeier. David has a B.S. from St. Mary's College and an M.S. From Golden Gate University, and has numerous years in Strategic Enterprise Security, Designing, Developing and Implementing various Enterprise Policies and Procedures, Enterprise-wide Security Awareness Training, Business Continuity, Project Management, and Technical Consultation experience, where he has provided professional judgments and advice to all levels of management. As a consultant, he has worked on insuring compliance with Industry Best Practices, Business Continuity, Disaster Recovery Planning, ISO 17799, NIST standards, OCC, Basel II and Basel III, and BITS regulation, and has offered Enterprise Security Management perspective for executives seeking an unbiased source of education, insight and expertise in order to ensure the success of their business. In addition, he has consulted with (ISC)2, where he was both part of the team that developed/modified the training to prepare security professionals for the CISSP exam and then was/is a Supervisor during the CISSP exams, wrote the Strategic Security Plan for one of the major departments of the State of California, speaks at International Enterprise Security Conferences, an on-going attendee of the U.S. Secret Service San Francisco Electronic Crimes Task Force, was a contributor of Risk Analysis: 1st Step in HIPAA Security Publication, *as well as a member of the High Technology Crime Investigation Association, Inc. David has received praise for his ability to explain complexity in lay terms from sources such as San Francisco Mayor's Criminal Justice Council, California Youth Authority and others.*

This case study provides a quick overview of IT Enterprise Risk Management analysis drawn from numerous local, national and international security reviews hc has completed, including, yet not necessarily limited to, third party service companies, mail services, various outsourcing functions/processes, venture capitalist projects, insurance companies, financial companies, and so forth from multimillion to multibillion dollar organizations, and as such the case study is an illustration of those robust review processes. Within the case study is a shorten, finalized, for space uses a single composite case, with a sample report that outlines both issues and possible solutions. Finally, adding the strategic real options and Integrated Risk Management such as applying Monte Carlo risk simulations offer solutions to the effective allocation of major funds on Enterprise Security projects. While the benefits of IT are clear, managing the risks that can be introduced to the business from IT processes, policies, and technology failures are not easily inferred and yet these risks can have serious impacts in terms of achieving compliance with:

- Regulations
- Protecting brand reputation
- Ensuring overall corporate performance

The process introduced in this case study is the *Risk Assessment Process* (RAP) process, which helps facilitate excellence in governance by aligning:

- IT policy, risk, and operations management

- Corporate business initiatives

- Strategy

- Operational standards

- Enterprise security

RAP is a comprehensive solution that reduces the cost, complexity and cumbersome nature of complying with numerous regulatory mandates. RAP facilitates the ongoing review, attestation and remediation process, while helping to identify similarities between regulations to reduce redundancy and duplication of effort and provides the confidence that compliance is achievable, risks are mitigated and corporate policies and procedures are enforced. As regulatory pressures continue to mount, businesses that take a more practical, cross-regulatory approach to managing compliance will alleviate increasing cost and complexity while gaining valuable insight into risks to key business processes that could affect the company's performance in the form of legal action, fines, penalties, and damage to a company's reputation.

Enterprise Risk Management is a complex and difficult problem that can be made efficient and manageable through RAP's consolidation, identification and harmonization of overlapping regulatory demands—interdependencies that cannot be seen using spreadsheets—and enables transparency and visibility to stakeholders throughout the organization. The process ensures that risks are properly associated to business strategy and needs while it helps to manage a multitude of technology risks. Such processes have become increasingly more difficult and require a holistic approach where the interdependencies between risk and business performance is easily understood and manageable. For example, currently organizations in general have had to rely on a fragmented and disparate approach to managing supplier risks. Reliance on a silo risk management approach is not only costly and inefficient, it lacks the contextual understanding of the real impacts that risk in technology processes and policies have on the business.

In today's highly regulated business environment, companies are required to comply with a multitude of global regulatory mandates, including privacy, industry, and process regulations. Regardless of a company's current compliance environment, similarities across regulations create overlapping management, documentation and audit demands, which can overwhelm efforts to effectively identify and manage risk. RAP makes governance practicable, enabling a company to sustain compliance across multiple best practice frameworks and regulations while managing IT control and risk according to the business processes they support. With RAP, a company will instill risk management and governance as part of the corporate culture, making procedures more effective and efficient while providing management with peace-of-mind that the corporate brand is protected providing management with the visibility, control, and decision support required to manage supplier risk and optimize business performance. RAP is a key building block in implementing an enterprise-wide risk management approach as it delivers a policy-driven, process-centric way to manage risk through:

- Control assessments

- User surveys

- Logical and repeatable workflow

- Industry standard best practices criteria

We are able to apply Risk Simulator input assumptions to both BAROV and Client Company's subject matter expert risk rankings, and then run simulations on the matrices in order to determine the total grand risk score for the Client Company (see Figure 168). Furthermore, we are able to develop optimization models where each element may be subject to a decision variable in terms of the cost required to correct any outstanding issues, compared to possible benefits/losses obtained from having/not having an "in compliance" security level, and run it based on the Client Company's budget constraints. Using probabilistic distributions obtained from the simulation(s), we are now able to identify the chances that a specific category's risk and impact may exceed tolerable limits, as well as identify the critical success factors (sensitivity analysis and tornado analysis are usually run on these assessment matrices). A strategy is then created of multiple phases (sequential compound option) on when certain elements of the issue(s) identified can/needs to be first to be fixed, when it/they then becomes the less/more critical in other phase(s), all the while were so warranted accounting for interrelationships among any/all Enterprise projects; for example, if a certain project requires another as a prerequisite (say, some platform technology that first needs to be implemented before any subsequent projects can be implemented) or any mutually exclusive redundant projects (the implementation of one project makes another obsolete or unnecessary). At the end of the day, at what point does not stopping project A become cost effective and/or project B becoming cost-effective or ending project A completely or moving toward project B become the best and optimal overall strategy? As most companies have hundreds of these projects BAROV could demonstrate both the dependency and the costs between projects, thereby giving a pragmatic real-world risk of project A versus project B, and so forth.

Based on a company's business objectives, the inherent risks associated will determine the tier ranking system using a value of 1 to 5 Likert scale (the scale can also be color-coordinated such as: 1 = Green, 2 = Yellow, 3 = Orange, 4 = Red, 5 = Black), indicating the level of risk involved, from low to high. In general, compliance reviews dictate that formal reviews must be conducted on at least an annual basis, and more frequently, if warranted based on risk. Using a pragmatic, real-world-based stance in conducting reviews, we understand how policy, procedures, and management controls mitigate risk. Based on a comprehensive and customizable risk-assessment approach, this RAP methodology can be used across multiple industries and functions. It can be used as the basis for performing up-front due-diligence, a one-time controls review, or an annual assessment of controls and/or best practices (Figure 165 illustrates this compliance core methodology).

A Sample Implementation

This sample implementation is derived from extensive on-site reviews (companies' names and proprietary information are intentionally kept confidential and we only present a generic example case) in the United States, India and China, of due-diligence reviews across numerous industries including yet not limited to financial services, insurance companies, onshore/offshore IT service providers, manufacturing, and other functional areas for compliance issues in general, while specifically reviewing Enterprise Security of internal, external, outsourced and offshore service security, highlighting the needs for BAROV and Real Options Valuation, Inc.'s (BAROV) methodologies to ensure enterprise security that meet or exceed industry-standard security practices that are cost-effective, robust, functionally effective, and real-time. Information systems are designed and deployed to support business and legal requirements, leverage cost efficiencies, and improve internal and external communication. However, organizations, like the people they are designed to serve, are organic—they grow, evolve, and change continuously. It is impossible for the infrastructures supporting such environments to maintain its secure integrity and cost effectiveness without persistent vigilance and wisely spent renewed investment which BAROV allows and facilitates. Striking the balance between sharing information among all necessary parties and maintaining adequate protection for the company's proprietary information is crucial in any business environment. In a networked world, information is the central nervous system for the organization with the risk of proprietary knowledge and confidential information being exposed to potential perpetrators. These perpetrators prey on the vulnerabilities that are inevitable in an IT system. Opportunities emerging from such vulnerabilities range from defacing corporate websites to stealing valuable assets where infrastructure resources are appropriated covertly for seditious activities. Eradicating all threats would make the infrastructure useless. System security and performance objectives tend to be at odds. However, steps can be taken to optimize and balance these seemly diametrically opposed poles. BAROV has developed the process and assessment methods to help companies have a way to cost effectively identify, prioritize, and achieve its security goals without depleting system performance. A summary of the four phases applied and nine processes are shown later in this case study, providing a summary of BAROV's usual recommend tasks, using a prioritized approach that qualitatively considers security benefits, and levels of effort. The methodology is developed to help initiate discussions regarding which recommendations to implement immediately, in the future, or not at all, within the context of the company's business requirements, security goals, and budget constraints. Due to the limited scope of this case study, any company-specific requirements would need a unique and detailed analysis prior to the remediation efforts described here.

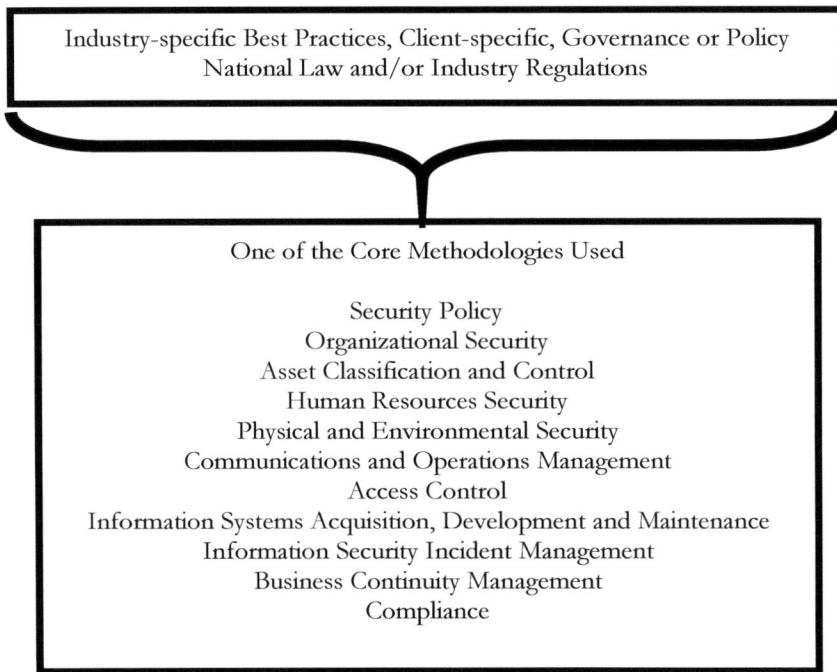

Industry-specific Best Practices, Client-specific, Governance or Policy
National Law and/or Industry Regulations

One of the Core Methodologies Used

Security Policy
Organizational Security
Asset Classification and Control
Human Resources Security
Physical and Environmental Security
Communications and Operations Management
Access Control
Information Systems Acquisition, Development and Maintenance
Information Security Incident Management
Business Continuity Management
Compliance

Figure 165 Assurance of Compliance with Legal Requirements

Sample Analysis Report

This section shows a sample BAROV analysis report issued to a company based on answers provided during personnel interviews with the company's staff and on independent examination of documents and facilities by the BAROV team. The company analyzed is a multinational billion-dollar organization that is currently outsourcing a relatively small quantity of work items to Outsourced Company and before expanding its activities, hired BAROV to review the risks, if any, related to this business expansion and outsourcing activities, with a detailed report that outlines the risks and steps to either remove or mitigate the said risks that are identified.

Approach

BAROV identified certain risks in its contract operations using agreed on work programs to address the risks. We also reviewed more than four dozen presentations and hundreds of documents in both English and Chinese, covering all the major policies and procedures within the scope of this engagement. Furthermore, we interviewed more than 42 company employees and the results of our review are presented in the form of an assessment report.

Findings

After careful review of our findings and recommendations regarding the activities supporting Outsourced Company combined with their staffs' responses, we present the following overall finding. With minor correction actions, as pointed out by the team and completed while on-site, no instances of substantial non-conformance to the expectations matrix in the methodology were found in our review of Outsourced Company. This does not mean there is absolutely no risk, but our review did not uncover any significant risks within Outsourced Company's operations or systems of internal control. In our professional judgment, the management controls operated by Outsourced Company mitigate the risks identified by the Client Company.

Recommendations

During our review process, we made numerous recommendations to Outsourced Company regarding process improvements that could increase mitigation of risk, reduce the opportunity for error or generally improve Outsourced Company's policy and procedures. The fact that Outsourced Company agreed to implement all of the recommendations documented in this report showed their interest in being viewed as a world-class service provider ; most were done immediately, due to the effort needed a few remain to be completed as outline in the findings section. Although the responsiveness of Outsourced Company to the risks of the existing business relationship is both reasonable and adequate, it should be noted that differences in relevant law, regulations, standards and audit practices with the United States merit recommendation that Outsourced Company conduct annual external/independent reviews of the ongoing adequacy of operations. These annual reviews should demonstrate that no material risk exist, or have developed, with the business relationship and service. In our professional judgment, Outsourced Company provides the following characteristics essential to the Client Company:

- Management is dedicated to "Best of Breed" Security

- Environment is highly secure

- Infrastructure is robust and backed up

- Policy and procedures are adequate, with two caveats:
    - Translation to English would make them more accessible
    - Improvements in organization would make them more cohesive

- Material control processes are effective and followed.

Scope of Assessment and Report

This report is not an audit report or an internal controls certification. It is an independent assessment of specifically identified performance criteria agreed by Client Company and for the exclusive use of Client Company. It is the sole responsibility of Client Company to determine the adequacy of the controls, take steps to ameliorate any deficiencies as soon as practicable and conduct a follow-up review to verify remediation. This report provides a narrative of the review conducted by a team from BAROV on-site in Outsourced Company's factory during the specified contractual period. The report is based on answers provided during personal interviews with Outsourced Company's staff and on independent examination of documents and facilities by the BAROV team. BAROV employed the staff and proprietary methodology of its affiliates to conduct this review.

Background

Outsourced Company began its operations (on some specified date) and currently employs approximately 1,600 personnel in one plant. There are plans to build multiple plants over the next 10 years at the same campus. Current capacity is 1.25 million manufactured units per year, with plans to double capacity by 2015. Client Company is currently outsourcing a relatively small item to Outsourced Company. Client Company is concerned about security and controls in all of its operations, including those contracted to Outsourced Company. Client Company engaged BAROV to review enterprise security at Outsourced Company.

Our relationship with the Outsourced Company was at the highest professional level at all times. From time to time, this excellent working relationship seemed strained. We learned near the end of our visit that Outsourced Company had previously experienced a similar review from a different customer and during the review was told everything was going great; however, the final report to the customer's executives was less than flattering. In hindsight, what we perceived as a misunderstanding about the scope of our review was an understandable tension about our motivation. This underlying caution on the part of Outsourced Company, combined with the language difficulties and the disjointed structure of the documentation, required that we occasionally needed to review the same items more than once. In the end, the misunderstanding about our scope and working style was resolved.

Approach

We reviewed more than four dozen presentations and hundreds of documents in both English and Chinese covering all the major policies and procedures within the scope of this engagement. We interviewed over 42 Outsourced Company employees.

Risk Assessment

Following our methodology, the project scope is determined by performing an independent risk assessment of the services outsourced. For this project, Client Company directed the work toward those areas it deemed most important.

Scope of Review

Based on our understanding of Client Company's situation and underlying risk, we performed the following work programs for this review:

- Security Policies
- IT Security Infrastructure
- Access Control—both physical and logical

- Business Continuation Management

- Malicious Software

- Network Management

- Cryptology and Files

- Materials Management

- Inventory Controls

Prior Audits or Reviews

Internal Audit Report

We viewed a copy of the latest internal audit report. BAROV's translator read the cover page and told us that there were no outstanding issues, but since it was written in Chinese we were unable to validate the contents. After conferring with Client Company it was decided that a full translation was low-priority for our review.

Assessment Reports

Each work program is summarized in a stand-alone Assessment Report (AR) in the following format. Each work program begins with a set of definitions and expectations that are repeated in this section of the AR for clarity in reading the report:

- *Situation*—This section describes the current policy and procedures (P&P) environment, with references to relevant documents in the work papers.

- *Findings*—This section presents the results of our inspection, citing specific incidents of nonconformance or issues that require discussion. We will specifically identify these incidents or issues as Item A, Item B, or Item C.

- *Recommendations*—We recommend the following actions: Items A, B, and C.

- *Disposition*—With regard to Item A, the Service Provider agrees with our recommendation and has already made changes that mitigate Item A. With regard to Item B, the Service Provider agrees with our recommendation and will make appropriate changes that mitigate Item B. With regard to Item C, the Service Provider believes that this issue is adequately addressed in another manner.

- *Conclusions*—This section provides our overall impression of this area of the assessment.

- *Follow up*—We recommend that Client Company ask the Service Provider to provide documentation of changes that mitigate Item B within a certain period to confirm the agreed upon changes. We recommend that Client Company review the Item C issue with regard to Client Company's policy, procedures and governance framework. Client Company should promptly discuss the Service Provider position with regard to Item C and ratify the approach or request that the Service Provider make changes to mitigate Client Company's concern.

Work Papers

The report described above is fully supported by professional documentation or work papers (WP), which is maintained by BAROV. These work papers are contained in four folders with the contents as follows:

- Tab A—Work Program
- Tab B—Additional Pages to Work Program
- Tab C—Service Provider Documentation
- Tab D—Other Documents including Service Provider Policy

The following is a sample of a work paper, specifically on IT security policy.

WP 1: Security Policy

Suppliers should have adhered to a documented Enterprise Policy and Procedures (P&P) manual to ensure that only properly approved users are granted access to information systems and assets. Users should be granted access on a need-to-know basis, according to job responsibilities. There exists an information security policy, approved by management that is published and communicated to all personnel who are responsible for its maintenance and review according to a defined review process. As part of the report, we will provide a situational awareness document, list our findings, recommendations for correction, prescribed disposition of the problem, and any follow-up required. As an example of a follow up, we may recommend that the Client Company ask Outsourced Company to provide a copy of the agreed changes to the P&P within six months to confirm the changes required. We recommend that Client Company review the identified issues with regard to Client Company policy, procedures and governance framework. Client Company should promptly discuss Outsourced Company's position and ratify the P&P approach or request that Outsourced Company make changes to mitigate Client Company's concerns.

Quantitative Risk Simulation, Real Options Analysis and Portfolio Optimization

WP2 to WP11 have been left out in this case study, but the sample seen in Figure 166 through Figure 167 and 14.77 illustrate a Pre-Assessment Ranking Matrix used to understand the specific risk within a specific industry and rate those risks in order of risks to be reviewed. Using the example matrix in Figure 167, we apply Risk Simulator input assumptions to the subject matter expert risk rankings, and we run simulations on the matrix in order to determine the total grand risk score for the Client Company. Using probabilistic distributions obtained from the simulation, we are now able to identify the chances that a specific category's risk and impact may exceed tolerable limits, as well as identify the critical success factors (sensitivity analysis and tornado analysis were run on this assessment matrix). Furthermore, we developed an optimization model where each element was subject to a decision variable in terms of the cost required to correct any outstanding issues, compared to the benefit obtained from having an in compliance security level, and ran it based on the Client Company's budget constraints. We were then able to create a strategy of multiple phases (sequential compound option) on when certain elements of the issues identified can first be fixed. Following this is the less critical next phase, all the while accounting for interrelationships among IT projects; for example, if a certain project requires another as a prerequisite (some platform technology that first need to be implemented before any subsequent projects can be implemented) or mutually exclusive redundant projects (the implementation of one project makes another obsolete or unnecessary).

In keeping with the belief that neither "cookie-cutter" nor "boil the ocean" approaches are cost-effective or appropriate, we use the following enterprise security assessment methodology to plan for a customized program. Our security assessment consists of four phases and nine processes. Phase 1 has four processes, Phase 2 has two processes, Phase 3 has two processes and Phase 4 has one process (Table 19).

Assumptions:

Manager's information has been received

Rated for an on-site review

After all eleven (11) domains are completed, the draft report will be completed. If issues need to be resolved, do so, else publish draft. After draft has been approved, the Executive Summary needs to be completed, and once approved, publish.

Fill out each of the sections below:

1. Security Policy
2. Organizational Security
3. Asset Classification and Control
4. Human Resources Security
5. Physical and Environmental Security
6. Communications and Operations Management
7. Access Control
8. Information Systems Acquisition, Development, and Maintenance
9. Information Security Incident Management
10. Business Continuity Management
11. Compliance

Figure 166: List of Working Papers

	Overall Rating		2.82	
	Strategic	Reputation	Compliance	Transactional
Probability Risk Assessment				
1 Security Policy	1	1.25	1.5	1.75
2 Organizational Security	2	2.25	2.5	2.75
3 Asset classification and control	3	3.25	3.5	3.5
4 Human Resources Security	4	4.25	4.5	4.75
5 Physical and Environmental Security	5	3	3	3
6 Communications and Operations Management	3	3	3	3
7 Access Control	3	3	3	3
8 Information Systems Acquisition, Development, Maintenance	3	3	3	3
9 Information Security Incident Management	3	3	3	3
10 Business Continuity Management	3	3	3	3
11 Compliance	3	3	3	3
Impact Risk Assessment				
1 Security Policy	5	2	2	1
2 Organizational Security	5	3	2	3
3 Asset classification and control	5	2	1	2
4 Human Resources Security	5	1	2	2
5 Physical and Environmental Security	5	1	1	3
6 Communications and Operations Management	5	2	2	2
7 Access Control	5	2	3	1
8 Information Systems Acquisition, Development, Maintenance	5	3	2	1
9 Information Security Incident Management	5	1	2	1
10 Business Continuity Management	5	1	1	2
11 Compliance	5	2	2	3

Risk free score is One (1) and the highest risk is Five (5)

1 2 3 4 5

Values that are accepted	1	1.25	1.5	1.75	2
Values that are accepted	2.25	2.5	2.75	3	3.25
Values that are accepted	3.5	3.75	4	4.25	4.5
Values that are accepted					

Figure 167: Assessment Matrix

	Overall Rating		1=lowest	10=highest	
Probability/Impact//Raw Score -- (5=highest risk, 1=no risk)					
Executive Summary Prioritization Criteria Matrix	**Strategic**	**Reputation**	**Compliance**	**Transactional**	**Priority**
Security Policy	3.0	1.6	1.8	1.4	1
Organizational Security	3.5	2.6	2.3	2.9	4
Asset classification and control	4.0	2.6	2.3	2.8	8
Human Resources Security	4.5	2.6	3.3	3.4	11
Physical and Environmental Security	5.0	2.0	2.0	3.0	9
Communications and Operations Management	4.0	2.5	2.5	2.5	5
Access Control	4.0	2.5	3.0	2.0	5
Information Systems Acquisition, Develop and Maint	4.0	3.0	2.5	2.0	5
Information Security Incident Management	4.0	2.0	2.5	2.0	2
Business Continuity Management	4.0	2.0	2.0	2.5	2
Compliance	4.0	2.5	2.5	3.0	9

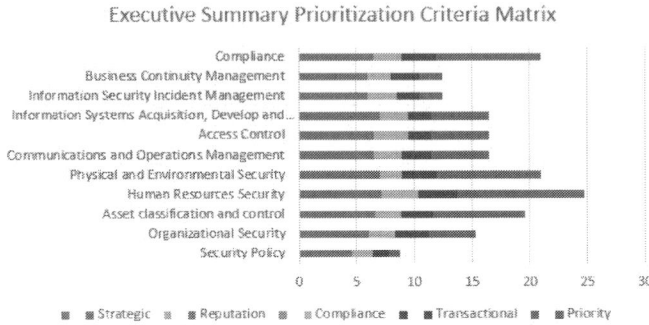

Figure 168: Ranking Matrix

Table 19: Summary of Four Phases and Nine Processes

Phase 1	Enterprise-Wide Security Requirements
Process 1	Identify Enterprise Knowledge
Process 2	Identify Operational Area Knowledge
Process 3	Identify Staff Knowledge
Process 4	Establish Security Requirements
Phase 2	Identify Infrastructure Issues
Process 5	Map Information Assets to Information Infrastructure
Process 6	Perform Infrastructure Vulnerability Evaluation
Phase 3	Determine Security Management Strategy
Process 7	Conduct Multi-Dimensional Risk Analysis
Process 8	Develop Protection Strategy
Phase 4	Develop Customized Training Program
Process 9	Develop Security Knowledge Gap Strategy

Each phase is designed to produce meaningful results for the organization. Please see the sample forms described in Figure 168 to get a flavor of the details that might be requested. Phase 1 examines the enterprise by eliciting information from people working in multiple levels of the enterprise. Phase 1 also derives the security requirements of the enterprise, based on the need for confidentiality, integrity, and/or availability of the key information assets. This phase is important because it helps in integrating unique perspectives and knowledge from multiple organizational levels and helps to build an enterprise-wide view of assets, threats, protection strategies, and risk indicators. This information can then be used to establish the security requirements of the enterprise, which is the goal of the first phase. Phase 2 is then applied to identify infrastructure issues and builds on the information identified during Phase 1. It uses the asset and threat information from Phase 1 to identify the high-priority components of the information infrastructure. Phase 2 also evaluates the information infrastructure to identify infrastructure vulnerabilities that are exposing the enterprise's assets as well as missing policies and practices. At the conclusion of Phase 2, the high-priority information infrastructure components, missing policies and practices, and vulnerabilities would have been identified. Phase 3 is then applied to determine the security risk management strategy, which involves analysis of assets, threats, and vulnerability information in the context of intrusion scenarios to identify and prioritize the information security risks to the organization. In addition, it develops and implements a protection strategy in the organization to reduce the risk to the enterprise. In addition, Phase 3 creates a comprehensive risk management plan for implementing the protection strategy and managing risks on a continual basis. The prioritized list of risks generated is used in conjunction with information from the previous phases to develop a protection strategy for the enterprise and to establish a comprehensive plan for managing security risks, which are among the goals of Phase 3. In addition, should the information supplied by staff-level employees indicate that there was some dissatisfaction among some of the employees in the company, specifically, any technical issues, these disgruntled insiders might have both the motive and the means to steal the information and would add to the risks, thereby in all probability adding to the complexity of the project. By performing a comprehensive risk assessment that considers asset, threat, and vulnerability information and puts it into the context of the enterprise, the risks facing the enterprise can be identified. In addition, personnel from all levels can understand risks when they are put into the context of the enterprise, and can make sensible decisions concerning a protection strategy.

Phase 1

- Process 1: Identify Enterprise Knowledge. This process identifies what senior managers perceive to be the key assets and their values, the threats to those assets, indicators of risk, and the current protection strategy employed by the enterprise.

- Process 2: Identify Operational Area Knowledge. This process identifies what operational area managers perceive to be the key assets and their values, the threats to those assets, indicators of risk, and the current protection strategy employed by the enterprise.

- Process 3: Identify Staff Knowledge. This process identifies what staff-level personnel perceive to be the key assets and their values, the threats to those assets, indicators of risk, and the current protection strategy employed by the enterprise.

- Process 4: Establish Security Requirements. This process integrates the individual perspectives identified in the first three processes to produce an enterprise view of the assets.

Phase 2

Uses the asset and threat information from Phase 1 to identify the high-priority components of the information infrastructure (both the physical infrastructure and the computing infrastructure). It also evaluates the information infrastructure to identify vulnerabilities. Standard catalogs of information about intrusion scenarios and vulnerabilities are used as a basis for evaluating the infrastructure. The ultimate goal of Phase 2 is to identify missing policies and practices as well as infrastructure vulnerabilities. The following two processes comprise Phase 2:

- Process 5: Map Information Assets to Information Infrastructure. This process combines Phase 1 asset and threat information with staff knowledge about the information infrastructure to establish asset locations, access paths, and data flows. This leads to the identification of the high-priority infrastructure components.

- Process 6: Perform Infrastructure Vulnerability Evaluation. This process combines the knowledge about assets, threats, risk indicators, and security requirements determined in Phase 1 with staff knowledge about the information infrastructure and standard catalogs of intrusion scenarios and vulnerabilities to identify missing policies and practices as well as infrastructure vulnerabilities.

Phase 3

This phase is applied to determine the security risk management strategy, and has two subprocesses. They analyze the assets, threats, and vulnerability information in the context of intrusion scenarios to identify and prioritize the risks to the enterprise. In addition, a protection strategy is developed and implemented in the enterprise. The ultimate goal of Phase 3 is to identify risks to the enterprise and develop a protection strategy to mitigate the highest priority risks. The following two processes comprise Phase 3:

- Process 7: Conduct Multidimensional Risk Analysis. This process analyzes the assets, threats, and vulnerability information identified in Phases 1 and 2 using intrusion scenarios to produce a set of risks to the enterprise. The risk attributes of impact and probability are estimated and then used to prioritize the risks.

- Process 8: Develop Protection Strategy. This process develops the protection strategy by identifying candidate mitigation strategies and then selecting the appropriate ones based on factors such as cost and available resources. This process also develops a comprehensive security risk management plan for implementing the protection strategy and managing risks on a continual basis.

Phase 4

This phase is used to develop customized training programs by analyzing the assets, threats, and vulnerability information in the context of intrusion scenarios, an organization can begin to understand what information is at risk. With this understanding, it can create and implement a protection strategy designed to reduce the overall risk exposure of its information assets. This phase comprises a single subprocess:

- Process 9: Develop Security knowledge Gap Strategy. This process combines all the above information and industry specific issues to tailor a training program that "fits" the organization and its current situation to meet current best practices as well as due diligence in its security practices.

CASE STUDY 17: BASEL II/III CREDIT RISK AND MARKET RISK—ANALYTICAL TECHNIQUES FOR MODELING PROBABILITY OF DEFAULT, LOSS GIVEN DEFAULT, ECONOMIC CAPITAL, VALUE AT RISK, PORTFOLIO OPTIMIZED VALUE AT RISK, INTEREST RATES AND YIELD CURVE, DELTA-GAMMA HEDGING, FLOATING AND FIXED RATES, FOREIGN EXCHANGE RISK HEDGING, VOLATILITY, COMMODITY PRICES, AND OVER-THE-COUNTER EXOTIC OPTIONS

This case study is written by the author based on consulting projects that he had performed on banks globally, and the case illustrations apply the Risk Simulator, Modeling Toolkit, and Real Options SLS software applications. For more details on some of these applications, please see two of the author's books, Advanced Analytical Models, *(Wiley Finance, 2008) and* The Banker's Handbook on Credit Risk: Implementing Basel II, *(Elsevier Science Academic Press, 2008). This is only meant to be a case study illustrating sample implementations at banks using risk analytic methods and the discussions are not meant to be step-by-step instructions.*

With the new Basel II and Basel III Accords, internationally active banks are now required to compute their own risk capital requirements using the internal ratings based (IRB) approach. Not only is adequate risk capital analysis important as a compliance obligation, it provides banks with the ability to optimize their capital through the ability to compute and allocate risks, perform performance measurements, execute strategic decisions, increase competitiveness, and enhance profitability. This case discusses the various *scientific risk management* approaches required to implement an IRB method, as well as the step-by-step models and methodologies in implementing and valuing economic capital, Value at Risk (VaR), probability of default, and loss given default, the key ingredients required in an IRB approach, through the use of advanced analytics such as Monte Carlo and historical risk simulation, portfolio optimization, stochastic forecasting, and options analysis. This case shows the use of Risk Simulator and the Modeling Toolkit software in computing and calibrating these critical input parameters. Instead of dwelling on theory or revamping what has already been written many times over, this case focuses solely on the practical modeling applications of the key ingredients to the Basel II and III Accords.

To follow along the analyses in this case, we assume that the reader already has *Risk Simulator*, *Real Options SLS*, and the *ROV Modeling Toolkit* installed, and are somewhat familiar with the basic functions of each software program. If not, please refer to www.realoptionsvaluation.com (click on the Downloads link) and watch the getting started videos, read some of the getting started case studies, or to install the latest trial versions of these software programs and their extended licenses. You can download and install the demo version of Modeling Toolkit from the website and use the password: "heteroskedasticity" when prompted. There is no trial version available; only demo versions or permanent and fully functional versions are currently available.

Probability of Default

Probability of default measures the degree of likelihood that the borrower of a loan or debt (the obligor) will be unable to make the necessary scheduled repayments on the debt, thereby defaulting on the debt. Should the obligor be unable to pay, the debt is in default, and the lenders of the debt have legal avenues to attempt a recovery of the debt, or at least partial repayment of the entire debt. The higher the default probability a lender estimates a borrower to have, the higher the interest rate the lender will charge the borrower as compensation for bearing the higher default risk.

Probability of default models are categorized as *structural* or *empirical*. Structural models look at a borrower's ability to pay based on market data such as equity prices, market and book values of asset and liabilities, as well as the volatility of these variables, and, hence, are used predominantly to estimate the probability of default of *companies* and *countries*, most applicable within the areas of commercial and industrial banking. In contrast, empirical models or credit scoring models are used to quantitatively determine the probability that a loan or loan holder will default, where the loan holder is an individual, by looking at historical portfolios of loans held, where individual characteristics are assessed (e.g., age, educational level, debt to income ratio, and so forth), making this second approach more applicable to the retail banking sector.

Structural Models of Probability of Default

Probability of default models is a category of models that assesses the likelihood of default by an obligor. They differ from regular credit scoring models in several ways. First of all, credit scoring models are usually applied to smaller credits—individuals or small businesses— whereas default models are applied to larger credits—corporations or countries. Credit scoring models are largely statistical, regressing instances of default against various risk indicators, such as an obligor's income, home renter or owner status, years at a job, educational level, debt to income ratio, and so forth, something that will be shown later in this case. Structural default models, in contrast, directly model the default process, and are typically calibrated to market variables, such as the obligor's stock price, asset value, book value of debt, or the credit spread on its bonds. Default models have many applications within financial institutions. They are used to support credit analysis and for finding the probability that a firm will default, to value counterparty credit risk limits, or to apply financial engineering techniques in developing credit derivatives or other credit instruments.

The example illustrated next uses the Merton probability of default model. This model is used to solve the probability of default of a publicly traded company with equity and debt holdings, and accounting for its volatilities in the market (Figure 169). This model is currently used by KMV and Moody's to perform credit risk analysis. This approach assumes that the book value of asset and asset volatility are unknown and solved in the model, and that the company is relatively stable and the growth rate of the company's assets are stable over time (e.g., not in startup mode). The model uses several simultaneous equations in options valuation theory coupled with optimization to obtain the implied underlying asset's market value and volatility of the asset in order to compute the probability of default and distance to default for the firm.

Illustrative Example: Structural Probability of Default Models on Public Firms

It is assumed that at this point, the reader is well versed in running simulations and optimizations in Risk Simulator. The example model used is the *Probability of Default – External Options Model* and can be accessed through *Modeling Toolkit | Prob of Default | External Options Model (Public Company)*.

To run this model (Figure 169), enter in the required inputs such as the market value of equity (obtained from market data on the firm's capitalization, that is, stock price times number of shares outstanding), equity volatility (computed in the Volatility or LPVA worksheets in the model), book value of debt and liabilities (the firm's book value of all debt and liabilities), the risk-free rate (the prevailing country's risk-free interest rate for the same maturity as the debt), and the debt maturity (the debt maturity to be analyzed, or enter 1 for the annual default probability). The comparable option parameters are shown in cells G18 to G23. All these comparable inputs are computed except for Asset Value (the market value of asset) and the Volatility of Asset. You will need to input some rough estimates as a starting point so that the analysis can be run. The rule of thumb is to set the volatility of the asset in G22 to be one fifth to half of the volatility of equity computed in G10, and the market value of asset (G19) to be approximately the sum of the market value of equity and book value of liabilities and debt (G9 and G11).

Then, an optimization needs to be run in Risk Simulator in order to obtain the desired outputs. To do this, set Asset Value and Volatility of Asset as the decision variables (make them continuous variables with a lower limit of 1% for volatility and $1 for asset, as both these inputs can only take on positive values). Set cell G29 as the objective to minimize as this is the absolute error value. Finally, the constraint is such that cell H33, the implied volatility in the default model is set to exactly equal the numerical value of the equity volatility in cell G10. Run a static optimization using Risk Simulator.

If the model has a solution, the absolute error value in cell G29 will revert to zero (Figure 170). From here, the probability of default (measured in percent) and distance to default (measured in standard deviations) are computed in cells G39 and G41.

Then, using the resulting probability of default, the relevant credit spread required can be determined using the *Credit Analysis – Credit Premium* model or some other credit spread tables (such as using the *Internal Credit Risk Rating* model).

The results indicate that the company has a probability of default at 0.87% with 2.37 standard deviations to default, indicating good creditworthiness (Figure 170).

Illustrative Example: Structural Probability of Default Models on Private Firms

In addition, several other structural models exist for computing the probability of default of a firm. Specific models are used depending on the need and availability of data. In the previous example, the firm is a publicly traded firm, with stock prices and equity volatility that can be readily obtained from the market. In this next example, we assume that the firm is privately held, meaning that there would be no market equity data available. It essentially computes the probability of default or the point of default for the company when its liabilities exceed its assets, given the asset's growth rates and volatility over time (Figure 171). It is recommended that before using this model, the previous model on external publicly traded companies is first reviewed. Similar methodological parallels exist between these two models, whereby this example builds upon the knowledge and expertise of the previous example.

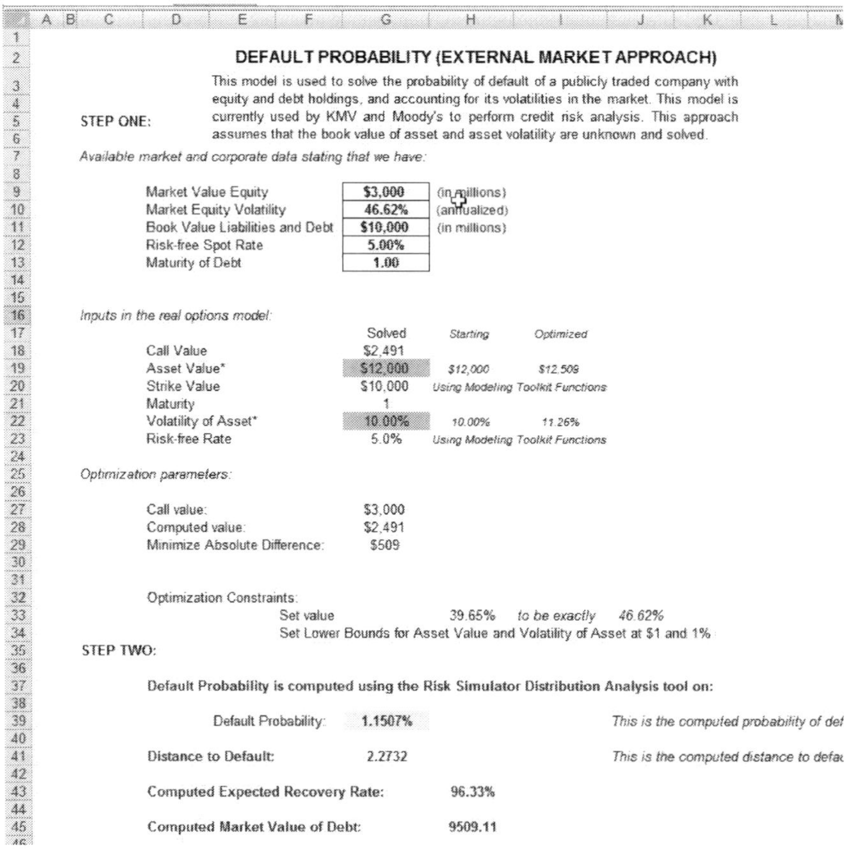

Figure 169: Probability of Default Model for External Public Firms

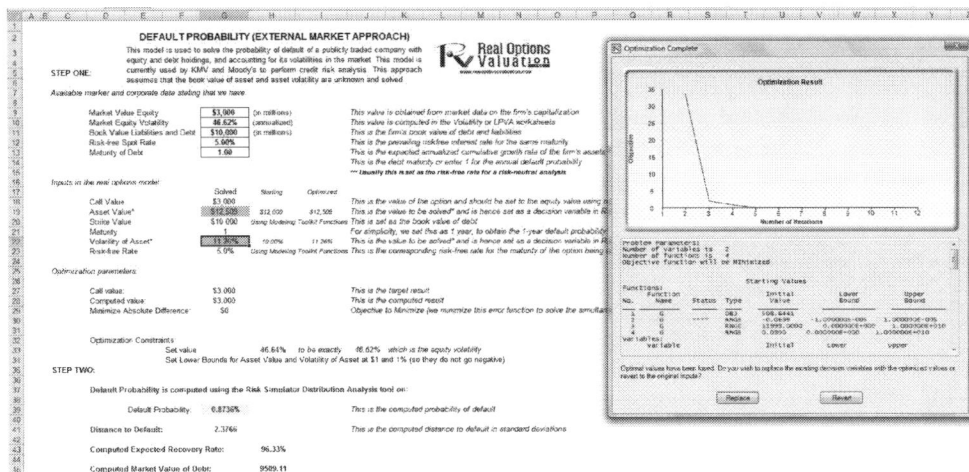

Figure 170: Optimized Model Results Showing Probability of Default

In Figure 171, the example firm with an asset value of $12M and a book value of debt at $10M with significant growth rates of its internal assets and low volatility returns a 0.67% probability of default. In addition, instead of relying on the valuation of the firm, external market benchmarks can be used if such data is available. In Figure 172, we see that additional input assumptions such as the market fluctuation (market returns and volatility) and relationship (correlation between the market benchmark and the company's assets) are required. The model used is the *Probability of Default – Merton Market Options Model* accessible from *Modeling Toolkit | Prob of Default | Merton Market Options Model (Industry Comparable)*.

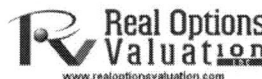

CREDIT RISK DEFAULT PROBABILITY (OPTIONS APPROACH)

VALUING DEFAULT PROBABILITY AND DISTANCE TO DEFAULT BASED ON OPTIONS MODELING OF INTERNAL DEBT

Input Assumptions	
Asset Book Value	$12.0000
Debt Book Value	$10.0000
Maturity	1.0000
Risk-free Rate	7.00%
Volatility of Asset	10.00%

This is the options approach to computing the probability of default and distance to default of a company assuming that the book values of asset and debt are known, as are the asset volatilities and anticipated annual growth rates. If the book value of assets or volatility of assets are not known and the company is publicly traded, use the External Markets model instead. This model assumes these inputs are known or the company is privately held and not traded.

Probability of Default	0.6695%
Distance to Default	2.4732

Function: B2ProbabilityDefaultMertonII (Asset Value, Strike, Maturity, Riskfree, Asset Volatility)
Function: B2ProbabilityDefaultMertonDefaultDistance(Asset Value, Strike, Maturity, Asset Volatility, Riskfree Rate)

Figure 171: Probability of Default of a Privately Held Company

MERTON MODEL OF DEBT DEFAULT PROBABILITY
VALUING THE PROBABILITY OF DEFAULT BASED ON MARKET RELATIONSHIPS

Real Options Valuation
www.realoptionsvaluation.com

Input Assumptions

Asset Value	$100.0000
Debt Value	$50.0000
Time to Maturity	1.00
Risk-free Rate	5.00%
Volatility of Asset	20.00%
Market Volatility	10.00%
Market Return	8.00%
Correlation	0.00

This models the probability of default for both public and private companies using an index or set of comparables (the market), assuming that the company's asset and debt book values are known, as well as the asset's annualized volatility. Based on this volatility and the correlation of the company's assets to the market, we can determine the probability of default.

Probability of Default   0.0150%

Function: B2ProbabilityDefaultMertoni (Asset, Debt, Maturity, Riskfree, Asset Volatility, Market Volatility, Market Return, Correlation)

Figure 172: Default Probability of a Privately Held Entity Calibrated to Market Fluctuations

Empirical Models of Probability of Default

As mentioned previously, empirical models of probability of default are used to compute an individual's default probability, applicable within the retail banking arena, where empirical or actual historical or comparable data exists on past credit defaults. The dataset in Figure 173 represents a sample of several thousand previous loans and credit or debt issues. The data shows whether each loan had defaulted or not (0 for no default, and 1 for default), as well as the specifics of each loan applicant's age, education level (1-3 indicating high school, university, or graduate professional education), years with current employer, and so forth. The idea is to model these empirical data to see which variables affect the default behavior of individuals, using Risk Simulator's *Maximum Likelihood Estimation* (MLE) tool. The resulting model will help the bank or credit issuer compute the expected probability of default of an individual credit holder of having specific characteristics.

Illustrative Example on Applying Empirical Models of Probability of Default

The example file is *Probability of Default – Empirical* and can be accessed through *Modeling Toolkit | Prob of Default | Empirical (Individuals)*. To run the analysis, select the dataset (include the headers) and make sure that the data have the same length for all variables, without any missing or invalid data points. Then, using Risk Simulator, click on *Risk Simulator | Forecasting | Maximum Likelihood Models*. A sample set of results are provided in the MLE worksheet, complete with detailed instructions on how to compute the expected probability of default of an individual.

The MLE approach applies a modified binary multivariate logistic analysis to model dependent variables to determine the expected probability of success of belonging to a certain group. For instance, given a set of independent variables (e.g., age, income, education level of credit card or mortgage loan holders), we can model the probability of default using MLE. A typical regression model is invalid because the errors are heteroskedastic and nonnormal, and the resulting estimated probability forecast will sometimes be above 1 or below 0. MLE analysis handles these problems using an iterative optimization routine. The computed results show the coefficients of the estimated MLE intercept and slopes.[33]

---

[33] For instance, the coefficients are estimates of the true population β values in the following equation: $Y = \beta_0 + \beta_1 X_1 + \beta_2 X_2 + ... + \beta_n X_n$. The standard error measures how accurate the

The coefficients estimated are actually the logarithmic odds ratios, and cannot be interpreted directly as probabilities. A quick but simple computation is first required. The approach is simple. To estimate the probability of success of belonging to a certain group (e.g., predicting if a debt holder will default given the amount of debt he or she holds), simply compute the estimated Y value using the MLE coefficients. Figure 174 illustrates an individual with 8 years at a current employer and current address, a low 3% debt to income ratio and $2,000 in credit card debt has a log odds ratio of −3.1549. Then, the inverse antilog of the odds ratio is obtained by computing:

$$\frac{\exp(estimated\ Y)}{1 + \exp(estimated\ Y)} = \frac{\exp(-3.1549)}{1 + \exp(-3.1549)} = 0.0409$$

So, such a person has a 4.09% chance of defaulting on the new debt. Using this probability of default, you can then use the *Credit Analysis – Credit Premium* model to determine the additional credit spread to charge this person given this default level and the customized cash flows anticipated from this debt holder.

PROBABILITY OF DEFAULT (EMPIRICAL METHOD USING MAXIMUM LIKELIHOOD MODELS ON HISTORICAL DATA)

Defaulted	Age	Education Level	Years with Current Employer	Years at Current Address	Household Income (Thousands $)	Debt to Income Ratio (%)	Credit Card Debt (Thousands $)	Other Debt (Thousands $)
1	41	3	17	12	176	9.3	11.36	5.01
0	27	1	10	6	31	17.3	1.36	4
0	40	1	15	14	55	5.5	0.86	2.17
0	41	1	15	14	120	2.9	2.66	0.82
1	24	2	2	0	28	17.3	1.79	3.06
0	41	2	5	5	25	10.2	0.39	2.16
0	39	1	20	9	67	30.6	3.83	16.67
0	43	1	12	11	38	3.6	0.13	1.24
1	24	1	3	4	19	24.4	1.36	3.28
0	36	1	0	13	25	19.7	2.78	2.15
0	27	1	0	1	16	1.7	0.18	0.09
0	25	1	4	0	23	5.2	0.25	0.94
0	52	1	24	14	64	10	3.93	2.47
0	37	1	6	9	29	16.3	1.72	3.01
0	48	1	22	15	100	9.1	3.7	5.4
1	36	2	9	6	49	8.6	0.82	3.4
1	36	2	13	6	41	16.4	2.92	3.81
0	43	1	23	19	72	7.6	1.18	4.29
0	39	1	6	9	61	5.7	0.56	2.91
0	41	3	0	21	26	1.7	0.1	0.34
0	39	1	22	3	52	3.2	1.15	0.51
0	47	1	17	21	43	5.6	0.59	1.82
0	28	1	3	6	26	10	0.43	2.17
0	29	1	8	6	27	9.8	0.4	2.24
1	21	2	1	2	16	18	0.24	2.64
0	25	4	0	2	32	17.6	2.14	3.49
0	45	2	9	26	69	6.7	0.71	3.92
0	43	1	25	21	64	16.7	0.95	9.74

Real Options Valuation
www.realoptionsvaluation.com

The data here represents a sample of several hundred previous loans, credit, or debt issues. The data show whether each loan had defaulted or not, as well as the specifics of each loan applicant's age, education level (1-3 indicating high school, university, or graduate professional education), years with current employer and so forth. The idea is to model these empirical data to see which variables affect the default behavior of individuals, using Risk Simulator's Maximum Likelihood Models. The resulting model will help the bank or credit issuer compute the expected probability of default of an individual credit holder of having specific characteristics.

To run the analysis, select the data on the left or any other data set (include the headers) and make sure that the data have the same length for all variables, without any missing or invalid data. Then, click on **Risk Simulator | Forecasting | Maximum Likelihood Models**. A sample set of results are provided in the MLE worksheet, complete with detailed instructions on how to compute the expected probability of default of an individual.

Figure 173: Empirical Analysis of Probability of Default

predicted coefficients are, and the Z-statistics are the ratios of each predicted coefficient to its standard error. The Z-statistic is used in hypothesis testing, where we set the null hypothesis (H_o) such that the real mean of the coefficient is equal to zero, and the alternate hypothesis (H_a) such that the real mean of the coefficient is not equal to zero. The Z-test is very important as it calculates if each of the coefficients is statistically significant in the presence of the other regressors. This means that the Z-test statistically verifies whether a regressor or independent variable should remain in the model or should be dropped. That is, the smaller the p-value, the more significant the coefficient. The usual significant levels for the p-value are 0.01, 0.05, and 0.10, corresponding to the 99%, 95%, and 90% confidence levels.

MLE Results

Log Likelihood Value   -200.507

Variable	Coefficients	Standard Error	Z-Statistic	p-Value	Sample Inputs
	-1.7003	0.7512	-2.2634	0.0236	
Age	0.0279	0.0205	1.3588	0.1742	
Education Level	0.0728	0.1447	0.5028	0.6151	
Years with Current Employer	-0.2528	0.0391	-6.4644	0.0000	8.000
Years at Current Address	-0.0952	0.0271	-3.5064	0.0005	8.000
Household Income (Thousands	0.0009	0.0125	0.0754	0.9399	
Debt to Income Ratio (%)	0.0750	0.0396	1.8934	0.0583	3.000
Credit Card Debt (Thousands $)	0.5521	0.1324	4.1697	0.0000	2.000
Other Debt (Thousands $)	0.0461	0.1005	0.4592	0.6461	

Log Odds Ratio   -3.1549

Default Probability   **4.09%**

Figure 174: MLE Results

Loss Given Default and Expected Losses

As shown previously, probability of default is a key parameter, for computing credit risk of a portfolio. In fact, the Basel II and III Accords require the probability of default as well as other key parameters such as the loss given default (LGD) and exposure at default (EAD), be reported as well. The reason is that a bank's expected loss is equivalent to:

Expected Losses = (Probability of Default) × (Loss Given Default) × (Exposure at Default)

or simply : $EL = PD \times LGD \times EAD$

PD and LGD are both percentages, whereas EAD is a value. As we have shown how to compute PD in the previous section, we will now revert to some estimations of LGD. There are again several methods used to estimate LGD. The first is through a simple empirical approach where we set *LGD = 1 – Recovery Rate*. That is, whatever is not recovered at default is the loss at default, computed as the charge off (net of recovery) divided by the outstanding balance:

$LGD = 1 - Recovery\ Rate$

or

$$LGD = \frac{Charge\ Offs\ (Net\ of\ Recovery)}{Outstanding\ Balance\ at\ Default}$$

Therefore, if market data or historical information is available, LGD can be segmented by various market conditions, types of obligor, and other pertinent segmentations (use Risk Simulator's segmentation tool to perform this). LGD can then be readily read off a chart.

A second approach to estimate LGD is more attractive in that if the bank has available information it can attempt to run some econometric models to create the best-fitting model under an ordinary least squares approach. By using this approach, a single model can be determined and calibrated, and this same model can be applied under various conditions, and no data mining is required. However, in most econometric models, a normal-transformation will have to be performed first. Suppose the bank has some historical LGD data (Figure 175), the best-fitting distribution can be found using Risk Simulator by first selecting the historical data, and then clicking on *Risk Simulator | Analytical Tools | Distributional Fitting (Single Variable)* to perform the fitting routine. The example's result is a beta distribution for the thousands of LGD values. The p-value can also be evaluated for the goodness-of-fit of the theoretical distribution (i.e., the higher the p-value, the better the distributional fit, so in this example, the historical LGD fits a beta distribution 81% of the time, indicating a good fit).

Past LGD	Normalized
49.69%	28.54%
25.76%	18.27%
14.61%	11.84%
26.91%	18.83%
18.47%	14.33%
21.29%	15.95%
26.00%	18.39%
11.84%	9.76%
51.85%	29.41%
19.35%	14.84%
24.74%	17.76%
15.68%	12.57%
14.35%	11.66%
21.36%	15.98%
35.31%	22.65%
50.71%	28.95%
28.58%	19.63%
5.96%	3.77%
3.84%	0.38%
21.70%	16.17%
71.28%	37.64%
23.49%	17.12%
20.25%	15.36%
44.01%	26.26%
31.27%	20.87%
40.86%	24.98%
26.54%	18.65%
25.29%	18.04%
28.51%	19.60%
55.40%	30.84%
31.57%	21.00%
16.30%	12.98%
24.37%	17.57%
8.46%	6.70%
77.08%	40.52%

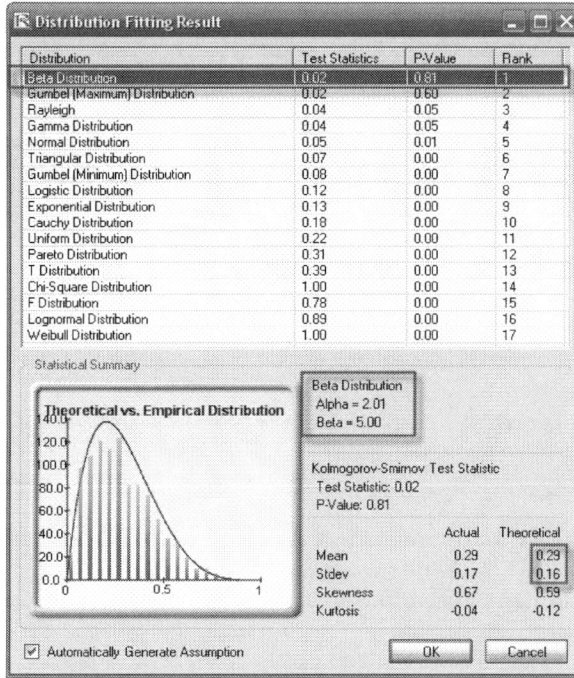

Distribution Fitting Result

Distribution	Test Statistics	P-Value	Rank
Beta Distribution	0.02	0.81	1
Gumbel (Maximum) Distribution	0.02	0.60	2
Rayleigh	0.04	0.05	3
Gamma Distribution	0.04	0.05	4
Normal Distribution	0.05	0.01	5
Triangular Distribution	0.07	0.00	6
Gumbel (Minimum) Distribution	0.08	0.00	7
Logistic Distribution	0.12	0.00	8
Exponential Distribution	0.13	0.00	9
Cauchy Distribution	0.18	0.00	10
Uniform Distribution	0.22	0.00	11
Pareto Distribution	0.31	0.00	12
T Distribution	0.39	0.00	13
Chi-Square Distribution	1.00	0.00	14
F Distribution	0.78	0.00	15
Lognormal Distribution	0.89	0.00	16
Weibull Distribution	1.00	0.00	17

Statistical Summary

Beta Distribution
Alpha = 2.01
Beta = 5.00

Kolmogorov-Smirnov Test Statistic
Test Statistic: 0.02
P-Value: 0.81

	Actual	Theoretical
Mean	0.29	0.29
Stdev	0.17	0.16
Skewness	0.67	0.59
Kurtosis	-0.04	-0.12

☑ Automatically Generate Assumption   [OK] [Cancel]

Figure 175: Fitting Historical LGD Data

Next, using the Distribution Analysis tool in Risk Simulator, obtain the theoretical mean and standard deviation of the fitted distribution (Figure 176). Then, transform the LGD variable using the *MTNormalTransform* function in the Modeling Toolkit software. For instance, the value 49.69% will be transformed and normalized to 28.54% (Figure 175). Using this newly transformed dataset, you can now run some nonlinear econometric models to determine LGD.

The following is a partial list of independent variables that might be significant for a bank, in terms of determining and forecasting the LGD value:

- Debt to capital ratio
- Profit margin
- Revenue
- Current assets to current liabilities
- Risk rating at default an done year before default
- Industry
- Authorized balance at default
- Collateral value
- Facility type
- Tightness of covenant
- Seniority of debt
- Operating income to sales ratio (and other efficiency ratios)
- Total asset, total net worth, total liabilities

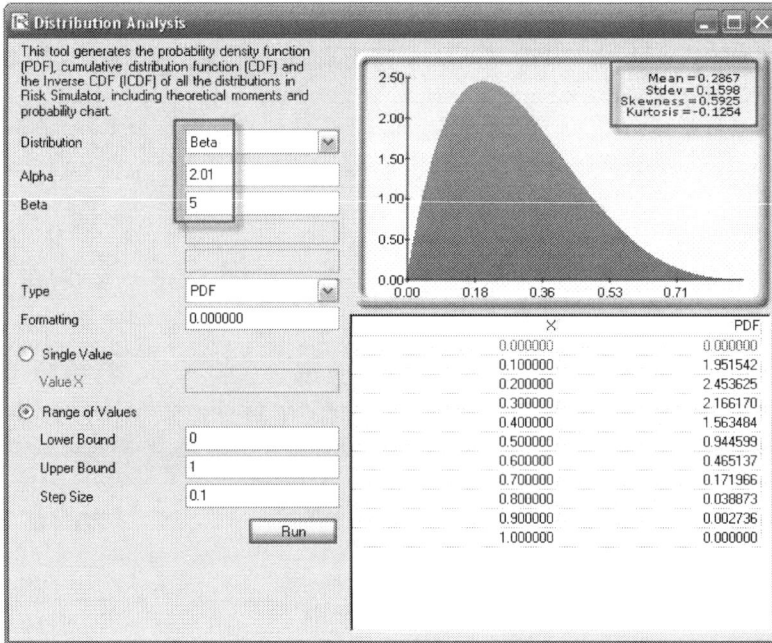

Figure 176: Distributional Analysis Tool

Economic Capital and Value at Risk

Economic capital is critical to a bank as it links a bank's earnings and returns to risks that are specific to a business line or business opportunity. In addition, these economic capital measurements can be aggregated into a portfolio of holdings. Value at Risk or (VaR) is used in trying to understand how the entire organization is affected by the various risks of each holding as aggregated into a portfolio, after accounting for their cross-correlations among various holdings. VaR measures the maximum possible loss given some predefined probability level (e.g., 99.90%) over some holding period or time horizon (e.g., 10 days). The selected probability or confidence interval is typically a decision made by senior management at the bank and reflects the board's risk appetite. Stated another way, we can define the probability level as the bank's desired probability of surviving per year. In addition, the holding period is usually chosen such that it coincides with the time period it takes to liquidate a loss position.

VaR can be computed several ways. Two main families of approaches exist: structural closed-form models and Monte Carlo risk simulation approaches. We will showcase both methods in this case, starting with the structural models.

The second and much more powerful approach is the use of Monte Carlo risk simulation. Instead of simply correlating individual business lines or assets in the structural models, entire probability distributions can be correlated using more advanced mathematical copulas and simulation algorithms in Monte Carlo simulation methods, by using Risk Simulator. In addition, tens to hundreds of thousands of scenarios can be generated using simulation, providing a very powerful stress testing mechanism for valuing VaR. In addition, distributional fitting methods are applied to reduce the thousands of data points into their appropriate probability distributions, allowing their modeling to be handled with greater ease.

Illustrative Example: Structural VaR Models

The first VaR example model shown is the *Value at Risk – Static Covariance Method,* accessible through *Modeling Toolkit | Value at Risk | Static Covariance Method.* This model is used to compute the portfolio's VaR at a given percentile for a specific holding period, after accounting for the cross-correlation effects between the assets (Figure 177). The daily volatility is the annualized volatility divided by the square root of trading days per year. Typically, positive correlations tend to carry a higher VaR compared to zero correlation asset mixes, whereas negative correlations reduces the total risk of the portfolio through the diversification effect (Figures 177–178). The approach used is a portfolio VaR with correlated inputs, where the portfolio has multiple asset holdings with different amounts and volatilities. Each asset is also correlated to each other. The covariance or correlation structural model is used to compute the VaR given a holding period or horizon and percentile value (typically 10 days at 99% confidence). Of course, the example only illustrates a few assets or business lines or credit lines for simplicity's sake. Nonetheless, using the functions in the Modeling Toolkit, many more lines, asset, or businesses can be modeled (the function MTVaRCorrelationMethod is used in this example).

VALUE AT RISK (VARIANCE-COVARIANCE METHOD)

Asset Allocation	Amount	Daily Volatility
Asset A	$1,000,000.00	1.20%
Asset B	$2,000,000.00	2.00%
Asset C	$3,000,000.00	1.89%
Asset D	$4,000,000.00	3.25%
Asset E	$5,000,000.00	4.20%

Correlation Matrix	Asset A	Asset B	Asset C	Asset D	Asset E
Asset A	1.0000	0.1000	0.1000	0.1000	0.1000
Asset B	0.1000	1.0000	0.1000	0.1000	0.1000
Asset C	0.1000	0.1000	1.0000	0.1000	0.1000
Asset D	0.1000	0.1000	0.1000	1.0000	0.1000
Asset E	0.1000	0.1000	0.1000	0.1000	1.0000

Horizon (Days)	10
Percentile	99.00%

Value at Risk (Daily)	**$655,915.30**
Value at Risk (Horizon)	**$2,074,186.30**

Daily Value at Risk (Positive Correlations)	**$2,074,186.30**
Daily Value at Risk (Zero Correlations)	**$1,889,345.26**
Daily Value at Risk (Negative Correlations)	**$1,684,340.28**

Figure 177: Computing Value at Risk Using the Structural Covariance Method

Correlation Matrix	Asset A	Asset B	Asset C	Asset D	Asset E
Asset A	1.0000	0.1000	0.1000	0.1000	0.1000
Asset B	0.1000	1.0000	0.1000	0.1000	0.1000
Asset C	0.1000	0.1000	1.0000	0.1000	0.1000
Asset D	0.1000	0.1000	0.1000	1.0000	0.1000
Asset E	0.1000	0.1000	0.1000	0.1000	1.0000

Correlation Matrix	Asset A	Asset B	Asset C	Asset D	Asset E
Asset A	1.0000	0.0000	0.0000	0.0000	0.0000
Asset B	0.0000	1.0000	0.0000	0.0000	0.0000
Asset C	0.0000	0.0000	1.0000	0.0000	0.0000
Asset D	0.0000	0.0000	0.0000	1.0000	0.0000
Asset E	0.0000	0.0000	0.0000	0.0000	1.0000

Correlation Matrix	Asset A	Asset B	Asset C	Asset D	Asset E
Asset A	1.0000	-0.1000	-0.1000	-0.1000	-0.1000
Asset B	-0.1000	1.0000	-0.1000	-0.1000	-0.1000
Asset C	-0.1000	-0.1000	1.0000	-0.1000	-0.1000
Asset D	-0.1000	-0.1000	-0.1000	1.0000	-0.1000
Asset E	-0.1000	-0.1000	-0.1000	-0.1000	1.0000

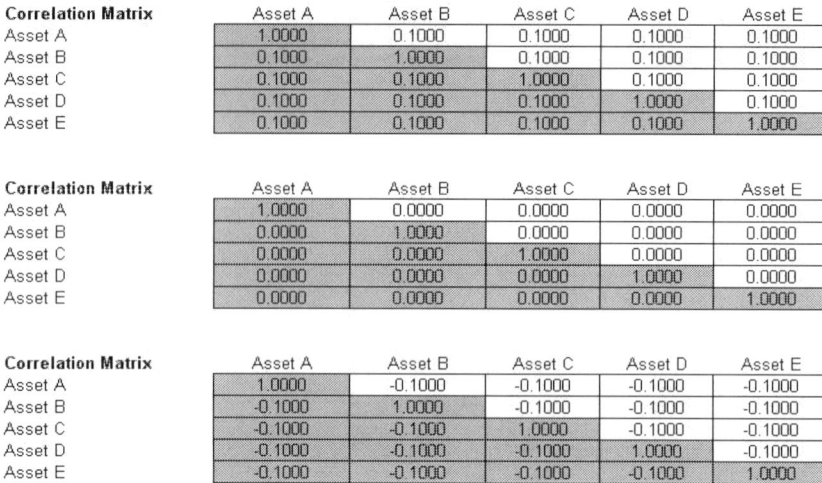

Figure 178: Different Correlation Levels

Illustrative Example: VaR Models using Monte Carlo Risk Simulation

The model used is Value at Risk – Portfolio Operational and Capital Adequacy and is accessible through *Modeling Toolkit | Value at Risk | Portfolio Operational and Capital Adequacy*. This model shows how operational risk and credit risk parameters are fitted to statistical distributions and their resulting distributions are modeled in a portfolio of liabilities to determine the Value at Risk (e.g., 99.50th percentile certainty) for the capital requirement under Basel II and III requirements. It is assumed that the historical data of the operational risk impacts (Historical Data worksheet) are obtained through econometric modeling of the Key Risk Indicators.

The *Distributional Fitting Report* worksheet is a result of running a distributional fitting routine in Risk Simulator to obtain the appropriate distribution for the operational risk parameter. Using the resulting distributional parameters, we model each liability's capital requirements within an entire portfolio. Correlations can also be inputted if required, between pairs of liabilities or business units. The resulting Monte Carlo simulation results show the Value at Risk or VaR capital requirements.

Note that an appropriate empirically-based historical VaR cannot be obtained if distributional fitting and risk-based simulations were not first run. Only by running simulations will the VaR be obtained. To perform distributional fitting, follow the steps below:

1. In the Historical Data worksheet (Figure 179), select the data area (cells C5:L104) and click on *Risk Simulator | Analytical Tools | Distributional Fitting (Single Variable)*.

2. Browse through the fitted distributions and select the best-fitting distribution (in this case, the exponential distribution with a particularly high p-value fit, as shown in Figure 180) and click *OK*.

3. You may now set the assumptions on the *Operational Risk Factors* with the exponential distribution (fitted results show *Lambda* = 1) in the Credit Risk worksheet. Note that the assumptions have already been set for you in advance. You may set them by going to cell *F27* and clicking on *Risk Simulator | Set Input Assumption*, selecting *Exponential* distribution and entering *1* for the *Lambda* value and clicking *OK*. Continue this process for the

remaining cells in column F or simply perform a *Risk Simulator Copy* and *Risk Simulator Paste* on the remaining cells:

    a.   Note that since the cells in column F have assumptions set, you will first have to clear them if you wish to reset and copy/paste parameters. You can do so by first selecting cells *F28:F126* and clicking on the *Remove Parameter* icon or select *Risk Simulator | Remove Parameter.*

    b.   Then select cell F27, click on the Risk Simulator Copy icon or select Risk Simulator | Copy Parameter, and then select cells F28:F126 and click on the Risk Simulator Paste icon or select Risk Simulator | Paste Parameter.

4.   Next, additional assumptions can be set such as the probability of default using the Bernoulli distribution (column H) and *Loss Given Default* (column J). Repeat the procedure in Step 3 if you wish to reset the assumptions.

5.   Run the simulation by clicking on the *Run* icon or clicking on *Risk Simulator | Run Simulation.*

6.   Obtain the Value at Risk by going to the forecast chart once the simulation is done running and selecting *Left-Tail* and typing in *99.50*. Hit *Tab* on the keyboard to enter the confidence value and obtain the VaR of $25,959 (Figure 181).

Another example on VaR computation is shown next, where the model Value at Risk – Right Tail Capital Requirements is used and available through *Modeling Toolkit | Value at Risk | Right Tail Capital Requirements.*

This model shows the capital requirements per Basel II and III requirements (99.95th percentile capital adequacy based on a specific holding period's Value at Risk). Without running risk-based historical and Monte Carlo simulation using Risk Simulator, the required capital is $37.01M (Figure 182) as compared to only $14.00M is required using a correlated simulation (Figure 183). This is due to the cross-correlations between assets and business lines, and can only be modeled using Risk Simulator. This lower VaR is preferred as banks can now be required to hold less capital and can reinvest the remaining capital in various profitable ventures, thereby generating higher profits.

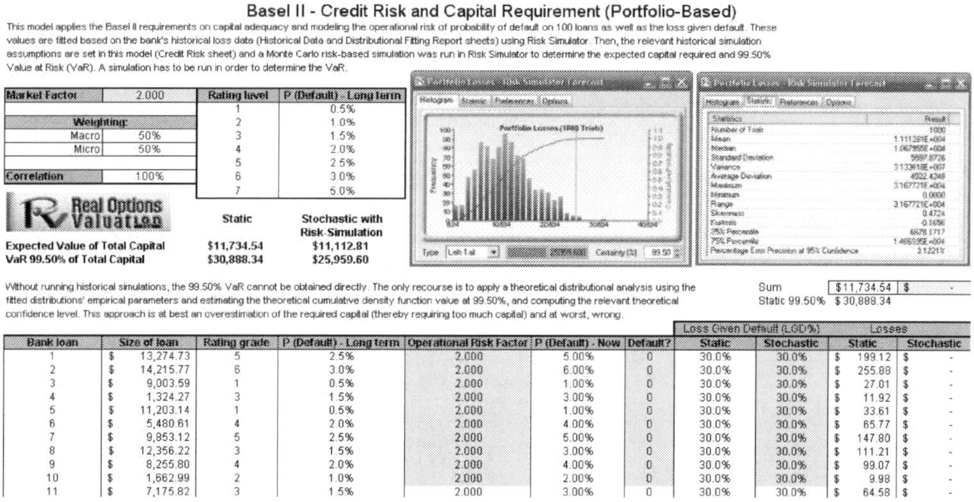

Figure 179: Sample Historical Bank Loans

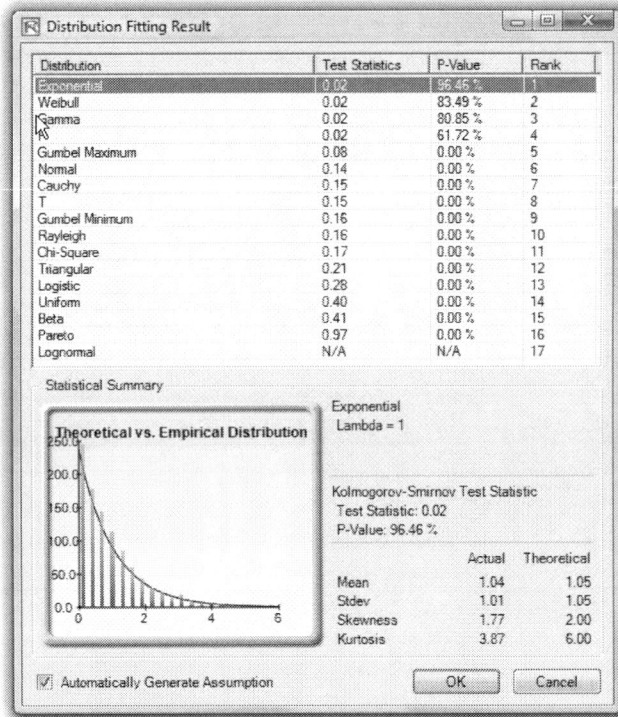

Figure 180: Data Fitting Results

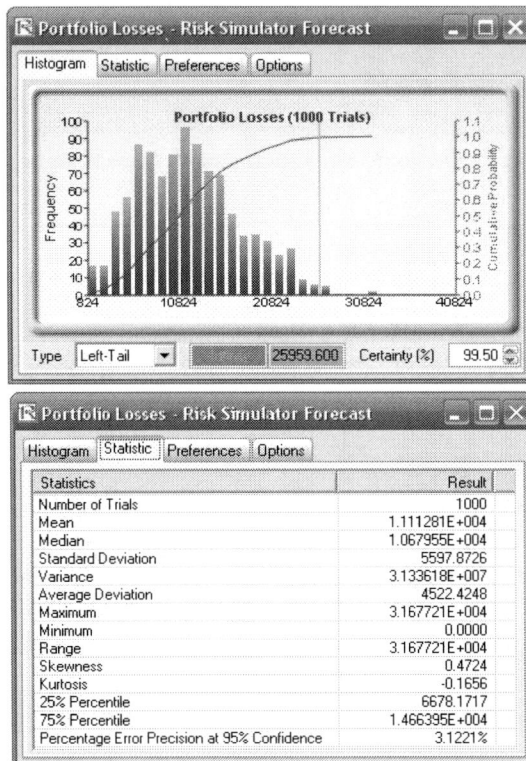

Figure 181: Simulated Forecast Results and the 99.50% Value at Risk Value

TAIL VALUE AT RISK MODEL (BASEL II REQUIREMENT)

Correlation Matrix

Line of Business	Mean Required Capital	99.95th Percentile	Capital Required	Allocation Weights	Minimum Allowed	Maximum Allowed			1	2	3	4	5	6	7	8	9	10
Business 1	$10.50	$36.52	$26.01	10.00%	5.00%	15.00%	3.48	1										
Business 2	$11.12	$47.52	$36.39	10.00%	5.00%	15.00%	4.27	2	-0.20									
Business 3	$11.77	$48.99	$37.22	10.00%	5.00%	15.00%	4.16	3	-0.13	0.35								
Business 4	$10.77	$37.34	$26.56	10.00%	5.00%	15.00%	3.47	4	-0.05	0.01	0.00							
Business 5	$13.49	$49.52	$36.03	10.00%	5.00%	15.00%	3.67	5	0.23	0.50	0.15	0.00						
Business 6	$14.24	$55.59	$41.35	10.00%	5.00%	15.00%	3.91	6	0.00	0.00	-0.15	0.00	0.03					
Business 7	$15.60	$60.24	$44.64	10.00%	5.00%	15.00%	3.86	7	0.25	0.00	-0.26	0.01	0.10	-0.10				
Business 8	$14.95	$64.69	$49.74	10.00%	5.00%	15.00%	4.33	8	0.36	-0.25	-0.60	-0.30	0.00	0.00	-0.15			
Business 9	$14.15	$61.02	$46.87	10.00%	5.00%	15.00%	4.31	9	-0.01	-0.20	0.16	0.04	-0.01	0.01	0.00	0.00		
Business 10	$10.08	$35.37	$25.29	10.00%	5.00%	15.00%	3.51											
Portfolio Total	**$12.67**	**$49.68**	**$37.01**	**100.00%**														
Total Capital Required			**$14.00**															

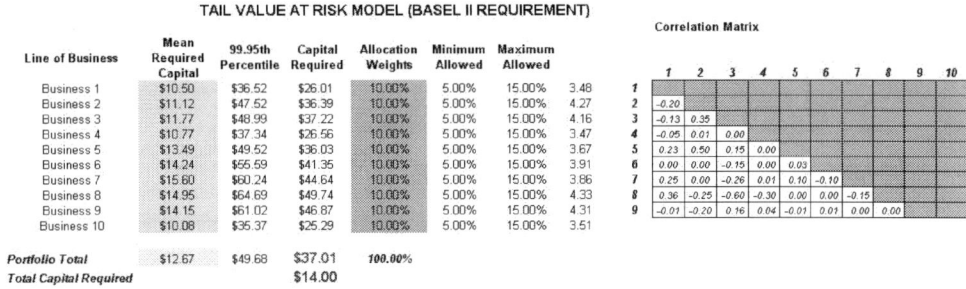

Figure 182: Right-tail VaR Model

1. To run the model, click on *Risk Simulator | Run Simulation* (if you had other models open, make sure you first click on *Risk Simulator | Change Simulation | Profile*, and select the *Tail VaR* profile before starting).

2. When simulation is complete, select *Left-Tail* in the forecast chart and enter in *99.95* in the *Certainty* box and hit *TAB* on the keyboard to obtain the value of $14.00M Value at Risk for this correlated simulation.

3. Note that the assumptions have already been set for you in advance in the model in cells *C6:C15*. However, you may set them again by going to cell *C6* and clicking on *Risk Simulator | Set Input Assumption*, selecting your distribution of choice or using the default *Normal Distribution* or perform a distributional fitting on historical data and click *OK*. Continue this process for the remaining cells in column C. You may also decide to first *Remove Parameters* of these cells in column C and setting your own distributions. Further, correlations can be set manually when assumptions are set (Figure 184) or by going to *Analytical Tools | Edit Correlations* (Figure 185) after all the assumptions are set.

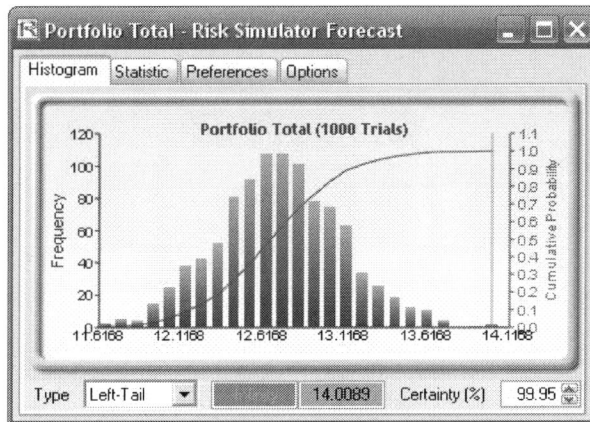

Figure 183: Simulated Results of the Portfolio VaR

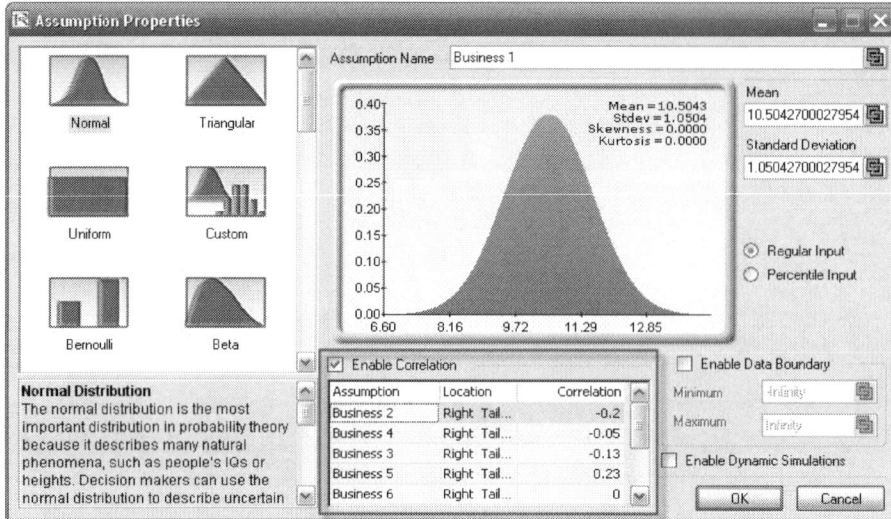

Figure 184: Setting Correlations One at a Time

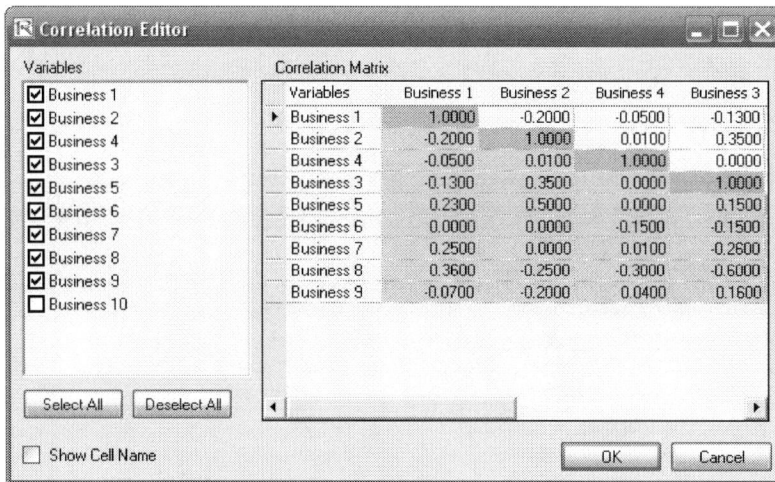

Figure 185: Setting Correlations Using the Correlation Matrix Routine

If risk simulation was not run, the VaR or economic capital required would have been $37M, as opposed to only $14M. And all cross-correlations between business lines have been modeled, as are stress and scenario tests, as well as thousands and thousands of possible iterations are run. Individual risks are now aggregated into a cumulative portfolio level VaR.

Efficient Portfolio Allocation and Economic Capital VaR

As a side note, by performing portfolio optimization, a portfolio's VaR can actually be reduced. We start by first introducing the concept of stochastic portfolio optimization through an illustrative hands-on example. Then, using this portfolio optimization technique, we apply it to four business lines or assets to compute the VaR or an unoptimized versus an optimized portfolio of assets, and see the difference in computed VaR. You will note that at the end, the optimized portfolio bears less risk and has a lower required economic capital.

Illustrative Example: Portfolio Optimization and the Effects on Portfolio VaR

Now that we understand the concepts of optimized portfolios, let us see what the effects are on computed economic capital through the use of a correlated portfolio VaR. This model uses Monte Carlo simulation and optimization routines in Risk Simulator to minimize the VaR of a portfolio of assets (Figure 186). The file used is *Value at Risk – Optimized and Simulated Portfolio VaR* which is accessible via *Modeling Toolkit | Value at Risk | Optimized and Simulated Portfolio VaR*. In this example model, we intentionally used only 4 asset classes to illustrate the effects of an optimized portfolio, whereas in real life, we can extend this to cover a multitude of asset classes and business lines. In addition, we now illustrate the use of a left-tail VaR, as opposed to a right-tail VaR, but the concepts are similar.

First, simulation is used to determine the 90% left-tail VaR (this means that there is a 10% chance that losses will exceed this VaR for a specified holding period). With an equal allocation of 25% across the 4 asset classes, the VaR is determined using simulation (Figure 187). The annualized returns are uncertain and, hence, simulated. The VaR is then read off the forecast chart. Then, optimization is run to find the best portfolio subject to the 100% allocation across the 4 projects that will maximize the portfolio's bang-for-the-buck (returns to risk ratio). The resulting optimized portfolio is then simulated once again and the new VaR is obtained (Figure 188). The VaR of this optimized portfolio is a lot less than the not optimized portfolio. That is, the expected loss is $35.8M instead of $42.2M, which means that the bank will have a lower required economic capital if the portfolio of holdings is first optimized.

VALUE AT RISK WITH ASSET ALLOCATION OPTIMIZATION MODEL

Asset Class Description	Annualized Returns	Volatility Risk	Allocation Weights	Required Minimum Allocation	Required Maximum Allocation
S&P 500	7.10%	9.80%	10.00%	10.00%	40.00%
Small Cap	9.51%	14.35%	27.30%	10.00%	40.00%
High Yield	15.90%	22.50%	22.70%	10.00%	40.00%
Govt Bonds	4.50%	7.25%	40.00%	10.00%	40.00%
		Total Weight:	100.00%		

Correlation Matrix	S&P 500	Small Cap	High Yield	Govt Bonds
S&P 500	1.0000	0.7400	0.6500	0.5500
Small Cap	0.7400	1.0000	0.4200	0.3100
High Yield	0.6500	0.4200	1.0000	0.2300
Govt Bonds	0.5500	0.3100	0.2300	1.0000

Covariance Matrix	S&P 500	Small Cap	High Yield	Govt Bonds
S&P 500	0.0096	0.0104	0.0143	0.0039
Small Cap	0.0104	0.0206	0.0136	0.0032
High Yield	0.0143	0.0136	0.0506	0.0038
Govt Bonds	0.0039	0.0032	0.0038	0.0053

Starting Value	$1,000,000.00
Term (Years)	5.00

Annualized Return	8.72%	Profit/Loss	$87,151.94
Portfolio Risk	9.84%	Return to Risk Ratio	88.59%
Ending Value	$1,087,151.94		

Specifications of the optimization model:

Objective:	*Maximize Return to Risk Ratio (E28)*
Decision Variables:	*Allocation Weights (E6:E9)*
Restrictions on Decision Variables:	*Minimum and Maximum Required (F6:G9)*
Constraints:	*Portfolio Total Allocation Weights 100% (E10 is set to 100%)*

Figure 186: Computing Value at Risk (VaR) with Simulation

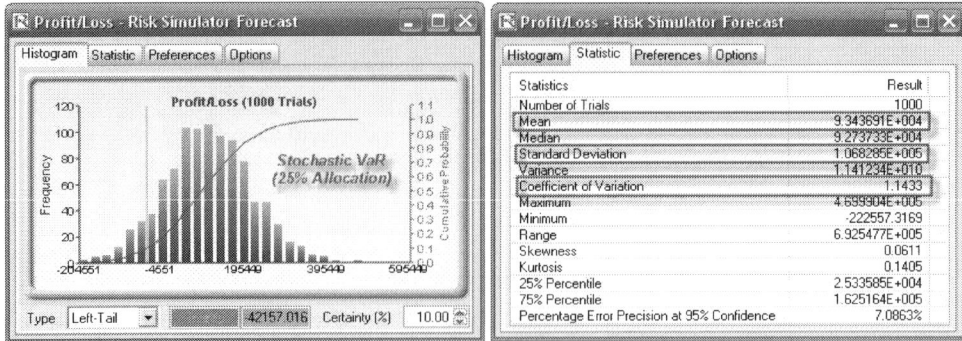

Figure 187: Unoptimized Value at Risk

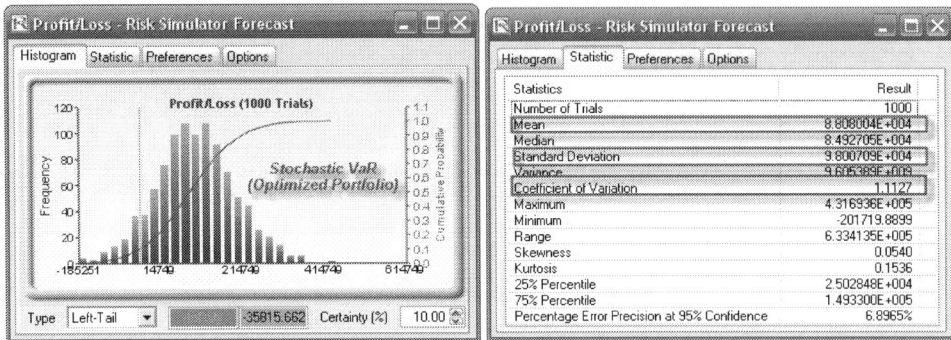

Figure 188: Optimal Portfolio's Value at Risk through Optimization and Simulation

Illustrative Example: Risk Analysis – Interest Rate Risk

File Name: Risk Analysis – Interest Rate Risk

Location: *Modeling Toolkit | Risk Analysis | Interest Rate Risk*

Brief Description: Applies duration and convexity measures to account for a bond's sensitivity and how interest rate shifts can affect the new bond price, and how this new bond price can be approximated using these sensitivity measures

Requirements: Modeling Toolkit, Risk Simulator

Modeling Toolkit Functions Used: *MTBondPriceDiscrete, MTModifiedDuration, MTConvexityDiscrete*

Banks selling fixed income products and vehicles need to understand interest rate risks. This model uses duration and convexity to show how fixed income products react under various market conditions. To compare the effects of interest rate and credit risks on fixed income investments, this model uses modified duration and convexity (discrete discounting) to analyze the effects of a change in interest rates on the value of a bond or debt (Figure 189).

Duration and convexity are sensitivity measures that describe exposure to parallel shifts in the spot interest rate yield curve, applicable to individual fixed income instruments or entire fixed income portfolios. These sensitivities cannot warn of exposure to more complex movements in the spot curve, including tilts and bends, only parallel shifts. The idea behind duration is simple. Suppose a portfolio has a duration measure of 2.5 years. This means that the portfolio's value will decline about 2.5% for each 1% increase in interest rates—or rise about 2.5% for each 1% decrease in interest rates. Typically, a bond's duration will be positive but exotic instruments such as mortgage backed securities may have negative durations, or portfolios that short fixed income instruments or pay fixed for floating on an interest rate swap. Inverse floaters tend to have large positive durations. Their values change significantly for small changes in rates. Highly leveraged fixed income portfolios tend to have very large (positive or negative) durations.

In contrast, convexity summarizes the second-most significant piece of information, or the nonlinear curvature of the yield curve, whereas duration measures the linear or first-approximation sensitivity. Duration and convexity have traditionally been used as tools for immunization or asset-liability management. To avoid exposure to parallel spot curve shifts, an organization (such as an insurance company or defined benefit pension plan) with significant fixed income exposures might perform duration matching by structuring its assets so that their duration matches the duration of its liabilities so the two offset each other. Even more effective (but less frequently practical) is duration-convexity matching, in which assets are structured so that durations and convexities match.

INTEREST RATE RISK

Face Value	$100.00
Coupon Rate	5.50%
Maturity	30.00
Current Interest Rate	5.50%
Interest Rate Shift	0.25%

Original Bond Price	$100.00	
Modified Duration	14.5337	
Convexity	321.0265	
	Duration and Convexity	**Using New Rates**
New Price After Shift	$96.47	$96.46
Price Change After Shift	-3.53%	-3.54%

Cash Flow	Interest Rates	Year	Shifted Interest Rates
$5.50	5.50%	1	5.75%
$5.50	5.50%	2	5.75%
$5.50	5.50%	3	5.75%
$5.50	5.50%	4	5.75%
$5.50	5.50%	5	5.75%
$5.50	5.50%	6	5.75%
$5.50	5.50%	7	5.75%
$5.50	5.50%	8	5.75%
$5.50	5.50%	9	5.75%
$5.50	5.50%	10	5.75%

Figure 189: Interest Rate Risk

Illustrative Example: Risk Hedging – Delta-Gamma Hedging

File Name: Risk Analysis – Delta Gamma Hedge

Location: *Modeling Toolkit | Risk Analysis | Delta Gamma Hedge*

Brief Description: Sets up a delta-gamma riskless and costless hedge in determining the number of call options to sell and buy, number of common stocks to buy and the borrowing amount required, to setup a perfect arbitrage-free hedge

Requirements: Modeling Toolkit

Modeling Toolkit Functions Used: *MTDeltaGammaHedgeCallSold,*
MTDeltaGammaHedgeSharesBought,
MTDeltaGammaHedgeMoneyBorrowed

The Delta-Gamma hedge (Figure 190) provides a hedge against larger changes in the asset value. This is done by buying some equity shares and a call option, which are funded by borrowing some amount of money and selling a call option at a different strike price. The net amount is a zero sum game, making this hedge completely effective in generating a zero delta and zero gamma for the portfolio, just like in a delta hedge, where the total portfolio's delta is zero (e.g., to offset a positive delta of some underlying assets, call options are sold to generate sufficient negative delta to completely offset the existing deltas to generate a zero delta portfolio). The problem of delta neutral portfolios is that secondary changes, that is, larger shocks, are not hedged. Delta-gamma hedged portfolios, on the contrary, hedge both delta and gamma risk, making it a much more expensive to generate. The typical problem with such a hedging vehicle is that in larger quantities, buying and selling additional options or underlying assets may change the market value and prices of the same instruments used to perform the hedge. Therefore, typically, a dynamic hedge, or continuously changing hedge portfolios might be required.

DELTA-GAMMA HEDGE

Asset	$100.00
Strike for Call Sold	$95.00
Strike for Call Bought	$100.00
Maturity for Call Sold	0.50
Maturity for Call Bought	0.75
Riskfree	8.00%
Volatility	20.00%
DividendRate	3.00%

Sell Calls	**$9.7258**
Shares to Buy	**($6.9058)**
Buy Calls	**($9.1991)**
Borrow This Amount	**$6.3791**
Delta-Gamma-Neutral Position Sum	**$0.0000**

Figure 190: Delta-gamma Hedging

Illustrative Example: Risk Hedging – Delta Hedging

File Name: Risk Analysis – Delta Hedge

Location: *Modeling Toolkit | Risk Analysis | Delta Hedge*

Brief Description: Sets up a delta riskless and costless hedge in determining the number of call options to sell, number of common stocks to buy and the borrowing amount required, to setup a costless hedge

Requirements: Modeling Toolkit

Modeling Toolkit Functions Used: *MTDeltaHedgeCallSold, MTDeltaHedgeSharesBought, MTDeltaHedgeMoneyBorrowed*

The Delta hedge (Figure 191) provides a hedge against small changes in the asset value by buying some equity shares of the asset and financing it through selling a call option and borrowing some money. The net should be a zero sum game to provide a hedge where the portfolio's delta is zero. For instance, an investor computes the portfolio delta of some underlying asset, and offsets this delta through buying or selling some additional instruments such that the new instruments will offset the delta of the existing underlying assets. Typically, say an investor holds some stocks or commodity like gold in the long position, creating a positive delta for the asset. To offset this, he or she sells some calls to generate negative delta, such that the amount of the call options sold on the gold is sufficient to offset the delta in the portfolio.

DELTA HEDGE

Asset	$100.00
Strike	$95.00
Maturity	0.50
Riskfree	8.00%
Volatility	20.00%
DividendRate	3.00%

Sell 1 Call	**$9.7258**
Shares to Buy	**($71.8275)**
Borrow This Amount	**$62.1018**
Delta-Neutral Position Sum	**$0.0000**

Figure 191: Delta Hedging

Illustrative Example: Risk Hedging – Effects of Fixed versus Floating Rates (Swaps)

File Name: Risk Hedging – Effects of Fixed versus Floating Rates

Location: *Modeling Toolkit | Risk Hedging | Effects of Fixed versus Floating Rates*

Brief Description: Sets up various levels of hedging to determine the impact on earnings per share

Requirements: Modeling Toolkit

This model illustrates the impact to financial earnings and earnings before interest and taxes (EBIT) on a hedged versus unhedged position (Figure 192). The hedge is done through an interest rate swap payments. Various scenarios of swaps (different combinations of fixed rate versus floating rate debt are tested and modeled) can be generated in this model to determine the impact to earnings per share (EPS) and other financial metrics. The foreign exchange cash-flow hedge model (shown next) goes into more detail on the hedging aspects of foreign exchange through the use of risk simulation.

IMPACTS OF FIXED VERSUS FLOATING RATE INTEREST PAYMENTS

Assumptions

EBIT	$3,000,000
Shares Outstanding	$500,000
Tax Rate	40.00%
Total Debt	$8,000,000
Fixed Interest Rate	7.00%
LIBOR	6.00%
10-Year Swap Rate	5.00%

		Scenarios		
Initial Debt Structure (before swap)	Current	1	2	3
% of Total Debt in Fixed-rate Debt	50.00%	50.00%	50.00%	50.00%
% of Total Debt in Floating-rate Debt	50.00%	50.00%	50.00%	50.00%
Desired Debt Structure (after swap)				
% of Total Debt in Fixed-rate Debt	50.00%	30.00%	100.00%	0.00%
% of Total Debt in Floating-rate Debt	50.00%	70.00%	0.00%	100.00%
Change in Interest Rates	0.00%	1.00%	0.50%	0.10%
Financials				
Fixed-rate Debt	7.00%	7.00%	7.00%	7.00%
Floating-rate Debt	8.00%	9.00%	8.50%	8.10%
EBIT	3,000,000	3,000,000	3,000,000	3,000,000
Interest Expense	(600,000)	(672,000)	(560,000)	(648,000)
Net Income before Taxes	2,400,000	2,328,000	2,440,000	2,352,000
Earnings	1,440,000	1,396,800	1,464,000	1,411,200
EPS	2.8800	2.7936	2.9280	2.8224
Change in Interest Expense		72,000	(40,000)	48,000
Change in Earnings		(43,200)	24,000	(28,800)

Figure 192: Impacts of an Unhedged Versus Hedged Position

Illustrative Example: Risk Hedging – Foreign Exchange Cash Flow Model

File Name: Risk Hedging – Foreign Exchange Cash Flow Model

Location: *Modeling Toolkit | Risk Hedging | Foreign Exchange Cash Flow Model*

Brief Description: This model illustrates how to use Risk Simulator for simulating foreign exchange rates to determine if the value of a hedged fixed exchange rate or floating unhedged rate is worth more

Requirements: Modeling Toolkit, Risk Simulator

This is a cash flow model used to illustrate the effects of hedging foreign exchange rates (Figure 193). The tornado sensitivity analysis illustrates that foreign exchange rate, or forex, has the highest effects on the profitability of the project (shown in the Excel model). Suppose for the moment that the project undertaken is in a foreign country (FC) and the values obtained are denominated in FC currency, and the parent company is in the United States (U.S.) and requires that the net revenues be repatriated back to the U.S. The question we try to ask here is what is the appropriate forex rate to hedge at and the appropriate costs for that particular rate? Banks will be able to provide your firm with the appropriate pricing structure for various exchange forward rates but by using the model here, we can determine the added value of the hedge and, hence, can decide if the value added exceeds the cost to obtain the hedge. This model is already preset for you to run a simulation on.

The *Forex Data* worksheet shows historical exchange rates between the FC and U.S. Dollar. Using these values, we can create a *custom* distribution (we simply used the rounded values in our illustration) which is already preset in this example model.

However, should you wish to replicate creating the simulation model, you can follow the steps below:

1. Start a new profile (*Risk Simulator | New Profile*) and give it an appropriate name.

2. Go to the *Forex Data* worksheet and select the data in cells *K6:K490* and click on *Edit | Copy* or *Ctrl + C*.

3. Select an empty cell (e.g., cell *K4*) and click on *Risk Simulator | Set Input Assumption* and select *Custom Distribution*.

4. Click on *Paste* to paste the data into the custom distribution, then *Update Chart* to view the results on the chart. Then, *File | Save* and save the newly created distribution to your hard drive. Close the set assumption dialog.

5. Go to the *Model* worksheet and select the *Forex* cell (*J9*) and click on *Risk Simulator | Set Input Assumption*, and choose *Custom*, then click on *Open* a distribution and select the previously saved custom distribution.

6. You may continue to set assumptions across the entire model, and set the *NPV* cell (*G6*) as a forecast (*Risk Simulator | Set Output Forecast*).

7. *RUN* the simulation with the custom distribution to denote an unhedged position. You can then rerun the simulation but this time, delete the custom distribution (use the *Delete Simulation Parameter* icon and not Excel's delete function nor hitting the keyboard's delete key) and enter in the relevant hedged exchange rate, indicating a fixed rate. You may create a report after each simulation to compare the results.

From the sample analysis, we see the following:

	Mean ($'000)	Stdev ($'000)	% Confidence ($'000)	CV (%)
Unhedged	2292.82	157.94	2021 to 2550	6.89%
Hedged at 0.85	2408.81	132.63	2199 to 2618	5.51%
Hedged at 0.83	2352.13	129.51	2147 to 2556	5.51%
Hedged at 0.80	2267.12	124.83	2069 to 2463	5.51%

From this table, several things are evident:

- The higher the hedged exchange rate is, the more profitable the project (e.g., 0.85 USD/FC is worth more than 0.80 USD/FC).

- The relative risk ratio, computed as the coefficient of variation (CV, or the standard deviation divided by the mean) is the same regardless of the exchange rate, we long as it is hedged.

- The CV is lower for hedged positions than unhedged positions, indicating that the relative risk is reduced by hedging.

- It seems that the exchange rate hedge should be above 0.80, such that the hedged position is more profitable than the unhedged.

- In comparing a hedged versus unhedged position, we can determine the amount of money the hedging is worth, for instance, going with a 0.85 USD/FC means that on average, the hedge is worth $115,990,000 (computed as $2,408.81 – $2,292.82 denominated in thousands). This means that as long as the cost of the hedge is less than this amount, it is a good idea to pursue the hedge.

Cash Flow Model

Base Year	2006	Sum PV Net Benefits	FC 3,809.62		
Start Year	2006	Sum PV Investments	FC 1,389.08		
Discount Rate	15.00%	Net Present Value	FC 2,420.54		
Private-Risk Discount Rate	5.00%	Internal Rate of Return	54.64%		
Terminal Period Growth Rate	2.00%	Return on Investment	174.25%		
Tax Rate	40.00%	Profitability Index	2.74	Forex Rate (USD/FC)	0.85000

	2006	2007	2008	2009	2010	2011	2012	2013	2014	2015
Prod A Price	FC 10.00	FC 10.50	FC 11.00	FC 11.50	FC 12.00	FC 12.00	FC 12.00	FC 12.00	FC 12.00	FC 12.00
Prod B Price	FC 12.25	FC 12.50	FC 12.75	FC 13.00	FC 13.25	FC 13.25	FC 13.25	FC 13.25	FC 13.25	FC 13.25
Prod C Price	FC 15.15	FC 15.30	FC 15.45	FC 15.60	FC 15.75	FC 15.75	FC 15.75	FC 15.75	FC 15.75	FC 15.75
Prod A Quantity	50	50	50	50	50	50	50	50	50	50
Prod B Quantity	35	35	35	35	35	35	35	35	35	35
Prod C Quantity	20	20	20	20	20	20	20	20	20	20
Total Revenues (Local Currency)	FC 1,231.75	FC 1,268.50	FC 1,305.25	FC 1,342.00	FC 1,378.75	FC 1,378.75	FC 1,378.75	FC 1,378.75	FC 1,378.75	FC 1,378.75
Direct Cost of Goods Sold	FC 184.76	FC 190.28	FC 195.79	FC 201.30	FC 206.81	FC 206.81	FC 206.81	FC 206.81	FC 206.81	FC 206.81
Gross Profit	FC 1,046.99	FC 1,078.23	FC 1,109.46	FC 1,140.70	FC 1,171.94	FC 1,171.94	FC 1,171.94	FC 1,171.94	FC 1,171.94	FC 1,171.94
Operating Expenses	FC 157.50	FC 157.50	FC 157.50	FC 157.50	FC 157.50	FC 157.50	FC 157.50	FC 157.50	FC 157.50	FC 157.50
Sales, General and Admin. Costs	FC 15.75	FC 15.75	FC 15.75	FC 15.75	FC 15.75	FC 15.75	FC 15.75	FC 15.75	FC 15.75	FC 15.75
Operating Income (EBITDA)	FC 873.74	FC 904.98	FC 936.21	FC 967.45	FC 998.69	FC 998.69	FC 998.69	FC 998.69	FC 998.69	FC 998.69
Depreciation	FC 10.00	FC 10.00	FC 10.00	FC 10.00	FC 10.00	FC 10.00	FC 10.00	FC 10.00	FC 10.00	FC 10.00
Amortization	FC 3.00	FC 3.00	FC 3.00	FC 3.00	FC 3.00	FC 3.00	FC 3.00	FC 3.00	FC 3.00	FC 3.00
EBIT	FC 860.74	FC 891.98	FC 923.21	FC 954.45	FC 985.69	FC 985.69	FC 985.69	FC 985.69	FC 985.69	FC 985.69
Interest	FC 2.00	FC 2.00	FC 2.00	FC 2.00	FC 2.00	FC 3.00	FC 4.00	FC 5.00	FC 6.00	FC 7.00
EBT	FC 858.74	FC 889.98	FC 921.21	FC 952.45	FC 983.69	FC 982.69	FC 981.69	FC 980.69	FC 979.69	FC 978.69
Taxes	FC 343.50	FC 355.99	FC 368.49	FC 380.98	FC 393.48	FC 393.08	FC 392.68	FC 392.28	FC 391.88	FC 391.48
Net Income	FC 515.24	FC 533.99	FC 552.73	FC 571.47	FC 590.21	FC 589.61	FC 589.01	FC 588.41	FC 587.81	FC 587.21
Depreciation/Amort	FC 13.00	FC 13.00	FC 13.00	FC 13.00	FC 13.00	FC 13.00	FC 13.00	FC 13.00	FC 13.00	FC 13.00
Net Working Capital	FC 0.00	FC 0.00	FC 0.00	FC 0.00	FC 0.00	FC 0.00	FC 0.00	FC 0.00	FC 0.00	FC 0.00
Capital Expenditures	FC 0.00	FC 0.00	FC 0.00	FC 0.00	FC 0.00	FC 0.00	FC 0.00	FC 0.00	FC 0.00	FC 0.00
Free Cash Flow	FC 528.24	FC 546.99	FC 565.73	FC 584.47	FC 603.21	FC 602.61	FC 602.01	FC 601.41	FC 600.81	FC 4,709.36
Investments	FC 500.00		FC 1,500.00							
Net Free Cash Flow	-FC 1,105.97	FC 546.99	FC 565.73	FC 584.47	FC 603.21	FC 602.61	FC 602.01	FC 601.41	FC 600.81	FC 4,709.36

Figure 193: Hedging Foreign Exchange Risk Cash Flow Model

Illustrative Example: Risk Hedging – Hedging Foreign Exchange Exposure

File Name: Risk Hedging – Hedging Foreign Exchange Exposure

Location: *Modeling Toolkit | Risk Hedging | Hedging Foreign Exchange Exposure*

Brief Description: This model illustrates how to use Risk Simulator for simulating foreign exchange rates to determine the value of a hedged currency option position

Requirements: Modeling Toolkit, Risk Simulator

This model is used to simulate possible foreign exchange spot and future prices and the effects on the cash flow statement of a company under a freely floating exchange rate versus using currency options to hedge the foreign exchange exposure (Figure 194).

Hedging Foreign Exchange Exposure with Currency Options

Months	Jan	Feb	Mar	April	May	June	July
FX Spot Rate (HKD/USD)	7.80	7.40	7.60	7.30	7.10	7.20	7.40
FX Strike Rate (HKD/USD)	7.80	7.80	7.80	7.80	7.80	7.80	7.80
Maturity (Years)	0.5833	0.5000	0.4167	0.3333	0.2500	0.1667	0.0833
Risk Free Rate US	6.08%	6.08%	6.08%	6.08%	6.08%	6.08%	6.08%
Risk Free Rate HK	5.06%	5.06%	5.06%	5.06%	5.06%	5.06%	5.06%
Volatility	15.00%	15.00%	15.00%	15.00%	15.00%	15.00%	15.00%
Quantity of Options Hedge Position	10,000,000	10,000,000	10,000,000	10,000,000	10,000,000	10,000,000	10,000,000
Currency Put Option Value (HKD/USD)	0.3229	0.5191	0.3795	0.5533	0.7012	0.6034	0.4102
Market Value of Hedge	3,229,135	5,191,009	3,794,813	5,532,845	7,012,229	6,034,435	4,102,320
Intrinsic Value	0	4,000,000	2,000,000	5,000,000	7,000,000	6,000,000	4,000,000
Time Value	3,229,135	1,191,009	1,794,813	532,845	12,229	34,435	102,320

FINANCIAL STATEMENTS IMPACTS - MARK TO MARKET

Balance Sheet (in 000's)	Jan	Feb	Mar	April	May	June	July
Option Contract	3,229,135	5,191,009	3,794,813	5,532,845	7,012,229	6,034,435	4,102,320
Other Comp Income (SE)		4,000,000	2,000,000	5,000,000	7,000,000	6,000,000	4,000,000

Income Statement (in 000's)							
Hedge Effectiveness gain or loss per period		(2,038,126)	603,805	(1,261,969)	(520,615)	22,206	67,884
Hedge Effectiveness sum of all periods							(3,126,816)
Market Cost of Hedge (Current Period)							3,229,135
Income from Option Exercise							4,000,000
Net Valuation of Hedging							770,865
Income from Hedging							74,770,865
Income from No Hedge							74,000,000
Loss Distribution from Hedging							3,229,135
Loss Distribution from No Hedge							4,000,000

Figure 194: Hedging Currency Exposures with Currency Options

Figure 195 shows the effects of the Value at Risk (VaR) of a hedged versus unhedged position. Clearly the right-tailed VaR of the loss distribution is higher without the currency options hedge. Figure 195 shows that there is a lower risk, lower risk to returns ratio, higher returns, and less swing in the outcomes of a currency hedged position than an exposed position, with Figure 196 showing the simulated forecast statistics of the loss distribution. Finally, Figure 197 shows the hedging effectiveness, that is, how often the hedged is in the money and become usable.

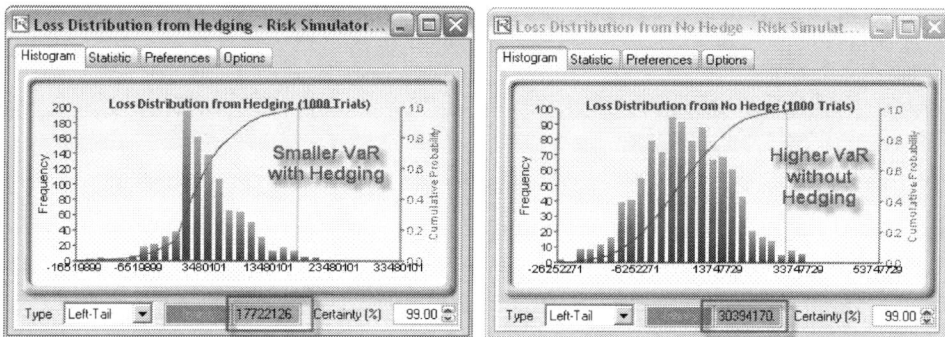

Figure 195: Values at Risk (VaR) of Hedged Versus Unhedged Positions

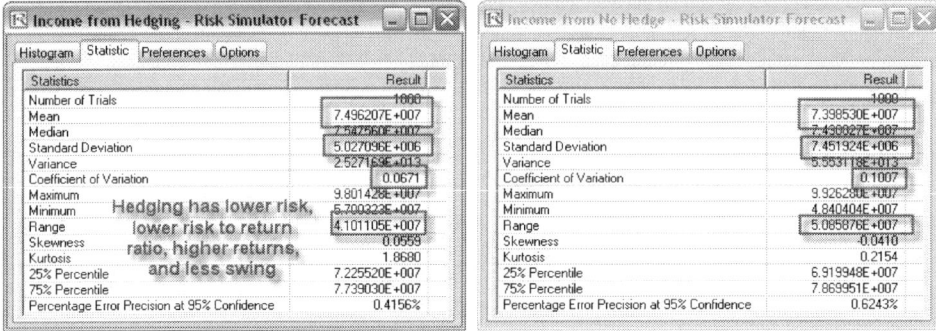

Figure 196: Forecast Statistics of the Loss Distribution

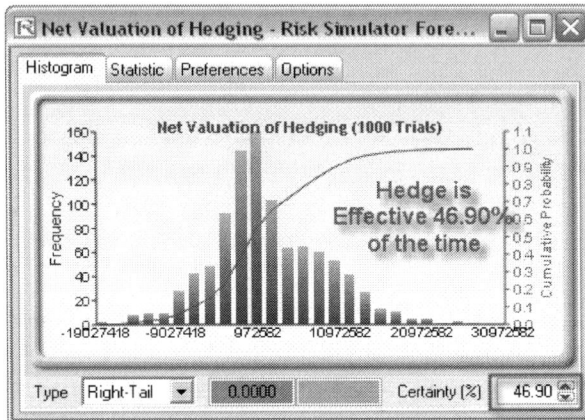

Figure 197: Hedging Effectiveness

Illustrative Example: Volatility – Implied Volatility

File Name: Volatility – Implied Volatility

Location: *Modeling Toolkit | Volatility | Implied Volatility*

Brief Description: This model computes the implied volatilities using an internal optimization routine, given the values of a call or put option, as well as all their required inputs

Requirements: Modeling Toolkit, Risk Simulator

Modeling Toolkit Function Used: *MTImpliedVolatilityCall, MTImpliedVolatilityPut*

This implied volatility computation is based on an internal iterative optimization, which means it will work under typical conditions (without extreme volatility values, i.e., too small or too large). It is always good modeling technique to recheck the imputed volatility using an options model to make sure the answers coincide with each other before adding more sophistication to the model. That is, given all the inputs in an option analysis as well as the option value, the volatility can be imputed (Figure 198).

IMPLIED VOLATILITY FUNCTION

Asset	$100.00
Strike	$95.00
Maturity	0.50
Riskfree	8.00%
Volatility	25.00%
DividendRate	3.00%

Call Option	$10.9126
Put Option	$3.6764

Implied Volatility Calculation

Call Option	25.00%
Put Option	25.00%

Figure 198 Getting the Implied Volatility from Options

Illustrative Example: Volatility – Volatility Computations

File Name: Volatility – Volatility Computations

Location: *Modeling Toolkit | Volatility | Volatility Computations*

Brief Description: This model uses Risk Simulator to apply Monte Carlo simulation in order to compute a project's volatility measure

Requirements: Modeling Toolkit, Risk Simulator

There are several ways to estimate the volatility used in the option models. The most common and valid approaches are:

Logarithmic Cash Flow Returns Approach or Logarithmic Stock Price Returns Approach: This method is used mainly for computing the volatility of liquid and tradable assets such as stocks in financial options; however, it is sometimes used for other traded assets such as price of oil and price of electricity. The drawback is that discounted cash flow models with only a few cash flows will generally overstate the volatility and this method cannot be used when negative cash flows occur. This means that this volatility approach is only applicable for financial instruments and not for real options analysis. The benefits include its computational ease, transparency, and modeling flexibility of the method. In addition, no simulation is required to obtain a volatility estimate. The approach is simply to take the annualized standard deviation of the logarithmic relative returns of the time series data as the proxy for volatility. The Modeling Toolkit function *MTVolatility* is used to compute this volatility, where the time-series of stock prices is arranged in time-series (can be chronological or reverse chronological). See the **Log Cash Flow Returns** example model under the Volatility section of Modeling Toolkit for details.

Exponentially Weighted Moving Average (EWMA) Models: This approach is similar to the previous logarithmic cash flow returns approach, using the *MTVolatility* function, to compute the annualized standard deviation of the natural logarithms of relative stock returns. The difference here is that the most recent value will have a higher weight than values further in the past. A *lambda* or weight variable is required (typically, industry standards set this at 0.94), where the most recent volatility is weighted at this lambda value, and the period before that is (1 – lambda), and so forth. See the **EWMA** example model under the Volatility section of Modeling Toolkit for details.

Logarithmic Present Value Returns Approach: This approach is used mainly when computing the volatility of assets with cash flows. A typical application is in real options. The drawback of this method is that simulation is required to obtain a single volatility and is not applicable for highly traded liquid assets such as stock prices. The benefit includes the ability to accommodate certain negative cash flows and applies more rigorous analysis than the logarithmic cash flow returns approach, providing a more accurate and conservative estimate of volatility when assets are analyzed. In addition, within, say, a cash flow model, multiple simulation assumptions can be set up (we can insert any types of risks and uncertainties such as related assumptions, correlated distributions and non-related inputs, multiple stochastic processes, and so forth), and we allow the model to distill all the interacting risks and uncertainties in these simulated assumptions, and we obtain the single value volatility, which represents the integrated risk of the project. See the **Log Asset Returns** example model under the Volatility section of Modeling Toolkit for details.

Management Assumptions and Guesses: This approach is used for both financial options and real options. The drawback is that the volatility estimates are very unreliable and are only subjective best guesses. The benefit of this approach is its simplicity—this method is very easy to explain to management the concept of volatility, both in execution and interpretation. That is, most people understand what probability is, but have a hard time understanding what volatility is. Using this approach, we can impute one from another. See the **Probability to Volatility** example model under the Volatility section of Modeling Toolkit for details.

Generalized Autoregressive Conditional Heteroskedasticity (GARCH) Models: These models are used mainly for computing the volatility on liquid and tradable assets such as stocks in financial options, this model is sometimes used for other traded assets such as price of oil and price of electricity. The drawback is that a lot of data is required, advanced econometric modeling expertise is required, and this approach is highly susceptible to user manipulation. The benefit is that rigorous statistical analysis is performed to find the best-fitting volatility curve, providing different volatility estimates over time. The EWMA model is a simple weighting model whereas the GARCH model is a more advanced analytical and econometric model that requires advanced algorithms such as generalized method of moments to obtain the volatility forecasts.

Illustrative Example: Yield Curve – CIR Model

File Name: Yield Curve – CIR Model

Location: *Modeling Toolkit | Yield Curve | CIR Model*

Brief Description: This is the CIR model for estimating and modeling the term structure of interest rates and yield curve approximation assuming the interest rates are mean-reverting

Requirements: Modeling Toolkit, Risk Simulator

Modeling Toolkit Function Used: *MTCIRBondYield*

The yield curve is the time-series relationship between interest rates and the time to maturity of the debt. The more formal mathematical description of this relationship is called the term structure of interest rates. The yield curve can take on various shapes. The normal yield curve means that yields rise as maturity lengthens and the yield curve is positively sloped, reflecting investor expectations for the economy to grow in the future (and, hence, an expectation that inflation rates will rise in the future). An inverted yield curve occurs when the opposite happens, where the long-term yields fall below short-term yields, and long-term investors will settle for lower yields now if they think the economy will slow or even decline in the future, indicative of a worsening economic situation in the future (and, hence, an expectation that inflation will remain low in the future). Another potential situation is a flat yield curve, signaling uncertainty in the economy. The yield curve can also be humped or show a smile or a frown. The yield curve over time can change in shape through a twist or bend, a parallel shift, or a movement on one end versus another.

As the yield curve is related to inflation rates as discussed above, and central banks in most countries has the ability to control monetary policy to target inflation rates, inflation rates are mean-reverting in nature. This also implies that interest rates are mean-reverting, as well as stochastically changing over time.

This section shows the Cox–Ingersoll–Ross (CIR) model that is used to compute the term structure of interest rates and yield curve (Figure 199). The CIR model assumes a mean-reverting stochastic interest rate. The rate of reversion and long-run mean rates can be determined using Risk Simulator's statistical analysis tool. If the long-run rate is higher than the current short rate, the yield curve is upward sloping, and vice versa.

CIR MODEL
YIELD CURVE CONSTRUCTION

Input Assumptions

Time to Maturity of the Bond or Debt (Years)	1.00
Riskfree Rate (Short Rate)	3.00%
Long-run Mean Rate	8.00%
Annualized Volatility of Interest Rate	6.00%
Market Price of Interest Rate Risk	0.00%
Rate of Mean Reversion	25.00%

Yield of Zero Coupon Bond   3.5744%

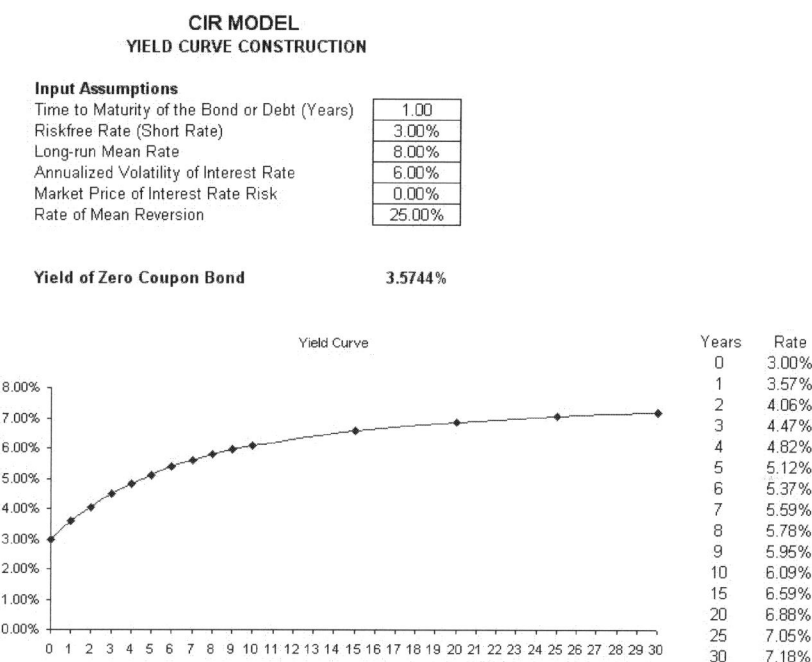

Years	Rate
0	3.00%
1	3.57%
2	4.06%
3	4.47%
4	4.82%
5	5.12%
6	5.37%
7	5.59%
8	5.78%
9	5.95%
10	6.09%
15	6.59%
20	6.88%
25	7.05%
30	7.18%

Figure 199: CIR Model

Illustrative Example: Yield Curve – Curve Interpolation BIM Model

File Name: Yield Curve – Curve Interpolation BIM

Location: *Modeling Toolkit | Yield Curve | Curve Interpolation BIM*

Brief Description: This is the BIM model for estimating and modeling the term structure of interest rates and yield curve approximation using curve interpolation methods

Requirements: Modeling Toolkit, Risk Simulator

Modeling Toolkit Function Used: *MTYieldCurveBIM*

A number of alternative methods exist for estimating the term structure of interest rates and the yield curve. Some are fully-specified stochastic term structure models while others are simply interpolation models. The former are models such as the CIR and Vasicek models (illustrated in other sections in this book), while the latter are interpolation models such as the Bliss or Nelson approach. This section looks at the Bliss interpolation model (Figure 200) for generating the term structure of interest rates and yield curve estimation. This model requires several input parameters whereby their estimations require some econometric modeling techniques to calibrate their values. The Bliss approach is a modification of the Nelson–Siegel method by adding an additional generalized parameter. Virtually any yield curve shape can be interpolated using these models, which are widely used at banks around the world.

YIELD CURVE - INTERPOLATION MODEL

Beta 0	0.0500
Beta 1	0.1000
Beta 2	0.1000
Lambda 1	0.2000
Lambda 2	0.2000

Time	Rate
1	8.91%
2	7.00%
3	6.33%
4	6.00%
5	5.80%
6	5.67%
7	5.57%
8	5.50%
9	5.44%
10	5.40%
11	5.36%
12	5.33%
13	5.31%
14	5.29%
15	5.27%
16	5.25%
17	5.24%
18	5.22%
19	5.21%
20	5.20%
21	5.19%
22	5.18%
23	5.17%
24	5.17%
25	5.16%
26	5.15%
27	5.15%
28	5.14%
29	5.14%
30	5.13%

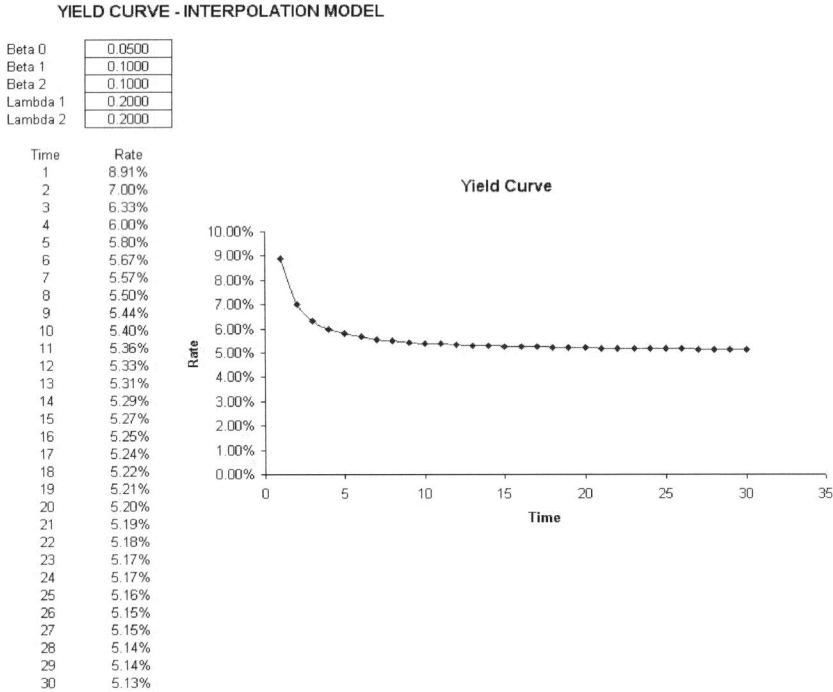

Figure 200: BIM Model

Illustrative Example: Yield Curve – Curve Spline Interpolation and Extrapolation Model

File Name: Yield Curve – Spline Interpolation and Extrapolation

Location: *Modeling Toolkit | Yield Curve | Spline Interpolation and Extrapolation*

Brief Description: This is the multidimensional cubic spline model for estimating and modeling the term structure of interest rates and yield curve approximation using a curve interpolation and extrapolation methods

Requirements: Modeling Toolkit, Risk Simulator

Modeling Toolkit Function Used: *MTCubicSpline*

The cubic spline polynomial interpolation and extrapolation model is used to "fill in the gaps" of missing spot yields and term structure of interest rates whereby the model can be used to both interpolate missing data points within a time series of interest rates (as well as other macroeconomic variables such as inflation rates and commodity prices or market returns) and also used to extrapolate outside of the given or known range, useful for forecasting purposes.

In Figure 201, the actual U.S. Treasury risk-free rates are shown, and entered into the model as known values. The timing of these spot yields are entered as Years (the known X value inputs), whereas the known risk-free rates are the known Y values. Using the "MTCubicSpline" function, we can now interpolate the in-between risk-free rates that are missing as well as the rates outside of the given input dates. For instance, the risk-free Treasury rates given include 1-month, 3-month, 6-month, 1-year, and so forth, until the 30-year rate. Using these data, we can interpolate the rates for say, 5 months or 9 months, and so forth, as well as extrapolate beyond the 30-year rate.

Years	Spot Yields
0.0833	4.55%
0.2500	4.47%
0.5000	4.52%
1.0000	4.39%
2.0000	4.13%
3.0000	4.16%
5.0000	4.26%
7.0000	4.38%
10.0000	4.56%
20.0000	4.88%
30.0000	4.84%

These are the yields that are known and are used as inputs in the Cubic Spline Interpolation and Extrapolation model

Spline Interpolation and Extrapolation Results

Years	Yield	Notes
0.5	4.52%	Interpolate
1.0	4.39%	Interpolate
1.5	4.21%	Interpolate
2.0	4.13%	Interpolate
2.5	4.13%	Interpolate
3.0	4.16%	Interpolate
3.5	4.19%	Interpolate
4.0	4.22%	Interpolate
4.5	4.24%	Interpolate
5.0	4.26%	Interpolate
5.5	4.29%	Interpolate
6.0	4.32%	Interpolate
6.5	4.35%	Interpolate
7.0	4.38%	Interpolate
7.5	4.41%	Interpolate
8.0	4.44%	Interpolate
8.5	4.47%	Interpolate
9.0	4.50%	Interpolate
9.5	4.53%	Interpolate
10.0	4.56%	Interpolate
10.5	4.59%	Interpolate
11.0	4.61%	Interpolate
11.5	4.64%	Interpolate
12.0	4.66%	Interpolate
12.5	4.68%	Interpolate
13.0	4.70%	Interpolate
13.5	4.72%	Interpolate
14.0	4.74%	Interpolate

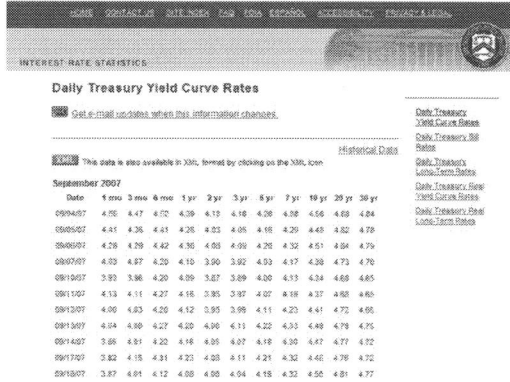

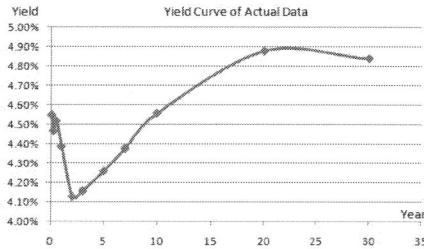

Figure 201: Cubic Spline Model

Illustrative Example: Yield Curve – Forward Rates from Spot Rates

File Name: Yield Curve – Forward Rates from Spot Rates

Location: *Modeling Toolkit | Yield Curve | Forward Rates from Spot Rates*

Brief Description: This is a bootstrap model used to determine the implied forward rate given two spot rates

Requirements: Modeling Toolkit, Risk Simulator

Modeling Toolkit Function Used: *MTForwardRate*

Given two spot rates (from Year 0 to some future time periods), you can determine the implied forward rate between these two time periods. For instance, if the spot rate from Year 0 to Year 1 is 8%, and the spot rate from Year 0 to Year 2 is 7% (both yields are known currently), the implied forward rate from Year 1 to Year 2 (that will occur based on current expectations) is 6%. This is simplified by using the MTForwardRate function in Modeling Toolkit (Figure 202).

FORWARD RATES
COMPUTING FORWARD RATES FROM SPOT RATES

Input Assumptions

Spot Rate 1	8.00%
Spot Rate 2	7.00%
Time of Spot Rate 1	1.00
Time of Spot Rate 2	2.00

Forward Rate   **6.00%**

Figure 202: Forward Rate Extrapolation

Illustrative Example: Yield Curve – Vasicek Model

File Name: Yield Curve – Vasicek Model

Location: *Modeling Toolkit | Yield Curve | Vasicek Model*

Brief Description: The Vasicek model is used to create the term structure of interest rates and to reconstruct the yield curve assuming the underlying interest rates are mean-reverting and stochastic

Requirements: Modeling Toolkit, Risk Simulator

Modeling Toolkit Function Used: *MTVasicekBondYield*

This is the Vasicek model used to compute the term structure of interest rates and yield curve. The Vasicek model assumes a mean-reverting stochastic interest rate (Figure 203). The rate of reversion and long-run mean rates can be determined using Risk Simulator's statistical analysis tool. If the long-run rate is higher than the current short rate, the yield curve is upward sloping, and vice versa.

The yield curve is the time-series relationship between interest rates and the time to maturity of the debt. The more formal mathematical description of this relationship is called the term structure of interest rates. As discussed previously, the yield curve can take on various shapes. The normal yield curve means that yields rise as maturity lengthens and the yield curve is positively sloped, reflecting investor expectations for the economy to grow in the future (and, hence, an expectation that inflation rates will rise in the future). An inverted yield curve occurs when the opposite happens, where the long-term yields fall below short-term yields, and long-term investors will settle for lower yields now if they think the economy will slow or even decline in the future, indicative of a worsening economic situation in the future (and, hence, an expectation that inflation will remain low in the future). Another potential situation is a flat yield curve, signaling uncertainty in the economy. The yield curve can also be humped or show a smile or a frown. The yield curve over time can change in shape through a twist or bend, a parallel shift, or a movement on one end versus another.

As the yield curve is related to inflation rates as discussed above, and central banks in most countries has the ability to control monetary policy to target inflation rates, inflation rates are mean-reverting in nature. This also implies that interest rates are mean-reverting, as well as stochastically changing over time.

A Czech mathematician, Oldrich Vasicek, in a 1977 paper proved that bond prices on a yield curve over time and various maturities are driven by the short end of the yield curve, or the short-term interest rates, using a risk-neutral martingale measure. In his work the mean-reverting Ornstein–Uhlenbeck process was assumed; hence the resulting Vasicek model requires that a mean-reverting interest rate process be modeled (rate of mean reversion and long-run mean rates are both inputs in the Vasicek model).

VASICEK MODEL
YIELD CURVE CONSTRUCTION

Input Assumptions

Time to Maturity of the Bond or Debt (Years)	1.00
Riskfree Rate (Short Rate)	2.00%
Long-run Mean Rate	8.00%
Annualized Volatility of Interest Rate	2.00%
Market Price of Interest Rate Risk	0.00%
Rate of Mean Reversion	20.00%

Yield of Zero Coupon Bond   **2.5562%**

Years	Rate
1	2.56%
2	3.03%
3	3.45%
4	3.81%
5	4.12%
6	4.40%
7	4.64%
8	4.86%
9	5.05%
10	5.22%
15	5.83%
20	6.21%
25	6.46%
30	6.63%

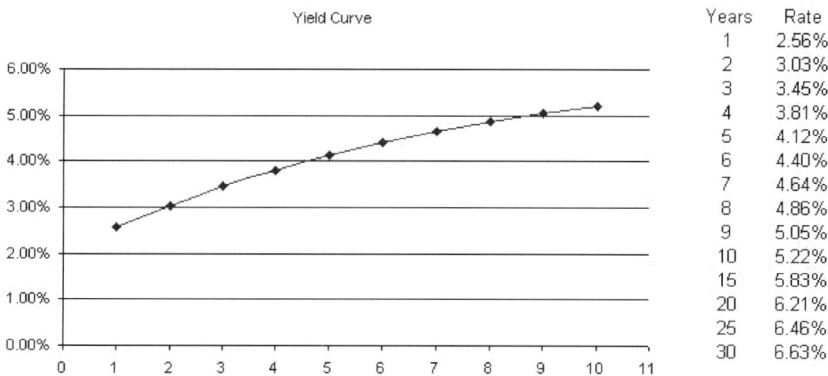

Figure 203: Using the Vasicek Model to Generate a Yield Curve

Illustrative Example: Stochastic Forecasting of Interest Rates and Stock Prices

File Name: Forecasting – Stochastic Processes

Location: *Modeling Toolkit | Forecasting | Stochastic Processes*

Brief Description: This sample model illustrates how to simulate Stochastic Processes (Brownian Motion Random Walk, Mean-Reversion, Jump-Diffusion, and Mixed Models)

Requirements: Modeling Toolkit, Risk Simulator

A stochastic process is a sequence of events or paths generated by probabilistic laws. That is, random events can occur over time but are governed by specific statistical and probabilistic rules. The main stochastic processes include Random Walk or Brownian Motion, Mean-Reversion and Jump-Diffusion. These processes can be used to forecast a multitude of variables that seemingly follow random trends but yet are restricted by probabilistic laws. We can use Risk Simulator's *Stochastic Process* module to simulate and create such processes. These processes can be used to forecast a multitude of time-series data including stock prices, interest rates, inflation rates, oil prices, electricity prices, commodity prices, and so forth.

Stochastic Process Forecasting

To run this model, simply:

1. Select *Simulation | Forecasting | Stochastic Processes.*

2. Enter a set of relevant inputs or use the existing inputs as a test case (Figure 204).

3. Select the relevant process to simulate.

4. Click on *Update Chart* to view the updated computation of a single path or click *OK* to create the process.

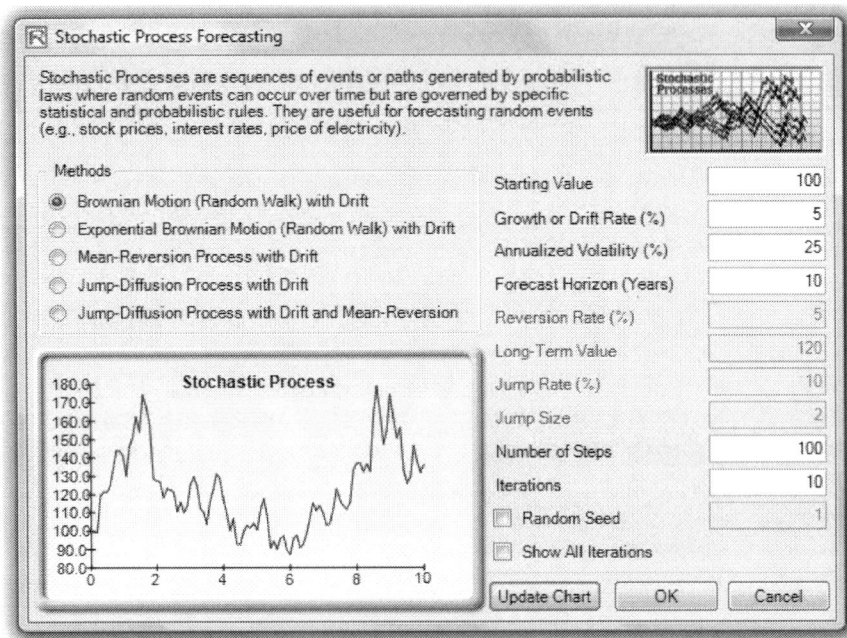

Figure 204: Running a Stochastic Process Forecast

For your convenience, the analysis Report sheet is included in the model. A stochastic time-series chart and forecast values are provided in the report as well as each step's time period, mean, and standard deviation of the forecast. The mean values can be used as the single-point estimate or assumptions can be manually generated for the desired time period. That is, finding the appropriate time period, create an assumption with a normal distribution with the appropriate mean and standard deviation computed. A sample chart with 10 iteration paths is included to graphically illustrate the behavior of the forecasted process.

18

CASE STUDY 18: IT INFORMATION SECURITY INTRUSION RISK MANAGEMENT

This case study looks at information systems security attack profile as well as provides decision analysis and support on the optimal investment. This case is contributed by Mark A. Benyovszky, Managing Director of Zero Delta Center for Enterprise Alignment. Zero Delta CfEA is a research and development organization that specializes in helping companies to align their strategic and tactical efforts.

There are several models illustrated in this case study and available in the Modeling Toolkit. First, the IT Bandwidth Requirements for Streaming Media model shows how to create forecasts for media streaming environments for off-peak and peak media consumptions cycles. The model explains how to use historical time series data to establish an understanding of the future demand for media consumption. This model also explores how the Delphi Method can be used when historical data does not exist or when there is significant uncertainty surrounding the demand for new media types that require more bandwidth or have 'chattier' communication channels.

The IT Intrusion Management model shows how to create an information systems security attack profile, determine the probabilities of occurrence of different types of attacks, assess the financial and operational impact that an attack has on an organization, and how to arrive at the level of investment (in technology security solutions (e.g., Intrusion Detection Systems, Intrusion Prevention Systems, Network Behavior Analysis solutions, etc.)) necessary to mitigate the profiled attacks.

Finally, the IT Storage and CPU Demand model illustrates how to create forecasts for future information system storage and CPU demand. The model explains how to use historical time series data to establish an understanding of the future demand for media storage and computing cycles. This model also explores how the Delphi Method can be used when historical data does not exist or when there is significant uncertainty surrounding the demand for new media types that require more storage space and where CPU cycles are being consumed by expensive encoding and decoding processes.

Organizations of all sizes rely upon technology to support a wide-range of business processes that span the spectrum from back-office finance and accounting to mid-office manufacturing, distribution, and other operational support functions, to front-office sales, marketing, and customer support functions. As a general rule of thumb, larger organizations have more complex system environments and significantly greater volumes of data along with a wide range of different types of information.

If you were to look across industries, there are different degrees of sensitivity of both the systems and information that are employed. For example, financial and insurance companies store critical and very sensitive information (financial transactions and personal medical histories) about their customers, and an energy company engaged in gas transmission and distribution relies upon critical technology systems that control the flow of gas through complex pipeline networks.

Regardless of the specific industry an organization is involved with or the size of the company, the underlying technology systems and the data and information they consume and produce are significant business assets. Like any asset, they must be protected. In order to protect these assets, we must understand what their individual and collective risk profiles look like.

Protecting these assets is of paramount concern. Technology systems are interconnected across private, semi-private, and public networks. Every second (perhaps you prefer nanoseconds, picoseconds, or attoseconds—depending upon your "geekiness factor") of every day, information moves across these networks—most of the time the information moves about intentionally, on other occasions it does not.

We can think of this information and these systems in the context of an information security asset portfolio. It is important for us to quantify the value of each class of system or set of information, which will help us to understand, according to a scale of sensitivity, which assets require greater protection. As higher value assets are likely to be greater targets for attack (based on the basic risk/reward equation).

We can then apply various methods against the portfolio to determine the composite (a high-level view) risk level of the portfolio; risk profiles of categories of assets; and individual asset risk profiles (detailed view). This approach enables us to gain a better grasp on our information and technology asset portfolio, and provides us with the ability to determine how much to invest to protect each class of assets.

While the specific approaches and processes that are required to perform this initial portfolio structuring is beyond the scope of this case study, determining the probabilities of events occurring against these assets and what the resultant outcomes are likely to be is at the center of our discussion. This case study will assume that this structuring process has already been completed. Specifically, there are five steps to undergo, including:

- Step 1: Create Environment Details

- Step 2: Create Attack Models

- Step 3: Create Attack Scenarios

- Step 4: Determine Financial Impact

- Step 5: Arrive at Investment Decision

Now, let us get on with the heart of our discussion. Monte Carlo simulation provides us with an effective way to estimate losses associated with a given attack. Mote Carlo simulation addresses the "flaw of averages" problem that plagues many single-point estimates or estimates based upon standard averages.

For the sake of this discussion, we will explore how we applied this approach to a large gas transmission and distribution company. The company (which we will refer to as Acme T&D) is one of the largest natural gas transmission and distribution companies in North America. Acme T&D has an extensive gas pipeline network that supplies natural gas to wholesalers and retailers in some of the largest markets throughout North America.

Energy companies fit in a unique category of organizations that use technology at the core of their business operations. Acme T&D relies upon an extensive industrial control system known in the industry as SCADA (Supervisory Control and Data) and PCM (Process Control System) systems. These systems are composed of a number of devices that are distributed throughout the gas pipeline network; these components are used to control the flow of gas through the network. It supplies critical information, such as gas flow-rate, temperature of the gas, and pressure at various points through the network, to a system operator who then makes certain decisions of what to do to keep the pipeline at an operationally efficient level—always supplying gas where it's needed and when it's needed in a dynamic environment that changes on a consistent basis.

These systems are critical not only to the operations of Acme T&D but they are critical also to the greater infrastructure of the United States. If the transmission and distribution of natural gas is interrupted for a significant period of time it can have downstream effects that could be economically (the suspended operations of manufacturing companies that rely upon natural gas) or personally (lack of gas to run a furnace in the cold of winter) devastating.

Clearly, these SCADA systems would be categorized as business critical assets with the highest priority placed on them vis-à-vis their protection.

STEP 1: Create Environment Details

When we consider the extent to which an attack will cause damage, we must identify the factors that drive the top end of our model. These factors will be different for each company (with similarities for companies within the same industry).

For Acme T&D our greatest concerns, from an operational perspective, are the count and types of networks in the environment, and employee productivity (we will take into account separately how operations are impacted when a threat impacts a SCADA network). The reason for using employee productivity as a factor is due to the fact that when networks are down or systems are unreachable (for whatever reason), employees are directly impacted (we use this in this example because of its universal relevance across industry domains).

ACME T&D Network Counts	
Enterprise Network Count	16
SCADA Network Count	4
PCN Network Count	1
Total Networks	21

As an aside, and as previously eluded to, the factors that drive the model will change based upon industry characteristics. For example, a financial institution may wish to use the economic losses associated with stolen credit card data as a primary factor to drive the model, in addition to employee productivity losses, and so forth.

Acme T&D has approximately 10,000 employees. We must determine the payroll expenses (fully burdened) per hour. We are simplifying this model intentionally—it is not likely that 10,000 employees are working all at once (e.g. some % of employees may be on a shift rotation schedule). A sample computation is shown next:

Total Employee Cost/Hour = Employee Count × (Salary/2,000) where 2000 is the number of hours worked per employee each calendar year or 2,080 less 80 hours for holidays, and the Salary input is the fully-burdened at the average of all employees.

The model is based upon various types of attack. We determine the probability that each attack will occur and to what extent it will cause damage (economic and operational) to the organization. We then create a separate model (our attack portfolio), which will allow us to simulate multiple attacks occurring against different networks in the environment and the resultant impacts in aggregate. We classify attacks based upon two variables—the frequency and impact of the attack.

An attack as profiled in Class I is considered an average attack. An average attack could be considered a low-impact worm, a Trojan horse, or virus that may affect various network systems and employee computers. Acme T&D has a variety of tools deployed in the network to mitigate these types of attacks; however no tool is 100% effective. This is where the value of Monte Carlo simulation is realized.

Minimum 0.7

Most Likely 0.8

Maximum 1.0

Now we construct the remaining elements of the model. We will use standard (and very conservative) estimates for the probability of occurrence of an attack.

Table 20 illustrates how the top-end of the model comes together. We place the attack types across the columns of the model and we create the network structure and impact structure components.

STEP 2: Create Attack Models

We must first create a common attack model and categorize the different types of attacks that exist. The classes of attacks are based upon the severity level of the attack (from average to extreme). We also indicate the extent of damage that an attack produces and the recovery details associated with each class of attack. This classification structure provides us with a basic framework we can leverage throughout the analysis exercise. We have five classes of attacks structured in our model. The descriptors are qualitative in nature (Table 20).

We create current state and future state models for the classes of attacks. The purpose for creating current and future state models is so that we can compare the models to each other. The current state model is based upon the technology and approaches that are currently in use (our pre-existing investments) to detect, mitigate, and recover from each respective type of attack. The future state model is based upon a set of new technologies (our future investments) that can be deployed in the environment to enhance the security of the environment, mitigate a wider range of attacks, and more rapidly recover from various types of attacks.

These types of attacks will be consistent across our current and future state models. There are a number of variables that are a part of our attack models. They include:

- % of Network Impacted
- % of Employees Impacted
- Productivity Loss (hours/employee)
- Costs to Recover Employees
- Hours to Recover Employees

Note that the models are populated with static values which are single-point estimates and averages. For example, a Class I Attack in the current state attack model has a 10% Network Impacted value and a 5-hour Productivity Loss value.

How can we be absolutely certain that a Class I Attack will always impact 10% of the networks and result in a productivity loss of 5 hours per employee (along with the other variables included in the model)? We cannot be sure with a reliable degree of confidence. As such, any analysis based upon single-point estimates or averages is flawed.

Table 20 Qualitative Assessments of Attack Classes

Attack Class	Severity Level of Attack	Type of Attack	Extent of Damage	Recovery Approach
Class I	Average	Benign worm, Trojan horse, virus, or equivalent.	Limited. Most damage occurs at host level.	Mostly automated, but may require some human intervention.
Class II	Slightly Above Average	Worm, Trojan horse, virus, or equivalent designed to create some damage or consume resources.	Limited. Damage can occur at the host and network level.	Human intervention is required. Humans use tools that require interaction and expertise.
Class III	Moderately Above Average	Worm, Trojan horse, or equivalent designed to create significant damage and consume resources.	Noticeable damage at host and network levels. Automated tools have limited affect to combat attacker.	Significant human intervention is required. Personnel require physical access to host machines and network environments.
Class IV	Significantly Above Average	Concentrated attack by hacker using a variety of tools and techniques to compromise systems.	Significant damage to important or sensitive data. May also include damage to host machines as Trojans and other tools are used to circumvent detection and mitigation techniques.	Extensive human intervention is required. Data and systems recovery necessary. Multiple techniques and methods necessary to fully recover.
Class V	Extreme Case	Concentrated attack by hacker or groups of hackers who are trying to compromise information or systems and have malicious intent.	Critical damage to important or sensitive information. Irreversible damage to systems or hardware.	Extensive human intervention is required. External experts required to assess and recover environment.

Monte Carlo simulation allows us to refine our assumptions and provides us with a mechanism to perturb these variables in a dynamic fashion. While we have solved the problem of dealing with averages, we are faced with a new challenge—what are the appropriate ranges to use to perturb the values and how should these perturbations behave throughout the simulation?

To gather these values we leveraged the Delphi Method. Following the Delphi Method approach, we interviewed a number of technical experts in the environment who had knowledge of prior attacks and the extent to which tools are used to mitigate them. The expert panel provided the details necessary to determine how the model variables might behave and what their respective upper and lower boundary values may be.

Figure 205 illustrates how we have adapted the % of Network Impacted value for a Class I attack. The original value was based upon an average of 10%. Upon closer inspection and after some discussion, our panel of experts determined that such an attack is unlikely to impact less than 10% of the network and may in fact impact a greater percentage of the network before it is identified and a stopped before further damage can occur. Using Monte Carlo simulation, we create an assumption for this value and select a normal distribution. We truncate the left side (or minimum value) of the distribution to take into account the 10% floor and provide some movement towards the right side (or maximum value) of the distribution. We set the mean to 10% and standard deviation to 5%. The resultant distribution indicates a minimum value of 10% a mean of 10% (our average) and a maximum value of approximately 25%.

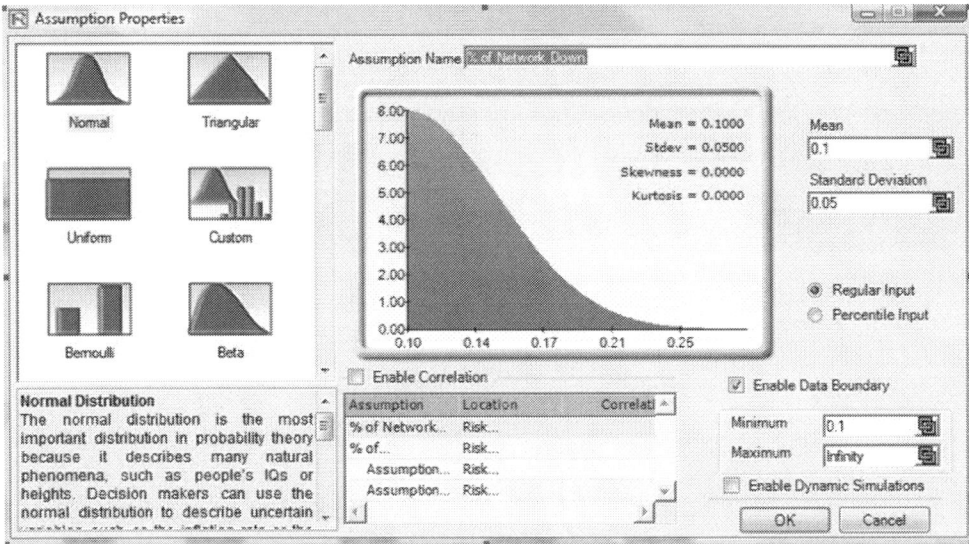

Figure 205: Truncated Percent of Network Impacted Simulation Assumption

We have introduced into our model a very powerful feature. Our model better reflects reality by taking into account the uncertainty associated with this value. We use this same approach for the other values and select and adjust the distributions accordingly. To further illustrate this point Figure 206 is taken from the Class V attack column. A Class V attack is considered an extreme event. The probability of occurrence is very low and the damage caused is expected to be extreme or catastrophic in nature. An analogous event would be a volcano eruption or an earthquake (they may evoke a tsunami wave, for example, if located in the South Pacific) that occurs once every one hundred years.

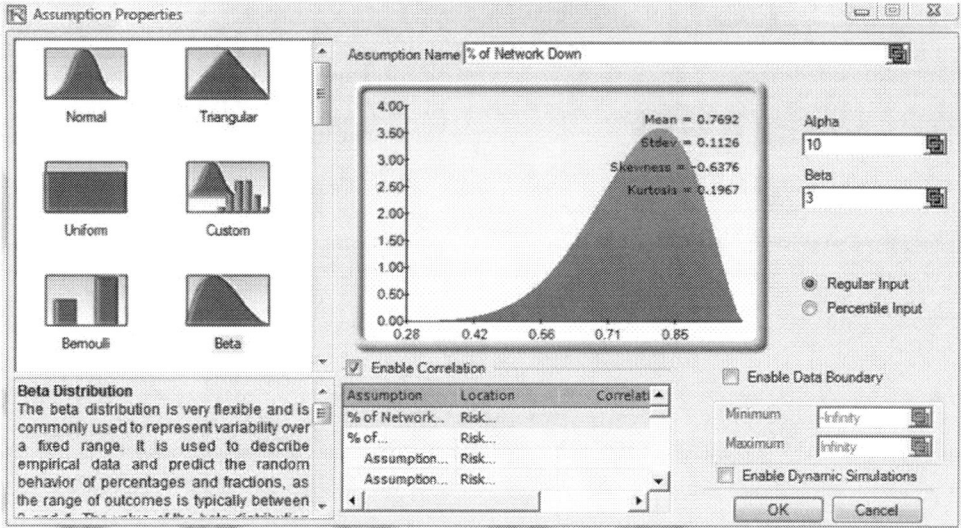

Figure 206: Percent of Network Impacted Simulation Assumption of a Class V Attack

The Gumbel Maximum Distribution is ideally suited for this type of catastrophic event. This distribution model is positively skewed and is designed to produce a higher probability of lower numbers and a lower probability of extreme values. We set the Alpha value to 70 and the Beta to 10. This results in a mean of 75.7722 and a standard deviation of 12.8255. It is important to note the third and fourth moments of this distribution. Skewness coefficient is 1.1395 (indicating the positively skewed nature of the distributions) and Kurtosis coefficient is 2.400 (indicating the extent to which extreme events should occur in the distribution).

This distribution model better reflects reality vis-à-vis extreme attacks. We can see that in Figure 207 that there are higher probabilities to the left of the mean than to the right. However, the model has taken into account the extreme distributions to the far right of the median.

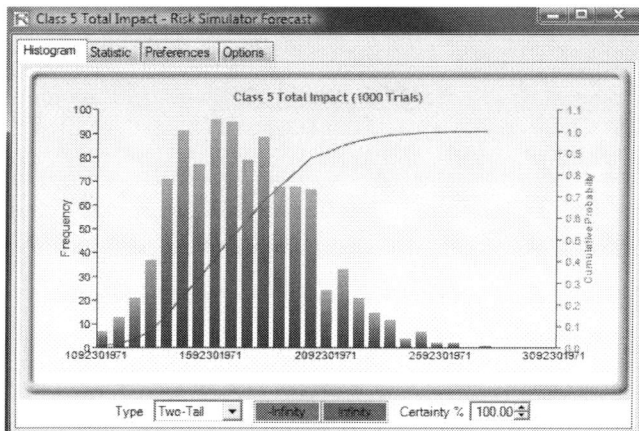

Figure 207: Forecast Distribution of a Class V Impact

The original analysis based upon averages indicated that for this scenario, the total financial losses are $21,741,176. If we follow our "1 in 3" approach, we find that the number is adjusted downward to $18,0174,729 or by a little over 12%. As you explore the model in more detail you will note the use of various distributions for each class of attack.

We adjust these figures for each scenario to take into account the greater variability of more advanced and staged attacks. We know that as attacks gain more sophistication there are more unknowns about how far reaching or to what extent damage will occur. Hence, the mean and standard deviation parameters can be adjusted to take into account this variability.

MODEL RESULTS

Impact to Operational Productivity

We have determined that the average fully-burdened salary per employee is $80,000. For Scenario I, we estimate that an attack that affects each employee results in 5 hours of lost productivity. It costs Acme T&D $39.22 per employee per hour of lost productivity. For an attack profile, we modeled in Scenario I where 10% of the networks and 10% of employees are impacted results in a total productivity loss of $196,078.43 (Table 21).

Table 21: Modeling Results from Scenario I

Lost Revenues	
Impact to Operational Productivity	$196,078.43
Assumption -- Avg. Salary/Employee (fully burdened)	$80,000
Assumption - Total Time to Fully Recover/employee (hours)	5
Productivity Cost/hour	$39.22
Costs to Recover/employee	$50
Assumption (hours to recover)	1
Costs to Recover Networks	$4,800
Assumption -- Hours to Recover	12
Resources per network	5
Cost per Hour	$50
Total Costs to Recover Employees	$50,000
Total Costs to Recover Networks	$4,800
Total Impact	$246,078.43

Recovery Costs

Attacks generally result in some form of damage (more often than not the damage is non-physical in nature). It is often necessary to deploy technical personnel to remediate the impacted environments and systems. There are two dimensions to this remediation. There is network remediation (resetting/reconfiguring network routers, switches, firewalls, etc.) and client remediation (ghosting client machines, patching software, re-installing/reconfiguring software, etc.).

Our model takes into account the number of resources and time necessary to recover the networks and the same for recovering employees. For Scenario I the costs are $50,000 and $4,800, respectively.

Total Impact

We now sum up all of the separate loss components of the model:

Loss(Productivity) + Loss (Network Recovery) + Loss (Employee Recovery)

For Scenario I, we have total losses of $147,647

In the model, there are 4 additional scenarios. For each scenario we tweak the assumptions to better fit the attack profiles. The percentage of networks down and employees impacted increase for each scenario:

	Class I Attack	Class II Attack	Class III Attack	Class IV Attack	Class V Attack
			Exposing the Flaw of Averages		
Total Impact (original)	147,647	616,471	1,933,235	5,223,529	21,741,176
Total Impact (revised)	310,616	714,145	1,679,616	7,507,908	23,817,256
Variance (%)	210.38%	115.84%	86.88%	143.73%	109.55%

The next step of our modeling efforts involves creating a portfolio of attacks. This step will provide us with the answer to the question: "How much should Acme T&D invest in security solutions to mitigate the risks associated with the attacks profiled?"

STEP 3: Create Attack Scenarios

Now that we have determined the estimated costs associated with different types of attacks we are ready to move on to creating the attack scenarios. The attack scenarios will provide us with the total losses realized during a specified period of time.

We have created six attack scenarios. The attack scenarios consider the occurrence of different types of attacks over a five year period. By creating different scenarios, we can consider different foreseeable futures. This approach allows an organization to determine how it wishes to view the world from a risk planning and risk mitigation standpoint.

The degree to which an organization will tolerate risk varies greatly. Some organizations are more tolerant of risk and will invest less in mitigating technologies and approaches while other organizations that are more risk averse will invest substantially more in order to reduce their risk profile.

One can think of this type of investment as an insurance policy—juggling premium with payout or from a strategic real options perspective of risk mitigation. The scenarios provide us with a landscape view—from lowest to highest possible losses. We will explore two different approaches to determining the probability of attacks occurring across a specified timeline. The first approach involves the use of the Delphi Method. We interview a number of subject matter and technical experts who are asked to produce five different likely scenarios for various attack profiles. We provide some guidance and suggest to each expert that the scenarios should range from a most likely scenario to a least likely scenario. This team of experts is then brought together to discuss the ranges across the spectrum. After various conversations and some debate, the team collectively determines to reduce the total scenarios (25 – 5 experts × 5 scenarios) to the *final 5*. These scenarios are reflected as Scenarios I through V on the Attack Scenarios spreadsheet.

Figure 208 illustrates a Scenario I attack profile. On our defined scale of least likely to most likely, this scenario is most likely to be realized. The experts provided the count of each type of attack that occurs within our 5 year period and further determines the years in which they will occur.

We have carried over our financial impact information from our previous exercise. For each class of attack we have current state and future state impact costs.

Scenario I						
	Year 1	Year 2	Year 3	Year 4	Year 5	TOTALS
Class I Attacks	1	0	1	1	0	3
Class II Attacks	0	0	0	0	1	1
Class III Attacks	0	0	0	0	0	0
Class IV Attacks	0	0	0	0	0	0
Class V Attacks	0	0	0	0	0	0
Class I Attack Impact CS	309,579	0	309,579	309,579	0	928,737
Class I Attack Impact FS	44,632	0	44,632	44,632	0	133,896
Class II Attack Impact CS	0	0	0	0	713,288	713,288
Class II Attack Impact FD	0	0	0	0	303,871	303,871
Class III Attack Impact CS	0	0	0	0	0	0
Class III Attack Impact FS	0	0	0	0	0	0
Class IV Attack Impact CS	0	0	0	0	0	0
Class IV Attack Impact FS	0	0	0	0	0	0
Class V Attack Impact CS	0	0	0	0	0	0
Class V Attack Impact FS	0	0	0	0	0	0
Impact based on Current State	309,579	0	309,579	309,579	713,288	1,642,025
Impact based on Future State	44,632	0	44,632	44,632	303,871	437,767
Variance	85.58%	#DIV/0!	85.58%	85.58%	57.40%	73.34%
Risk Adjustment	264,947	0	264,947	264,947	409,417	1,204,258

Figure 208: Scenario I Attack Profile of a Future State

The first section of the model includes the classes of attacks. For Scenario I, we have determined that three Class I attacks will occur in years 1, 3, and 4. In addition we have determined that one Class II attack will occur in year 5.

The second section of the model includes the impact values from the attack models. We include in this model both the current state and future state impact values. These values are computed for each year and are summed in the totals column. The variance value indicates the percentage reduction from current to future state loss values. By investing in the proposed technologies we can reduce by 73.34% the total losses for this scenario. The risk adjustment value is the difference of the current state impact and future state impact values. This value is carried over to the next step of our analysis.

We use this same model to create the other attack scenarios. Figure 209 illustrates the Scenario IV attack profile. This scenario represents the opposite end of the spectrum. In this scenario the company is successful in preventing all classes of attacks until year 5, where a Class V attack occurs. This is the infamous hacker with malicious intent scenario who makes a concentrated effort to circumvent intrusion management technologies with the specific desire to cause significant harm to the organization. For Acme T&D this scenario could perhaps reflect the sentiments of a terrorist who has a desire to gain access to the critical gas pipeline systems in order to cause a catastrophic failure to the pipeline network.

Scenario IV						
	Year 1	Year 2	Year 3	Year 4	Year 5	TOTALS
Class I Attacks	0	0	0	0	0	0
Class II Attacks	0	0	0	0	0	0
Class III Attacks	0	0	0	0	0	0
Class IV Attacks	0	0	0	0	0	0
Class V Attacks	0	0	0	0	1	1
Class I Attack Impact CS	0	0	0	0	0	0
Class I Attack Impact FS	0	0	0	0	0	0
Class II Attack Impact CS	0	0	0	0	0	0
Class II Attack Impact FD	0	0	0	0	0	0
Class III Attack Impact CS	0	0	0	0	0	0
Class III Attack Impact FS	0	0	0	0	0	0
Class IV Attack Impact CS	0	0	0	0	0	0
Class IV Attack Impact FS	0	0	0	0	0	0
Class V Attack Impact CS	0	0	0	0	23,791,472	23,791,472
Class V Attack Impact FS	0	0	0	0	16,095,255	16,095,255
Impact based on Current State	0	0	0	0	23,791,472	23,791,472
Impact based on Future State	0	0	0	0	16,095,255	16,095,255
Variance					32.35%	32.35%
Risk Adjustment	0	0	0	0	7,696,217	7,696,217

Figure 209: Scenario IV Attack Profile of a Future State

One could argue that such an approach to determining these probabilities lacks scientific rigor or can be significantly biased—either intentionally or unintentionally. Consider the technical expert who firmly believes that his skills are second to none with respect to effectively deploying and managing an armory of intrusion management technology. He may be biased to create scenarios that are on the conservative end of the spectrum, significantly coloring the reality of the environment or threat landscape. If we pin our decision on this approach, a crafty hacker who has superior skills to this individual may easily circumvent these technologies and successfully realize his attack objectives and goals.

Conversely, consider the doomsday character who is constantly pondering the worst case scenario and has a strong voice in the room. He or she may be overly aggressive with the attack scenarios, creating unrealistic models that result in doom and gloom.

How can one test for these biases? Is there a way to independently determine the probabilities and likelihoods of events? Indeed there is a way and it is again found in Monte Carlo simulation.

Scenario VI represents our independent attack scenario. You may consider this the control model. This is our expert who is neutral to all biases. The probabilities of occurrence are factually driven and leverage a distribution model that is focused on the discrete nature of these events—an event either happens or it doesn't.

The Poisson distribution provides us with the ability to address the unique aspects of occurrence probabilities. Figure 210 illustrates how we can leverage the Poisson distribution for the Class I Attack. These events are discrete in nature—they either occur or don't occur. For a Class I attack we set the Lambda value to 1.5984. This creates a distribution model that ranges from 0 to 6. Note on the left side of the model the probability scale. We can see that this Lambda value results in a 20% non-occurrence outcome. Or, in other words, 80% of the time a class I attack will occur at least one time (at a rate of approximately 33%) and may occur up to 6 times within our time interval at a rate of say .01%.

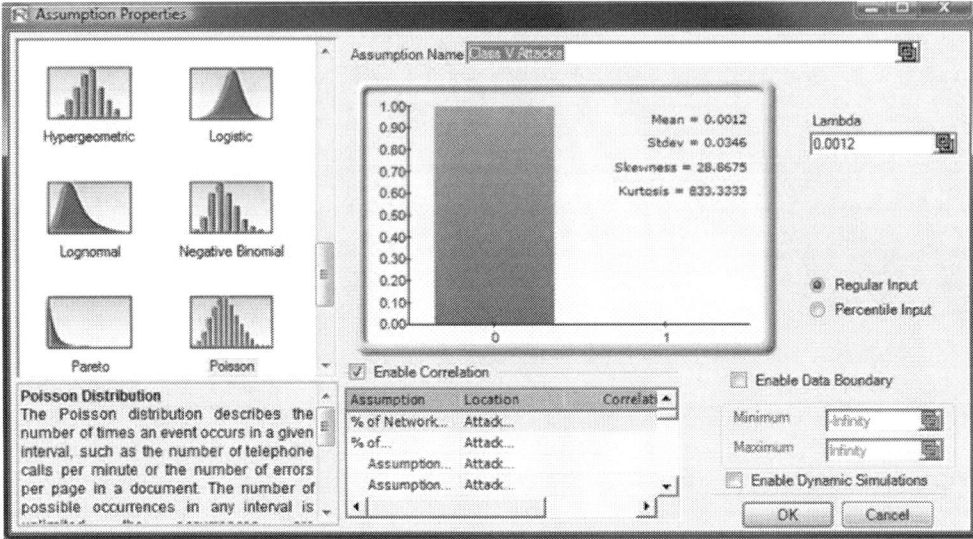

Figure 210: Poisson Distribution Assumption

Compare this to a Poisson distribution model for a Class V extreme attack. We set the Lambda value to 0.0012 to reflect this. It results in a distribution model where this event will not occur 99.9988% of the time. There is only a .0012% chance that the event will occur in any given trial.

You may wonder why, if Monte Carlo simulation can be used reliably to arrive at probabilities of occurrence, we choose two use two different methods for determining probabilities. There are three primary reasons.

- To reduce the "fear of the black box" phenomenon. People who are not familiar with analytical techniques or the details associated with statistical methods have a tendency to treat analysis and the resultants outputs as black box generated values. There is a natural fear to mistrust the unknown. By leveraging both statistical methods and expert opinion interviews, the layman observing the analysis and output can rationalize in their mind how the results were generated and how they were validated or refuted. It also provides an avenue for the layman to provide input (vis-à-vis his or her own opinions) into the equation.

- To spur additional dialogue and debate. The interview process inherently spurs additional dialogue among the expert panel. My experience has been that the more divergence of opinions the more debate occurs, which results in more robust and more refined models. The process may require more work, but, more often than not, the value of the outcome is greater than the additional effort.

- As a litmus test of expert opinions. Conversely, if we relied solely on the input of expert opinions without thinking through and modeling out the statistical side of the equation, we may fall victim to tunnel vision.

While it's beyond the scope of this case study, these models could be further enhanced by creating forecasts for different types of attacks and determining the probabilities of becoming a victim for each attack. These enhancements could be realized by using historical data (what is published in the public domain along with an organization's own data).

For the purposes of simplicity, we leveraged the Delphi Method to create the various attack scenarios. The attack scenario total impact values range from $1,547,895 to $23,791,472 is quite a significant range. How do we determine how much to invest to mitigate the risks associated with attacks?

STEP 4: Determine Financial Impact

We are now ready to explore different investment scenarios to offset the risks of attacks. We now have more reliable estimates for the various classes of attacks and can take this financial information and turn it through a classical Net Present Value (NPV) and Discounted Cash Flow (DCF) analysis.

Our NPV/DCF analysis will also have six different scenarios that will follow the same scenario structure as those previously defined. We follow this same approach through the entire analysis. It allows us to see multiple sides of the problem and arrive at a more reliable outcome.

We will return to our original investment estimate (as provided by the client) of $2,000,000, which was previously arrived at through a variety of network and systems analysis. This amount reflects the investment necessary to upgrade and enhance the intrusion management systems currently distributed throughout the environment.

At a high level, this investment will result in:

- The replacement of Intrusion Detection Systems (IDS) with Intrusion Prevention Systems (IPS).

- An increased deployment of IPS devices at additional points throughout the network—from network perimeter to network core.

- The deployment of Network Behavior Analysis (NBA) solutions are various points throughout the network along with data collection and analysis engines necessary to detect anomalies and suspect network and traffic behavior.

The logical question is, "Does a $2,000,000 investment adequately address the risks associated with the attacks and their likelihood of occurrence in this environment?" Add to this, "Is it too much or too little?"

If you recall from the previous steps we created two different aspects of our models. Current state and future state views. The basic premise of our argument is that no technology or set of technologies can provide 100% protection from all classes of attacks. However, we can intelligently place technology throughout the environment that mitigates these attacks. And, these technologies will have varying degrees of success with respect to eliminating all together the attack or significantly reducing the damage produced or the amount of time necessary to recover from an attack. What is important to us then is the reduction of losses. The investment decision is how much we should invest to reduce our losses. This is the basis behind our current state and future state views. We now move on to create our DCF and NPV analysis scenarios. Figure 211, below illustrates Scenario I.

SCENARIO I

	Year 1	Year 2	Year 3	Year 4	Year 5	TOTALS
Capital Investments	(2,000,000)	(300,000)	(300,000)	(300,000)	(300,000)	
Risk Adjustment	264,947	0	264,947	409,417	409,417	1,348,728
Net Cash Flow	(1,735,053)	(300,000)	(35,053)	109,417	109,417	
					NPV	($1,708,918.00)
					IRR	-42.36%

Figure 211: DCF and NPV Analysis

We create our 5-year time horizon and determine the timing and intensity of capital investments (our intrusion management technology solutions). The Risk Adjustment value is the difference of the Current State Impact less the Future State impact for each year in this scenario (as modeled previously during the attack scenario step). We compute our net cash flows for each year, sum up the values and then apply our NPV and Internal Rate of Return (IRR) calculations (note: we use the MIRR function in Excel to better adapt to negative values). We also have unknowns associated with this model. We don't know precisely a few critical inputs into the model. We must account for these uncertainties. The following lists the additional inputs required to run the NPV analysis:

DCF/NPV INPUT PARAMETERS

Discount Rate	10%
Finance Rate	5%
Reinvestment Rate	7%
Equipment Annual Maintenance	15.00%

where we definite the following parameters:

Discount Rate. The standard discount rate on the cash flows.

Finance Rate. The cost of capital or financing rate used to acquire the desired assets.

Reinvestment Rate. The return on the free cash flows that are reinvested.

Equipment Annual Maintenance. The annual maintenance fees and service fees associated with keeping current (software upgrades, signature updates) the various technology solutions.

We apply Monte Carlo based distributions to each value. For example, we may have varying degrees of success negotiating annual maintenance fees on the various equipment we decide to purchase. For this value we use a normal distribution with the mean set to 15% (industry average for a company of Acme T&D's size) and the standard deviation set to 0.015%, which gives us a range of between just less than 12% and slightly more than 18% (both of which are realistic outer limits). Next, Figure 212 represents what the expert team believed to be the planning case—in others words the team agreed that they should plan their efforts and investments based upon this scenario. This is also the scenario we use for our unbiased expert.

Based upon this case we are expecting a total of eight attacks during a five-year period. Our current state model suggests that we would incur losses of $11,650,567 in this scenario; our future state model suggests losses of $4,600,118. As mentioned above, our DCF/NPV analysis is concerned with the net difference, which in this case is $6,990.449. The model takes into account when these losses occur and when the difference is realized. We then compute the NPV and IRR values. Using the $2,000,000 assumption as our capital investment in intrusion management technologies, we can see that this scenario results in a positive NPV of $2,228,925.15, which results in a 35.32% IRR on our investment. Clearly, this model supports a $2,000,000 investment. This model in isolation would suggest that we could nearly double the initial investment and still have a positive NPV and IRR (the threshold to negative NPV is $3,666,000 year 1 expense following standard computations for all other variables in the model).

SCENARIO VI

	Year 1	Year 2	Year 3	Year 4	Year 5	TOTALS
Capital Investments	(2,000,000)	(300,000)	(300,000)	(300,000)	(300,000)	
Risk Adjustment	264,947	264,947	813,973	5,381,635	264,947	6,990,449
Net Cash Flow	(1,735,053)	(35,053)	513,973	5,081,635	(35,053)	

NPV	$2,228,925.12
IRR	35.32%

Figure 212: DCF and NPV Analysis on Scenario VI

STEP 5: Arrive at Investment Decision

We are now near the end of our analysis. We now have a solid understanding of what our current and future risks are vis-à-vis the losses we are likely to incur across a variety of attack scenarios. We know that a $2,000,000 investment is within the range of reason. However, we also know that we could invest more and as a result further reduce our risk of losses. Alternatively, we could invest less and rely upon the relatively low probability of being a target of a severe or catastrophic event.

We are at a crossroad. There is no absolute right or wrong decision for all or any organization. The decision makers in your organization must choose the right decision based upon all of the available facts, expert opinion, and in light of the organization's culture. Consider that the analysis is relatively conservative in nature. Consider that the most conservative and least biased model (the model generated by our independent expert) suggests that 80% of the time losses will be greater than $1,857,474 (current state) and if we implement our proposed future state technology plan these losses will reduce to $267,792, resulting in a total loss reduction of $1,589,742. Follow this same mode of thinking and be on the greater side of a betting man—51% of the time losses will be greater than $2,570,762 (current state) and $401,688 (future state), yielding $2,169,074 in loss reductions. Figure 213 illustrates an example set of risk tolerance and required investment levels, and the resulting simulation forecast distributions shown in Figure 214 further illustrates the probabilistic levels of these risk tolerances.

Loss Reduction	$813,973	$7,696,217
Investment IRR	35.32%	-100%
Total Loss	$23,791,472	$813,973
Investment	$0	$3,666,000

More Risk Tolerant   More Risk Averse

Figure 213: Risk Tolerance Levels

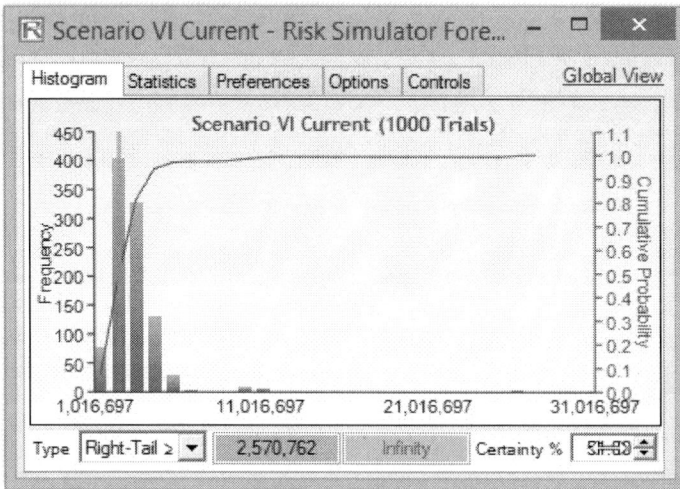

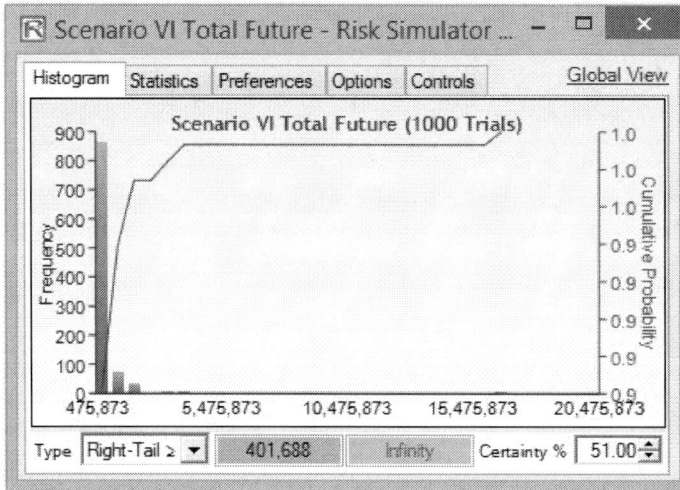

Figure 214: Simulation Forecast Risk Tolerance Levels

19

CASE STUDY 19: DYNAMIC EVALUATION OF ENTERPRISE RISK MANAGEMENT AT ELETROBRAS FURNAS IN BRAZIL

This case study was written by Dr. Nelson Albuquerque and Dr. Johnathan Mun, with the cooperation of Eletrobrás Furnas SA, which allowed us access to this enterprise risk management project and its officers, Welington Cristiano Lima and José Roberto Teixeira Nunes. We would like to also acknowledge the thorough review conducted by Professor Pedro Bello, also of Eletrobrás. It is intended to describe the methodology applied in automating Enterprise Risk Management (ERM) for Eletrobrás Furnas, the largest utility company in Brazil. The ERM approach uses Real Options Valuation, Inc. (ROV) PEAT software's ERM module, and adapts the Risk Matrix model currently used by the Eletrobrás group to the concept of expected value of risk, pushing the envelope from qualitative risk assessment to more quantitative risk management.

The PEAT ERM module was built according to the concept of Expected Risk—which uses the concept of quantification of risks—enabling plans for risk mitigation, statistical evaluation, strategic real options, and analysis of alternatives, as well as optimizing the portfolios of multiple projects.

To get started, ERM requires a two-dimensional input of the Likelihood (L) or Frequency of a risk event occurring and the Impact (I) or the Severity in terms of financial, economic, and noneconomic effects of the risk. These L and I concepts are industry standard and used even in regulatory environments such as the Basel II and Basel III Accords (initiated by the Bank of International Settlements in Switzerland and accepted by most Central Banks around the world as regulatory reporting standards for operational risks).

However, Eletrobrás is a utility company and is not subject to stringent banking and financial regulations; therefore, in place of the probability scale of Likelihood or Frequency, Eletrobrás uses the concept of *Vulnerability* (V). Consequently, the typical ERM risk matrix is modified slightly as shown in Figure 215.

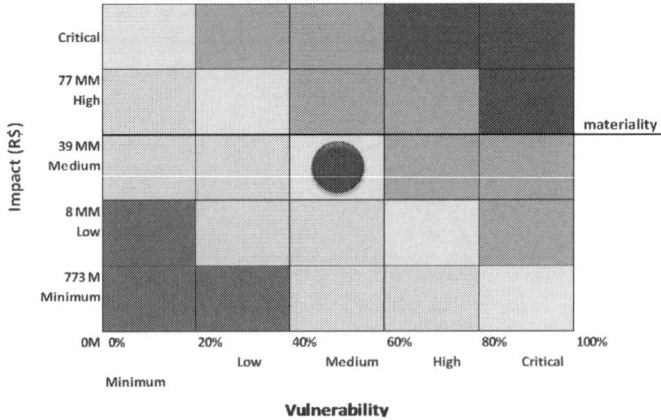

Figure 215: Modified Eletrobrás Risk Matrix

Using Likelihood or Vulnerability produces similar results and the choice of which to use is entirely up to the organization. However, we do observe several advantages to using the concept of Vulnerability, especially as it facilitates the existing audit activity in Eletrobrás because the degree of vulnerability metric within the company has already been associated with the evaluation of easily auditable controls and has been in use for several years.

This case study explores how the PEAT ERM module was customized and applied at Eletrobrás, allowing its managers to not only document the major risk factors but to also push the envelope of risk analytics and perform sensitivity analysis, Monte Carlo risk simulation, and quantitative analytics and to assess the dynamics of its business risks, risk controls, and overall enterprise risk management. See Chapter 16 of *Modeling Risk* (Third Edition) for more details and expanded examples or PEAT's ERM module.

For the sole purpose of this case study, we will adapt and use the concept of Vulnerability associated with items related to internal control standards and guidelines already established in Brazil and internationally (e.g., ISO-31000, COSO, COBIT, and SOX or Sarbanes–Oxley Act). The purpose of this customization is to make it possible to qualify and quantify the degree of implementation in each of the Risk Elements (RE) attached to specific Eletrobrás' company-wide programs.

Uncertainty, Risk, and Vulnerability

In enterprise risk assessment of the quantitative risk environment, the concept of *uncertainty* is associated with the Likelihood (L) of an event happening in the future. The uncertainties of repetitive events observed in nature over a long period of time can sometimes become predictable but usually not with absolute certainty. Such observances can be associated with mathematical functions that reflect the statistical properties of something likely to occur at a future time.

The risk of an event occurring is connected to two parameters: the Impact (I) caused by an uncertain event and the probability of an event occurring or its Likelihood (L). Given some known probability of a risk event occurring, the higher the impact, the greater the risk. If the impact is zero, the risk will be zero even though the event has a high probability of occurring. The reverse argument is also true. If the probability of a risk event occurring is equal to zero, the risk is zero (this is an environment of pure certainty), regardless of the magnitude of the impact.

In other words, uncertainty is measured in terms of Likelihood of occurrence, and unless there is some financial or noneconomic but observable Impact, there is no risk, just uncertainty.

Within the realm of Eletrobrás, the concept of Vulnerability (V) is associated with the risk of an event. Put another way, Vulnerability is associated with an organization's susceptibility to the consequences of a risk event. Risk is reduced through the mitigation of risk, either by decreasing the Likelihood of an event occurring (e.g., rather than leaving the car parked on a deserted street at night, put it in a garage under camera surveillance) or by reducing its Impact (e.g., purchasing auto theft insurance) to protect your capital.

The mitigation of the risk consequences can be scaled according to the predictable value of risk. For example, say we have a specific risk event where its maximum financial impact is valued at $100, with a 10% probability of occurring. Further suppose that there is a minimum or residual value of $5 with 90% probability, which implies that there is an expected value of $14.5. Thus, mitigation measures can be designed to try to neutralize this exposure. Clearly, there are two ways to reduce the risk: reduce the Impact or reduce the Likelihood.

Impact reduction means taking preventive measures (e.g., entering into contractual agreements to reduce legal liability), and Likelihood reduction may mean changing organizational processes and behaviors (e.g., changing processes that have a high probability of disaster). Nevertheless, regardless of the steps used to reduce the Likelihood or Impact, if the possibility still exists of the risk event occurring, the risk should be assessed on two levels: the mitigated risk and the residual risk. Mitigation measures are meant to reduce the first level of risk to its residual risk whenever possible.

Proposed Mechanism for Dynamic Risk Indicators

Institutional rules or guidelines that address business risk with only a qualitative view do not indicate a method to evaluate this exposure quantitatively. In the traditional qualitative analysis, the measure of the riskiness of a company is a snapshot at a point in time. Mitigation measures are evaluated later, often from audits to verify the degree of compliance on previous snapshots. The effort to implement these mitigation measures is typically not dynamically evaluated, nor are its results compared to what was expected within the range of risks vis-à-vis the cost of mitigation.

The PEAT ERM module intends not only to document the state of vulnerability of a company to the events that may lead to risk losses, whether economic or noneconomic, but also to quantify and measure the uncertainties of the risks and their mitigation costs. All of this is done dynamically, whereby the company may periodically make adjustments to achieve its targeted goals for reducing exposure, and pushes the envelope from qualitative assessment to quantitative risk analysis.

PEAT ERM allows dynamic assessments and measures the degree of vulnerability of the company over time using the "% Risk Mitigation Currently Completed" parameter for each risk control and their respective weights in the Risk Register window (see Figure 219), which assumes the function of the measurement parameter of Vulnerability as applied within Eletrobrás. This percentage parameter is interpreted as "% Mitigation Completed = 100% − % Vulnerability" indicating a reduction in risk exposure due to the company having implemented measures to reduce its exposure to the risks identified.

This parameter ranges from 0% Complete (i.e., 100% Vulnerable), indicating that the company is exposed to the Total Risk Value, up to 100%; whereas a 100% Complete indicates a 0% Vulnerability measure, where the risk is reduced to an exposure at its minimum level, also known as the Residual Value Risk.

Accounting for Corporate Risk

The set of Key Risk Indicators (KRI) provides an overview of financial risk to which the company is subject. Figure 216 shows an example of the residual risk exposure in PEAT ERM. In the following example, we present the risk exposure of the Finance Department due to the Risk Element of Cost Overrun. In the example, the Gross Value of Risk is $1,000,000 and its Residual Value is $500,000. The Corporate Risk, composed of all the risk factors of the company, is $1,480,000.

In this example, KRI Overrun is measured as $(L = 4) \times (I$ or $V = 4) = (KRI = 16)$ and can be shown in the Risk Matrix. In this case, it is classified as a Moderate Risk, and a reduction factor of 50% will reduce the risk exposure to $750,000 or a KRI of 12.

The model of dynamic measurement of exposure to corporate risk has the graphical representation as shown in Figure 217.

In this case, the company can assess its risk exposure dynamically by implementing the mitigation of Risk Factors, which may be marked by international standards and controls (e.g., SOX, COBIT). Thus, the Vulnerability used by Eletrobrás is associated with compliance with the controls. Dynamically this can be represented by Figure 218.

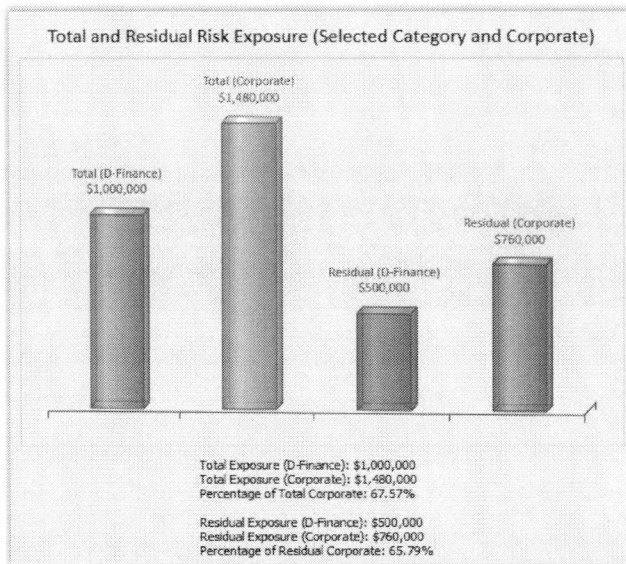

Figure 216: Financial Impact Associated with KRI and for the Full Corporation

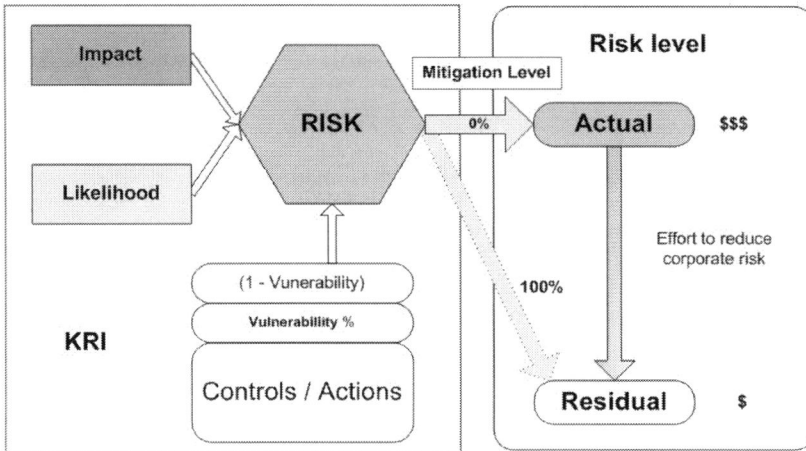

Figure 217: Model of Dynamic Measurement of Exposure to Corporate Risk

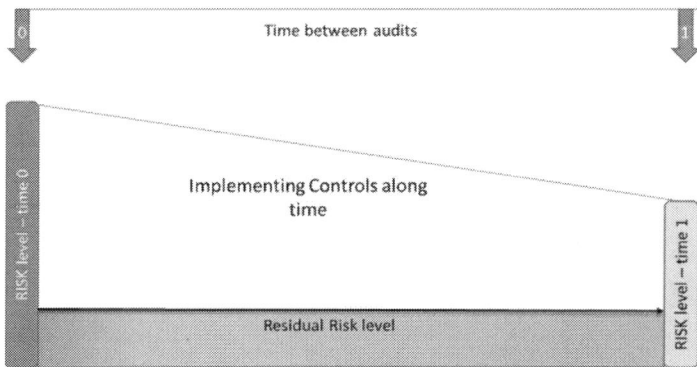

Figure 218: Dynamic Mitigation of Risk Factors

By means of the audit, be it external or internal, the company can show the evolution of the measures taken to mitigate the risk and reduce the financial exposure of the company.

Dynamic Assessment of Vulnerability: An Illustration

The Vulnerability Factor (VF) is associated with a set of controls (Cr_{ij}), based on international standards or internal rules that must be fulfilled to reduce the Risk Element (RE_j) to a level of residual risk. Each control (Cr_{ij}) by RE_j selected should be associated with a weight (w_{ij}) equal to one, two, or four, depending on the degree of importance attached to it. The use of weights allows us to distinguish between controls that are more difficult to be implemented or which would have a much greater impact on risk mitigation. Our suggestion is to rank the controls by the degree of impact: minor impact should be classified as having a weight identical to unity; the average impact, a weight equal to 2 (two); and, finally, if any, high impact with a weight of 4 (four), providing a sense of geometric growth. After an audit, controls may have different degrees of conformity (GC_{ij}), namely, implemented (0%), partially implemented (50%), and nondeployed (100%). The RE_j audited Vulnerability Factor (VF_{ij}) is calculated using the following formula:

$$VF_j = \frac{\sum_{i=1}^{n} Cr_{i,j} * w_{i,j} * GC_{i,j}}{\sum w_j}$$

Case Illustration

Figure 219 illustrates a manual computation of several sample Risk Elements, their respective Risk Controls, Weights, Vulnerability %, and the computed Vulnerability Factor (%VF) and Degree of Mitigation (%DM). It also shows a screen shot of the PEAT ERM Risk Register tab showing how these assumptions can be entered and the subsequent simple steps required to set up the ERM Risk Register.

- A Risk Register comprises multiple Risk Elements. Figure 219's PEAT ERM shows three sample saved Risk Registers, with the highlighted Risk Register being actively edited (e.g., Risk Register *Project DGS728* is currently selected).

- A Risk Element means an actual or anticipated risk. In the table, we see there are *n* Risk Elements in a single Risk Register. The first Risk Element example is a catastrophic fire risk event at one of the plants or utility facilities, another risk is employee accidents at the plants (Risk Element 2), and so forth, ending with legal risks (Risk Element *N*).

- In the first Risk Element, the catastrophic fire, let's say, for illustration purposes, there are three problems relating to this fire: destruction and loss of assets (Assets), loss of production and output (Production), and loss of human productivity (Productivity).

- Each problem is mitigated by a control. Control 1 mitigates losses in Assets by purchasing fire insurance; Control 2 mitigates losses in Production by installing capacitors and storage areas in a different off-site location that can store excess production and handle demand for the next 90 days after a catastrophic fire; and Control 3 mitigates Productivity losses by initiating a joint venture with a partner company to house all the employees at a temporary workplace while at the same time migrating all IT systems to a cloud-based environment for instant restoration of proprietary data such that employees can get back to work almost immediately.

Risk Element 1 (Catastrophic Fire)	Control 1	Control 2	Control 3	Vulnerability Factor (%VF)	Degree of Mitigation (%DM)
Weight	6	3	1	40%	60%
Vulnerability %	0%	100%	100%		
Risk Element 2 (Plant Accidents)	Control 1	Control 2	Control 3	Vulnerability Factor (%VF)	Degree of Mitigation (%DM)
Weight	6	1	3	65%	35%
Vulnerability %	55%	65%	85%		
. . .					
Risk Element N (Legal Problems)	Control 1	Control 2	Control 3	Vulnerability Factor (%VF)	Degree of Mitigation (%DM)
Weight %	60%	10%	30%	65%	35%
Vulnerability %	55%	65%	85%		

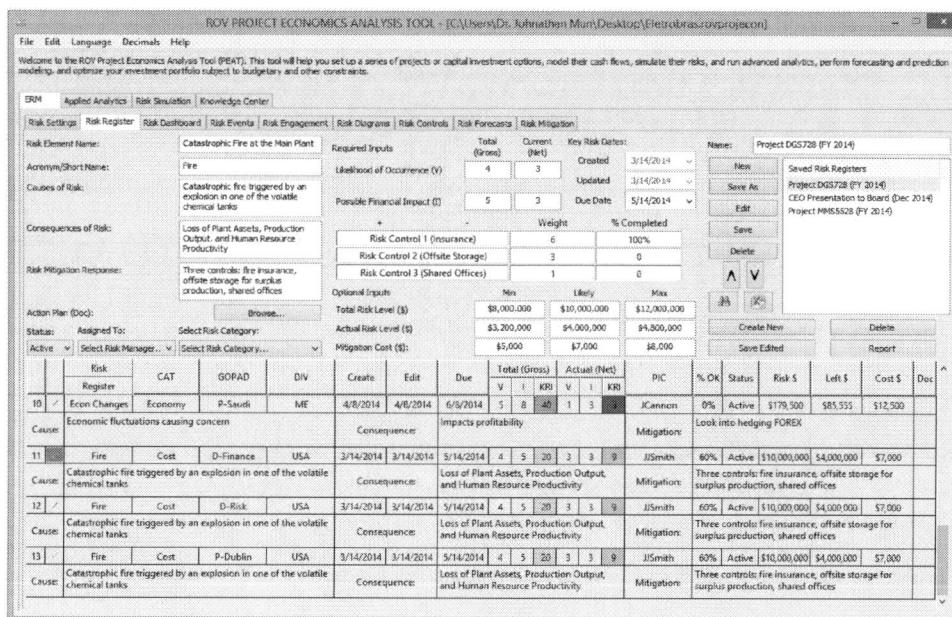

Figure 219: PEAT ERM Risk Register

- Let's further assume a simple scenario involving Risk Element 1 where the estimated total and complete catastrophic fire event will mean a loss of $6M in Assets, $3M in Production, and $1M in Productivity. These amounts were obtained through an audit by the risk personnel by performing inventory of the assets, financial analysis of production rates and loss revenues, and human resource estimations. Using these estimates, we can enter the relevant weights, either as numerical values or percentages. For instance, Control 1 has a weight of 6, Control 2 has a weight of 3, and Control 3 has a weight of 1, commensurate with the total gross risk covered and impact mitigated by each control for this single Risk Element. Of course, each company may have its own paradigm in setting the weights, as long as it is consistent throughout its ERM implementation. In this simple example we look at weighting the risk-reduction impact, whereas different organizations who do not have such impact numbers may similarly use degree of difficulty to execute the control, complication, or cost to implement (in which case the weights will be different than in the example above).

- Furthering our example, let's say that Control 1 (fire insurance) is very simple to execute and coverage was already purchased for the full amount of the Assets, which means that the % Mitigation Completed (%M) is 100% or, alternatively, % Vulnerability (%V) is 0%. Controls 2 and 3 are more difficult to complete and take time and money, and, as of right now, they are 0% completed (0% mitigated or 100% vulnerable if a fire occurs).

- As a side note, %M and %V are complementary to each other (i.e., 1 − %V = %D), and expressing either vulnerability or degree of mitigation is a matter of preference (%M takes a more optimistic point of view whereas %V takes a more pessimistic point of view, but converting from one measure to another is very simple).

- See the table for Risk Element 2 (employee accidents at the plant) for another sample set of inputs. Finally, Risk Element N intentionally showcases the same weighting levels but here a percentage weight is used instead. Therefore, instead of a numerical weight of 6, 1, 3 (which sums to 10), we can alternatively input these as 60%, 10%, and 30% (this is equivalent to 6/10, 1/10, and 3/10). This is a user preference and can be set in PEAT ERM's *Global Settings* tab.

- Then, the PEAT ERM module automatically computes the Vulnerability Factor (%VF) and Degree of Mitigation (%DM) for each of the Risk Elements. The following shows their respective calculations:

- Risk Element 1: Catastrophic Fire.

    o $\%VF = (6 \times 0\% + 3 \times 100\% + 1 \times 100\%) \div (6 + 3 + 1) = 40\%$

    o $\%DM = 1 - \%VF = 100\% - 40\% = 60\%$, or, similarly, we have:

    o $\%DM = 1 - (6 \times 0\% + 3 \times 100\% + 1 \times 100\%) \div (6 + 3 + 1) = 60\%$

- Risk Element 2: Plant Accidents.

    o $\%VF = (6 \times 55\% + 1 \times 65\% + 3 \times 85\%) \div (6 + 1 + 3) = 65\%$

    o $\%DM = 1 - \%VF = 100\% - 65\% = 35\%$, or, similarly, we have:

    o $\%DM = 1 - (6 \times 55\% + 1 \times 65\% + 3 \times 85\%) \div (6 + 1 + 3) = 35\%$

- Risk Element N: Legal Issues. In this example, we use % weights instead.

    o $\%VF = (60\% \times 55\% + 10\% \times 65\% + 30\% \times 85\%) = 65\%$

    o $\%DM = 1 - \%VF = 100\% - 65\% = 35\%$, or, similarly, we have:

    o $\%DM = 1 - (60\% \times 55\% + 10\% \times 65\% + 30\% \times 85\%) = 35\%$

- As a side note, the numerical weight can take on any positive integer and does not have any further restrictions, whereas the % weight each needs to be between 0% and 100%, and the total weights for each Risk Element must sum to 100%.

- The monetary Gross Risk for Risk Element 1 (catastrophic fire) is, of course, $6M + $3M + $1M = $10M. And in the example above, we see that only Control 1 (fire insurance) was 100% mitigated (0% vulnerable). This means the entire $6M has been mitigated and the risk no longer exists, at least financially speaking. Thus, the Remaining or Residual Risk is $3M + $1M = $4M. Alternatively, we can compute the *Residual Risk = Gross Risk × % Vulnerability Factor*. Of course, this is the same as saying *Residual Risk = Gross Risk × (1 − % Degree of Mitigation)*. That is, we can compute *Residual Risk* = $10M × 40% = $10M × (1 − 60%) = $4M. This $4M is the Remaining or Residual Risk or the risk that remains after the Risk Controls are in place. As a side note, COSO requirements specifically state to use Impact and Likelihood measures and define Gross Risk as Inherent Risk, and Residual Risk as the remaining risks after management executes whatever controls they have executed. (See Chapter 16 of *Modeling Risk* [Third Edition] for specifications of how PEAT complies with Basel II/III, ISO 31000:2009, and COSO global standards.) Regardless of the definitions used in the example here, clearly, different companies have different paradigms; the important things is to be consistent in defining them. If we compute the Remaining Risk in the example above, the user has the option to change the name "Residual Risk" to something like "Actual or Remaining Risk" in the PEAT ERM's *Global Settings* tab to avoid any confusion.

Procedures

The following shows how simple it is to use PEAT ERM to input Risk Elements and Risk Controls into a Risk Register (Figure 219):

- Step 1: In the relevant Risk Register, users can input new Risk Elements in the data grid or edit an existing Risk Element (click on the pencil icon in the data grid for the relevant row to edit). Each Risk Element is a row in the Risk Register's data grid.

- Step 2: Enter the *Risk Controls, Weight,* and *% Mitigation Completed* for each control item (weights can be entered as integers or percent depending on user settings in the *Global Settings* tab). The *% Degree of Mitigation* is automatically computed and shown in the data grid under the *%OK* column.

- Step 3: Users can optionally enter the monetary Gross Risk amounts if required and known, as well as a spread that will be used later in running Monte Carlo risk simulations. For instance, enter $8M, $10M, and $12M, where the most likely Gross Risk is $10M as illustrated in this example (the sum of the Assets, Production, and Productivity).

- Step 4: Users can then optionally enter the monetary Residual Risk amounts if required. This is very simple to enter: simply take the Gross Risk amounts and multiply by $(1 - \%DM)$. In this example, the Residual Risk spreads will be:

  - *Minimum Residual Risk* $= \$8M \times (1 - 60\%) = \$3.2M$.

  - *Most Likely Residual Risk* $= \$10M \times (1 - 60\%) = \$4.0M$.

  - *Maximum Residual Risk* $= \$12M \times (1 - 60\%) = \$4.8M$.

- Step 5: Depending whether the user has previously selected the *Impact and Vulnerability* or the *Impact and Likelihood* settings for the Risk Matrix in the *Global Settings* tab of PEAT ERM, users can either use the $4M computed Actual Risk or Residual Risk amount or the %OK (i.e., % Vulnerability Factor for the Risk Element after performing the weighted average computation of the various Risk Controls), or they can use their own specified categories and enter either the V or I value. For example, the following is a simple example of company-specific V and I values, which can be tied to net income, revenues, or other financial metrics, and are obviously unique to each company and may change over time. These categorizations will be decided by the risk committee (the example below is a 5×5 risk matrix):

Risk Categories	When Net Income = $6.24M	
Critical Risk (I = 5)	> 1.0%	≥ 62M
High Risk (I = 4)	≥ 0.1%	6.2M – 62M
Medium Risk (I = 3)	≥ 0.01%	0.6M – 6.2M
Low Risk (I = 2)	≥ 0.001%	62K – 0.6M
Minimal Risk (I = 1)	< 0.001%	≤ 62K

Vulnerability Factor	V Index
≪ 20%	V = 1
20% – 40%	V = 2
40% – 60%	V = 3
60% – 80%	V = 4
≫80%	V = 5

- Step 6: Continue adding more Risk Elements in the Risk Register, perform the tornado and scenario analyses, and simulation analysis, as well as run the various Risk Dashboard reports.

Dynamic Evaluation of the Impact

The impact is always associated with the wealth of the decision maker. For example, a company that moves billions of dollars every month in its business of mining or oil extraction has a very different risk appetite than a bakery or pharmacy. The levels of impact designed in the Risk Matrix should be associated with the appropriate financial impact scale. These financial ranges can be indexed, for example, to the turnover of the company, so that the monetary values of risk are related to or are always updated with the size of the company, since the KRIs are absolute and its evolution will depend only on the implementation of the risk mitigation measures and the nonvolatile wealth of the company.

Dynamic Evaluation of Probability

The probability of an event is associated with a measure of whether it will occur regardless of the actions of the company's managers. It may be the result of a Monte Carlo risk simulation (in the case of measuring the VaR [Value at Risk] or other associated probability and confidence intervals) or a subjective evaluation of those responsible for its management. Usually, experts have some sensitivity, based on their experience, about the chances of a risk event occurring. This value can then be the result of an analytical assessment or research and expert consensus. An example of setting the levels of event probability can be established by the following table:

Range of Probability		Qualitative Classification		Equivalent Scale
> 80%	→	critical	↔	5
60% - 80%	→	high	↔	4
40% - 60%	→	medium	↔	3
20% - 40%	→	low	↔	2
< 20%	→	minimum	↔	1

Dynamic Evaluation of the Measurement of KRI (Risk)

A quantitative assessment of the risk or the KRI is associated with mitigation or reduction of risk exposure. These measures can be understood or organized in a listed group, whereby risks are assessed as "OK" or "Low" for those events, if they occur, that are not relevant to the financial health or the image of the company, or "Critical" to "Acceptable" for those that are very severe and may compromise the survival of the company. The group's risk managers should define measures of exclusion or mitigation of risks so that they are always on the "Critical" to "Acceptable" level, and the level of investment to be made by the company in mitigating actions should be less than the decrease of the expected risk.

CASE STUDY 20: ANALYSIS OF SALES FORECAST AND PERFORMANCE RISK

This case study was written by the author and Larry Blair, a partner at Goals HQ, Inc. Prior to cofounding Goals HQ, Inc., Larry spent 8 years as the Vice President of Sales for MAM Software, Inc., and was Managing Director of Triad Systems Europe with offices in Coventry, England; Longford, Ireland; and Orleans, France. He holds a BS in Business and MBA degrees from Pepperdine University and is Certified in Risk Management.

Sales Plan Uncertainty

The lifeblood of every commercial organization is the revenue stream that pays its expenses and funds its growth. No organization can survive for long if the capture of new revenues does not surpass the accumulation of costs sustained from its operations. The designation of *sales* as the essential task of a business must be understood and applied as the mantra of management if a healthy organization is to be able to support all of its operations and goals.

The need for sales of a company's products is continual (i.e., necessary every day, week, month, quarter, year), but no sale is actually attained until a customer has decided to buy the products or services presented and the company has received payment in exchange for said products or services. The customer decision is ultimately beyond the control of the company and can only be solicited, cajoled, and requested by sales staff. Nevertheless, every company needs assurances of what sales level will be attained and if that level will be sufficient to support the costs of the company. There is, by definition, an element of uncertainty and risk associated with the forecasts reported for what sales will occur within a specified future period, and every organization needs to understand the risks that the reported sales forecasts will not be met. No company likes to receive the bad news that forecasts have not been met, especially when no thought was given to the possibility of underperformance prior to its occurrence. End-of-period actions are too late to provide assistance in making sales goals. In a world of uncertainty, knowing the level of risks contained within sales forecasts is essential for management to be able to tactically act in time to have a significant effect on final sales results.

How confident will a CEO be when providing sales forecasts for the next quarter to Wall Street analysts, the board of directors, or shareholders in general? Are the risks and uncertainties affecting these sales projections known? What are the risks and probabilities the sales goals will never be attained? Is the sales force optimized to maximize potential pipeline sales? Is the sales team converting enough potential clients into tangible sales? What is the sales cycle or pipeline conversion rate? In this case study, we answer these questions by applying the Integrated Risk Management (IRM) methods to sales projections and pipeline analysis, namely, the applications of Monte Carlo risk simulation, stochastic forecasting, decision analytics, probabilistic mechanics, statistical analysis, and portfolio optimization.

Sales Management Case: Automotive Replacement Parts, Inc.

This case study is based on the actual experience of Automotive Replacement Parts, Inc.'s application of software tools created by Real Options Valuation, Inc. (ROV). Fictional names and data have been used to protect the privacy of the organization.

Automotive Replacement Parts, Inc. (ARP) is a national provider of systems used by U.S. and Canadian parts manufacturers whose products are included in automobiles and light trucks. To serve its customers, ARP has sales staff located in seven territories: Northeast, Northcentral, Northwest, Southwest, Southcentral, Southeast, and Canada. ARP believes that its sales personnel are most successful when they know what the corporate goals for total sales are and the part that each salesperson plays in making that goal (the individual quota). To provide this information, ARP has employed ROV's Sales Performance Indicator, Data, Event, and Reporting (SPIDER) cloud-based application. SPIDER is a Web-based Software as a Service (SaaS) that allows companies to post their sales goals at each level of an organization via a secured online portal; from the total headquarters' goal to the goals of particular Departments, Teams, and Sales Individuals. Each salesperson is appraised on a regular basis (at least daily or weekly) of their status vis-à-vis the status of the rest of the organization. Studies have shown that persons who know their relative roles in the accomplishment of a goal actually achieve better results (higher numbers, more consistently, over more periods). ARP then uses ROV's Sales Performance Evaluation Analysis and Reporting (SPEAR) analytical tool to evaluate the sales performance of its staff. SPEAR is a desktop application that uses the data created within SPIDER to reveal the characteristics of the actual sales, forecasts, and sales pipeline. ARP believes it can better manage its staff and allow them to be more successful by keeping them informed of each period's sales target and by enabling each sales individual to make personal updates to his or her status as those sales successes occur. The entire organization sees the accomplishments in real time while corporate headquarters is supplied with the necessary data to predict final period outcomes and the risks of underperformance well before a period ends.

Several problems exist with most sales incentive programs: they are post-event oriented, they are inequitable, and they can be inaccurate. Regarding the problem of being too late to help, SPEAR is a statistically based program that can harvest data based on the frequency desired by management and certainly during the period when there are still opportunities to review and take actions if necessary to ensure that goals are achieved. Regarding being unfair in some cases, SPEAR allows the company to see sales staff within their respective teams as well as comparisons among each individual's contribution toward the corporate goal across regions and departments. Regarding accuracy, SPEAR provides complete oversight of not just actual sales contributions but also accuracy of forecasts and the health and volatility of the pipeline. All these benefits are initiated by the use of SPIDER and then realized by the application of the conclusions produced in SPEAR.

ARP Implementation of SPIDER

The setup of SPIDER is accomplished through the Goals HQ website (www.goalshq.com). There is a public home page but also a Login portal. Staff of Goals HQ assign a login per client company such as ARP, and create a Local Administrator (LA) account and multiple End-User (EU) accounts. The security level on all LA and EU users as well as the pertinent company-specific information is entered (Figure 220).

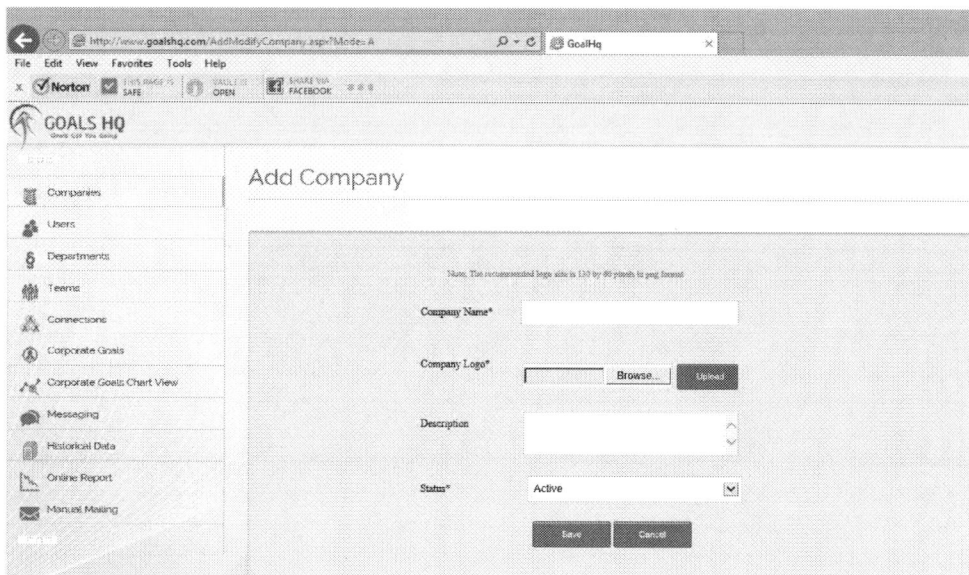

Figure 220: Goals HQ's Global Administration of a New Company

After the unique corporate identity and LA/EU accounts have been created, the ARP LA uses its secure login to establish the basic structure of the sales organizations and who will participate in the program (Figure 221). The information entered by the LA includes the territorial arrangement of the sales areas and the individuals themselves with their contact details, as well as who will have access to and be tracked by the program (Figures 222–224).

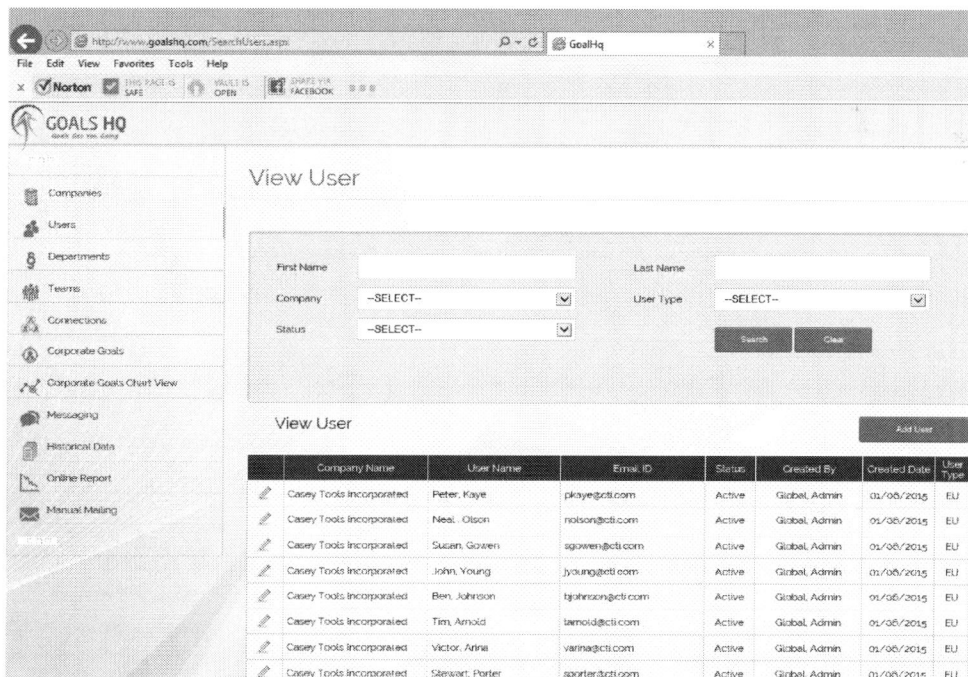

Figure 221: Individuals Participating in the Goals Program Are Entered

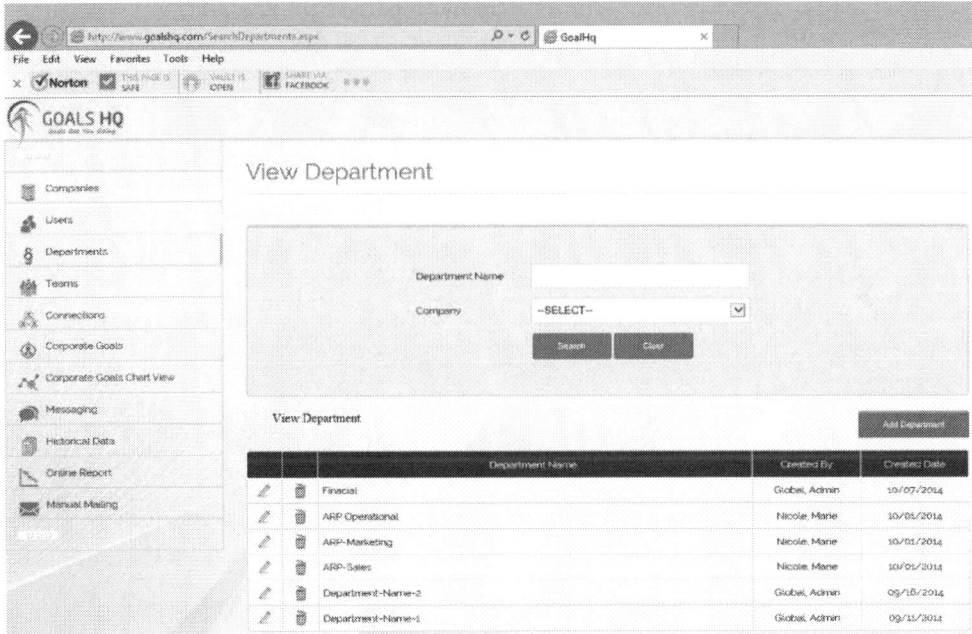

Figure 222: Assignment of Departments Per Company

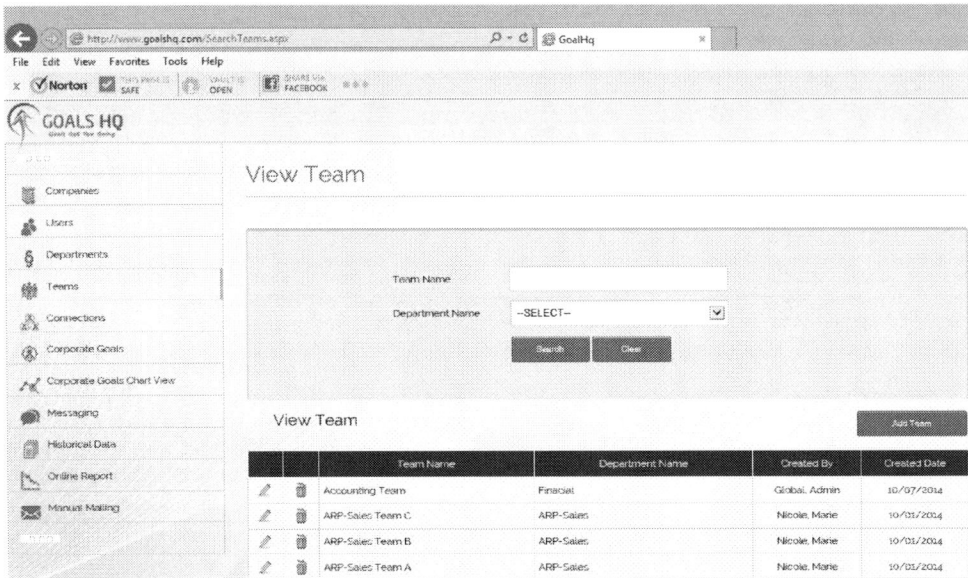

Figure 223: Team Designations Such As Specific Sales Territory Assignments

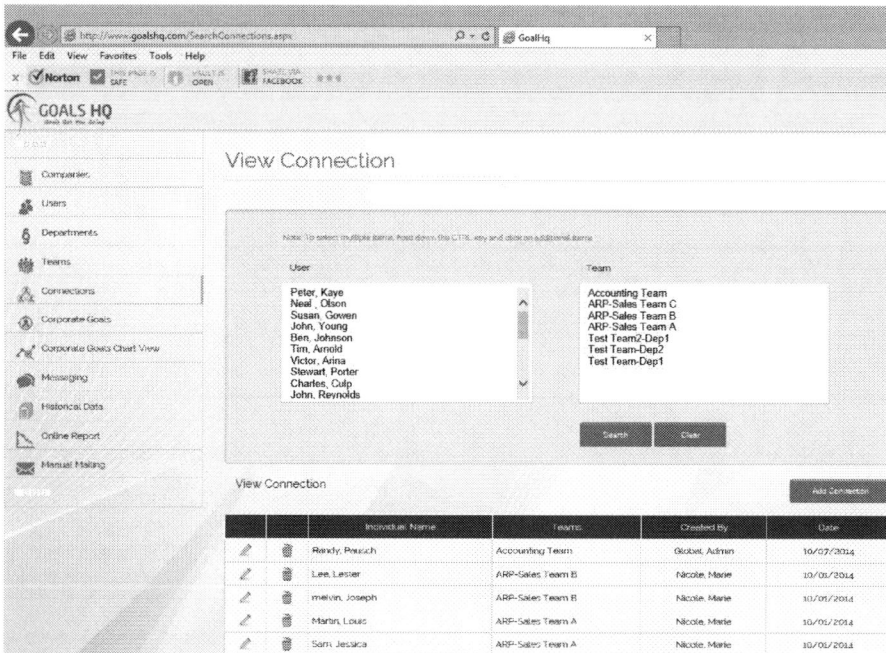

Figure 224: Individual Staff Members Are Assigned to Their Respective Teams

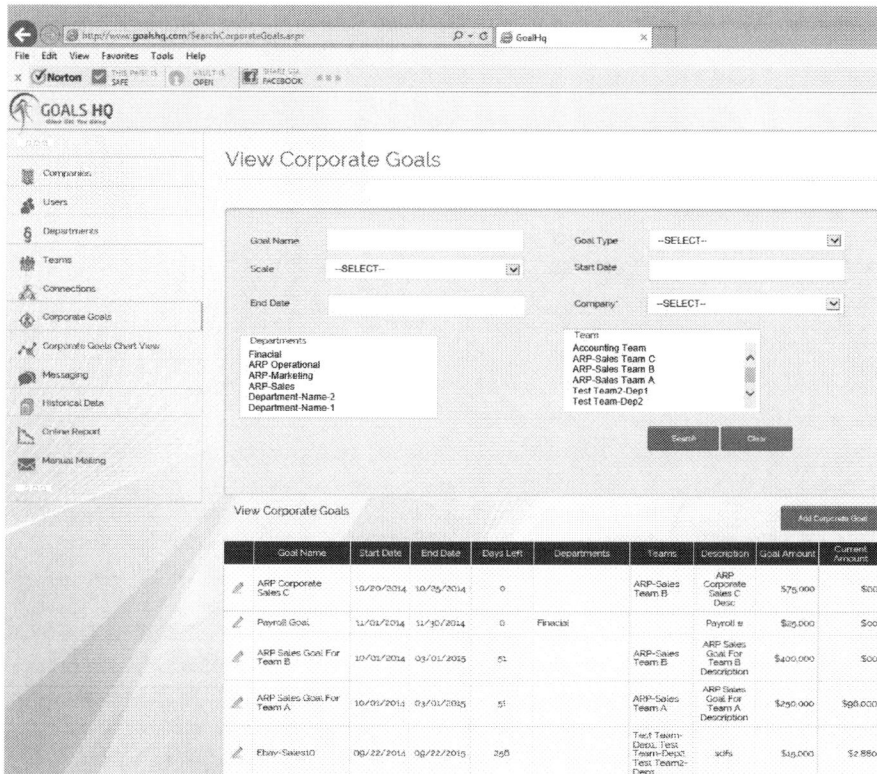

Figure 225: Entry of the Goal Relative to Each Department

Each individual participating in the program signs into the Goals HQ website and accepts the individual goal per period that is assigned per Department/Team (territory), as shown in Figure 225. The individual sign-in provides an instant view of the Goal status of the organization in four charts as shown in Figure 226. The Goals HQ program also sends a status of sales performance to each participant in the sales chain via email per the frequency determined by the LA.

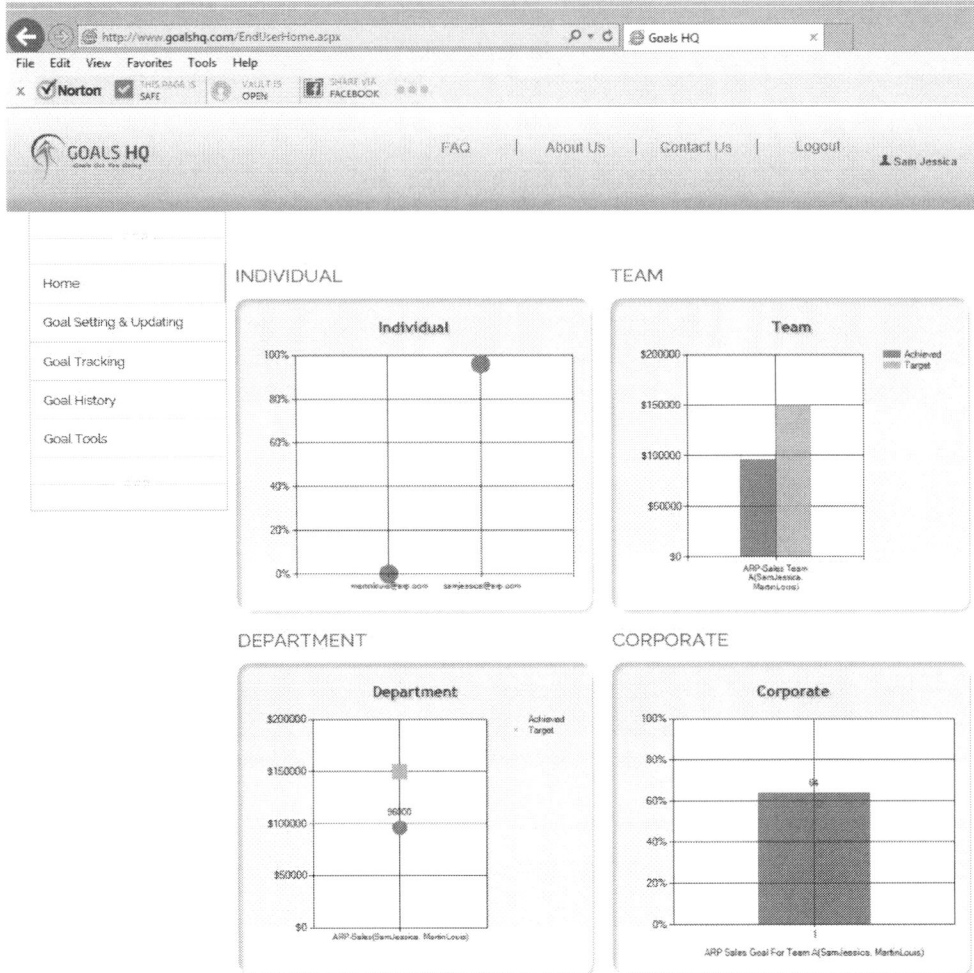

Figure 226: Status Screen Per Individual

The Goals HQ status and communications service, SPIDER, is a SaaS program that provides easy online access and ensures private and secure use by each corporate client. Use of the program benefits all levels of a sales organization through continuous communication, broad and specific perspectives, and a sense of urgency by tracking the remaining work days and remaining sales deficit pertaining to the target per period. SPIDER also is the database creation engine for the essential information that is used by the next phase of the program, SPEAR. Transfer of data between the two services is simple using preprogrammed import/export functions. Excel is an output option of SPIDER available at the LA account level for use on demand. Of course, the LA can review sales status whenever desired at any level of the organization.

The spreadsheet in Figure 227 shows the detailed ARP individual sales results by period. Each row has all the data for all the salespersons included in the program for a particular period. The columns per salesperson are Actual Sales, Sales Forecast, Pipeline, and Sales Goal. The column variables are repeated for different salespersons across the spreadsheet.

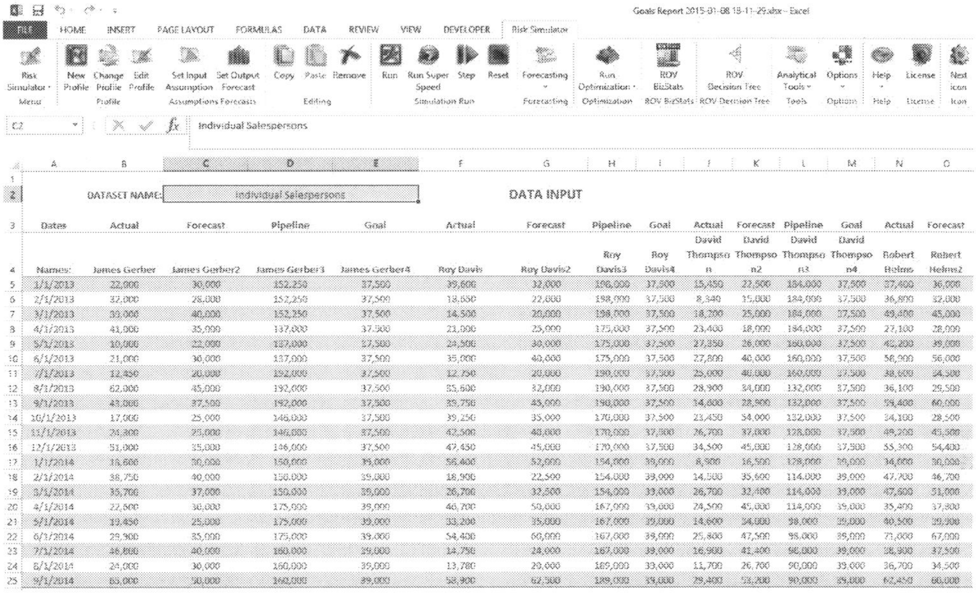

DATASET NAME: Individual Salespersons — DATA INPUT

Dates	Actual	Forecast	Pipeline	Goal	Actual	Forecast	Pipeline	Goal	Actual	Forecast	Pipeline	Goal	Actual	Forecast
Names:	James Gerber	James Gerber2	James Gerber3	James Gerber4	Roy Davis	Roy Davis2	Roy Davis3	Roy Davis4	David Thompson	David Thompson2	David Thompson3	David Thompson4	Robert Helms	Robert Helms2
1/1/2013	22,000	30,000	152,250	37,500	39,600	32,000	196,000	37,500	15,450	22,500	184,000	37,500	37,400	36,000
2/1/2013	32,000	28,000	152,250	37,500	18,650	22,000	198,000	37,500	8,340	15,000	184,000	37,500	36,800	32,000
3/1/2013	39,000	40,000	152,250	37,500	14,500	20,000	198,000	37,500	18,200	25,000	184,000	37,500	49,400	45,000
4/1/2013	41,000	35,000	137,000	37,500	21,000	25,000	175,000	37,500	23,400	18,000	184,000	37,500	27,100	28,000
5/1/2013	10,000	22,000	137,000	37,500	24,500	30,000	175,000	37,500	27,350	26,000	160,000	37,500	42,200	39,000
6/1/2013	21,000	30,000	137,000	37,500	35,000	40,000	175,000	37,500	27,800	40,000	160,000	37,500	58,900	56,000
7/1/2013	12,450	20,000	192,000	37,500	12,750	20,000	190,000	37,500	25,000	40,000	160,000	37,500	38,600	34,500
8/1/2013	62,000	45,000	192,000	37,500	55,600	32,000	190,000	37,500	28,900	34,000	132,000	37,500	36,100	29,500
9/1/2013	43,000	37,500	192,000	37,500	33,750	45,000	190,000	37,500	14,000	28,900	132,000	37,500	59,400	60,000
10/1/2013	17,000	25,000	146,000	37,500	39,250	35,000	170,000	37,500	23,450	54,000	132,000	37,500	34,100	28,500
11/1/2013	24,300	25,000	146,000	37,500	42,500	40,000	170,000	37,500	26,700	37,000	128,000	37,500	49,200	45,500
12/1/2013	51,000	35,000	146,000	37,500	47,450	45,000	170,000	37,500	34,500	45,000	128,000	37,500	55,300	54,400
1/1/2014	16,600	30,000	150,000	39,000	56,400	52,000	154,000	39,000	8,900	16,500	128,000	39,000	34,000	30,000
2/1/2014	38,750	40,000	150,000	39,000	18,900	22,500	154,000	39,000	14,500	35,600	114,000	39,000	47,700	46,700
3/1/2014	35,700	37,000	150,000	39,000	26,700	32,500	154,000	39,000	26,700	32,400	114,000	39,000	47,600	51,000
4/1/2014	22,600	30,000	175,000	39,000	46,700	50,000	167,000	39,000	24,500	45,000	114,000	39,000	35,400	37,300
5/1/2014	19,450	25,000	175,000	39,000	33,200	35,000	167,000	39,000	14,600	34,000	98,000	39,000	40,500	39,300
6/1/2014	29,300	35,000	175,000	39,000	54,400	60,000	167,000	39,000	25,300	47,500	98,000	39,000	71,000	67,000
7/1/2014	46,800	40,000	160,000	39,000	14,750	24,000	167,000	39,000	16,900	41,400	98,000	39,000	38,900	37,500
8/1/2014	24,000	30,000	160,000	39,000	13,780	29,000	169,000	39,000	11,700	26,700	90,000	39,000	36,700	34,500
9/1/2014	65,000	50,000	160,000	39,000	58,900	62,500	169,000	39,000	29,400	53,200	90,000	39,000	62,450	60,000

Figure 227: Exported Spreadsheet of Data Generated by SPIDER

ARP Implementation of SPEAR

The data generated by SPIDER allows ARP to see the trends at each level of the sales organization. However, the in-depth examination of sales performance is the job of the various analysis suites included in the program called SPEAR. Section A of SPEAR's setup screen under the *Sales Data | Global Settings* tab allows for the selection of period and weightings of performance factors. Section B is a list of the individuals within their various sales territories (team and department assignments). Figure 228 shows the ARP sales organization assignments for all the Individuals, Teams, and Department designations. This information can be entered or pasted into the SPEAR program from other software sales performance management (SPM) software applications.

In the *Sales Data | Individuals* tab, further analysis details are selected to identify the data. All the details have been imported, entered, or copy and pasted from SPIDER or other software applications such as Salesforce.com. Figure 229 is a screen in SPEAR showing the detailed data from ARP by Individuals that had been in Excel format as was shown in Figure 227 but is now within the program and ready for analysis. The view shown is the Individuals tab but data may also be reviewed and summarized by Teams and Departments.

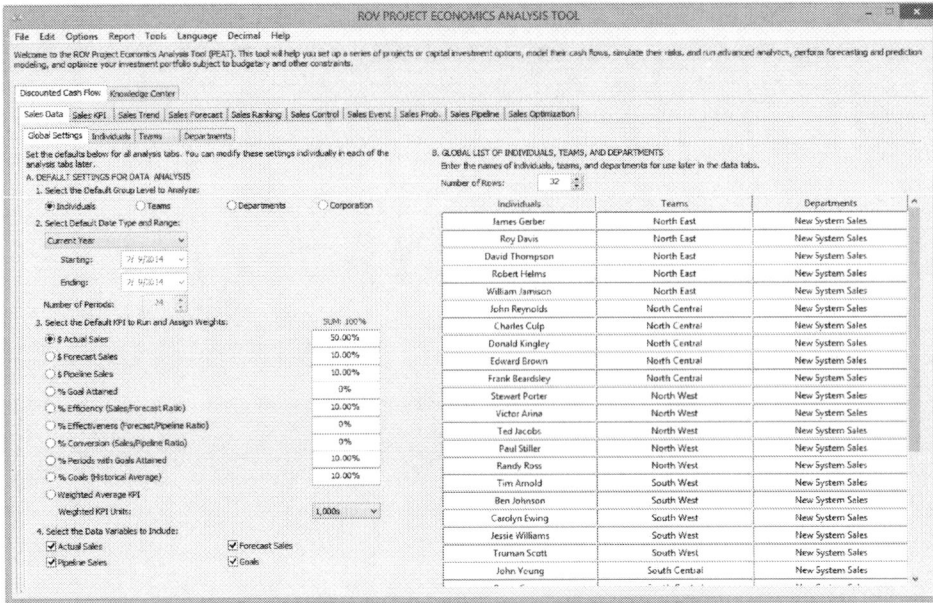

Figure 228: SPEAR Initial Data Setup

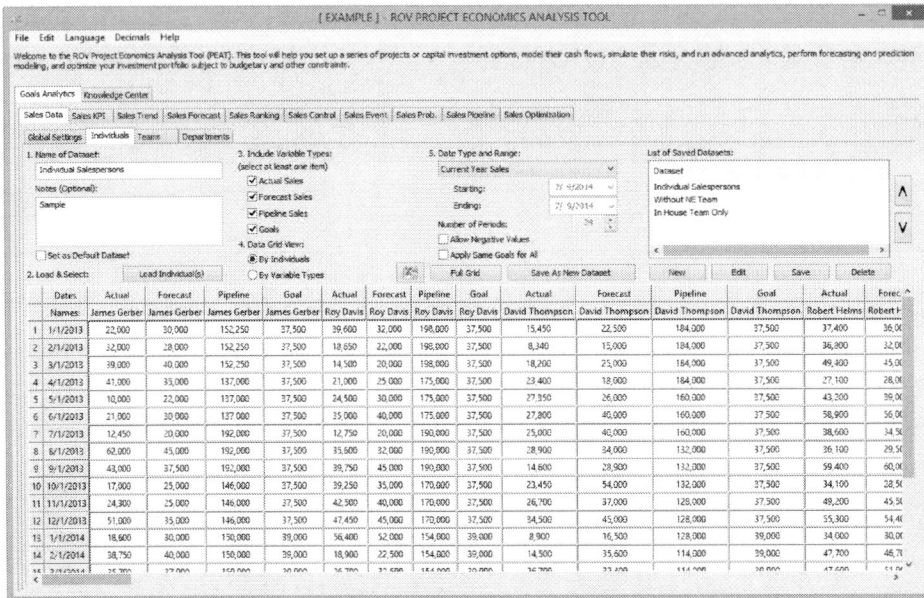

Figure 229: Detailed Data by Individuals

SPEAR Analysis Options

After setup, the analysis can proceed. When the data is loaded, the organizational hierarchy and the particular elements that will be scrutinized will also automatically load. SPEAR was developed to emphasize ease of use so that a user's only qualification is not background knowledge of the mathematical and statistical intricacies that are necessary to reveal the trends and nuances present in the data, but simply an understanding of the company's products and market.

SPEAR analysis tools have different uses and should be applied as the need arises per the functionality required. The analysis tasks are divided into nine areas of focus: Sales KPI, Sales Trend, Sales Forecast, Sales Ranking, Sales Control, Sales Event, Sales Probability, Sales Pipeline, and Sales Optimization.

- Sales KPI—Individual and Team performance comparison for Efficiency, Effectiveness, Conversion, and the weighted operational index.

- Sales Trend—Individual and Team performance trending analysis of key sales elements.

- Sales Forecast—Individual and Team predictive modeling and forecasts of key sales elements highlighting changes in performance per period.

- Sales Ranking—Individual and Team Pareto sequencing and ranking of sales performance with graphical representation.

- Sales Control—Individual and Team statistical process analysis of the elements in the KPI by dollars or percentage contribution to see if dips and spikes in KPIs and sales revenues occur due to randomness and regular business fluctuations or are statistically significant and represent a structural shift in the market and sales cycle, and so forth.

- Sales Event—Analysis of date-based sales support actions to evaluate worth and to test and identify the statistical effects of certain marketing and sales campaigns.

- Sales Probability—Calculates the probability of hitting goals per Individual, Team, or Department.

- Sales Pipeline—Individual and Team assessment of pipeline health, volatility, conversion, and staleness.

- Sales Optimization—Modeling the optimal sales staffing thresholds with the objective of maximizing the probability of hitting the corporate sales goals.

Sales KPI

A Key Performance Indicator (KPI) is important for comparison of accomplishments across any organization in which there is more than one active supplier of results. A KPI can be unique per person or team and provides a qualifier of actual results against a number best comprising the desired goal. Efficiency, Effectiveness, and Conversion are the KPIs calculated per salesperson.

- *Efficiency* is a ratio of *Sales to Forecast*, which measures both how *accurate* the salesperson's forecast performed in advance is to actual sales that were attained, as well as assuming the sales forecast was performed with proper due diligence and represents the universe of potential sales, and how *efficient* the salesperson is in closing all the forecast sales opportunities within the specified period. Clearly, the higher the efficiency ratio, the better the salesperson or sales team.

- *Effectiveness* is a ratio of *Forecast to Pipeline*, which measures how much of the sales pipeline (conceivably the entire known universe of potential clients, both current and future, that have been identified as potential candidates to purchase the company's products and services) the salesperson or sales team predicts it can *effectively* capture and convert during the specified period. Clearly, the higher the effectiveness ratio, the better the salesperson or sales team.

- *Conversion* is a ratio of *Sales to Pipeline*, which measures how many of the sales in the pipeline were closed as actual sales. Clearly, the higher the conversion ratio, the better the salesperson or sales team. If the conversion ratio is close to or equals the effectiveness ratio, this also indicates that the efficiency ratio is high (specifically, the ratio of conversion to effectiveness is equal to the efficiency KPI).

Using these KPIs, sales management will be able to understand the relative value of each individual and team based on real reported and accomplished results.

Figure 230 is an ARP example of the total sales results for all the sales staff by period. Goals HQ has created several operational indices for judging sales success that are shown in this screen. First, the actual numbers per period across the horizontal rows for Actual Sales, Forecast, Pipeline, and the Sales Goal (shown as a percent of Actual) are shown. Then the ratios of Efficiency, Effectiveness, and Conversion are displayed. These ratios, which are shown as percentages, will vary by client, but their comparisons between periods provide ARP an indication of the rate of transition of prospects to customers. The KPI number provided in the far right column is determined by the formula of weightings as selected in the Sales Data screen (Figure 228) and the actual results for the period.

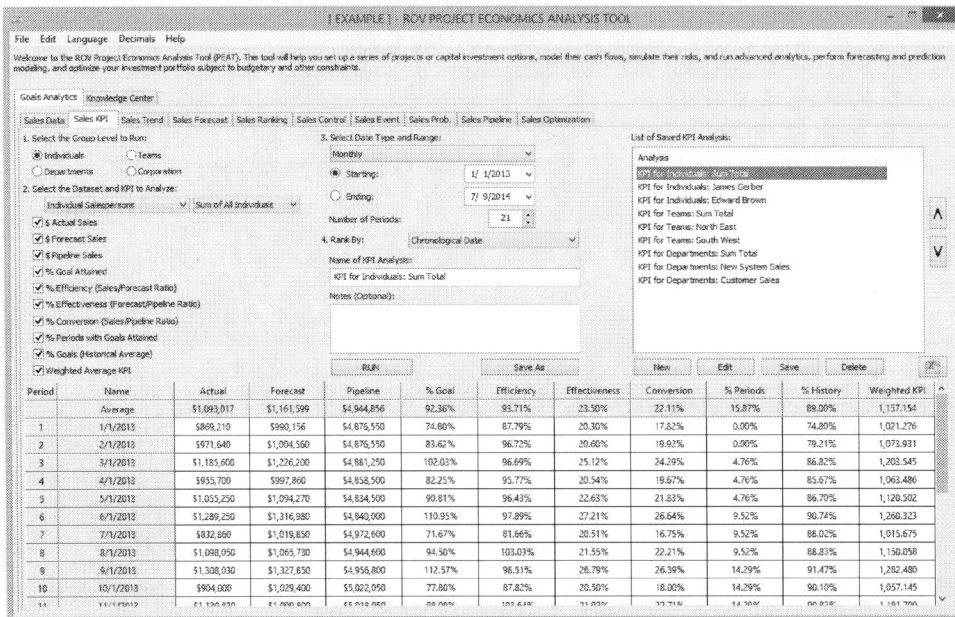

Figure 230: Selection and Weighting of KPIs

Sales Trend

The time-series trend within the elements of sales performance provides management a map of sales direction and velocity, and an understanding of the rate of success or lack thereof. Any element of sales performance can be included or excluded to isolate and zoom in on significant issues that may be affecting particular sales individuals or teams. The information is then graphically displayed for a real-time view of the past to present sales status.

Figure 231 is an example of ARP Actual Sales with the chart showing 21 months of information. The accumulation of data for multiple periods adds to the value of the analysis by allowing the significance of the fluctuations between periods to become apparent. ARP's example shows that quarterly period-ending months have a predominately higher sales figure. Therefore, management's tasks for increasing sales would be best focused on what actions would increase sales in the first two months of each quarter.

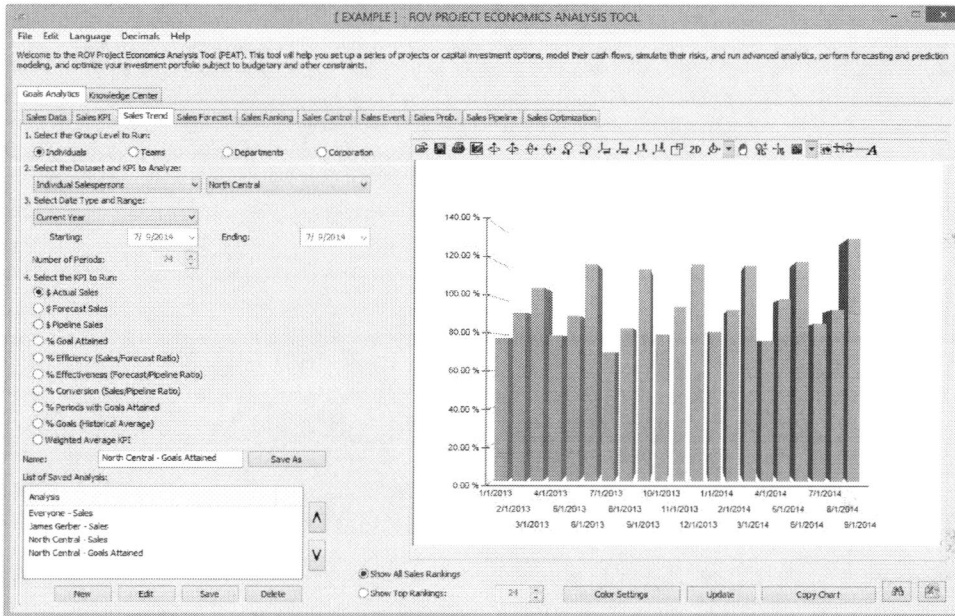

Figure 231: Selection of Sales Elements for Graphical Display of Sales Trends

Sales Forecast

Sales Forecast is the examination of the change occurring per period within the forecasts of individuals or teams. The time-series data for sales performance are combined and charted for analysis. The importance of the review is to understand what progress is being made in the market by the sales team towards growing the market share or success level. The software applies a variety of ROV forecast methods (e.g., ranging from ARIMA, Basic Econometrics, GARCH, and Nonlinear Multivariate Regressions, to Combinatorial Fuzzy Logic, Neural Networks, Stochastic Processes, Trend Analysis, and Time-Series Decomposition). The algorithms use self-selection by applying historical data to backcast and backfit existing sales or KPI data, and then uses the best-fitting model to predict and forecast the future. Clearly this approach is much more powerful than management guesstimates as it employs historical data on sales and sales performance metrics, applying advanced analytics and Monte Carlo risk simulations of thousands of scenarios and returning results with confidence intervals and probability distributions.

Figure 232 is an example of ARP Forecasts totaled for all salespersons and displayed graphically for 21 consecutive periods with a backcast and forecast model. The selection criteria in the screen determines the presentation of data by Individual, Team, or Department, or for the entire company. The user can choose the computational criteria (e.g., sales elements, periodicity, and groupings) to forecast. The chart reveals increasing trends for ARP Sales Forecasts and for Actual Sales. After seeing this chart, the task of ARP Sales Management would be to learn why forecasts increase for the third month per quarter but remain lower for the first two months.

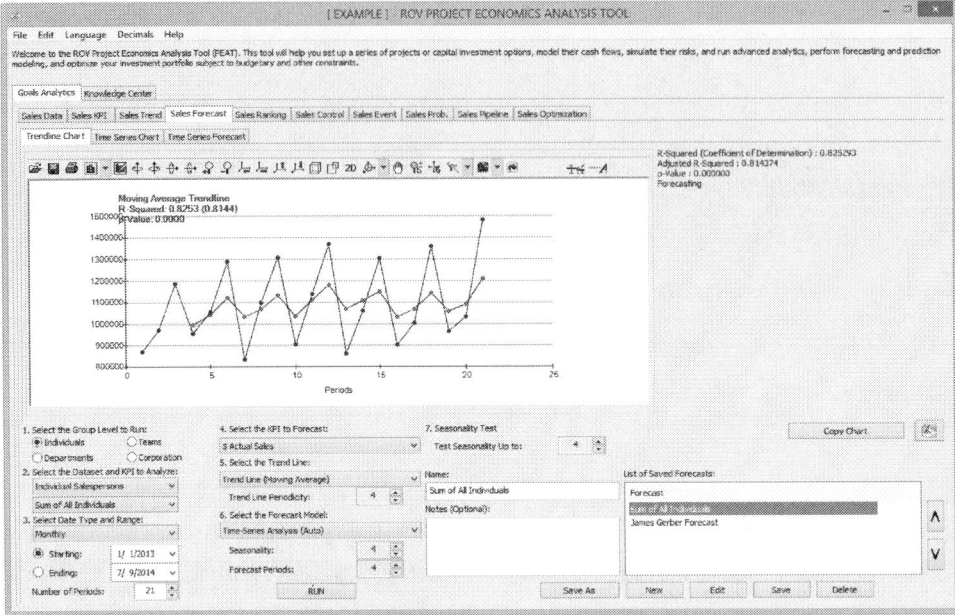

Figure 232: Selection and Graphing Sales Forecast Variations

Sales Ranking

Sales management needs an accurate identification of the most successful and least successful individuals within the sales force. Rewards can then be provided based on real performance, and the best contributors can be presented as role models for the rest of the team to emulate. Ranking provides a graphical depiction of results after sequencing the performance of individuals or teams.

Figure 233 is an example of ARP sales ranking for the top 10 salespersons across all sales territories. The selection criteria in steps 1–4 provide the identification of data for analysis, and step 5 involves selecting the methodology for display of the results. In this ARP example, the user has selected to show the top 10 rankings and depict the same in the format of bubble and bar charts. These alternative methods illuminate the achievements of the star contributors and show their relative relationship in contributions. Obviously, these are the salespersons who should be emulated by the rest of the sales team, and their factors for Efficiency, Effectiveness, and Conversion are particular indices of how they make the numbers that they do.

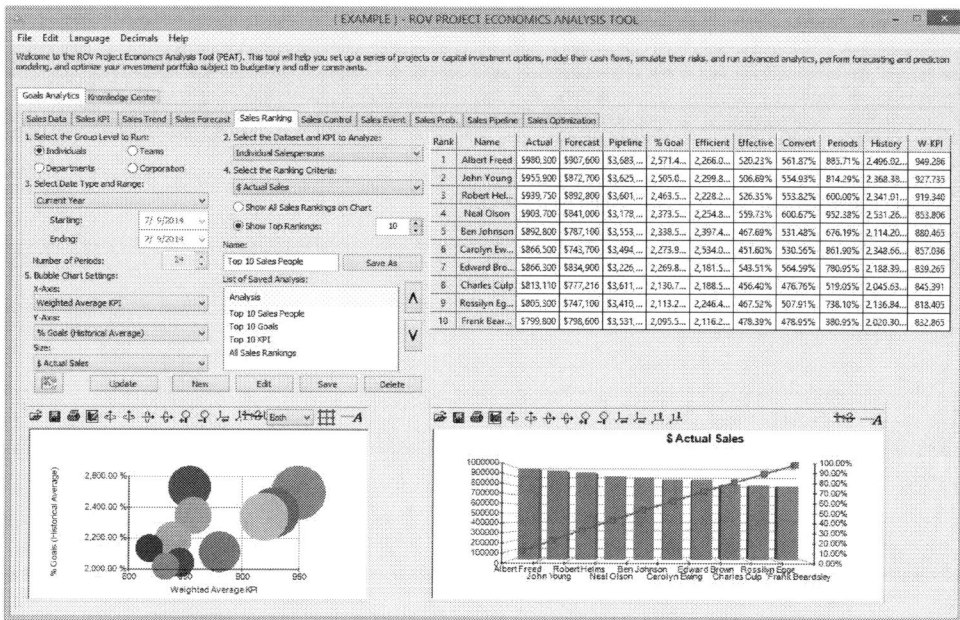

Figure 233: Selection and Ranking of Best or Worst Performers

Sales Control

Sales Control is a tool for examining the fluctuations and volatility within a specific team's or individual's performance over time. End results per period do not always tell the correct story of how sales staff approach the accomplishment of their sales goal. Variations between periods can be related to the time or position in the quarter or position within a fiscal year that are deemed most relevant to sales staff. Sales management needs to know if motivation for performance lags in particular periods and who amongst the sales team is best and worst in performance.

A Statistical Process Control analysis and control chart are employed on the time-series of historical and current sales and sales performance KPIs to determine if any spikes or valleys (i.e., extreme events where sales are suddenly at a low point or experienced a sudden and immediate increase) are entirely random given the volatile history of the KPI or can be deemed as a statistically significant event, signifying that intervention may be required (e.g., start of an economic downturn, a structural shift in the market with some new competitive entrant, etc.).

Figure 234 is an example of the Sales Control screen selected for all salespersons and for 21 periods of historical and current results. The selection options shown in steps 1–4 provide the user the ability to pick the dataset summary level to be reviewed and the charting type desired. In the case shown in Figure 234, the volatility of ARP sales is charted using a Statistical Process Control chart for sales totals. What the graph indicates is that ARP sales are fluctuating within 1 sigma of variance for 13 of the 21 periods reported. This may be considered an allowable fluctuation, but the other 8 periods are a different matter and specific occurrences that can be isolated should be reviewed for these other, out of bounds, periods. In fact, 3 of these periods are positive but the remaining 5 periods are negative.

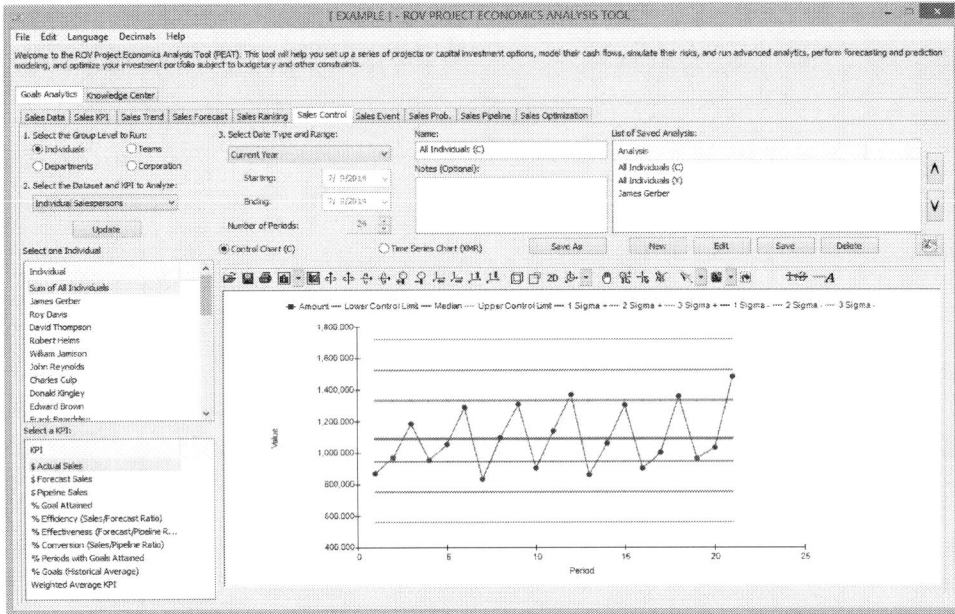

Figure 234: Selection and Computation of Sales Volatility

Sales Event

How effective are your sales trainings, new sales methodologies, conventions, sales events, conferences, marketing mailers, or search engine optimizations? You can enter the sales revenue or any sales KPI before the triggering event as a stand-alone variable and the post-event sales or KPI as a new variable and run statistical tests to determine if the differences between the two variables are due to random chance or if there is a statistically significant effect. In other words, did the new sales strategies have an impact?

Figure 235 is an example of the Sales Event screen populated with ARP data for multiple salespersons (each salesperson's data is entered as a row). The dataset loaded was for actual sales results for a certain number of periods before and after sales training was given to the group. The analysis revealed that no significant changes in sales were seen and, therefore, the sales training provided cannot be judged as being helpful in increasing sales. Obviously, the benefit to ARP is knowing whether or not investments of this nature are helpful for increasing sales because this analysis is a good *proof of concept test* to see if a certain event or sales training is worth its cost.

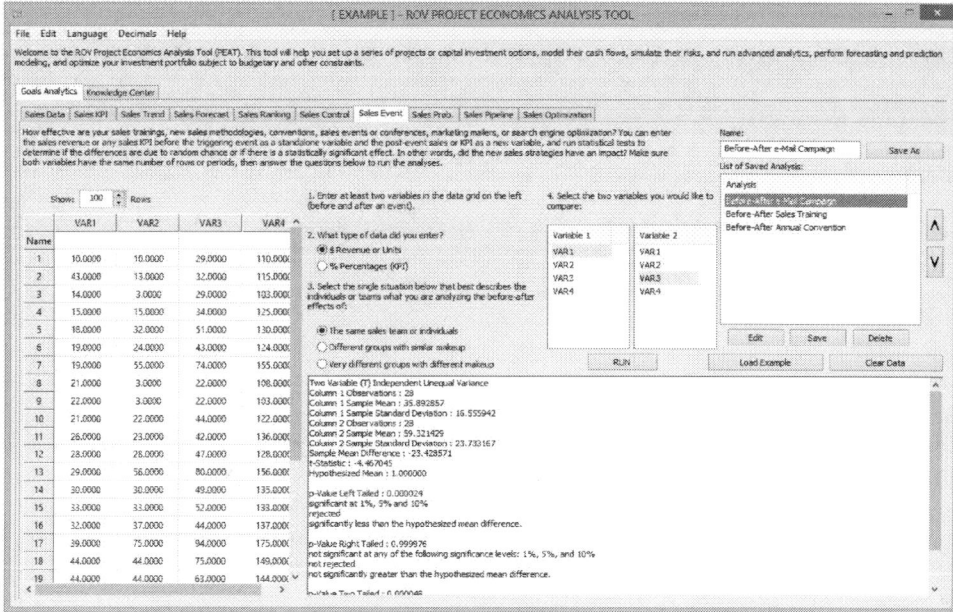

Figure 235: Data for Analysis of Event Effectiveness

Sales Probability

Your sales department, team, or individuals have just submitted their sales forecasts for the next few periods just as in the past, and corporate management wants to know the true likelihood that the forecasts submitted will be accomplished. The Sales Probability analysis allows for entry of past average performance to approximate and model the probability for success. The probability distribution outcomes are charted and a probability table is provided for further interpretation.

Figure 236 is an example of ARP sales data graphically depicting the probability that a sales goal will be achieved. The screen is designed for an interactive session for the LA using the sales projections of the sales staff. The sales forecast is entered along with the confidence level for attainment. The program calculates the cumulative probability of sales thresholds and charts the normal curve distribution. Both methods of calculation reveal sales potential and probability. In the ARP case, the percent confidence and the minimal variance between the actual forecast and the confidence level have yielded charts in which the sales probability is a clear example of how reality seldom follows commitments prior to the event. The most telling is the *Probability of Selling At Least Amount or More* chart. It is a reminder that forecasts must be factored before management decisions or financial forecasts are given to investors.

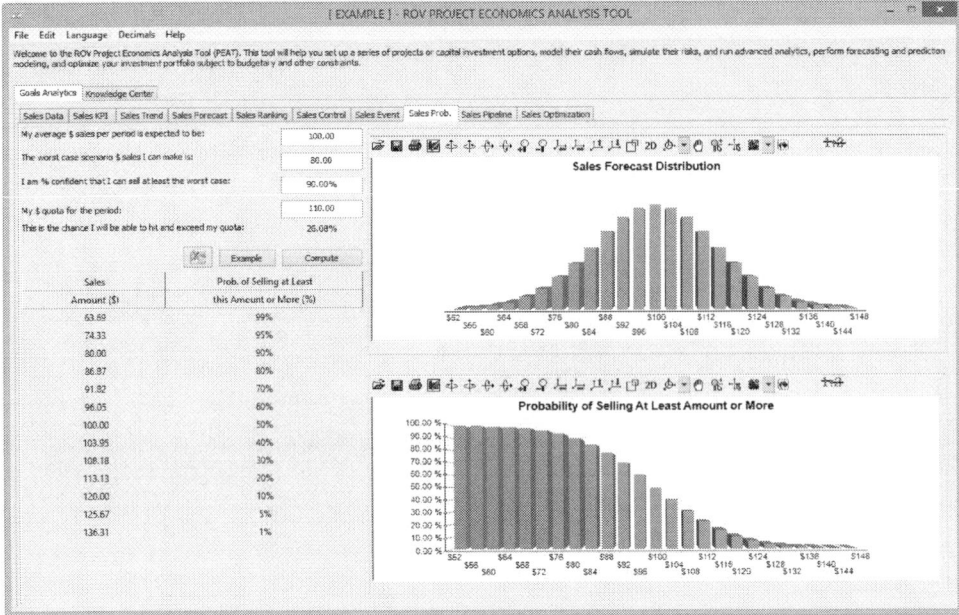

Figure 236: Probability That Sales Projections Will Be Attained

Sales Pipeline

Sales pipeline analysis allows you to enter the potential market and sales target opportunities over time and track how the sales pipeline is progressing (turnover rates, pipeline staleness, velocity and movement, growth, seasonality, etc.). Users start by setting the periodicity (we recommend the same periodicity going forward for better comparison) and entering the required pipeline data (Figure 237). Users then save the pipeline and keep adding pipelines for analysis and comparison over time.

Figure 237 is an example of ARP data for pipeline analysis (i.e., Pipeline Data tab). This area of sales is a significant precursor to success but is often the most overlooked aspect of sales development. The screen example for ARP shows the pipeline for just one salesperson. Each prospect is listed and the status of each is tracked as they are converted to customers or if the prospect is lost. The data grid alone is indicative of the activity of a salesperson. Pipelines should change over time with prospects discovered and added while others are deducted from the list because they were won or lost. For prospects to stay in the pipeline excessively long would indicate that either they are not truly a prospect or that the salesperson is possibly not working on converting them. This screen's data feeds the subsequent tab, Pipeline Analysis, which is not shown in this review (the charting of pipeline volatility). This chart is of similar construction to the other time-series charts in the program.

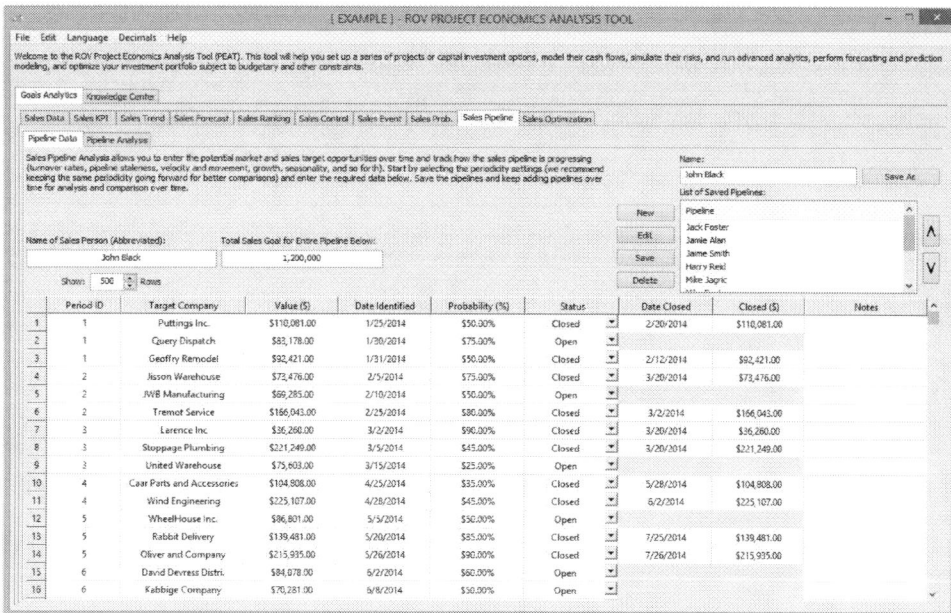

Figure 237: Comparison of the Pipeline Data Per Sales Individual

Sales Optimization

What is the probability your company will hit and exceed the targeted sales goals this period? Should you revise your sales targets to something more realistic (reduce the goals for a higher probability of attainment)? Should you add additional sales associates to help increase your chances of hitting the target (i.e., is the higher cost worth it)? Enter the typical salesperson's worst-case, most-likely, and best-case sales amounts; the targeted corporate sales goal; and the total number of sales associates available currently, and then run a Monte Carlo risk simulation to see your chances. In addition, the levels of diminishing marginal returns can be determined. That is, adding additional salesperson in theory would allow the company to sell more, but market saturation can occur, pipelines can overlap, internal sales competition can happen, and sales cannibalization of product lines can develop. With additional salespersons, the chances of hitting the company's sales goals increase, but at a decreasing rate. Therefore, sales optimization analysis looks at the nonlinear cost and return trade-offs. For example, hiring an additional salesperson may increase the probability of achieving your goals by 10%, but hiring a second person may only increase it by 17% (instead of 20%), and a third by only 22% (instead of 30%). And if the second new staffer will increase the total probability of achieving target at a 99.9% chance, hiring the third, fourth, or fifth person really does not contribute much if all that is required is that the sales target be attained, but the additional hires will cause the total costs to skyrocket (in fact, this action may even cause a spiraling effect of requiring an upward adjusted sales goal to cover the higher operational costs of the company).

Figure 238 is an example of the Sales Optimization screen with ARP data. The screen is interactive allowing the user to play *what-if* staffing games. The charts show the Simulated Sales Forecast for ARP with the probability declining as the sales projection increases. How much risk does ARP Sales Management want to take with upper management? The *Standard Analysis* tab reveals forecasts that are achievable and risk can be known. Included in the screen is the

Simulated Probabilities of Achieving Target chart that shows the staffing necessary based on actual productivity. For ARP, the chart indicates that sales probability jumps to 100% between the staffing levels of 9 to 11. Certainly it is not possible to instantly add sales personnel at will to meet the sales goals of the company, but it is necessary to see productivity calculated as a component of average staff productivity. Working in this tab also allows sales management to understand the capability of the company's staff and initiate any staff requests with firm numbers for productivity.

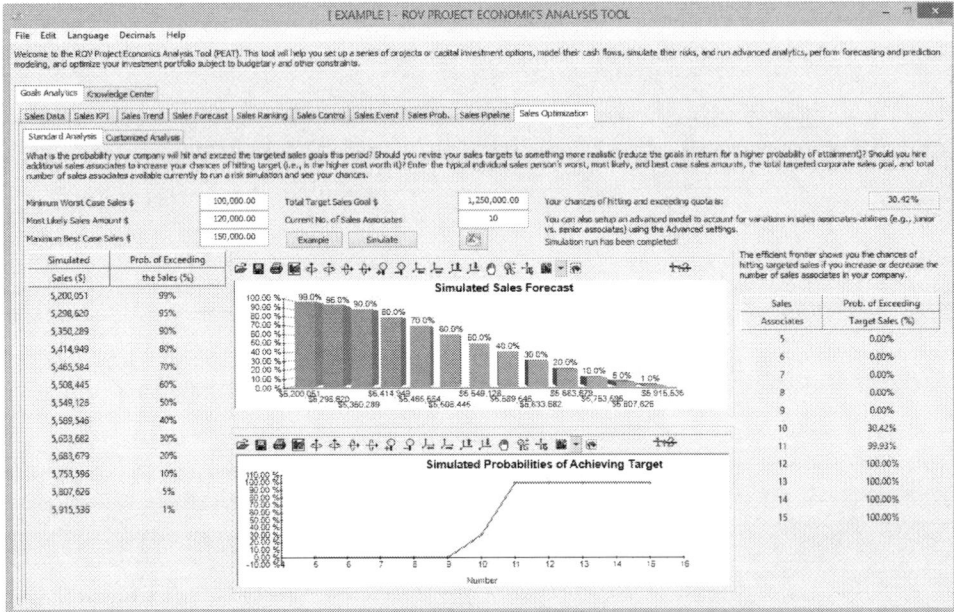

Figure 238: Sales Actuals Against Computed Future Sales Outcomes

Figure 239 is an ARP example of *Customized Optimization* with functionality for optimization analysis of the sales performance for particular salespersons. The current tab is a slight variation of the previous *Standard Analysis* tab in which the current tab models sales teams or departments individually, with unique sales capabilities. For example, an individual's salesperson's historical or anticipated performance for *worst-case*, *most-likely*, and *best-case* scenarios can be entered, Monte Carlo risk simulation is run, and the results are charted to show the cumulative probabilities of hitting given sales targets. The results of Figure 239 for ARP indicate that given the assumptions of the sales team, there is a 99% confidence that ARP can sell at least $1.42M, an 80% confidence of selling $1.54M, and less than a 5% confidence of exceeding $1.73M in sales that particular period.

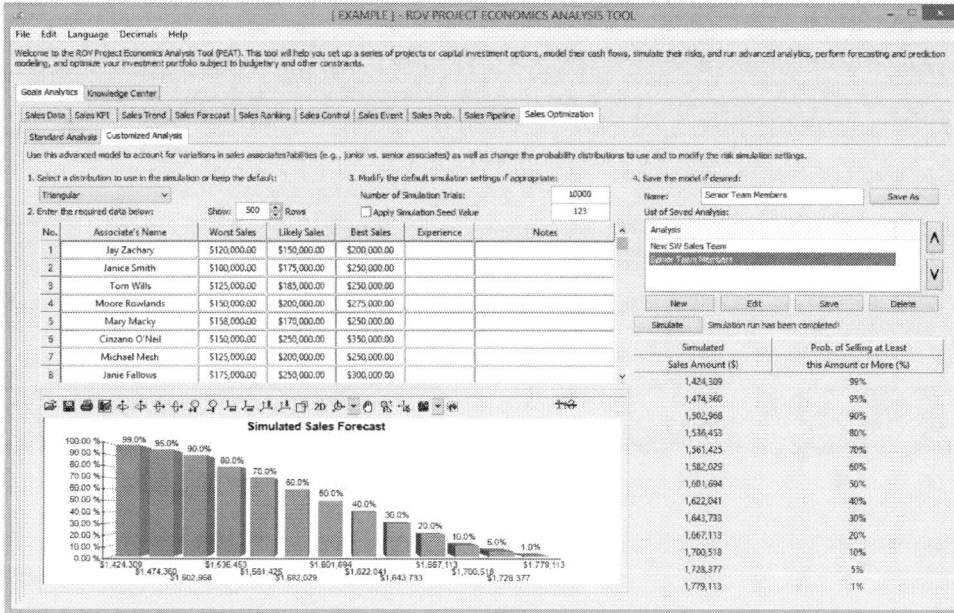

Figure 239: Sales Actual Potential with Customized Probability Settings

Conclusion

The combination of SPIDER and SPEAR is intended to provide a comprehensive service in assisting sales performance analysis for any organization seeking to improve sales and to also better understand the nuances that are unique to its products, markets, and sales staff. The overall goals of the service are significant and varied: to demystify the profession of sales, to provide actual improvement per sales staff member, to reveal the inhibitors and facilitators of good sales practice, and to alert management to sales performance trends and risk thresholds on a timely basis. All of these goals lead to a better understanding of present risks based on quantifiable metrics. Where SPIDER is the facility to drive improved sales and smoother communications of sales status, SPEAR is the facility for understanding the characteristics of the company's sales performance.

The benefits of SPEAR can be applied to compensation, hiring, severance, and the overall communication of sales information to all interested parties, including board-level oversight, C-level management, and the operational management tasked with fulfillment of sales plans.

For ARP, the use of both products has provided significant value. Its cost to use SPIDER has been repaid with a sales force completely knowledgeable of their sales goals and a sense of urgency for accomplishment. Compensation has been adjusted to recognize performers with consistent sales for all periods per quarter, and the star contributors have been recognized as model sales staff for all sales departments to emulate. Needless to say, the habitual underperformers have been identified and actions taken to address their issues or remove them from their role in sales. Overall, ARP claims a significant sales growth for which they credit the use of Goals HQ analytics.

The value of SPEAR is part and parcel of the overall results. ARP's upper management is now more comfortable with the forecasts received since they are backed by the analysis of

SPEAR. Sales-related costs are more carefully invested, and investment has actually increased since the *Event* analysis provides real understanding of effectiveness of certain marketing campaigns and sales efforts. The concept of sales surprises has been virtually removed since the trend analysis can predict end results more accurately than intuition. Surprises still occur but they are generally positive with the capture of a few *blue birds* from time to time. The human element is not ignored through any of the analysis now available to the sales management staff, but the ability to now ask pertinent questions and see real-time reports juxtaposed with historical data and then modeled by the SPEAR tools has removed the adversarial relationship between field and in-house staff.

Sales can be the most exciting aspect of a company's operations. The fulfilling nature of adding new customers or new revenue to the firm and winning the battle of ideas for a company's products should be one of the most satisfying tasks that any employee can have. SPIDER and SPEAR are two tools matched to the profession of sales for the salesperson and for his or her sales management.

CASE STUDY 21: EMPLOYER-SPONSORED HEALTHCARE INSURANCE; REAL OPTIONS STRATEGIES, ANALYTICS, AND INSIGHTS INCLUDING THE U.S. AFFORDABLE CARE ACT

This business case is contributed by Thomas Schmidt, MBA, MIM, CEBS, CPCU, CRM. Tom is a boutique management consultant and CEO of Health Quant focused on employee benefits and the deployment of healthcare-data-driven decision strategies, predictive modeling, evidence-based guidelines, and financial analytics in the large employer group market. He is the co-developer of ROV Health Quant Data Modeler with Dr. Johnathan Mun that is a software application used to quantify and model a comprehensive suite of insurance and noninsurance options for employer-sponsored health insurance and operationalizes key provisions of the Affordable Care Act into its modeling. This case is an overview of how modeling risk in such a dynamic environment is valuable.

The United States passed major healthcare reform legislation in March 2010, hereafter referred to as the Affordable Care Act (ACA). It is complicated and has many moving parts. Figure 240 identifies the key healthcare finance stakeholders and their moving parts. What makes this so important is that public and private healthcare spending within the United States is 17.6% of a $15.8 trillion gross domestic product, which equates to $8,233 per person. As such, the changes brought about by this legislation have created a monumental disruption opportunity as employers strategize what to do with respect to their employer-sponsored insurance offerings. Our focus here is on the employer-sponsored health insurance portion of the ACA because even though this system is currently subsidized through the tax code with the deductibility of the employers' contributions from the corporation and the exclusion from the taxable income of the employee for these employers' contributions, employers need to assess and determine what option is optimal in creating value as they define it. Figure 241 illustrates a sampling of strategic real options an employer may review when managing its healthcare exposure.

AFFORDABLE CARE ACT
Circa 2015

INDIVIDUAL MANDATE TAX
Greater-of Calculation
Fee per Individual + ¼ Fee per Child /
Capped at (3X Fee per Family)
2015 – Fee ($325) | Percent (2%)
2016 – Fee ($695) | Percent (2.5%)
OR Percent of Excess Income
(Gross Income – Filing Threshold)
Lesser-of Calculation
Prior Result OR National Average
Bronze ($2,484 I, $12,420 F) 2015

PREMIUM TAX CREDITS
Premium Tax Credits are Matched to the
Percentage of Income to the Federal
Poverty Level from 133% to 400% and
Cap the Cost of Coverage from 2% to
9.5% of Household Income.

COST-SHARING REDUCTIONS
1/2 | 73% AV | 201 to 250% FPL
2/3 | 87% AV 151 to 200% FPL
2/3 | 94% AV 100 to 150% FPL

ADDITIONAL MEDICARE TAX
+ .9% HI Tax > $250K [J] | $200K [I]

MINIMUM VALUE TEST
60% Actuarial Value
No Annual | Lifetime Maximums

AFFORDABILITY TEST
9.5% Income | Self-Only Premium

TRANSITIONAL REINSURANCE
$5.25 Fee Per Member Per Year

COMPARATIVE EFFECTIVENESS
$2 Fee Per Member Per Year

HIGH-COST PLAN EXCISE TAX
40% Nondeductible Excise Tax
$10,200 Single | $27,500 Family

Employee

Individual Mandate
Employer Sponsored

On or Off Exchange
Network Providers

PREMIUM TAX CREDITS
Directly to Insurance Carrier
Administered by Exchange

COST-SHARING REDUCTIONS
OOP Limit Reductions
70% to 93% Actuarial Value

MINIMUM VALUE THRESHOLD
Minimum Value Calculator
Design-Based Safe Harbors
Actuarial Certification
Plan's Share ≥ 60% of Costs

Federal Government

Large | 50 FTE
Provide Coverage
or Pay Penalty

Employer

PENALTY CALCULATION
Total Full-Time Employees – 30
Multiplied by $2,000 | Annual | 2015

ASSESSABLE PAYMENT
Fails MV and/or Affordability Tests
1 EE Receives Premium Tax Credit
$3,000 | Annual | Capped | 2015

Capped

Marketplace Types
Types of Exchanges

Insurance Company

ESSENTIAL HEALTH BENEFITS
1. Ambulatory
2. Emergency
3. Hospitalization
4. Maternity | Newborn
5. Mental Health | SA | BH
6. Prescription Drugs
7. Rehabilitative | Habilitative
8. Laboratory
9. Preventive | Wellness | CDM
10. Pediatric (incl. Oral + Vision)

NETWORKS
On Exchange – Narrowed Networks
Off Exchange – Existing Networks

State

MARKETPLACES
14 State-Based (SBM)
7 State Partnership (SPM)
27 Federally Facilitated (FFM)
3 Federally Supported (FSM)

MEDICAL LOSS RATIO
Individual and Small Group – 80%
Large Group – 85%

ACTUARIAL VALUE TEST
Individual and Small Group Only
60% | Bronze
70% | Silver
80% | Gold
90% | Platinum

SUBSIDY
Advance Premium Tax Credits
Cost-Sharing Reductions

STATE-MANDATED BENEFITS
Individual
Fully Insured Small Group
Fully Insured Large Group

MINIMUM VALUE TEST
Fully Insured Large Group
60% Actuarial Value
No Annual | Lifetime Maximums

LEVEL PLAYING FIELD
On or Off Exchange | Rates

RISK ADJUSTMENT PAYMENTS
Risk Corridor ± 3% HHS | 3 Years
Risk Adjustment – Low to High Risk
Insurance Carriers | Permanent

MULTISTATE PLAN PROGRAM
Office of Personnel Management
Two Options in Each Exchange

MEDICAID EXPANSION
30 Yes | 2 Open Debate | 19 No

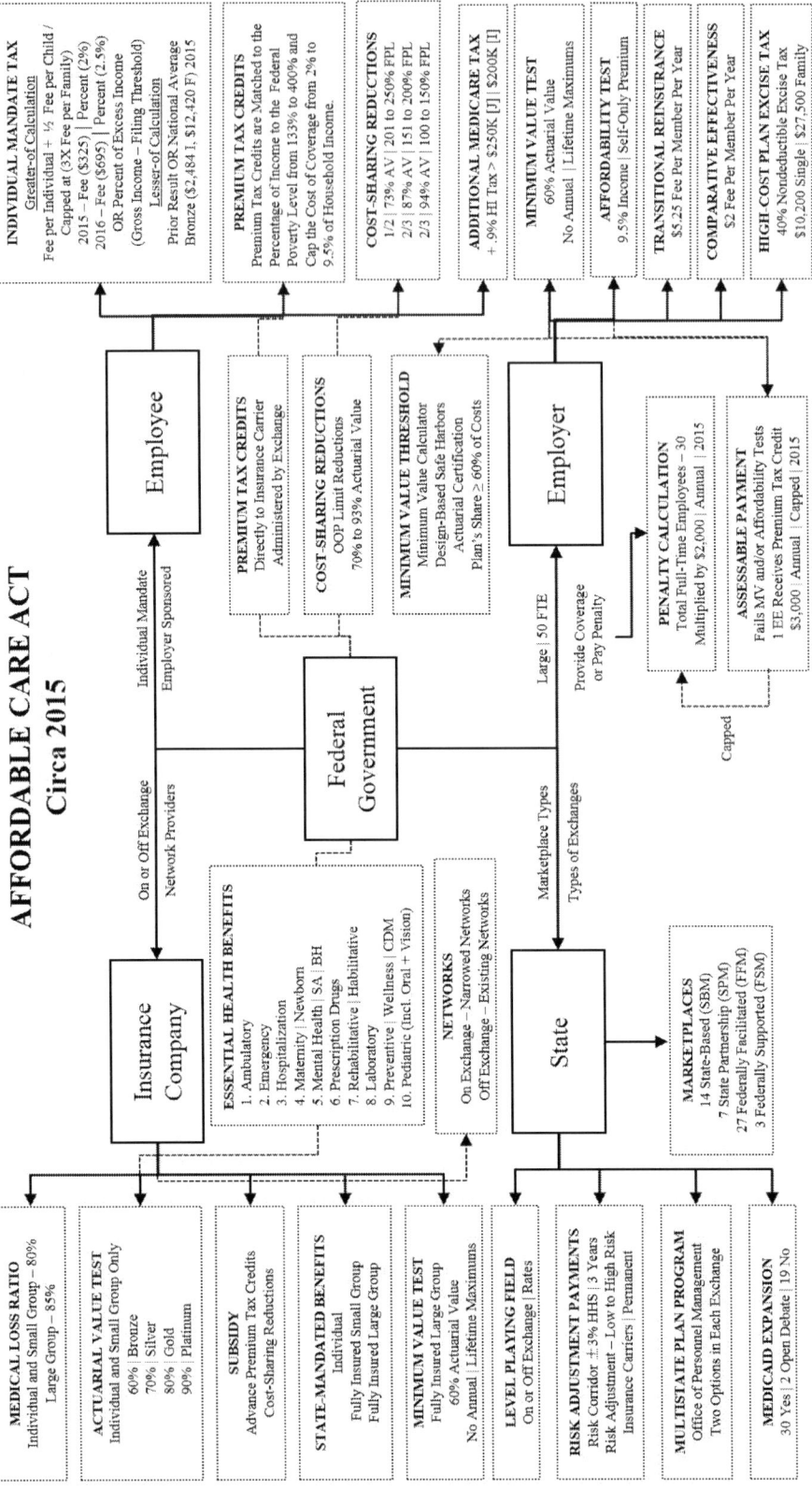

Figure 240: Structure of the U.S. Affordable Care Act

Current + Renewal Plan Offerings	Comparative Plan Offerings + Plan Options | Minimum Essential Coverage (MEC), Value (MV), Affordability (MAF)
Terminate + Realize	Employer Elects to Terminate Employer Sponsored Insurance Pays Annual 4980H(a) Penalty | Loses Tax Shields | Employer Realizes Savings
Terminate + Distribute	Employer Elects to Terminate Employer Sponsored Insurance Pays Annual 4980H(a) Penalty | Loses Tax Shields | Employer Distributes Savings
High Deductible Health Plan	Employer Provides Qualified High Deductible Health Plan Employer Realizes Savings | Employee Funds Health Savings Accounts
Consumer Driven Health Plan	Employer Provides Higher Deductible Health Plan Employer Funds Integrated Health Reimbursement Arrangements
Controlled Group Considerations	Single Plan | Affiliated Service Groups and Employer Shared Responsibility Applicable Large Employer and/or Applicable Large Employer Member
Special Enrollment Triggers	Funding Back Stop | Off-Anniversary Enrollment Window Part-Time Employee Eligibility | Strategically Priced to Trigger Premium Tax Credits
Strategic Firewall	Lowest Cost Self-Only Premium and 9.5% Employee Only Safe Harbor Family Member Premium Tax Credit Access + Prevents Dependent Surge
Retain + Minimize	Employer Elects to Retain Employer Sponsored Insurance Designed to Avoid 4980H Penalties and Meet Minimum Affordability Test
Retain + Maximize	Employer Elects to Retain Employer Sponsored Insurance Designed as an Attraction + Retention Option | 100% All Tiers
Defined Contribution – Employer	Defined Contribution Approach – Employer Control | Single or Dual Carriers Defined % or $ Contribution Amount | Health Reimbursement Arrangements
Defined Contribution – Exchange	Adopt Defined Contribution Approach – Private Exchange Control Single or Multiple Carriers | Group Platform | ESI | Minimum Value

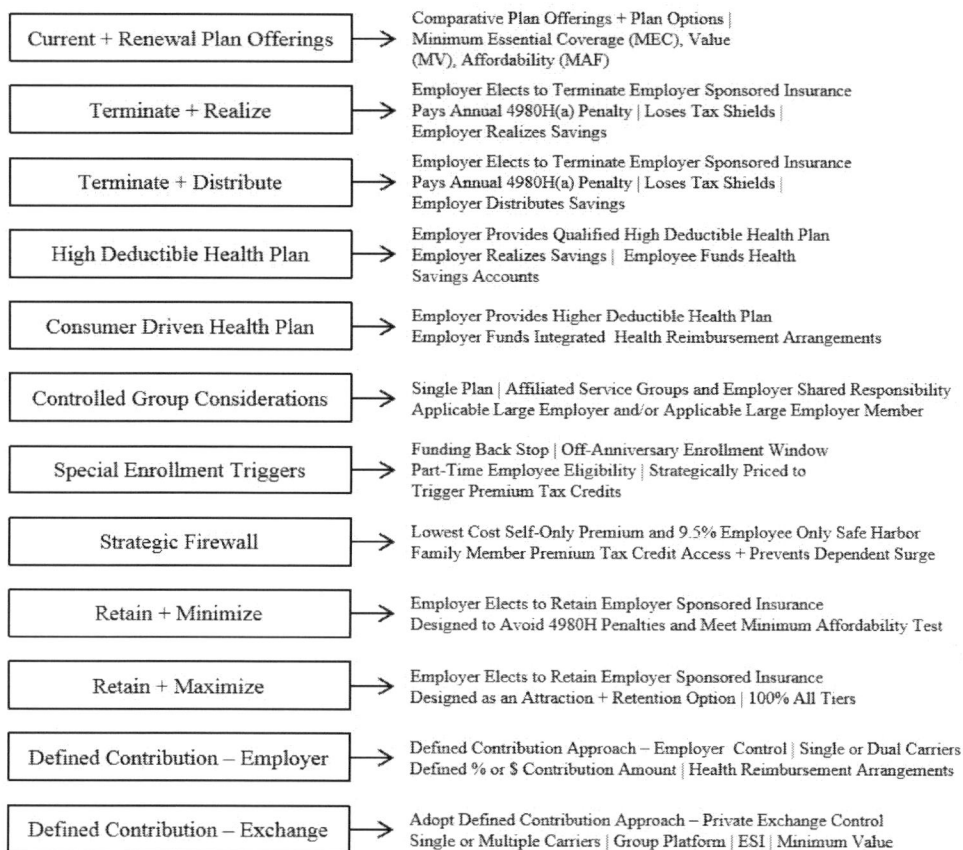

Figure 241: Description of Employer-Sponsored Insurance Strategic Real Options

The Decision-Making Process

The economic pressures to know, quantify, select, and execute are critical in the control of healthcare costs. However, the process begins with setting the goals (Goals), outlining the strategy (Strategy), selecting the tactics (Tactics), implementing the strategy (Implementation) and applying the controls (Control). What follows is a discussion of the interrelationship of these elements and how, as we speak to the strategic options development, financial analytics, and modeling, they are integrated into the overall process.

Goals—Setting goals involves the systematic approach of developing an understanding of the sources of company value. This activity identifies trade-offs between monetary and nonmonetary benefits, increasing revenues versus decreasing expenses, and attempting to attract and retain human capital while trying to effectively manage plans to the market, and so on. The key considerations in alignment may be cost-focused, revenue-focused, market-focused, customer-focused, and employee-focused goals.

- Review Corporate Mission Statement
- Identify Business Strategy
- Discover Key Business Objectives
- Align Plan Objectives
- Establish Key Performance Metrics

Strategy—Developing a strategy outlines the logic of the organization's approach directed at achieving its goals and involves the identification and understanding of the underlying issues, the development and quantification of strategic options, the narrowing of the options for consideration, and the presentation of these options for selection and evaluation.

- Issue Identification
- Strategic Options Development
- Strategy Identification
- Strategy Evaluation

Tactics—Tactics comprise the mix of actionable elements that are deployed in support of the desired strategy with the three-fold objective to create, communicate, and deliver value. Value creation defines the processes used to capture the value for organization and its employees, value communication brings the awareness of the value to the stakeholders, and value delivery transfers the captured value to the organization and its employees.

- Financial Analytics and Modeling
- Health Plan Analytics
- Health Risk Management
- Networks and Network Effectiveness
- Pharmacy Analytics

Implementation—Developing an implementation plan provides an outline of the timeline for executing the strategy and tactics. The two key factors in implementation are the processes that enable the company to implement its strategy and tactics and the people managing the processes. The underlying processes are the logistics that support the company to achieve its goal and deliver value. The people are the human-resources dimension of implementation and the identification of the core skills and knowledge of the people involved.

Control—The policy for evaluating the performance and monitoring of the effectiveness of the strategy to ensure the adequate progress toward the set goal involves applying controls. A control is designed to continually assess the viability of the strategies and tactics through the use of key performance metrics and to provide environmental updates from the market that educate and inform as to newly issued regulations or legislation, plan design considerations, and emerging technologies for assessment.

- Reporting
- Per Capita Results
- Plan Utilization Metrics
- Productivity Costs
- Aggregate Financials

This is no small task as there are multiple stakeholders involved in the process (see Figure 242) and each participant does not have the exact same finance or benefits background or understanding of the nuances for each option, yet each is still accountable and responsible for the decisions. Thus it is even more critical to convert any analysis into the level of understanding for the decision makers to make it clear, concise, and actionable.

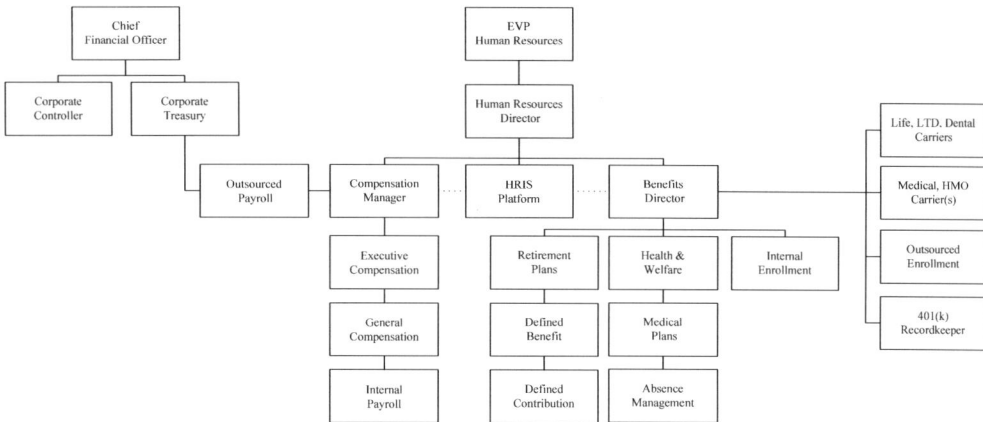

Figure 242: Organizational Chart

Strategic Options Development

As noted earlier, the ACA has generated many opportunities for an employer's consideration:

- A fully insured employer may elect to *self-fund* to avoid state-mandated benefits requirements, eliminate insurance premium taxes and take advantage of the favorable experience and pay-as-you go cash flow funding flexibility through Employee Retirement Income Security Act (ERISA) preemption and gain more control over their plan design that meets the minimum value actuarial requirements under the ACA.

- An employer may elect to not offer or to *terminate* its employer-sponsored insurance coverage as an enterprise paying the 4980H(a) annual penalty of $2,000 for each full-time employee not being offered coverage (less the first 30 full-time employees), losing its tax shield (penalty is non-deductible), retaining or distributing the savings in the event the cost is lower than their current arrangement, and shifting the decision to its employees as to whether they will elect to pay the individual mandate penalty, gain coverage as a dependent on another group plan, secure coverage in the private insurance market or opt for coverage in the state-based, state-partnership, federally facilitated or federally supported marketplaces.

- An employer may elect to continue to provide employer-sponsored insurance through the group platform, but decide to adopt a *defined contribution* strategy for its employees. This may take the form of continuing with the current level of coverage and multiple plan options with one or multiple carriers, contracting with a carrier to gain access to its private exchange and networks, or directly contracting with a private exchange to gain access to multiple carriers and networks.

- An employer may elect to continue to provide employer-sponsored insurance, but look at a strategy that looks at the implications of dramatically altering coverage geographically as the cost of coverage may no longer be sustainable in a particular region of the country. This may mean either a *hybrid funding* arrangement to shift high-cost users into a fixed cost environment, plan design changes, or a termination strategy that anti-selects against the public exchange.

- An employer may decide to no longer allow the *working spouses* of eligible employees to be covered as dependents under the health care plan. Non-working spouses and dependent children to age 26 remain eligible for dependent coverage. However, utilizing both eligibility definitions and contribution strategies, the objectives may range from eliminating working spouses only to adopting a pricing strategy that effectively lowers all dependent participation without violating the requirements of the Affordable Care Act.

Employers need to know how to model these types of options and risks. One way is to take the demographic and financial data of the company, integrate it with the marketplace data and illustrate the financial impact of the options by comparing it to the current structure and program. Figure 243 shows how the modeling process is initiated by mapping the data to calculate the options using the Health Quant Data Modeler (HQDM) utility.

File Variables Tools Help

| Data | Mapping | Model | Options | Forecasts | Optimization | Cohorts | Charts | Simulation | Benchmarks | Dashboard |

Map Variables   Add Table   Delete Table   Options...

Visualize | Demographics | Experience

N	VAR1	VAR2	VAR3	VAR4	VAR5	VAR6	VAR7	VAR8	VAR9	VAR10	VAR11	VAR12	VAR13	VAR14	VAR1
NOTES	DL_UEID	DL_ST...	DL_FTE	DL_CY...	DL_DOB	DL_AGE	DL_AG...	DL_AG...	DL_AG...	DL_AG...	DL_ZIP	DL_4TI...	DL_DP...	DL_4TI...	DL_4T
1	1.00	TN	FTE	44000.00	3/4/19...	51.00	0.00	0.00	0.00	0.00	36689.00	EE Only	1.00	451.64	451.6
2 / 3	Unique Employee ID	State	Full Time or Part Time	Annual Salary	Date of Birth	Employee Age	Spouse Age	Child 1 Age	Child 2 Age	Child 3 Age	5 Digit Zip Code	Four Tier Rating Structure	Number of Dependents	Four Tier Total Rate	Four Tier EE Only Rate
4	4.00	NE	FTE	52000.00	11/7/1...	28.00	0.00	0.00	0.00	0.00	97731.00	EE Only	1.00	312.55	312.5
5	5.00	NY	FTE	37000.00	12/5/1...	27.00	0.00	0.00	0.00	0.00	30824.00	EE Only	1.00	533.43	533.4
6	6.00	PA	FTE	59000.00	7/7/19...	31.00	0.00	0.00	0.00	0.00	41168.00	EE Only	1.00	311.86	311.8
7	7.00	NY	FTE	61000.00	5/4/19...	51.00	0.00	0.00	0.00	0.00	48267.00	EE Only	1.00	949.29	949.2
20	20.00	MA	FTE	62000.00	4/11/1...	45.00	0.00	0.00	0.00	0.00	78118.00	EE Only	1.00	469.80	469.8
21	21.00	CA	FTE	50000.00	3/7/19...	51.00	0.00	0.00	0.00	0.00	95133.00	EE Only	1.00	622.35	622.3
22	22.00	MI	FTE	52000.00	7/19/1...	35.00	0.00	0.00	0.00	0.00	41347.00	EE Only	1.00	397.32	397.3
23	23.00	NC	FTE	38000.00	5/11/1...	53.00	0.00	0.00	0.00	0.00	12540.00	EE Only	1.00	656.05	656.0

Figure 243: Sample of Required Data Elements in a Data Grid

After the options have been calculated and the option variables have been settled (i.e., whether to include or exclude part-time employees, to expand premium tax credits to those with family coverage or illustrate for the employee only, to illustrate the individual income tax impact resulting from the loss of the IRC § 106 tax-favored employer contribution towards employer-sponsored insurance coverage that means the gross income of an employee does not include the contributions that the employer makes to an accident or health plan, etc.), things get more interesting. First we review the strategic options developed and their cost (Figure 244) and then progress to the next stage of additional analytics and modeling.

- *Current Option.* This is the net cost to the employer under the current employer-sponsored insurance arrangement. It is calculated by deducting employee contributions and the corporate tax shield from the total cost of coverage (Figure 244, Reference A).

- *Termination Option.* The option is to not offer minimum essential coverage to full-time employees (FTEs). The net cost is the sum of the Employer-Shared Responsibility assessable payments of $2,000 per full-time employee multiplied by the total number of FTEs minus the first 30 FTEs with the lost tax shield resulting from the non-tax-deductibility of the assessable penalty payments added back (Figure 244, Reference B).

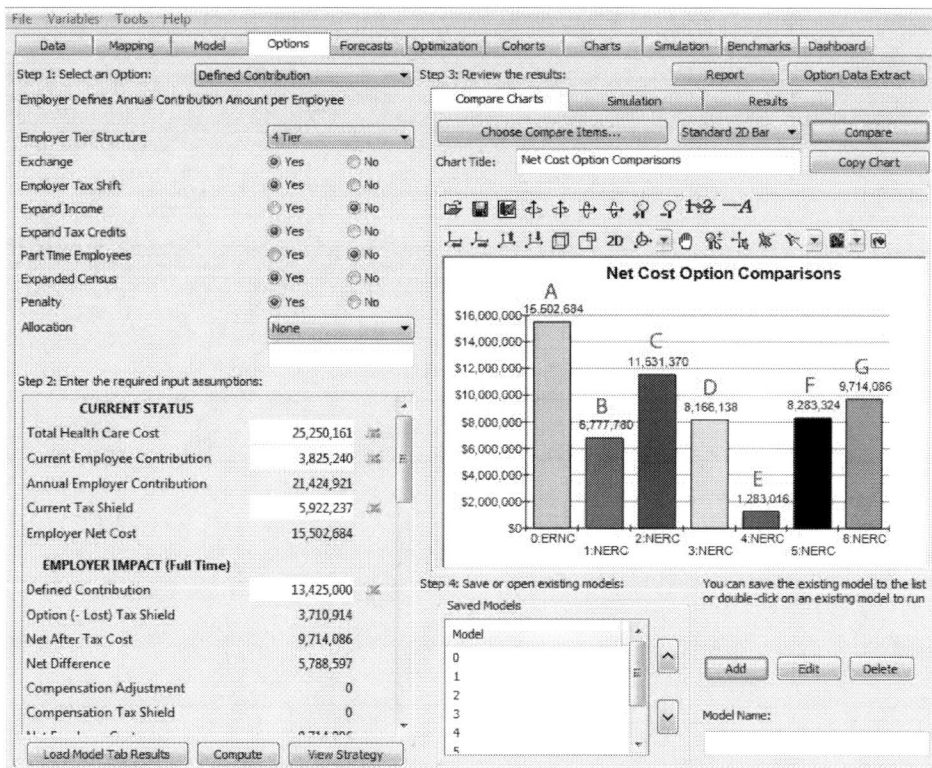

Figure 244: Employer-Sponsored Insurance and Noninsurance Options

- *Consumer-Driven Health Plan Option.* The option is to offer employer-sponsored insurance for all employees using a qualified high deductible health plan (HDHP) with a health savings account (HSA) or a higher-deductible health plan using an integrated health reimbursement arrangement (HRA) with the employer funding $500 in the account for each participant. The net cost for the option is gross premium for the coverage plus the account contribution less employee contributions and corporate tax shields (Figure 244, Reference C).

- *Strategic Firewall Option.* This option is to offer employer-sponsored insurance to employees, non-working spouses and dependent children up to age 26. The net cost to the employer under the current employer-sponsored insurance arrangement is calculated by deducting employee contributions and the corporate tax shield from the total cost of coverage (Figure 244, Reference D).

- *Minimum Compliance Option.* This option is to offer employer-sponsored insurance for employees only and dependent children up to age 26 and minimize the employer's contribution toward the cost of coverage to the level that meets the minimum affordability requirement established by the IRS, that is, the level where the employee's contribution for self-only premium for the lowest-cost coverage that provides minimum value that is less than 9.5% of the employee's W-2. The net cost to the employer under the employer-sponsored insurance arrangement is calculated by deducting employee contributions and the corporate tax shield from the total cost of coverage (Figure 244, Reference E).

- *Attraction and Retention Option.* This option is to offer employer-sponsored insurance coverage and use it as a talent attraction and retention instrument. It offers coverage with the employer contributing 100% for all tiers of coverage. The net cost to the employer is the total cost of coverage less the corporate tax shields (Figure 244, Reference F).

- *Defined-Contribution Option.* This option is for the employer to define an amount as a percentage of salary, a flat dollar, or a combination toward the cost of employer-sponsored insurance. This illustration uses a formula with a cap of $5,000 per participant. The employer continues to offer coverage on a group basis with its contributions structured under a tax-favored approach (i.e., integrated health reimbursement arrangements [HRA], employer-funded health savings accounts [HSA], or a credit-based cafeteria plan [IRC § 125]). The coverages offered are assumed to be multiple options administered by one carrier directly contracting with the employer where the actuarial values of the options range from 60% to 80%. The net cost to the employer under this option is the employer's defined contribution amount less the corporate tax shields (Figure 244, Reference G).

Strategic options development is an important first step, but additional steps are required in the review process for each option before a decision can be made. In other words, the options create the framework and the additional modeling and analytics assist in facilitating a decision. To provide one illustration, we will focus on the termination option with the understanding that the other options also create similar types of derivatives.

Termination Option Example

We see in Figure 245 that the net cost of this option is $6,777,780 compared to the current net cost of coverage at $15,502,684. In what follows (see Figure 245), this cost includes the penalty plus the cost of the lost tax shield. As shown, there is a net savings of $8,724,903, and should an employer continue to sponsor health coverage this spread would be perennially realized as the difference between the trended healthcare costs and the cost for termination (the required penalty and lost tax shield).

In short, a large employer must either offer at least 95% of its full-time employees the opportunity to enroll in an employer-sponsored health insurance program or pay an annual penalty of $2,000 for each full-time employee less the first 30 full-time employees. If the employer offers such coverage, it is considered to have met the definition of an "offer" of minimum essential coverage. If the full-time employees elect not to take up the coverage, this has no impact on the penalty calculation because the only issue is whether coverage has been offered.

Notwithstanding the offer of coverage as previously noted, if the offer of coverage is either not affordable (i.e., the employee-only contribution for the "lowest cost self-only coverage" is greater than 9.5% of the employee's W-2 income) or it does not meet the minimum value requirement (i.e., the value of the coverage is less than an actuarial value of 60%), the employer will be responsible for a 4980H(b) assessable payment penalty of $3,000 for each full-time employee to which these conditions apply and who also receives a premium tax credit. However, the accumulation of these penalties will never exceed the penalty amount that would be assessed if the employer did not offer coverage (4980H(a) penalty amount), which, as noted, is the total number of full-time employees less the first thirty full-time employees multiplied by $2,000. This termination option illustrates the cost for the employer if it elected to not offer coverage.

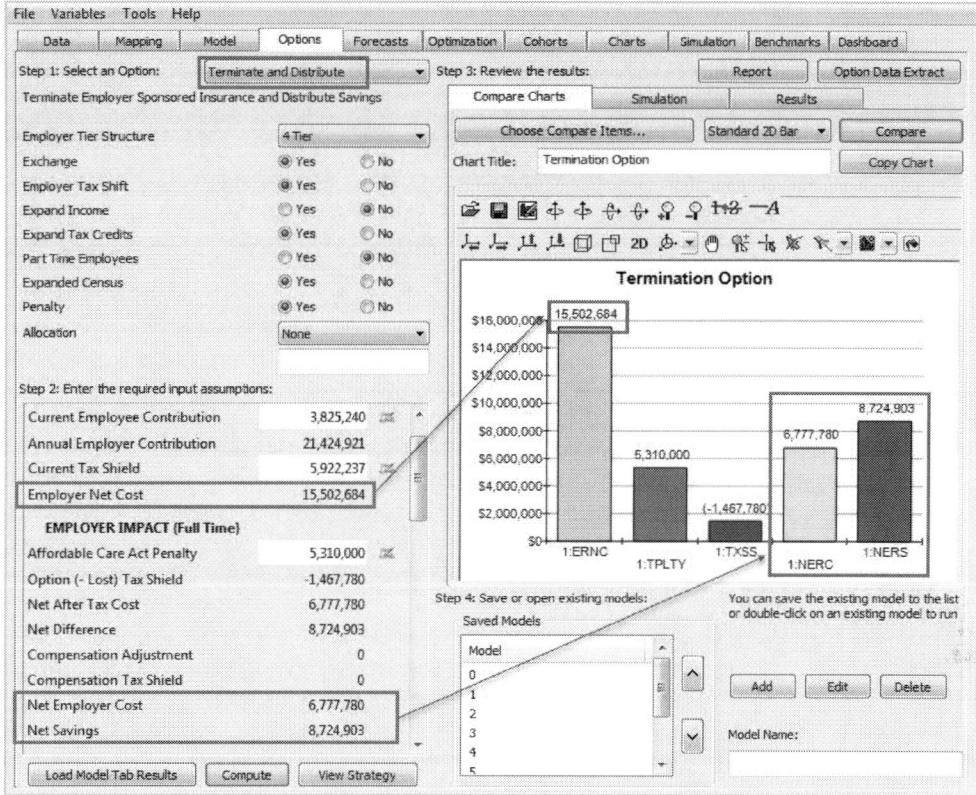

Figure 245: Termination Option

What the modeling illustrates are the added dimensions to such a decision. For example, what if an employer offers minimum essential coverage (MEC), but prices it such that it is not affordable? What if coverage is offered, but it does not meet the minimum value test? An important note is that an employer is not assessed a penalty unless at least on full-time employee receives a premium tax credit from a state-based, state-partnership, federally-facilitated or federally-supported marketplace. (This application was upheld June 25, 2015 by the Supreme Court affirming the US Court of Appeals Fourth Circuit decision in David King, et al., petitioners v. Sylvia Burwell, Secretary Health and Human Services, et al., that the IRS may extend tax-credit subsidies to coverage purchased through exchanges established by the federal government under Section 1321 of the Patient Protection and Affordable Care Act.)

There are multiple reasons when a full-time employee would never realize the premium tax credit. The chart in Figure 246 shows the low end of the range (i.e., 100% of the federal poverty level) and the high end of the range (i.e., 400% of the federal poverty level) for each dependent (meaning a tax dependent) level that is the basis for determining premium tax credit eligibility and subsequent calculation. An illustration of a household eligible for and not eligible for the premium tax credit follows where an employee earns $50,000 per year and has two tax dependents (i.e., employee + spouse). If household income was employee only income, the household would be eligible for a premium tax credit because $50,000 is between $15,730 (100% of FPL) and $62,290 (400% of FPL) for two tax dependents. If household income was modified adjusted gross income of $85,000 (employee and spouse) the household would not be eligible for a premium tax credit because $85,000 is greater than $62,290 (400% of FPL).

What if the employees opted for coverage on their spouse's plan? What if they opted to pay the higher contributions and remain on the employer's plan? What if they elected to go uninsured and pay the individual mandate tax? The following examples (see Figure 247) illustrate:

- The employer elects not to offer the minimum essential coverage. It has 2,685 full-time employees and its calculated penalty is $5,310,000 (2,685 − 30 = 2,655 x $2,000). This represents the employer's maximum liability and is referred to as the 4980H(a) penalty.

- The employer elects to offer an employer-sponsored group plan. This meets the requirement to offer minimum essential coverage, but the plan itself does not meet the minimum 60% actuarial value requirement. In addition, of the 2,685 full-time employees it is determined that 1,877 could be eligible for some kind of premium tax credit based solely on the salary from the employer and comparing it to the range of 100% to 400% of the federal poverty level tables (see Figure 246). If we assume in this example that all premium tax credit–eligible full-time employees were certified as recipients of a premium tax credit, this would mean the employer would be liable for a $3,000 assessable payment per person and is referred to as the 4980H(b) penalty. This penalty would calculate to $5,631,000 (1,877 x $3,000), but the law caps this liability to not exceed the 4980H(a) amount which, in this example, is $5,310,000.

- Let's further assume that the employer has made an estimate that of the 1,877 premium tax credit–eligible employees, a certain percentage goes to the state-based, state-partnership, federally facilitated or federally supported marketplaces and realizes the premium tax credit, another percentage gets covered under their spouse's plan, another percentage remains uninsured and pays the individual mandate penalty, and the largest percentage actually represents dual-income households whose modified adjusted gross income will make them ineligible for the premium tax credits. This estimate would leave the total number of certified premium tax credit–eligible full-time employees at 608. The result of this estimate would be a 4980H(b) liability calculation of $1,824,000 (608 x $3,000).

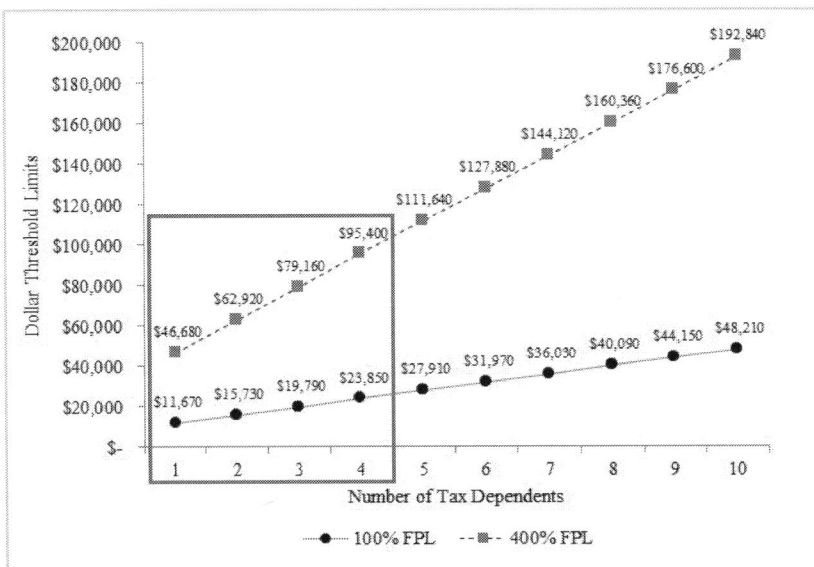

Figure 246: Premium Tax Credit Federal Poverty Level Calculation Range

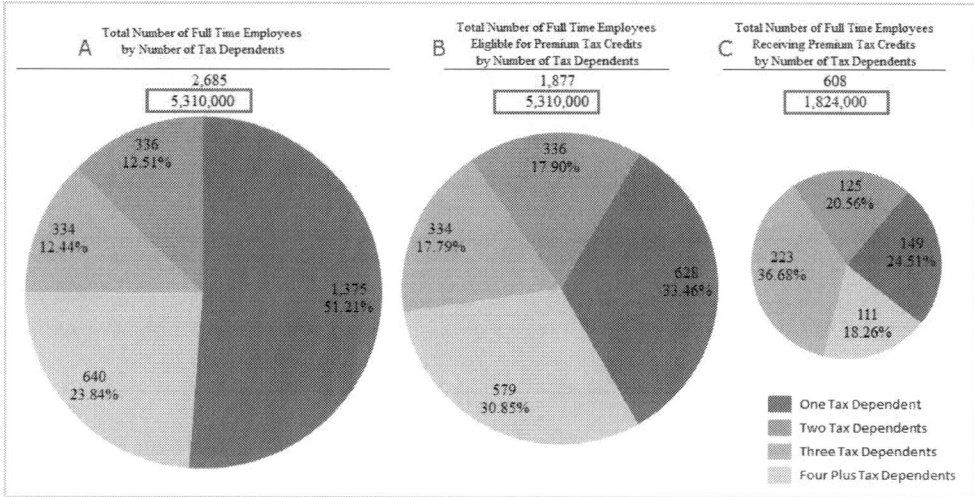

Figure 247: Penalty Calculations for Three Scenarios

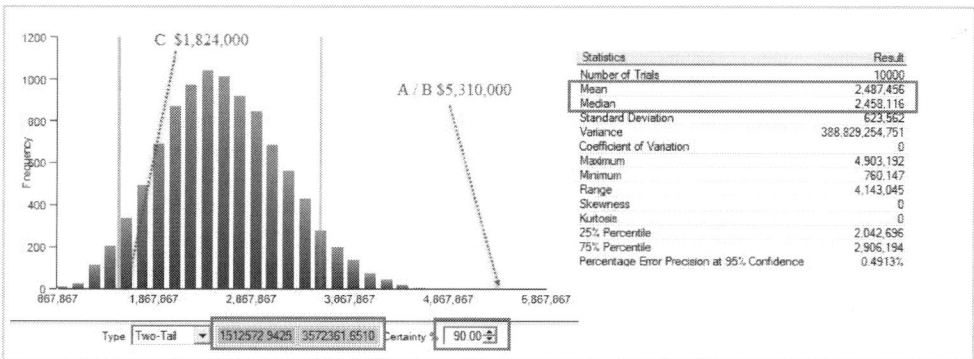

Figure 248: Simulating 4980H(b) Assessable Payment Penalties

However, all three examples are based on estimates. The first example represents the maximum liability and the third example, a single-point estimate for one calculated guess. This is where using Monte Carlo risk simulation adds value in getting a better view of the possibilities. The chart in Figure 248 is a histogram of a probability distribution of possible outcomes based on a set of input assumptions for this option (i.e., for each tier of coverage whether none, an educated guess, or all would receive a premium tax credit).

The Monte Carlo risk simulation uses 10,000 trials and exhibits a 90% confidence interval that the expected penalty range is between $1.5M and $3.6M with a mean of $2.5M. This example illustrates the potential to save an additional $2.8M ($5.3M − $2.5M) on top of the $8,700,000 if the employer offers coverage and creates a design strategy with some level of risk assumption that may or may not be of interest to the employer. What is important to note from this exercise is that the identification, quantification, and simulation of the option allows the employer to know what can be done, have an opportunity to review it, and accept it or veto it.

In parallel, the employer reviews each additional option with its special considerations as well and models its current arrangement to see what has happened in the past, what is expected to happen in the future, and some of the considerations in the analysis. Figures 249–255 are examples of considerations in this parallel process. Figure 249 is a 36-month control chart that calculates the per capita cost of the total healthcare cost on a per-employee per-month (PEPM) basis. Figure 250 is a 36-month control chart that calculates the per capita cost of the total healthcare cost on a per-member per-month (PMPM) basis.

Figure 16.160 is an example of a forecast for future healthcare costs using historical data and forecasting expected medical claims liability on per-employee per-month per-capita basis. Figure 252 is an example of the monthly aggregate dollar forecast of the medical claims liability for future healthcare costs using historical data. Figure 253 is an example of comparing eight plan options and their respective per-capita cost on per-employee per-year basis using demographic data and cost factors for each option.

Figure 254 is an example of the current employer contribution structure (i.e., 100% for employee and 50% for all other tiers of coverage) and the net cost of coverage to the employer of $23.6M, which is 80.6% of the total cost of coverage. Figure 255 is an example of a revised employer contribution structure where the target is set at 78% of coverage, which allows for the adjustment of whatever tiers of coverage are selected. In this case the employer contributes $22.8M at 78% of the total cost, which represents a reduction of $760,000 from its current cost of coverage.

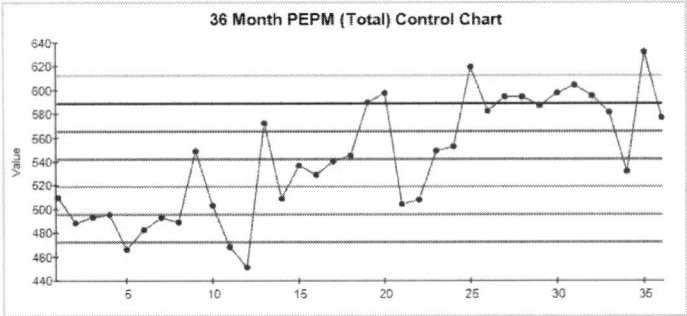

Figure 249: PEPM Control Chart

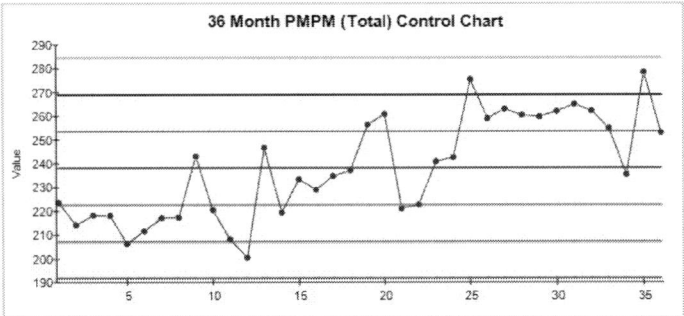

Figure 250: PMPM Control Chart

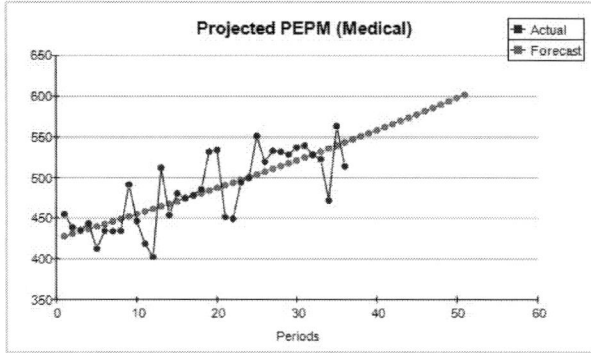

Figure 251: PEPM Forecast

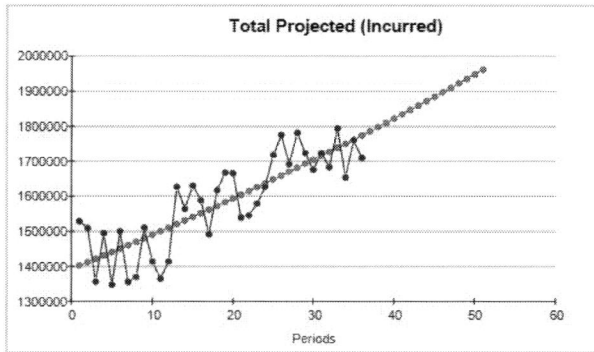

Figure 252: Incurred Medical Forecast

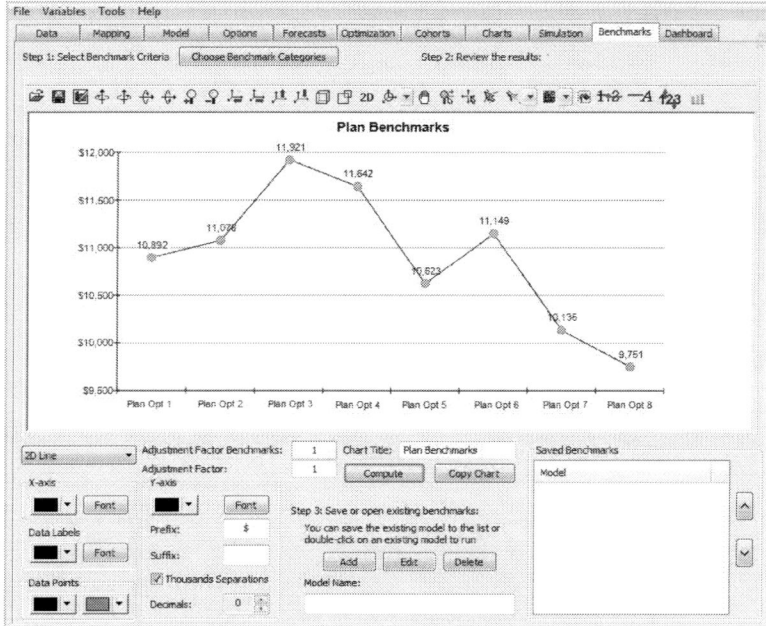

Figure 253: Plan Option Benchmarks

File Variables Tools Help

| Data | Mapping | Model | Options | Forecasts | Optimization | Cohorts | Charts | Simulation | Benchmarks | Dashboard |

Step 1: [Select Tier Variable]

Step 2: Enter the model specifications below: (Tiers: 4)   Forecasted Total Healthcare Cost ($):   29219539

	Tier	Ratio(>1)	Distribution	Monthly Premium	Annual Premium	Employer Contributio...	?	Min (%)	Max (%)
1	EE Only	1	1,375	$496.79	$8,197,018	100			
2	EE+SP	2	571	$993.58	$6,807,996	50			
3	EE+CH	1.8	648	$894.22	$6,953,456	50			
4	Family	3	406	$1,490.37	$7,261,068	50			
TOTAL			3,000		$29,219,539				

	Employer Contribution Monthly	Employer Contribution Annual	Employee Contribution Monthly	Employee Contribution Annual
1	$496.79	$8,197,018	$0.00	$0
2	$745.18	$5,105,997	$248.39	$1,701,999
3	$695.50	$5,408,244	$198.72	$1,545,212
4	$993.58	$4,840,712	$496.79	$2,420,356
TOTAL		$23,551,971		$5,667,568

[Compute]

*Total employee count: 3000   (validated)

Step 3: Optimization (optional):
Target Effective Employer Contribution (%):   30.60

[Optimize]

Step 4: Saved Optimization Models
Model Name: Revised
[Add] [Delete]

Original
Revised

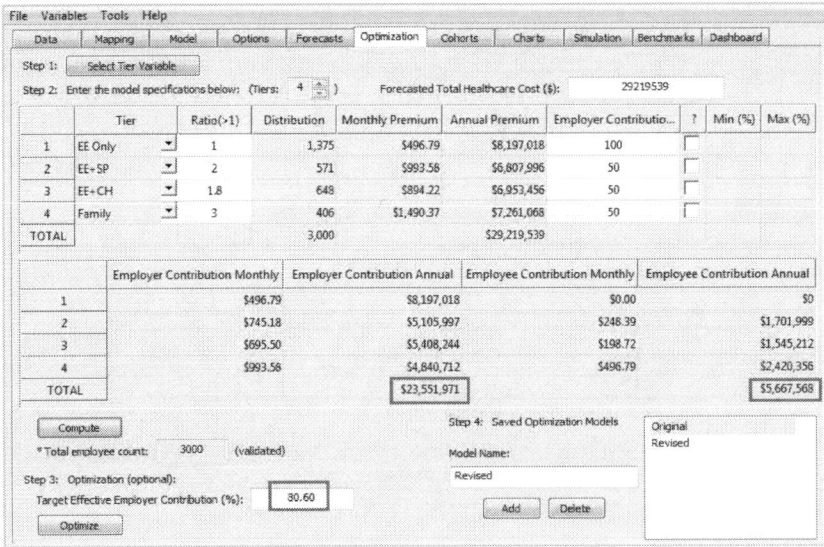

Figure 254: Original Optimization

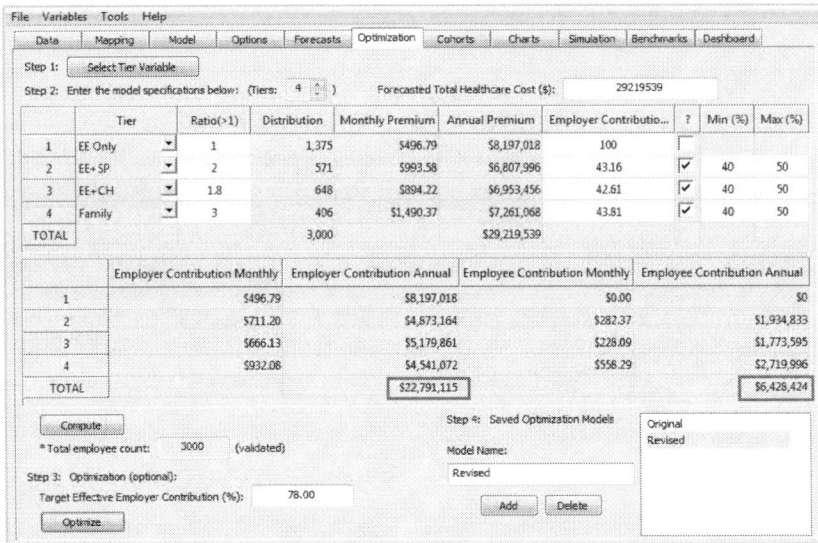

File Variables Tools Help

| Data | Mapping | Model | Options | Forecasts | Optimization | Cohorts | Charts | Simulation | Benchmarks | Dashboard |

Step 1: [Select Tier Variable]

Step 2: Enter the model specifications below: (Tiers: 4)   Forecasted Total Healthcare Cost ($):   29219539

	Tier	Ratio(>1)	Distribution	Monthly Premium	Annual Premium	Employer Contributio...	?	Min (%)	Max (%)
1	EE Only	1	1,375	$496.79	$8,197,018	100			
2	EE+SP	2	571	$993.58	$6,807,996	43.16	✓	40	50
3	EE+CH	1.8	648	$894.22	$6,953,456	42.61	✓	40	50
4	Family	3	406	$1,490.37	$7,261,068	43.81	✓	40	50
TOTAL			3,000		$29,219,539				

	Employer Contribution Monthly	Employer Contribution Annual	Employee Contribution Monthly	Employee Contribution Annual
1	$496.79	$8,197,018	$0.00	$0
2	$711.20	$4,873,164	$282.37	$1,934,833
3	$666.13	$5,179,861	$228.09	$1,773,595
4	$932.08	$4,541,072	$558.29	$2,719,996
TOTAL		$22,791,115		$6,428,424

[Compute]

*Total employee count: 3000   (validated)

Step 3: Optimization (optional):
Target Effective Employer Contribution (%):   78.00

[Optimize]

Step 4: Saved Optimization Models
Model Name: Revised
[Add] [Delete]

Original
Revised

Figure 255: Revised Optimization

Conclusion

This business case is intended as an overview of how the modeling of risk is valuable in the field of employee benefits. There is so much more to each of the options as each has its own special considerations, but by focusing on one and comparing it the employer's current arrangement, we trust the point has been sufficiently made about how important this process is in providing insight into very costly decisions.

CASE STUDY 22: MAKE OR BUY— ANALYSIS OF THE IMPACTS OF 3D PRINTING OPERATIONS, 3D LASER SCANNING TECHNOLOGY, AND COLLABORATIVE PRODUCT LIFECYCLE MANAGEMENT ON SHIP MAINTENANCE AND MODERNIZATION IN THE U.S. NAVY

This case is contributed by Dr. Tom Housel (he is currently a tenured Full Professor for the Information Sciences Department at the U.S. Naval Postgraduate School); Dr. David Ford (he is currently an Associate Professor in the Construction Engineering and Management Program, Zachry Department of Civil Engineering, Texas A&M University, with a Ph.D. from the Massachusetts Institute of Technology); and the author, Dr. Johnathan Mun. A special thanks to RADM Jim Greene (Ret.) for his expert review of the case study. A more detailed case and other related case applications can be found at the Acquisition Research Program, Graduate School of Business & Public Policy, U.S. Naval Postgraduate School, California (www.acquisitionresearch.net).

Executive Summary

Fleet maintenance and modernization are critical for the U.S. Navy to achieve expected service life of assets. With 288 ships in 12 ship-classes and numerous variations within those classes based at over 10 homeports, and the material condition of each ship being so different, managing maintenance is extremely complicated and challenging. Service lives of ships range from 25 years for smaller, less-complex ships, and up to 50 years for aircraft carriers. With lower spending on defense, the Navy must also continue to maintain weapons systems past their intended life while reconfiguring its depots to meet the maintenance needs of new systems designed for the evolution to the next generation of warfare.

Modernization often entails a ship being out of service for several years. Certain assets such as nuclear-powered submarines and aircraft carriers, for example, require lengthy and costly midlife refueling overhaul, removing them from service. Guided-missile destroyers or cruisers getting a midlife modernization overhaul are also unavailable for deployment for extended periods. For Aegis cruisers and destroyers to be installed with "Advanced Capability Build 12," the process requires significant modifications to the ship's combat systems.

Traditional ship maintenance and modernization tools and methods employ extensive acquisition processes, reverse engineering, and manufacturing of replacement parts when performed by outside contractors. In-sourcing these operations using 3-Dimensional Printing (3DP), 3-Dimensional Laser Scanning Technology (3DLST), and Collaborative Product Lifecycle Management (CPLM) can reduce fleet maintenance costs. Whether to outsource or in-source parts manufacturing using these technologies requires estimates of potential savings using different make/buy strategies. A comparison of in-sourcing and outsourcing 3DLST and 3DP for fleet maintenance and upgrading is needed to capture all the available cost and performance benefits of these technologies in either condition.

Primary and secondary data were collected on current operations and costs. Primary research data was collected on U.S. Navy 3DP operations at the Naval Surface Warfare Center, Port Hueneme Division. Secondary research was collected from publicly available sources. Based on this research, cost models were developed to estimate start-up costs, potential operations costs and cost savings, and estimates of cycle time reductions in fleet maintenance and modernization possible under five make/buy strategies. The models were then used to simulate different levels of outsourcing to estimate the initial costs, potential cost savings, and cycle time reductions in fleet maintenance and upgrading possible under five scenarios to be discussed in the case study.

The project addressed several important issues:

1. What are the relative costs of in-sourcing 3DLST and 3DP fleet maintenance and modernization compared to outsourcing those same operations with contractors using these two technologies?

2. What are the impacts of in-sourcing 3DLST and 3DP on fleet maintenance and modernization compared to outsourcing those operations with contractors using the two technologies?

3. How does in-sourcing versus outsourcing, using 3DP and 3DLS, affect cost and fleet readiness?

Introduction

Ship maintenance and modernization—repairs and improvements to the existing fleet—are central to U.S. Naval operations. The current cost-constrained environment within the federal government and the U.S. Department of Defense (DOD), as well as evolving threats, require Naval leadership to maintain and modernize the fleet to retain technological superiority while simultaneously balancing budget cost constraints and extensive operational commitments. Downsizing forces potentially threatens fleet readiness. At the same time, Navy leadership must navigate a complex technology acquisition process. The Navy spends billions annually on ship maintenance programs. Maintenance programs play a critical role in meeting Navy objectives.

New technologies can facilitate meeting fleet readiness requirements within cost constraints, but only if those technologies are adopted and applied effectively and efficiently. One of the most important issues in addressing these challenges concerns what work to in-source within Navy organizations and what work to outsource, that is, the "make versus buy" decision. As will be described, both in-sourcing (make) and outsourcing (buy) have been promoted as cost-savings tools. Currently, the impact of new technology adoption on the make/buy decision is unclear.

DOD maintenance accounted for 12% of the total DOD resource allocation of $652.3 billion—about $79.5 billion in FY2012. As seen in Figure 256, this $79.5 billion effort required approximately 645,000 military and civilian maintainers and thousands of commercial firms— all devoted to the maintenance of roughly 14,800 aircraft; 896 strategic missiles; 386,600 ground combat and tactical vehicles; 256 ships; and a myriad of other DOD weapon systems to maintain strategic materiel readiness (OASD [L&MR], 2013, page i).

Performed at several levels, DOD materiel maintenance ranges in complexity from daily system inspections to rapid removal and replacement of components to complete overhauls or rebuilds of a weapon system. Levels of maintenance are largely distinguished largely by their relative capabilities, flexibility, agility, and capacity and include the following.

- *Depot*—the most complex and extensive work. This level of maintenance encompasses materiel maintenance requiring major repair, overhaul, or complete rebuilding of weapon systems, end items, parts, assemblies, and subassemblies; manufacture of parts; technical assistance; and testing. Each military service manages and operates its own organic depot-level maintenance infrastructure. The majority of depot maintenance, approximately three quarters, is associated with ships and aircraft; aircraft work amounts to more than half of the overall total, while ship work accounts for about a third. The remaining work includes missile, combat vehicle, tactical vehicle, and other ground equipment system workloads.

- *Intermediate*—less complex maintenance performed by operating unit back shops, basewide activities, or consolidated regional facilities. Intermediate or shop-type work includes limited repair of commodity-oriented assemblies and end items (e.g., electronic "black boxes" and mechanical components); job shop, bay, and production line operations for special requirements; repair of subassemblies such as circuit boards; software maintenance; and fabrication or manufacture of repair parts, assemblies, and components.

- *Organizational (or on-equipment)*—more time-sensitive work performed in the field, on the flight line, or at the equipment site. This type is normally performed by an operating unit on a day-to-day basis to support operations of its assigned weapon systems and equipment. It encompasses many categories, including inspections, servicing, handling, preventive maintenance, and corrective maintenance.

- *Field*—signifies the combination of the organizational and intermediate levels. It comprises shop-type work as well as on-equipment maintenance activities at maintenance levels other than depot.

Ship Maintenance

In support of the Fleet Response Plan (Plan) that allows Fleet Commanders to control maintenance priorities in order to provide the right match of capabilities to requirements, the Navy's organic ship maintenance program is performed by its public shipyards, regional maintenance centers, and intermediate maintenance facilities, in conjunction with private vendors and shipyards. Under the plan, fleets support the nation's maritime strategy by quickly and efficiently allocating work to ships that are required to "provide sea control, forward presence and power projection in order to influence actions and activities both at sea and ashore."

In addition, "the ship maintenance budget supports an integrated capabilities-based force through the maintenance and modernization of the right portfolio of ships to provide the optimum mix of force application and logistics ensuring ships are warfighting ready and well-maintained to operate forward." For FY2015, the Navy requested $6.6 billion for total ship maintenance.

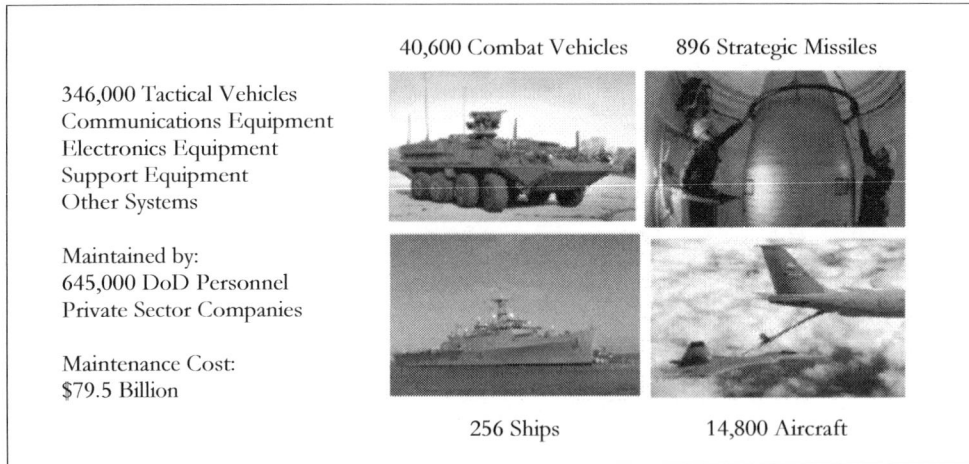

346,000 Tactical Vehicles
Communications Equipment
Electronics Equipment
Support Equipment
Other Systems

Maintained by:
645,000 DoD Personnel
Private Sector Companies

Maintenance Cost:
$79.5 Billion

40,600 Combat Vehicles   896 Strategic Missiles

256 Ships   14,800 Aircraft

Figure 256: Systems Supported by DOD Maintenance (OASD [L&MR], 2013, p. 3)

Issues with Ship Maintenance

DOD cost-reduction imperatives have forced a review of ship maintenance and modernization tools and methods. The review has found that a particularly acute problem is how to acquire one-off (or few-off) parts. In ship maintenance, often the parts required were originally manufactured by now-defunct businesses. Often only one, or a few copies, of a given part is required for ship repair, maintenance, or improvement. Another challenge is the duration and cost of the traditional acquisition process when applied to parts, especially when old, unique, or few parts are needed. When outsourced, fabricating parts involves an extensive acquisition process in addition to reverse engineering and manufacturing the replacement parts. Acquiring just a few parts of a kind from organizations that are not the original equipment manufacturer (OEM), and sometimes from the OEM, tends to take longer and cost more than acquiring many copies of a currently manufactured part. Manufacturing small numbers of parts such as customized or obsolete components can be very expensive. The loss of the small- and medium-size industrial base to support ship maintenance and upgrades leads to very expensive manufacturing of custom parts; hence, the proverbial $1,000 bolt. In addition, in the current manufacturing base, custom parts are very expensive to design and produce in job shops using traditional methods. Also, engineering design changes balloon the costs of projects by creating large numbers of customized parts or modifications of existing parts.

Drew, McGarvey, and Buryk (2013) of the RAND Corporation studied make/buy decisions by the U.S. Air Force. They describe parts with two parameters: how frequently the part is needed (frequency) and its specificity (uniqueness). Their analysis identified specific types of aircraft maintenance work (e.g., penetrating aids, fire control, and propulsion) that are currently being performed externally but might be better performed by the U.S. Air Force. Given the fast evolution of manufacturing technologies, similar studies are needed that include the impacts of the adoption and use of new technologies on DOD make or buy decisions.

Problem Description

Issues in the Use of 3DLST and 3DP in Ship Maintenance and Upgrading

Commercially available new technologies such as 3DLST and additive manufacturing (AM), can improve ship maintenance and modernization. They can be used to improve the distant support of the fleet. The website of the NAVSEA distance support operations at Port Hueneme provides an example of the benefits of distance support and the potential benefits of 3DLST and 3DP:

Resolving Problems at Sea, from Shore

It is 0700 (7:00 am) and a Navy destroyer, underway in the Persian Gulf, has a problem with its primary radar system. The radar technician has run all the appropriate equipment tests, but is still unable to pinpoint the fault. Political unrest means that tensions are high in the area and the ship may be called into action at any time. The radar problem needs to be resolved, and quickly.

The technician calls upon experts at Navy Shore Command for support. On the other side of the world, engineers use a Navy Distance Support Web Portal to research all the engineering and historical information needed to understand the problem. They are able to connect to the ship's system and remotely run system tests.

Within minutes they have monitored the system's performance, analyzed test results, and isolated the faulty component. The part is replaced from onboard spare parts or spares from another ship in the battle group. The ship is once again mission-ready, without ever having left its designated battle arena. (NSWC, 2013)

Notice that, in this scenario, "The part is replaced from onboard spare parts or spares from another ship in the battle group." This solution may not be available if the part required is not in the fleet's inventory, is a custom part, is an obsolete part, or must be customized to fit specific conditions. In these cases the part must be provided from a shore inventory, if it is available, or redesigned, then fabricated, and then manufactured. New technologies can facilitate accomplishing these tasks quickly and without excess costs.

Issues Related to Costs

In a 2013 report on U.S. Air Force sourcing titled "Enabling Early Sustainment Decisions, Application to F-35 Depot-Level Maintenance," Drew, McGarvey, and Buryk (2013) of the RAND Corporation proposed and applied a method for recommending sourcing with two dimensions: *frequency* of need and asset *specificity* (Figure 257). In this framework, "OEM" (upper left) is outsourcing to the original equipment manufacturer, "Organic" (upper right) is in-sourcing by the U.S. military, "Spot-market contract" (lower left) is outsourcing for one or a few of a single part type, and "Longer-term contract" (lower right) is long-term outsourcing and oftentimes to a different private manufacturer for many parts.

3DLST and 3DP have the potential to generate large cost savings by, for example:

- Reducing labor and material costs by reducing wasted material required by traditional manufacturing methods.

- Reducing manufacturing costs by eliminating the need for traditional manufacturing equipment such as large lathes and drill presses.

- Reducing or eliminating parts inventories and the infrastructures required to maintain those inventories by making parts on demand.

- Reducing the space needed on ships to carry inventories and fabricating equipment.

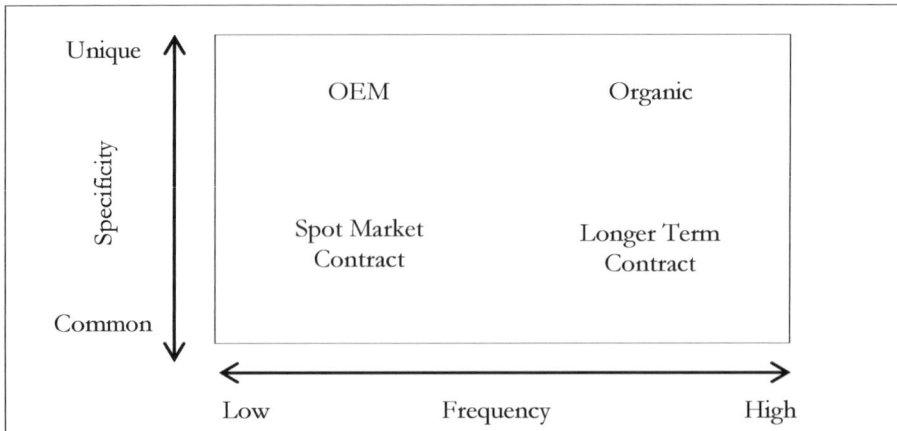

Figure 257: A Conceptual Sourcing Framework (Drew, McGarvey, and Buryk, 2013)

However, it is not clear whether the Navy will capture the potential savings if new technologies are outsourced to private industry, which has historical design and manufacturing costs as a benchmark and traditional manufacturing infrastructure costs. More savings may accrue if the new technologies are adopted and these operations performed by Navy organizations. However, building these internal capabilities, skilled workforce, and capacity will require an initial investment. A cost comparison of outsourcing versus in-sourcing fleet maintenance and upgrading operations with new technologies can provide insight for developing a technology adoption strategy.

Current research has investigated the adoption of the 3DLST, 3DP, and CPLM technologies for fleet maintenance and modernization. A critical implementation issue is whether to develop 3DLST, 3DP, and CPLM capabilities within the service (i.e., in-sourcing) or to have industry do this for the Navy (i.e., outsourcing). This study creates the needed make/buy comparison for implementing 3DLST, 3DP, and CPLM. The work addresses these important issues by investigating the following questions:

1. What are the relative costs of in-sourcing 3DLST, 3DP, and CPLM fleet maintenance and modernization compared to outsourcing those same operations with contractors using these technologies?

2. What cost savings may be captured by the use of 3DLST, 3DP, and CPLM for fleet maintenance and modernization if those operations are in-sourced?

Successful In-Sourcing Examples

The literature reviewed several examples of federal agencies successfully bringing projects back in-house. Examples include the following:

- Fleet and Industrial Supply Center (FISC) Puget Sound, Bremerton, WA, completed the first Navy conversion of contract operations to government work in 2009, saving the Navy $2.7 million over five years.

- Federal Aviation Association (FAA) Tech Center in-sourcing saves between $52 and $203 million in data system costs over the life of the project. Prior to the new NADIN Message Switch Rehost (NMR), the FAA used a National Airspace Data Interchange Network (NADIN) to exchange critical information. Customers of the network included FAA National Airspace System, Department of Interior, National

Weather Service, DOD, Department of Homeland Security, commercial airlines, the general aviation community, and airline data service providers. Completed in 2009, the replacement process required seamless migration of over 2,000 domestic and international users to the new system. The in-house team was responsible for all phases of the project development lifecycle (requirements definition through design, software development, hardware integration, documentation, test and evaluation, deployment, and training). Estimates from external contractors to replace the system ranged from $90 million to $240 million over a 10-year service life (USDT, 2009).

- The Contractor Inventory Process used at the U.S. Army claimed that in-sourcing resulted in savings of 16% to 30% and that in-sourcing was largely responsible for reducing the Army's contract services obligations from $51 billion in 2008 to $36 billion in 2010 (Aronowitz, 2012).

- The information technology division of U.S. Customs and Border Protection at the Department of Homeland Security estimated that it saved $27 million in 2010 out of a budget of $400 million by taking 200 private contractors and giving those same individuals government jobs (Lipowicz, 2011).

In addition, the U.S. Internal Revenue Service abandoned experiments with outsourcing debt collection after the agency calculated that contractors brought in less revenue than federal employees (GAO, 1997).

Additive Manufacturing, Collaborative Product Lifecycle Management, and 3-Dimensional Laser Scanning Technologies

This section introduces additive manufacturing, product lifecycle management, and 3-dimensional laser scanning technologies. It begins with a discussion of additive manufacturing, also commonly referred to as 3-dimensional scanning, one of the most promising technologies.

Additive Manufacturing

Additive manufacturing (AM) is the youngest and most diverse technology addressed in this research. AM has quickly moved through technology development into the mainstream, with websites now offering services that allow the public to design and use AM to produce products of their own design (e.g., see Kronsberg, 2013).

The following descriptions, based primarily on Gibson, Rosen, and Stucker (2010) and Lipson and Kurman (2013), first describe the principles and techniques, followed by an overview of the potential market size of 3D technology. Also included in this section are potential adoption rates and applications of the technology. Finally, a comparison of conventional manufacturing to specific AM technologies is provided.

Principles and Techniques

Additive manufacturing is defined by the American National Standards Institute (ASTM, 2013) as the "process of joining materials to make objects from 3D model data, usually layer upon layer, as opposed to subtractive manufacturing methodologies. Synonyms: additive fabrication, additive processes, additive techniques, additive layer manufacturing, layer manufacturing and freeform fabrication" (Wohlers, 2013). 3D printing is also another common synonym.

AM differs radically from the currently dominant manufacturing methodologies. Most current methods use subtractive processes (e.g., machining), but AM builds a 3D object by gradually adding successive layers of material that are laid down exactly in their final location.

AM does this by fabricating objects directly from 3D computer-aided design (3D CAD) models. The 3D model is disaggregated into multiple horizontal layers, each of which is produced by the machine and added to the preceding layers.

AM generally involves a number of steps that move from a virtual 3D CAD model to a physical 3D object, as follows:

- *CAD:* A 3D CAD model of the target object is built in software. The 3D CAD model determines only the geometry of the target object; 3D laser scanning can be used to create the model.

- *Conversion to Stereolithography STL Files:* The CAD model cannot be used directly by AM machines; it must be converted to STL format. An STL file describes the external closed surfaces of the original CAD model and forms a basis for calculation of layers. The STL model approximates surfaces of the model with a series of triangular facets.

- *Revision of STL Files:* STL files must often be manipulated before manufacturing. For example, multiple objects may be manufactured simultaneously from the same file, requiring that the STL files of the objects be integrated.

- *Machine Setup:* AM machines must be set up to accommodate specific materials, layer thicknesses, and timing.

- *Build:* Although all AM machines follow the layer-by-layer fabrication process, they utilize different techniques and technologies. For example, some of them use a high-power laser beam to melt a very fine metal powder in order to form a thin layer, while some others use UV light to solidify a specific kind of liquid polymer, called a photopolymer.

- *Post-Process:* Post-processing may be required due to the need to cure photopolymers.

Additive Manufacturing vs. Conventional Manufacturing Methods

Additive manufacturing is a relatively new technology that directly deposits materials to make products by sequentially laying down millions of particles in thousands of layers to "build up" the final component. 3-dimensional design documents direct manufacturing hardware. By controlling the movement of the material deposition equipment and the flow of material, the process controls where particles are deposited in each layer, thereby creating surfaces, shapes, and cavities. Materials can be plastic for fast prototyping, metals, ceramics, or human tissue. 3D printing has several advantages over traditional manufacturing methods. First, a primary advantage is the ability to create almost any shaped product, with the only limitation being the need for each layer of material to have a layer below it for support, although secondary materials can be used to provide support under overhanging component parts during manufacturing. Second, whereas traditional methods are subtractive, the AM process is additive, greatly reducing waste materials.

One of the greatest advantages of AM is the freedom it provides for designers. The more complex the design, the more advantage can be gained by using AM. A related advantage of AM is its accuracy. AM processes can operate with resolution of a few tens of microns. In other words, AM machines can produce layers as thin as the diameter of human hair.

AM also has limitations. A primary limitation concerns the materials that can be used. AM technologies were originally developed around polymer materials. Then materials such as metals were introduced. The current approach remains limited to a range of materials and their physical properties (e.g., strength). Some AM materials require careful handling. They usually have a limited shelf life and must be kept in conditions that prevent unwanted chemical reactions. Exposure to moisture, excessive light, and so forth may degrade or destroy some materials.

Additive Manufacturing Methods

Although all AM methods use layer-by-layer production, they differ in terms of procedures, technologies, materials, and applications.

- *Photopolymerization:* Photopolymerization solidifies a special type of liquid polymer using UV light. Stereolithography (SL or SLA) is a well-known photopolymerization technique. In SL, a vat of liquid photopolymer sits in an AM machine. A UV light source above the vat emits a narrow beam of light. Once the UV beam touches the photopolymer, the liquid hardens. This process is repeated with each sweep of the surface, layering the object until the whole is fabricated. Photopolymerization can also use visible lights or other radiations, depending on the photopolymer's properties.

- *Powder Bed Fusion:* Powder bed fusion (PBF), also widely referred to as selective laser sintering (SLS), is similar to SL in terms of procedure, but uses steel powder materials (instead of liquid polymer) and a heating source, usually a high-power laser (instead of UV light). The fabrication process is done in an enclosed chamber filled with nitrogen gas (or in a vacuum chamber) because the hot powder is highly vulnerable to oxidation.

- *3-Dimensional Printing:* 3DP currently refers to both the whole AM process and one of its techniques. The 3DP technique, which was developed by MIT researchers, is a powder-bed approach, similar to PBF, but 3DP does not use a heating-based sintering system. Instead, a high-power laser beam touches a thin layer of powder material, and the print head (nozzle) squeezes adhesive to bind the powder particles together.

- *Beam Deposition:* The beam deposition (BD) process is referred to as laser engineered net shaping (LENS), laser metal deposition or laser-based metal deposition, laser freeform fabrication, construction laser additive direct, directed light fabrication, and directed metal deposition. Beam deposition is predominantly used for metal powders.

- *Polyjet Printing:* Polyjet printing is one the newest AM techniques. It can be considered to be a combination of LENS and SL techniques. A polyjet printing system utilizes a deposition head like LENS, using a photopolymer and UV light instead of metal powder and a laser.

- *Laminated Object Manufacturing (LOM):* LOM or sheet lamination involves layer-by-layer lamination of very thin sheets of material. Each sheet represents one cross-sectional layer in the CAD model. In LOM, each layer is cut—using laser or mechanical tools—from a larger sheet of material.

- *Extrusion-Based Systems:* Extrusion, also called fused deposition modeling (FDM), is a simple form of AM. It is quite similar to putting icing on a cake. A creamy (semisolid) substance is gradually extruded through a nozzle by applying pressure. The extruded material forms a track of the material. Thermoplastic polymers are also excellent materials for this approach as they are easily liquefied by heat and solidify instantly.

AM technologies use a variety of materials, including plastics, metals, ceramics, and composites, and deploy multiple different processes to address a variety of issues (i.e., unit cost, speed of operations, design complexity). Aerospace companies such as Boeing, Airbus, Lockheed Martin, Pratt & Whitney, Rolls-Royce, Honeywell, and MTU Aero Engines are accelerating involvement and investments in AM. Lockheed Martin estimates that some complex satellite components can be produced 48% cheaper and 43% faster with 3D. Moreover, production costs could be reduced by as much as 80%. Aerospace applications and demonstrations of 3D include:

- NASA's Juno satellite has 3D printed parts that are lighter and less costly, manufactured by Lockheed Martin in its final assembly. Lockheed is preparing to use 3D printing processes to manufacture production parts for other aircraft and spacecraft.

- Engineers at NASA's Marshall Space Flight Center in Huntsville, AL, have also been testing 3D-printed components for rocket engines. Printing a rocket-engine injector piece reduced the cost of the $300,000 part by 80%, according to a report by *Nature* magazine.

- Boeing has installed environmental control system ducting made by AM for its commercial and military aircraft for many years. Tens of thousands of AM parts are flying on 16 different production aircraft models and types—both commercial and military (Wohlers, 2013).

- Airbus has 20 AM projects underway, with a few hundred part numbers currently flying or soon will be, on the new A350 airplane. A structural cabin bracket made by AM in the titanium alloy Ti-6Al-4V will fly on an A350.

- Airbus is also using 3D printing to produce a seat-belt mold as a spare part for the A310 jet. According to the head of research and technology for industrial systems in the Manufacturing Engineering Centre of Competence at Airbus, the company plans to use 3D printed plastic parts for the A350 aircraft by early 2015. Even with small components, a 50% weight savings and a cost savings of 60% to 70% on production parts is anticipated (Mitchell, 2014).

GE Aviation is investing heavily into AM and other advanced technologies. For example, it will open a new $100 million assembly plant that will employ 200 people by 2020, to build the world's first passenger jet engine with 3D printed fuel nozzles and next-generation materials. Although the engine, called LEAP, will not enter service until 2016 on the Airbus A320, it has already become GE Aviation's bestselling engine, with more than 6,000 confirmed orders from 20 countries, valued at over $78 billion (GE, 2014). Each LEAP engine has 19 3D-printed fuel nozzles inside, fourth-generation carbon-fiber composite blades, and parts made from CMCs. In addition to the 3D-printed nozzles being five times more durable than the previous model, 3D printing allowed engineers to use a simpler design that reduced the number of brazes and welds from 25 to just 5. There are currently more than 300 3D printing machines in use across GE. Moreover, GE Aviation predicts that 100,000 additive parts will be manufactured by 2020.

The United States has been the global leader in AM since its beginning, having launched many of the most successful companies in the field, including 3D Systems, Stratasys, Z Corporation, and Solidscape. In an analysis conducted by the Science & Technology Institute (IDA), IDA found that the U.S. government has played a role in the early development of AM. The following are some examples.

- *Department of Defense*: Office of Naval Research (ONR) and the Defense Advanced Research Projects Agency (DARPA) were some of the earliest investors in AM by providing steady streams of funding for both academic and industry-based researchers.

- *National Science Foundation:* NSF funded precursors of AM technologies in the 1970s (development of computer numerical controlled machining and solid modeling tools) and turned early AM patents in the 1980s into proof-of-concept and prototype machines in two major commercial technology areas (binder jetting and laser sintering). NSF also later funded application development (e.g., medical) and academically oriented networking activities. It has supported research efforts related to new processes, new applications for existing processes, and benchmarking and roadmapping activities as AM technologies matured. NSF has awarded almost 600 grants for AM research and other activities, amounting to more than $200 million (2005 dollars) in funding.

- *Other support*: The Department of Energy (DOE), NASA, and the National Institute of Standards and Technology (NIST) have also been involved in aspects of developing the AM field. DOE in particular played a role in developing directed energy deposition technologies.

The U.S. Navy has supported research into 3D printing for more than 20 years and has approximately 70 additive manufacturing projects underway at dozens of different locations. The Chief of Naval Operations (CNO) is in the process of developing the Navy's additive manufacturing vision and strategy.

The following projects demonstrate how AM is transforming Navy logistics and maintenance capabilities through reduced costs, efficiency gains, and parts replacement.

- Norfolk Naval Shipyard's Rapid Prototype Lab is saving thousands of dollars on the Gerald R. Ford-class of aircraft carriers. The lab prints much cheaper plastic polymer models in hours versus days or weeks, rather than the traditional wood or metal mockups of ship alterations. All four Navy shipyards have 3D printers working on similar and other ways to benefit the Navy.

- Navy's Fleet Readiness Center Southeast uses AD for more complicated designs and unique material properties to develop an enhanced hydraulic intake manifold for the V-22 Osprey. This manifold has fewer leak points than its traditionally manufactured counterpart, is 70% lighter, and improves fluid flow.

- Walter Reed National Military Medical Center (WRNNMC) uses AM to meet a range of medical needs and delivers personalized patient care. With easily customizable 3D printed parts, WRNNMC produces items including tailor-made cranial plate implants, medical tooling, and surgical guides.

- Naval Undersea Warfare Center at Keyport used additive manufacturing to create a supply of replacement parts to keep the Fleet ready. Certain critical OEM parts installed onboard Los Angeles-class nuclear-powered guided-missile submarines, and Ohio-class nuclear-powered guided-missile submarines are no longer produced by its original manufacturer.

- CNO's Rapid Innovation Cell Print the Fleet project installed a 3D printer aboard USS *Essex* this year, demonstrating the ability to develop and print a variety of shipboard items, from oil reservoir caps, plastic syringes, and deck drain covers to training aids and silhouettes of planes that are used on the mock-up of the flight deck to keep the flight deck organized.

Collaborative Product Lifecycle Management

Product lifecycle management (PLM) address the issues related to a product throughout its life. Collaborative product lifecycle management (CPLM) works to integrate product lifecycle management across project participants, time, and technologies. CPLM technology provides a common platform to electronically integrate other technologies, such as 3DLST images and manufacturing files for Additive Manufacturing, to enable collaboration among all parties involved in a given project across project phases and regardless of their geographic location (e.g., on a ship at sea and at a land-based depot). Schindler (2010) illustrated the potential of CPLM to facilitate integration of the development of material solutions.

CPLM tools also provide a means to store the images and all related maintenance work within a common database accessible by all participants in a ship alteration or modernization project. PLM is defined by CIMdata as a strategic business approach applying a consistent set of business solutions in support of the collaborative creation, management, dissemination, and use of product definition information across the extended enterprise, from concept to end of life (CIMdata, 2007).[34] It integrates people, processes, and information.

Specific CPLM tools include technologies that support data exchange, portfolio management, digital manufacturing, enterprise application integration, and workflow automation. A range of industries has invested in CPLM solutions, including those involved in aerospace and defense, automotive and transportation, utilities, process manufacturing, and high-tech development and manufacturing. The CPLM market is poised for further growth with vendors expanding product offerings as the industry evolves.[35]

3-Dimensional Laser Scanning Technology

3D scanners create a *point cloud* of the surface of an object. Similar to cameras in some ways, they have a cone-shaped field of view, but can also collect distance information about each point, allowing each point to be located in a 3-dimensional space. Usually, multiple scans are required from different directions to capture adequate information to create a description of the object. Most manufacturers' scanners work by scanning a target space with a laser light mounted on a highly articulating mount, enabling data capture in virtually any orientation with minimal operator input. Some also incorporate a digital camera that simultaneously captures a 360° field-of-view color photo image of the target. Once the capture phase is complete, the system automatically executes proprietary point-processing algorithms to process the captured image. The system can generate an accurate[36] digital 3D model of the target space, automatically fuse image texture onto 3D model geometry, export file formats ready for commercial, high-end design, and import them into 2D/3D computer-aided design (CAD) packages.

Terrestrial laser scanning technology is well established as a valuable tool in practice and is currently used in a variety of industries. According to industry analysts, laser scanner manufacturers and related software and service providers report strong activity across many markets, including shipbuilding, offshore construction and repair, onshore oil and gas, fossil and nuclear power, civil and transportation infrastructure, building, automotive and construction equipment, manufacturing, and forensics (Greaves & Jenkins, 2007). In the latest data available, sales of terrestrial 3D laser scanning hardware, software, and services reached $253 million in 2006—a growth of 43% over 2005 (Greaves & Jenkins, 2007).

---

[34] CIMdata is a consulting firm with over 20 years of experience in strategic IT applications and is an acknowledged leader in the application of PLM and related technologies.

[35] The two largest U.S. shipyards that construct aircraft carriers and submarines are also transitioning into CPLM solutions. Typically, PLM vendors do not focus efforts on the shipbuilding industry because of its size relative to other products, such as automotive or aerospace. Having a PLM tool designed specifically for an industry has a significant impact on the tool's efficiency within that industry.

[36] The National Shipbuilding Research Program's (NSRP) studies (2006) requirement was within 3/16 of an inch to actual measurements.

Research Approaches and Methods

This research developed estimates of the impacts of the three technologies (3DLST, 3DP, and CPLM) on fleet maintenance costs by comparing the costs of different make/buy strategies. The background, issues, and cost estimates were then used in the real options approach.

To estimate the make/buy strategy costs, the traditional investment analysis approach was reverse-engineered using the following steps:

- Describe the make/buy strategies.
- Estimate revenues that reflect benefits using market-comparables. approach.
- Estimate a return on investment (ROI) for each strategy using Knowledge Value Added (KVA) models to generate return on knwoledge (ROK), a proxy for ROI.
- Estimate costs of each make/buy strategy using the ROI estimates and estimates of benefits.
- Estimate potential cost savings by comparing costs of make/buy strategies.

Integrated Risk Management and Strategic Real Options Analysis

Integrated Risk Management (IRM) is an eight-step, quantitative software-based modeling approach for the objective quantification of risk (cost, schedule, technical), flexibility, strategy, and decision analysis. The method can be applied to program management, resource portfolio allocation, and return on investment to the military (maximizing expected military value and objective value quantification of nonrevenue government projects), analysis of alternatives or strategic flexibility options, capability analysis, prediction modeling, and general decision analytics. The method and toolset provide the ability to consider hundreds of alternatives with budget and schedule uncertainty, and provide ways to help the decision maker maximize capability and readiness at the lowest cost. This methodology is particularly amenable to resource reallocation and has been taught and applied by the authors for the past 10 years at over 100 multinational corporations and over 30 projects at the DOD.

IRM provides a structured approach that will yield a rapid, credible, repeatable, scalable, and defensible analysis of cost savings and total cost of ownership while ensuring that vital capabilities are not lost in the process. The IRM + KVA methods do this by estimating the value of a system or process in a common and objective way across various alternatives and providing the return on investment (ROI) of each in ways that are both comparable and rigorous. These ROI estimates across the portfolio of alternatives provide the inputs necessary to predict the value of various options. IRM incorporates risks, uncertainties, budget constraints, implementation, lifecycle costs, reallocation options, and total ownership costs in providing a defensible analysis describing management options for the path forward. This approach identifies risky projects and programs, while projecting immediate and future cost savings, total lifecycle costs, flexible alternatives, critical success factors, strategic options for optimal implementation paths/decisions, and portfolio optimization. Its employment presents ways for identifying the potential for cost overruns and schedule delays and enables proactive measures to mitigate those risks. IRM provides an optimized portfolio of capability or implementation options while maintaining the value of strategic flexibility.

In the extant case, IRM provides a way to differentiate among various alternatives for implementation of 3DLST, CPLM, PDF, and Logistics Team Center with respect to ship maintenance processes, and to postulate where the greatest benefit could be achieved for the available investment from within the portfolio of alternatives. As a strategy is formed and a plan developed for its implementation, the toolset provides for inclusion of important risk factors, such as schedule and technical uncertainty, and allows for continuous updating and evaluation by the program manager to understand where these risks come into play and make informed decisions accordingly.

IRM Modeling Approach

Through the use of Monte Carlo simulation, the resulting stochastic KVA ROK model yielded a distribution of values rather than a point solution. Thus, simulation models analyze and quantify the various risks and uncertainties of each program. The result is a distribution of the ROKs and a representation of the project's volatility.

In real options, the analyst assumes that the underlying variable is the future benefit minus the cost of the project. An implied volatility can be calculated through the results of a Monte Carlo simulation. The results for the IRM analysis will be built on the quantitative estimates provided by the KVA analysis. The IRM will provide defensible quantitative risk analytics and portfolio optimization suggesting the best way to allocate limited resources to ensure the highest possible value over time.

The first step in real options is to generate a strategic map through the process of framing the problem. Based on the overall problem identification occurring during the initial qualitative management screening process, certain strategic options would become apparent for each particular project. The strategic options could include, among other things, the option to wait, expand, contract, abandon, switch, stage-gate, and choose.

Risk analysis and real options analysis assume that the future is uncertain and that decision makers have the ability to make midcourse corrections when these uncertainties become resolved or risk distributions become known. The analysis is usually done ahead of time and, thus, ahead of such uncertainty and risks. Therefore, when these risks become known, the analysis should be revisited to incorporate the information in decision making or to revise any input assumptions. Sometimes, for long-horizon projects, several iterations of the real options analysis should be performed, where future iterations are updated with the latest data and assumptions. Understanding the steps required to undertake IRM is important because the methodology provides insight not only into the methodology itself but also into how IRM evolves from traditional analyses, showing where the traditional approach ends and where the new analytics start.

The risk simulation step required in the IRM provides us with the probability distributions and confidence intervals of the KVA methodology's resulting ROI and ROK results. Further, one of the outputs from this risk simulation is volatility, a measure of risk and uncertainty, which is a required input into the real options valuation computations. In order to assign input probabilistic parameters and distributions into the simulation models, we relied on the U.S. Air Force Cost Analysis Agency's (AFCAA) handbook. In the handbook, the three main distributions recommended are the triangular, normal, and uniform distributions. We chose the triangular distribution because the limits (minimum and maximum) are known, and the shape of the triangular resembles the normal distribution, with the most likely values having the highest probability of occurrence and the extreme ends (minimum and maximum values) having considerably lower probabilities of occurrence. Also, the triangular distribution was chosen instead of the normal distribution because the latter's tail ends extend toward positive and negative infinities, making it less applicable in the model we are developing. Finally, the AFCAA also provides options for left skew, right skew, and symmetrical distributions. In our analysis, we do not have sufficient historical or comparable data to make the proper assessment of skew and, hence, revert to the default of a symmetrical triangular distribution.

Strategic Real Options

As described previously, an important step in performing IRM is the application of Monte Carlo risk simulation. By applying Monte Carlo risk simulation to simultaneously change all critical inputs in a correlated manner within a model, researchers can identify, quantify, and analyze risk. The question then is, what next? Simply quantifying risk is useless unless it can be managed, reduced, controlled, hedged, or mitigated. This is where strategic real options analysis comes in. Think of real options as a strategic road map for making decisions.

The real options approach incorporates a learning model, such that the decision maker makes better and more informed strategic decisions when some levels of uncertainty are resolved through the passage of time, actions, and events. The combination of the KVA methodology (to monitor the performance of given options) and the adjustments to real options as leaders learn more from the execution of given options provides an integrated methodology to help military leaders hedge their bets while taking advantage of new opportunities over time. Traditional analysis assumes a static investment decision, and assumes that strategic decisions are made initially with no recourse to choose other pathways or options in the future. Real options analysis can be used to frame strategies to mitigate risk, to value and find the optimal strategy pathway to pursue, and to generate options to enhance the value of the project while managing risks. Imagine real options as a guide for navigating through unfamiliar territory, providing road signs at every turn to direct drivers in making the best and most informed driving decisions. This is the essence of real options. From the options that are framed, Monte Carlo simulation and stochastic forecasting, coupled with traditional techniques, are applied. Then, real options analytics are applied to solve and value each strategic pathway and an informed decision can be made.

Cost Saving Estimates

Several challenges arise in expanding previous research on Navy investment strategies in new technologies to investigate make/buy strategies. One challenge is that previous research was often based on a specific portion of the parts used in Naval ship maintenance (e.g., high-, medium-, or low-complexity parts). These product types differ in their costs and market comparable values and, therefore, in their contributions to fleet readiness. Make/buy analysis should consider the potential for in-sourcing all three types of parts. A second challenge is differentiating costs generated by industry from costs generated by parts production by the Navy. These costs differ due primarily to differences in labor costs. A third challenge is the description of the make/buy strategies.

Describing Make/Buy Strategies

Estimates of annual production rates are based on data collected for one depot that manufactures approximately 27,000 parts per year, of which 25% were high complexity, 50% were medium complexity, and 25% were low complexity (Mackley, 2014). Table 22 shows the estimated industry and Navy production rates for five make/buy strategies ranging from all-buy (100% by industry) to all-make (100% by Navy). These estimates assume that the Navy would produce highly complex parts first (in the lowest "make" strategy), then add medium-complexity parts as it increased the fraction of parts made, and produce low-complexity parts only in strategies that have the Navy making all the parts (in the highest "make" strategy).

The production rates reflect two extreme strategies and three shared-production strategies. The first strategy (0% Navy production) is the extreme strategy in which all parts are made by industry. This strategy is relatively close to the current conditions in which most parts production is outsourced to industry. The second strategy (25% Navy production) reflects the Navy producing all complex parts and outsourcing all medium-complexity and low-complexity (aka "simple") parts to industry. The third strategy (50% Navy production) reflects the Navy producing all high-complexity parts and half of the medium-complexity parts, while outsourcing half of the medium complexity parts and all simple parts to industry. The fourth strategy (75% Navy production) reflects the Navy producing all high- and medium-complexity parts and outsourcing all simple parts. The last strategy (100% Navy production) is the extreme strategy in which all parts are made by the Navy.

As shown in the Total Parts Produced by Industry and Total Parts Produced by Navy columns, the Navy increases production as the make/buy strategies shift from low percentage made by the Navy to higher percentages made. The Total Parts Produced column shows that these strategies reflect shifts in production between industry and the Navy, not changes in the total number of parts produced.

Estimating Revenues That Reflect Benefits

Benefits were estimated by multiplying the production rates in Table 22 by the average part values. The conservative $6,000 average value of a complex part is supported by an interview of an expert by one of the research team. That expert said, "Externally we see charges anywhere between $6,000 to $8,000 dollars and upwards of $15,000 per model" and later confirmed that $12,000 was "at the upper end of your range" (personal interview summarized in Kenney, 2013). The modelers assumed that medium-complexity parts had an average value of $3,000 each and that low-complexity parts had an average value of $1,000 each. Table 23 shows the estimated values of produced parts for each make/buy strategy.

Table 22: Annual Production Rate Estimates of Five Make/Buy Strategies

% by Navy	High Complexity 25%		Medium Complexity 50%		Low Complexity 25%		Total Parts Produced		Industry & Navy
	Industry	Navy	Industry	Navy	Industry	Navy	Industry	Navy	Total
0%	6,750		13,500		6,750		27,000		27,000
25%		6,750	13,500		6,750		20,250	6,750	27,000
50%		6,750	6,750	6,750	6,750		13,500	13,500	27,000
75%		6,750		13,500	6,750		6,750	20,250	27,000
100%		6,750		13,500		6,750		27,000	27,000

Table 23: Estimated Annual Benefits of Five Make/Buy Strategies

% by Navy	High Complexity 25%		Medium Complexity 50%		Low Complexity 25%		Total Parts Produced		$'000
	Indus.	Navy	Indus.	Navy	Indus.	Navy	Indus.	Navy	Total
0%	$40,500		$40,500		$6,750		$87,750		$87,750
25%		$40,500	$40,500		$6,750		$47,250	$40,500	$87,750
50%		$40,500	$20,250	$20,250	$6,750		$27,000	$60,750	$87,750
75%		$40,500		$40,500	$6,750		$6,750	$81,000	$87,750
100%		$40,500		$40,500		$6,750		$87,750	$87,750

Estimating Returns on Investment

Estimated Returns on Investment (ROI) were generated with KVA models using the methodology described previously. Each KVA model reflected the appropriate average 2013 labor costs (Navy) based on work by Mackley (2014) and market value of the common unit of output (high-, medium-, or low-complexity parts). The estimated Returns on Investment are shown in Table 24. The relatively large returns are consistent with the savings found by industry.

Table 24: Estimated Returns on Investment (ROI) of Five Make/Buy Strategies

% Made by Navy	High Complexity 25%		Medium Complexity 50%		Low Complexity 25%	
	Industry	Navy	Industry	Navy	Industry	Navy
0%	573%		151%		12%	
25%		1120%	151%		12%	
50%		1120%	236%	510%	12%	
75%		1120%		358%	12%	
100%		1120%		358%		103%

Estimating Production Costs and Cost Savings

Costs for each make/buy scenario can be estimated using the definition of Return on Investment:

$$ROI = (Benefits - Costs) / Costs$$

The equation above was used with the benefits (Table 23) and Returns on Investment (Table 24) to estimate the costs of each make/buy strategy. The total cost of each make/buy scenario (rows in Table 25) is the sum of six costs: the costs generated by industry to produce high-, medium-, and low-complexity parts plus the costs generated by the Navy to produce high-, medium-, and low-complexity parts. In some strategies some of these costs are zero, such as the Navy cost when 100% of parts are produced by industry or industry cost when 100% of parts are produced by the Navy. Capturing all six cost components for each strategy assures the inclusion of all relevant production costs.

Table 25: Estimated Annual Costs of Five Make/Buy Strategies

% Navy	High Complexity 25%		Medium Complexity 50%		Low Complexity 25%		Parts Produced		$'000
	Industry	Navy	Industry	Navy	Industry	Navy	Industry	Navy	Total
0%	$6,022		$16,109		$6,022		$28,153		$28,153
25%		$3,319	$16,109		$6,022		$22,131	$3,319	$25,450
50%		$3,319	$6,022	$3,319	$6,022		$12,044	$6,638	$18,682
75%		$3,319		$8,841	$6,022		$6,022	$12,160	$18,182
100%		$3,319		$8,841		$3,319		$15,479	$15,479

Figure 258 shows these results in graphical form by plotting the costs in the Parts Cost by Industry, Parts Cost by Navy, and Total Parts Production Cost columns of Table 25.

Savings increase with the volume of parts manufactured by the Navy (more in-sourcing). Savings at the depot studied by having the Navy instead of industry produce all parts are estimated to be $12.67M (i.e., $28.15M − $15.48M) per year at the depot investigated. Assuming 10 depots that apply this strategy implies savings that exceed $120M annually. For context, these estimated savings can be compared to the threshold set by the National Defense Authorization Act for Fiscal Year 2012:

> (e) Determination relating to the conversion [from outsourcing to in-sourcing] of certain functions…in determining whether a function should be converted to performance by Department of Defense civilian employees, the Secretary of Defense shall - …

> (C) Ensure that the difference in the cost of performing the function by a contractor compared to the cost of performing the function by Department of Defense civilian employees would be equal to or exceed the lesser of …
> (I) 10 percent of the personnel-related costs for performance of the function; or

> (ii)) $10,000,000

The potential savings forecasted above far exceed the $10M threshold set by the statute, thereby supporting the adoption and use of these technologies.

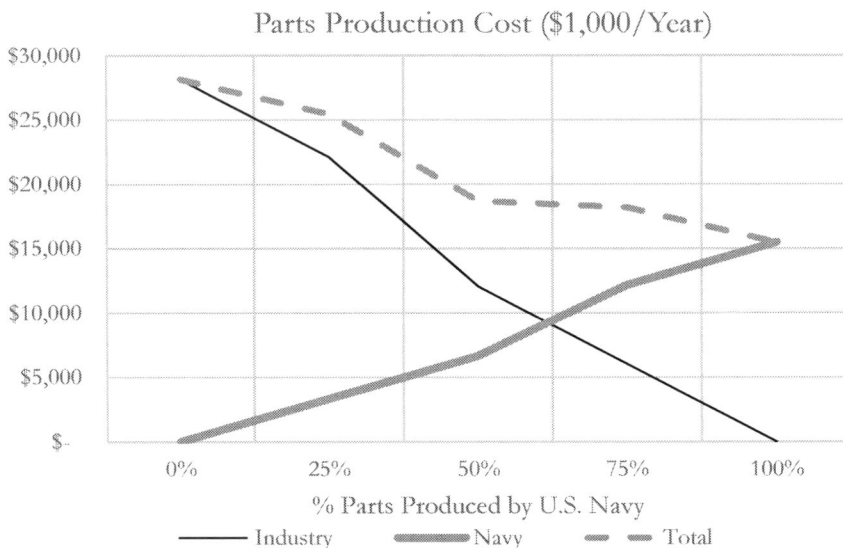

Figure 258: Estimated Annual Costs of Five Make/Buy Strategies

Real Options Analysis

Risk Analysis and Real Options Valuation techniques allow a new way of approaching the problems of estimating return on investment (ROI) and the risk-value of various strategic real options. ROV technology was used to both provide preliminary analyses and build a strategy that is financially optimal and reduces the risks of financial losses in given circumstances and to provide flexibility in changing decisions when new information becomes available. An important point is that, in contrast, the traditional discounted cash flow (DCF) approach assumes a single decision pathway with fixed outcomes, and all decisions are made in the beginning without the ability to change over time. The strategic real options approach considers multiple decision pathways as a consequence of high uncertainty coupled with management's flexibility in choosing the optimal strategies or options along the way when new information becomes available. That is, management has the flexibility to make midcourse strategy corrections when there is uncertainty involved in the future. As information becomes available and uncertainty becomes resolved, management can choose the best strategies to implement.

Benefits and ROI were used to estimate the costs of each make/buy strategy. Benefits were estimated by multiplying the production rates by the average parts values. Monte Carlo risk simulation was used to create artificial futures by generating hundreds of thousands of sample paths of outcomes and analyzing their prevalent characteristics. In the Monte Carlo simulation process, triangular distribution was used as the base case per the AFCAA handbook as described previously.

ROV methodology is used in:

- Identifying different investment decision pathways that management can navigate given the highly uncertain conditions.

- Valuing each of the strategic decision pathways and what it represents in terms of financial viability and feasibility.

- Prioritizing these pathways or projects based on a series of qualitative and quantitative metrics.

- Optimizing the value of strategic investment decisions by evaluating different decision paths under certain conditions or determining how using a different sequence of pathways can lead to the optimal strategy.

- Managing existing and developing new strategic decision pathways for future opportunities.

As illustrated in Figure 259, four major strategies were identified and solved using ROV SLS technology as options for the decision-making process concerning planning for further action.

- Strategy A: Base case. Keep purchasing vast majority of Inventory. This is a risky strategy. Opportunity losses are occurring due to missed financial savings and control over the process in the long run.

- Strategy B: Outsource. Buy All 100%: Outsource all manufacturing to outside contractors. This strategy is risky because it leads to dependency on organizations that are outside the control of the Navy.

  - Open Architecture. To reduce the risk of dependency on a few vendors, the Navy could implement an Open Architecture principle that provides interchangeability of critical parts on a ship without any loss of functionality. That gives the Navy the flexibility to choose vendors based on objective parameters (price, frequency, availability).

  - Exit. This Strategy is not expensive to abandon. The Navy can easily go to other options without any substantial costs.

- Strategy C: In-source. Make All 100%: Option is to manufacture everything "in-house" immediately. The ROI is high but cost and risks are very high if it does not work out.

- o Invest 100%. Pros: savings may be captured by the use of 3DLST, 3DP, and CPLM for fleet maintenance and modernization. Cons: high costs and risks of immediate in-sourcing.

- o Exit. This option is very costly to abandon because of the high investment costs.

- Strategy D: Sequential Compound Option

  - o Phase I. 25% PLM: Implement PLM. This is a strategic business approach applying a consistent set of business solutions in support of the collaborative creation, management, dissemination, and use of product definition information across the extended enterprise.

  - o Phase II. 50%: 3D Laser Scanning Technology. This is a small-scale investment over time with the ability to exit and walk away should the technology not work out as expected. Phasing investments over time hedges any downside risks and reduces any risks of large lump-sum investments.

  - o Exit. This technology could still be useful for other Options.

  - o Phase III. 75%: Additive Manufacturing. This includes 3D CAD models, Conversion to Stereolithography STL, Revision of STL Models, AM Machine Setup and implementation.

  - o Exit. 3D Technology could be still applied in other operations of the Navy.

  - o Phase IV. 100%: Final Phase. Implement the PLM, 3DLST technology for all required inventory parts. At this point the project is too costly to abandon. The Navy will choose to implement the technology limited to the most critical parts of its operations.

To calculate Volatility for use in the Real Option Valuation process, the Risk Simulator software was used. Monte Carlo simulation was applied for estimating Volatility. The result is shown in Figure 260. The Coefficient of Variation of 33.61% for the High Risk and 23.62% for the Medium Risk AFCAA settings are the volatilities used in the analyses.

Calculations performed by ROV SLS software (Figure 261) illustrate that the Strategy D, Sequential Compound Option, is the most obvious choice with the highest total strategic value. The results (Figure 262) show that Strategy D has the highest value. This Sequential Compound Option involves implementing new technologies in phases, thus giving Navy leadership the ability to exit at any stage of the project while minimizing the risk of losses.

It has now become evident that the U.S. Navy leadership can take advantage of more advanced analytical procedures when making strategic investment decisions and when managing portfolios of projects. In the past, due to the lack of technological maturity, businesses and the government had to resort to relying on experience and managing by gut feel. Now, with the assistance of technology and more mature methodologies, analysis can be taken a step further. The only barrier to implementation, simply put, is the lack of exposure to the potential benefits of the methods. In order to be ready for the challenges of the 21st century, and to create a highly effective and efficient force, strategic real options and risk analysis are available to aid leadership with critical decision making.

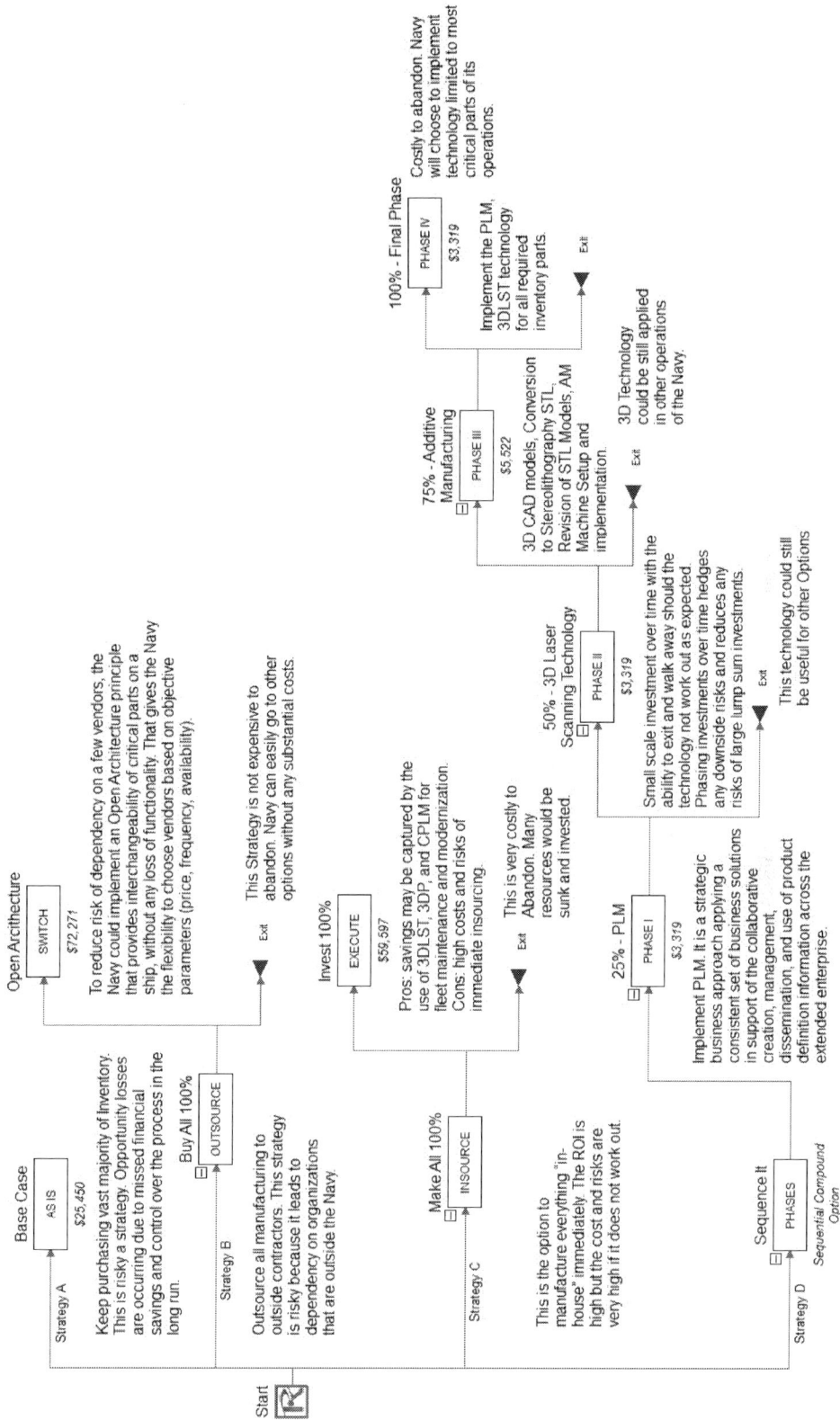

Base Case

Strategy A → AS IS — $25,450

Keep purchasing vast majority of Inventory. This is risky a strategy. Opportunity losses are occurring due to missed financial savings and control over the process in the long run.

Open Arcitheture

SWITCH — $72,271

To reduce risk of dependency on a few vendors, the Navy could implement an Open Architecture principle that provides interchangeability of critical parts on a ship, without any loss of functionality. That gives the Navy the flexibility to choose vendors based on objective parameters (price, frequency, availability).

Buy All 100% → OUTSOURCE

Strategy B

Outsource all manufacturing to outside contractors. This strategy is risky because it leads to dependency on organizations that are outside the Navy.

Exit — This Strategy is not expensive to abandon. Navy can easily go to other options without any substantial costs.

Invest 100%

EXECUTE — $59,597

Pros: savings may be captured by the use of 3DLST, 3DP, and CPLM for fleet maintenance and modernization. Cons: high costs and risks of immediate insourcing.

Make All 100% → INSOURCE

Strategy C

This is the option to manufacture everything "in-house" immediately. The ROI is high but the cost and risks are very high if it does not work out.

Exit — This is very costly to Abandon. Many resources would be sunk and invested.

25% - PLM

PHASE I — $3,319

Implement PLM. It is a strategic business approach applying a consistent set of business solutions in support of the collaborative creation, management, dissemination, and use of product definition information across the extended enterprise.

50% - 3D Laser Scanning Technology

PHASE II — $3,319

Small scale investment over time with the ability to exit and walk away should the technology not work out as expected. Phasing investments over time hedges any downside risks and reduces any risks of large lump sum investments.

Exit — This technology could still be useful for other Options

75% - Additive Manufacturing

PHASE III — $5,522

3D CAD models, Conversion to Stereolithography STL, Revision of STL Models, AM Machine Setup and implementation.

Exit — 3D Technology could be still applied in other operations of the Navy.

100% - Final Phase

PHASE IV — $3,319

Implement the PLM, 3DLST technology for all required inventory parts.

Exit — Costly to abandon. Navy will choose to implement technology limited to most critical parts of its operations.

Sequence It → PHASES

Strategy D

Sequential Compound Option

Start

Figure 259: Schema of Four Strategies

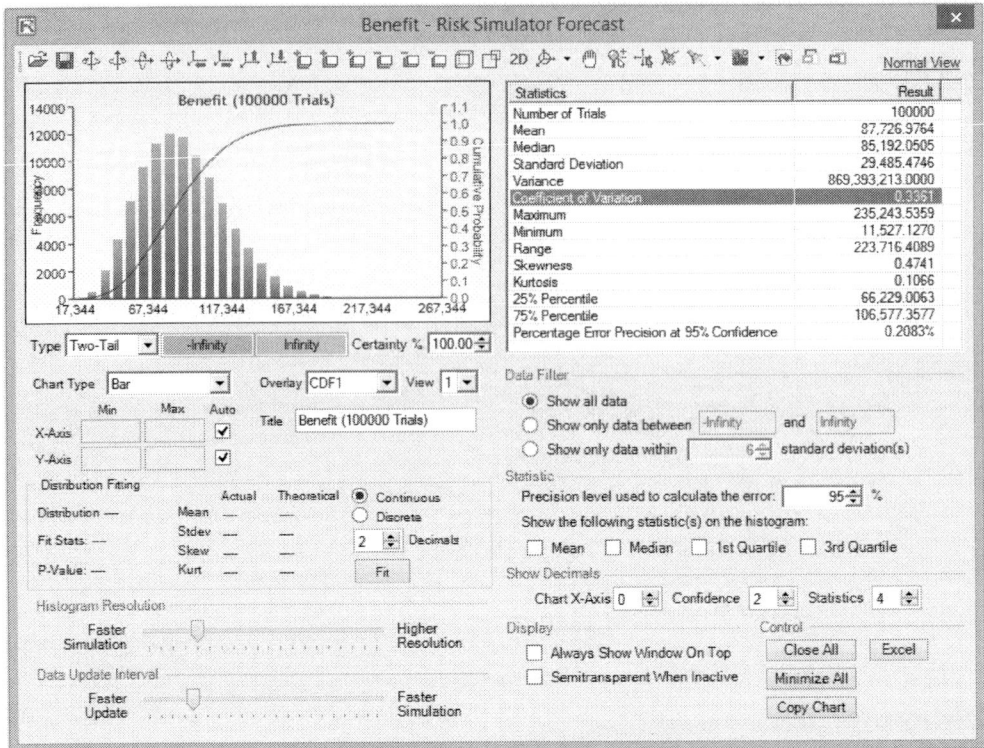

Figure 260: Risk Simulator Monte Carlo Simulation Results Window

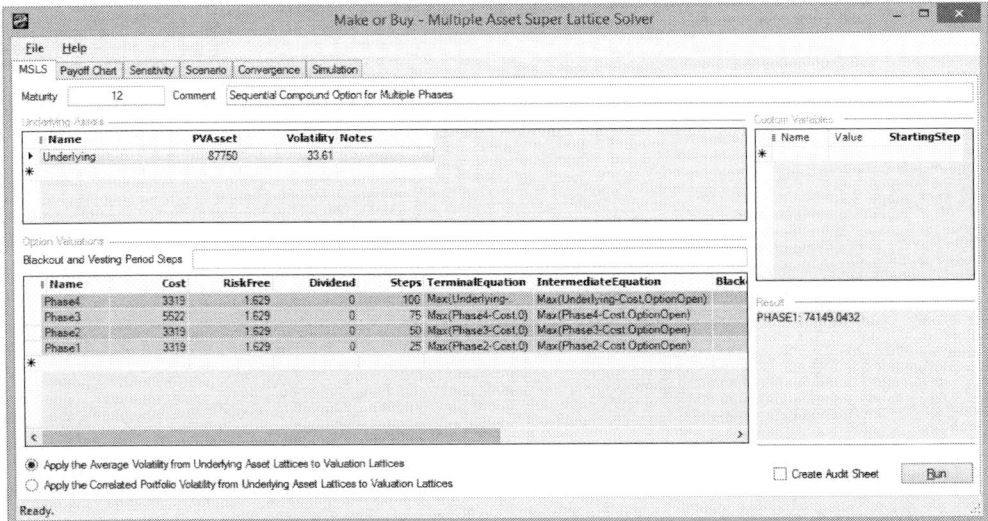

Figure 261: ROV SLS Inputs

STRATEGY PATH	DECISION	STRATEGIC VALUE	NOTES
Strategy A	25% Navy As-Is	$62.30M	AS-IS 25%
Strategy B	Buy 100%	$59.60M	Buy 100%
Strategy C	Make 100%	$72.27M	Make 100%
Strategy D	Phased	$74.15M	Stepwise
PHASES	COST	TIMING	
Phase 1 Cost	$3.32M	2 Years	
Phase 2 Cost	$3.32M	4 Years	
Phase 3 Cost	$5.52M	6 Years	
Phase 4 Cost	$3.32M	8 Years	
Total Costs	$15.48M		

Figure 262: Strategic Real Options Results

Conclusions and Recommendations

The current work investigated the potential of three emerging technologies, namely the 3D Printing Operations, 3D Laser Scanning Technology, and Collaborative Product Lifecycle Management to generate cost saving in U.S. Naval ship maintenance and modernization. The challenges posed by fleet maintenance and modernization and an introduction to in-sourcing and its history within the U.S. federal government were described as a context for the work. An extensive introduction to the three technologies was followed by a description of the research approach and methods. Then cost savings using the technologies under different in-sourcing (make/buy) scenarios were estimated. Real options were used to investigate several in-sourcing versus outsourcing alternatives.

Potential cost savings due to the adoption and use of the three technologies was estimated to increase as more parts were manufactured the U.S. Navy (i.e., in-sourced), with savings over $12 million annually if all parts were in-sourced. In-house manufacture of complex parts was found to generate the largest savings. In combination with other research this suggests that complex parts for which few copies are needed are the best candidates for initial in-sourcing using the technologies. Of the four make/buy strategies analyzed, Strategy D of the phased implementation approach has the highest strategic value. This strategy involves implementing new technologies in phases, thus giving management the ability to exit at any stage of the project, while minimizing the risk of losses.

The results have several significant implications for fleet maintenance and modernization practice. The finding of significant potential savings with in-sourcing suggests that the three technologies have created a potential shift in the optimal acquisition modes for fleet parts. Based on the RAND model of in-sourcing and outsourcing acquisition, as the costs of producing few more different types of parts (e.g., simple vs. complex and frequent vs. rare) drop with the new technologies, the Navy will be able to capture more benefits by in-sourcing more parts. Recommendations include that the U.S. Navy should:

- Adopt the three technologies investigated.
- Test in-sourcing with these technologies starting with low-volume complex products.
- Plan to increase the scale of in-sourcing after developing processes and a track record to justify expansion.
- Work to change acquisition regulations and procedures that impede the use of in-sourcing for parts manufacturing.

References

American Federation of Government Employees (2014). Defcon 2014 fact sheet on in-sourcing. Retreived from https://www.afge.org/?documentID=3975

Aronowitz, J. (2012, March 29). Contractors: How much are they worth? Hearing before the Subcommittee on Contracting Oversight, Committee on Homeland Security and Governmental Affairs, Senate. 112th Cong 2 (2012) (testimony of Jay D. Aronowitz). Retreived from http://www.gpo.gov/fdsys/pkg/CHRG-112shrg73681/html/CHRG-112shrg73681.htm

ASTM, American Society for Testing and Materials (2013). *Annual Book of ASTM Standards* (Vol. 10.04).

Brodsky, R. (2011, February 3). Army suspends all ongoing in-sourcing plans. *Government Executive.* Retreived from http://www.govexec.com/defense/2011/02/army-suspends-all-ongoing-insourcing-plans/33242/

CIMdata. (2007). All about PLM. Retrieved from https://www.cimdata.com/en/resources/about-plm

Drew, J., McGarvey, R., & Buryk, P. (2013). "Enabling Early Sustainment Decisions, Application to F-35 Depot-Level Maintenance (RR-397-AF)." Santa Monica, CA: RAND.

GAO, Government Accountability Office (1997, July). *Internal Revenue Service: Issues affecting IRS' private debt collection* (GGD-97-129R). Retrieved from http://www.gao.gov/assets/90/86658.pdf

GE, General Electric (2014, June 23). Fit to Print: New Plant Will Assemble World's First Passenger Jet Engine With 3D Printed Fuel Nozzles, Next-Gen Materials. Retrieved from http://www.gereports.com/post/80701924024/fit-to-print.

Gibson, I., Rosen, D. W., & Stucker, B. (2010). *Additive Manufacturing Technologies: Rapid Prototyping to Direct Digital.* New York (NY): Springer Science+Business Media, LLC.

Greaves, T., & Jenkins, B. (2007). 3D laser scanning market red hot: 2006 industry revenues $253 million, 43% growth. *SparView, 5*(7). Retrieved from http://www.sparllc.com/archiveviewer.php?vol=05&num=07&file=vol05no07-01

Kenney, M. (2013). *Cost reduction through the use of additive manufacturing (3D printing) and collaborative product life cycle management technologies to enhance the Navy's maintenance programs* (Master's thesis). Monterey, CA: Naval Postgraduate School.

Kronsberg, Matthew (2013) "3-D Printing for All" Wall Street Journal, Oct. 20, 2013. p D14.

Lipowicz, A. (2011, February 22). Converting contract IT workers to employees saved $27M, official says. *Federal Computer Week.*

Lipson, H., & Kurman, M. (2013). *Fabricated: The New World of 3D Printing.* Somerset (NJ): Wiley.

Mackley, C. J. (2014, March). *Reducing costs and increasing productivity in shop maintenance using product lifecycle management, 3D laser scanning, and 3D printing* (Master's thesis). Monterey, CA: Naval Postgraduate School.

Mitchell, Robert L. (2014, August 13).l 3D printing makes its move into production. Computerworld. Retrieved from http://www.computerworld.com/article/2490930/enterprise-applications-3d-printing-makes-its-move-into-production.html

NSRP, National Shipbuilding Research Program (2006). Retrived from www.nsrp.org

NSWC, Naval Surface Warfare Center. Port Hueneme Division (2013). Distance support: Distance support in depth. Retrieved from http://www.navsea.navy.mil/nswc/porthueneme/whatWeDo/distanceSupport/inDepth.aspx

OASD, Office of the Assistant Secretary of Defense (Logistics and Materiel Readiness) (2013). *DOD Maintenance 2013 Factbook.* Retrieved from http://www.acq.osd.mil/log/mpp/factbooks/Fact_Book_2013_10-15-2013_Final_ecopy.pdf

Schindler, C. (2010). *Product lifecycle management: A collaborative tool for defense acquisitions* (Master's thesis). Monterey CA: Naval Postgraduate School.

USDT, U.S. Department of Transportation (2009, August 14). FAA Tech Center in-sourcing saves between $52 and $203 million in data system costs. Retrieved from http://usdotblog.typepad.com/secretarysblog/2009/08/faa-tech-center-in-sourcing-saves-between-52-and203-million-in-data-system-costs.html#.VEgHuGfRppF

Wohlers Associates, Inc. (2013). Retrieved from http://wohlersassociates.com/brief07-10.htm

SOFTWARE DOWNLOAD & INSTALL

As current versions of the software are updated all the time, we highly recommend that you visit the Real Options Valuation, Inc., website and follow the instructions below to install the latest software applications.

- **Step 1**: Visit **www.realoptionsvaluation.com** and click on **Downloads** and **Download Software** (Figure A). You will be prompted to log in. Please first register if you are a first-time user (Figure B) and an automated e-mail will be sent to you within several minutes. (If you do not receive a registration e-mail after you register, then please send a note to support@realoptionsvaluation.com.) While waiting for the automated e-mail, browse this page and see the free getting started videos, case studies, and sample models you can download.

- **Step 2**: Return to this site and LOGIN using the login credentials you received via e-mail. Download and install the latest versions of **Risk Simulator** and **Real Options SLS** on this Web page. The download links, installation instructions, and Hardware ID information are also presented on this page (Figure C).

- **Step 3**: After installing the software, start Excel and you will see a Risk Simulator ribbon. Follow the instructions provided on the Web page to obtain and e-mail support@realoptionsvaluation.com your Hardware ID and mention the code **"MR3E 30 Days"** and you will be sent a free extended 30-day license to use both the Risk Simulator and Real Options SLS software.

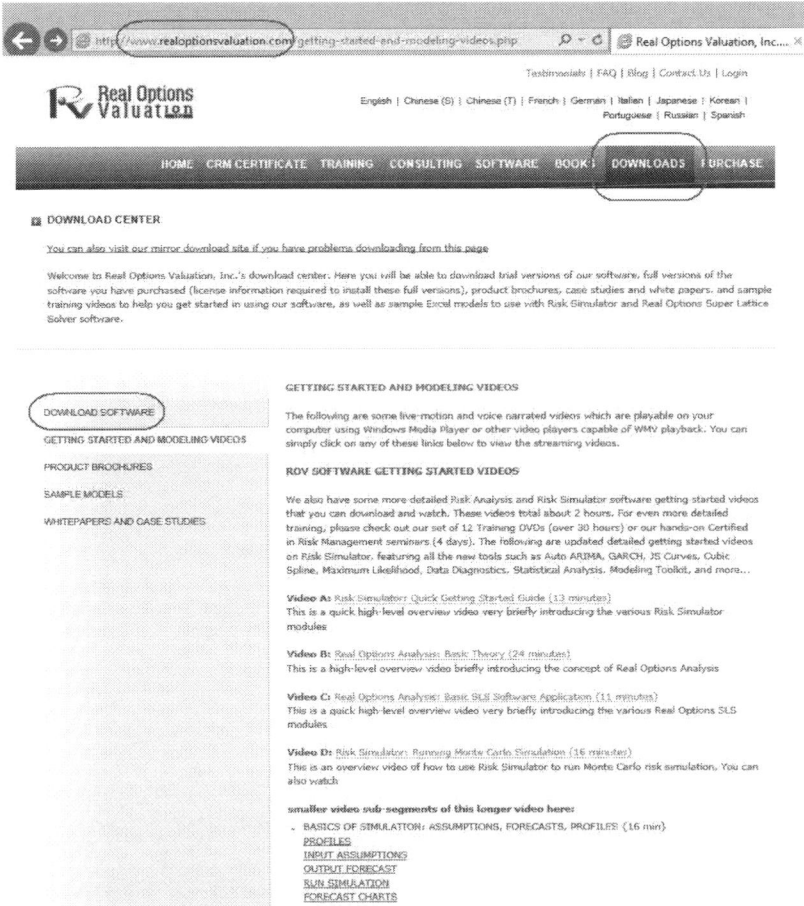

Figure A: Step 1 – Software download site

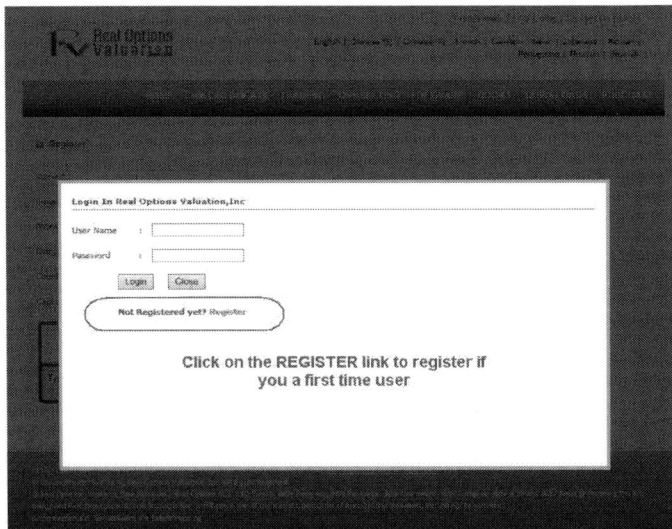

Figure B: Register if you are a first-time visitor

Real Options Valuation

Testimonials | FAQ | Blog | Contact Us | Logout

English | Chinese (S) | Chinese (T) | French | German | Italian | Japanese | Korean | Portuguese | Russian | Spanish

HOME   CRM CERTIFICATE   TRAINING   CONSULTING   SOFTWARE   BOOKS   DOWNLOADS   PURCHASE

DOWNLOAD CENTER

You can also visit our mirror download site if you have problems downloading from this page

Welcome to Real Options Valuation, Inc.'s download center. Here you will be able to download trial versions of our software, full versions of the software you have purchased (license information required to install these full versions), product brochures, case studies and white papers, and sample training videos to help you get started in using our software, as well as sample Excel models to use with Risk Simulator and Real Options Super Lattice Solver software.

DOWNLOAD SOFTWARE

GETTING STARTED AND MODELING VIDEOS

PRODUCT BROCHURES

SAMPLE MODELS

WHITEPAPERS AND CASE STUDIES

SOFTWARE DOWNLOADS

Risk Simulator

SOFTWARE DOWNLOADS SOFTWARE DOWNLOAD: RISK SIMULATOR 2014
(ENGLISH, FRENCH, GERMAN, ITALIAN, JAPANESE, KOREAN, PORTUGUESE, SIMPLIFIED CHINESE, TRADITIONAL CHINESE, SPANISH, RUSSIAN)

FULL & TRIAL VERSION DOWNLOAD:

Download Risk Simulator 2014 [WIN x32/x64 and Excel x32 most common edition]
Download Risk Simulator 2014 [WIN x32/x64 and Excel x32 most common edition] (mirror site)

Download Risk Simulator 2014 [WIN x64 and Excel x64 special edition]
Download Risk Simulator 2014 [WIN x64 and Excel x64 special edition] (mirror site)

This is a full version of the software but will expire in 15 days, during which time you can purchase a license to permanently unlock the software. Please first **uninstall all previous versions** of Risk Simulator before installing this newer version.

To permanently unlock the software, purchase a license and e-mail us your Hardware ID (after installing the software, start **Excel**, click on **Risk Simulator, License**, and e-mail admin@realoptionsvaluation.com the 16 to 20 digit **Hardware ID** located on the bottom left of the splash screen). We will then e-mail you a permanent license file. **Save** this file to your hard drive, start **Excel**, click on **Risk Simulator, License, Install License** and point to the location of this license file, restart Excel and you are now permanently licensed. Installing the license only takes a few seconds.

System requirements, FAQ, and additional resources:

- Windows XP, Vista (32 and 64 bit), Windows 7 (32 and 64 bit), or Windows 8 (32 and 64 bit)
- Microsoft Excel XP, 2003, 2007, 2010, or 2013
- 1GB RAM Minimum (2 GB minimum recommended)
- 350 MB Hard Drive
- Administrative Rights to install software
- Microsoft .NET Framework 2.0, 3.0, 3.5 or later
- MAC OS users will require either Virtual Machine or Parallels running Microsoft Excel

Figure C: Download links and hardware ID instructions

INDEX

BOOKS BY DR. JOHNATHAN MUN

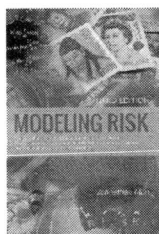

Modeling Risk: Applying Monte Carlo Risk Simulation, Strategic Real Options, Stochastic Forecasting, Portfolio Optimization, Data Analytics, Business Intelligence, and Decision Modeling, 3rd Edition
1112 Pages (2015)
ISBN: 9781943290000
Thomson-Shore & ROV Press

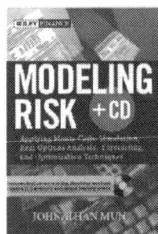

Modeling Risk: Applying Monte Carlo Simulation, Real Options Analysis, Stochastic Forecasting, and Optimization
610 Pages (2006)
ISBN: 0471789003
Wiley Finance

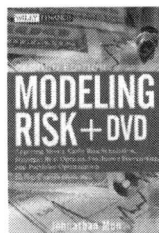

Modeling Risk: Applying Monte Carlo Risk Simulation, Strategic Real Options Analysis, Stochastic Forecasting, and Portfolio Optimization, 2nd Edition
986 Pages (2010)
ISBN: 9780470592212
Wiley Finance

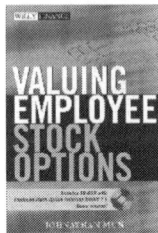

Valuing Employee Stock Options: Under 2004 FAS 123
320 Pages (2004)
ISBN: 0471705128
Wiley Finance

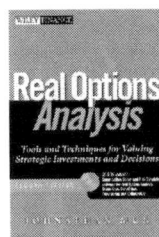

Real Options Analysis: Tools and Techniques for Valuing Strategic Investments & Decisions, 2nd Edition
670 Pages (2005)
ISBN: 0471747483
Wiley Finance

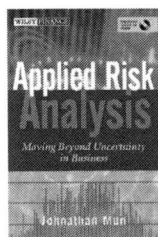

Applied Risk Analysis: Moving Beyond Uncertainty
460 Pages (2003)
ISBN: 0-471-47885-7
Wiley Finance

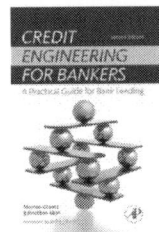

Credit Engineering for Bankers (With Morton Glantz)
1000 Pages (2010)
ISBN: 9780123785855
Elsevier Academic Press

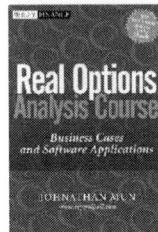

Real Options Analysis Course: Business Cases and Software Applications
360 Pages (2003)
ISBN: 0471430013
Wiley Finance

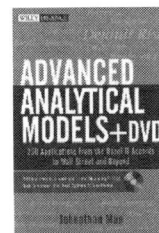

Advanced Analytical Models: Over 800 Models and 300 Applications from Basel II Accords to Wall Street and Beyond
1000 Pages (2008)
ISBN: 9780470179215
Wiley Finance

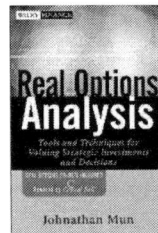

Real Options Analysis: Tools and Techniques for Valuing Strategic Investments & Decisions
416 Pages (2002)
ISBN: 0-471-25696-X
Wiley Finance

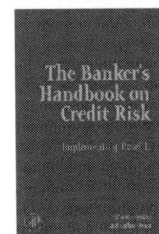

The Banker's Handbook on Credit Risk: Implementing Basel II (With Morton Glantz)
420 Pages (2008)
ISBN: 9780123736666
Elsevier Science

See Dr. Mun's other books, articles, whitepapers, technical papers, and academic journal publications on his company's website at www.rovusa.com and www.realoptionsvaluation.com.

26017818R00201

Printed in Great Britain
by Amazon